Work Group Learning

Understanding, Improving & Assessing How Groups Learn In Organizations

Work Group Learning

Understanding, Improving & Assessing How Groups Learn In Organizations

Edited by
Valerie I. Sessa
Manuel London

LEA Lawrence Erlbaum Associates
Taylor & Francis Group

New York London

Lawrence Erlbaum Associates
Taylor & Francis Group
270 Madison Avenue
New York, NY 10016

Lawrence Erlbaum Associates
Taylor & Francis Group
2 Park Square
Milton Park, Abingdon
Oxon OX14 4RN

Lawrence Erlbaum Associates is an imprint of Taylor & Francis Group, an Informa business

Printed in the United States of America on acid-free paper
10 9 8 7 6 5 4 3 2 1

International Standard Book Number-13: 978-0-8058-6022-1 (Softcover) 978-0-8058-6021-4 (Hardcover)

Library of Congress Cataloging-in-Publication Data

Work group learning : understanding, improving and assessing how groups learn in organizations / editors, Valerie Sessa and Manuel London.
p. cm.
Includes bibliographical references and index.
ISBN 978-0-8058-6022-1 (alk. paper)
1. Organizational learning. 2. Teams in the workplace. 3. Learning. 4. Group work in education. I. Sessa, Valerie I. II. London, Manuel. III. Title.

HD58.82.S473 2007
658.4'022--dc22 2007014986

Visit the Taylor & Francis Web site at
http://www.taylorandfrancis.com

Contents

Preface

This volume examines the meaning of group learning and how groups become high-performing teams. More specifically, it reviews how groups learn to use members' expertise, adapt to unexpected events and demands, prepare for the future, and occasionally, transform themselves to form new structures and processes in light of emerging opportunities and challenges.

Group learning is a function of the learning of the members of the group and the evolving interactions among them that produce mutual understanding and lead to task accomplishment. Groups that are able to capture their learning for the future, adopt new work methods, and formulate new interdependencies are likely to meet the expectations of their members and stakeholders. Successful groups "learn" as they discover and experiment with new task structures and processes and respond to changes, such as members coming and going, new goals imposed or adopted, advancing technologies, and resource constraints.

This book offers a state-of-the-art examination of group-learning processes, covering advancements in theory, research, and practice. It explores processes that affect group learning, such as members verifying their self-concepts through group interaction, developing a shared sense of how different members contribute to the group effort, and establishing routines that create a sense of psychological safety and build on members' expertise and interdependencies to get the job done. It suggests interventions that facilitate group learning at different stages of group development and under different and changing conditions.

Groups hold an intermediate position within the organization. They link individuals together and at the same time, they link to other groups to form organizations. Stated another way, groups link what might be thought of as lower order components of the organizational system (that is, individuals, who are systems themselves) to higher order components (organizations). One of the functions of groups is to pull together the behavior of their members and integrate this joint behavior with other groups in the system. Therefore, groups are the linking pin between individual learning and organizational learning. To further advance our understanding and practice of learning at all three levels, we need to delve more deeply into understanding learning at the group level.

Group learning is important to organizations. Project-based organizations may rely on a constant shift in work groups. Individuals in these organizations are likely to be part of multiple, often interdepartmental groups, which are changing continuously as work is completed and new projects begin. Flat organizational structures may broaden work group responsibilities and the diversity of group members. New communications technologies and means of sharing work alter interaction patterns and require participants to work in new ways. There is already considerable literature on learning at the individual level and a growing body of literature on organizational learning. Only recently has attention begun to focus on group learning.

This volume helps shape the emerging field of group learning by drawing on leading researchers in the field to explore some basic questions. We asked the authors to examine what is new in this emerging field with their prior work as a foundation. In particular, we address basic questions such as the following:

- What is group learning?
- Why is group learning important?
- What do groups need to do to be effective learners?
- How do groups learn?
- When and where do groups learn best?
- What are group learning processes?
- What conditions foster learning? How do external forces/situations and group/member readiness affect learning? What conditions hinder group learning?
- What facilitates group learning? What are the roles of the leader and facilitator in group learning? What interventions (e.g., leader coaching) work for group learning, and what interventions are most appropriate at different stages of group development?
- What is the relationship between group learning, individual member learning, and organizational learning?
- What is a continuous learning group? How does it relate to the concepts of a learning organization and individuals who are continuous learners? Are there ways to foster group learning orientation?

In Sessa and London (2006), we examined the interplay of individual, group, and organization learning. We argued that individuals, groups, and organizations are nested and iterative living systems. We offer a systems model of parallel processes between systems at each level of analysis. The type of learning mechanism used by the system (adaptive, generative, or transformative) depends on the external pressures and opportunities experienced by the system and internal readiness to learn. While learning at each level is similar, we need to understand how forces at one level impact learning at other levels. This volume complements our continuous learning book.

This book aggregates existing theory and research into one volume and goes beyond this foundation to examine new insights about group learning. As such, the authors' contributions will be new and important, and the book will be a unique contribution that sets direction for the field. The book is applicable to learning in many different types of groups in different settings.

This book is for those who are working in the area of group learning, including theoreticians, researchers, and professional level practitioners who want a solid grounding in group learning theory and research, including organizational development and change professionals, trainers, coaches, human resource professionals, and top-level executives who establish directions for training and development, and need to convince others that this is key to the ongoing success of their enterprise. Students of organizational behavior will benefit from having the nascent group-learning literature brought together in a single volume with chapters from leading researchers. Organization development and change professionals will benefit from understanding how groups learn, the different ways that learning occurs, and current practice in group learning. Trainers and those involved in corporate universities will benefit from recognizing how curricula and instructional design can meet needs for improved group interaction. Team leaders and coaches will benefit from seeing how they can enhance their contribution as guides, role models, and corporate educators for targeted behavior change within groups. Human resource professionals will learn how to integrate group training and development within a cohesive set of interrelated human resource processes that directly support business objectives.

The book is organized into four sections. In the first section, we consider how groups learn and what they learn. The second section turns to factors that influence group learning. The third section explores learning interventions, both those occurring in situ and more formal methods. The final section reviews team-learning assessment methods. This includes assessing the capacity and need for team learning, assessing learning outcomes, and evaluating team learning interventions. In chapter 1, we set the stages for the book by describing why there is a need for each of the sections and chapters. In our section introductions, we provide abstracts for each chapter.

Many of the chapter authors use the term "team." Others use "group." Generally, we refer to a group as two or more people who work together on a common goal. This may be a committee, council, board, or taskforce. Their task may be to solve a problem, make a decision or recommendation, plan an event, or develop a product. A team may be an ongoing, natural work group (all employees who report to the same supervisor and work together on interdependent efforts) or a group that meets and works together periodically, but in which members are highly interdependent (e.g., a sports team). Most of the concepts throughout this book apply to any type of group, whether they are cohesive teams of highly interdependent members or more loosely structured entities who meet periodically in person or through electronic communication media. The authors note when team is more applicable or when specific group characteristics influence the nature of group learning.

We want to thank all our authors for their valuable contributions, and Anne Duffy, our editor at Erlbaum, who has helped shape our own development and encouraged us to develop the concept of group learning.

Valerie I. Sessa
Manuel London

About the Authors

Andrea Amelinckx is Director of the International Management Programs Office in the Faculty of Management at the University of Lethbridge (Canada). She also serves as the Area Coordinator for the International Management Area. She received her JD from the State University of New York at Buffalo. Her teaching and research interests are in the areas of cross-cultural management, global virtual teams, international law and policy, and gender relations.

Holly Arrow is an Associate Professor of Psychology and a member of the Institute for Cognitive and Decision Sciences at the University of Oregon. She is coauthor, with Joseph McGrath and Jennifer Berdahl, of *Small Groups as Complex Systems: Formation, Coordination, Development, and Adaptation* (2000). She studies the emergence and transformation of group structure and the evolution of social capacities upon which the group dynamics that facilitate war depend.

Bradford S. Bell is an Assistant Professor of Human Resource Studies in the School of Industrial and Labor Relations at Cornell University. He received his BA in Psychology from the University of Maryland at College Park and his MA and PhD in Industrial and Organizational Psychology from Michigan State University. His research focuses on issues surrounding training and development, both at the individual and team levels, as well as the implications of job applicants' expectations of organizational justice. Currently, he is interested in issues surrounding active, self-directed learning as they apply to the design and implementation of different types of learning programs, including e-learning and embedded workplace learning. His work has appeared in a number of book chapters and journals, including the *Journal of Applied Psychology, Personnel Psychology,* and *Group and Organization Management.*

Clint A. Bowers is a Professor of Digital Media at the University of Central Florida. He is also Chief Scientist of the university's Augmented Cognition for Training in Virtual Environments Laboratory (ACTIVE). Dr. Bowers' research interests include team training, team performance, and the use of technology in complex workplaces.

David P. Brandon obtained his PhD in Speech Communication in 2003 from the University of Illinois at Urbana-Champaign and currently serves as Manager of the Theoretical and Computational Biophysics Group at that same institution.

C. Shawn Burke is a Research Scientist at the Institute for Simulation and Training of the University of Central Florida. Her expertise includes teams and their leadership, team adaptability, team training, measurement, evaluation, and team effectiveness. Dr. Burke has published more than 50 journal articles and book chapters related to the above topics, has presented at more than 70 peer-reviewed conferences, and has assisted organizations in evaluating aviation-related team-training programs and reducing medical errors. She is currently investigating team adaptability and its corresponding measurement, issues related to multicultural team performance, leadership, and training, and the impact of stress on team process and performance. Dr. Burke earned her doctorate in Industrial and Organizational Psychology from George Mason University. She serves as an ad hoc reviewer for *Human Factors, Leadership Quarterly, Human Resource Management*, and *Quality and Safety in Healthcare*. She has coedited a book on adaptability and is currently coediting a book on advances in team effectiveness research.

Janis A. Cannon-Bowers works at the Institute for Simulation and Training and Digital Media Department at the University of Central Florida as an Associate Professor and Research Scientist. She has also worked as the U.S. Navy's Senior Scientist for Training Systems. Her research interests are in technology-enabled learning and synthetic learning environments. To date, she has been awarded several grants to support this work, including two awards by the National Science Foundation. Dr. Cannon-Bowers has been an active researcher, with more than 100 publications in scholarly publications. She is on the Board of Directors of the Society for Simulation in Healthcare and advisor to the national Serious Games Initiative.

Jonathan Cook, a doctoral student at the University of Oregon, studies inter- and intragroup dynamics, particularly as they relate to diversity, power, and minority group identity.

David V. Day is Professor of Organisational Behaviour in the Lee Kong Chian School of Business, Singapore Management University. Prior to joining SMU, he was a Professor of Industrial-Organizational Psychology and Director of Graduate Training at The Pennsylvania State University, University Park. He has published more than 50 journal articles and book chapters, many pertaining to the core topics of leadership and leadership development. He serves on the editorial boards of *Human Performance, Journal of Applied Psychology, Journal of Management,* and *Personnel Psychology,* and as an Associate Editor of *Leadership Quarterly* and *Human Resource Management Review.* Dr. Day is the lead editor of *Leader Development for Transforming Organizations: Growing Leaders for Tomorrow* (Lawrence Erlbaum Associates, 2004). He is a Fellow of the American Psychological Association.

Thomas Diamante was Vice President, Corporate Strategy and Development in Global Securities Research and Economics reporting to the Chief Operating Officer of Merrill Lynch. Prior to Merrill Lynch, Dr. Diamante was Senior Manager and Lead Change Consultant for KPMG Consulting. Earlier in his career, he held executive Human Resource positions at Philip Morris Companies (Altria). Currently he is affiliated with Marist College School of Management. He has his PhD in Industrial and Organizational psychology from The Graduate Center, City University of New York. He complements the industrial degree with postdoctoral training in clinical psychology from the Institute for Behavior Therapy in New York. He is certified in employee relations law by the Institute for Applied Management and Law and is a licensed New York State psychologist. He is also a member of the American Psychological Association's Consulting, Industrial, and Law Divisions.

Deborah Diaz is a PhD student in the Industrial and Organizational Psychology program at the University of Central Florida, where she also received her MS in Industrial and Organizational Psychology. She received her BS degrees from the University of Houston. Her primary areas of study included management (specifically, hotel/restaurant management), business, and psychology, with an emphasis in industrial and organizational psychology and accounting. Ms. Diaz's areas of expertise include teams and training theory, motivation theory, performance measurement, and leadership. While at the University of Central Florida, Ms. Diaz has taught several undergraduate classes as an adjunct professor. She has multiple national conference publications and presentations to her credit. She also has served as a consultant to several companies, such as NAVAIR Orlando and other small businesses in the Orlando area.

Aleksander P. J. Ellis received his BA in Psychology from Cornell University and his MA and PhD in Industrial and Organizational Psychology from Michigan State University. He is currently an Assistant Professor at the Eller College of Management at the University of Arizona. His publications have appeared in numerous journals, including the *Journal of Applied Psychology, Personnel Psychology,* and the *Academy of Management Journal.* His research interests primarily involve team-effectiveness issues, and his recent work has focused on uncovering the nomological network surrounding the effects of stress in teams.

Katherine Ely is a doctoral student in Industrial and Organizational Psychology at George Mason University. She received her BA in Psychology from the College of William and Mary and her MA from George Mason University. Her research interests include leadership, training, and adaptability.

Theodore L. Gessner received his PhD in Social Psychology from the University of Maryland in 1971. He is an Associate Professor of Psychology at George Mason University. His research interests include anxiety, personality factors in human destructiveness, and sense of humor.

Andrea B. Hollingshead is Associate Professor of Communication in the Annenberg School for Communication at the University of Southern California. Her research concerns knowledge networks in work groups: how people in groups learn, store, retrieve, communicate, and use knowledge from others inside and outside the group. She seeks to identify the factors and processes that lead to effective knowledge sharing in groups including those that are technologically based. Her publications include two books, *Theories of Small Groups: Interdisciplinary Perspectives* (2005, co-edited with Marshall Scott Poole) and *Groups Interacting with Technology* (1994, with Joseph E. McGrath). Her articles have appeared in top-tier journals in the fields of psychology, communication, and management. Professor Hollingshead is currently Senior Editor at *Organization Science* and has served on many editorial boards including *Academy of Management Journal, Journal of Personality and Psychology, Journal of Experimental Social Psychology, Group Processes and Intergroup Relations, Small Group Research* and *Group Dynamics.*

Elizabeth Jacobs earned a master's degree from San Diego State University and is now an applied social psychology doctoral student at Loyola University, Chicago. Her major research interests are procedural justice, group decision making, and minority influence.

Karen A. Jehn is a Professor of Social and Organizational Psychology at Leiden University, the Netherlands. She received her PhD from Northwestern University. Her research interests include group processes, diversity, conflict, lying and deceit in organizations, and political organizing behavior. She has published in *Administrative Science Quarterly, Academy of Management Journal,* and the *Journal of Personality and Social Psychology.*

Richard J. Klimoski is Dean of the School of Management and Professor Psychology and Management at George Mason University in Fairfax, Virginia. His teaching and research interests revolve around the areas of organizational control systems in the form of performance appraisal and performance feedback programs and team performance. His research has appeared in the *Journal of Applied Psychology, Personnel Psychology,* the *Academy of Management Journal,* the *Journal of Management, Administrative Science Quarterly,* and the *Journal of Conflict Resolution.* He is coauthor with Neal Schmitt of *Research Methods in Human Resource Management* (1991) and coeditor with Stephen Zaccaro of *The Nature of Organizational Leadership* (2001). He is also coeditor with Robert G. Lord and Ruth Kanfer of *Emotions in the Work Place* (2002). He is on the editorial review board of *Human Resource Management Review,* and *Organizational Research Methods and Applied Psychology: An International Review Board.*

Steve W. J. Kozlowski is a Professor of Organizational Psychology at Michigan State University. Multilevel theory is at the core of his work, which focuses on the processes by which individuals, teams, and organizations learn and adapt to dynamic complexity. His research has spanned technological innovation, socialization and climate, adaptive performance, leadership, team development and team effectiveness, self-regulated learning, and training effectiveness. Dr. Kozlowski's current research program is focused on three related facets of learning and adaptation: (a) self-regulation, (b) the process of team learning and development, and (c) the active role of team leaders in promoting coherent, adaptive, and effective teams. The goal of this work is to generate knowledge and tools to promote the development of adaptive individuals, teams, and organizations. His work has been published in the leading journals of the field, including the *Academy of Management Journal, Human Performance,* the *Journal of Applied Psychology,* the *Journal of Vocational Behavior, Organizational Behavior and Human Decision Processes, Personnel Psychology,* and *Psychological Science in the Public Interest,* among others. He has published several theoretical chapters relating to his areas of expertise and has coedited books in the SIOP Frontiers Series: *Multilevel Theory, Research, and Methods* and *Learning, Training, and Development in Organizations.* Dr. Kozlowski is an Associate Editor for the *Journal of Applied Psychology* and has served on the editorial boards of the *Academy of Management Journal, Human Factors,* the *Journal of Applied Psychology,* and *Organizational Behavior and Human Decision Processes.* He is a Fellow of the American Psychological Association and the Society for Industrial and Organizational Psychology. Dr. Kozlowski received his BA in Psychology from the University of Rhode Island, and his MS and PhD degrees in Organizational Psychology from The Pennsylvania State University.

Krista L. Langkamer is a PhD student in the Industrial and Organizational Psychology program at George Mason University in Fairfax, Virginia. She is currently working on her dissertation, which is a longitudinal study examining factors that contribute to employee engagement in effective leader self-development activities. Other research areas include leader influences on employee organizational commitment, violated training expectations in relation to psychological contracts, and error-based learning within organizations.

Manuel London is Professor and Director of the Center for Human Resource Management in the College of Business at the State University of New York at Stony Brook. He previously taught at the University of Illinois at Champaign and was a researcher and human resource manager at AT&T. He received his PhD in Industrial and Organizational Psychology from The Ohio State University. His books include *Self and Interpersonal Insight: How People Learn about Themselves and Others in Organizations* (1995), *Leadership Development: Paths to Self-Insight and Professional Growth* (2002), and *Job Feedback: Giving, Seeking, and Using Feedback for Performance Improvement* (2004). He consults with business and government organizations on competency modeling, performance evaluation, employee attitude surveys, and management and career-development programs.

Christopher O. L. H. Porter received his BA in Psychology from Morehouse College. He received his MS in Criminal Justice and PhD in Business Administration from Michigan State University. He is an Associate Professor of Management and Mays Research Fellow at Mays Business School at Texas A&M University. His publications have appeared in a number of journals, including the *Academy of Management Journal*, the *International Journal of Conflict Management*, the *Journal of Applied Psychology*, the *Journal of Management*, and *Police Quarterly*. He also serves on the editorial board at the *Journal of Applied Psychology*. His research interests concern team composition and teamwork, performance appraisals and feedback interventions, workplace fairness, and police performance management.

Etiënne A. J. A. Rouwette holds a master's degree in psychology from Utrecht University, the Netherlands. In 1994, he started working at Radboud University Nijmegen, where he completed his PhD research in November 2003 in the Methodology Department of the Faculty of Management Sciences. At present, he is an associate professor. His research concentrates on the effects of participating in the use of these methods on beliefs, attitudes, and behavior. As part of this research, he participated in and conducted a large number of research projects in profit and nonprofit organizations, such as Dutch Telecom, Corus, Eurocontrol, and TNO Research, as well as a number of Dutch ministries and municipalities. He is a member of the System Dynamics Policy Council and was the local host for the 2006 International System Dynamics Conference. In 1996, 1999, and 2002, he was involved in organizing annual conferences for the International Association of Facilitators.

Joyce Rupert is a PhD student in Social and Organizational Psychology at Leiden University, the Netherlands. Her research interests include group composition, diversity faultlines, conflict asymmetry, and team learning, with a special emphasis on team learning types. She conducts multimethod field research and studies different types of work group entities.

Eduardo Salas is Trustee Chair and Professor of Psychology at the University of Central Florida. He also holds an appointment as Program Director for the Human Systems Integration Research Department at the Institute for Simulation and Training. Previously, he was a senior research psychologist and Head of the Training Technology Development Branch of NAVAIR-Orlando for 15 years. During this period, Dr. Salas served as a principal investigator for numerous R&D programs focusing on teamwork, team training, advanced training technology, decision making under stress, learning methodologies, and performance assessment. Dr. Salas has coauthored over 300 journal articles and book chapters and has coedited 15 books. He is on/has been on the editorial boards of the *Journal of Applied Psychology, Personnel Psychology, Military Psychology, the Interamerican Journal of Psychology, Applied Psychology: An International Journal,* the *International Journal of Aviation Psychology, Group Dynamics,* and the *Journal of Organizational Behavior* and is past editor of *Human Factors* journal. In addition, he has edited two special issues of the *Human Factors* journal, as well as other special issues for *Military Psychology, Journal of Organizational Behavior,* and *International Journal of Aviation Psychology.* He currently edits an annual series, *Advances in Human Performance and Cognitive Engineering Research.*

Dr. Salas has held numerous positions in the Human Factors and Ergonomics Society during the past 15 years. He is the past chair of the Cognitive Engineering and Decision Making Technical Group and of the Training Technical Group, and served on the Executive Council. He is also very active with the Society for Industrial and Organizational Psychology (SIOP). He is the past series editor for the Professional Practice Book Series and has served on numerous committees throughout the years. His expertise includes helping organizations on how to foster teamwork, design and implement team-training strategies, facilitate training effectiveness, manage decision making under stress, develop performance measurement tools, and design learning environments. He is currently working on designing tools and techniques to minimize human errors in aviation, law enforcement, and medical environments. He has consulted to a variety of manufacturing, pharmaceutical, industrial, and governmental organizations. Dr. Salas is a Fellow of the American Psychological Association (SIOP and Division 21) and the

Human Factors and Ergonomics Society. He received his PhD in Industrial and Organizational Psychology from Old Dominion University.

Alicia Sanchez's interests lie in the implementation of games and simulations into a variety of learning environments. Leveraging decades of research in Education and Simulations, her focus lies in the appropriate use of games within curriculum and emerging technologies that continuously redefine the potential of games-based learning options. After completing her PhD with the University of Central Florida's Modeling and Simulation program, she served as a Research Scientist and Educational Cluster Director at Virginia Modeling, Analysis and Simulation Center and recently joined Defense Acquisition University.

Valerie I. Sessa is an Assistant Professor of Industrial and Organizational Psychology in the Department of Psychology at Montclair State University. Prior to MSU, she worked as a Research Scientist and Director at the Center for Creative Leadership. Dr. Sessa has also worked as a consultant in a variety of areas, most recently assessing middle- and high-potential managers using instruments, behavioral assessment centers, and feedback. Consulting activities include Bellevue Medical Center, Ciba-Geigy Pharmaceuticals, Citibank, New York Hospital System, and Xerox. Her research interests include continuous learning at the individual, group, and organizational levels, managing team effectiveness, and executive selection. Her books include *Executive Selection: Strategies for Success* (with Jodi Taylor; 2000) and *Continuous Learning in Organizations: Individual, Group, and Organizational Perspectives* (with Manuel London; 2005). Her research publications have appeared in the *Consulting Psychology Journal, Industrial and Commercial Training, Human Resource Development Review,* the *Journal of Applied Behavioral Science,* the *Journal of Applied Psychology,* and *The Psychologist Manager Journal.* Her work has also appeared in such periodicals as *Business Week, Fast Company,* and *Harvard Business Review.* Dr. Sessa received her BA in Psychology from the University of Pennsylvania and her MS and PhD in Industrial and Organizational Psychology from New York University.

Marissa Shuffler is a doctoral student at the University of North Carolina at Charlotte. She holds an MA in industrial-organizational psychology from George Mason University. She is the 2006–2007 Organizational Science TIAA-CREF Fellow at UNCC and is focusing her research on issues related to leadership and distributed teams. From her previous work as a Consortium Fellow with the Army Research Institute, she is particularly interested in exploring issues of team mental models and shared cognition in association with leadership and team performance in dynamic environments.

Joyce Silberstang is an Assistant Professor of Management and Communications at Adelphi University. She has been advising senior executives on individual, team, and organizational effectiveness for the past 20 years. She specializes in team building and conflict management. Formerly the Director of Organizational Development Services at Burgess Levin & Co., Dr. Silberstang led large-scale change management projects and customer service workshops. As a personnel psychologist with the Department of the Navy, Dr. Silberstang was appointed the Technical Advisor to the Secretary of the Navy Group on Ethics and Character, and the Civilian Leadership Board. Prior to that, she developed crisis management manuals for the U.S. Department of State, and provided training, used in embassies worldwide, on how to negotiate with hostage takers. She also assisted in the development of a customized decision support system for American Red Cross disaster response managers. Dr. Silberstang's workshops on team building, organizational change, leadership and management skills, ethics, and customer service have been taught to more than 21,000 people worldwide. She has presented her research on job satisfaction and retention to academic and business audiences, and has given numerous presentations on teamwork and communications skills. Dr. Silberstang has her PhD in Industrial and Organizational Psychology from The George Washington University and her BA from New York University.

Kevin C. Stagl has partnered with dozens of organizations over the past decade to cultivate lasting business value via targeted human capital management solutions and decision support. In his current role as an Organizational Consultant with Assessment Technologies Group (ATG), and formerly, as a Research Scientist at the Institute for Simulation and Training (IST), Dr. Stagl has had the unique opportunity to learn from and collaborate with an influential list of individuals working on the leading edge of organizational science and practice. At IST, Dr. Stagl, with the guidance of his academic mentors, Drs. Eduardo Salas and Barbara A. Fritzsche, initiated a program of research that spans the spectrum of team issues, with an emphasis on fostering leadership, performance, development, and adaptation. The lessons learned and best practices distilled from this effort have appeared in three dozen scholarly outlets, including the *Journal of Applied Psychology, Leadership Quarterly, Organizational Frontiers Series, Research in Multilevel Issues,* and the *International Review of Industrial and Organizational Psychology.*

Sarah Stawiski is a doctoral candidate in the Applied Social Psychology program at Loyola University, Chicago. Her research interests include group processes within an organizational context. Specifically, she is interested in ethical climate and its effect on decision making at the group level. She teaches courses in social psychology, research methods, and industrial and organizational psychology.

R. Scott Tindale is a Professor of Psychology at Loyola University, Chicago. His major areas of research include small-group performance, socially shared cognitions, individual and group decision making, and social influence in groups. He is an associate editor of the *Journal of Personality and Social Psychology: Interpersonal Relations and Group Processes and Group Processes and Intergroup Relations* and has coedited six books and two journal special issues on various aspects of applied social psychology or group processes.

Jac A. M. Vennix holds a PhD from Nijmegen University. He is Professor of Research Methodology in the Department of Management of Nijmegen University. The main focus of his research is on managerial decision making in complex systems and (computer-based) tools for decision support. Research interests and areas of expertise include system dynamics computer simulation, problem structuring methodologies, scenario analysis, and group decision support systems. For his work in the field of system dynamics, he received the Jay W. Forrester Award in 1999. In addition, his paper "Group Model Building" (1999) was selected as one of the 76 most influential papers on "systems thinking" since the beginning of the field. He has guest lectured at MIT's Sloan School of Management, SUNY Albany, the London Business School, the University of Bergen, the University of Palermo, Nijenrode University, TIAS Business School, and SIOO. Over the years, he has conducted a large number of research projects for a variety of profit and nonprofit organizations, such as Royal Dutch Shell, Royal Dutch Airlines, Dutch Telecom, Corus, DSM, Eurocontrol, and the Royal Dutch Medical Association, as well as a number of Dutch ministries and municipalities.

David Wilemon is Snyder Professor of Innovation Management in the Whitman School of Management at Syracuse University. He cofounded the Snyder Innovation Management Research Center and the Entrepreneurship & Emerging Enterprises Program. He also is a cofounder of the international organization, the Product Development and Management Association (PDMA). He is an active researcher in the areas of corporate ventures, product development, project management, and high-performing teamwork. He was selected as the Syracuse University Scholar/Teacher of the Year and also received the Outstanding Teacher/Researcher award within the Whitman School of Management. He was recently named as one of the most prolific authors in the management of innovation and technology management field by *R&D Management Journal*. His research has appeared in the *Academy of Management Journal*, the *Journal of Marketing, Project Management Journal, California Management Review, Sloan Management Review, Columbia Journal of World Business, Transactions on Engineering Management*, the *Journal of Product Innovation Management, Technology & Engineering Management*, and *R&D Management*.

Sandra A. Wolverton received her BBA in Finance from the University of Texas at Austin. She is a doctoral student in the Department of

Management at Mays Business School at Texas A&M University. Her research interests include individual differences, ethics, and leadership in teams.

Stephen J. Zaccaro is a Professor of Psychology at George Mason University, Fairfax, Virginia. Previously, he served on the faculty of Virginia Polytechnic Institute and State University, and the College of the Holy Cross. He received his PhD in Social Psychology from the University of Connecticut. He has been studying, teaching, and consulting about teams and leadership for over 25 years. He has written over 100 articles, book chapters, and technical reports on group dynamics, team performance, leadership, and work attitudes. He has written *The Nature of Executive Leadership: A Conceptual and Empirical Analysis of Success* (2001) and coedited three other books, *Occupational Stress and Organizational Effectiveness* (1987), *The Nature of Organizational Leadership: Understanding the Performance Imperatives Confronting Today's Leaders* (2001), and *Leader Development for Transforming Organizations* (2004). He has also coedited a special issue of *Group and Organization Management* on the interface between leadership and team dynamics, and special issues of *Leadership Quarterly* on individual differences and leadership. He has directed funded research projects in the areas of team performance, shared mental models, leader-team interfaces, leadership training and development, leader adaptability, and executive leadership. He has consulted for projects on developing leader assessment tools, constructing leadership-training systems, and on measuring performance in human–robot team systems. He is also an experienced leadership coach.

Norhayati Zakaria is Assistant Professor at the Universiti Utara Malaysia in the Department of International Business, Faculty of International Studies. She received her PhD in Information Science & Technology from Syracuse University, her MSc in Information Transfer from Syracuse University, her MSc in Management of Technology from Rensselaer Polytechnic Institute, and her Bachelor's in Business Administration at Universiti Utara Malaysia, Malaysia. She has been engaged for many years in research pertaining to issues of cross-cultural and intercultural communication and its impact on the effectiveness of managing expatriates, building effective cross-cultural training, and global virtual teams and the use of computer-mediated communication technologies. She has also published in numerous journal articles, book chapters, and conference proceedings related to her field of expertise. She is currently an affiliated researcher in the Collaboratory on Technology Enhanced Learning Communities (Cotelco), a research laboratory located in Syracuse University that is built on the concept of "collaboration without walls." As a researcher, she brings her expertise in cross-cultural and intercultural communication issues by addressing concerns for designing and implementing culturally sensitive IT applications when building collaboratories for geographically distributed collaboration. Her ongoing research program includes impact of cultural values on the effectiveness of global virtual teams, cultural perspective on building credibility and trust when using the Internet for e-business, and testing and building new cross-culturally attuned theory for understanding globally distributed collaboration.

SECTION

I

How Groups Learn and What They Learn

This first section provides a view of how groups learn as well as a few samples of what groups learn. We introduce the book in the first chapter by describing our model of groups as learning systems. Propensity to learn depends on the triggers (pressures and opportunities) in the environment within and outside the group and the group's readiness to learn (its openness to new ideas, sensitivity to others, and stage of development). We define three types of learning: (a) Adaptive learning is making changes in reaction to environmental stimuli. (b) Generative learning is seeking and sharing new knowledge and information and applying it in new and different ways. (c) Transformative learning is making a major shift in group membership, goals, operations, and/or outcomes. We propose that generative learning and transformative learning require groups to be ready to learn and triggered to learn. The model suggests how groups learn to be adaptive, generative, and transformative. Overall, the approach has implications for designing interventions to improve group learning and performance at different stages of group development. After briefly reviewing this model, we raise the needs that led to this book—understanding groups as systems, identifying what groups learn, determining variables that affect group learning, exploring interventions that improve group learning, applying assessment methods to measure group outcomes and evaluate learning, and seeing whether this theory and research has value from a practitioner's perspective.

Kozlowski and Bell (chapter 2) develop a theoretical perspective on team learning, development, and adaptation. They describe emergent phenomena: how group-level properties emerge from member characteristics, conditions, tasks, and interactions. They examine different forms of emergence depending on these factors. They consider group cognitive and knowledge-based outcomes, motivation and behavioral competencies, and how these are linked to forms of emergence. They describe a multilevel, multiple-goal-regulation process for individual and group learning (multilevel multiple-goal regulation). Finally, they describe how groups compile a repertoire of capabilities through exploration and experimentation.

While Kozlowski and Bell focus on group learning from an emergent perspective, in the third chapter, Arrow and Cook consider group learning from a complex adaptive systems (CAS) perspective viewing learning as a dynamic process that is part of the interplay of change, stability, and structure in the group system. They integrate concepts such as fitness landscapes, attractors, and control parameters into a multilevel model of adaptive learning. They conceptualize group learning as a set of multilevel assessment, diagnosis, adjustment, and evaluation processes. For instance, they ask whether rewards are structured properly at the individual and group level? Is the group adapting to environmental changes and do we understand the group's learning needs in order to make adjustments to be successful? Does the group have a meaningful strategy for learning? What interventions will foster learning? Does the group have a system for monitoring its progress? Has the group increased its flexibility and learning capacity?

In the fourth and fifth chapters, we offer two examples of outcomes of group learning. In the fourth chapter, Tindale, Stawiski, and Jacobs consider how groups develop shared cognitions. They discuss what is currently known about shared cognitions in groups and how they affect learning and performance. Shared cognitions come from prior experiences and common context of group members. The group's actual experience builds on this foundation to further shape and reinforce a shared mental model. Members develop a common conceptualization of the task, how they work together, and the environment.

Ellis, Porter, and Wolverton (chapter 5) build on the concept of emerging shared cognitions by describing the development of transactive memory systems in groups. Members learn about each other's skills and expertise and how to draw on this when needed, particularly as unexpected situations emerge. They develop a directory of information about group members as individuals and about their capacity to work together. Not all group members need to know everything—they only need to know where to fine necessary information. The chapter reviews antecedents of transactive-memory systems and outcomes that may result from a fully functioning transactive-memory system.

CHAPTER

1

Group Learning: An Introduction

VALERIE I. SESSA
Montclair State University

MANUEL LONDON
State University of New York at Stony Brook

Groups are increasingly being called upon to make important decisions within organizations. Individuals need to learn to be group members—that is, move from a collective of individuals to a cohesive unit focused on the same goals and understanding of the methods used to achieve those goals. Groups often need to learn how to structure themselves, communicate with other groups, conduct work processes, make decisions, and put these decisions into action. As the organizational context shifts, groups must be fluid enough to shift with them—restructuring, adapting decisions, and updating plans. Groups and their members need to learn continuously or they will find themselves standing still in a continuously changing environment. This first chapter examines how successful groups learn, with an emphasis on factors that determine team readiness for learning, team-learning mechanisms (adaptive, generative, and transformative), and relationships between individual, group, and organizational learning. We set the stage for the other chapters in the book by exploring the need to understand factors affecting and enhancing group learning and ways to assess changes in group learning over time.

THE MEANING OF GROUP LEARNING

The purpose of most groups in organizations is to do work—to create something, manage a project, provide or deliver a product or service, work with customers, do research, solve a problem, or make a decision. Groups are expected to get work done efficiently and effectively, on time, and under budget. Two or more individuals comprise a group. Group members often differ in knowledge, skills, abilities, functions, expertise, and background and are brought together to work interdependently on a task because it is assumed that this is an efficient or better use of resources to get work done than having one person do the task alone. Group members are expected to know how to work together and get the group's work accomplished and often how to interact using a variety of options from face-to-face meetings to different-time-different-place technologies around the world. At different points in time, they are expected to be able to do different sorts of tasks such as define a problem, brainstorm, gather data, and evaluate alternatives.

Groups do not exist to learn, and often the idea of learning falls by the wayside unless the group finds that it is failing in some regard in fulfilling its purpose. However, learning is important in every aspect of group work and occurs whether the group members, the group leader, the group itself, or even the organization know or acknowledge it. Consider these examples: An internationally dispersed team receives a complaint from a valued customer while the group leader is on vacation. Without much discussion, the group restructures so that the highest-ranking group member from the nearest company location contacts the customer and passes the information on to group members who are beginning their workday in another part of the world. That subgroup works to solve the problem and recontacts the customer from across the world. The irate customer is satisfied. The group mentions it to its leader when she comes back from vacation but never really discusses it. However, group members find themselves using a similar process during another customer intervention. An architectural firm realizes that learning and using a new computer program is no longer a luxury but a necessity. The firm is losing its competitive edge and beginning to lose customers. Despite reluctance by the two senior architects, every architect in the small firm learns the new computer program and begins using it regularly—even the two senior members. The firm slowly regains its competitive advantage and wins a local award for one of its designs. A product-development team in a high-tech firm works night and day for months to launch a new doll that "learns" using a computer chip in time for Christmas. The doll is appealing to young girls—an unfilled niche in the marketplace. The doll is a hit and sells out during the holiday season and team members are excited about their accomplishment. The group is now expected to manage the product. The group quickly realizes that despite having the same members, it needs to change or transform completely from a product-development team into a product-management team. In each of these situations, some sort of learning has occurred. However, we typically only recognize the architectural firm as having engaged in learning.

In today's competitive workplace, the savvy group leader needs to know what group learning is, when it is needed, when it is occurring, and even how to harness it for the benefit of the group. Group learning includes learning how to be a group and how to do things, acquiring knowledge, skills, and behaviors, and learning how to become a whole new entity in order to survive. Groups learn how to take the fragmented outputs of each individual member, pool them, and over time, integrate them in a way that the individuals in the group could not do working alone (Kasl, Marsick, & Dechant, 1997). Groups that work effectively in organizations have learned and continue to learn ways to enhance their interactions, detect and correct errors, exploit opportunities, and meet or exceed standards of quantity, quality, and timeliness of performance (Hackman & Wageman, 2005). Groups that work less effectively are learning as well. For instance, they struggle to find smooth ways of interacting, fail to detect and correct errors (or correct errors in ways not in line with organizational needs), exploit opportunities that are self-serving rather than taking into account the needs of the organization, or have learned not to do anything risky so that they attract little attention. Some groups even learn not to learn.

GROUP AS A LIVING SYSTEM

Group learning has been defined in a variety of ways. It has been viewed as an aggregate of individual learning (Druskat & Wheeler, 2003; Ellis et al., 2003). According to this view, group learning occurs when individual group members create, acquire, and share unique knowledge and information. Group learning has been defined as a process in which a group takes action, obtains and reflects upon feedback, and makes changes to adapt or improve (Drach-Zahavy & Somech, 2001; Edmondson, Bohmer, & Pisano, 2001). Feedback allows the group to recognize the effects of its actions and choices and, if need be, to change those actions and choices over time to have a different effect (Locke & Latham, 1990). According to this perspective, group learning is assumed to occur when a group engages in behaviors such as asking questions, seeking feedback, experimenting, reflecting, and discussing options and errors. Another view is that group learning is a dynamic process in which learning processes, the conditions that support them, and group "behaviors" change as the group learns (Argote, Gruenfeld, & Naquin, 1999; Kasl et al., 1997; Sessa & London, 2006). For example, Kasl et al. (1997) suggested that groups progress from fragmented, individualistic behaviors to synergistic, group-as-a-whole interactions that foster continuous learning.

In line with this third view, a group can be viewed as an open, living system that continuously interacts with its environment (London & Sessa, 2006a, 2006b; Sessa & London, 2006). We use this analogy of the group as a living system as a heuristic to help conceptualize how groups learn. Although groups and organizations are social systems designed for a specific purpose and may follow a structured process with members having designated roles, many groups, particularly those that are unstructured, take on the characteristics of complex, living systems (Arrow, McGrath, & Berdahl, 2000; Capra, 2002; Senge, Scharmer, Jaworski, & Flowers, 2000). As such, a group may be thought of as a system with input, process, output, and feedback components. *Living* systems have three additional characteristics. First, they are self-organizing through their interactions with the environment. That is, living systems maintain and renew themselves (even forming new structures and new patterns) using energy and resources from their surroundings. Second, living systems are both closed and open. That is, they have forms or structures that remain stable as information, materials, or viewpoints are transformed. Third, living systems have an organizing activity or process involved in the continual embodiment of the system's pattern of organization and structure (Capra, 1997; Miller, 1978).

Living systems, whether individuals, groups, or organizations, exist to do work (Jaques, 2002). They (living systems) typically do not exist to learn, but they learn naturally as they work, and they can't help learning (Jaques, 2002). A group's purpose or work consists of three elements: (a) to complete group projects, (b) to fulfill member's needs, and (c) to maintain the structure and the integrity of the group as a system (Arrow et al., 2000). Thus, a group has some sort of goal or desired state it strives to achieve. It moves toward the desired state by coordinating members, tools, and tasks, processing information and generating meaning, managing conflict and developing consensus, and motivating, regulating, and coordinating group members' behavior. It monitors itself to determine whether it is moving toward its desired state (Kasl et al., 1997). Also, it has procedures to change direction if there is a gap between where it currently is and the goal it is trying to achieve (Arrow et al., 2000).

Group learning includes both the process of acquiring new ways of interacting, skills, knowledge, worldviews, and the changed outcome such as changing communications patterns between team members, standard operating procedures, and behavioral routines (Sessa & London, 2006; see also Argote, Gruenfeld, & Naquin, 2001). We define group continuous learning as a deepening and broadening of the group's capabilities in (a) (re)structuring to meet changing conditions, (b) adding and using new skills, knowledge, and behaviors, and (c) becoming an increasingly sophisticated system through feedback and reflection about its own actions and consequences (Sessa & London, 2006; London & Sessa, 2007).

Group learning is intertwined with individual and organizational learning. To fully understand group learning necessitates a multilevel perspective that examines characteristics, factors, and processes that unfold at the individual, group, and organizational levels. Individuals, groups, and organizations can be thought of as a nested hierarchy of living systems. Individuals are embedded in groups, and groups in organizations (Arrow et al., 2000). Individual members, the groups of which they are members, and their organizations are learning—at once and continuously. Individual members may influence the groups to which they belong to learn. Organizations may influence groups within them to learn. Groups respond to outside pressures, challenges, and opportunities and to the insights and motivation of the members.

Thus, while groups learn for themselves as they work (others cannot learn for them), individuals and organizations can stimulate and facilitate group learning. Outside forces disturb the group's status quo and thereby stimulate learning. However, as living systems, groups choose the forces or disturbances that get their attention, and they decide how to respond. Outside forces can facilitate or hinder learning, but here again, groups determine how to respond (Capra, 2002). In the end, groups learn when they perceive a need to learn, and they apply that learning when they see an opportunity. Because learning is driven by the group and cannot be wholly predicted, it can lead to unexpected outcomes such as forming dysfunctional habits of interaction that are counterproductive when new goals or tasks arise.

A MODEL OF CONTINUOUS GROUP LEARNING

In previous works (Sessa & London, 2006; London & Sessa, 2006a, 2006b; London & Sessa, 2007, in press), we articulated a theory of continuous group learning. We review this briefly here. Group learning is the emergence of revised and new patterns of interaction to increase the group's performance. Triggers for learning include external forces—pressures or opportunities that impinge on the group. Pressures might be tight deadlines, high demands and expectations, limited resources, and so forth. Opportunities may be the reverse. Triggers for learning can also be internal pressures, such as the group leader or one or more members' exuberance, capabilities, or desire to get the group to try something new—a new goal, activity, or method of production, for instance. Readiness for learning includes the group members' openness to new ideas, sensitivity to forces within and beyond the boundaries of the group, and desire to learn. These are also group characteristics as the individual members engage in and reinforce openness, boundary permeability, and mastery learning. Also at the group level, readiness to learn is a function of the group's maturity—for instance, knowledge of each other's capacity to contribute to the group and experience working with each other. Groups in which members feel a sense of interpersonal trust (psychological safety) will be more open to sharing knowledge, expressing ideas, developing those ideas, and testing out new patterns of interaction.

Triggers for learning and learning readiness prompt three types of learning: (a) adaptive, (b) generative, and (c) transformative. Adaptive learning is making an adjustment in the way members work together in response to a pressure or opportunity. The change might happen almost automatically without much thought. If triggers are high and readiness is low, then adaptive learning is likely. The group makes an adjustment in response to a change in the environment and moves on. That adjustment will continue as needed until the environment changes such that the adjustment no longer works. Generative learning is seeking new knowledge and information, learning new skills, and then finding new ways to apply it. Generative learning is mastery learning. There may be an immediate instrumental value or not. In our model, we argue that generative learning happens when there are triggers for learning and when the group is ready to learn. It can occur without triggers, as when individual members acquire new knowledge and skills and educate other members. However, receptivity will be higher when there are triggers to prompt the learning and when members are ready to learn. Transformative learning is making significant changes in the structure, goals, and/or operations of the group. Similar to generative learning, we hypothesized that transformative learning would occur only when there are strong triggers in the environment that demand transformation and when the group is ready to learn. If the triggers are present but readiness is not, the group is likely to ignore, misinterpret, or in other ways rationalize away the triggers and fail to seek new directions.

To summarize, our hypotheses boiled down to the following statements:

1. Low Triggers + Low Readiness = Little learning needed or accomplished
2. High Triggers + Low Readiness = Adaptive Learning
3. Low Triggers + High Readiness = Generative Learning possible
4. High Triggers + High Readiness = Generative Learning; Potential for transformative learning.

Adaptive learning can be functional, but probably not when the group needs to make a major change. Interventions for learning focus on ways to help the group recognize triggers, increase its readiness to learn, and then facilitate adaptive, generative, and/or transformative learning. The group can increase its awareness of the environment largely by analyzing information and examples of what is happening elsewhere. Group readiness can be increased by introducing group members to each other early on so they have similar perceptions of each other's background and ability to contribute to the group task (interpersonal congruence). Teambuilding exercises (e.g., icebreakers or games) can promote interpersonal trust. Training group members to brainstorm helps them understand the difference between generating ideas and evaluating them and teaches them how to encourage other members to express creative ideas and accept feedback about group behavior from outside sources. The group leader or facilitator can promote adaptation by making suggestions or asking group members for suggestions about ways to alter goals or operations. Ways to promote generative learning include giving and receiving feedback, teaching group members new skills, asking group members to instruct each other, and trying new methods and tracking their success. Ways to promote transformative learning include holding discussions about group process (asking members to reflect on how they feel about the group, barriers to learning, and ways they might improve their working relationships), obtaining benchmark information about changes other organizations have made, learning experimental and data-collection methods to assess change, and agreeing to take chances recognizing possible risks and gains in the short and long run.

Groups under less pressure or that are less prepared to learn will learn to adapt. Groups that learn to be generative engage in continuous learning. As they engage in generative learning, they learn to be generative—that is, they reinforce each other's generative behavior. At times, they may adapt. At other times, a transformation may be in order. Groups that have transformed learn to be transformative and are more likely to engage in transformative learning in the future. A basic goal of group facilitation is to enhance awareness of triggers, increase the group's readiness to learn, and train the group in generative and, if needed, transformative interactions.

SETTING THE STAGE: WHAT WE NEED TO KNOW ABOUT GROUP LEARNING

We began organizing this book by asking some general questions, such as, How do groups learn? What do they learn? What affects group learning, in particular, the context in which they learn? What interventions increase group learning? How can we assess whether and what groups are learning? Also, is the theory and research on group learning useful from a practitioner's viewpoint, and what are the implications of our knowledge in this area for future research and practice? Answering these questions led to the four sections of this book.

In this first section on how groups learn and what they learn, we started by analyzing how groups learn as well as a few samples of what they learn. An apt model seemed to be the group as a dynamic, open system that is continuously learning. To start with, a group consists of individual systems—that is, the members. The group is also a system in its own right. Moreover, the group is a system within a larger, organizational system. In the next chapter, Kozlowski and Bell (chapter 2) discuss how a group's knowledge and skills emerge over time and are shaped by the context, the leader, the members' characteristics, interaction among members, and the group's interactions. In the third chapter, Arrow and Cook take a multilevel, systems perspective in understanding groups as complex learning systems. They describe how group leaders and members guide the process of system change and introduce innovations that increase group learning. They argue that group learning occurs at the intersection of individual and organizational learning. Cross-learning dynamics suggest that undirected learning at one level will block learning at another. For example, if members do not acquire new interaction skills, the group is not likely to learn interaction patterns that rely on these skills. Learning is exchanged between levels to promote group development.

The remaining two chapters in this section address two outcomes of group learning. Tindale, Stawiski, and Jacobs (chapter 4) examine how groups, as processing systems, acquire information and establish a shared cognition that contributes to an optimal level of performance and aids in the group consensus process. Group members learn about the nature of the task they are performing and how the group operates. Ellis, Porter, and Wolverton (chapter 5) describe how groups develop a transactive memory system that explains how individuals in close relationships divide their combined workload. The members learn who in the group has specific expertise and how the group members can best work together. They can draw on this knowledge as situations change and unexpected conditions arise. Therefore, everyone in the group does not have to know everything, and the group does not have to start from scratch every time the context changes. Group members capitalize on distributing information efficiently and effectively within the group through information allocation and retrieval coordination.

Next, we wanted to address what factors influence group learning. We asked Jehn and Rupert (chapter 6) to describe the concept of group faultlines, which are hypothetical dividing lines that split a group into relative homogeneous subgroups based on the group members' alignment along one or more attributes. This is a way to explain the effects of group composition on group performance. Jehn and Rupert introduce a new learning typology of social learning that relates group faultlines to types of learning and how potential moderators, such as psychological safety and error culture, affect group learning. Porter (chapter 7) examines how groups develop a mastery learning orientation, focusing on generative learning rather than learning to accomplish a specific objective. Just as individual group members may be mastery learning, the group overall can learn to be generative, acquiring and sharing information, knowledge, and skills and then applying this new learning in new ways.

Culture and leadership are other factors that need to be taken into account in understanding group learning. Zakaria, Amelinckx, and Wilemon (chapter 8) deal with how groups work across cultures and distance in virtual environments. They describe global virtual groups whose members come from different geographical locations, may not have a common background, are organizationally dispersed, collaborate using asynchronous and synchronous technologies, and often assemble on an ad-hoc basis. These groups use new modes of learning and develop new patterns of knowledge sharing, communication, and social exchange in a computer-mediated team environment. Zaccaro, Ely, and Shuffler (chapter 9) examine the central pathways that group leaders follow to promote learning. They argue that leaders need to foster synergistic group processes that promote collective learning. Leaders can help the group learn performance regulatory processes, such as goal setting, performance monitoring, and feedback. They can develop task-related abilities that further the team's performance and development. The authors provide a systematic integration of leadership behaviors and strategies that foster group learning.

In section 3, we explore learning interventions. Some interventions focus on learning "in situ" while others focus on off-line training interventions. Burke, Salas, and Granados (chapter 10) place group learning as the fourth and final phase of their adaptive cycle within their group adaptation model. In the adaptive cycle, groups recognize a cue from the environment suggesting a need for adaptation. They formulate and execute a plan to adapt and finally learn from their adaptation. Using this model, authors focus on the question, "How can this information be used to delineate the methods and tools by which teams can learn from ongoing experience and in the process move one step closer to adaptive team performance and the corresponding distal outcome of team adaptation?" They focus on more novel available methods to do so "in situ" including storytelling, action learning, and communities of practice. Rouwette and Vennix (chapter 11) describe how groups learn as they work on messy problems. Groups are often called upon to handle complex problems that are defined differently by different members of the organization. Some members may not even perceive that there is any difficulty. They describe Problem Structuring Methods (PSMs) that structure and integrate information, help a group reach a decision, create commitment to specific actions, and tie these methods into relevant group learning theory.

Examining collaboration in online groups, Brandon and Hollingshead (chapter 12) apply collaborative learning concepts to online organizational groups. They show how groups become learning entities using information communication technologies (ICTs). These include commonplace Internet-communication technologies (e.g., e-mail, Websites, newsgroups) and more specialized information/knowledge-management tools (e.g., groupware, intranets, Lotus Notes). Cannon-Bowers, Bowers, and Sanchez (chapter 13) examine synthetic learn environments (SLEs) as vehicles for group training. These are simulations, games, and virtual worlds that are technology-enabled instructional systems. They provide instruction by augmenting, replacing, creating and/or managing a learner's experiences. They use realistic content and embed deliberate synthetic experiences and instructional features that enhance learning and performance.

Silberstang and Diamante (chapter 14) conclude this section by describing interventions that build general (transportable) group competencies and context-specific competencies that are related to specific situations groups face. Transportable competencies include conflict resolution, collaborative problem solving, communication, goal setting, and performance management. The chapter describes "phases" of a group's life cycle, and offers guidelines on the type of intervention groups can use during each cycle.

In the fourth section, we turn to assessment of group learning. Stagl, Salas, and Day (chapter 15) review the identification and measurement of group-learning outcomes. Outcomes may be affective, behavioral, and cognitive. Affective states include group efficacy, potency, and cohesion. Behavioral outcomes include a wide range of competencies that are reflected in group interactions, such as information sharing, giving and seeking feedback, brainstorming, and distribution of work. Cognitive outcomes may be knowledge of group methods, individual capabilities, and effective work processes (transactive memory systems) which can help coordinate members, solve problems, and make decisions in the future. Gessner, Langkamer, and Klimoski (chapter 16) suggest how to design research and measure variables for rigorous assessment, that is, research that gives us confidence in making inferences about learning.

REFERENCES

Argote, L., Gruengeld, D., & Naquin, C. (2001). Group learning in organizations. In M. E. Turner (Ed.), *Groups at work: Theory and research* (pp. 369–412). Mahwah, NJ: Erlbaum.

Arrow, H., McGrath, J. E., & Berdahl, J. L. (2000). *Small groups as complex systems*. Thousand Oaks, CA: Sage.

Capra, F. (1997). *The web of life: A new scientific understanding of living systems*. New York: Anchor Books.

Capra, F. (2002). *The hidden connections*. New York: Doubleday.

Drach-Nahavy, A., & Somech, A. (2001). Understanding team innovation: The role of team processes and structures. *Group Dynamics: Theory, Research, and Practice*, 5(2), 111–123.

Druskat, V. U., & Wheeler, J. V. (2003). Managing from the boundary: The effective leadership of self-managing work teams. *Academy of Management Journal*, *46*(4), 435–457.

Edmondson, A. C., Bohmer, R. M., & Pisano, G. P. (2001). Disrupted routines: Team learning and new technology implementation in hospitals. *Administrative Science Quarterly, 46,* 685–716.
Ellis, A. P. J., Hollenbeck, J. R., Ilgen, D. R., Porter, C. O. L. H., West, B. J., & Moon, H. (2003). Team learning: Collectively connecting the dots. *Journal of Applied Psychology, 88*(5), 821–835.
Hackman, J. R., & Wageman, R. (2005). A theory of team coaching. *The Academy of Management Review, 302,* 269–288.
Jaques, E. (2002). *The life and behavior of living organisms: A general theory.* Westport, CT: Praeger.
Kasl, E., Marsick, V. J., & Dechant, K. (1997). Team as learners: A research-based model of team learning. *Journal of Applied Behavioral Science, 33,* 227–246.
Locke, E. A., & Latham, G. P. (1990). *A theory of goal setting and task performance.* Englewood Cliffs, NJ: Prentice-Hall.
London, M., & Sessa, V. I. (2006a). Group feedback processes. *Human Resource Development Review, 5,* 303–329.
London, M., & Sessa, V. I. (2006b). Continuous learning in organizations: A living systems analysis of individual, group, and organization learning. In F. J. Yammarino, & F. Dansereau (Eds.), *Research in multi-level issues* (Vol. 5, 123–172). Greenwich, CT: Jai Press.
London, M., & Sessa, V. I. (in press). How groups learn, continuously. *Human Resource Management Journal.*
London, M., & Sessa, V. I. (2007). *The development of group interaction patterns: A dynamic, mid-level model of group learning.* Working paper. SUNY-Stony Brook.
Miller, R. B. (1978). The information system designer. In W. T. Singleton (Ed.), *The analysis of practical skills* (pp. 278–291), Baltimore: University Park Press.
Senge, P., Scharmer, C. O, Jaworski, J., & Flowers, B. S. (2000). *Presence: Human purpose and the field of the future* (pp. 5–7). Cambridge, MA: Society for Organizational Learning.
Sessa, V., & London, M. (2006). *Continuous learning: Directions for individual and organization development.* Mahwah, NJ: Erlbaum.

CHAPTER

2

Team Learning, Development, and Adaptation

STEVE W. J. KOZLOWSKI
Department of Psychology, Michigan State University

BRADFORD S. BELL
School of Industrial and Labor Relations, Cornell University

Increasing environmental turbulence driven by technological change, the challenges of globalization, clashes of culture, and political turmoil increasingly buffet organizations and upset their routines—often unexpectedly. Such change is not merely continuous—it is metamorphic, discontinuous, and unpredictable—placing a premium on organizational adaptability as a means for organizations to survive such disruptions and even thrive on the edge of chaos. Over the last two decades, organizations have responded to this turbulence by developing networks and alliances with other organizations, flattening structures, and reorganizing work around teams to push decisions closer to the problem source, decrease response time, and increase flexibility.

Work teams

> (a) are composed of two or more individuals, (b) who exist to perform organizationally relevant tasks, (c) share one or more common goals, (d) interact socially, (e) exhibit task interdependencies (i.e., workflow, goals, outcomes), (f) maintain and manage boundaries, and (g) are embedded in an organizational context that sets boundaries, constrains the team, and influences exchanges with other units in the broader entity. (Kozlowski & Bell, 2003, p. 334)

Although teams are often viewed as a means to enable organizational adaptability (Devine, Clayton, Phillips, Dunford, & Melner, 1999; Lawler, Morhman, & Ledford, 1995), it is important to recognize that merely restructuring work around teams rather than clusters of individual jobs does not ensure that effective and adaptive teams will be created. Indeed, many efforts to organize work around teams yields "phantom" teams of individuals working in parallel that, with process loss (Steiner, 1972), actually impedes performance and flexibility; a cluster of individuals that is a team in name only. A team-based work structure makes sense when no one person can accomplish the task and information, distinctive knowledge or expertise, and effort need to be coordinated. On the other hand, we do not mean to imply that teams are purely collective and holistic entities that are somehow disconnected from or independent of the characteristics of the members that compose them. Individuals possess a range of characteristics (Pulakos, Arad, Donovan, & Plamondon, 2000) that can influence team learning and adaptation, but that is not the focus of this chapter.

The creation of an adaptive team necessitates learning the capabilities that underlie team performance, developing collaboration and coordination skills to effectively combine member resources, and adapting capabilities, coordination, and performance to meet unexpected and novel challenges (Kozlowski, Gully, Nason, & Smith, 1999). It is a process of knowledge and skill compilation among team members that is shaped by organizational system factors that characterize the context (e.g., top-down influences), by actions of the team leader (e.g., team-level factors), and by interactions among members (e.g., bottom-up emergence) as the team develops its capabilities over time. Thus, our perspective is a multilevel one that simultaneously considers individuals—the team, its embedding task, and organizational context—and the interplay among these multiple levels over time as team adaptive capabilities develop, emerge, and manifest.

Our purpose is to explore conceptually these themes centered on team learning, development, and adaptation. We note at the onset that this chapter is not a comprehensive review of the literature. Indeed, solid conceptual and empirical work on these themes are sparse relative to the vast amount of work on team effectiveness more generally, and therefore a thematic set of topics that are ripe for conceptual development and integration (Kozlowski & Bell, 2003; Kozlowski & Ilgen,

2006). We draw on an ongoing stream of theory development and research in these areas to integrate and sculpt a distinct perspective on team learning, development, and adaptation.

We begin with a discussion of the nature of emergent phenomena; that is, how team-level properties emerge from the perceptions, knowledge, feelings, actions, and interactions among individuals (Kozlowski & Klein, 2000). The factors that determine the nature of emergence are directly relevant to conceptualizing team learning in terms of emergent states (Marks, Mathieu, & Zaccaro, 2001) or developmental outcomes (e.g., collective knowledge representations, cognitive structures) and dynamic processes (e.g., learning and development). Here we would note that the literature has been far more fascinated with conceptualizing team-learning outcomes or emergent states than with the processes by which collective knowledge is acquired and crystallized. Our primary purpose in this section is to establish that qualitatively different forms of emergence related to team performance and effectiveness are driven by the organizational system context, the team task, and resulting workflow interdependencies that link members. This is key to understanding the implications for the nature of team-learning outcomes and processes.

In the next section, we briefly review outcome representations of team learning with a particular focus on cognitive or knowledge-based outcomes and also a consideration of motivational states and behavioral competencies, and how different outcomes are linked to differing forms of emergence. Because this literature has been subject to extensive reviews (e.g., Ilgen, Hollenbeck, Johnson, & Jundt, 2005; Kozlowski & Bell, 2003; Kozlowski & Ilgen, 2006) and is covered elsewhere in this volume, in this chapter, we merely summarize, highlight, and inform.

We then turn attention to the processes underlying team learning, development, and adaptation. We first consider the "engine" for individual and team learning; that is, a psychological process of learning that underlies both individual and team learning and performance—multilevel multiple-goal regulation (DeShon, Kozlowski, Schmidt, Milner, & Wiechmann, 2004). We then address the "vehicle" for team development and adaptation; that is, developmental experience in the team context. Team compilation is a process that yields knowledge and skill outcomes at the individual and team levels and as team skills compile; exploration and experimentation by the team yields a repertoire of capabilities and response alternatives that enable team adaptability (Kozlowski et al., 1999).

Finally, we close with a brief consideration of some ways to enhance team learning, development, and adaptation. We consider how training experiences can be embedded in work systems and how team training, simulations, and other forms of "synthetic experience" can provide an infrastructure for team (and organizational) learning (Kozlowski, Chao, & Nowakowski, in press). We also consider the critical role of team leaders as shapers and developers of adaptive teams (Kozlowski, Watola, Nowakowski, Kim, & Botero, in press). Considered together, the distinct theory and research streams that we weave constitute an integrated perspective on the nature of team learning, development, and adaptation.

THE NATURE OF EMERGENCE

Our intent in this section is to sketch three fundamentals in our consideration of team learning, development, and adaptation as emergent phenomena. Emergence is a bottom-up and interactive process. It is shaped and constrained by the organizational and team task context, and it is patterned in different ways—which is to say that it can manifest in different forms. (See Kozlowski & Klein, 2000; Morgeson & Hoffman, 1999 for more detailed discussions.)

Bottom Up and Interactive

Kozlowski and Klein (2000) defined emergence as follows: "A phenomenon is emergent when it originates in the cognition, affect, behaviors, or other characteristics of individuals, is amplified by their interactions, and manifests as a higher-level, collective phenomenon" (p. 55). Applied to team learning, there are key assumptions inherent in this definition of emergence.

First, learning is a psychological change that takes place within the person and, thus, is fundamentally an individual-level property (Kozlowski & Salas, 1997). Individuals acquire a knowledge of facts (e.g., declarative knowledge) and they link the application of facts to enabling conditions (e.g., procedural knowledge) and, with experience, develop strategic knowledge to guide prioritization and resource allocation (Anderson, 1987; Ford & Kraiger, 1995), which ultimately impact performance. However, individuals do not learn in a social vacuum, and this is especially true in team contexts that also embody task exchanges. People share and exchange information, ideas, knowledge, and insights. They do so as informal social communication, as formal aspects of workflow interdependence, and as deliberate efforts to prompt knowledge acquisition, learning, and behavior change in teammates. Thus, products of individual learning are transmitted through a variety of social psychological mechanisms, such as vicarious observation, communication, exchange, collaboration, and deliberate coaching, so that they propagate across team members and emerge as a collective phenomenon.

Second, team learning embodies aspects of both process *and* structure. The nature of the process by which learning is transmitted has critical implications for the structure of the construct that emerges at the team level. At the individual level, learning is a process of psychological change that yields knowledge and skill (structure). Team learning results from a process of emergence as individual level knowledge and skill intersect, amplify, and compile to yield team-level manifestations of collective knowledge and skill (Kozlowski et al., 1999). Hence, we will treat team learning as a phenomenon with structure and process aspects, considering each aspect in turn.

Shaped by the Context

Patterns of interaction among individuals are shaped and constrained by a variety of organizational and team characteristics. With respect to team learning, proximal linkages among members within teams are largely dictated by workflow interdependencies that yield team performance. Such linkages pattern exchanges of information, knowledge, and skills needed to "get work done." In that sense, learning is more likely to propagate along direct, frequent, and proximal linkages in the network of workflow. Exchange linkages for boundary spanners—those members connecting between teams—also provide a conduit for knowledge and learning to flow into and out of a unit. Although we view these formal work-based linkages as the primary means for patterning the emergence of team learning, we acknowledge that informal social exchanges based on friendship or propinquity (but not workflow) also play a role (Campbell, 1959; Rentsch, 1990).

For example, Fig. 2.1 illustrates a range of workflow patterns that range from simple to complex—pooled, sequential, reciprocal, and team network (Van de Ven, Delbeq, & Konig, 1976). For pooled teams, one would expect team learning, if it emerges at all, to be patterned by friendship or proximity, since there are no real workflow links among members. For sequential teams, learning would tend to propagate across adjacent links and in one direction. For reciprocal teams, propagation

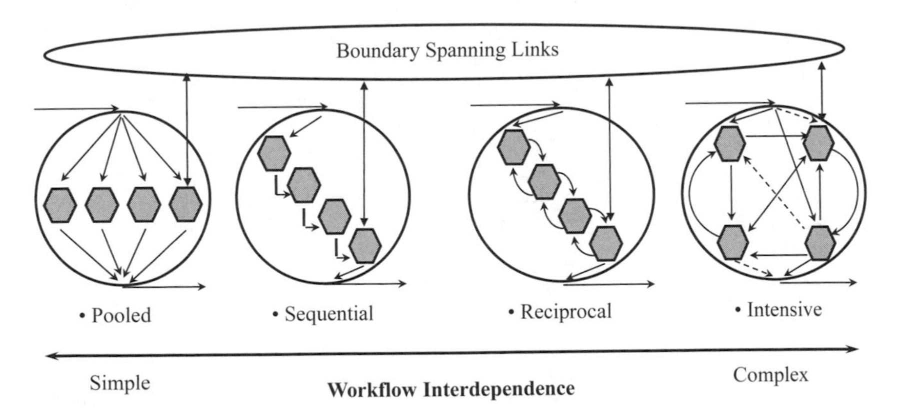

Figure 2.1 A continuum of team task workflow.

could be more uniform and bidirectional, whereas for team networks, centrality, transaction alternatives, and frequent contacts would pattern exchanges and, hence, the emergence of team learning.

Variable in Process and Form

Depending on the nature of the patterns of interaction and exchange that link members to the phenomenon of interest, emergence is not fixed but variable in form. In other words, "collective phenomena may emerge in different ways under different contextual constraints and patterns of interaction. Emergence is often equifinal, rather than universal in form" (Kozlowski & Klein, 2000, p. 59). As shown in Fig. 2.2, Kozlowski and Klein (2000) characterized two qualitatively distinct forms of emergence—composition and compilation—that anchor opposite ends of a quasi-continuum of emergence types that we can apply to our consideration of team learning.

The composition form of emergence pertains to a phenomenon that emerges via convergent processes in which the same elemental content is shared across team members. Composition captures essentially the same construct at the individual and team levels of analysis. Such a construct is structurally equivalent (e.g., is composed of the same elemental content) and functionally equivalent (e.g., performs the same role in a

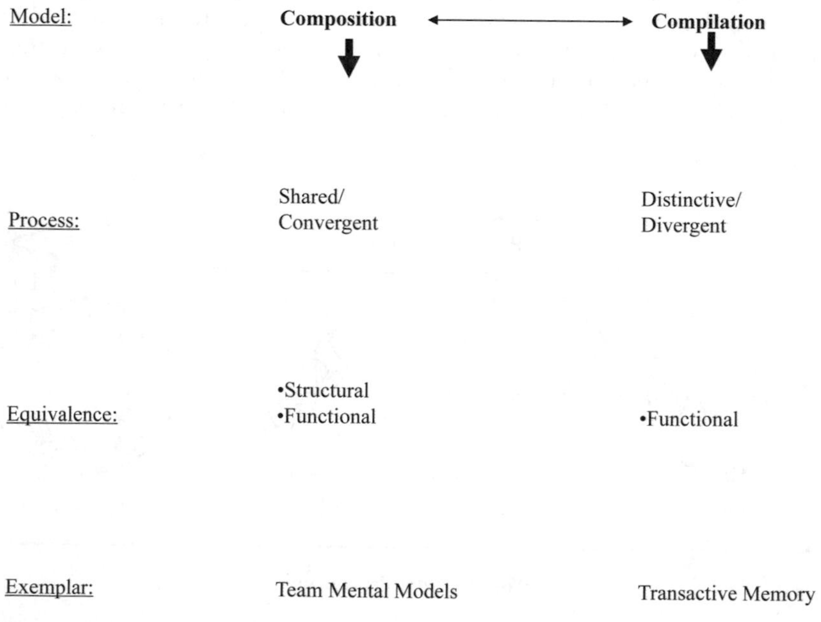

Figure 2.2 Composition and compilation forms of emergence.

model-linking constructs) at both levels of analysis (Kozlowski & Klein, 2000; Morgeson & Hofmann, 1999).

With respect to team learning, for example, researchers have postulated that team members develop shared mental models of the team, task, equipment, and interaction pattern that enable better coordination (Cannon-Bowers, Salas, & Converse, 1993). In this conceptualization, team members share *identical knowledge*, which should enable them to anticipate one another's needs and actions and, indeed, several research studies evidence such effects (Kozlowski & Bell, 2003).

The compilation form of emergence characterizes a phenomenon that emerges via a divergent process in which different elemental content held across team members forms a patterned whole. Like the nodes and links of a network or the pieces of a puzzle, each element is unique and yet combines to form a meaningful whole. Compilation captures a construct that is functionally equivalent, but not structurally equivalent across levels (Kozlowski & Klein, 2000; Morgeson & Hofmann, 1999).

Therefore, for example, researchers have suggested that team members may form a distributed and networked memory system—transactive memory—in which members hold distinctive knowledge and share knowledge of each member's unique expertise that enables the team to collectively access knowledge when needed (Mohammed & Dumville, 2001). Individuals do not share the same knowledge (e.g., elemental content) and therefore transactive memory is not structurally equivalent, but the team-level memory system performs a similar role in models and thus is functionally equivalent across levels. In this conceptualization, it is the configuration or pattern of distinct team-member knowledge that comprises the team-memory system.

This section has highlighted the distinction between composition and compilation processes of emergence, discussed their links to the team context (especially its workflow structure), and described their implications for the multilevel structure of the outcomes of emergence. We now turn our attention to consider in more detail the emergent states that represent outcomes of team-learning processes. We then consider team-process dynamics that give rise to collective emergent states and learning outcomes more directly.

TEAM LEARNING AS EMERGENT STATES OR OUTCOMES

In this section, we briefly review the outcome representations of team learning, with a particular focus on cognitive and knowledge-based outcomes that represent the most salient manifestations of learning as a psychological process. However, we also discuss a selective set of motivational states and behavioral capabilities that can be developed through team-learning processes and facilitate team performance and adaptability. It is important to note that our focus in this section is on the emergent outcomes that indicate that team learning has taken place, not on the learning process per se. The next section will detail the multilevel processes that underlie team learning and skill development and yield the emergent outcomes we discuss here.

We begin this section with a discussion of team climate and its role as an enabling condition for team learning. Although not an outcome of team learning per se, it is important to highlight the importance of team climate as a cognitive-contextual factor that shapes team learning through its impact on social interactions among team members. We then turn attention to several cognitive and knowledge-based emergent outcomes that have been prominently featured in prior research as indicators of team learning. Finally, we conclude with a brief discussion of a few key motivational and behavioral manifestations of team learning. As noted earlier, because this literature has been subject to many extensive reviews, our purpose is a focused discussion of these emergent states as key indicators of team learning distinct from the team-learning processes that will be examined in the next section.

Team Climate

Team climate represents cognitively based, collective perceptions of important contextual features that can influence team functioning and effectiveness (Kozlowski & Bell, 2003). One important implication of collective climates is that they characterize the "strategic imperatives" (Schneider, Wheeler, & Cox, 1992) of the organizational and team context. Kozlowski and Hults (1987), for example, showed that a shared organizational climate that emphasized the strategic imperative to stay technically current and innovative predicted individual performance, updating activity, and job attitudes among engineers in technological firms. In a recent study, Bunderson and Sutcliffe (2003) examined the relationship between management team members' climate perceptions of learning, what they referred to as team-learning orientation, and business-unit performance. They argued that, "A team learning orientation reflects a shared perception of team goals related to learning and competence development; goals that guide the extent, scope, and magnitude of learning behaviors pursued within a team" (p. 553). Their results revealed that an appropriate emphasis on learning, relative to the team's recent performance, could have positive consequences for team effectiveness. These examples highlight the role of team climate in establishing learning as a strategic imperative.

Team climates can also reflect the interpersonal context within a team, which can have important implications for the sharing and exchange of information, ideas, knowledge, and insights. Edmondson (1999), for example, examined how team learning is influenced by team psychological safety, which she defined as a shared belief that the team is safe for interpersonal risk taking. She argued that team psychological safety should facilitate learning behaviors, such as feedback seeking and experimentation, because it alleviates excessive concern about others' reactions to actions (e.g., mistakes) that have the potential for embarrassment or threat. Indeed, her results showed that team psychological safety positively influenced team-learning behaviors, which in turn influenced team performance. Smith-Jentsch, Salas, and Brannick (2001) also provided evidence that a supportive team climate is important for facilitating positive-learning behaviors. Specifically, the authors showed that trainees' transfer behavior was influenced by their perceptions of the team-transfer climate, or the degree to which a particular group of teammates accepts and expects the use of behaviors learned in a training program. It is important to note that in both of these studies the team leader had a significant influence on perceptions of the team climate.

Collective Knowledge

Conceptually, changes in a team's collective knowledge represent a direct indication that team learning has taken place. However, Kozlowski and Ilgen (2006) noted that team learning as an outcome is rarely assessed directly and instead is typically inferred from changes in team performance. For example, in a laboratory-based setting, Argote, Insko, Yovetich, and Romero (1995) examined the impact of individual turnover and task complexity on team learning. The authors found that group performance exhibited a learning curve, with output increasing significantly at a decreasing rate over six trials. Turnover and task complexity were both detrimental to group performance, with the detrimental effect increasing as groups gained experience, suggesting that turnover depleted aspects of collective knowledge. However, the problem with this approach is that many of the factors that influence team learning (e.g., turnover) are also likely to impact team performance via mechanisms other than learning. As a result, it is impossible to distinguish changes in team performance that are due to changes in a team's collective knowledge from those that result from changes in other team processes critical to team effectiveness. Thus, there is a need for research that directly measures changes in individual and team knowledge or provides some other direct evidence that learning has occurred (Ellis & Bell, 2005; Kozlowski & Ilgen, 2006).

A second important issue surrounding collective knowledge concerns the implications of different methods used to aggregate individual knowledge to create a team-level construct. A common approach is to operationalize collective knowledge as either the sum or average of individual team members' knowledge. Ellis et al. (2003), for example, assessed collective knowledge and skill by summing the effectiveness and efficiency with which individual team members prosecuted unknown tracks. Teams that were more effective and efficient on average could be inferred to have shared information or learned from one another. However, a focus on the average or sum of individual team members' knowledge does not provide insight into the distribution or pattern of content knowledge within the team. For example, the extent to which team members possess common or unique content knowledge influences the breadth of the team's information pool or the proportion of the total knowledge space covered by the team's collective knowledge (Hinsz, 1990). In addition, how a team's collective knowledge influences team performance may depend on who within the team knows what. Ellis, Bell, Ployhart, Hollenbeck, and Ilgen (2005) showed that the declarative knowledge of critical team members, or those most central to the workflow activities of the team, had a greater impact on team performance than the knowledge held by less critical team members. In the following sections, the distributional properties of collective knowledge are considered in more detail as we discuss team mental models and transactive memory. However, as Kozlowski and Ilgen (2006) noted, this raises the question as to whether team learning as a knowledge-based outcome can be meaningfully distinguished from mental models and transactive memory.

Team Mental Model

Team mental models are team members' shared, organized understanding and mental representation of knowledge about key elements of the team's task environment (Klimoski & Mohammed, 1994). Cannon-Bowers et al. (1993) outlined four content domains underlying team mental models: (a) knowledge of equipment and tools utilized by the team (equipment model); (b) understanding about the team's task, including its goals or performance requirements and the problems facing the team (task model); (c) awareness of team member characteristics, such as their knowledge, skills, preferences, and habits (member model); and (d) team members' understanding of or beliefs regarding appropriate or effective team processes (teamwork model).

Research in this area has tended to focus on the formation of common or shared team mental models as an important indicator of team development. Indeed, numerous studies have provided evidence that shared mental models are associated with team effectiveness (e.g., Marks, Mathieu, & Zaccaro, 2001; Mathieu, Heffner, Goodwin, Salas, & Cannon-Bowers, 2000; Minionis, Zaccaro, & Perez, 1995). However, there is growing recognition that team members do not necessarily possess identical knowledge structures, but possess some shared cognition and some unique structural information that is compatible with that of other member roles (e.g., Banks & Millward, 2000; Kozlowski, Gully, Salas, & Cannon-Bowers, 1996). This conceptualization of mental models takes into consideration the distributional properties of team knowledge discussed earlier. The shared and complementary cognitions emerge from both composition and compilation processes, involving the exchange of information, ideas, knowledge, and insights within a team over time. This exchange may occur through a variety of mechanisms, including informal social interaction, shared task experiences, and formal intervention. Shared and complementary cognitions provide a foundation for essential teamwork capabilities. Specifically, this shared comprehension, often referred to as team coherence, enables a team to adapt to variations in the task environment and to maintain synchronicity without explicit directives (Kozlowski, Gully, McHugh, et al., 1996). This sharing represents an integration of task work and teamwork capabilities.

Transactive Memory

Transactive memory is a group-level shared system for encoding, storing, and retrieving information that is distributed across group members (Wegner, 1986, 1995; Wegner, Giuliano, & Hertel, 1985). The concept was introduced to explain how intimate relationships foster the development of shared memory. In essence, each partner uses the other as an external memory aid and in so doing becomes part of a larger system. In a team context, each team member maintains a registry of other members' expertise, directs new information to appropriate team members, and accesses needed information from others in the system (Mohammed & Dumville, 2001).

Transactive memory offers teams the advantage of cognitive efficiency, because individual memories become more specialized and are organized into a differentiated collective memory. The knowledge specialization that develops in a transactive memory system should reduce the cognitive load on individuals, expand the pool of collective expertise, and decrease redundancy of effort (Hollingshead, 1998a, 1998b). A study by Austin (2003) identified the specialization of knowledge and accuracy of knowledge identification as two important dimensions of transactive memory that relate to team effectiveness. However, there are limits to the size of such a distributed memory system and errors can occur as individuals update and retrieve information in the system (Wegner, 1986; Pearsall, Ellis, & Bell, 2006). Further, there are time lags involved in acquiring needed information from the system, which can be detrimental to team effectiveness in time-critical situations (Kozlowski & Bell, 2003).

Nonetheless, the emergence of transactive memory systems is an important manifestation of team-learning processes. Transactive memory systems develop as a team gains experience and members communicate and update information each has about the areas of others' knowledge. Liang, Moreland, and Argote (1995), for example, compared the performance of groups whose members were trained individually to that of groups whose members trained together. Groups whose members were trained together outperformed groups whose members were trained individually, presumably due to the operation of a transactive memory system. A subsequent study by Moreland, Argote, and Krishnan (1996) showed that subjects who were trained in one group and performed in another exhibited inferior performance to subjects who trained and performed in the same group. This finding suggests that it is the experience of working with particular group members that develops transactive memory systems (Argote et al., 2001). Some work also suggests that face-to-face interaction is important for the emergence of transactive memory and that computer-mediated communication presents barriers (Hollingshead, 1998b; Lewis, 2003).

Behavioral Capabilities and Motivational States

In addition to the cognitive and knowledge-based outcomes just discussed, changes in a team's behavioral capabilities or motivational states can indicate that learning has taken place. In this section, we provide a focused examination of how team learning may manifest in several noncognitive, team-level emergent outcomes.

Prior research has identified three key behavioral capabilities that influence team effectiveness: (a) coordination, (b) cooperation, and (c) communication (Kozlowski & Bell, 2003). Coordination and cooperation are related in that both focus on the interdependence of team members' activities, although coordination possesses a temporal component that cooperation does not. Similarly, communication is often viewed as a means of enabling coordination and cooperation. The emergence of these behavioral capabilities can be directly linked to the intersection and integration of team members' knowledge and skills. Evidence suggests, for example, that teams that share and exchange their knowledge and information will be better equipped to coordinate their actions and be "in sync." Mathieu et al. (2000) examined the influence of shared mental models on team process and performance. In the study, the team process measure consisted of three dimensions: (a) strategy formation and coordination, (b) cooperation, and (c) communication. Their results indicated that the convergence, or sharedness, of team members' mental models was positively related to team process. Further, they found that both task and team mental models had unique effects on team process. In a study using a tank-battle simulation, Marks et al. (2000) also found a significant and positive relationship between the similarity of team members' mental models and the quality of team communication processes. As noted earlier, transactive memory systems can also enhance team process and performance by promoting specialization and reducing redundancy of effort (Hollingshead, 1998b).

Given that these behavioral capabilities have been positively linked to team performance (e.g., Guastello & Guastello, 1998; Stout, Salas, & Carson, 1994), their emergence is likely to also be accompanied by an increase in team efficacy. That is, the development of shared cognitions and coordinated action patterns should facilitate team performance and goal progress. A reduction in goal-performance discrepancies should increase the shared belief in the team's collective capability to organize and execute courses of action required to produce given levels of attainment. This pattern would be consistent with the notion that just as enactive mastery contributes to individual self-efficacy, teams who experience performance successes and master difficult challenges should experience higher levels of efficacy (Bandura, 1997; Kozlowski et al., 1999). The challenge, however, is linking changes in team efficacy directly to team learning and not simply spurious improvements in team performance. This necessitates a closer examination of the self-regulatory processes that underlie team learning, which we address in the next section.

TEAM-LEARNING PROCESSES AND ADAPTATION

The prior section addressed the emergent manifestations of team learning; the collective knowledge, motivational states, and behavioral capabilities that indicate learning has occurred. Here we consider the team *processes* underlying learning and skill development that occur over time to yield collective-learning outcomes.

Basic Assumptions

There are three central points that shape our perspective on team learning. First, it is axiomatic that learning, as a psychological process, occurs within the individual. Second, although learning is fundamentally an individual-level phenomenon, team learning occurs in a task and social context that shapes what is learned and how it is learned. Third, team learning is a process that unfolds dynamically through repeated interactions and engagements over time, thereby yielding emergent outcomes signaling that learning has occurred. Thus, key to our conceptualization of team learning is to (a) first understand individual learning processes in the context of a team task *and* how individual leaning processes yield parallel team-learning processes, and (b) then to understand how individual knowledge, skills, and other capabilities compile and emerge at the team level over time.

We describe the first aspect of this conceptualization as *multiple goal, multilevel regulation,* which is based on basic psychological theories addressing the self-regulation of learning, motivation, and performance and on the principles of multilevel theory (DeShon et al., 2004). The multiple-goal, multilevel regulatory process constitutes the engine of team learning.

We describe the second aspect of this conceptualization as *team compilation,* which is based on theories of team development and on the principles of multilevel theory (Kozlowski et al., 1999). Team compilation processes capture qualitatively distinct team-member capabilities as they develop over time and emerge across levels—individual, dyadic, and team—as collective capabilities. Team compilation constitutes the vehicle for team development and adaptation.

Multiple-Goal, Multilevel Regulatory Process

Models of self-regulation reference goals as mechanisms for directing attention and effort, and strategies as ways to direct the process of goal striving. Progress toward goal accomplishment is monitored, discrepancies revealed via feedback are diagnosed, and goals and strategies are revised in an iterative process directed toward performance improvement and goal accomplishment. Over time, this process of goal striving accounts for individual learning, skill acquisition, and performance (Bandura, 1991; Locke & Latham, 1990). This general model has amassed considerable support in the literature (Karoly, 1993).

Moreover, theorists have asserted that the process of self-regulation can be extended to the team level to account for team learning, skill acquisition, and performance (Kozlowski, Gully, McHugh, et al., 1996; Kozlowski et al., 1999; Kozlowski, Gully, Salas, et al., 1996; Zaccaro, Rittman, & Marks, 2001). In support of this assertion, recent research has developed and validated a multiple-goal, multilevel model of individual and team regulation (DeShon et al., 2004).

Although most research on self-regulation has focused on individuals striving to achieve a single goal, being on a team means that individual members have to regulate their cognitive, motivational, and behavioral resources around multiple goals, both individual and team. Although theorists have asserted that the process of self-regulation can be extended to the team level to account for team learning, skill acquisition, and performance, the process of how individuals dynamically allocate their resources around multiple goals has been a research focus. Moreover, the fact that individuals allocate attention and effort around multiple goals in the team context means that regulatory processes in teams are multilevel. Yet, most research about team learning and performance either focuses only on the individual level, ignoring the nesting of individuals within the team context, or on the team level as a collective, ignoring the distinctive contributions of individuals to the team.

The conceptualization developed by DeShon et al. (2004) treated team regulation, learning, and performance as parallel, multilevel phenomena. They considered the team task as embodying a discretionary structure (Steiner, 1972) consistent with the most general type of team task in which team members have latitude in terms of *how* and *how much* of their personal resources they allocate to accomplish team performance. This team-task structure requires team members not only to strive to achieve their own goals, but also to coordinate effort and provide assistance to other team members to accomplish related but distinct team objectives. Individual team members have to make resource-allocation decisions that balance individual goal striving while also contributing to the team by coordinating collective effort or backing up a teammate.

DeShon et al. (2004) first conceptualized the influence of these multiple goals— individual and team—on the goal-feedback loops underlying the regulation of individual attention and the allocation of behavioral resources. Fig. 2.3 illustrates a heuristic model of the interdependent goal-feedback loops that underlie individual and team-resource allocation. In this heuristic, the distinct individual and team goals and their associated feedback loops vie for behavioral control, and both goal-feedback loops cannot be influenced simultaneously; individual and team performance are distinct resource allocations. The individual goal-feedback loop monitors discrepancies between current performance and individual goals and activates behavioral outputs to reduce the discrepancy. The team-feedback loop operates on the individual's team goals to activate behavioral outputs to reduce team-level discrepancies. Because individual and team performance is distinct, the behavioral output from each of the feedback loops affects the performance levels being regulated by the other feedback loop. Minimizing discrepancies on one loop will typically yield larger discrepancies on the other loop. In addition, the nature of the situation or surrounding environmental context and changes in the context may sensitize individuals to one loop or the other by increasing the salience of discrepancies on that loop. In other words, situational factors may bias resource allocation toward either the team or individual level.

Next, the dynamic self-regulatory implications of the multiple-goal resource allocation model were extrapolated over time to develop a multilevel model that captured regulatory processes at both the individual and team levels. The multilevel regulation model is shown in Fig. 2.4. The essential characteristics required to validate a multilevel

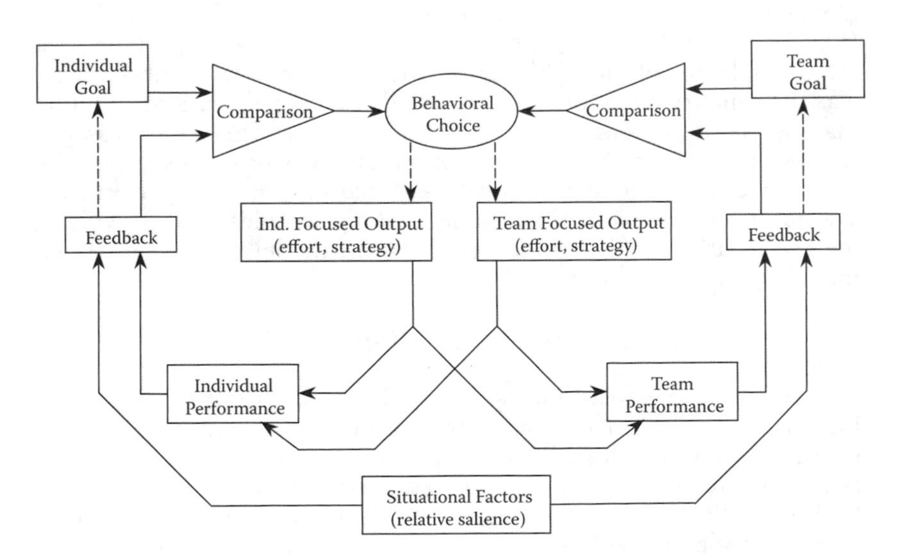

Figure 2.3 Multiple goal regulation: Individual and team goal-feedback loops.

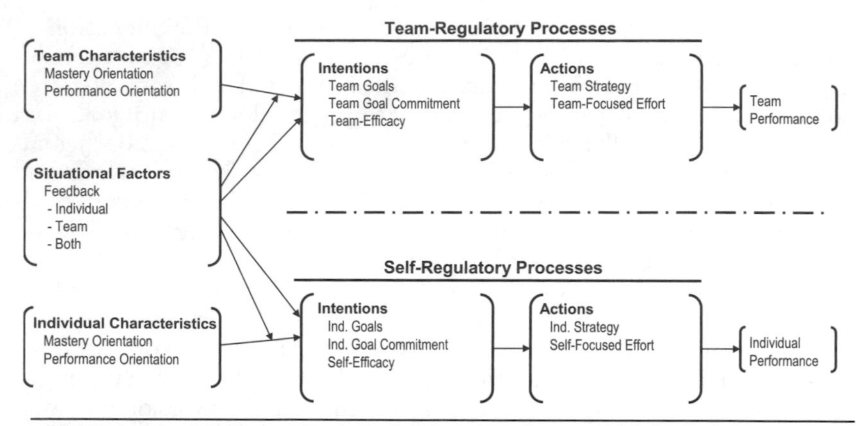

Figure 2.4 A multilevel homology of individual and team regulatory processes.

model are (a) that team-level constructs, conceptually parallel to those at the individual level, satisfy statistical criteria to support composition or aggregation to the team level, and (b) that the linkages among parallel constructs at both levels demonstrate functional equivalence or configural invariance (Kozlowski & Klein, 2000). In an experimental design that examined 237 trainees organized into 37 teams of three, DeShon et al. (2004) provided empirical support for the multiple-goal (Fig. 2.3), multilevel (Fig. 2.4) models. Of particular importance, the relative salience of either the individual or team goal-feedback loops was the primary factor driving individual resource allocations and, ultimately, manifestations of team learning and performance. In essence, the research demonstrated that the key regulatory processes responsible for individual resource allocation, skill acquisition, and performance also substantially hold at the team level. This provides validity evidence for the multiple-goal, multilevel-regulation model as a basic process model that accounts for team learning.

Team Compilation

Whereas multiple-goal, multilevel regulation constitutes the psychological engine of team learning, team compilation constitutes the emergent process by which such learning manifests as collective capabilities that enable teams to adapt to the unexpected. Kozlowski and colleagues (1999) applied a process perspective to develop a normative model of team compilation with self-regulatory underpinnings that integrates learning, team development, and team performance perspectives with the principles of multilevel theory. Their theoretical framework is characterized by three key conceptual features that center on (a) episodic task cycles, (b) temporal development with attention to distinct learning content and outcomes as development progresses, and (c) transitions in the focal level of learning and development.

First, task dynamics are viewed in terms of cyclical task episodes. Task cycles capture the effects of multiple task episodes and the individual and team regulatory processes discussed previously that energize individual and team learning. Variations in task episodes or cycles prompt individual regulatory processes, providing experiences for learning and skill acquisition (Kozlowski, Gully, McHugh, et al., 1996; Kozlowski, Gully, Salas, et al., 1996; Marks et al., 2001). With repeated experiences, skill acquisition in the team context begins to shift from individual regulation to multiple-goal, multilevel regulation (DeShon et al., 2004). This enables the compilation process.

Second, developmental processes and transitions capture the compilation of knowledge and skills. This is partly modeled on the way individual expertise is acquired. As novices make the transition to experts, they progress through a series of learning phases during which their knowledge and skills compile into qualitatively different forms—declarative, to procedural, to strategic (Anderson, 1987; Ford & Kraiger, 1995). Similarly, team capabilities improve developmentally, thereby prompting transition to more advanced phases of skill acquisition that entail distinct learning content and outcomes.

Third, team compilation is viewed as an emergent multilevel phenomenon. In a team context, knowledge and skill compilation have emergent manifestations at multiple levels of analysis. Knowledge, skills, and performance capabilities compile across focal levels from an individual self-focus to a focus on dyadic workflow exchanges to a focus on developing an adaptive team network. Team members transition from a focus on the self (e.g., What do I need to do to perform my task?) to a focus on those teammates with whom they have a direct link (e.g., With whom do I exchange inputs and outputs?) to focus on the team as an entity (e.g., How do we coordinate and adapt?). Teams become self-regulating and adaptive entities.

As shown in Fig. 2.5, the theory postulates four phase transitions as a set of individual team members develop into an adaptive team across content domains and levels. In the first phase, team formation, team members are socialized to the team as an entity, yielding outcomes of interpersonal knowledge and team orientation, providing a foundation for shared norms, goals, and climate perceptions. As they transition to the next phase, task compilation, team members acquire task knowledge, yielding outcomes of task mastery and self-regulation skills. The focal level transitions to dyads in the fourth phase, role compilation, as team members identify their role sets, negotiate role exchanges, and develop routines to guide task exchanges. In the last phase, team compilation, the focal-level transitions to team members develop a reconfigurable network of role linkages that enable incremental improvement

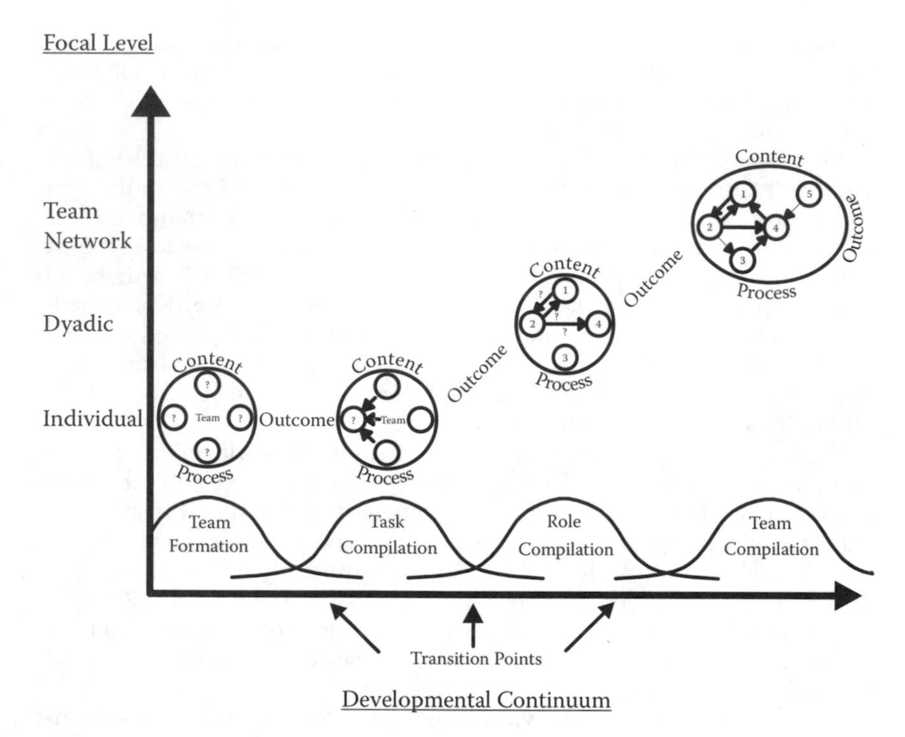

Figure 2.5 A process model of team compilation.

for routine tasks and capabilities for adaptation to novel and unexpected demands. Although there are no direct tests of the theory, it is synthesized from a diverse literature. Moreover, DeShon, Kozlowski, Schmidt, Wiechmann, and Milner (2001) provided preliminary support for the basic proposition that developmental shifts in focal level from individual to team contribute to team performance adaptability.

ENHANCING TEAM LEARNING, DEVELOPMENT, AND ADAPTATION

Our conceptualization of team learning as an emergent multilevel regulatory process means that interventions designed to influence and improve team learning should target the nature, focus, and quality of regulation at the individual and team levels of analysis. Here we highlight two primary types of interventions—training systems and team leadership—with high potential for enhancing team-learning processes and outcomes. Although theory and research in these two areas of theory and research are largely distinct in the literature, we believe that they have high potential for integration and will be increasingly entwined in the future as organizations focus on building an infrastructure to promote collective learning (Kozlowski, Chao et al., in press).

Training Systems

Many different training techniques can be used to deliver training to teams and to team members. Indeed, because both the delivery of individual knowledge and skills (e.g., task work), as well as the team skills that enable coordination (e.g., teamwork) are required, any number of techniques are potentially relevant. We do not intend to provide an exhaustive treatment. Readers are directed to Salas and Cannon-Bowers (1997) for a more complete summary of methods and approaches for training team members and teams.

Rather, consistent with our conceptualization of team learning as a process, we focus on techniques that have the potential to influence the nature, focus, and quality of self- and team regulation. Moreover, many scholars have suggested that teams learn best by doing (Dyer, 1984); that is, through practice and guided experiences that emulate their task and its performance setting. Thus, we focus on techniques that selectively stimulate regulatory processes and allow training to be delivered through computer simulations and/or are embedded in workplace technology systems to create synthetic learning environments (Cannon-Bowers & Bowers, in press; Kozlowski, Toney et al., 2001).

Note that although the *content* for knowledge and skill acquisition differs for individual (e.g., task work) and team (e.g., teamwork) training, the *principles* for designing an instructional experience (Cannon-Bowers & Bowers, in press) and stimulating the underlying regulatory processes (Kozlowski, Toney, et al., 2001) are largely the same. It is the same whether the training is delivered under simulated conditions or is embedded in a technology system that augments learning during real-time task performance. Thus, we do not make specific distinctions between individual and team training or embedded and synthetic training with regard to selectively stimulating regulation and sequencing instructional phases.

Cannon-Bowers and Bowers (in press) defined *Synthetic Learning Environments* (SLEs) as "… a variety of technology-based training media or approaches that have as an essential feature the ability to augment, replace, create and/or manage a learner's actual experience with the world by providing realistic content and embedded instructional features" …. [that include] simulations, games and virtual worlds" (p. 2). Drawing on an integrative review of instructional design by Sugure and Clark (2000), they proposed six instructional phases that need to be addressed in the design of an SLE: (a) articulate and clarify the instructional goals and supports for motivation and learning strategies, (b) instill declarative knowledge (knowledge of task facts), (c) create practice experiences to translated declarative knowledge to procedural skill, (d) monitor trainee progress, (e) diagnose trainee deficiencies, and (f) present appropriate feedback, adapt training, or give remediation. They then reviewed the literature and identified interventions that can be used to accomplish each of these instructional objectives for SLE design.

The theoretical model developed by Kozlowski, Toney et al. (2001) to guide the design of embedded and simulation-based training integrates these instructional objectives (Cannon-Bowers & Bowers, in press; Sugure & Clark, 2000) within the process of learning and adaptation. The model developed by Kozlowski and colleagues uses self-regulation as its core theoretical process. The basic logic of their design approach is that a training strategy is constructed from a combination of distinct training components—training design, information provision, and trainee orientation—designed to actively influence the self-regulation process. Training design refers to the nature of the experiences, such as practice experiences, simulation scenarios, or experiential exercises that are emulated by a simulation or embedded in a work technology system. This incorporates factors such as practice variability (e.g., the extent to which the goals, problem, or scenario complexity varies or is fixed), sequencing (e.g., the extent to which the goals, problem, or scenario complexity scaffolds skill acquisition), and scenario complexity (e.g., difficulty, interconnections, and dynamics). *Information provision* refers to the way that feedback information can be presented to shape how trainees interpret and calibrate their prior progress and whether it guides them to influence future self-regulatory focus, effort, and strategies. *Trainee orientation* references motivational frames, such as goal orientation, that affect the way the trainee perceives the training experience as one of mastering the task for its own sake or performing well relative to others (Dweck, 1986).

Experimental research has been supportive of the utility of this approach for constructing interventions that enhance self-regulatory processes during simulation-based training, with subsequent effects on learning (e.g., basic and strategic knowledge), performance (e.g., basic and strategic performance), and performance adaptation (see Bell & Kozlowski, in press, for a review summary). Although this work has been conducted at the individual level, given the findings of DeShon et al. (2004), its use of regulatory processes as the core theoretical process suggests that the design logic can be extend across multiple levels to encompass the team level. Indeed, work by Chen, Thomas, and Wallace (2005) examined how multilevel regulatory processes (individual and team) accounted for the relationship between outcomes at the end of training and subsequent performance adaptation during transfer. Their work represents an integration and extension of this regulation-based perspective on team learning and training, and further supports its applicability and promise.

The key distinction for team training is the shift from a primary focus on individual task proficiency to a focus on competencies that enable members to combine their expertise, information, resources, and effort to collectively accomplish the team task. For instance, team self-correction training has been identified as one strategy for fostering the development of team mental models (Blickensderfer, Cannon-Bowers, & Salas, 1997). By training team members on skills such as monitoring one another and exchanging feedback, team self-correction training leverages key elements of information provision to influence collective interpretation of the team's prior progress and planning for the future. Cross-training is another strategy that has received significant attention as a means of enhancing team processes. Marks, Sabella, Burke, and Zaccaro (2002), for example, found that positional modeling, which entails both verbal discussion and observation of different team members' roles, enhanced the development of shared team-interaction models. A somewhat different strategy for enhancing team process is teamwork-skills training, which focuses on providing individuals with the generic teamwork skills necessary across a variety of team and task settings (Salas & Cannon-Bowers, 1997). A recent study by Ellis et al. (2005) showed that generic teamwork-skills training enhanced individuals' declarative knowledge of teamwork competencies. Further, teams composed of trained members evidenced higher levels of planning and task coordination, collaborative problem solving, and communication.

A recent meta-analysis by Klein et al. (2005) of the effectiveness of team training techniques provided insights into techniques that evidence effectiveness for improving team processes, performance, and affective reactions. The team-training strategies with a sufficient number of studies to examine included cross-training; variants of team adaptation, coordination, or crew-resource-management (CRM) training; and different types of simulation-based training. The results provided evidence for training effectiveness for each of these strategies. Cross-training, in which team members get trained on other members' roles, evidenced an overall correlation of .47 with the outcomes (the 95% confidence interval ranged from .38 to .56) based on 6 studies and 13 effect sizes. Simulation-based training evidenced an overall correlation of .45 with the outcomes (the 95% confidence interval ranged from .38 to .50) based on 37 studies and 81 effect sizes. And, team adaptation, coordination, and CRM training had an overall correlation of .60 (the 95% confidence interval ranged from .48 to .70) based on 16 studies and 30 effect sizes. The bottom line: team-learning processes and outcomes can be enhanced through the use of team-training strategies. Moreover, the increasing sophistication of team simulations and other SLE's and the capability to embed training capabilities into work systems provides a means for organizations to develop an infrastructure to prompt, guide, and support the individual and team learning that form the basis for organizational learning systems (Kozlowski, Chao et al., in press).

Team Leadership

Most mainstream theories of leadership are intended to be universal, focusing on leadership across all contexts and levels of the organization (Kozlowski, Watola et al., in press). Functional-leadership theory (McGrath, 1962) has centered on level of the team and individuals embedded in teams. According to McGrath (1962), the leader is responsible for ensuring that all necessary functions for team-task accomplishment and the maintenance of member interpersonal and social relationships are accomplished. The leader does this by monitoring the team and taking necessary action to deal with internal or external challenges that might interfere with the task or social functions. A number of other scholars have contributed to the development of this perspective over the intervening years (e.g., Fleishman et al., 1991; Hackman & Walton, 1986; Komaki, Desselles, & Bowman, 1989; Lord, 1977; Zaccaro et al., 2001).

More recent work in this tradition has centered on leader functions that underlie team learning and development. For example, Edmondson (1999) viewed the primary role of the leader in promoting team learning as one of establishing a shared group climate for safety, so members could experiment, take risks, and stretch their skills. Drawing on Fleishman et al. (1991), Zaccaro et al. (2001) provided a broad framework encompassing four superordinate and thirteen subordinate leadership functions. Of interest is their attention to the leader's role in team learning by prompting the development of team-mental models, collective information processing, and team metacognitive processes. Hackman and Wageman (2005) proposed a model of team coaching in which they posit that leaders can positively influence team learning and development by providing motivational functions (getting familiar) early in a team's work cycle, consultative functions (task strategies) at the mid-point of its work, and educational functions (reflection) at the end of a meaningful *task* episode or piece of work. Note that this last aspect of the theory evidences an apparent temporal discontinuity because it references a work episode, which cycles more rapidly relative to the first two phases that reference development along a slower linear progression.

One line of theorizing in this tradition is designed to directly integrate with the perspective of team learning and development as a multilevel emergent regulatory process that we have highlighted throughout this chapter. A series of theoretical frameworks by Kozlowski, Gully, McHugh, et al. (1996), Kozlowski, Gully, Salas, et al. (1996), and Kozlowski, Watola et al. (in press) integrated functional leadership (McGrath, 1962), regulatory processes (Karoly, 1993), team development (Tuckman, 1965), and multilevel theory (Rousseau, 1985) to develop a normative theory of team leadership. Fig. 2.6 illustrates primary aspects of the theory. A key aspect of its conceptual approach is that it specifies dynamic environmental, developmental, and task-

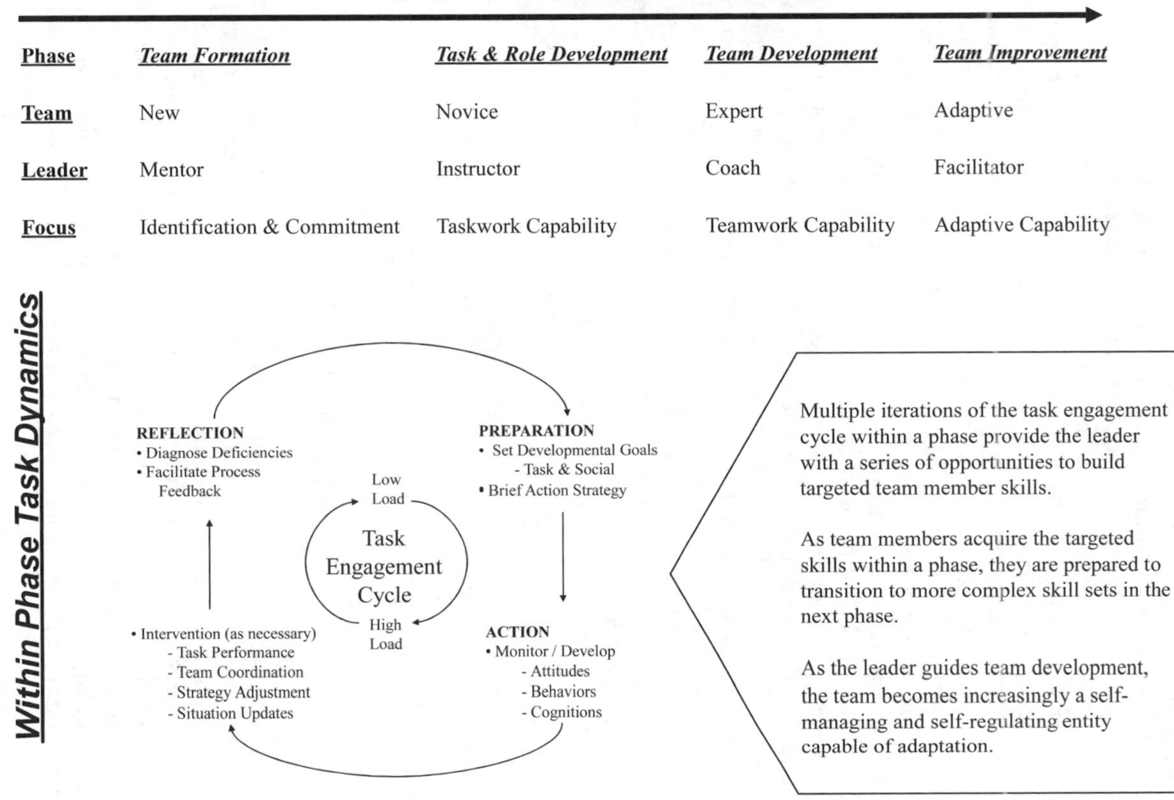

Figure 2.6 Task engagement cycles and developmental phase transitions.

episode contingencies that should influence that application of leader functions. Team tasks are viewed as linked to an embedding environment or broader organizational system that is a source of team-task demands, which necessitate appropriate team processes for resolution, which then yield team performance outputs that cycle back to the context in an adaptive loop. The overarching role of the leader is to guide and shape the acquisition of member capabilities, so the team can eventually regulate this systemic transformation process. One primary leader function is task based or instructional. The leader has to manage dynamic contingencies that arise from the environment (variations in environmentally driven task complexity) and link task variations to the regulatory processes of setting learning goals, monitoring progress, and intervening to aid the team as needed, diagnosing performance deficiencies, and guiding process feedback. This instructional function stimulates team-member regulation and the acquisition targeted knowledge and skills. A second primary leader function is developmental. As team members compile basic knowledge and skills, the leader prompts transitions to focus the team on acquiring progressively more advanced skills and capabilities (Kozlowski et al., 1999). Over time, this dynamic leadership process of shaping regulation and transitioning the focus of skill development is expected to yield team-level regulation and adaptive teams (Kozlowski, Watola et al., in press). Although there are no direct evaluations of the efficacy of this theory, research examining key aspects of the model including the regulatory process engine (Chen et al., 2005; DeShon et al., 2004) and the developmental shift in level (DeShon et al., 2001) have been supportive. The bottom line is that team leaders are key agents for creating learning experiences (e.g., using SLE's, creating exercises, harnessing ongoing tasks) for prompting, guiding, and shaping team learning and the development of adaptive teams.

CONCLUSION

The increasing push toward team-based work structures in organizations and the need to build human capital to respond to unexpected challenges, make salient the importance of the themes we explored in this chapter: team learning, development, and adaptation. Although the amount of theory and research devoted to these topics is quite small in relation to the vast literature on team effectiveness, these thematic areas are garnering increased attention from organizational scholars who are generating new, diverse, and innovative approaches (Kozlowski & Bell, 2003; Kozlowski & Ilgen, 2006). And, while diversity is a good thing, we also think that an integrated perspective can be useful for guiding productive lines of research.

Our purpose was to selectively focus on several streams of theory and research embedded in our themes and to weave them together into a perspective that integrates team learning, development, and adaptation.

We would not argue that the framework we offer is the only way to conceptualize team learning; other chapters in this volume offer alternative perspectives. However, we do believe that the theoretical breadth and interlocking features of our conceptualization—which encompasses self-regulation and multiple goal loops as the core psychological processes underlying learning, multilevel theory to characterize the compilation of emergent team-learning outcomes, and team leadership and training as levers that can be used to guide, shape, and enhance the development of team adaptability—provides our perspective with unique synergies, conceptual strengths, and research directions.

We have shown that early treatments of team learning as a simple aggregate of individual knowledge or performance, while a reasonable point of departure, are an inadequate foundation for the conceptualization of team learning. Such treatments neglect the interface between individual learning and team learning, and treat team learning as an outcome rather than a psychological process with effects at multiple levels. Although there is growing conceptual sophistication regarding distinctions between team-learning processes, emergent states as learning outcomes, and the compilation of team regulation, performance, and adaptive capabilities, more multilevel (e.g., individual and team) and temporally dynamic (e.g., task episodes and skill progression) research is needed. We have provided a theoretical integration and foundation, initial research findings, and a map to guide further research. We believe that team-learning processes can be shaped and show great promise for widespread application, and we hope the perspective we offer will help stimulate that effort.

Author Note: Work on this chapter was sponsored, in part, by the Air Force Office of Scientific Research (Grant F49620-01-1-0283; Kozlowski & DeShon, Principal Investigators) and the Army Research Institute for the Behavioral and Social Sciences (Grant 1435-04-03-CT-71272; Klein, Kozlowski, & Xiao, Principal Investigators). The U.S. Government is authorized to reproduce and distribute reprints for governmental purposes notwithstanding any copyright notation thereon.

The views and conclusions contained herein are those of the authors and should not be interpreted as necessarily representing the official policies or endorsements, either expressed or implied, of the Air Force Research Laboratory, the Army Research Institute for the Behavioral and Social Sciences, the Office of Naval Research, or the U.S. Government.

REFERENCES

Anderson, J. R. (1987). Skill acquisition: Compilation of weak-method problem situations. *Psychological Review, 94*(2), 192–210.

Argote, L., Gruenfeld, D. H., & Naquin, C. (2001). Group learning in organizations. In M. Turner (Ed.), *Groups at work: Theory and research* (pp. 369–411). Mahwah, NJ: Lawrence Erlbaum Associates.

Argote, L., Insko, C. A., Yovetich, N., & Romero, A. A. (1995). Group learning curves: The effects of turnover and task complexity on group performance. *Journal of Applied Social Psychology, 25,* 512–529.

Austin, J. R. (2003). Transactive memory in organizational groups: The effects of content, consensus, specialization, and accuracy on group performance. *Journal of Applied Psychology, 88*(5), 866–878.

Bandura, A. (1991). Social cognitive theory of self-regulation. *Organizational Behavior and Human Decision Processes, 50,* 248–287.

Bandura, A. (1997). *Self-efficacy: The exercise of control.* New York: Freeman.

Banks, A. P., & Millward, L. J. (2000). Running shared mental models as a distributed cognitive process. *British Journal of Psychology, 91,* 513–531.

Bell, B. S., & Kozlowski, S. W. J. (in press). Toward a theory of learner centered training design: An integrative framework of active learning. In S. W. J. Kozlowski & E. Salas (Eds)., *Learning, training, and development in organizations.* Mahwah, NJ: Lawrence Erlbaum Associates.

Blickensderfer, E., Cannon-Bowers, J. A., & Salas, E. (1997). Theoretical bases for team self-corrections: Fostering shared mental models. In M. M. Beyerlein, & D. A. Johnson (Eds.), *Advances in interdisciplinary studies of work teams* (Vol. 4, pp. 249–279). Greenwich, CT: JAI Press.

Bunderson, J. S., & Sutcliffe, K. A. (2003). Management team learning orientation and business unit performance. *Journal of Applied Psychology, 88*(3), 552–560.

Campbell, D. T. (1958). Common fate, similarity, and other indices of the status of aggregates of persons as social entities. *Behavioral Science, 3,* 14–25.

Cannon-Bowers, J. A., & Bowers, C. A. (in press). Synthetic learning environments: On developing a science of simulation, games and virtual worlds for training. In S. W. J. Kozlowski & E. Salas (Eds)., *Learning, training, and development in organizations.* Mahwah, NJ: Lawrence Erlbaum Associates.

Cannon-Bowers, J. A., Salas, E., & Converse, S. A. (1993). Shared mental models in expert team decision making. In J. N. J. Castellan (Ed.), *Current issues in individual and group decision making* (pp. 221–246). Hillsdale, NJ: Lawrence Erlbaum Associates.

Chen, G., Thomas, B., & Wallace, J. C. (2005). A multilevel examination of the relationships among training outcomes, mediating regulatory processes, and adaptive performance. *Journal of Applied Psychology, 90,* 827–841.

DeShon, R. P., Kozlowski, S. W. J., Schmidt, A. M., Milner, K. R., & Wiechmann, D. (2004). A multiple-goal, multilevel model of feedback effects on the regulation of individual and team performance. *Journal of Applied Psychology, 89*(6), 1035–1056.

DeShon, R. P., Kozlowski, S. W. J., Schmidt, A. M., Wiechmann, D., & Milner, K. A. (2001, April). *Developing team adaptability: Shifting regulatory focus across levels.* Paper presented at the 15th annual conference of the Society for Industrial and Organizational Psychology, New Orleans, LA.

Devine, D. J., Clayton, L. D., Phillips, J. L., Dunford, B. B., & Melner, S. B. (1999). Teams in organizations: Prevalence, characteristics, and effectiveness. *Small Group Research, 30*(6), 678–711.

Dweck, C. S. (1986). Motivational processes affecting learning. *American Psychologist, 41*(10), 1040–1048.

Dyer, J. C. (1984). Team research and team training: State-of-the-art review. In F. A. Muckler (Ed.), *Human factors review* (pp. 285–319). Santa Monica, CA: Human Factors Society.

Edmondson, A. (1999). Psychological safety and learning behavior in work teams. *Administrative Science Quarterly, 44*, 350–383.

Ellis, A. P. J., & Bell, B. S. (2005). Capacity, collaboration, and commonality: A framework for understanding team learning. In L. L. Neider, & C. A. Shriesheim (Eds.), *Understanding teams: A volume in research in management* (pp. 1–25). Greenwich, CT: Information Age.

Ellis, A. P. J., Bell, B. S., Ployhart, R. E., Hollenbeck, J. R., & Ilgen, D. R. (2005). An evaluation of generic teamwork skills training with action teams: Effects on cognitive and skill-based outcomes. *Personnel Psychology, 58*, 641–672.

Ellis, A. P. J., Hollenbeck, J. R., Ilgen, D. R., Porter, C. O. L. H., West, B. J., & Moon, H. (2003). Team learning: Collectively connecting the dots. *Journal of Applied Psychology, 88*(5), 821–835.

Fleishman, E. A., Mumford, M. D., Zaccaro, S. J., Levin, K. Y., Korotkin, A. L., & Hein, M. B. (1991). Taxonomic efforts in the description of leader behavior: A synthesis and functional interpretation. *Leadership Quarterly, 2*, 245–287.

Ford, J. K., & Kraiger, K. (1995). The application of cognitive constructs and principles to the instructional systems model of training: Implications for needs assessment, design, and transfer. In C. L. Cooper & I. T. Robertson (Eds.), *International review of Industrial and Organizational Psychology* (Vol. 10, pp. 1–48). New York: Wiley.

Guastello, S. J., & Guastello, D. D. (1998). Origins of coordination and team effectiveness: A perspective from game theory and nonlinear dynamics. *Journal of Applied Psychology, 83*(3), 423–437.

Hackman, J. R., & Wageman, R. (2005). A theory of team coaching. *Academy of Management Review, 30*, 269–287.

Hackman, J. R., & Walton, R. E. (1986). Leading groups in organizations. In P. S. Goodman & Associates (Eds.), *Designing effective work groups* (pp. 72–119). San Francisco: Jossey-Bass.

Hollingshead, A. B. (1998a). Communication, learning, and retrieval in transactive memory systems. *Journal of Experimental Social Psychology, 34*, 423–442.

Hollingshead, A. B. (1998b). Retrieval processes in transactive memory systems. *Journal of Personality and Social Psychology, 74*, 659–671.

Ilgen, D. R., Hollenbeck, J. R., Johnson, M., & Jundt, D. (2005). Teams in organizations: From I-P-O models to IMOI models. *Annual Review of Psychology, 56*, 517–543.

Karoly, P. (1993). Mechanisms of self-regulation: A systems view. *Annual Review of Psychology, 44*, 23–52.

Klimoski, R. J., & Mohammed, S. (1994). Team mental model: Construct or metaphor? *Journal of Management, 20*, 403–437.

Komaki, J. L., Desselles, M. L., & Bowman, E. D. (1989). Definitely not a breeze: Extending an operant model of effective supervision to teams. *Journal of Applied Psychology, 74*, 522–529.

Kozlowski, S. W. J., & Bell, B. S. (2003). Work groups and teams in organizations. In W. C. Borman, D. R. Ilgen, & E. J. Klimoski (Eds.), *Handbook of psychology: Industrial and organizational psychology* (Vol. 12, pp. 333–375). London: Wiley.

Kozlowski, S. W. J., Chao, G. T., & Nowakowski, J. M. (in press). Organizational learning systems. In S. W. J. Kozlowski & E. Salas (Eds)., *Learning, training, and development in organizations.* New York: Lawrence Erlbaum Associates.

Kozlowski, S. W. J., Gully, S. M., McHugh, P. P., Salas, E., & Cannon-Bowers, J. A. (1996). A dynamic theory of leadership and team effectiveness: Developmental and task contingent leader roles. In G. R. Ferris (Ed.), *Research in personnel and human resource management* (Vol. 14, pp. 253–305). Greenwich, CT: JAI Press.

Kozlowski, S. W. J., Gully, S. M., Nason, E. R., & Smith, E. M. (1999). Developing adaptive teams: A theory of compilation and performance across levels and time. In D. R. Ilgen, & E. D. Pulakos (Eds.), *The changing nature of work performance: Implications for staffing, personnel actions, and development* (pp. 240–292). San Francisco: Jossey-Bass.

Kozlowski, S. W. J., Gully, S. M., Salas, E., & Cannon-Bowers, J. A. (1996). Team leadership and development: Theory, principles, and guidelines for training leaders and teams. In M. Beyerlein, D. Johnson, & S. Beyerlein (Eds.), *Advances in interdisciplinary studies of work teams: Team leadership* (Vol. 3, pp. 251–289). Greenwich, CT: JAI Press.

Kozlowski, S. W. J., & Hults, B. M. (1987). An exploration of climates for technical updating and performance. *Personnel Psychology, 40,* 539–563.

Kozlowski, S. W. J., & Ilgen, D. R. (2006). Enhancing the effectiveness of work groups and teams. *Psychological Science in the Public Interest, 7,* 77–124.

Kozlowski, S. W. J., & Klein, K. J. (2000). A multilevel approach to theory and research in organizations: Contextual, temporal, and emergent processes. In K. J. Klein, & S. W. J. Kozlowski (Eds.), *Multilevel theory, research, and methods in organizations: Foundations, extensions, and new directions* (pp. 3–90). San Francisco: Jossey-Bass.

Kozlowski, S. W. J., & Salas, E. (1997). An organizational systems approach for the implementation and transfer of training. In J. K. Ford, S. W. J. Kozlowski, K. Kraiger, E. Salas, & M. Teachout (Eds.), *Improving training effectiveness in work organizations.* (pp. 247–287). Mahwah, NJ: Lawrence Erlbaum Associates.

Kozlowski, S. W. J., Toney, R. J., Mullins, M. E., Weissbein, D. A., Brown, K. G., & Bell, B. S. (2001). Developing adaptability: A theory for the design of integrated-embedded training systems. In E. Salas (Ed.), *Advances in human performance and cognitive engineering research* (Vol. 1, pp. 59–123). Amsterdam: JAI/Elsevier Science.

Kozlowski, S. W. J., Watola, D., Nowakowski, J. M., Kim, B., & Botero, I. (in press). Developing adaptive teams: A theory of dynamic team leadership. In E. Salas, G. F. Goodwin, & C. S. Burke (Eds.), *Team effectiveness in complex organizations: Cross-disciplinary perspectives and approaches* (SIOP Frontiers Series). New York: Lawrence Erlbaum Associates.

Lawler, E. E., Mohrman, S. A., & Ledford, G. E. (1995). *Creating high performance organizations: Practices and results of employee involvement and total quality management in Fortune 1000 companies.* San Francisco: Jossey-Bass.

Lewis, K. (2003). Measuring transactive memory systems in the field: Scale development and validation. *Journal of Applied Psychology, 88*(4), 587–604.

Liang, D. W., Moreland, R. L., & Argote, L. (1995). Group versus individual training and group performance: The mediating role of transactive memory. *Personality and Social Psychology Bulletin, 21,* 384–393.

Locke, E. A., & Latham, G. P. (1990). *A theory of goal setting and task performance.* Englewood Cliffs, NJ: Prentice Hall.

Lord, R. G. (1977). Functional leadership behavior: Measurement and relation to social power and leadership perceptions. *Administrative Science Quarterly, 22*(1), 114–133.

Marks, M. A., Mathieu, J. E., & Zaccaro, S. J. (2001). A temporally based framework and taxonomy of team processes. *Academy of Management Review, 26*(3), 356–376.

Marks, M. A., Sabella, M. J., Burke, C. S., & Zaccaro, S. J. (2002). The impact of cross-training on team effectiveness. *Journal of Applied Psychology, 87*(1), 3–13.

Marks, M. A., Zaccaro, S. J., & Mathieu, J. E. (2000). Performance implications of leader briefings and team-interaction training for team adaptation to novel environments. *Journal of Applied Psychology, 85*(6), 971–986.

Mathieu, J. E., Heffner, T. S., Goodwin, G. F., Salas, E., & Cannon-Bowers, J. A. (2000). The influence of shared mental models on team process and performance. *Journal of Applied Psychology, 85*(2), 273–283.

McGrath, J. E. (1962). Leadership behavior: *Some requirements for leadership training.* Washington, DC: U.S. Civil Service Commission.

Minionis, D. P., Zaccaro, S. J., & Perez, R. (1995). *Shared mental models, team coordination, and team performance.* Paper presented at the 10th annual meeting of the Society for Industrial and Organizational Psychology, Orlando, FL.

Mohammed, S., & Dumville, B. C. (2001). Team mental models in a team knowledge framework: Expanding theory and measurement across disciplinary boundaries. *Journal of Organizational Behavior, 22*, 89–106.

Moreland, R. L., Argote, L., & Krishnan, R. (1996). Socially shared cognition at work: Transactive memory and group performance. In J. L. Nye, & A. M. Brower (Eds.), *What's social about social cognition? Research on socially shared cognition in small groups* (pp. 57–84). Thousand Oaks, CA: Sage.

Morgeson, F. P., & Hofmann, D. A. (1999). The structure and function of collective constructs: Implications for multilevel research and theory development. *Academy of Management Review, 24*(2), 249–265.

Pearsall, M. J., Ellis, A. P. J., & Bell, B. S. (2007). Slippage in the system: The effects of errors in transactive memory behavior on team performance. Manuscript submitted for publication.

Pulakos, E. D., Arad, S., Donovan, M. A., & Plamondon, K. E. (2000). Adaptability in the workplace: Development of a taxonomy of adaptive performance. *Journal of Applied Psychology, 85*(4), 612–624.

Rentsch, J. R. (1990). Climate and culture: Interaction and qualitative differences in organizational meanings. *Journal of Applied Psychology, 75*(6), 668–681.

Salas, E., & Cannon-Bowers, J. (1997). Methods, tools, and strategies for team training. In M. A. Quinones, & A. Ehrenstein (Eds.), *Training for a rapidly changing workplace* (pp. 249–280). Washington, DC: American Psychological Association.

Schneider, B., Wheeler, J. K., & Cox, J. F. (1992). A passion for service: Using content analysis to explicate service climate themes. *Journal of Applied Psychology, 77*(5), 705–716.

Smith-Jentsch, K. A., Salas, E., & Brannick, M. T. (2001). To transfer or not to transfer? Investigating the combined effects of trainee characteristics, team leader support, and team climate. *Journal of Applied Psychology, 86*(2), 279–292.

Steiner, I. D. (1972). *Group process and productivity.* New York: Academic Press.

Stout, R. J., Salas, E., & Carson, R. (1994). Individual task proficiency and team process behavior: What's important for team functioning. *Military Psychology, 6*, 177–192.

Sugrue, B. & Clark, R. E. (2000). Media selection for training. In S. Tobias & J. D. Fletcher (Eds.), Training and retraining: A handbook for business, industry, government, and the military (pp. 208–234). New York: Macmillan.

Tuckman, B. W. (1965). Developmental sequence in small groups. *Psychological Bulletin, 63,* 384–399.

Van De Ven, A. H., Delbecq, A. L., & Koenig, R. (1976). Determinants of coordination modes within organizations. *American Sociological Review, 41,* 322–338.

Wegner, D. M. (1986). Transactive memory: A contemporary analysis of the group mind. In B. Mullen, & G. R. Goethals (Eds.), *Theories of group behavior* (pp. 185–205). New York: Springer-Verlag.

Wegner, D. M. (1995). A computer network model of human transactive memory. *Social Cognition, 13,* 319–339.

Wegner, D. M., Giuliano, T., & Hertel, P. (1985). Cognitive interdependence in close relationships. In W. J. Ickes (Ed.), *Compatible and incompatible relationships* (pp. 253–276). New York: Springer-Verlag.

Zaccaro, S. J., Rittman, A. L., & Marks, M. A. (2001). Team leadership. *Leadership Quarterly, 12*(4), 451–483.

CHAPTER

3

Configuring and Reconfiguring Groups as Complex Learning Systems

HOLLY ARROW AND JONATHAN COOK

University of Oregon

Change over time is observable in all aspects of life, from the process of birth, growth, aging, and death, to the cycles of seasonal change and the march of human history. Groups, too, change over time. As a group forms, its members learn about one another and develop structures that allow them to coordinate their behavior. Over time, norms and roles evolve, tasks change, groups expand—all of which requires a new wave of learning about the group, one another, and new tasks (Levine & Moreland, 1991). Changes that increase group knowledge and the group's capacity to achieve group goals merit the term *learning.* Originally studied as an individual process, the term learning has more recently been applied to changes in systems of interacting individuals such as organizations and groups (Bapuji & Crossan, 2004).

In groups, as in other systems of living things, stability and change both have costs and benefits. Learning does not necessarily improve performance: "learning efforts are not efficient—they consume resources and divert attention from existing initiatives" (Sessa & London, 2006, p. 114). Groups may "compromise performance in the near term by overemphasizing learning" (Bunderson & Sutcliffe, 2003, p. 552). The relative costs and benefits vary with the type of changes involved and the contexts in which the group and its members operate. A multilevel understanding of group learning can help leaders and other group members guide the process of change and stabilize useful innovations so that the net effect of learning is positive. Without this guidance, costly increases in group knowledge may have little effect on group efficacy, resulting in a group performing badly even if many or even all of its members "know better."

In this chapter, we consider group learning from a complex adaptive systems (CAS) perspective (Arrow, McGrath, & Berdahl, 2000), treating it as a dynamic process that is part of the interplay of change, stability, and structure in the group system. We integrate concepts such as fitness landscapes, attractors, and control parameters (defined and discussed later in the chapter) into a multilevel model of adaptive learning. Our focus is on how a CAS approach can help groups and leaders diagnose the type of mismatches that learning can address and select tactics that promote cost-effective group learning. From a CAS perspective, groups are characterized by nonlinear, recursive interactions that create and adjust structure as groups adapt to their embedding contexts. A pervasive feature of nonlinear dynamics is that small actions have the potential to create large effects, while large actions may have little or no impact. Clearly, the former is to be preferred in any cost-effective learning strategy.

A core insight of systems theory (von Bertalanffy, 1976) is the multileveled nature of systems, which are arranged hierarchically, with smaller units partially or fully nested within larger units. Groups are systems with memory and history. They can configure themselves to channel and stabilize member behavior, and they can reconfigure themselves in response to changes in the smaller systems (e.g., the members) embedded within them and the larger systems (e.g., organizations) within which they are embedded (Arrow et al., 2000, p. 34). Flows of information and feedback among components within and across levels allow these components to adjust in ways that improve capacity and performance—in other words, to learn.

Groups can be viewed as having two primary functions: to (a) complete group projects and (b) fulfill member needs. Success in fulfilling these two functions helps develop and maintain system integrity, a third function, which in turn supports the group's ability to serve its primary functions (Arrow et al., 2000, p. 47; see also Hackman & Morris, 1975; McGrath, 1991). Change and adaptation, including learning at multiple levels, help systems build complexity, and more complex systems tend to be more robust (Holland, 1995); in other words, they have greater system integrity.

A major challenge in writing this chapter was to integrate complexity concepts with the existing literature on groups and organizations so that readers gain something of value beyond a greater facility with some CAS catch phrases. We chose to start by defining learning without reference to CAS concepts, and then organize the rest of the chapter around a cycle model that breaks group learning into conceptually distinguishable processes. We introduce and explain key CAS concepts within the sections on a need-to-know basis. Numerous figures complement the verbal explanations. We have also used case studies and other examples to make the usefulness of the CAS concepts as concrete as possible. We turn now to the definitions.

LEARNING AT MULTIPLE LEVELS

Learning at every level (individual, group, organizational) includes both *process* and *outcomes*. The learning process involves (a) attention systems, (b) information flows and exchanges, and (c) the generation and adjustment of structures. Learning outcomes are the improvements in knowledge, capacity, and performance that result from learning processes. We distinguish between *directed* and *undirected* learning, which correspond to the CAS idea of directed and undirected adaptation (Arrow et al., 2000, p. 47).

In directed learning, explicit goals direct the focus of attention and deliberately shape the outcome of learning. Monitoring and feedback are used to track progress toward desired outcomes. A basketball team, for example, may set out to learn and practice a new defensive strategy. The coach's monitoring and the group's own performance in practice provide feedback about the group's developing skills.

Undirected learning occurs tacitly when group members notice salient environmental cues and come to associate certain actions (or states) with good or bad outcomes. The same basketball team, for example, will tend to form positive associations with strategies employed in games they win, and negative associations in games they lose. Undirected learning can also occur when watching other teams play. In individuals, groups, and organizations, both directed and undirected learning can and do occur simultaneously.

Our systems approach assumes that group learning can best be understood in the context of learning that is occurring in adjacent levels in a hierarchy of systems. Group learning occurs at the intersection of individual and organizational learning and occupies a unique position in the confluence of systems. Individuals rely on groups to help them make sense of information and events (Weick, 1995). Organizations rely on individuals and groups to incorporate and implement the changes that constitute organizational learning.

The meaning of learning shifts as one moves from organisms, which are living systems, to organized aggregates of organisms, which are not themselves living systems but are systems of living things. Although learning at every level involves both process and outcome, we view the specific processes and outcomes differently across levels. We use the following definitions of learning at each level to anchor our discussion.

Individual learning. At the individual level, learning is a directed or undirected process of attention to information resulting in an outcome of increased knowledge (including unlearning), improved understanding (including expanded awareness of one's ignorance), or expanded ability. As new military recruits progress through basic training, for example, they are challenged mentally and physically as they learn and practice fighting techniques. Learning to break down and clean a rifle is directed learning, because it is characterized by conscious motivation and active practice. In field exercises, recruits learn, again in a directed fashion, how to execute specific tactics. Undirected learning occurs in actual combat experience. While the focus of conscious attention is on the mission, soldiers continue to hone their skills and discover more about what works and does not work in a particular operational setting.

Organizational learning. Organizational learning is a directed or an undirected process of adjusting organizational structures and culture (both formal and informal) that results in an outcome of increased access to relevant knowledge across multiple levels, improvements in collective systems, and expanded ability to satisfy organizational goals. The Center for Army Lessons Learned (CALL; http://call.army.mil/) provides an example of directed learning at the organizational level, aimed at the goal of improving military effectiveness. CALL collects and analyzes data to inform adjustments in organizational policies and strategies. An example of undirected organizational learning might be ad hoc local adjustments to policy based on unforeseen features of a situation. Those higher up in the organization may not be aware of these adjustments.

Group learning. At the group level, learning is a directed or undirected process of shared attention to information that results in an outcome of increased collective access to knowledge, development of shared mental models, and expanded ability to satisfy the implicit and explicit goals of the group. "After-action" reviews by military units are an example of directed group learning, designed to help the unit be more effective in similar combat situations. As members assemble their perceptions of events into a collective account, the group's shared mental model is adjusted and elaborated. As this occurs, the group will be better able to determine, for example, whether an undesirable outcome resulted from a poor plan or from coordination problems in carrying out an otherwise sound plan. Common in the military, after-action reviews have also been adopted in civilian organizations (Baird, Holland, & Deacon,

1999). Undirected group learning might occur if groups are punished for providing unwanted negative information to superiors. The group learns to tell leaders only what they want to hear.

Cross-level learning. In the example just given, undirected learning at the group level will likely inhibit organizational learning by restricting information flows. It illustrates how cross-level learning can be thwarted by undirected and unintended learning outcomes. Cross-level learning is the directed or undirected process of multilevel information exchange and integration that results in an outcome of individual, group, and/or organizational learning. In a complex system, information flows not only within boundaries but also across boundaries between units at different levels. The after-action review, for example, allows the group to draw upon individual learning to assemble a broader picture of an event. Discussion builds a shared understanding of events that becomes part of the group mental model. CALL analyzes after-action reviews submitted by groups and also interviews soldiers returning from combat assignments, allowing the organization to benefit from both individual and group learning (http://usacac.army.mil/cac/lessons.asp).

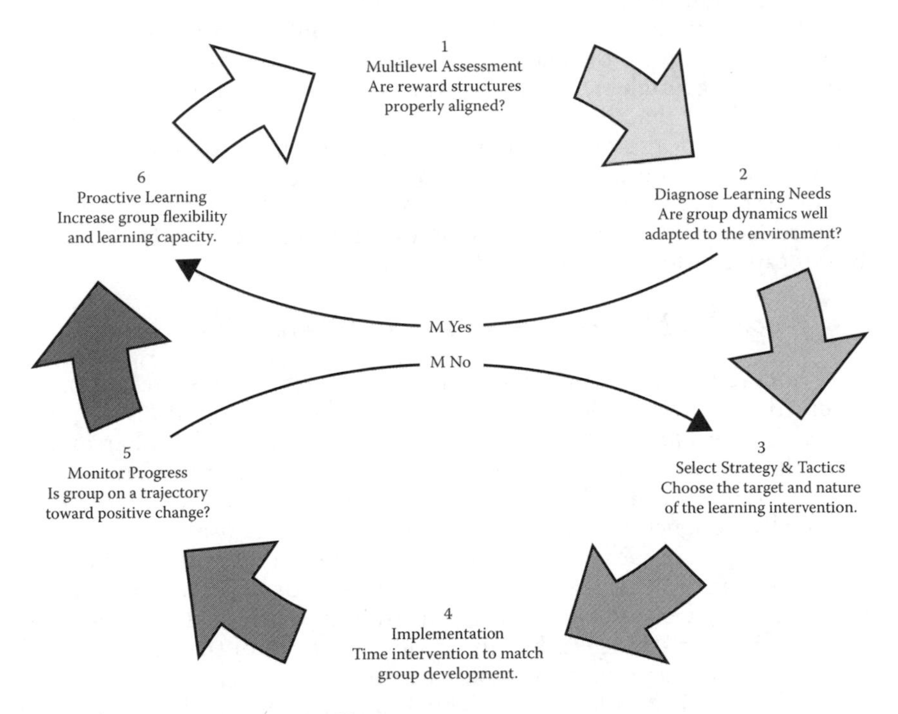

Figure 3.1 Cycle model of learning processes.

A CYCLE MODEL OF LEARNING PROCESSES

The remainder of this chapter is organized around a framework that conceptualizes group learning as a set of multilevel assessment, diagnosis, adjustment, and evaluation processes. We believe the cycle model (see Fig. 3.1) can serve as a useful device for leaders and other group members interested in learning about and guiding group learning. Readers should keep in mind that groups can and do shift from one process to another without following the sequence described. In other words, the cycle is a conceptual tool and is not meant as a descriptive linear stage model of how groups in general learn.

We start with a multilevel assessment of the reward structures that shape member behavior in the group context and group behavior in its embedding context(s). Knowledge gained in this assessment informs a diagnosis of learning needs based on both group dynamics and reward structures. High-functioning groups in currently stable environments may have little need to reconfigure group structure or practices. Instead, they will likely benefit from a focus on proactive learning. Proactive learning is anticipatory and future oriented and enhances the ability to adapt to change.

If group dynamics and external demands are not well matched or if reward structures at different levels create conflicting pressures, this diagnosis will inform the choice of a learning strategy to improve alignment. During implementation of the strategy, monitoring provides feedback about whether the desired changes are taking place. When monitoring indicates an unpromising trajectory, the group may reconsider learning strategies and implement any corrections, cycling through the lower half of the model as needed. When immediate challenges have been addressed, this frees up resources for proactive learning, which builds capacity for challenges to come.

Process 1. Multilevel Assessment: Where Are We Now?

Assessing reward structures across multiple levels provides insight into where the undirected learning process may be working at cross purposes. A *fitness landscape* is a useful conceptual device that characterizes relations across levels. It indicates how well different behaviors or other system attributes “fit” the context in which the system operates. Originally designed to represent the “fitness” of organisms (likelihood of surviving and reproducing) within a natural environment, a fitness landscape can by extension represent the rewards and punishments a member or a group evokes from its embedding context based on different attributes or strategies. In this section, we explain the fitness landscape concept and provide examples at two levels.

Fig. 3.2 is a fitness landscape. The X-axis represents some variable that affects group outcomes. The Y-axis represents the favorability of outcomes when the system is at different levels of the variable. The line

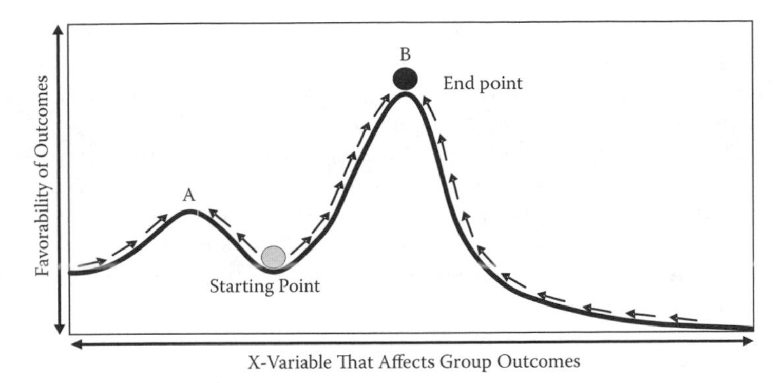

Figure 3.2 A group fitness landscape.

that shows the outcomes for every level of X represents a "landscape" of peaks and valleys that a group can traverse by changing the value of X. Higher peaks in the landscape represent more rewarding states, and movement uphill yields the improved results that are the desired outcome of any learning process. In Fig. 3.2, there are two possible performance "peaks," one higher than the other, and a deep valley on the right. The arrows indicate the likely movement of a group, via undirected learning, toward the points A or B. The dark ball is a group that has moved from a valley of poor outcomes (the light ball) to a fitness peak of good outcomes.

Group fitness: A conflict and performance example. Assume that X is group task conflict and Y is group performance quality. Moderate levels of task conflict are expected to benefit group performance by stimulating more careful analysis of issues, better decisions, more creativity, and attention to problems that may be ignored by conflict-avoidant groups (Jehn, 1997; Wall & Callister, 1995). The group in Fig. 3.2 has attained this ideal, improving its performance and the associated rewards.

A recent review of the literature on conflict and performance (De Dreu & Weingart, 2003), however, documents that task conflict tends to be correlated with relationship conflict, which damages performance. If low levels of task conflict fail to trigger relationship conflict, this could create an alternate performance peak in the nonzero-but-low conflict area, as illustrated. If task conflict gets too high, collateral interpersonal clashes can quickly absorb so much member time and energy that performance crashes and the fitness landscape falls off sharply.

Earlier, we described undirected learning as associative learning that links member or group states or actions with positive or negative outcomes. The shaping effect of rewards and punishments drives undirected adaptation. The process is governed by an evolutionary motor of change (van de Ven & Poole, 1995) based on variation, selection, and retention. Assume a group starts at the conflict level where the light ball is. Any variation in task conflict—either an increase or a decrease—will improve group outcomes. This desirable result reinforces the shift, moving the group farther in that direction and pushing it "uphill" toward a fitness peak. Undirected learning is "blind," however, in that it serves equally well to push the group toward point A or point B. Knowledge of the fitness landscape takes off the blinders and allows for the more conscious steering of directed learning. An obvious goal is B, the higher fitness peak.

Group performance quality is typically assessed based on how well group behavior "fits" the demands of its embedding context (organization, audience, customers). Hence, this fitness landscape represents the cross-level group-embedding context interchange. Of course, the group is also an embedding context for members. The next example focuses on the member-group interchange.

Member fitness: A learning-from-mistakes example. Within a group, each member has a fitness landscape that represents how the group rewards (or punishes) that member based on his or her attributes, strategies, or activities. A study of error reporting in hospital units (Edmondson, 2004) found that the fitness landscape for members differed from group to group, depending primarily on the climate defined by the nurse manager.

Fig. 3.3 shows two contrasting member fitness landscapes. The X variable is the percentage of medication errors that are detected and reported to the nurse manager. The Y variable (fitness) is the quality of unit relationships, one of the outcome variables Edmondson measured. The first landscape (Fig. 3.3a) illustrates a punitive climate. Interviews revealed that "nurses are blamed for mistakes" and one nurse said the manager made her feel like she was "on trial; it was degrading" (p. 84). Under these circumstances, the only way to maintain positive relations is to report as few errors as possible. Nurses learn to move toward the left of the graph toward the only fitness peak. On the right side, as more errors are detected and reported, the quality of interpersonal relations is liable to deteriorate to a point that the nurse is either fired or quits, so the curve bottoms out. No undirected learning takes place in flat regions of a fitness landscape.

In Fig. 3.3b, which shows a learning-from-mistakes climate, nurses are not punished for reporting errors. Instead, the nurse manager understands that "it is essential to deal with this error productively" and the nurses report that there is an "unspoken rule here to help each other and check each other" (pp. 83–84). In this climate, reporting errors is positive; it improves the quality of interpersonal relations. Nurses who do not check each other and discover errors are out of step with the group norm, so they are at a lower fitness level with poorer interpersonal relations. We have assumed that the curve dips at very high levels of

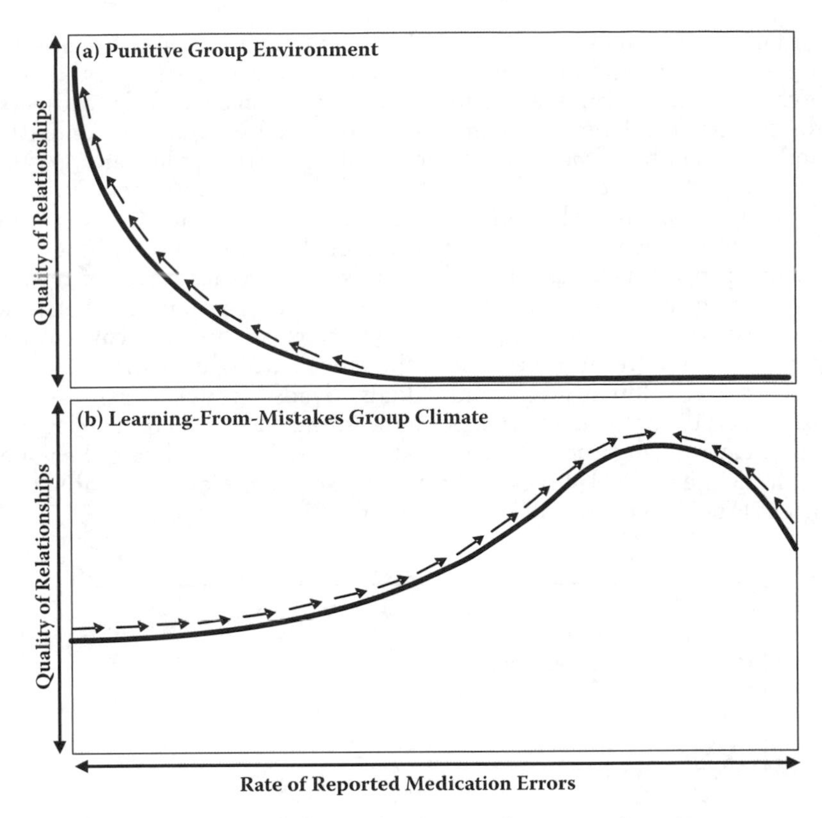

Figure 3.3 Two member fitness landscapes for reported medication errors, based on (a) a punitive group climate and (b) a learning-from-mistakes group climate.

reporting, as this may spark perceptions that the nurse is either making too many mistakes or is overzealous in reporting on the errors of others.

Multilayered fitness landscapes. So far, we have discussed a fitness landscape at the group level, where the activity involved is group task conflict (Fig. 3.2), and fitness landscapes at the member level, where the action involved is members reporting errors to the group leader (Fig. 3.3). Of course, the organization in which a group is embedded also operates within a broader context—an industry, a sports league, a war zone—and hence experiences varying results depending on organizational activities, strategies, and attributes. The medical units studied by Edmondson (2004) were, in turn, embedded in hospitals, which have their own climate for detecting and reporting errors.

The fitness landscape of rewards, incentives, and punishments for a given unit is typically defined by the immediate context at the next level up. A fitness landscape assessment should consider the landscape(s) for the group relative to its most consequential embedding context(s) and the member fitness landscapes relative to the group and (where relevant) broader embedding contexts that impact members directly. Outcomes for group leaders who report to others outside the group, for example, may be strongly determined by levels above the group. Member fitness landscapes will be shaped by several sources of reward and punishment, including the responses of other group members, the responses of a group leader (which may differ), and in some cases, other people outside the group to whom the member might report.

Units at different levels (individuals, dyads, groups, organizations) are generally not operating within the same fitness landscape, which can create misalignment in reward structures. To complicate the issue, both the meaning of "fitness" (the Y-axis) and the relevant factor(s) that affect fitness (the X-axis) often differ at different levels.

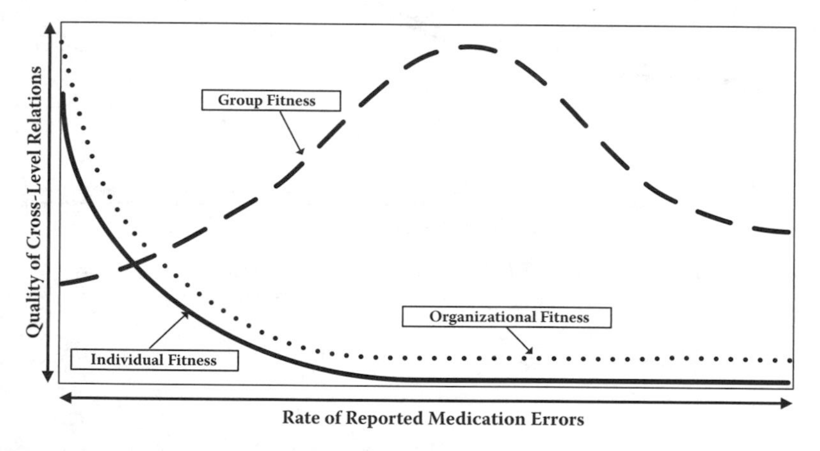

Figure 3.4 A hypothetical multilevel fitness landscape for reporting medication errors, showing individual, group, and organizational fitness.

To illustrate multiple fitness landscapes, we build on the hospital error example by focusing on a single X variable—rate of medication errors detected and reported to the next level up—that remains meaningful at each level. The Y variable—fitness—can also represent the quality of cross-level relations in each case, whether member-group, group-organization, or organization-surrounding community. In Fig. 3.4, the fitness landscape for members, groups, and the organization are superimposed, using the punitive-climate group from Edmondson (2004) for the member fitness landscape (solid line), and making some simplifying assumptions about plausible fitness landscapes for the other two levels.

The fitness landscape for the group, represented by the dashed line, indicates that the group has the best relations with the hospital administration at moderate levels of error detection and reporting. This level demonstrates (from the organizational perspective) that groups are monitoring and learning from errors, but do not appear to be making an unusually high number of errors. The organization rewards groups that are safe (thus catching errors) and relatively effective (not making too many errors). The response is negative if no errors are reported (this shows poor compliance with a culture that values error reporting) or if there is an unusually high rate of reported errors.

Being unschooled in the complex economic, legal, and political climate within which hospitals operate, and that impose costs or bestow rewards on hospitals for detecting and reporting medication errors, we make a simplifying assumption that allows us to sketch a hypothetical curve. We assume that the relations of a hospital with the public it serves suffer (via bad press, malpractice suits, and reduced community trust) for errors that get reported to the community, even if their own internal system of error detection and reporting supports a learning environment that promotes patient safety. Hence, the dotted line shows a punitive climate. Clearly, the curves do not all match.

Landscape misalignment. Fitness landscapes show where undirected learning will tend to push members and the group as a whole. When peaks at one level correspond to valleys at another, it creates conflicting "pushes" in different directions and encourages members or groups to learn behaviors that are, at a different level, counterproductive. For the group depicted in Figure 3.4, the leader created a climate for members that was not aligned with the group-fitness landscape defined by the organization. Similarly, the internal organizational climate (e.g., group-fitness landscape) does not match the (hypothesized) broader context in which the hospital operates. Within the hospital, groups are rewarded for a moderate rate of error reporting, but the hospital itself is rewarded for having the lowest possible rate of reported error.

Both situations provide examples of a problematic fit between fitness landscapes operating at multiple levels. The issue of what, if anything, should be done about such mismatches is addressed in the section on learning strategies. First, however, we need to consider another complicating issue: the internal dynamics of a group.

Process 2. Diagnose Learning Needs Based on Landscapes and Topologies

The undirected learning that tends to push members or groups toward nearby peaks does not operate in a "frictionless" landscape. Even when peaks line up across multiple levels, a group may fail to adapt and improve. Species do go extinct, and many groups perform poorly despite clear and seemingly compelling incentives to improve. The dynamics of interaction also create a "pull" toward familiar and easily performed collective actions, which may or may not correspond to fitness peaks. Group dynamics that can prevent, complicate, or facilitate learning are the topic of this section.

To visualize the dynamic forces that pull a group in one direction or another, we first introduce another kind of graphical and conceptual device, the *topology of attractors.* We then put together the attractor topology and the fitness landscapes to assess alignments and misalignments that define the agenda for learning interventions.

Internal group dynamics: The topology of attractors. As groups form and members interact, they develop routines and norms that structure subsequent group behavior (Gersick & Hackman, 1990). Routines that are constantly repeated and reinforced can become like engrained habits or ruts—easy to fall into and difficult to escape. Other routines will evolve and change or be abandoned and replaced over time (Feldman, 2000). The way that such routines interact with fitness landscapes can be understood using the concept of *attractors.*

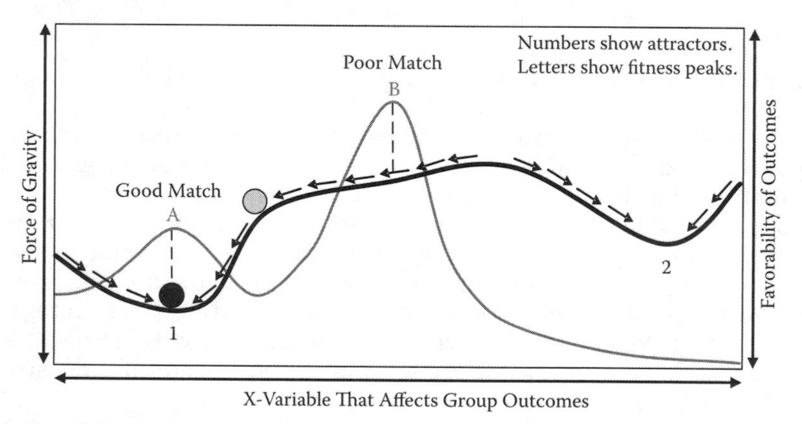

Figure 3.5 Group topology of attractors with superimposed fitness landscape and lines illustrating fitness/topology alignment.

The propensity of a group to gravitate naturally toward a particular state as members interact indicates that that state is an *attractor* for the group. The topology of attractors (see Fig. 3.5, solid line) represents the difficulty or ease of being in an array of different states, indexed by different values on an X factor. While the conceptual device of a fitness landscape comes from evolutionary biology, with evolution pushing species *up* fitness peaks, attractors and related concepts hail originally from physics, where the currency is energy. The tendency of objects to move from higher to lower states of energy is like the force of gravity, which causes objects to roll *down* into energy wells.

Thus, one focuses on peaks when looking at a fitness landscape; for attractor topologies, one focuses on depressions toward which the dynamics at play in the system drive an object, and by extension an organism, a group, or an organization. In Fig. 3.5, the dark line and arrows represent the topology of attractors. There are two attractors, labeled 1 and 2, with 1 being a "deeper" and thus stronger attractor than 2. The dark ball shows where a group would tend to end up if it started where the light ball is shown.

The reader may be wondering, at this point, what justifies the increased learning load of adding attractor topologies to fitness landscapes, requiring us to switch between up-oriented and down-oriented graphics. The answer is that attractors provide different and complementary information about the learning challenges and needs of a group. An attractor topology is not just a mirror image of the group's fitness landscape. Both provide insight into the dynamics of global variables that indicate the state of a system—for example, conflict, cohesion, or information flow in a group. However, the fitness landscape focuses on *outcomes* based on being in a particular state (a point on the X-axis). In contrast, the topology of attractors focuses on what states a group will naturally gravitate to in the *process* of interaction, regardless of whether those states yield good, bad, or indifferent outcomes.

Landscape-topology fit. Previously, we discussed alignment and misalignment between fitness landscapes across multiple levels. Within a particular level (e.g., member, group, organization), a different sort of misalignment may result when the attractor topology for a particular X variable (conflict, for example) does not mirror the fitness landscape for that variable. This is illustrated in Fig. 3.5, in which the fitness landscape from Fig. 3.2 (gray line) is superimposed on the attractor topology (black line). Fitness peak A shows a good match to Attractor 1. (Recall that a mirror image—fitness peak and attractor well—is a match.) However, fitness peak B, which is higher and thus theoretically yields the best outcomes for the group, does not correspond to an attractor. Hence, the internal dynamics of the group will tend to push the group away from that point on the X-axis.

In contrast to Attractor 1's good match, Attractor 2 is a bad match to the fitness landscape: It is located at the lowest point. This undesirable attractor can cause trouble for the group. If conflict is the X variable, a group may find it very easy to fall into an "attractor" of constant bickering and fighting (Attractor 2) that is so disruptive that the group can get nothing else done.

The match or mismatch between states that are more rewarding (e.g., fitness peaks) and states that are readily achieved and maintained (e.g., attractors) determines the dynamics of group performance. Stable optimal performance (an idealized state) occurs when the configurations match. When they do not, high performance will be a fleeting experience. The tendency for groups to settle into an attractor space is comparable to the process of homeostasis in the physical sciences. Biological organisms maintain a variety of set points that remain stable despite changes in the external environment. Heart rate, for example, changes from moment to moment with exertion and stress. The resting heart rate set point, however, is much more stable.

Given a fixed context, set points help sustain the health of the organism—and by extension, a homeostatic system of attractors can stabilize effective group behaviors. However, what works well in one context may be maladaptive if conditions change. Crossan, Lane, White, and Djurfeldt (1995) noted that, "existing systems and procedures appropriate at one time may inhibit individuals from exhibiting new and different behaviors that may be required for the future" (p. 347). Group learning includes alterations in the attractor topology that establish more functional set points. Such changes are discussed in more detail in the next section.

Putting the pieces together. Sketches of the group's attractor topology and multilevel fitness landscapes will help the group and its leaders ascertain how well they all "match" and to locate points of misalignment. This will then inform decisions about whether it is appropriate to increase the directed learning load in the service of change and/or to make some adjustments that will allow undirected learning to steer the group in a different direction. We turn next to learning strategies that address various misalignment scenarios.

Process 3. Select Strategy and Tactics

Misalignments, whether between fitness landscapes at different levels, or between a fitness landscape and attractor topology at the same level, provide "learning opportunities" for a group. The target of intervention in the latter case may be the attractor topology, the fitness landscape, or both. For fitness landscape mismatches, one or more of the landscapes will be the target for change.

The recommended strategies for improving alignment differ (see Table 3.1) by type of mismatch involved and target of intervention. The severity of the mismatch and the corresponding costs and benefits of learning should inform the choice of strategy. A group that has two attractors, for example, one that aligns with a fitness peak, and one that corresponds to a fitness valley (as in Fig. 3.5), has a less daunting learning task than one with a single deep attractor far from any fitness peak. In the former case, a more modest intervention is warranted; in the latter case, a more dramatic strategy such as shifting to an alternative attractor topology will likely be more cost effective.

Strategy choice will also depend on other features special to the situation. Groups differ, for example, in how much they are able to influence those features of their embedding context that define the group-fitness landscape. If the problem landscape is not malleable, it may be feasible

TABLE 3.1 Available Learning Strategies Based on Mismatch Type and Target of Change

	Target of Change	
Type of Misalignment	**Fitness Landscape**	**Topology of Attractors**
Among Fitness Landscapes	• Align current landscapes • Move to a different landscape	(Not applicable)
Landscape-Topology	• Adjust fitness landscape • Move to a different landscape	• Improve navigation skills • Use training to adjust attractors • Move to a different topology

to shift to another landscape. Next, we discuss concrete examples to illustrate the strategies in Table 3.1 and the challenges involved.

Interventions That Target the Fitness Landscape

Align mismatched fitness landscapes. A common mismatch between fitness landscapes, well known to organizational scholars, is the folly of "rewarding A while hoping for B" (Kerr, 1975). The obvious cure is to redesign the landscape to create a peak at "B" and remove the "A" peak.

In the case of the medication errors example illustrated in Fig. 3.4 (Edmondson, 2004) both member and organizational fitness landscapes are in conflict with the behavior that the organization would like to promote in groups. The easiest way to achieve alignment, and one clearly within the control of the organization, would be to change the group landscape and punish error reporting. Because patient safety is best served by a learning-from-mistakes culture, however, abandoning an effort to inculcate this culture is clearly at odds with the greater good.

The challenge is thus twofold: Adjust both the individual and organizational landscapes to better match the group fitness curve. Alignment of individual landscapes can be achieved by replacing or retraining the nurse leader whose leadership style is creating a punitive climate. Changing the climate under which the hospital is operating is more difficult. Administrators will need to work at a broader political level to educate "upwards" and help change the social and regulatory structures that constrain their actions. In the meantime, the hospital might adjust its own structures (which falls within our definition of organizational learning) to cope with the misalignment. For example, a system that enables individuals and groups to report incidents anonymously would help "buffer" them from the misaligned fitness landscape the organization faces.

Adjust fitness landscape to match the topology better. Landscape adjustments are also an option in addressing a group landscape-topology misalignment that discourages learning. For example, a reward system that offers a bonus for improvements in group performance that are so far from existing attractors as to seem unattainable is unlikely to spur group learning. The literature on goal setting suggests that challenging but attainable goals are best (Locke, Shaw, Saari, & Latham, 1981; Weldon & Weingart, 1993). Fitness landscapes with sharp cliffs (as opposed to slopes) make learning less likely, because undirected learning operates best on gradients. A graduated system of small rewards for small improvements, and increasing rewards for each increment of improvement, provides a gradient for the group to climb. As the group becomes more successful, the attractor topology will shift accordingly. What formerly was difficult becomes not just possible but relatively easy for the group to maintain.

The literature on goal setting, which focuses on the fitness landscape of rewards, indicates that it is most effective for less complex tasks. When topology-landscape mismatches are dramatic, shifting to a different attractor topology or a different landscape may work better than a landscape-adjusting, goal-setting approach.

Move to a different fitness landscape. When a problematic fitness landscape is also not malleable, the most cost-effective solution to a landscape-topology mismatch may not be group learning but a change of group or setting (e.g., change in the organizational structure that assigns groups to tasks). Consider a task in which building trusting, cooperative relationships with suspicious and potentially hostile out-group members (rather than in-group members) is the key to success. A key X variable linked to positive group outcomes might be the group's ability to inspire trust in out-group members. A reassuring, nonthreatening presence would clearly be helpful. Now assume the group assigned to this task has been rigorously trained to quickly and efficiently overpower, subdue, and immobilize out-group members by the application of overwhelming force: A platoon of U.S. Marines, for example. The result is a serious landscape-topology misalignment.

Team behaviors that have been practiced and reinforced through both training and experience create deep, stable attractors. For the Marine platoon to excel at building cooperative out-group relations, it must resist the pull of a strong attractor, a very difficult "unlearning" task. The cost/benefit profile for retraining the group (changing the attractor topology) is quite unattractive. A less-experienced group without deep attractors would have an easier learning task in conforming to the fitness landscape. The platoon should be reassigned to a different fitness landscape that better matches its skills.

Interventions That Target the Attractor Topology

Improve navigation skills. When the misalignment between fitness landscape and attractors is not too serious, strategies that attempt to change one or the other may be unnecessary. Instead, improving collective knowledge of the topology and honing navigation skills is probably the most cost-effective strategy. The group conflict and performance example (Fig. 3.5) is a good example. The "safe" attractor of low task conflict yields reasonably good performance (Attractor 1, Peak A), while the "hazardous" high-conflict Attractor 2 yields very poor outcomes. The dynamics underlying these attractors are processes that prevent or dampen down conflict when it occurs (keeping or returning the group to Attractor 1) or that feed conflict via, for example, negative spirals of escalation (Glasl, 1982), which trap the group in Attractor 2. The "critical point" for group conflict is where the basin to Attractor 2 begins, and the group's ability to dampen conflict (moving it back to Attractor 1) gets overwhelmed. When the group falls into Attractor 2, it will likely require outside assistance to climb out.

The first learning task for the group is to reach a shared understanding of where the critical point separating the two attractor basins is, and then to be vigilant about down-regulating the level of conflict whenever the group gets too close to the tipping point. In essence the group has to learn how "not to go there." Attractors that are not visited tend to weaken and flatten, making the problem state easier and easier to avoid. Collective awareness of the relative location of the highest fitness peak and the critical point should also reassure conflict-averse members that for important decisions, the group can "safely" engage in more heated debate to improve performance. The attractor topology ensures that the increased conflict will be temporary, as long as they don't overshoot and end up in the basin for Attractor 2.

Use training to adjust attractors. The expanded mental model provided by greater awareness of the existing topology should help the group avoid the really bad outcomes of Attractor 2. A next, somewhat more ambitious step would be to use training to change the topology. The main goal of a learning initiative such as this would be to improve topology alignment with Fitness Peak B. To develop a new attractor at this point, coaching or facilitation of group discussion of "hot" topics may help the group engage in substantive debate without spilling over into interpersonal attacks. Practice using ground rules that support "fighting fair" and sticking to the issues will help the group stabilize a new way of interacting at a higher level of task conflict. The existing low-conflict attractor will likely remain the more comfortable and easily accessible state for the group. However, a new, moderate-conflict attractor, even if it is shallow and not particularly stable, would still be very useful in enabling the group to process information thoroughly for those issues where the quality of decision making is critical.

Move to a different topology. Earlier, we discussed the option of moving to a different fitness landscape as a way of resolving a serious landscape-topology mismatch. When the group assigned to a fitness landscape has an incompatible attractor topology but is nevertheless clearly the right group for the job, the group needs a new topology. This was the situation for interdisciplinary operating room (OR) teams trying to learn a new minimally invasive cardiac surgery (MICS) technique (Edmondson, 2003). The well-practiced and powerful attractor for such teams in traditional open-heart surgery was for the surgeon to give orders and the other members of the team—nurses, anesthesiologists, and perfusionists (who run the heart-lung machine)—to pay attention to what the surgeon was doing and respond immediately to whatever he or she said. Their job was to listen but not to speak up.

The new MICS technique promised many potential advantages for patients, but required a very different type of interaction for the OR team. Because the heart is not exposed, the surgeon needs to rely on vital information communicated by other team members. The team must coordinate by talking rather than via the shared visual field available in open-heart surgery. Hence, for an X variable of "conversing during operations" the fitness peak was at the high end, while the team's existing attractor was at the low end. Retraining involved, in essence, making a new attractor appear in the place where a *repellor* (an inaccessible value) existed in the group's current topology.

Hospitals adopting the new procedure were required to send OR teams to a three-day training. While this may have been adequate training in learning the technical requirements, it was clearly inadequate training for groups to learn a completely different way of interacting. At one hospital, for example, a surgeon lamented that "after 50 cases…I'm not getting that much better at it." Members of all 16 teams studied reported "being amazed at the extent of change…required. The difficulty…was more behavioural than technical" (Edmondson, 2003, p. 1434). Knowledge of the attractor topology makes the daunting nature of the learning task clear. However, the ability to work effectively in more traditional surgery situations was not a skill that members would want to lose. What the group needed was the capacity for *bistability:* the ability to access two incompatible stable states, each appropriate in a different setting.

In such situations, which call for a radical reconfiguration of the attractor topology, the most cost-effective learning solution is to discover and adjust a *control parameter* that moves the group from one topology to another—and that can be readjusted to move the group back. The group needs to access a different topology.

Control parameters and bifurcations: The topology reformed. Because attractors are determined by the internal dynamics of a group, factors that affect these dynamics can also alter the attractor topology. Parameters that shape the contours of attractors are called *control parameters*

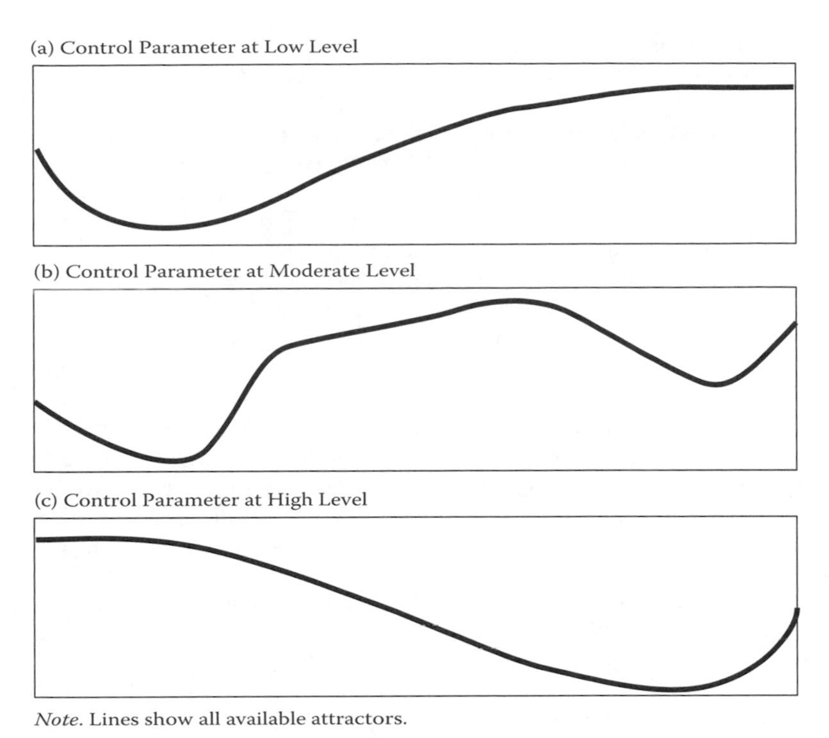

Figure 3.6 Group topology of attractors at (a) low, (b) moderate, and (c) high levels of a control parameter.

(also known as contextual parameters; Arrow et al., 2000, p. 44). When the control parameters change, attractors appear, disappear, or change their nature. What was easy becomes difficult, and vice versa. Just as reassigning the Marine platoon moves the group from one fitness landscape to another, adjusting a control parameter can move a group from one attractor topology to another.

Consider the three topologies displayed in Fig. 3.6. Fig. 3.6b replicates the attractor topology for conflict used in Fig. 3.5, which is determined by the dynamics that amplify and dampen conflict in a particular group. A different group, with somewhat different dynamics, would have a different picture. However, if the dynamics that create the attractors with a particular group are altered, that same group may find itself navigating a different topology. An example of a control parameter that might alter the dynamics in this way would be the level of stress or threat under which a group is operating. Under the normal range of stress conditions, the group operates in topology 3.6b. Under high-threat conditions, however, the topology of attractors may be deformed so that the low-conflict attractor disappears (Fig. 3.6c). If stress is radically reduced (for example, when group members interact outside of work in a social setting), the high conflict attractor may disappear (Fig. 3.6a). Changes in control parameters move the group to a qualitatively different set of operating conditions.

To get control of the topology, a leader or group needs to discover what parameters shift the group from one set of dynamics to another and in this way control the topology's shape. Instead of constantly struggling to enact previously forbidden behaviors (speaking to the surgeon during an operation), the MICS teams need to shift to a topology in which speaking up seems natural. The people who made up the team all presumably operate effectively in other arenas of their life in which they have open conversations. What was the key to access this dynamic?

Edmondson (2003) focused on the power differential in the groups. In a traditional OR setting, the power differential between surgeon and other team members was very steep. Surgeons in teams that were successful in learning and executing the new technique changed this parameter. One tactic was to emphasize to the other members that MICS is a team project; another was to invite nurses and perfusionists to seminars that had formerly been for surgeons only (p. 1439), a setting in which all team members would interact as colleagues rather than as "dictator" and subordinates. Without "unlearning" the behaviors appropriate to a traditional OR (which would be immediately cued by the power stance of the surgeon in that setting), MICS team members together developed the ability to switch to a different mode of operating, with an attractor of constant communication appropriately aligned to the MICS fitness landscape.

Processes 4 & 5. Implement and Monitor

From a CAS perspective, successful intervention in a dynamic system depends on the dynamics already operating in a group. In this section, we focus on *group development*, the pattern of systematic global changes in a group over time. Group development is relevant to learning for three reasons. First, changes that improve a group's ability to complete group projects and fulfill member needs may occur as a natural effect of development with no need for intervention. Second, the "same" intervention, implemented at different times in a group's development, can have a positive impact, a negative impact, or no effect whatsoever. In other words, timing matters. Third, developmental patterns have implications for monitoring and feedback. After what length of time should improvements be expected? Premature course corrections can derail learning; delaying too long can make getting back on track harder.

From the perspective of CAS theory, group development is a process of successively establishing and stabilizing attractor topologies, and then destabilizing those patterns to replace them with new ones (cf. Hsu & Fogel, 2003, for a similar perspective on developmental processes in infants). It refers to global changes that happen over the life course of a group, rather than to changes in shorter-term cycles, such as phases of group decision making. Although many developmental models have been proposed (for some overviews, see Arrow, 1997; Arrow, Henry, Poole, Wheelan, & Moreland, 2005; McCollom, 1995; Mennecke, Hoffer, & Wynne, 1992), all assert that groups shift over time from one state to another. The models differ in the number and nature of states (in our terms, attractor topologies) characterized, in endorsing a fixed or a flexible sequence of states, and in whether they view triggers for change as endogenous to the group, exogenous, or both. At the most abstract level of configuration, stabilization, and reconfiguration, most models can fit under the umbrella of three logically ordered modes: (a) *formation,* (b) *operation,* and (c) *metamorphosis* (Arrow et al., 2000, p. 54).

During formation, a group configures itself as a coordinated network of members, tasks, and tools. Members learn about one another and the group tasks. Roles and status hierarchies emerge. Norms may be imported from the group context or may need to be negotiated if members have different notions of how the group should operate (Bettenhausen & Murnighan, 1985). Some groups move through this mode quickly, in a matter of hours or days (e.g., Gersick, 1988; Ginnett, 1990); others may take weeks or months to configure the relevant networks (e.g., Wheelan, 1994).

In operation mode, a group is functioning (well or poorly) in service of group projects and member needs. Ongoing operations tend to stabilize the group, deepen existing attractors, and in the process make member and group behavior predictable. However, the attractor topology may also shift (gradually or abruptly) in response to events occurring in embedding contexts. Gersick (1988; 1989), whose punctuated equilibrium model emphasizes stability within phases and abrupt shifts to instability between phases, called the restructuring period the transition. During a *transition,* the attractor topology is destabilized, altered, and then stabilized into a new pattern.

Metamorphosis is a transition mode of reconfiguration in which a destabilized group is undergoing profound change. A group in metamorphosis may dissolve, change into a different social entity (e.g., split into two groups), or emerge with some aspect (structure, culture, mission, membership) transformed. The outcome is uncertain.

In formation mode, group members devote conscious attention to sorting out how they will interact with one another and who will do what. Groups in formation require time for their attractor topology to emerge and stabilize before learning strategies are implemented that modify the topology or alter the fitness landscape. Too much change in the early stages of a group life can make it harder for the group to develop a stable attractor topology (e.g., Arrow, 1997). If the fitness landscape in which the group forms is aligned with organizational objectives, this can help avoid costly "unlearning" later on.

Just as children naturally acquire language without special training, groups naturally develop attractor topologies without special training programs. However, the context strongly shapes what children and groups learn. If the group fitness landscape is both salient and reasonably compatible with member fitness landscapes as the group forms, the emerging attractor topology is unlikely to be seriously out of alignment.

Openness to learning within the operation mode should change systematically as a group moves from one configuration of attractors to another. Within inertial states or phases, Gersick (1988) found that groups were inattentive to external information about performance—i.e., to the group-fitness landscape. During transitions, however, groups suddenly paid a great deal of attention to their embedding context, searching for new information and reconsidering previously ignored information (Gersick, 1990).

This shift of attention between inertial phases and transition periods yields insight into timing issues for implementing and monitoring. During inertial states, interventions focused either on improving navigation skills to avoid troublesome attractors or shifting the locus of attractors via training are appropriate. Changes to the group fitness landscape, however, are unlikely to motivate short-term undirected learning. In the longer term, after a transition that focuses attention outward, undirected learning strategies based on changes to the fitness landscape implemented during an inertial state may still become effective. Thus, even for the "same" intervention, expectations for the timing of learning, and thus judgments about the success or failure of an intervention, should take the developmental state of the group into account.

Transitions also offer a promising opportunity for more ambitious change efforts. As the group alters its trajectory, even small inputs can have a substantial impact on the shape of a new attractor structure. Gersick (1989) suggested that the midpoint is a natural transition point for task groups with defined lifespans. For these groups, the midpoint may be a promising occasion to implement a directed-learning intervention.

Worchel (1994) has proposed a six-stage recurrent cycle model of group development that does not assume a fixed beginning or ending point for a group. Ongoing groups lack the strong midpoint trigger that task forces experience. According to Worchel's model, a transition (or a metamorphosis) is triggered by a *precipitating event* that occurs after the group system has fallen into decay and discontent, with declining member commitment and energy. This description suggests a group with a deeply rutted attractor topology that is not well matched to member fitness landscapes.

The precipitating event may be externally generated (e.g., threat by powerful outsiders, or an imposed change in members) or an internally generated event such as interpersonal conflict (Gersick, 1991; Gersick & Hackman, 1990). Worchel's model suggested timing tips for shifting a group to a different attractor topology: Implement the strategy early in the decay/discontent part of the cycle, and actively engineer a dramatic event to pull member energy back into the group and precipitate change. "Unlearning" is easiest during metamorphosis, when structure is erased and the group is ready for reconfiguration into a new mold.

Monitoring and feedback should be part of any intervention. Changes in the group's emotional climate may be apparent relatively quickly. If the intervention imposes a significant learning load, the first noticeable change in task performance is likely to be negative, as attention and resources are redirected, and established routines are disrupted. Planning for disruption can help ease stress. The tension between learning and performance is also a theme in the last process we discuss, proactive learning.

Process 6. Proactive Learning

Proactive learning involves changes in knowledge, capacity, and interaction patterns that increase system integrity, making groups both more robust against shocks and disruptions and more nimble in adapting to change. For some groups, proactive learning is a waste of time and energy. Project groups with a relatively short and finite lifespan, for example, might better focus on completing their project as well as possible using its available repertoire of skills. Groups that tackle well-learned tasks for which efficiency is paramount may also find sacrificing short-term effectiveness in the service of flexibility to be a bad tradeoff. Proactive learning *is* worthwhile for groups with an indefinite lifespan, which expect to tackle a succession of tasks in operating conditions that will likely change over time—in other words, for *teams* (Argote & McGrath, 1993). Investing in future capacity makes sense if the group has a future.

Proactive learning comes naturally to groups with a high "learning orientation," which can be assessed by asking members about the extent to which their team seeks "opportunities to develop new skills and knowledge," likes challenging assignments, is willing to experiment, and considers learning important (Bunderson & Sutcliffe, 2003, p. 555). Translated into CAS terms, such groups seek out tasks with fitness landscapes not aligned to their current attractor topology. Experimentation moves groups away from familiar attractors. Through exploration, groups discover alternate attractors in their repertoire of topologies and learn to form and stabilize new attractors, multiplying the number of topologies they can shift to as needed.

Groups high in learning orientation respond to disruptions differently than groups with a high performance orientation, especially when a group has difficult goals (LePine, 2005). Faced with a change in operating conditions, high-learning orientation groups were "more cooperative, shared problem-relevant information with one another, and made and evaluated suggestions about alternative ways of doing the task" (LePine, 2005, p. 1164), while groups high in performance orientation focused on how they were doing relative to their goal (not well, given the disruption) and failed to adapt effectively.

Having many members with a high-learning orientation is helpful in establishing this as the group culture (LePine, 2005). However, as shown by the impact of nurse managers in the units studied by Edmondson (2004), learning orientation can also be strongly affected by a group leader. Like other aspects of climate, it can be adjusted. Membership change and variation in settings and group activities can promote proactive learning by increasing the volume and diversity of information flow and boosting behavioral variability. People pay closer attention to novel cues compared to familiar cues (Daffner et al., 2006), and change introduces novelty. To develop and maintain adaptability, groups need change.

Membership change. Communication tends to decrease over time in groups, especially if the group membership is stable for a matter of years (Katz, 1982). Periodic membership change, whether permanent or temporary, helps combat this decay and keep communication channels active. Newcomers promote information flow by asking questions that elicit explanations (Sutton & Louis, 1987). This draws explicit attention to taken-for-granted attractors that may no longer be well adapted to the group-fitness landscape. The presence of guest members can promote more creative thinking (Arrow & McGrath, 1993), and temporary member transfer to other groups can yield benefits in increased involvement and more debate and new thinking after the "itinerant" member returns (Gruenfeld, Martorana, & Fan, 2000).

Along with importing and exporting members, changing member roles (job switching) also promotes information exchange and learning. The short-term decrease in performance efficiency builds the group's capacity to substitute for missing members and handle other disruptions to group composition in the future.

Promote variability in settings and interactions. The opportunity to interact in new settings extends the group's experience with different attractor topologies and helps members discover more about one another's knowledge and expertise (Littlepage, Robison, & Reddington, 1997). Socializing outside of work, for example, extends the range of who talks to whom about what. Collective awareness of the outside lives of group members expands the group's mental model of who knows what, who has what skills, and who is potentially connected to people and resources beyond group boundaries. This knowledge could prove useful if the group needs to rapidly access informational resources beyond its usual repertoire. When work requires a shift in attractors, as was true for the OR team members (Edmondson, 2003), experience in other settings can facilitate the shift.

"Off-task" group activity during work hours also diversifies information flows. Though often viewed negatively, gossip is an enjoyable information transfer activity that can help strengthen and maintain bonds within a community (Dunbar, 1996). It tends to flow along different routes than formal reporting lines, enriching the informal network. A culture of practical jokes and other improvised off-task activities also helps keep a group fresh in performing routine tasks, as members try to stay alert for "surprises" that other group members may have prepared (Roy, 1960).

Concluding Thoughts

Our goal in this chapter has been to demonstrate how a complex systems perspective can provide insight into group learning. Awareness of fitness landscapes, and of how undirected learning moves systems from one point to another on these landscapes, can provide insight into why groups sometimes "learn" the wrong thing when landscapes are out of alignment. It also provides ideas for how to reorient groups by fixing such misalignments. Awareness of how attractor topologies govern behavior can provide insight into why, even when all the fitness landscapes seem to be properly aligned, groups sometimes seem to be incapable of learning from experience, but instead remain stuck in unproductive patterns. Suggested strategies for improving navigation, shifting attractors, and using control parameters to catapult the group into alternative topologies provide a toolbox for constructive change.

Group learning strategies should be grounded in a realistic assessment of costs and benefits. To avoid wasted effort, interventions should take a group's developmental state into account. "Change agents" should pay attention to group development to pinpoint windows of instability. At these times interventions can have a big impact, even in groups that previously seemed impervious to change, because the nonlinearity of complex systems can magnify impact instead of dampening and canceling it out.

For groups that are already performing well, proactive learning can build capacity for future performance. Groups that focus too strongly on performance goals can become "brittle" and prove maladaptive should change become necessary. Of course, strategies such as membership change, off-task activity, and socializing can also divert energy emphasis away from immediate performance goals. "Continuous learning" is not a good strategy for groups that will only be together briefly and have a looming deadline to meet.

Our intent has not been to propose a normative or descriptive model of how groups do or should learn. Our more modest goal was to use the complex adaptive systems perspective to offer a fresh look at how to assess learning needs and implement strategies to "configure" and "reconfigure" groups as complex learning systems.

Author Note: We are grateful to Valerie Sessa and Manuel London for the invitation to write the chapter, and to Valerie and Joe McGrath for helpful comments on drafts. We also would like to express our deep appreciation for Skype, which allowed us to have many lengthy transatlantic phone conversations for free.

REFERENCES

Argote, L., & McGrath, J. E. (1993). Group processes in organizations: Continuity and change. In C. Cooper, & I. T. Robertson (Eds.), *International review of industrial & organizational psychology* (Vol. 18, pp. 333–389). New York: John Wiley.

Arrow, H. (1997). Stability, bistability, and instability in small group influence patterns. *Journal of Personality & Social Psychology, 72*(1), 75–85.

Arrow, H., Henry, K. B., Poole, M. S., Wheelan, S. A., & Moreland, R. L. (2005). Traces, trajectories, and timing: The temporal perspective on groups. In M. S. Poole, & A. B. Hollingshead (Eds.), *Theories of small groups: Interdisciplinary perspectives* (pp. 313–367). Thousand Oaks, CA: Sage.

Arrow, H., & McGrath, J. E. (1993). Membership matters: How member change and continuity affect small group structure, process, and performance. *Small Group Research, 24*, 334–361

Arrow, H., McGrath, J. E., & Berdahl, J. L. (2000). *Small groups as complex systems: Formation, coordination, development, and adaptation*. Thousand Oaks, CA: Sage.

Baird, L., Holland, P., & Deacon, S. (1999). Learning from action: Imbedding more learning into the performance fast enough to make a difference. *Organizational Dynamics, 27*(4), 19–32.

Bapuji, H., & Crossan, M. (2004). From questions to answers: Reviewing organizational learning research. *Management Learning, 35*(4), 397–417.

Bettenhausen, K., & Murnighan, J. (1985). The emergence of norms in competitive decision-making groups. *Administrative Science Quarterly, 30*(3), 350–372.

Bunderson, J. S., & Sutcliffe, K. M. (2003). Management team learning orientation and business unit performance. *Journal of Applied Psychology, 88*(3), 552–560.

Crossan, M. M., Lane, H. W., White, R. E., & Djurfeldt, L. (1995). Organizational learning: Dimensions for a theory. *International Journal of Organizational Analysis, 3*(4), 337–360.

Daffner, K. R., Ryan, K. K., Williams, D. M., Budson, A. E., Rentz, D. M., Wolk, D. A., et al. (2006). Age-related differences in attention to novelty among cognitively high performing adults. *Biological Psychology, Electronic,1*, 67–77.

De Dreu, C. K. W., & Weingart, L. R. (2003). Task versus relationship conflict, team performance, and team member satisfaction: A meta-analysis. *Journal of Applied Psychology, 88*(4), 741–749.

Dunbar, R. (1996). *Grooming, gossip, and the evolution of language*. Cambridge, MA: Harvard University Press.

Edmondson, A. C. (2003). Speaking up in the operating room: How team leaders promote learning in interdisciplinary action teams. *Journal of Management Studies, 40*(6), 1419–1452.

Edmondson, A. C. (2004). Learning from mistakes is easier said than done. *The Journal of Applied Behavioral Science, 40*(1), 66–90.

Feldman, M. S. (2000). Organizational routines as a source of continuous change. *Organization Science, 11*(6), 611–629.

Gersick, C. J. (1988). Time and transition in work teams: Toward a new model of group development. *Academy of Management Journal, 31*(1), 9–41.

Gersick, C. J. (1989). Marking time: Predictable transitions in task groups. *Academy of Management Journal, 32*(2), 274–309.
Gersick, C. J. (1990). The students. In J. R. Hackman (Ed.), *Groups that work (and those that don't)* (pp. 89–111). San Francisco: Jossey-Bass.
Gersick, C. J. (1991). Revolutionary change theories: A multilevel exploration of the punctuated equilibrium paradigm. *Academy of Management Review, 16*(1), 10–36.
Gersick, C. J., & Hackman, J. (1990). Habitual routines in task-performing groups. *Organizational Behavior & Human Decision Processes, 47*(1), 65–97.
Ginnett, R. C. (1990). Airline cockpit crew. In J. R. Hackman (Ed.), *Groups that work (and those that don't)* (pp. 427–448). San Francisco: Jossey-Bass.
Glasl, F. (1982). The process of conflict escalation and roles of third parties. In G. B. J. Bomers, & R. Peterson (Eds.), *Conflict management and industrial relations* (pp. 119–140). Boston: Kluwer-Nijhoff.
Gruenfeld, D. H., Martorana, P. V., & Fan, E. T. (2000). What do groups learn from their worldliest members? Direct and indirect influence in dynamic teams. *Organizational Behavior and Human Decision Processes, 82*(1), 45–59.
Hackman, J. R., & Morris, C. G. (1975). Group tasks, group interaction process, and group performance effectiveness: A review and proposed integration. *Advances in Experimental Social Psychology, 8*, 45–99.
Holland, J. H. (1995). *Hidden order: How adaptation builds complexity.* Reading, MA: Addison-Wesley.
Hsu, H. C., & Fogel, A. (2003). Stability and transitions in mother-infant face-to-face communication during the first 6 months. A microhistorical approach. *Developmental Psychology, 39*, 1061–1082.
Jehn, K. (1997). Affective and cognitive conflict in work groups: Increasing performance through value-based intragroup conflict. In C. K. W. De Dreu, & E. V. d. Vliert (Eds.), *Using conflict in organizations* (pp. 87–100). London: Sage.
Katz, R. (1982). The effects of group longevity on project communication and performance. *Administrative Science Quarterly, 27*(1), 81–104.
Kerr, S. (1975). On the folly of rewarding A, while hoping for B. *Academy of Management Journal, 18*(4), 769–783.
LePine, J. A. (2005). Adaptation of teams in response to unforeseen change: Effects of goal difficulty and team composition in terms of cognitive ability and goal orientation. *Journal of Applied Psychology, 90*(6), 1153–1167.
Levine, J. M., & Moreland, R. L. (1991). Culture and socialization in work groups. In L. B. Resnick, J. M. Levine, & S. D. Teasley (Eds.), *Perspectives on socially shared cognition* (pp. 257–279). Washington, DC: American Psychological Association.
Littlepage, G., Robison, W., & Reddington, K. (1997). Effects of task experience and group experience on group performance, member ability, and recognition of expertise. *Organizational Behavior & Human Decision Processes, 69*(2), 133–147.
Locke, E. A., Shaw, K. N., Saari, L. M., & Latham, G. P. (1981). Goal setting and task performance: 1969–1980. *Psychological Bulletin, 90*(1), 125–152.
McCollom, M. (1995). Reevaluating group development: A critique of the familiar models. In J. Gillette, & M. McCollom (Eds.), *Groups in context* (pp. 133–154). Lanham, MD: University Press of America.

McGrath, J. E. (1991). Time, interaction, and performance (TIP): A theory of groups. *Small Group Research, 22*(2), 147–174.

Mennecke, B. E., Hoffer, J. A., & Wynne, B. E. (1992). The implications of group development and history for group support system theory and practice. *Small Group Research, 23*(4), 524–572.

Roy, D. F. (1960). "Banana time" job satisfaction and informal interaction. *Human Organization, 18,* 158–168.

Sessa, V. I., & London, M. (2006). *Continuous learning in organizations: Individual, group, and organizational perspectives.* Mahwah, NJ: Lawrence Erlbaum.

Sutton, R. I., & Louis, M. R. (1987). How selecting and socializing newcomers influences insiders. *Human Resource Management, 26*(3), 347–361.

van de Ven, A. H., & Poole, M. S. (1995). Explaining development and change in organizations. *The Academy of Management Review, 20*(3), 510–540.

von Bertalanffy, L. (1976). *General system theory: Foundations, development, applications* (Rev ed.). New York: George Braziller.

Wall, J. A. Jr., & Callister, R. R. (1995). Conflict and its management. *Journal of Management, 21*(3), 515–558.

Weick, K. E. (1995). *Sensemaking in organizations.* Thousand Oaks, CA: Sage Publications.

Weldon, E., & Weingart, L. R. (1993). Group goals and group performance. *British Journal of Social Psychology, 32,* 307–334.

Wheelan, S. A. (1994). *Group processes: A developmental perspective.* Boston: Allyn & Bacon.

Worchel, S. (1994). You can go home again: Returning group research to the group context with an eye on developmental issues. *Small Group Research, 25*(2), 205–223.

CHAPTER

4

Shared Cognition and Group Learning

R. SCOTT TINDALE, SARAH STAWISKI,
AND ELIZABETH JACOBS
Loyola University Chicago

Over the past few decades, behavioral scientists have begun to view groups less as task performance vehicles and more as information processing systems (Brauner & Scholl, 2000; Hinsz, Tindale, & Vollrath, 1997). Task performance remains an important outcome variable, but the assumptions and hypotheses concerning how groups reach different levels of performance tend to focus on the social and cognitive aspects of information processing. Hinsz et al. (1997) defined group information processing as "the degree to which information, ideas, or cognitive processes are *shared* [italics added], and are *being shared* [italics added], among the group members" (p. 43). The italicized aspects of the aforementioned definition are the key components that distinguish group-level from individual-level information processing. Information that is shared a priori by the group's members sets the context for the group's behavior and often plays an inordinate role in both group processes and outcomes (Kameda, Tindale, & Davis, 2003; Tindale & Kameda, 2000; Wittenbaum & Stasser, 1996). The sharing of information while the group is working on its task helps to insure optimal levels of performance and aids in the group consensus process (Stasser, 1992; Winquist & Larson, 1998).

The notion of a priori "sharedness" (Tindale & Kameda, 2000) and the sharing that goes on during group discussion are also intricately linked to one of the most important aspects of group information processing: group learning. Group learning involves the acquisition and use of information by the group in order to reach a group goal. Although many of the same issues are involved in group and individual learning, the group context adds multiple levels of complexity. First, each group member can act as an information-acquisition site for the group, which allows the group to acquire and use a much larger base of information in a smaller time frame; however, simply because a given group member has acquired a relevant piece of information does not mean that the group has the information at its disposal. The information must first be perceived as relevant, and then shared with other group members in order for it to truly be considered acquired (Stasser, 1999). Thus, critical variables for group—as opposed to individual—learning are which group member has the relevant information for the task, as well as whether or not other group members recognize this individual as having task-relevant information. Second, at least two levels of learning or understanding must happen at the group level in order for the group to operate smoothly (Cannon-Bowers, Salas, & Converse, 1993). Like individuals, groups must understand the basic characteristics of the task on which they are working; however, they must also understand the basics of effective group processes and how such processes interact with the idiosyncrasies of their own groups. All of the aforementioned knowledge must be shared among the group members, at least to some degree, in order for the group to put it to good use. Finally, much recent research has shown that a shared group identity is quite useful, if not necessary, for the effective execution of group information processing (Hogg, 2001; Kramer, Hanna, Su, & Wei, 2001). Thus, sharedness and sharing infiltrate group learning from many different directions. As the following discussion will show, however, when it comes to sharedness, more is not always better; group learning often requires a balance of shared and unshared information for its occurrence.

In the following sections, we will discuss what is currently known about shared cognitions in groups and how they affect learning and performance. Two types of learning will be addressed. One involves how group members learn in a group context, which is sometimes referred to as "group-to-individual transfer" (Laughlin & Adamopoulos, 1982). The second focuses on the group level, in terms of both how and when a group learns to behave differently in a new or changing environment. Obviously, individual learning among group members is involved in this second type of learning as well, but the focus is on what is learned by the group as a whole rather than what any given individual can take away from the group for use at a later point in time. We will finish with a discussion of potentially fruitful arenas for future research on shared cognition and group learning.

Where Shared Cognitions Originate

Shared cognitions are present to some degree when any group forms, and can be at least part of their reason for forming (Moreland, 1987). Groups often form because of shared interests or a shared commitment to solving a particular problem. Even most organizational groups or teams are formed based on common areas of expertise or associations to the same department or product. In addition, through processes such as common experience, and cultural transmission and assimilation, group members who are drawn from the same culture or society share many basic assumptions about the world (Tindale, Meisenhelder, Dykema-Engblade, & Hogg, 2001). Shared cognitions also derive from the basic social encounters experienced in everyday life (Festinger, 1954). Whenever a situation develops where individuals encounter uncertainty, they look to the people around them for cues as to appropriate responses and beliefs to hold. Members and norms of our salient in-group are particularly likely to help resolve such uncertainties (Hogg & Mullen, 1999). A social comparison process known as "modeling" is probably the most basic aspect of learning in groups (Bandura, 1986). This process seems to be a natural consequence of social interaction at many levels, from small groups to societies and nations (Latanè & Bourgeois, 2001).

The literature on shared mental models discusses two different aspects of sharedness: (a) shared representations of the task and (b) shared representations of the group (Cannon-Bowers et al., 1993). Shared representations of the task involve both the equipment and the behaviors necessary to carry the task to completion. Much of the literature on learning in groups focuses on task mental models and how individual members learn from these models how to accomplish the task. Group task performance, however, often requires knowledge about how the group operates and appropriate norms for "good" group behavior; this knowledge is what comprises the team mental model. Models of the group will involve member roles and responsibilities, role interdependence, information sources, and typical interaction and communication patterns. They may also involve prescriptive ideas as to how the group should operate (Wiener, Kanki, & Helmreich, 1993).

One particular type of shared mental model that has received considerable research attention is a transactive memory system (Wegner, 1987). Transactive memory involves the shared understanding of who knows what within the context of the group. In other words, it involves the distribution of information among the group members and the shared metaknowledge of how that information is distributed. Without the shared metaknowledge, a group could possess information that is never used because those members who need it are not the ones who possess it. Transactive memory systems allow groups to store and use considerably more information than could be held in memory by a single individual. The distributed nature of the information allows for considerably greater memory load at the group level, while helping to keep memory load for each individual member at a reasonable level. Recent research on group memory has shown that reducing the cognitive load of the individual members tends to increase the group's ability to later recall and use information (Dykema-Engblade & Tindale, 2006; Tindale & Sheffey, 2002).

Shared mental models and transactive memory systems tend to form naturally through group interaction (Baumann & Bonner, 2006; Peterson, Mitchell, Thompson, & Burr, 2000). Peterson et al. (2000) found that groups working on semester-long class projects showed greater degrees of sharedness of task and group knowledge as the semester progressed, with those groups showing the most sharedness performing the best at the end of the semester. Baumann and Bonner (2006) found that groups expecting to be together longer showed more well-formed transactive memory systems than groups with a short-term expectation. In addition, they found that the transactive memory systems tended to form naturally without any special planning by the group. Research by Hollingshead (1996; 1998) and others also showed that dating and married couples both have and use transactive memory systems, mainly due to their shared knowledge of each other's interests and experiences. Research by Moreland and associates (Liang, Moreland, & Argote, 1995; Moreland, Argote, & Krishnan, 1998) showed that a simple 30-minute training session with intact groups was enough for the groups to form transactive memory systems that subsequently led to better performance compared to groups in which members were individually trained.

Groups can be explicitly trained to develop shared mental models of both the task and the group, however, and such training can substantially improve performance (Cannon-Bowers et al., 1993). Probably one of the most successful team-training programs is Cockpit Resource Management (CRM; Wiener et al., 1993). The basic premise of CRM is that each member of the team should have not only a thorough understanding of his or her own role and duties, but also a working knowledge of what other members of the team do, should know, and need to know in order for them to do their tasks effectively. In addition, CRM involves creating an environment for trust and risk-free communication so that any member of the team can question and inform other members, regardless of status considerations. Research using both airline cockpit crews and medical operating teams has shown that the shared knowledge and open communication channels can significantly reduce errors, even in high-stress environments (Helmreich, 1997).

Individual Learning in Groups

In many ways, shared cognitions provide the context for learning in groups. Early theorists in the symbolic interactionist framework (e.g., Mead, 1934) argued that shared meanings were necessary for any type of meaningful social exchange. More recently, Moscovici (1984) argued that shared meanings, termed "social representations," provide the context for the learning of social norms and belief structures that are considered "givens" in society. These shared representations are both proliferated and reinforced by social interaction. Consider a comment during a casual discussion that expresses a belief such as, "Well, they have always had a reputation of thinking they are better than others." If such a statement receives either explicit approval or no direct refutation, it becomes strengthened in the cognitive framework of those already familiar with the belief, and plants a seed of the belief in anyone for whom it is unfamiliar. As such beliefs gain validity, they become more likely to be shared in further conversations. In this manner, such beliefs slowly become part of the social representation of those exposed to them. Later, when someone uses the belief to draw an inference about the aforementioned out-group, the inference seems plausible within the already-shared representation, and thus remains unquestioned. Additional reactions to the out-group that are consistent with the shared representation are also interpretable and expected (Turner & Oakes, 1989), and they help to form the social representation associated with that out-group. Thus, casual social interaction can lead to incidental learning in groups, even when the interaction is not purposefully oriented toward learning.

Much of the laboratory work on learning in groups has focused on the degree to which successful group performance transfers to individual members after their group experience (Laughlin & Adamopoulos, 1982; Laughlin & Sweeney, 1977; Stasson, Kameda, Parks, Zimmerman, & Davis, 1991). Laughlin and colleagues (e.g., Laughlin & Adamopoulos, 1982) demonstrated that for certain types of tasks, solving problems as a member of a group helps members to solve the same problems at a later point in time. In addition, a number of studies have shown that as a function of group discussion, individual group-member preferences change to become more like those of the other group members (Davis, 1980; Hinsz et al., 1997). For decision problems where no correct or optimal answer exists, majority factions tend to define the final group choice, and postdiscussion convergence among group member preferences is largely due to majority influence (Kameda et al., 2003). For problems with "demonstrably correct" solutions, however, such convergence is more likely to reflect learning, at least in terms of the specific problem addressed by the group (Laughlin, 1980). In some cases, even a single group member with the correct answer can convince all other members to change their preference (Laughlin & Ellis, 1986). Such learning is at least partly a function of background knowledge shared among the group members (Tindale, Smith, Thomas, Filkins, & Sheffey, 1996).

Laughlin and Ellis (1986) defined four criteria that should be met in order for a task to have a "demonstrably correct solution." First, group members must share a verbal or mathematical system for solving the problem. Second, sufficient information must be available to demonstrate the correctness of the response within the shared system. Third, the group members who do not solve the problem correctly must have sufficient knowledge of the shared system to recognize a correct solution when it is proposed. Finally, members who do solve the problem correctly must have the requisite ability, motivation, and time to demonstrate the correct solution to the incorrect members. The first and third criteria are most relevant to learning in groups. Without a shared knowledge structure, a correct solution proposed in the group will not be understood by all group members, even if it is adopted by the group. This has been empirically demonstrated with children in groups (Mugney & Doise, 1982). In their experiments, children who could solve a problem were paired with children who either could almost solve the problem or were completely incapable of solving the problem. In such settings, learning only occurred for children with at least some understanding of the problem. The children with no understanding deferred to the child in the group who could solve the problem, but showed no evidence of learning on subsequent trials.

It would seem that demonstrability could refer to both the correct solution of a specific problem and to one or more strategies that aid in solving a problem. Group-to-individual transfer has been consistently demonstrated when the postgroup individuals work on the exact same problems solved by the group (Laughlin & Adamopoulos, 1982). Postgroup individual performance, however, often shows considerably less improvement if the individuals are asked to work on different problems in the same genre (Budescu & Maciejousky, in press; Laughlin & Sweeney, 1977). For example, a group member may learn the appropriate answer to a particular analogy problem and may remember the answer for subsequent testing, though knowing that answer will not be of much help for solving different analogy problems. That said, some group experiences allow for the learning of strategies that can be used later.

Recent research by Laughlin, Hatch, Silver, and Boh (2006) used a "letters-to-numbers" mapping task in which individuals and groups must learn the correct number-letter mapping for each numeric digit. Participants are allowed to develop equations using the letters, and they are given feedback in terms of the letters that would correctly and numerically solve the equation. When first faced with this problem, most individuals (and groups) use a trial-and-error method that revolves around simple two-letter equations. Although this strategy will eventually lead to discovery of the correct mapping, some simple strategies lead to much quicker solutions. For example, adding all 10 letters together will lead to the answer 45. Feedback in terms of letters will then instantly provide information about which letter represents 4 and which represents 5. With this knowledge, one can compose new equations with known solutions in order to discover the numeric values for the other letters (Laughlin, Bonner, & Miner, 2002). If any of the individual group members discovers this strategy, virtually every other member should quickly understand its usefulness and apply it on subsequent problems. Evidence for this type of "strategy learning" in groups has been documented using simple geometry and algebra problems (Stasson et al.,1991), and more recently with the Wason selection task (Budescu & Maciejousky, in press). Processes such as strategy learning are examples of the development of a shared task representation (Tindale et al., 1996). Formally, a shared task representation is any task/situation-relevant concept, norm, perspective, or cognitive process shared by most or all of the group members.

Through what is basically the same aforementioned process, group members can also learn erroneous strategies (Tindale, 1993; Tindale et al., 1996). Although there is plenty of evidence that people acquire bad habits from peer groups (Lorenzi-Cioldi & Clèmence, 2001), most studies on group transfer show either positive transfer or no transfer at all. A series of studies by Tindale et al. (1996), however, showed that whenever a shared task representation is present, group members who favor responses or strategies consistent with the shared representation are overly influential, thus affecting both group processes and outcomes. Importantly, shared task representations are helpful in task performance only to the extent that they are accurate. In Laughlin and Ellis' (1986) definition of demonstrability, a shared verbal or mathematical system used for solving a problem is a shared task representation. In most group contexts, such shared task representations are either generally accurate or at least normative in terms of the particular task.

There are situations, however, in which a shared task representation is inaccurate from either a normative or a logical perspective. For example, when people are asked to estimate the probability of a conjoint event in which the two events differ substantially in their individual likelihoods, they often estimate the conjoint probability as the numeric average of the two single event probabilities (Kahneman, Slovic, & Tversky, 1982). Such a strategy is very intuitive and seems plausible to virtually everyone, even if it was not the initially preferred strategy. According to probability theory, however, this is an error in logic. When groups are asked to work on such tasks, they are more likely than individuals to make this error (Tindale, 1993). In addition, groups will make errors even when a majority of their members did not individually make the error. Moreover, some of the individuals who were initially correct in their conjoint estimates before group discussion end up making conjunctive errors after participating in the group (Tindale, Sheffey, & Filkins, 1990). Similar results have been found for other types of probabilistic tasks (Tindale, 1993). Thus, group members use shared cognitions to guide their behavior while in the group, and often are influenced by them after they leave. Whether the influence is positive or negative depends on what shared representations are salient during group discussion.

Sharing Information and Learning by Groups

In terms of task performance, one of the major advantages often attributed to groups, as opposed to individuals, is that groups bring a greater amount of information, as well as information that is highly diverse to the task. By combining information and expertise contributed by each member, groups can consider a greater amount of relevant information and develop more informed solutions than is the case for individuals working alone. Although these assumptions are true in theory, research has now convincingly demonstrated that groups are notoriously poor at taking advantage of the information that is at their disposal. In a now-seminal paper by Stasser and Titus (1985), information was distributed among group members such that some information was shared by all members, whereas other pieces of information were held by only a single group member. The bulk of the shared information favored one alternative, but if all of the information (e.g., shared and unshared) was taken into account, a different "best" candidate emerged. Stasser and Titus found that groups rarely uncovered this "hidden profile," and chose the alternative favored by the shared information most of the time. Their "shared versus unshared, hidden profile" paradigm has become a standard research approach in the field, and the basic finding has been replicated many times (Wittenbaum & Stasser, 1996).

Two factors that have been found to help promote the sharing of unshared information are (a) a shared orientation toward the problem and (b) a shared transactive memory system (Stasser & Stewart, 1992; Stasser, Stewart, & Wittenbaum, 1995; van Ginkel, Tindale, & van Knippenberg, 2005). Stasser & Stewart (1992) found that telling groups that they were working on a problem-solving task with a correct solution increased the amount of unshared information brought up during the discussion relative to groups told that there was not a single correct solution. Van Ginkel et al. (2005) found that groups with a shared task representation emphasizing that good performance depended on information exchange exchanged more information and performed better than groups without such a shared representation. Interestingly, even when all three members of the group had the same task representation, the observed increase in information sharing depended upon whether or not group members were aware that they all had the same task representation.

A number of studies have now shown that a well-defined and recognized transactive memory system can also lead to greater information sharing (Hollingshead, 1998; Stasser et al., 1995). Stasser et al. (1995) distributed information in the groups such that each member had unique pieces of information about a particular response option. In some cases, they told the individual members that they had unique information about a specific alternative, but did not inform other members about this distributed expertise. In other cases, the information or expertise distribution was made public; thus, it was shared among the group members. It was only when both the members knew for which alternative they had additional information and when the information distribution was collectively known did groups both share more unshared information and improve their performance. These findings point to a key aspect of the role that sharedness plays in group learning. Groups, in order to learn, need access to information that is not currently shared—either from other group members or from the environment—and that they can use to alter, change, improve, and so forth their current positions and practices. The group must be collectively aware, however, of the diversity of information and how it might be useful in order for it to be used.

Mohammed (2001; Mohammed & Dumville, 2001) used the term cognitive consensus in relation to shared cognition and group learning. Cognitive consensus is the degree of similarity among the mental models held by the group members. It is a natural function of group interaction that tends to increase over time, though can also decrease if group interaction decreases as the task nears completion (Levesque, Wilson, & Wholey, 2001). Thus, if group members spend more time with each other, their level of cognitive consensus should be greater. Such consensus helps to establish how the group should operate and what aspects of the task are important. It also allows group members to respond to new information in similar ways.

The usefulness of cognitive consensus, however, may depend on the ways in which the initial cognitive conflicts were resolved (Ensley & Pearce, 2001). Cognitive conflicts reflect differences among members in terms of their mental representations of the problem rather than differences in terms of goals or outcomes (McGrath, 1984). Many theorists have argued that cognitive conflict is good in groups, at least early on, so that groups do not reach consensus too fast and fail to discuss important information or possible alternatives (Jehn, 1994; Schulz-Hardt, Jochims, & Frey, 2002). Recent evidence implies that preference differences between members need not include the best solution in order for it to lead to improved performance (Schulz-Hardt, Brodbeck, Mojzisch, Kershreiter, & Frey, in press). A recent meta-analysis indicates, however, that cognitive conflict and relationship conflict (interpersonal conflicts between members) tend to be correlated and both seem to inhibit performance (De Dreu & Weingart, 2003). It may be that only cognitive conflicts that do not lead to (or become interpreted in terms of) relationship conflicts are beneficial to group learning.

Conflicts created by minority factions have also been shown to influence group learning and creativity (De Dreu & West, 2001; Smith, in press). Nemeth (1986) argued that the presence of a minority faction in a group leads to divergent thinking on the part of majority members. Divergent thinking involves thinking about different sides of an issue or different possible alternatives; it generally includes a greater number of thoughts or more effortful processing. According to this view, it is not only conflict per se, but also the source of the conflict that is important for learning, creativity, and adaptation in groups. Both De Dreu and West (2001) and Smith (in press) showed that conflict created by a minority position tends to lead to greater innovation and creativity on both current and future tasks. In addition, Smith found that conflict created from a minority position led to a more robust and thorough discussion of the issues involved. Thus, it appears that only certain types of cognitive conflict are useful for group learning.

Another way that new ideas and information can be brought into a group is through the addition of new members (Levine, Moreland, & Choi, 2001). New members bring to the group knowledge and experience that current members may not possess. To the degree that new members share their unique information and experiences with the other group members, groups can learn from them. A number of barriers, however, can make it difficult to learn from new members. First, new members often attempt to assimilate to the current norms and procedures in the group in order to be accepted. Thus, they may not share their unique knowledge for fear of being alienated. In addition, current members may be less likely to use unique information from newcomers if they feel the newcomer has not yet earned the right to contribute (Levine et al., 2001).

Recent research has shown that the relationship between newcomers and group learning is rather complex. Some research has shown that if members expect a newcomer to be different, due to being from a different group or social category, their discrepant positions are accepted better than if the same position was espoused by an in-group member (Phillips, 2003). Groups made up of divergent members also seem more willing to tolerate discrepant positions, even by in-group members (Phillips & Loyd, 2006). Kane, Argote, and Levine (2005) found, however, that new members rotating in from different groups had very little influence in their new groups, even if they espoused a superior way to perform the task, unless they shared a superordinate identity. Such differences may be a function of how long the current group has been together, as well as the general diversity of its membership. New members to recently formed groups, particularly those seen as bringing new and useful resources, may foster divergent thinking and acceptance of new ideas, whereas groups with a long history may require newcomers to assimilate first before attempting to create change.

Leadership can also affect how well groups learn from new information. Recent research by van Ginkel (2006) showed leaders with a team mental model that encourages information exchange can lead groups to share such a model, resulting in better information sharing and performance. Leaders do not, however, necessarily create more information exchange. Larson, Foster-Fishman, and Franz (1998) found that participative leaders led to greater information exchange, including both shared and unshared information. Directive leaders, however, repeated more information, but did not create greater information exchange. In addition, if they did not prefer the optimal alternative, they tended to prevent correct members of lesser status from influencing the group.

Thus, whereas leaders that believe in and promote participation will increase information sharing, leaders with different team mental models may actually inhibit it.

Social scientists have long known that trust is a central concept to functional interpersonal behavior (Pruitt, 1998). More recent work has begun to show that trust is often involved in productive group behavior as well (Kramer et al., 2001). Van Ginkel et al. (2005) argued that trust is a key component to understanding how shared mental models can lead to more information sharing and better performance. In line with previous research, they found that not only do members of a group each need task representations that promote sharing, but they also need to know that other members share this representation. They argued that knowledge of the sharedness of the representation leads to a greater level of trust among the group members. This allows them to share information—even unique information—without fearing that other members will doubt the veracity of the information.

Social identity has been shown to be a key aspect of trust in a variety of circumstances. Persuasive communications are typically only influential if the source is perceived to be an in-group member (Crano, 2001). Related to trust, cooperation in social dilemmas has been found to increase when perceptions of social identification increase (Dawes, van de Kragt, & Orbell, 1988). Thus, it appears that a shared identity allows group members to be more open to the opinions of other in-group members, and to trust them to cooperate in the best interests of the group. Trust in a small in-group, however, can lead to less information exchange with members outside the group, and thus may actually inhibit the ultimate success of the group (Burt, 1999). Burt argued that dense networks with high trust among in-group members and low trust toward members outside the group lead to information deprivation within the group. Less dense networks with lower criteria for moderate levels of trust allow for more social connections within an organization, leading to better information flow. The greater information flow across members allows the group to learn and adapt faster, and this leads to better overall performance. The key aspect seems to be that the shared distrust of outsiders that is engendered in dense social groups prevents the sharing of information with noncentral group members.

Virtually all of the research findings and examples discussed thus far have involved groups whose members share cooperative goals and exchange information through some type of direct communication. Most conceptualizations of information sharing and group learning presuppose both cooperative goals and direct information exchange. A recent study by Budescu and Maciejousky (in press), however, found that neither of these assumptions need be met in order for group information sharing and learning to occur. In fact, they studied a competitive environment with no direct information exchange among members, and found effective information sharing and levels of performance at least as high as interacting, cooperative groups. They compared four-person, cooperative, interacting groups to four-person competitive auctions in their ability to solve the Wason selection task. They also assessed group-to-individual transfer in both settings.

The Wason selection task involves having people choose the fewest number of cards necessary to test an "if p then q" conditional rule. For example, a person might be given four cards with the following letters or numbers on the side facing up: a, 2, c, 7. The hypothesis to test is "when a card has a vowel on one side, it has an even number on the other." In order to effectively test this hypothesis, one would need to turn over the "a" card and the "7" card, and thus attempt to disconfirm it. Most people, however, choose the "a" and "2" cards. Research using the Wason selection task converges upon the finding that individuals, when faced with such tasks, are far more likely to act in a manner resulting in evidence that confirms an existing hypothesis than they are to operate in a manner that disconfirms it. Indeed, on average, only about 10% of individuals choose the correct card combination that disconfirms the hypothesis (Griggs & Cox, 1983).

First, Budescu and Maciejousky (in press) had individuals attempt to solve one instance of the Wason selection task. Following the individual solutions, some individuals were assigned to four-person groups and were then asked to solve the problem for a second time as a group. Others were allowed to bid on the four cards in a "combinatorial auction" (see Budescu & Maciejousky for further details of the auction process). Individuals in the auction condition simply bid on the cards, and then received feedback regarding who won and which cards they received. They also received a payoff for choosing the cards that could best test the hypothesis. Thus, by seeing who won and how much the winners received, participants could use this information to ascertain the correct strategy. The individuals were in direct competition and had no motivation to provide information to others. Yet by bidding to win, individuals who had figured out how to solve the problem provided others with information about the solution. Budescu and Maciejousky (in press) found that auctions with public feedback produced solution rates as good or better than interacting groups. They also showed that individuals who participated in such auctions learned how to solve additional problems as well or better than individual who participated in cooperative groups. Taken together, these findings indicate that learning can occur in groups even when members have competitive (as opposed to cooperative) motives.

SUMMARY AND FUTURE DIRECTIONS

In our discussion, we have attempted to show that initially shared cognitions and the process of sharing cognitions during group activities both play a role in group learning. The types of information and representations that group members share a priori provides the context in which both groups and group members learn from task performance experiences. Ideas brought up during group discussion are more influential if they resonate with the shared ideas and experiences of the group members (Tindale et al., 1996). Previously shared ideas and information are more likely to be mentioned in group discussions, and are more likely to be perceived as valid compared to their unique counterparts (Stasser, 1999). Groups and their members learn more, however, when new information is mentioned during the discussion, and this can only really happen if at least some information remains unshared among the group members. Thus, both the sharedness and the uniqueness of information are important for group learning to occur.

Although there is now a large body of research on the role both shared and unshared information in group performance and learning, very little research has emphasized the degree to which different levels of sharedness and unsharedness are useful for such endeavors. Obviously, some amount of shared knowledge is necessary for groups to operate, but how much is enough? When does it become too much? The same questions can be applied to appropriate amounts of unshared information as well. Research on individual decision making has shown that having too much information can be just as detrimental to decision quality as having too little (Baron, 2000). Such questions have not yet received much attention at the group level. A recent study by Tindale and Sheffey (2002) showed that assigning information to group members in partially redundant ways (based on a model proposed by Zajonc and Smoke, 1959) improved group recall compared to that observed in total redundancy conditions. Optimal amounts of shared and unshared information, however, will probably vary depending on the different aspects and characteristics of both the task and the group.

Another interesting line of research that we hope continues to flourish involves sharedness along various dimensions (Larson, 2006; Phillips, 2003; Phillips & Loyd, 2006). Much of this research has dealt with the pros and cons of diversity in groups. The focus has begun to shift, however, to the type of diversity and how more versus less diversity across different dimensions influences group process and performance. Diversity on a particular dimension and the positive value it can bring may depend in part on how much sharedness on some other dimension is present in the group. In many ways, research on shared cognitions in groups has only scratched the surface of the many issues involved, and we hope that future research will continue to explore this interesting and important topic.

Author Note: Preparation of this chapter was supported by the National Science Foundation (Grant #0621632).

REFERENCES

Bandura, A. (1986). *Social foundations of thought and action: A social cognitive theory.* Englewood Cliffs, NJ: Prentice Hall.

Baron, J. (2000). *Thinking and deciding.* New York: Cambridge University Press.

Baumann, M. R., & Bonner, B. L. *Effects of temporal perspective on the development of transactive memory systems.* Paper presented at the 1st Annual Conference of the Interdisciplinary Network for Group Research, Pittsburgh, PA.

Brauner, E., & Scholl, W. (2000). The information processing approach as a perspective for group research. *Group Processes and Intergroup Relation, 3,* 115–122.

Budescu, D., & Maciejousky, B. (in press). Collective induction without cooperation? Learning and knowledge transfer in cooperative groups and competitive auctions. *Journal of Personality and Social Psychology.*

Burt, R. S. (1999). Entrepreneurs, distrust, and third parties: A strategic look at the dark side of dense networks. In L. L. Thompson, J. M. Levine, & D. M. Messick (Eds.), *Shared cognitions in organizations: The management of knowledge* (pp. 213–244). Florence, KY: Lawrence Erlbaum Associates.

Cannon-Bowers, J. A., Salas, E., & Converse, S. (1993). Shared mental models in expert team decision making. In N. J. Castellon (Ed.), *Individual and group decision making: Current directions* (pp. 221–246). Hillsdale, NJ: Lawrence Erlbaum Associates.

Crano, W. D. (2001). Social influence, social identity, and ingroup leniency. In C. K. W. De Dreu, & N. K. De Vries (Eds.), *Group consensus and minority influence: Implications for innovation* (pp. 122–143). Oxford, U.K.: Blackwell Publishers.

Davis, J. H. (1980). Group decision and procedural justice. In M. Fishbein (Ed.), *Progress in social psychology* (Vol. 1, pp. 157–229). Hillsdale, NJ: Lawrence Erlbaum Associates.

Dawes, R. M., van de Kragt, A. J. C., & Orbell, J. M. (1988). Not me or thee but we: The importance of group identity in eliciting cooperation in dilemma situations: Experimental manipulations. *Acta Psychologica, 68,* 83–97.

De Dreu, C. K. W., & Weingart, L. R. (2003). Task vs. relationship conflict, team performance and team member satisfaction: A meta-analysis. *Journal of Applied Psychology, 88,* 741–749.

De Dreu, C. K. W., & West, M. A. (2001). Minority dissent and team innovation: The important of participation in decision making. *Journal of Applied Psychology, 86,* 1191–1201.

Dykema-Engblade, A., & Tindale, R. S. (2006). The roles of redundancy and expertise in group decision making and recall. In T. Nielsen (Chair), *Information sharing within teams: Dynamics and performance effects.* Symposium conducted at the Academy of Management Annual Convention, Atlanta, GA.

Ensley, M. D., & Pearce, C. L. (2001). Shared cognition in top management teams: Implications for new venture performance. *Journal of Organizational Behavior, 22,* 145–160.

Festinger, L. (1954). A theory of comparison processes. *Human Relations, 7,* 117–140.

Griggs, R. A., & Cox, J. R. (1983). The effects of problem content and negation on Wason's selection task. *Quarterly Journal of Experimental Psychology, 35A,* 519–533.

Helmreich, R. L. (1997). Managing human error in aviation. *Scientific American, 276,* 62–67.

Hinsz, V. B., Tindale, R. S., & Vollrath, D. A. (1997). The emerging conceptualization of groups as information processors. *Psychological Bulletin, 121,* 43–64.

Hogg, M. A. (2001). Social categorization, depersonalization, and group behavior. In M. A. Hogg, & R. S. Tindale (Eds.), *Blackwell handbook of social psychology: Group processes* (pp. 56–85). Oxford, U.K.: Blackwell Publishers.

Hogg, M. A., & Mullen, B. A. (1999). Joining groups to reduce uncertainty: Subjective uncertainty reduction and group identification. In D. Abrams & M. A. Hogg (Eds.), *Social identity and social cognition* (pp. 249–279). Oxford, U.K.: Blackwell.

Hollingshead, A. B. (1996). The rank order effect in group decision making. *Organizational Behavior and Human Decision Processes, 68,* 181–193.

Hollingshead, A. B. (1998). Retrieval processes in transactive memory systems. *Journal of Personality and Social Psychology, 74,* 659–671.

Jehn, K. (1994). Enhancing effectiveness: An investigation of advantages and disadvantages of value-based intra-group conflict. *International Journal of Conflict Management, 5,* 223–238.

Kahneman, D., Slovic, P., & Tversky, A. (Eds.). (1982). *Judgment under uncertainty: Heuristics and biases.* Cambridge, U.K.: Cambridge University Press.

Kameda, T., Tindale, R. S., & Davis, J. H. (2003). Cognitions, preferences, and social sharedness: Past, present, and future directions in group decision making. In S. L. Schneider, & J. Shanteau (Eds.), *Emerging perspectives on judgment and decision research.* Cambridge, U.K.: Cambridge University Press.

Kane, A. A., Argote, L., & Levine, J. M. (2005). Knowledge transfer between groups via personnel rotation: Effects of social identity and knowledge quality. *Organizational Behavior and Human Decision Processes, 96,* 56–71.

Kramer, R. M., Hanna, B. A., Su, S., & Wei, J. (2001). Collective identity, collective trust, and social capital: Linking group identification and group cooperation. In M. E. Turner (Ed.), *Groups at work: Theory and research* (pp. 173–196). Mahwah, NJ: Lawrence Erlbaum Associates.

Larson, J. R., Jr., (2006). *Cognitive diversity and strong synergy: Modeling the impact of variability in members' problem-solving strategies on group problem-solving performance.* Paper presented at the International Network of Group Research annual conference, Pittsburgh, PA.

Larson, J. R., Jr., Foster-Fishman, P. G., & Franz, T. M. (1998). Leadership style and the discussion of shared and unshared information in decision-making groups. *Personality and Social Psychology Bulletin,* 24, 482–495.

Latane, B., & Bourgeois, M. J. (2001). Dynamic social impact and the consolidation, clustering, correlation, and continuing diversity of culture. In M. A. Hogg, & R. S. Tindale (Eds.), *Blackwell handbook of social psychology: Group processes* (pp. 235–258). Oxford, U.K.: Blackwell Publishers.

Laughlin, P. R. (1980). Social combination processes of cooperative, problem solving groups on verbal intellective tasks. In M. Fishbein (Ed.), *Progress in social psychology* (Vol. 1, pp. 127–155). Hillsdale, NJ: Erlbaum.

Laughlin, P. R., & Adamopoulos, J. (1982). Social decision schemes on intellective tasks. In H. Brandstatter, J. H. Davis, & G. Stocker-Kreichgauer (Eds.), *Group decision making* (pp. 81–96). London: Academic Press.

Laughlin, P. R., Bonner, B. L., & Miner, A. G. (2002). Groups perform better than their best member on letters-to-numbers problems. *Organizational Behavior and Human Decision Processes, 88*, 605–620.
Laughlin, P. R., & Ellis, A. L. (1986). Demonstrability and social combination processes on mathematical intellective tasks. *Journal of Experimental Social Psychology, 22*, 177–189.
Laughlin, P. R., Hatch, E. C., Silver, J. S., & Boh, L. (2006). Groups perform better than the best individuals on letters-to-numbers problems: Effects of group size. *Journal of Personality and Social Psychology, 90*, 644–651.
Laughlin, P. R., & Sweeney, J. D. (1977). Individual-to-group and group-to-individual transfer in problem solving. *Journal of Experimental Psychology: Human Learning and Memory, 3*, 246–254.
Levesque, L. L., Wilson, J. M., & Wholey, D. R. (2001). Cognitive divergence and shared mental models in software development projects. *Journal of Organizational Behavior, 22*, 135–144.
Levine, J. M., Moreland, R. L., & Choi, H. (2001). Group socialization and newcomer innovation. In M. A. Hogg, & R. S. Tindale (Eds.), *Blackwell handbook of social psychology: Group processes* (pp. 86–106). Oxford, U.K.: Blackwell Publishers.
Liang, D. W., Moreland, R. L., & Argote, L. (1995). Group vs. individual training and group performance: The mediating role of transactive memory. *Personality and Social Psychology Bulletin, 21*, 384–393.
Lorenzi-Cioldi, F., & Clemence, A. (2001). Group processes and the construction of social representations. In M. A. Hogg, & R. S. Tindale (Eds.), *Blackwell handbook of social psychology: Group processes* (pp. 311–333). Oxford, U.K.: Blackwell Publishers.
McGrath, J. E. (1984). *Groups: Interaction and performance.* Englewood, NJ: Prentice Hall.
Mead, G. H. (1934). *Mind, self, and society from the standpoint of a social behaviorist.* Chicago: University of Chicago Press.
Mohammed, S. (2001). Toward an understanding of cognitive consensus in a group- decision making context. *The Journal of Applied Behavioral Science, 37*, 408–425.
Mohammed, S., & Dumville, B. C. (2001). Team mental models in a team knowledge framework: Expanding theory and measurement across disciplinary boundaries. *Journal of Organizational Behavior, 22*, 89–106.
Moreland, R. L. (1987). The formation of small groups. In C. Hendrick (Ed.), *Group processes* (pp. 80–110). Newberry Park, CA: Sage Publications.
Moreland, R. L., Argote, L., Krishnan, R. (1998). Training people to work in groups. In R. S. Tindale, L. Heath, E. J. Posavic, F. B. Bryant, E. Henderson-King, Y. Suarez-Balcazar, et al. (Eds.), *Social psychological application of social issues: Applications of theory and research on groups* (Vol. 4, pp. 37–60) New York: Plenum Press.
Moscovici, S. (1984). The phenomenon of social representations. In R. M. Farr, & S. Moscovici (Eds.), *Social representations* (pp. 3–69). Cambridge, U.K.: Cambridge University Press.
Mugny, G., & Doise, W. (1982). Social interaction in cognitive development. In H. Brandstatter, J. H. Davis, & G. Stocker-Kreichgauer (Eds.), *Group decision making* (pp. 241–256). London: Academic Press.
Nemeth, C. (1986). Differential contributions of majority and minority influence. *Psychological Review, 93*, 23–32.

Peterson, E., Mitchell, T., Thompson, L., & Burr, R. (2000). Collective efficacy and aspects of shared mental models as predictors of performance over time in work groups. *Group Processes & Intergroup Relations, 3,* 296–316.

Phillips, K. W. (2003). The effects of categorically based expectations on minority influence: The importance of congruence. *Personality and Social Psychology Bulletin, 29,* 3–13.

Phillips, K. W., & Loyd, D. L. (2006). When surface and deep-level diversity collide: The effects on dissenting group members. *Organizational Behavior and Human Decision Processes, 99,* 143–160.

Pruitt, D. G. (1998). Social conflict. In D. Gilbert, S. T. Fiske, & G. Lindsey (Eds.), *Handbook of social psychology* (4th ed., Vol. 2, pp. 89–150).

Schulz-Hardt, S., Brodbeck, F., Mojzisch, A., Kerschreiter, R., & Frey, D. (in press). Group decision making in hidden profile situations: Dissent as a facilitator for decision quality. *Journal of Personality and Social Psychology.*

Schulz-Hardt, S., Jochims, M., & Frey, D. (2002). Productive conflict in group decision making: Genuine and contrived dissent as strategies to counteract biased information seeking. *Organizational Behavior and Human Decision Processes, 88,* 563–586.

Smith, C. M. (in press). Adding minority status to a source of conflict: An examination of influence processes and product quality in dyads. *European Journal of Social Psychology.*

Stasser, G. (1992). Information salience and the discovery of hidden profiles by decision-making groups: A "thought experiment." *Organizational Behavior and Human Decision Process, 52,* 156–181.

Stasser, G. (1999). The uncertain role of unshared information in collective choice. In L. L. Thompson, J. M. Lavine, & D. M. Messick (Eds.), *Shared cognition in organizations: The management of knowledge* (pp. 49–70). Mahwah, NJ: Lawrence Erlbaum Associates.

Stasser, G., & Stewart, D. D. (1992). The discovery of hidden profiles by decision making groups: Solving a problem versus making a judgment. *Journal of Personality and Social Psychology, 63,* 426–434.

Stasser, G., Stewart, D. D., & Wittenbaum, G. M. (1995). Expert roles and information exchange during discussion: The importance of knowing who knows what. *Journal of Experimental Social Psychology, 31,* 1–22.

Stasser, G., & Titus, W. (1985). Pooling of unshared information in group decision making: Biased information sampling during discussion. *Journal of Personality and Social Psychology, 48,* 1467–1478.

Stasson, M. F., Kameda, T., Parks, C. D., Zimmerman, S. K., & Davis, J. H. (1991). Effects of assigned group consensus requirement on group problem solving and group member learning. *Social Psychology Quarterly, 54,* 25–35.

Tindale, R. S. (1993). Decision errors made by individuals in groups. In N. Castellan, Jr. (Ed.), *Individual and group decision making: Current issues* (pp. 109–124). Hillsdale, NJ: Erlbaum.

Tindale, R. S., & Kameda, T. (2000). Social sharedness as a unifying theme for information processing in groups. *Group Processes and Intergroup Relations, 3,* 123–140.

Tindale, R. S., Meisenhelder, H. M., Dykema-Engblade, A. A., & Hogg, M. A. (2001). Shared cognition in small groups. In M. A. Hogg, & R. S. Tindale (Eds.), *Blackwell handbook of social psychology: Group processes.* Malden, MA: Blackwell.

Tindale, R. S., & Sheffey, S. (2002). Shared information, cognitive load, and group memory. *Group Processes and Intergroup Relations, 5,* 5–18.
Tindale, R. S., Sheffey, S., & Filkins, J. (1990). *Conjunction errors in individuals in groups.* Paper presented at the Annual Meeting of the Society for Judgment and Decision Making, New Orleans, LA.
Tindale, R. S., Smith, C. M., Thomas, L. S., Filkins, J., & Sheffey, S. (1996). Shared representations and asymmetric social influence processes in small groups. In E. Witte, & J. H. Davis (Eds.), *Understanding group behavior: Consensual action by small groups* (Vol. 1, pp. 81–103). Mahwah, NJ: Lawrence Erlbaum Associates.
Turner, J. C., & Oakes, P. J. (1989). Self-categorization and social influence. In P. B. Paulus (Ed.), *The psychology of group influence* (2nd ed., pp. 233–275). Hillsdale, NJ: Lawrence Erlbaum Associates.
van Gindel, W. P. (2006) *The use of distributed information in decision making groups: The role of shared task representations.* Unpublished doctoral dissertation, Erasmus University, Rotterdam, the Netherlands.
van Ginkel, W. P., Tindale, R. S., & van Knippenberg, D. (2005). *Reflexivity, development of shared task representations, and group decision making.* Paper presented at SIOP 2006, Dallas, TX.
Wegner, D. M. (1987). A transactive memory: A contemporary analysis of the group mind. In B. Mullen, & G. R. Goethals (Eds.), *Theories of group behavior* (pp. 185–208). New York: Springer-Verlag.
Weiner, E. L., Kanki, B., & Helmreich, R. L. (1993). *Cockpit resource management.* San Diego, CA: Academic Press.
Winquist, J. R., & Larson, J. R. (1998). Information pooling: When it impacts group decision making. *Journal of Personality and Social Psychology, 74,* 371–377.
Wittenbaum, G. M., Hubbel, A. P., & Zuckerman, C. (1999). Mutual enhancement: Toward an understanding of collective preference for shared information. *Journal of Personality and Social Psychology, 77,* 967–978.
Wittenbaum, G. M., & Stasser, G. (1996). Management of information in small groups. In J. L. Nye, & A. M. Brower (Eds.), *What's social about cognition?* Thousand Oaks, CA: Sage Publications.
Zajonc, R. B., & Smoke, W. H. (1959). Redundancy in task assignment and group performance. *Psychometrica, 24,* 361–369.

CHAPTER

5

Learning to Work Together: An Examination of Transactive Memory System Development in Teams

ALEKSANDER P. J. ELLIS
The Eller College of Management, The University of Arizona

CHRISTOPHER O. L. H. PORTER
Texas A&M University

SANDRA A. WOLVERTON
Texas A&M University

In today's knowledge economy, an organization's ability to assemble, integrate, and exploit its knowledge assets represents a significant source of competitive advantage for firms of more highly industrialized nations (McGaughey, 2002; Teece, 1998). One way to leverage the power of employee knowledge is through the use of team-based work structures, where two or more employees interact interdependently toward a common and valued goal or objective and each has been assigned specific roles or functions to perform (e.g., Ilgen, Major, Hollenbeck, & Sego, 1993). As evidence, organizations have placed increased emphasis on the use of team-based work structures (Lawler, Mohrman, & Ledford, 1992, 1995). Researchers estimate that half of all U.S. organizations and more than 80% of Fortune 500 companies utilize teams (Devine, Clayton, Philips, Dunford, & Melner, 1999; Robbins, 2003). Cross-functional, project, and product-development teams are a few types of teams utilized by organizations to capitalize on the specialized expertise of individual team members (Lewis, 2003).

The successful use of team-based work structures depends on team members' ability to utilize their own specialized expertise while integrating the differentiated expertise of their teammates (Lewis, 2003; Nonaka & Takeuchi, 1995). This can be achieved through the development of a transactive memory system (TMS), which represents a cooperative division of labor for learning, remembering, and communicating relevant team knowledge (e.g., Hollingshead, 2001; Lewis, 2003; Wegner, 1987). TMSs represent efficient team-level systems for collaborating and combining team members' unique knowledge, which creates new knowledge that becomes imbedded in the teams' structures and processes (Lewis, Lange, & Gillis, 2005).

Although previous research has documented the effectiveness of TMS in teams (e.g., Austin, 2003; Cannon-Bowers & Salas, 2001; Ellis, 2006; Lewis, 2003; Moreland & Myaskovsky, 2000), we know little about how the construct itself develops over time. This limits our ability to understand the full potential of TMSs in teams and the impact TMSs may have within organizations. In this chapter, we develop a model of TMS development in teams, paying particular attention to the crucial role of learning in the process (see Figure 5.1).

We begin by first discussing the two primary conceptualizations of transactive memory that have arisen in the organizational literature. We then combine these two complementary perspectives into a model describing how the system develops in newly formed teams. In doing so, we suggest that learning plays a crucial role during two phases of the developmental process. We then introduce a number of antecedents that have the potential to affect each specific learning phase as well as the process as a whole. Finally, we discuss several outcomes that may result from a fully functioning transactive memory system in teams and the theoretical and practical implications of our model.

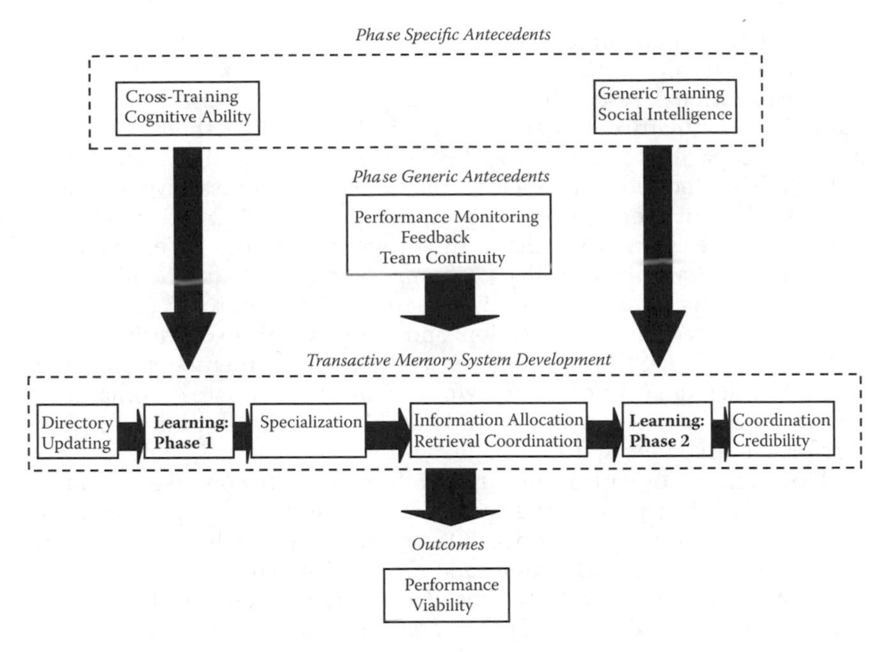

Figure 5.1 A framework of transactive memory system development in teams.

TMS DEVELOPMENT

Transactive memory was originally conceived by Wegner (e.g., 1987) to describe how individuals in close relationships divide their combined workload. Rather than any one person cluttering his or her memory by attempting to retain all relevant information, each partner takes responsibility for specific pieces of relevant information. Any pertinent information (e.g., information related to one's specialty) is then sent to or retrieved from that individual. Wegner labeled this system "transactive memory," as it allowed couples to efficiently and effectively process information (e.g., Wegner, 1987; Wegner, Erber, & Raymond, 1991; Wegner, Giuliano, & Hertel, 1985).

To illustrate the inner workings of TMSs, Lewis (2003) described a typical couple, John and Jane, who need to remember friends' and family members' birthdays. John cannot remember any of the dates, but because Jane is responsible for remembering birthdays, he can access her memory and retrieve the information whenever needed. In addition, when new friends or family members are added to the list, John can send birthday information to Jane without encoding any of it into his memory. Such a system clearly benefits John because he is no longer required to remember certain types of information, yet he still has access to that information when necessary.

Organizational researchers have adopted the concept of TMSs to describe how team members synergistically combine their individual memory capacities (e.g., Hinsz, Tindale, & Vollrath, 1997; Moreland, 1999). Like individuals in close relationships, "transactive memory allows different members of [a] group to process information, so they remember the information that is directly related to their area of expertise" (Hinsz et al., 1997, p. 48). Utilizing their TMS, team members can rely on their teammates' expertise, enabling the team to access a larger pool of task-relevant information and avoid wasting cognitive effort (Hollingshead, 1998b). A TMS exists when team members possess a shared understanding of their own and their teammates' domains of expertise and actively draw on and combine specialized knowledge to perform a task (Lewis, 2003).

However, as organizational researchers have become more interested in TMSs in groups and teams, two different conceptualizations of the construct have developed. One group of researchers has focused on specialization, coordination, and credibility, which are considered emergent cognitive manifestations of transactive memory (Ilgen, Hollenbeck, Johnson, & Jundt, 2005). *Specialization* refers to the level of memory differentiation within the team, *coordination* refers to team members' perceptions of their ability to work together efficiently, and *credibility* refers to team members' beliefs about the reliability of other members' knowledge (e.g., Lewis, 2003; Moreland & Myaskovsky, 2000).

A second group of researchers has focused on directory updating, information allocation, and retrieval coordination, which are considered independent behavioral indicators of transactive memory and fall under the category of action processes (e.g., Ellis, 2006). Through *directory updating,* team members become aware of each other's areas of expertise and "who knows what" by sharing or requesting information from their teammates. Through *information allocation,* information is communicated to the team member possessing the relevant area of expertise, allowing other team members to pass information to each other without storing anything into memory. Through *retrieval coordination,* team members utilize their "directory of directories" to request information known to be held within a teammate's areas of expertise (e.g., Hollinghead, 1998a, 1998b).

While some may view these two conceptualizations of the construct as contradictory, we view them as complementary. Moreover, we believe that both conceptualizations are interwoven into the developmental process of TMSs in teams. In support of our perspective, Marks, Mathieu, and Zaccaro (2001), when developing their temporally based framework and taxonomy of team processes, noted that emergent cognitive states "are products of team experiences (including team processes) and become new inputs to subsequent processes" (p. 358). We argue that during TMS development, action processes drive cognitive states, which then drive action processes, which feed into additional cognitive states. Therefore, TMSs represent a blend of both cognitive and behavioral components (see Ellis, 2006). For example, Wegner et al. (1985) stated that they "envision transactive memory to be a combination of individual minds and the communication among them" (p. 256).

Inherent in the interplay between cognitive states and action processes during TMS development is *team learning,* which can be defined as "a relatively permanent change in the team's collective level of knowledge and skill produced by the shared experience of the team members" (Ellis et al., 2003, p. 822). Team learning represents an integral component of TMS development as team members gain an understanding of the location of knowledge within the team and learn how to utilize that knowledge effectively and efficiently. In fact, Lewis et al. (2005) conceptualized TMSs as learning systems that produce knowledge relevant for the current task through a series of learning cycles.

To further illustrate the relationship between the two conceptualizations of the construct and the role of team learning, we present a model of TMS development in Fig. 5.1. As previous research suggests, the developmental process begins as team members engage in directory updating (e.g., Wegner, 1995). Before team members can begin distributing information within the team, they need to know where it can come from and where it should go. In other words, they first need to set up modules of specialized expertise within the team that all the team members agree upon and are aware of. According to Wegner et al. (1991), directory updating behavior can include the use of simple defaults based on stereotypes, negotiation (e.g., one team member accepts responsibility for a certain domain of knowledge), self-disclosure of previous expertise, and/or the sharing of knowledge regarding a team member's access to information.

While team members update their directories, they are expanding their knowledge of differentiated expertise within the team and learning who is associated with what area of expertise, permanently changing the team's collective knowledge and skill. Therefore, as shown in Fig. 5.1, we believe that directory updating stimulates Phase 1 learning during TMS development. Through directory updating, team members memorize the location of expertise within the team and learn "who knows what"—cognitions that become useful in later stages of TMS development.

By learning through directory updating, team members are free to develop additional knowledge in their own specialty areas (Wegner et al., 1991), become more involved and more focused on their specific areas of expertise, and worry less about information falling outside of their knowledge domain, further differentiating the memory of one team member from another. As noted by Lewis (2004), "such exchanges help members learn more about the content and depth of one another's knowledge and help to elaborate, refine, and clarify members' perceptions of member-expertise associations" (p. 1522). As a result, we argue that learning during Phase 1 leads to specialization, where members perceive a high degree of memory differentiation within the team.

Team members can then capitalize on their high levels of specialization by distributing information efficiently and effectively within the team through information allocation and retrieval coordination. Lewis et al. (2005) referred to the team's knowledge base as location information, which, according to the authors, allows team members to allocate information to and retrieve accurate information from the appropriate team members. Information allocation and retrieval coordination represent the active behavioral manifestations of the collective knowledge held by the team. Team members use information allocation and retrieval coordination as a system of information distribution and workload allocation in the team based on team members' areas of expertise. Without information allocation and retrieval coordination, a TMS cannot become fully functional and the team will not be able to utilize and integrate information, ultimately rendering the TMS ineffective in assisting team members' in the achievement of their collective goals.

While team members set up an information distribution system through information allocation and retrieval coordination, their repeated interactions stimulate the Phase 2 of learning during TMS development. While team members are exchanging information, they develop patterns of interactions based on the feedback they receive. They are learning what works and what does not work, initiating a pattern of interaction that becomes established within the team (Lewis et al., 2005). In effect, team members are permanently changing the way they approach and complete tasks as a collective unit; they are learning how to deal with information efficiently and effectively through their use of specialized knowledge within the team.

Finally, by reinforcing the efficiency and effectiveness of information sharing based on specialized areas of expertise within the team, Phase 2 learning positively affects coordination and credibility within the team. For example, researchers have shown that, by developing patterns of interaction, uncertainty about how team interactions ought to proceed is greatly reduced (Gersick & Hackman, 1990). Team members will likely feel more confident in their ability to work together efficiently and in the reliability of their teammates' expertise when they have learned how to successfully utilize their information network. When team members receive information they need from their teammates and see information that they send utilized effectively within the team, they will likely feel more efficacious in the collective capabilities of their team.

As an illustration of the developmental process of TMSs, consider the example of a cross-functional product team in the pharmaceutical industry. The team combines experts from R&D, sales, marketing, and manufacturing to develop and sell a new class of drugs aimed at pain management. In the first meeting, team members sit down to determine who can do what. However, even before the meeting begins, each team member has made some assumptions about what other members should know based on those members' membership in particular divisions (e.g., it is assumed that the manufacturing representative has expertise in procurement). Collectively, they learn that Dan specializes in all aspects of R&D around this new class of drug, Rachel specializes in all aspects of sales, Bill specializes in both professional and customer marketing, and Lisa does not specialize in procurement, but rather in distribution and planning. However, Lisa does have strong network ties to a procurement specialist, which can serve the team indirectly by helping the team develop its plans regarding the supply of materials and services needed to complete the project. Once they have established specialization within the team, they begin to work on developing, manufacturing, and selling the new drug. Throughout the process, team members frequently communicate with one another to ensure that things are running smoothly. For example, Dan from R&D immediately allocates information regarding the drug's chemical composition to Lisa who is overseeing the manufacture of the drug. Soon thereafter, Rachel from sales retrieves projections of next month's production volume from Lisa. By coordinating with and trusting their teammates' expertise, team members manage to get shipments of the drug to the market as scheduled.

In conclusion, once team members have achieved high levels of coordination and credibility, we argue that the team's TMS is running efficiently and effectively. However, the model presented in Fig. 5.1 is merely designed to represent a framework of TMS development that integrates a number of interrelated concepts over time. We do not mean to portray TMS development as a simple, linear process. Teams are inherently open systems (see Johnson et al., 2006), with energy flowing in a number of different directions and from a number of sources. For example, the use of information allocation and retrieval coordination may feed back into specialization as team members continue to focus on providing and receiving information in their particular area of expertise. While we recognize that Fig. 5.1 ignores any cyclical or nonlinear effects, our intention is to focus on portraying the primary drivers of TMS development over time.

ANTECEDENTS OF TMS DEVELOPMENT

Based on our model, a number of antecedents have the potential to impact the learning processes inherent in TMS development. In this chapter, we focus on those antecedents that we feel are particularly relevant for the learning components of the model. First, we focus on two variables that are specific to Phase 1 and Phase 2 learning: (a) intelligence and (b) team training. In particular, we suggest that cognitive ability and cross-training will impact Phase 1 learning while social intelligence and generic teamwork-skills training will impact Phase 2 learning. Second, we examine three phase-generic variables that are likely to affect Phase 1 and Phase 2 learning equally: (a) performance monitoring, (b) feedback, and (c) team continuity.

Phase-specific antecedents: Phase 1. During Phase 1 learning, team members need to recognize and memorize their teammates' areas of expertise. Cognitive ability may be particularly influential during the initial phase of learning in TMS development. Researchers have defined cognitive ability as "acquiring, storing in memory, retrieving, combining, comparing, and using in new contexts information and conceptual skills" (Humphreys, 1979, p. 115). Researchers have shown that cognitive ability predicts learning at the individual level (Jensen, 1986) and at the team level (Ellis et al., 2003).

This is likely because teams composed of members with higher levels of cognitive ability have a larger capacity to collectively process information. One of the basic tenets of information-processing theory is the idea that there are limits on attentional resources and immediate memory capacity (e.g., Dempster, 1981; Shiffrin, 1976). Team members possess a certain attentional span, which determines the maximum number of mental elements they can attend to at one time (e.g., Baldwin, 1894). Team members' storage capacities are also restricted in their ability to handle large amounts of information (e.g., Baddeley, 1986; Baddeley & Hitch, 1974). The processing and storing of information must compete for the limited capacity in the working memory (e.g., Daneman & Carpenter, 1980, 1983). In their resource-allocation model, Kanfer and Ackerman (1989) proposed that task demands, such as having to deal with a novel task, consume valuable cognitive resources. Team members who are high in cognitive ability have greater cognitive capacity and their pool of cognitive resources may be deeper than team members with low levels of cognitive ability (Ackerman, 1986, 1987). Concomitantly, as the overall level of cognitive ability within a team increases, so does a team's collective capacity to process and store valuable information.

Cognitive ability has important implications for Phase 1 learning, as team members are charged with attending to and storing large amounts of information regarding the distribution of expertise within the team. Team members with increased attentional resources will have the capacity to more efficiently and effectively learn "who knows what" in the team. This should help team members develop specialization more quickly, easing transitions between each stage of the model and increasing the fluidity of TMS development.

During Phase 1 learning, team members may also benefit from the introduction of a cross-training program. Researchers have suggested that a well-developed training program can influence information processing capabilities at the individual (e.g., Ford & Kraiger, 1995; Howell &

Cook, 1989) and team (e.g., Cannon-Bowers, Salas, & Converse, 1993; Hinsz et al., 1997) levels. As a result, it has been argued that team training may be an effective strategy for promoting team learning (Ellis & Bell, 2005; Feldman, 1989; Levine & Moreland, 1991).

We suggest that cross-training may be particularly effective at stimulating Phase 1 learning in the development of TMSs in teams. Cross-training is defined as "an instructional strategy in which each team member is trained in the duties of his or her teammates" (Volpe, Cannon-Bowers, Salas, & Spector, 1996, p. 87). Blickensderfer, Cannon-Bowers, and Salas (1998) identified three different cross-training methods: (a) positional clarification, (b) positional modeling, and (c) positional rotation. Positional clarification offers information about each role through a brief presentation, positional modeling employs both discussion and observation of each role in action, and positional rotation provides hands-on training in each role. In other words, cross-training provides team members with a first-hand preview of their teammates' expertise that reduces or eliminates the need for information sharing and self-disclosure within the team. Cross-training, in effect, reduces the amount of cognitive resources that team members need to allocate to the directory updating process. Team members can update their directories through their own observation rather than trying to ensure that they have located and identified the expertise of each team member—a search process that takes both time and cognitive effort. With cross-training, the information is provided for them.

Consequently, we expect that cross-trained team members will be able to learn more efficiently and effectively during Phase 1 of the developmental process. A number of studies have supported these propositions and indicates that cross-training directly affects interpositional knowledge. This, in turn, allows team members to more quickly develop an accurate picture of their teammates' roles and responsibilities (e.g., Cannon-Bowers, Salas, Blickensderfer, & Bowers, 1998; Marks Sabella, Burke, & Zaccaro, 2002).

Phase-specific antecedents: Phase 2. During Phase 2 learning, team members need to figure out how to utilize information allocation and retrieval coordination to establish a coherent communication structure within the team. Social intelligence may be particularly influential during this second stage of learning in TMS development. According to Thorndike (1920), social intelligence can be defined as "the ability to understand and manage men and women, boys and girls—to act wisely in human relations" (p. 228). Walker and Foley (1973) broke social intelligence down into two key elements: "the ability to (a) understand others and (b) act or behave wisely in relating to others" (p. 842). In organizational terms, employees high in social intelligence are more likely to cooperate with others and help their coworkers (Drasgow, 2003).

While researchers have yet to investigate the role of social intelligence in team-based work structures, we suggest that social intelligence will promote Phase 2 learning during TMS development. Social intelligence represents an individual's skill in recognizing situations that require their assistance and the knowledge of what steps to take. Individuals high in social intelligence recognize the needs of others, predict how others will perceive situations, maintain recognition of others' perspective (even if they conflict with one's own views), and apply this understanding to one's behavior in a given situation (Drasgow, 2003). Given that team members need to utilize information allocation and retrieval coordination to learn how to work together, social intelligence can help connect the various pieces of information contained within a team into a coherent information-sharing system. Team members high in social intelligence will be better able to perform according to their role in the network and will more readily recognize interconnections between team members. Social intelligence can shift team members' attention away from their individual roles and responsibilities and toward the collective goals and objectives of the team. In sum, team members who are high in social intelligence will learn how to work together more quickly and more effectively than team members who are low in social intelligence.

Phase 2 learning may also benefit from the introduction of a generic teamwork skills training program for team members. While cross-training is task and team specific, generic teamwork skills training focuses on developing the task- and team-generic skills that can then be applied in a variety of contexts (Cannon-Bowers, Tannenbaum, Salas, & Volpe, 1995). Generic teamwork skills training can focus on a number of different skills or competencies, which include "(a) the requisite knowledge, principles, and concepts underlying the team's effective task performance; (b) the repertoire of required skills and behaviors necessary to perform the team task effectively; and (c) the appropriate attitudes on the part of team members (about themselves and the team) that foster effective team performance" (Cannon-Bowers et al., 1995, pp. 336–337).

We suggest that the second category of skills will be most effective in promoting Phase 2 learning during TMS development. Such skills include communication and planning-and-task coordination skills. *Communication* refers to team members' capacity to understand information exchange networks, and to utilize these networks to enhance information sharing. *Planning-and-task coordination* refers to team members' capacity to effectively sequence and orchestrate activities, as well as manage procedural interdependencies among team members (Stevens & Campion, 1994). Skills such as these may help team members develop a comprehensive system of information sharing more efficiently and effectively. If team members understand how to exchange information and sequence their actions, they will be able to more easily translate information allocation and retrieval coordination into an information network with clear links between team members' expertise. In other words, generic teamwork skills training should help team members learn how to work together better within their TMS.

Several studies support these assertions. For example, Smith-Jentsch, Salas, and Baker (1996) trained 60 undergraduates in team performance-related assertiveness, or the ability of team members to share their opinions with their teammates in a manner that is persuasive to others. Trained individually, participants in the experimental condition were introduced to one of three training methods: (a) behavioral-role modeling, (b) lecture with demonstration, and (c) lecture-based training. Participants were then paired to complete a PC-based flight simulation task as a two-person team. Relative to a control group that received no training, Smith-Jentsch et al. found that behavioral role modeling had a significant positive effect on performance-related assertive behavior. Similarly, Ellis, Bell, Ployhart, Hollenbeck, and Ilgen (2005) examined 65 four-person teams participating in an interdependent command-and-control simulation. Half of these teams went through a half-hour training program focusing on skills related to planning and task coordination, collaborative problem solving, and communication. The teams were then given a task that was unrelated to the content of the training program. Results indicated that trained teams exhibited significantly higher levels of planning-and-task coordination, collaborative problem solving, and communication behavior.

Phase-generic antecedents: Performance monitoring. Regardless of the specific phase of learning, we believe that it is critical that team members monitor each other's performance. Performance monitoring is primarily a cognitive activity (Marks et al., 2001; Marks & Panzer, 2004; Porter, Gogus, Keng, & Yu, 2005), as it involves regular observation and concern with the performance of teammates (Serfaty, Entin, & Johnston, 1998). When team members monitor each other's performance, they observe fellow team members while at the same time devoting attention to their specific roles and tasks.

Performance monitoring is important to the development of TMS in teams across both Phase 1 and Phase 2 learning. When team members are aware of each other's performance, they are better able to recognize strengths and weaknesses (Porter et al., 2005). Rather than just assuming that team members are performing adequately, performance monitoring allows members to observe each other during task enactment. This allows them to better coordinate their individual actions into a meaningful whole. For example, Marks and Panzer (2004) found that team members who engaged in monitoring were better prepared to evaluate the pace of others' actions and make adjustments in the coordination of their individual efforts to more quickly accomplish interdependent tasks. Performance monitoring also allows team members to identify each other's errors and performance deficiencies. Although performance monitoring does not necessarily imply that members will take immediate action by reacting to what they observe (Porter et al., 2005), when team members take note of other's effectiveness, they develop a more accurate assessment regarding each other's knowledge, skills, and abilities (KSAs; e.g., credibility). In addition, when team members monitor each other's performances, it enables them to better identify areas of overlapping expertise.

We believe that performance monitoring facilitates the development of TMSs in teams because it helps teams become aware of both gaps and redundancies in their members' knowledge and expertise. In situations where team members identify knowledge and expertise gaps, the team may take steps to address the deficiencies. In situations in which team members identify redundancies, the team may decide where members' limited attentional resources could be better devoted. In the latter case, the opportunity to reallocate some subset of members' resources could potentially lead to opportunities for members to gain additional expertise in more appropriate areas or devote more of their attention to areas in which team members already possess expertise.

Phase-generic antecedents: Feedback. The provision of feedback in teams should also promote the development of TMS in teams across both Phase 1 and Phase 2 learning because, similar to performance monitoring, feedback helps team members understand their strengths and weaknesses. Although researchers have identified a number of forms of feedback (see Conlon & Barr, 1989; DeNisi, 2000; Ilgen, Fisher, Taylor, 1979; Kluger & DeNisi, 1996; Nadler, 1979), we focus specifically on the provision of information to and from members of the team regarding each other's performance (or what Marks & Panzer, 2004, referred to as intrateam feedback).

In their developmental model, Kozlowski, Gully, Nason, and Smith (1999) suggested that during earlier stages of team development (what they refer to as *task compilation*), members focus on their individual performance and specific task mastery. We believe that when members provide feedback to one another, they acknowledge effective and ineffective behavior and pass information to and from one another regarding each other's performance. In addition, similar to DeNisi's (2000) suggestion regarding individual level performance appraisals, when members give each other feedback, it should help them more accurately perceive their inputs relative to the inputs of other team members. Taken together, the provision of feedback among team members helps members more accurately assess their individual performance and make better judgments regarding the uniqueness of their expertise. Thus, like performance monitoring, the provision of feedback helps members identify gaps and redundancies in their members' knowledge and expertise. However, unlike performance monitoring, feedback ensures greater levels of accountability among team members for their individual performance.

Finally, it is worth noting that both performance monitoring and feedback are considered aspects of teamwork behaviors (e.g., McIntyre & Salas, 1995). Although teamwork is generally considered multidimensional and there are a number of other important aspects of teamwork (e.g., backing up behavior), we believe that these two particular aspects of teamwork are likely to have important effects on the development of TMS in teams. In addition, both performance monitoring and feedback are conceptually and empirically distinct from our previous discussion regarding teamwork-skills training. Whereas teamwork-skills training represents initiatives to train members in how to best coordinate their individual performances, performance monitoring and feedback are but two processes that teams can engage in that allow them to combine their individual cognitive, verbal, and behavioral activities to ensure that their teams reach collective goals (Marks et al., 2001). Because teamwork is discretionary (Marks et al., 2002; Porter et al., 2003), teams often vary in the extent to which they actually engage in teamwork behaviors, regardless of whether or not they have received teamwork-skills training. Thus, although TMS in teams may be fostered by teamwork-skills training, we believe that the extent to which teams actually engage in performance monitoring and provide and share feedback with one another will have unique effects on the development and maintenance of those TMSs.

Phase-generic antecedents: Team continuity. Team continuity refers to the relative stability of team composition. Today's work environment is constantly changing and the composition of the team may change due to promotions, lay-offs, transfers, etc. (e.g., Ilgen & Pulakos, 1999). We believe the effects of team continuity span both Phase 1 and Phase 2 learning during TMS development. When team members are replaced, the team's collective set of KSAs usually changes. Team members have to learn their new teammates' knowledge domain and determine the degree of overlap in information and expertise. With the change in directories, team members then have to change the way they utilize their communication network to retrieve and allocate information to team members. The location of each knowledge domain and the linkages between them will likely shift. As a result, the team's TMS needs time to redevelop as team members learn the contingencies associated with the addition of a new team member.

A number of studies support these assertions. Moreland and Argote (2003) found that member turnover can disrupt the team's TMS and decrease performance. The more team members work together, the more exposure they have to each other and the more they are able to accurately judge each other's competencies and skills (Austin, 2003). Performance in teams has been shown to improve over time as groups learn to utilize each other's specialized knowledge (Hollingshead, 2001). Moreland, Argote, and Krishnan (1996) found that teams trained together tend to develop a stronger transactive memory system than those trained apart. In their experiment involving the assembly of AM radios, teams that were trained together had better information recall and made fewer errors.

However, it is worth noting that although we believe that a lack of team continuity will likely have short-term negative implications for the development of TMS, it may not necessarily have negative long-term effects. When team members are replaced, newcomers may hold differentiated knowledge that team members can capitalize on during task completion. If properly managed, new additions to a team may eventually lead to a more efficient and effective TMS. For example, researchers have shown that turnover can rejuvenate and encourage innovation within teams (Thompson, 1999).

OUTCOMES OF TMS DEVELOPMENT

The impact of TMS development on team effectiveness has been well established in the literature. In fact, Moreland (1999) noted that "the potential benefits of transactive memory for a work group's performance are clear" (p. 5). A number of studies have supported this assertion, finding that transactive memory positively affects team performance (e.g., Austin, 2003; Cannon-Bowers & Salas, 2001; Hollingshead, 1998a; Lewis, 2003; Moreland & Myaskovsky, 2000). For example, Ellis (2006) found that directory updating, information allocation, and retrieval-coordination behaviors were all significantly and positively related to team performance.

However, a comprehensive assessment of team effectiveness must capture both current team effectiveness (e.g., present performance) and future team effectiveness (e.g., team viability) (e.g., Hackman, 1987). As a result, researchers have begun to investigate the link between TMS development and team viability, or the team's capability to continue functioning as a unit (e.g., Phillips, 2001). Lewis et al. (2005) found that TMSs stimulated learning that transferred across task domains, particularly when the division of cognitive labor remained constant. As further support, Lewis (2004) found that the implementation of a TMS during task completion accounted for more than half the variance in perceptions of team viability.

In sum, these results suggest that TMSs play a crucial role in the continued success or failure of team-based work structures. The development and maintenance of the TMS, which is the subject of this chapter, is both individual and group-oriented in nature. While research has shown that TMS is beneficial to group learning and ultimately team effectiveness, it is important to remember that TMS is a complex process that needs to be learned. The more efficiently and effectively team members can learn how to capitalize on differentiated expertise, the better they will perform over time.

MODEL IMPLICATIONS

In organizational literature, researchers have treated transactive memory as an emergent cognitive construct (e.g., Lewis, 2003) and as a behavioral construct in line with Marks et al.'s (2001) definition of action processes (e.g., Ellis, 2006). We assert that these two perspectives are not mutually exclusive and have the potential to coexist during TMS development. As indicated in our developmental model, we suggest that TMSs represent a blend of both cognitive and behavioral components. Each of these components is held together by learning processes occurring within the team. Without learning, team members would be unable to shift from directory updating to specialization or from information allocation-and-retrieval coordination to coordination and credibility. Our model helps to combine the divergent perspectives regarding transactive memory that have developed within the literature and provides an integrative picture of TMS development in teams.

Because we suggest that learning occurs at two distinct phases during TMS development, our model takes into account both the emergent cognitive and behavioral components and suggests that each can operate independently of one another. This has implications for the nature of the construct as a whole. In the past, researchers have assumed that transactive memory represents a latent construct, where the dimensions are merely manifestations of some deeper, more embedded construct (Law, Wong, & Mobley, 1998). There is empirical support for the latent perspective (e.g., Lewis, 2003). However, much of that support is based on teams that already developed a fully functioning TMS. Researchers that have focused on the initial development of TMSs in teams have found that the dimensions exhibit varying levels of overlap with each other (Ellis, 2006). This supports our model, which suggests that transactive memory represents an aggregate construct, where the arrows point from each dimension to the construct, and not away from it, and dimensions can be weighed and combined algebraically (LePine, Erez, & Johnson, 2002).

Our model suggests that the importance of each dimension for the efficient and effective functioning of the team's TMS varies depending on the type of team, type of task, and phase of learning involved. For example, if a team has been together for an extended period and team members' areas of expertise remain static, as is the case with production teams like those at Saturn (see Sundstrom, 1999), it may be useful to weigh information allocation-and-retrieval coordination more heavily than directory updating. At that point, team members have already passed the first learning phase and have established differentiated expertise within the team. Furthermore, if team members' areas of expertise significantly overlap, as is the case with most service teams (see Sundstrom, 1999), their level of specialization may be lower than teams with high levels of differentiated expertise, yet their TMS may function equally well. Such teams may also need lower levels of coordination to sustain a fully functioning TMS, as team members are able to perform a large portion of their teammates' tasks.

Researchers have examined the components of TMSs individually in the past (see Hollingshead, 1998a, 1998b). For example, Hollingshead (1998c) focused on retrieval coordination and found that both nonverbal and paralinguistic communication can be utilized by intimate couples to aid them in the retrieval of information from localized directories. We suggest that focusing on specific components of transactive memory is conceptually accurate given the aggregate nature of the construct. Further work on TMSs in teams should examine the component(s) that fit with the type of task, type of team, and phase of learning that team members face. By examining the most applicable components, organizations can get a more accurate picture of the operation of the team's TMS.

Our introduction of two specific learning phases can also help the organization direct its human resource activities to select and train team members to maximize TMS development. Organizations should first examine which learning phase is of most immediate concern. For example, if the team members are coming together for the first time with highly differentiated expertise, they will likely need to spend a significant amount of time in the first learning phase updating their directories and establishing a level of specialization within the team. In such situations, organizations could increase the speed at which the team proceeds through the first learning phase by selecting team members with high cognitive ability (*g*) or by providing a cross-training program to better establish team members' directories. The exact cross-training method used depends on the resources available. With significant resources, organizations can opt for positional rotation, which represents the highest degree of immersion in the task. However, the decision also depends on the type of team and task. For example, a surgical team comprised of doctors and nurses would likely be unable to allow nurses to gain "hands-on" experience, no matter how many resources were at the organization's disposal. However, given that the effects of all three methods appear to be similar (Marks et al., 2002), it may be possible for organizations to improve learning during the first phase of TMS development by utilizing a less intense form of cross-training, such as positional clarification.

If team members have a history with one another or have significant overlap in expertise, the first learning phase should progress more quickly and without incident. Team members will likely spend the majority of their time developing coordination and credibility through information allocation-and-retrieval coordination. Organizations could aid the process by selecting team members with high levels of social intelligence or by providing a generic teamwork-skills training program before or during task completion. According to the results of Ellis et al. (2005), team members can increase skills in a variety of teamwork competencies such as communication and collaborative problem solving through a brief lecture session. These skills are critical for the interdependent interaction occurring in the second phase of learning during TMS development.

Our model also highlights the crucial role of performance monitoring, feedback, and team continuity in stimulating both phases of learning during TMS development. Turning first to performance monitoring and feedback, both lead to a greater awareness of resource deficiencies and redundancies within teams. Performance monitoring, in particular, provides opportunities for members to gain more accurate perceptions of other members' expertise. Organizations can promote such opportunities by creating situations in which members are less likely to hide ineffective performances. This might be especially important during the early phases of team development and in situations in which new members are added to teams as members' expectations are likely to be especially high during these times (e.g., Chen, 2005). This recommendation is also consistent with research suggesting the importance of psychological safety climates in teams (Edmondson, 1999). Even before a team begins to work together, it might be possible to structure it so that it is composed of members more likely to have open discourse about the scope and level of their respective expertise, strengths, and weaknesses. Some research has suggested that members can be selected who are more likely to request help and other forms of assistance from team members (e.g., Porter et al., 2003). Therefore, it may be possible for managers, leaders, and teams themselves to select members who are more likely to allow their performance to be observed by other members of the team.

As it relates specifically to the provision of feedback in team settings, although we advocate initiatives that encourage team members to share feedback with one another, we also should acknowledge that feedback provided at the individual level (e.g., member-level feedback) has the potential to have unintended negative effects. For instance, Ilgen et al. (1993) noted that member-level performance assessments may encourage within-group competition because such individual level assessments may run counter to group-oriented goals. In addition, member-level performance feedback may not always be easily accessible. Consider, for instance, situations in which one team member's performance is highly dependent on the performance of another team member or the behaviors of the team as a whole. In such situations, it may be difficult if not impossible for members to distinguish the performance of one member from another member, thus rendering member-level-performance feedback ambiguous and useless. Although we readily acknowledge that it may be challenging to create situations in which members can assess one another without some potential for negative effects, we nevertheless believe that benefits for TMS development may outweigh these negatives.

One important step that organizations can take is to distinguish between individual-level appraisals in team settings and the provision of performance feedback among team members. Unlike appraisals that are typically linked to rewards and other forms of compensation, feedback provided by team members (e.g., intrateam feedback) should be used more developmentally. We believe that when not associated with rewards and compensation, the provision and exchange of feedback within teams can create a less-threatening opportunity for team members to engage in constructive dialogue with one another about each other's inputs and to best combine these inputs to increase the effectiveness of the team. We should also note that members may be more likely to perceive such feedback as nonthreatening and consistent with attempts to foster teamwork if the feedback is shared within the team only and supervisors or others external to the team are not privy to the feedback.

Another step we believe organizations can take to mitigate the potentially negative effects of members providing feedback to one another is to encourage members to not only assess each other's performance but also the performance of the team as a whole. Nothing about team settings precludes the provision of both team- and member-performance feedback (DeNisi, 2000). We believe that when team members assess and are accountable to each other for both their individual and team performance, it helps them understand the relationship between their individual inputs and team outcomes. In addition, members will learn that a concern with member performance does not negate the importance of teamwork.

Turning next to team continuity, researchers note that, given the dynamic nature of organizations, both voluntary and involuntary turnover are common (Moreland & Argote, 2003). This turnover, as discussed earlier, can have severe effects on TMS development, especially when there is little warning given by members about their turnover intentions. Researchers have suggested that the detrimental effects of turnover can be lessened with certain organizational actions. One action the organization could take is to structure teams with assigned roles and procedures (Devadas & Argote, 1995). In this way, it is relatively easy to identify the knowledge that has been lost and the roles that need to be filled. However, not all team environments require highly specialized and differential roles, and a high degree of specialization may not be appropriate given some team environments and demands (e.g., Hollenbeck et al., 2002; Wagner, 2000). Moreover, much of what individual members do may not fall under their formal role requirements but may nevertheless be important for successful team functioning. Nevertheless, we believe it would be advantageous for teams to document not only what each member does but also what each member does well. Where there is adequate documentation, newcomers may be better able to determine what unique expertise they need to develop and how they can best fill gaps that may exist when they join teams. This should speed up both phases of the learning process during TMS development, mitigating the negative effects of turnover.

A second action that the organization can take to minimize the effects of turnover is to engage the employees in a formalized socialization process, where newcomers and old-timers have the opportunity to familiarize themselves with each other (Moreland, 1999). One way to accomplish this is for newcomers to "shadow" old-timers. This can prove very effective in training newcomers and gives both old-timers and newcomers the opportunity to learn more about each other's strengths and weaknesses, reducing the length of the learning process involved in TMS development.

Finally, managers might consider creating opportunities for team members to learn about each other's individual expertise in settings in which task accomplishment is not of primary importance. In other words, we suggest that team members have opportunities to learn more about one another when they are not working toward the team's goals or objectives. By providing opportunities to interact outside the traditional working environment, team members may have a better chance to develop closer relationships, which may improve trust and credibility. This is particularly important when the team traditionally works under time pressure and/or threat with limited opportunity for more informal (nontask) interaction (Ellis, 2006; Staw, Sandelands, & Dutton, 1981). The additional time with one another should provide opportunities for members to move beyond and/or reconcile inaccurate default settings (e.g., stereotypes; Wegner et al., 1991) regarding each other's expertise. The challenge, however, is for managers to develop novel opportunities for team members to interact in and out of the work environment in order to facilitate the learning needed for TMS development to run smoothly and efficiently.

CONCLUSION

Given the recognized value of TMS development in team-based work structures, our objective in this chapter was to delineate the specific steps involved in the process. By bringing together the two dominant conceptualizations of transactive memory, we created a model of TMS development that highlighted the role learning plays at two distinct times. Our model helps clarify the nature of the construct during development and identifies phase-specific and phase-generic variables that can be used to impact the system at various times, adding to our understanding of what makes an efficient and effective TMS in teams.

REFERENCES

Ackerman, P. L. (1986). Individual differences in information processing: An investigation of intellectual abilities and task performance during practice. *Intelligence, 10,* 101–139.

Ackerman, P. L. (1987). Individual differences in skill learning: An integration of psychometric and information processing perspectives. *Psychological Bulletin, 102,* 3–27.

Austin, J. R. (2003). Transactive memory in organizational groups: The effects of content, consensus, specialization, and accuracy on group performance. *Journal of Applied Psychology, 88*(5), 866–878.

Baddeley, A. (1986). Modularity, mass-action, and memory. *Quarterly Journal of Experimental Psychology, 38,* 527–533.

Baddeley, A. D., & Hitch, G. J. (1974). Working memory. In G. A. Bower (Ed.), *Recent advances in learning and motivation* (Vol. 8, pp. 47–89). New York: Academic Press.

Baldwin, J. M. (1894). *Mental development in the child and the race.* New York: Macmillan.

Blickensderfer, E., Cannon-Bowers, J., & Salas, E. (1998). Cross-training and team performance. In J. A. Cannon-Bowers, & E. Salas (Eds.), *Making decisions under stress: Implications for individual and team training* (pp. 299–311). Washington, DC: American Psychological Association.

Cannon-Bowers, J. A., & Salas, K. (2001). Reflections on shared cognition. *Journal of Organizational Behavior, 22,* 195–202.

Cannon-Bowers, J. A., Salas, E., Blickensderfer, E. L., & Bowers, C. A. (1998). The impact of cross-training and workload on team functioning: A replication and extension of initial findings. *Human Factors, 40,* 92–101.

Cannon-Bowers, J. A., Salas, E., & Converse, S. A. (1993). Shared mental models in expert team decision making. In N. J. Castellan, Jr. (Ed.), *Individual and group decision making: Current issues* (pp. 221–246). Hillsdale, NJ: Erlbaum.

Cannon-Bowers, J. A., Tannenbaum, S. I., Salas, E., & Volpe, C. E. (1995). Defining competencies and establishing team training requirements. In R. A. Guzzo, & E. Salas (Eds.), *Team effectiveness and decision making in organizations* (pp. 333–380). San Francisco: Jossey-Bass.

Chen, G. (2005). Newcomer adaptation in teams: Multilevel antecedents and outcomes. *Academy of Management Journal, 48,* 101–116.

Conlon, E., & Barr, S. (1989). A framework for understanding group feedback. In E. J. Lawler, & B. Markovsky (Eds.), *Advances in group processes* (Vol. 6, pp. 27–48). Greenwich, CT: JAI Press.

Daneman, M., & Carpenter, P. A. (1980). Individual differences in working memory and reading. *Journal of Verbal Learning and Verbal Behavior, 19,* 450–466.

Daneman, M., & Carpenter, P. A. (1983). Individual differences in integrating information between and within sentences. *Journal of Experimental Psychology: Learning, Memory, and Cognition, 9,* 561–584.

Dempster, F. N. (1981). Memory span: Sources of individual and developmental differences. *Psychological Bulletin, 89,* 63–100.

DeNisi, A. (2000). Performance appraisal and performance management: A multilevel analysis. In K. J. Klein, & S. W. J. Kozlowski (Eds.), *Multilevel theory, research, and methods in organizations: Foundations, extensions, and new directions* (pp. 121–156). San Francisco: Jossey-Bass.

Devadas, R., & Argote, L. (1995, May). *Organizational learning curves: The effects of turnover and work group structure.* Paper presented at the annual meeting of the Midwestern Psychological Association, Chicago, IL.

Devine, D. J., Clayton, L. D., Philips, J. L., Dunford, B. B., & Melner, S. B. (1999). Teams in organizations: Prevalence, characteristics, and effectiveness. *Small Group Research, 30,* 678–711.

Drasgow, F. (2003). Intelligence and the workplace. In W. C. Borman, D. R. Ilgen, & R. J. Klimoski (Eds.), *Handbook of psychology: Industrial and organizational psychology* (Vol. 12, pp. 107–130). Hoboken, NJ: John Wiley & Sons, Inc.

Edmondson, A. (1999). Psychological safety and learning behavior in work teams. *Administrative Science Quarterly, 44*(2), 350–383.

Ellis, A. P. J. (2006). System breakdown: The role of mental models and transactive memory in the relationship between acute stress and team performance. *Academy of Management Journal, 49*(3), 576–589.

Ellis, A. P. J., & Bell, B. S. (2005). Capacity, collaboration, and commonality: A framework for understanding team learning. In C. Schrieshiem, & L. L. Neider (Eds.), *Understanding teams* (p. 1–26). Greenwich, CT: Information Age Publishing.

Ellis, A. P. J., Bell, B. S., Ployhart, R. E., Hollenbeck, J. R., & Ilgen, D. R. (2005). An evaluation of generic teamwork skills training with action teams: Effects on cognitive and skill-based outcomes. *Personnel Psychology, 58*(3), 641–672.

Ellis, A. P. J., Hollenbeck, J. R., Ilgen, D. R., Porter, C. O. L. H., West, B. J., & Moon, H. (2003). Team learning: Collectively connecting the dots. *Journal of Applied Psychology, 88,* 821–835.

Feldman, D. C. (1989). Socialization, resocialization, and training: Reframing the research agenda. In I. L. Goldstein (Ed.), *Training and development in organizations* (pp. 376–416). San Francisco: Jossey-Bass.

Ford, J. K., & Kraiger, K. (1995). The application of cognitive constructs and principles to the instructional systems model of training: Implications for needs assessment, design, and transfer. In C. I. Cooper, & I. T. Robertson (Eds.), *International review of industrial and organizational psychology* (Vol. 10, pp. 1–48). New York: Wiley.

Gersick, C. J. G., & Hackman, J. R. (1990). Habitual routines in task-performing teams. *Organizational Behavior and Human Decision Processes, 47,* 65–97.

Hackman, J. R. (1987). The design of work teams. In J. W. Lorsch (Ed.), *Handbook of organizational behavior* (pp. 315–342). Englewood Cliffs, NJ: Prentice Hall.

Hinsz, V. B., Tindale, R. S., & Vollrath, D. A. (1997). The emerging conceptualization of groups as information processors. *Psychological Bulletin, 121,* 43–64.

Hollenbeck, J. R., Moon, H., Ellis, A. P. J., Ilgen, D. R., Sheppard, L., West, B., et al. (2002). Structural contingency theory and individual differences: Examination of external and internal person-team fit. *Journal of Applied Psychology, 87,* 599–606.

Hollingshead, A. B. (1998a). Communication, learning, and retrieval in transactive memory systems. *Journal of Experimental Social Psychology, 34*(5), 423–442.

Hollingshead, A. B. (1998b). Distributed knowledge and transactive processes in decision-making groups. In M. A. Neale, E. A. Mannix, & D. H. Gruenfeld (Eds.), *Research on managing groups and teams* (Vol. 1, pp. 103–123). Greenwich, CT: JAI Press.

Hollingshead, A. B. (1998c). Retrieval processes in transactive memory systems. *Journal of Personality & Social Psychology, 74*(3), 659–671.

Hollingshead, A. B. (2001). Cognitive interdependence and convergent expectations in transactive memory. *Journal of Personality & Social Psychology, 81*(6), 1080–1089.

Howell, W. C., & Cooke, N. J. (1989). Training the human information processor: A review of cognitive models. In I. L. Goldstein (Ed.), *Training and development in organizations* (pp. 121–182). San Francisco: Jossey-Bass.

Humphreys, L. G. (1979). The construct of general intelligence. *Intelligence, 3,* 105–120.

Ilgen, D. R., Fisher, C. D., & Taylor, M. S. (1979). Consequences of individual feedback on behavior in organizations. *Journal of Applied Psychology, 64,* 349–371.

Ilgen, D. R., Hollenbeck, J. R., Johnson, M., & Jundt, D. (2005). Teams in organizations: From I-P-O models to IMOI models. *Annual Review of Psychology, 56,* 517–543.

Ilgen, D. R., Major, D. A., Hollenbeck, J. R., & Sego, D. J. (1993). Team research in the 1990s. In M. M. Chemers, & R. Ayman (Eds.), *Leadership theory and research: Perspectives and directions* (pp. 245–270). San Diego, CA: Academic Press.

Ilgen, D. R., & Pulakos, E. D. (Eds.). (1999). *The changing nature of performance: Implications for staffing, motivation, and development.* San Francisco: Jossey-Bass.

Jensen, A. R. (1986). g: Artifact or reality? *Journal of Vocational Behavior, 29,* 301–331.

Johnson, M. D., Hollenbeck, J. R., Humphrey, S. E., Ilgen, D. R., Jundt, D., & Meyer, C. J. (2006). Cutthroat cooperation: Asymmetrical adaptation of team reward structures. *Academy of Management Journal, 49,* 103–119.

Kanfer, R., & Ackerman, P. L. (1989). Motivation and cognitive abilities: An integrative/aptitude-treatment interaction approach to skill acquisition. *Journal of Applied Psychology, 74,* 657–690.

Kluger, A. N., & DeNisi, A. S. (1996). Effects of feedback interventions on performance: A historical review, a meta-analysis, and a preliminary feedback intervention theory. *Psychological Bulletin, 119,* 254–284.

Kozlowski, S. W. J., Gully, S. M., Nason, E. R., & Smith, E. M. (1999). Developing adaptive teams: A theory of compilation and performance across levels and time. In D. R. Ilgen, & E. D. Pulakos (Eds.), *The changing nature of work and performance: Implication for staffing, personnel actions, and development* (pp. 240–292). San Francisco: Jossey-Bass.

Law, K. S., Wong, C., & Mobley, W. H. (1998). Toward a taxonomy of multidimensional constructs. *Academy of Management Review, 23,* 741–755.

Lawler, E. E., III, Mohrman, S. A., & Ledford, G. E., Jr. (1992). *Employee involvement and total quality management.* San Francisco: Jossey-Bass.

Lawler, E. E., III, Mohrman, S. A., & Ledford, G. E., Jr. (1995). *Creating high performance organizations: Practices and results of employee involvement and total quality management in Fortune 1000 companies.* San Francisco: Jossey-Bass.

LePine, J. A., Erez, A., & Johnson, D. E. (2002). The nature and dimensionality of organizational citizenship behavior: A critical review and meta-analysis. *Journal of Applied Psychology, 87,* 52–65.

Levine, J. M., & Moreland, R. L. (1991). Culture and socialization in work groups. In L. B. Resnick, J. M. Levine, & S. D. Teasley (Eds.), *Perspectives on socially shared cognition* (pp. 257–279). Washington, DC: American Psychological Association.

Lewis, K. (2003). Measuring transactive memory systems in the field: Scale development and validation. *Journal of Applied Psychology, 88*(4), 587–604.

Lewis, K. (2004). Knowledge and performance in knowledge-worker teams: A longitudinal study of transactive memory systems. *Management Science, 50*(11), 1519–1533.

Lewis, K., Lange, D., & Gillis, L. (2005). Transactive memory systems, learning, and learning transfer. *Organization Science, 16*(6), 581–598.

Marks, M. A., Mathieu, J. E., & Zaccaro, S. J. (2001). A conceptual framework and taxonomy of team processes. *Academy of Management Review, 26,* 356–376.

Marks, M. A., & Panzer, F. J. (2004). The influence of team monitoring on team processes and performance. *Human Performance, 17,* 25–41.

Marks, M. A., Sabella, M. J., Burke, C. S., & Zaccaro, S. J. (2002). The impact of cross training on team effectiveness. *Journal of Applied Psychology, 87,* 3–13.

McGaughey, S. L. (2002). Strategic interventions in intellectual asset flows. *Academy of Management Review, 27,* 248–274.

McIntyre, R. M., & Salas, E. (1995). Measuring and managing for team performance: Lessons from complex environments. In R. A. Guzzo, & E. Salas (Eds.), *Team effectiveness and decision-making in organizations* (pp. 9–45). San Francisco: Jossey-Bass.

Moreland, R. L. (1999). Transactive memory: Learning who knows what in work groups and organizations. In L. L. Thompson, J. M. Levine, & D. M. Messick (Eds.), *Shared cognition in organizations: The management of knowledge* (pp. 3–31). Mahwah, NJ: Lawrence Erlbaum Associates.

Moreland, R. L., & Argote, L. (2003). Transactive memory in dynamic organizations. In R. S. Peterson, & E. A. Mannix (Eds.), *Leading and managing people in the dynamic organization* (pp. 135–162). Mahwah, NJ: Lawrence Erlbaum Associates.

Moreland, R. L., Argote, L., & Krishnan, R. (1996). Socially shared cognition at work: Transactive memory and group performance. In J. L. Nye, & A. M. Brower (Eds.), *What's social about social cognition? Research on socially shared cognition in small groups* (pp. 57–84). Thousand Oaks, CA: Sage Publications.

Moreland, R. L., & Myaskovsky, L. (2000). Exploring the performance benefits of group training: Transactive memory or improved communication? *Organizational Behavior & Human Decision Processes, 82*(1), 117–133.

Nadler, D. A. (1979). The effects of feedback on task group behavior: A review of the experimental research. *Organizational Behavior and Human Performance, 23,* 309–338.

Nonaka, I., & Takeuchi, H. (1995). *The knowledge-creating company.* Oxford, U.K.: Oxford University Press.
Phillips, J. M. (2001). The role of decision influence and team performance in member self-efficacy, withdrawal, satisfaction with the leader, and willingness to return. *Organizational Behavior and Human Decision Processes, 84*(1), 122–147.
Porter, C. O. L. H., Gogus, C. I., Keng, J. C., & Yu, R. C. (2005, April). *The moderating effects of legitimacy of need on the effects of teamwork on team performance.* Poster presented at the 20th annual Conference for the Society of Industrial & Organizational Psychology, Los Angeles, CA.
Porter, C. O. L. H., Hollenbeck, J. R., Ilgen, D. R., Ellis, A. P. J., West, B. J., & Moon, H. (2003). Backing up behaviors in teams: The role of personality and legitimacy. *Journal of Applied Psychology, 88,* 391–403.
Robbins, S. P. (2003). *Organizational behavior.* Upper Saddle River, NJ: Prentice Hall.
Serfaty, D., Entin, E. E., & Johnston, J. H. (1998). Team coordination training. In J. A. Cannon-Bowers, & E. Salas (Eds.), *Making decisions under stress: Implications for individual and team training* (pp. 221–245). Washington, DC: American Psychological Association.
Shiffrin, R. M. (1976). Capacity limitations in information processing, attention, and memory. In W. K. Estes (Ed.), *Handbook of learning and cognitive processes* (Vol. 4, pp. 177–236). Hillsdale, NJ: Erlbaum.
Smith-Jentsch, K., Salas, E., & Baker, D. P. (1996). Training team performance-related assertive-ness. *Personnel Psychology, 49,* 909–936.
Staw, B. M., Sandelands, L. E., & Dutton, J. E. (1981). Threat-rigidity effects in organizational behavior: A multilevel analysis. *Administrative Science Quarterly, 26,* 501–524.
Stevens, M. J., & Campion, M. A. (1994). The knowledge, skill, and ability requirements for teamwork: Implications for human resource management. *Journal of Management, 20,* 503–530.
Sundstrom, E. (1999). The challenges of supporting work team effectiveness. In E. Sundstrom, & associates (Eds.), *Supporting work team effectiveness* (pp. 3–23). San Francisco: Jossey-Bass.
Teece, D. J. (1998). Capturing value from knowledge assets: The new economy, markets for know-how, and intangible assets. *California Management Rev., 40,* 55–79.
Thompson, L. (1999). *Making the team: A guide for managers.* Upper Saddle River, NJ: Prentice Hall.
Thorndike, R. (1920). Intelligence and its issues. *Harpers Magazine, 140,* 227–235.
Volpe, C. E., Cannon-Bowers, J. A., Salas, E., & Spector, P. (1996). The impact of cross training on team functioning. *Human Factors, 28,* 87–100.
Walker, R. E., & Foley, J. M. (1973). Social intelligence: Its history and measurement. *Psychological Reports, 33,* 839–864.
Wagner, J. A. (2000). Organizations. In A. E. Kazdin (Ed.), *Encyclopedia of psychology* (Vol. 6, pp. 14–20). New York & Washington, DC: Oxford University Press & American Psychological Association.
Wegner, D. M. (1987). Transactive memory: A contemporary analysis of the group mind. In B. Mullen, & G. R. Goethals (Eds.), *Theories of group behavior* (pp. 185–208). New York: Springer-Verlag.

Wegner, D. M. (1995). A computer network model of human transactive memory. *Social Cognition, 13*(3), 319–339.
Wegner, D. M., Erber, R., & Raymond, P. (1991). Transactive memory in close relationships. *Journal of Personality & Social Psychology, 61*(6), 923–929.
Wegner, D. M., Giuliano, T., & Hertel, P. T. (1985). Cognitive interdependence in close relationships. In W. J. Ickes (Ed.), *Compatible and incompatible relationships* (pp. 253–276). New York: Springer-Verlag.

SECTION

II

Member, Group, and Organizational Factors Influencing Group Learning

Now that we have considered how groups learn and what they learn, we turn to variables that affect group learning positively and negatively. Jehn and Rupert (chapter 6) introduce a learning typology that centers on the concept of group faultlines affecting social, process, and task learning. *Social learning* is the process through which team members get to know each other better as individuals and learn to interpret each other's behavior in the context of their personal lives and personalities. *Task learning* is the process of improving the team's understanding of the content of the task, by sharing and reflecting upon knowledge, ideas, and insights through interaction with each other in order to improve team performance. *Process learning* is the pattern of interaction through which team members create work routines and develop procedures about how to organize their work, such as delegating issues and role definitions (e.g., the development of a transactive-memory system). *Faultlines* are hypothetical dividing lines that split a group into relatively homogeneous subgroups based on one or more characteristics. Faultlines explain the effects of group composition on team functioning better than traditional heterogeneity theories of group composition. Jehn and Rupert propose that social category faultlines lead to low levels of social and task learning and high levels of process learning. Informational faultlines produce high task learning and high process learning but low social learning. Further, they propose that the negative effect of social category faultlines on tas k and social learning is weakened when team members feel their group is psychologically safe and the positive effect of social category faultlines on process learning will be strengthened. The positive relationship between information faultlines and task and process learning is enhanced when groups have an error management culture. Therefore, we need to know the basis for how faultlines form (information or social) and measure different learning criteria (social, process, and task) in order to understand group learning.

Porter's chapter on group learning orientation (chapter 7) emphasizes the importance of understanding members' individual learning orientation (their desire to become mastery learners as opposed to goal-oriented learners) and the group's learning orientation (their learning mastery-oriented, generative-interaction patterns). He identifies deficiencies in the literature on goal orientation among individuals working alone and discusses the need for research on group learning orientation. Learning and goal orientation are loosely related, suggesting that an individual can be simultaneously high or low on both of these dimensions. Goal orientation is a relatively stable individual trait that can be influenced by the state the individual is in at the moment. We can think of groups as collections of members who possess their own individual learning goal dispositions that influence the group. Since goal orientation can be a state or state-like phenomenon, it can be influenced by both bottom-up and top-down processes—that is, individual members can affect the group's learning-goal orientation and a group leader or facilitator can create conditions that affect the group's learning-goal orientation. The chapter shows how goal orientation affects both individual and group behavior.

Zakaria, Amelinckx, and Wilemon (chapter 8) discuss teams working in global virtual settings. Electronic communication media allow group members to work long distance. Global virtual teams navigate across distance and culture. This chapter considers the nature, structure, and composition of global virtual groups and how cultural complexities affect group dynamics and learning. They consider when it is important to assess the performance of effective global virtual teams. Finally, they conclude by presenting how new patterns of communication and positive social exchange can emerge in computer-mediated group environments that can provide cross-national companies with important competitive advantages.

Zaccaro, Ely, and Shuffler (chapter 9) outline ways that leaders aid in group learning. They consider how leaders inculcate a learning climate within the group, how they develop individual and group-level learning tools, and how they act as a learning partner, coaching, mentoring, and providing feedback to the group. The result is that members learn how to work together collaboratively, how to educate each other, and how to take advantage of the synergies among members' abilities and interactions to learn and perform effectively.

CHAPTER

6

Group Faultlines and Team Learning: How to Benefit from Different Perspectives

KAREN A. JEHN AND JOYCE RUPERT
Leiden University

The extent to which teams learn and how they perform partly depends on their group composition. Although there is ample research on the effects of diversity on team functioning and performance (for reviews and meta-analyses, see Jackson, Joshi, & Erhardt, 2003; Mannix & Neale, 2005; Stewart, 2006; Webber & Donahue, 2001; Williams & O'Reilly, 1998), little research has been done on the effects of group composition on team learning. Team learning is a relatively new concept that is starting to crystallize. Likewise, new theories of group composition have been introduced, such as group faultlines (Lau & Murnighan, 1998). Group faultlines are hypothetical dividing lines that split a group into relative homogeneous subgroups based on the group members' alignment along one or more attributes (adapted from Lau & Murnighan, 1998). Group faultlines are assumed to better explain the effects of group composition on team functioning than traditional heterogeneity theories of group composition (Bezrukova, Thatcher, & Jehn, in press).

In this chapter, we further the understanding of the concept of team learning by reviewing past typologies and definitions, by introducing a new learning typology that includes the concept of social learning, and by proposing a model in which we relate group faultlines to these learning types. In this model, we will explore what factors influence the realization of a team's learning potential and examine the role of potential moderators, such as psychological safety and error culture. We propose that a better understanding of how team members interact and how group processes evolve in teams with various group compositions will help fully utilize the team's learning potential.

TEAM LEARNING DEFINITIONS

In this chapter, we define *team learning* as a process of reflection and interaction in which team members actively acquire, process, and share knowledge and information in order to improve team performance (based on Argote, Gruenfeld, & Naquin, 2001). In this definition, we explicitly link the process of team learning to the goal of task improvement, since we assume that teams are usually oriented toward team performance or outcomes in their efforts to learn from each other. Before we introduce our new team learning typology, we first give a short review of past team learning definitions (see Table 6.1 for a summary).

Although much research has been done on teams and learning in organizations, we know relatively little about learning in teams (cf. Edmondson, 1999). Researchers have defined team learning in different ways; some have emphasized the process of learning (e.g., Edmondson, 1999, 2002; Gibson & Vermeulen, 2003; Tsjosvold, Yu, & Chun, 2004), while others have stressed the outcomes of learning (e.g., Ellis et al., 2003; see Table 6.1). Process definitions of team learning often capture aspects such as reflection and action (Edmondson, 1999, 2002; Tjosvold et al., 2004; Gibson & Vermeulen, 2003), sharing and processing knowledge, and making improvements (Edmondson, 2002; Argyris & Schön, 1978; Gibson, 2001; Kolb, 1984). Some researchers have described concrete team learning behaviors associated with these concepts, such as (a) asking questions, (b) challenging assumptions, (c) evaluating alternatives, (d) seeking feedback, (e) experimenting, (f) reflecting on results, (g) detecting, discussing, and correcting errors, and (h) reflective communication (Argyris & Schön, 1978; Edmondson, 1999; Gibson & Vermeulen, 2003; Van der Vegt & Bunderson, 2005). Outcome definitions of team learning are often described in terms of changes in knowledge resulting from team-member interactions (e.g., Argote et al., 2001; Ellis et al., 2003). An emerging field of literature examines the concept of team innovation and the factors that influence it (e.g., Ancona & Caldwell, 1992; De Dreu & West, 2001; Drach-Zahavy & Somech, 2001; Hambrick, Cho, & Chen, 1996; O'Reilly, Williams, & Barsade, 1997), which can be regarded as a team learning outcome.

TABLE 6.1 Overview of Past Definitions of Team Learning

Reference	Label	Definition	Process/ outcome	Learning typology
Argote, Guenfeld, & Naquin, 2001	Group learning	"We define group learning in terms of both the processes and outcomes of group interaction. As a process, group learning involves the activities through which individuals acquire, share and combine knowledge through experience with one another. Evidence that group learning has occurred includes changes in knowledge, either implicit or explicit, that occur as a result of such collaboration" (p. 370)	Process and outcome	Task, process, & social
Edmondson, 1999	Team learning behavior	"…an ongoing process of reflection and action, characterized by asking questions, seeking feedback, experimenting, reflecting on results and discussing errors or unexpected outcomes of actions" (p. 353)	Process	Task & process
Edmondson, 2002	Team learning	"Team learning has been defined as a process in which a team takes action, obtains and reflects upon feedback and makes changes to adapt or improve (Edmondson, 1999; Argote et al., 2001)" (p. 2002)	Process	Task, process, & social
Edmondson, Bohmer, & Pisano, 2001	Collective learning process	"Interdependence requires people to communicate and coordinate to create new routines, thereby participating in a collective learning process. This may involve learning about others' roles (Levine & Moreland, 1999), improvising (Orlikowski & Hofman, 1997), and making numerous small adjustments that facilitate technology implementation (Leonard-Barton & Deschamps, 1988)" (p. 688)	Process	Task & process

(Continued)

TABLE 6.1 (Continued)

Reference	Label	Definition	Process/ outcome	Learning typology
Ellis, Hollenbeck, Ilgen, Porter, West, & Moon, 2003	Team learning	"We define team learning as a relatively permanent change in the team's collective level of knowledge and skills produced by the shared experience of the team members" (pp. 821–822)	Outcome	Task, process, & social
Gibson & Vermeulen, 2003	Team learning behavior	"The exploration of knowledge through experimentation, the combination of insights through reflective communication, and the explication and specification of what has been learned through codification" (pp. 203–204)	Process and outcome	Task & process
Hinsz, Tindale, & Vollrath (1997)	Group level information processing	"We defined group level information processing as the degree to which information, ideas or cognitive processes are shared, and are being shared, among the group members and how this sharing of information affects both individual- and group level outcomes. The shared information can relate to the task at hand, characteristics of the group, aspects of group members, the pattern of group interaction, or the context within which the task, group and its members exist" (p. 53)	Process	Task, process, & social

(Continued)

TABLE 6.1 (Continued)

Reference	Label	Definition	Process/ outcome	Learning typology
Liang, Moreland, & Argote, 1995	Transactive memory	'This system is a combination of the knowledge possessed by particular group members and an awareness of who knows what" (p. 385)	System/ Process	Process learning
Moreland & Myaskovsky (2000)	Transactive memory	". . . transactive memory systems develop in many groups to ensure that important information is recalled. These systems combine what individual group members know with a shared awareness of who knows what. When group members need information, but cannot recall it themselves or mistrust their own memories, they can turn to each other for help. In this way, a transactive memory system can provide a group's members with more and better information than any of them could recall alone" (p.118)	System/ Process	Process learning
Stasser & Stewart (1995)	Transactive memory	Refer to the work of Wegner (1986) and emphasize the effect of expert roles and role structure in teams as a way to stimulate this transactive memory system	System/ process	Process learning
Sarin & McDermott (2003)	Team Learning	"We define learning as occurring when the processing of experience changes the range of potential behaviors/actions (Huber, 1991)" (p.709)	Process/ outcome	Task, process, & social

(Continued)

TABLE 6.1 (Continued)

Reference	Label	Definition	Process/ outcome	Learning typology
Tsjosvold, Yu, & Hui, (2004)	Team learning	"…learning involves understanding new ideas and incorporating them into one's own thinking (Crossan, et al., 1999). (…) Team members reflect on their performance and its consequences, discover cause and effect relationships, and identify weaknesses and strengths in their own efforts. They gain insight into their own behavior, develop and implement changes, and prepare for future challenges" (p. 1224)	Process	Task, process, & social
Van der Vegt & Bunderson, 2005	Team learning behaviors	"We define team learning behaviors as activities by which team members seek to acquire, share, refine, or combine task-relevant knowledge through interaction with one another (Argote, Gruenfeld, & Naquin, 2001: 370). These activities may include asking questions, challenging assumptions, seeking different perspectives, evaluating alternatives, and reflecting on past actions (Edmondson, 1999; Gibson & Vermeulen, 2003). We therefore view team learning behavior as one aspect of a group's 'interaction process' (Hackman & Morris, 1975), or as an example of a 'group action 'process' (Marks, Mathieu, & Zacarro, 2001)" (p. 534)	Process	Task learning
Wegner (1986)	Transactive memory	'The transactive memory system begins when individuals learn something about each other's domains of expertise" (p. 191)	System	Process learning

Innovation can be defined as the initiation or discovery of a technology, process, or idea that is new in the particular context of the organization and which is often followed by the development and implementation of this idea or technology (adapted from Amabile, 1988). Although the team-innovation literature can improve our understanding of team learning as an outcome, unfortunately, a lack of cross-fertilization still exists between this field and the literature field on team learning. We will therefore incorporate this literature in our later review on group composition and team learning.

What, however, makes team learning a group- or team-level construct? First, what is a group or team? A *group* or *team* can be defined as a social system of at least two members who (a) recognize themselves as a group, (b) are recognized by others as a group, (c) have a shared responsibility for a team product or service, and (d) operate in an organization (Hackman, 1987; Alderfer, 1987). In research on group composition and diversity faultlines, the term *group* is mainly used to refer to this definition (e.g., Gruenfeld, Mannix, Williams, & Neale, 1996; Jehn, Northcraft, & Neale, 1999; Lau & Murnighan, 1998). In the literature on team learning, however, the term *team* is mainly used, but often to refer to the same definition. We believe that the integration of these fields and terminologies is an important contribution to the literature, and therefore, we use the terms interchangeably, thereby referring to the previous definition.

The process of learning becomes a group- or team-level process when the ability to acquire knowledge and skills is collectively shared by group members (Ellis et al., 2003). Teams can do this by developing a transactive memory, which ensures that important information is recalled. In this system, the knowledge of individual group members is combined with a shared awareness of who knows what and who has certain abilities and skills (Liang, Moreland, & Argote, 1995; Moreland & Myaskovsky, 2000; Wegner, 1986). By effectively using this system, teams can become more efficient.

To summarize, team learning is a rich concept that can be seen as both a process and an outcome, and past researchers in different fields have discussed and emphasized the different aspects of this concept. In the following sections, we will extend the concept of team learning by proposing a new typology.

A TEAM LEARNING TYPOLOGY

As previously outlined, most past team learning definitions describe a process of interaction and reflection, in which information or knowledge is being shared, acquired, and combined (e.g., Argote et al., 2001; Edmondson, 1999, 2002; Hinsz, Tindale, & Vollrath, 1997; see Table 6.1). It remains largely unclear, however, exactly *what* this information or knowledge is about, and thus, what the *subject* of learning entails

(Rupert & Jehn, 2006). As Hinsz et al. (1997) pointed out, shared information can be related to the task, characteristics of the group, or patterns in the team's interaction. The broad and undefined scope of subjects that team learning can be about calls for a typology, which further refines our understanding of team learning.

We propose that different aspects of the group process are associated with different types of learning. For instance, past research on group conflict has shown (Amason, 1996; Jehn, 1995, 1997; Pelled, 1996) that group members can have *relationship* conflicts and fight about nonwork issues, such as social events, clothing preferences, and hobbies. Group members can also have *task* conflict, which are disagreements regarding the task being performed, such as writing a report or developing a product (De Dreu & Weingart, 2003; Jehn, 1995, 1997). Recent studies (e.g., Behfar, Mannix, Peterson, & Trochin, 2005; Jehn & Mannix, 2001) have also distinguished *process* conflict as a separate conflict type, which can be defined as conflict about how to accomplish a task and who is doing what (Jehn, 1997; Kramer, 1991).

Corresponding with this conflict typology, we propose a similar framework for distinguishing types of team learning (Rupert & Jehn, 2006). First, we distinguish *task learning,* which we define as the process of improving the team's understanding of the content of the task, by sharing and reflecting upon knowledge, ideas, and insights through interaction with each other, in order to improve team performance. Some of the definitions given in Table 6.1 already refer to task learning; for instance, the definitions that describe "reflecting on results" (Edmondson, 1999) and "activities by which team members seek to acquire, share, refine, or combine *task* [italics added] relevant knowledge through interaction with each other" (Argote, Gruenfeld, & Naquin, 2001: 370).

Consider the example in which a four-person research group is developing a measurement instrument to test some new constructs. The group is composed of a statistician, two experts who know the field in which the concepts have originated, and one researcher who has experience with the methodology. In several meetings, they bring in their specific areas of expertise and discuss conceptual and methodological problems to develop an effective instrument to measure their constructs. This is an example of what we label "task learning," since the team members improve their understanding of the task by interacting with each other and sharing each other's knowledge and expertise about the content of the task.

Some of the past team learning definitions describe *process* activities, such as reflecting on performance (Tjosvold et al., 2004), creating routines, and learning about each other's roles (Edmondson et al., 2001).Gibson and Vermeulen (2003) proposed and found that team members often come up with ideas about how their work should be done, and they labeled this as "experimentation." Additionally, *codification* is the process by which tacit knowledge becomes explicit through, for instance, recording what has been discussed (e.g., meeting minutes;

Gibson & Vermeulen, 2003). These activities, through which members learn about *how* to do their work, we refer to as "process learning." We define *process learning* as the pattern of interaction through which team members create work routines and develop procedures about how to organize their work, such as delegating issues and role definitions. An important aspect of process learning is the development of a transactive memory. By working together, team members get to know each other's abilities, fields of expertise, and knowledge. Based on this information, they develop a system in which important information is recalled and in which members know who knows what, and thus, whom they can turn to with questions, which will make team processes more efficient.

To continue with our example of the research group, process learning would occur when, after a meeting, the research group divides the tasks based on what they have learned about each other's abilities and knowledge. For instance, the group decided that the two researchers who know the literature fields will do some more research and will come up with very detailed descriptions of the constructs. In turn, the statistician and the person having the experience with the methodology will give input and feedback regarding methodological issues. The process through which they learn who is best and most knowledgeable in doing what, and dividing the work based on their information about this, are examples of process learning.

An important omission in most definitions of team learning is learning about other team members as individuals with a personality, hobbies, family life, and so forth. Similarly, the literature on interdependency in teams has predominantly focused on functional and cognitive interdependency, ignoring interdependency between employees that has a more friendly nature (Rispens, 2006). Rispens extended this literature by distinguishing affect-based interdependency, which refers to the interdependency people experience in their search for a feeling of well-being and social acceptance, such as friendship relationships at work. These friendship relationships can have an important impact on individual and group effectiveness and job satisfaction (Rispens, 2006). Also, as a recent review of empirical research on group-personality composition and team effectiveness showed, personality can have an important impact on the team process as well (Halfhill, Sundstrom, Lahner, & Calderone, 2005). We therefore propose that team members can learn about each other's personality, family life, and social relationships at work as well.

Similarly, the literature on family-work balance shows that a supportive environment in which supervisors and colleagues have empathy for the employees' needs to balance work and family responsibilities positively influenced job satisfaction (Thomas & Ganster, 1995) and commitment (Thompson, Jahn, Kopelman, & Prottas, 2004). This type of environment, however, negatively influenced absenteeism (Goff, Mount, & Jamison, 1990), work stress (Frone, Yardley, & Markel, 1997) and work-family conflict (Anderson, Coffey, & Byerly, 2002). For effective team performance to occur, it can therefore be important to take into account personal characteristics such as personality and family situation when interpreting each other's actions. This is what we label "social learning," which we define as the process through which team members get to know each other better as individuals and learn to interpret each other's behavior in the context of personal life and personality. Referring to our example of the research group, social learning would occur when team members show some consideration for each other's personal situation and family life. For instance, the statistician in our example is a woman who has two little children, and she often has to leave at three o'clock to pick them up from school, which means that the team cannot meet in the late afternoon. In addition, this person is often in the office very early and prefers not to be disturbed or have coffee breaks in the morning, since she has to get a lot of work done at that time. Knowledge about these aspects of a team member's personal life can make it easier to interpret the relationships and interactions at work.

In our theoretical model, which we introduce later in this chapter, we link group composition to the different types of learning. Before we discuss this, we first give a short review of the literature on the effects of group composition and faultlines on team learning. We specifically focus on studies that have empirically tested the construct of team learning or related concepts (e.g., innovation, information sharing).

GROUP COMPOSITION AND TEAM LEARNING: A REVIEW

The extent to which teams have the potential to learn partially depends on how the team is composed in terms of social-category characteristics and informational characteristics. Past diversity research has categorized diversity into these different types of characteristics to provide a better understanding of the effects of diversity in teams on outcomes. We will briefly discuss the difference between these types of heterogeneity and review what is known about their effects on team learning. After that, we will discuss what is known about the effects of faultlines on team learning and propose a model in which we link social category versus informational faultlines to the team learning types.

Diversity and Organizational Outcomes

Diversity is a very broad concept, commonly defined as any attribute that a person may use to discover individual differences (Jackson, 1992; Mannix & Neale, 2005; Williams & O'Reilly, 1998). As a result, researchers have begun to classify diversity into similar attributes, such as social-category diversity and informational diversity (Jehn, Chadwick, & Thatcher, 1997; Jehn et al., 1999; Milliken & Martins, 1996; Polzer, Milton, & Swann, 2002). *Social-category diversity* refers to explicit and often observable differences in social-category memberships, such as race, sex, and age (Jackson, 1992; Jehn et al., 1999; Pelled, 1996). *Informational diversity* refers to differences in knowledge bases and perspectives that members bring to a team, which are likely to arise from differences in educational background, training, and work experiences (Jehn et al., 1999). Since social-category diversity often refers to more visible, readily observable characteristics, and informational diversity is less visible and more job related (Van Knippenberg, De Dreu, & Homan, 2004), we believe that the distinction between social-category versus informational diversity reflects previous diversity distinctions, such as visible versus nonvisible diversity (Jackson, May, & Whitney, 1995; Tsui & Gutek, 1999) and surface- versus deep-level diversity (Phillips & Loyd, 2006; Harrison, Price, & Bell, 1998; Harrison, Price, Gavin, & Florey, 2002).

Researchers have suggested that these two categories of diversity may have a different impact on group processes due to their job-relatedness (Pelled, Eisenhardt, & Xin, 1999; Webber & Donahue, 2001). Researchers in many domains (e.g., organizational and social psychology, sociology, anthropology, education) have studied the effects of gender, race, cultural diversity, age, tenure, educational background, and personality on performance (e.g., Allport, 1954; Blau, 1977; Ely & Thomas, 2001; Hallinan & Smith, 1985). Some scholars endorse the optimistic view of diversity (cf. Mannix & Neale, 2005), arguing that diversity can be beneficial for organizations and can improve team outcomes, which is known as the "value-in-diversity hypothesis" (Cox, Lobel, & McLeod, 1991). In contrast, scholars who endorse the pessimistic view of diversity argue that diversity can create social divisions that can, in turn, lead to social disintegration and poor cohesion, thus decreasing group performance. Research has found support for both arguments, illustrating that diversity appears to be a "double-edged sword" (Milliken & Martins, 1996), increasing the opportunity for productive task conflict and creativity, as well as the likelihood that group members will become dissatisfied and have low identification with the group.

Despite this ample amount of research on the effects of diversity on organizational group outcomes (for reviews and meta-analyses, see Jackson et al., 2003; Mannix & Neale, 2005; Stewart, 2006; Webber & Donahue, 2001; Williams & O'Reilly, 1998), little research has linked group composition to the concept of team learning. Some studies examined the effects of heterogeneity on concepts that are highly related to team learning, such as creative problem solving and innovation (e.g., Jackson, 1992; Drach-Zahavy & Somech, 2001) For instance, Drach-Zahavy and Somech found that teams with members who were heterogeneous in their roles were more innovative than homogeneous teams. In another study, Jackson (1992) found that teams with members who were heterogeneous on functional characteristics outperformed homogeneous teams on tasks that required creative problem solving and innovation. Consistently, other studies showed that heterogeneous teams generated more arguments (Smith, Tindale, & Dugoni, 1996), detected more novel solutions (Nemeth & Kwan, 1987), and were better able to integrate multiple perspectives (Gruenfeld, 1995; Peterson & Nemeth, 1996) than groups without conflicting perspectives.

Some other studies looked at the effects of group composition on information sharing (e.g., Phillips, Mannix, Neale, & Gruenfeld, 2004; Gruenfeld et al., 1996), which can be regarded as an aspect of team learning behavior (e.g., Edmondson, 1999; Ellis et al., 2003; Hinsz et al., 1997; Table 6.1). For instance, Gruenfeld et al. (1996) examined the effects of member familiarity and information distribution on performance and found that teams in which team members were familiar with each other outperformed groups consisting of strangers when the distribution of knowledge was diverse. In contrast, teams of strangers outperformed teams with members familiar to each other when the distributed information was redundant. This finding is consistent with past research by Shah and Jehn (1993), who found that groups of friends have better conflict-management strategies, which helps them improve task performance compared to groups of strangers.

Although the studies discussed above provide useful insights into the concept of knowledge and information management in groups, most studies did not hypothesize and test the specific link between group composition and team learning. A theoretical model is therefore needed to further our understanding of the complex relationship between group composition and team learning. Before introducing our theoretical model, we first briefly discuss two different approaches to group composition—dispersion versus alignment—and introduce the concept of faultlines.

Dispersion Versus Alignment Theories of Group Composition

Most past diversity research is based on the dispersion view of group composition (cf. Bezrukova et al., in press), which focuses on the individual distribution of characteristics in a group (McGrath, 1998; Moreland & Levine, 1992) and how this influences group and organizational outcomes. Studies based on this view have often predicted the effect of heterogeneity on group processes (e.g., conflict) through mechanisms explained by social identity and social categorization theory (Tajfel & Turner, 1986; Turner, 1987), the similarity attraction paradigm (Byrne, 1971), and an information/decision making perspective (Gruenfeld et al., 1996; Wittenbaum & Stasser, 1996). This dispersion approach of group composition has been criticized because of the assumption that members' attributes are independent (cf. Bezrukova et al., in press). For instance, if one is examining race, gender is often ignored, leading to the assumption that the experiences of black men in a group would be similar to those of black women in an otherwise identical group. Thus, the heterogeneity concept captures the degree to which a group differs on only one demographic characteristic at a time, while ignoring the interaction with other demographic characteristics (McGrath, 1998).

Alignment theories of group composition, such as group faultline theory (e.g., Lau & Murnighan, 1998) and compositional gaps (Hambrick, Li, Xin, & Tsui, 2001; Li & Hambrick, 2005), however, argue that the interaction of multiple attributes affects group processes more than separate characteristics. Group *faultlines* are defined as hypothetical dividing lines that split a group into relatively homogeneous subgroups based on each group member's alignment along one or more attributes (adapted from Lau & Murnighan, 1998). An example of a faultline group would be a four-person team consisting of two white male technicians and two black female sales managers. In this group, the alignment among members is clear because there are two homogeneous subgroups based on race, gender, and functional background. Group faultline theory predicts that the compositional dynamics of multiple characteristics has a greater effect on group processes and performance than the separate demographic attributes (e.g., Lau & Murnighan, 1998; Thatcher, Jehn, & Zanutto, 2003). Members that are similar on several demographic attributes are likely to align and form subgroups, differentiating themselves from other subgroups in a team (Early & Mosakowski, 2000; Cramton & Hinds, 2005).

Two recent studies theorized about and tested the relationship between group faultlines and team learning. Gibson and Vermeulen (2003) found a curvilinear relationship between subgroup strength and learning behavior, such that teams with moderately strong demographic subgroups displayed more learning behavior than teams with weak or strong subgroups. Additionally, they found that both teams that were highly homogeneous or heterogeneous tended to display more learning behavior, but this was only when they controlled for the simultaneous effect of subgroup strength.

In their experimental field study, Lau and Murnighan (2005) found that gender and ethnicity faultlines explained more variance in perceptions of team learning than single-attribute heterogeneity indices. Although they did not find support for their hypothesis that strong faultlines would negatively impact team members' perceptions of group learning, they found that cross-sex and cross-ethnicity work communications positively influenced perceptions of group learning and were particularly effective for weak faultline groups. Based on this finding, Lau and Murnighan suggested that past research on group effectiveness needs to be revised, since the effectiveness of intragroup communications may depend on whether or not groups have strong faultlines.

As we can conclude from these recent studies, more sophisticated theories are coming up to deepen our understanding of the effects of group composition on outcomes, still little research has been done on the effects of group composition on team learning. We further our theoretical understanding of this relationship, by proposing a theoretical model explaining the complex relationship between group composition and team learning.

A THEORETICAL MODEL LINKING FAULTLINES TO TEAM LEARNING

To examine which type of group composition has the highest potential for team learning to occur, we propose a model in which we apply the social-category versus informational distinction to faultlines, and then link these faultline types to the proposed types of team learning (see Fig. 6.1 for an overview of propositions). In this model, we will draw specific attention to the moderating role of psychological safety and error management culture on the relationship between faultlines and team learning (see Fig. 6.2 for propositions).

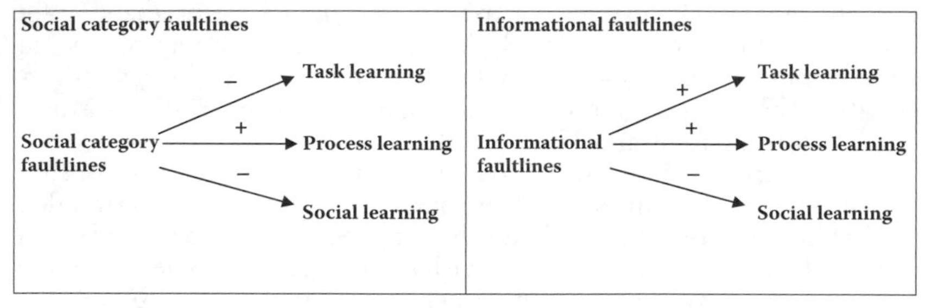

Figure 6.1 Proposed relations between faultlines and team learning.

Social-Category Faultlines and Task Learning

We propose that the bases of the faultline subgroups are crucial to group functioning (Jehn et al., in press). Subgroups formed along social-category characteristics, such as race, gender, or age, are more likely to set in motion mechanisms such as stereotyping and prejudice (Messick & Mackie, 1989). Consequently, members in teams with social-category faultlines may feel less comfortable, and subgroup members are less likely to interact with members from the other subgroup. They may dislike and distance members who belong to the other social-category subgroup (Byrne, 1971). This polarization based on social-category dimensions can prevent subgroup members from sharing task-relevant information across subgroups (Milliken & Martins, 1996), and it will be less likely that group members will take task-related comments of members of the other subgroup seriously. For instance, past research has found that groups heterogeneous on age and race had less frequent and more formal task related communications with each other than members of homogeneous groups (Hoffman, 1985; Zenger & Lawrence, 1989). It is likely that the inhibited, task-related interactions with members from the other subgroup due to stereotyping and prejudice will prevent team members from displaying task learning.

Moreover, self-verification theory (Swann, Polzer, Seyle, & Ko, 2004) proposes that people seek to confirm their thoughts and feelings about themselves. In groups with social-category faultlines it is more likely that this confirmation of thoughts is mainly taking place within subgroups, rather than across subgroups, creating different thought worlds based on social-category faultlines. During task-related discussions, subgroup members might stick to their opinions since they feel supported by the shared beliefs of their subgroup members (cf. Lau & Murnighan, 1998). For task learning to occur, however, it is important that *all* group members share each other's expertise, knowledge, and information in order to perform the task and that they are willing to adjust and change their ideas, based on the expertise of other group members. Therefore, we expect that social-category faultlines will inhibit a team from engaging in task learning and have made the following proposition:

> Proposition 1a: Teams with social-category faultlines will experience *low* levels of task learning.

Social-Category Faultlines and Process Learning

Team members who have different social-category characteristics may face "interpretive barriers" due to members' different language systems, life experiences, or values acquired from varying socialization experiences (Dougherty, 1992; Jehn et al., in press). Based on certain social groups such as, for instance, men and women, individuals can have different conventions regarding social interactions at work and task accomplishment (Jehn et al., 1999; Von Glinow, Shapiro, & Brett, 2004). In groups in which these social groups are aligned with each other, it is more likely that members of subgroups develop their own routines and procedures to carry out their work. Priorities and work might not be aligned within the team, and thus, they may spend more time arguing who does what, when, and how (Behfar et al., 2005). These process conflicts about who should do what, however, can ultimately improve group members' understanding of how the work should be done. By arguing about the best way to carry out the work and by having discussions about responsibilities, the different roles of group members are being clarified, and better processes can result from these conflicts. So although there may be some polarization and conflict about routines in teams with social-category faultlines, these conflicts can ultimately turn into learning about the process of how to carry out the work. When team members know who is good in what and how tasks are being assigned, coordination should improve as well, since team members can anticipate rather than simply react to each other's behavior (Moreland, 1999). This leads us to the following proposition:

Proposition 1b: Teams with strong social-category faultlines will experience *high* levels of process learning.

Social-Category Faultlines and Social Learning

As we proposed earlier, differences based on highly visible social-category characteristics, such as race, gender, and age, can evoke negative responses, giving rise to stereotyping and prejudice. These stereotypes and biases can distort the information that group members acquire about each other, which can lead to misinterpretations about each other's behaviors. Consequently, heterogeneity based on social-category characteristics can cause feelings of discomfort, interpersonal tension, and hostility that can even result in relationship conflict (e.g., Alagna, Reddy, & Collins, 1982; Jehn, 1997; Jehn et al., 1997; Pelled, 1996), which will inhibit social learning.

Based on faultline theory (Lau & Murnighan, 1998), we argue that if social-category attributes align, similar members will interact with each other more often and are more likely to form strong subgroupings (Stevenson, Peacre, & Porter, 1985; Prentice & Miller, 2002). The salience of in-group versus out-group can trigger stereotypes and biases about the other subgroup, causing polarization between subgroups (Hogg, Turner, & Davidson, 1990). We expect that the inhibited communication between members from different subgroups based on social categories will inhibit team members from learning about each other's differences in personality, background, and lifestyle. Impressions that team members build about the personality and lifestyle differences can easily become distorted by stereotypes and biases. It will be less likely, therefore, that group members will be open to learn from each other's backgrounds and value the diversity that surrounds them. This leads us to the following proposition:

Proposition 1c: Teams with social-category faultlines will experience *low* levels of social learning.

Informational Faultlines and Task Learning

Teams with informational faultlines split into relatively homogeneous subgroups based on functional and educational background and/or position. These informational differences are less visible and less prone to interpersonal prejudice and stereotyping. Subgroup formation caused by informational faultlines may result in coalitions of opposing thoughts, which can operate in workgroups as "healthy divides," stimulating effective decision-making processes and team learning (Gibson & Vermeulen, 2003). Research shows that one of the mechanisms through which diversity can lead to better results is by the confrontation of different ideas (cf. Van den Bossche, Van Gennip, Gijselaers, & Segers, 2006). Van der Vegt and Bunderson (2005) showed that the potential benefits of diversity were realized through "the cross-fertilization of ideas," which can originate from task conflict; this, in turn, can lead to task learning. Especially when solving complex, nonroutine problems, teams are more effective when they are composed of team members with a variety of skills, knowledge, abilities, and perspectives (Bantel & Jackson, 1989).

The alignment along informational characteristics in teams with informational faultlines stimulates team members to exhibit similar viewpoints within each subgroup and display different opinions across subgroups. In this situation, subgroup members may find social support from other subgroup members due to mutual liking, perceived similarity, and shared experiences (Phillips et al., 2004). Literature on minority influence shows that this social support from other group members can have an important impact on information sharing in diverse groups (cf. Allen & Levine, 1971; Bragg & Allen, 1972). In groups with strong informational faultlines, members may engage in open discussions of different viewpoints across subgroups because they feel supported by their subgroup members (Lau & Murnighan, 1998; Phillips, 2003; Swann et al., 2004). We therefore argue that individuals within informational faultline groups will experience high levels of communication over task-related issues. These task-related discussions will, in turn, improve the team's understanding of the content of the task, since knowledge, ideas, and insights are openly shared through interaction with each other. We therefore propose the following:

> Proposition 2a: Teams with informational faultlines will experience *high* levels of task learning.

Informational Faultlines and Process Learning

As we suggested, informational faultlines are less prone to stereotyping and biases. In fact, they are highly relevant for the work context, and group members get to know each other's fields of expertise and functional backgrounds through interaction with each other. These interactions play an important role in developing expectations about each other's behavior in the workplace.

According to expectancy violation theory, people make inferences about, for instance, values and work attitudes based on characteristics that they know, such as informational differences (Bettencourt, Dill, Greathouse, Charlton, & Mulholland, 1997). Team members in groups with informational faultlines expect to be different along characteristics such as educational and functional background and experience. Since these informational differences often align in teams with informational faultlines, these expectancies are often confirmed, which should lead to positive affect (Rink & Ellemers, in press). When expectations are consistent, there is less confusion about each other's roles and how task accomplishment should proceed in the team. We therefore expect that although there might be different opinions between subgroups about how the task should be accomplished, there is clarity about each other's roles and work procedures, which will make it more likely that team members will be effective in dealing with, for instance, logistical problems or other process issues (Jehn et al., in press).

Additionally, when the expectations that group members have about each other's functional background and experiences are confirmed, group members are better able to build their transactive memory system, which clarifies who is good at what and how tasks should be divided. Team members know each other's strengths and weaknesses and will therefore be better prepared to divide and delegate the work tasks to enable effective team performance. We therefore expect that team members in groups with informational faultlines are likely to display process learning. We therefore propose the following:

> Proposition 2b: Teams with informational faultlines will experience *high* levels of process learning.

Informational Faultlines and Social Learning

As we have previously argued, due to expectancy effects, there is less confusion about task accomplishment and procedures. The confirmation of team members' expectancies regarding the alignment of informational characteristics in teams with informational faultlines creates a stable and certain environment, one in which members are more likely to cooperate. This sense of stability and clarity about the environment will give less rise to questions about other members' personal lives and hobbies; it will also inhibit the communication about these subjects. Work-related attributes are likely to dominate social-category differences, and since highly job-related differences are more related to the task, these attributes are more likely to impact task performance (Pelled, 1996; Pelled et al., 1999). Consequently, team learning efforts will be more focused on the task than on social or interpersonal issues. We therefore expect that in teams with informational faultlines, group members will not frequently communicate about lifestyle and personality issues, which leads to less social learning. We now make the following proposition:

> Proposition 2c: Teams with informational faultlines will experience *low* levels of social learning.

THE MODERATING ROLE OF PSYCHOLOGICAL SAFETY AND ERROR MANAGEMENT CULTURE

As suggested in past research (e.g., Lau & Murnighan, 2005), it can be important to consider group beliefs when explaining the relationship between faultlines and team functioning. In our theoretical model we introduce two potential moderators—(a) psychological safety and

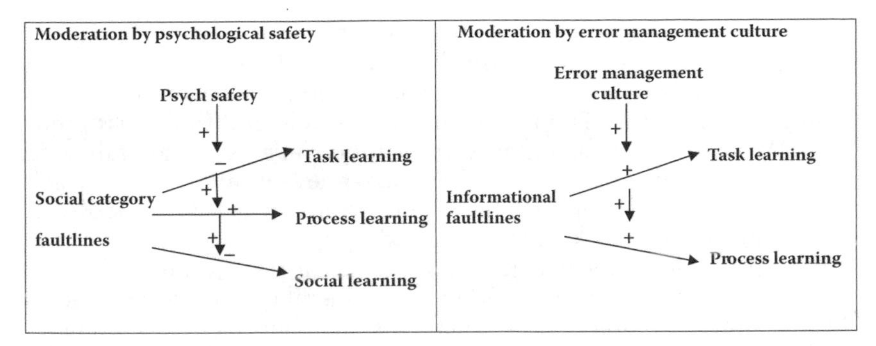

Figure 6.2 Proposed moderation on relationships between faultlines and team learning.

(b) error culture—to further specify the relationship between faultlines and the different types of team learning (see Fig. 6.2 for an overview of propositions).

Social-Category Faultlines and the Moderating Role of Psychological Safety

Edmondson (1999) suggested that team members who are in the position to display learning behavior may feel that they are placing themselves at risk, for instance, by admitting an error or asking for help, because other group members may interpret these behaviors as an indication of incompetence. She therefore argued that it is important for team members to feel that the group is a safe place to express ideas and opinions, and that members will not be punished or rejected for making mistakes. Edmondson introduced this as the concept of *psychological safety*, which can be defined as shared beliefs of team members about how safe the group is for interpersonal risk taking (definition adapted from Edmondson, 1999). Indicators of psychological safety are openness to discuss mistakes and bring up problems, openness for diversity, room to ask for help, and value of each other's skills and differences (Edmondson, 1999). Research has shown that psychological safety is an important condition that facilitates learning behavior (Edmondson, 1999; Tjosvold et al., 2004) and performance (Baer & Frese, 2003).

As we previously argued, teams with social-category faultlines are highly divisive and tend to split into relatively homogeneous subgroups based on characteristics such as age, gender, and race. These groups are likely to suffer from stereotypes and biases between subgroups, which can inhibit task and social learning, in particular. Since the concept of psychological safety does not specify the *content* of the problems or mistakes that people discuss, we propose that it can be about task and process issues, as well as social issues, which, in turn, can influence the different types of learning. Specifically, we propose that psychological safety can inhibit the negative effects of social-category faultlines on *task* and *social* learning. In a psychologically safe environment, team members are more open to diversity. They value and respect each other's differences, and there is openness to ask for help and to discuss problems. We therefore expect that team members in a psychologically safe climate will be less likely to withdraw task-relevant information, which will tone down the proposed negative relationship between social-category faultlines and task learning. In addition, when the climate of the team is psychologically safe, it is less likely that stereotypes and biases will distort information about other group members, which can lead to misinterpretations and interpersonal tension. Team members are more likely to build accurate impressions of each other, which will lessen the proposed negative relationship between social-category faultlines and *social* learning. We also expect that psychological safety will enhance the proposed positive relationship between social-category faultlines and process learning, since a psychologically safe climate will promote open discussion about routines and procedures across subgroups. Therefore, we argue the following:

> Proposition 3a: Psychological safety will moderate the relationship between social-category faultlines and task, social, and process learning, such that the proposed negative effect of social-category faultlines on task and social learning will be *weakened* when team members feel their team is psychologically safe, and the proposed positive effect of social-category faultlines on process learning will be *strengthened*.

Informational Faultlines and the Moderating Role of Error Management Culture

The concept of psychological safety enhances the quality of social relationships between team members and emphasizes the importance of trust and respect between team members. Since these aspects are particularly relevant and influential for teams in which it is likely that stereotypes and biases may occur, we proposed psychological safety to be a moderator of the relationship between *social-category* faultlines and team learning. Teams with informational faultlines split on more job-related characteristics, and therefore, we propose a more job-related moderator for the relationship between informational fautlines and team learning, which is error management culture.

Van Dyck, Frese, Baer, and Sonnentag (2005) introduced the concept of *error management culture*, which can be conceptualized as a system of shared norms, values, and common practices in an organization regarding individual reactions to errors that is aimed at reducing negative error consequences and increasing potentially positive error outcomes. Examples of concrete behaviors associated with this are communicating about errors, sharing error knowledge, helping each other in error situations, and detecting and handling errors. The ways in which individuals deal with errors and the content of the errors that they make are often interrelated with members' knowledge about and experience with the specific task. For instance, to continue with our example of the research group, when the statistician has much experience with developing the instrument that the team is working on, it is less likely that the team will make errors regarding the statistical part of the instrument. In addition, when they have a climate in which errors can be openly discussed, it will be more likely that they will successfully deal with errors, increasing the positive aspects and decreasing the negative aspects. We therefore propose that in teams with an error management culture, members communicate about errors and share their knowledge about errors, which will enhance the proposed positive relationship between informational faultlines and task learning. In an environment in which mistakes are being shared, team members will be better able to use each other's knowledge and expertise (Cannon & Edmondson, 2001), which will increase their understanding of the task and, in turn, increase task learning. Similarly, when a team climate promotes open discussion of error detection and handling, team members will be better able to find routines and procedures to improve task accomplishment, which will enhance process learning as well. Teams that have an open climate for sharing knowledge about mistakes will also be better able to develop a transactive memory system in which the team's knowledge about error handling is saved, and that specifies who knows how to handle particular errors, which, in turn, enhances process learning. Since error management culture and informational faultlines are highly work related, we expect that their interaction will have no substantial effect on social learning. We therefore only develop a proposition for the moderating effect of error culture on the relationship between informational faultlines and task and process learning:

> Proposition 3b: Error management culture will moderate the relationship between informational faultlines and task and process learning, such that the positive relationship between information faultlines and task and process learning will be *enhanced* when teams have an error *management* culture.

DIRECTIONS FOR FUTURE THEORY AND RESEARCH

The proposed typology of task, process, and social learning may help researchers to deepen their understanding of the concept of team learning. The team learning typology also suggests new avenues for research on team learning and group composition, which we address in this section. First, the new concept of *social* learning, which we introduced in this chapter, needs to be further crystallized and validated, and future research should investigate how it is affected by group composition and demographic faultlines. Secondly, our typology may be extended in the future by considering additional types of team learning that refer to other subjects that teams can learn about, such as their relationship with the external environment (e.g., clients, competitors).

Another direction for future research regarding the team typology is to examine the dynamic nature of different types of team learning in groups at different stages. The team learning types might evolve over time, and their impact on team functioning might change depending on the group's stage. For instance, when a group of individuals is recently formed to accomplish a task, it is likely that it starts with some form of task and process learning. The group's common goal is to perform the task, and it is likely that team members will discuss the task and start to develop routines and procedures to accomplish it. Learning about each other's hobbies and lifestyles might be more likely to develop later on in the process of getting to know each other better, for instance, during a happy-hour outing or during lunch. When working together over time, individuals develop a more elaborated and integrated picture of their team members' personalities and personal lives, which facilitates interpreting each other's behavior and work relationships. It might therefore be that social learning is more likely to have its beneficial effects on team functioning when teams are more developed. Future research should examine this dynamic nature of team learning types and investigate how they influence group processes and team performance over time.

The ways that demographic group faultlines influence team functioning is a relatively new researched topic as well. In the theoretical model proposed in this chapter, we distinguished social-category and informational faultlines and linked these faultlines types to the proposed types of team learning. In this model, we made propositions about how faultlines based on different characteristics can potentially influence group processes and team learning. Faultlines in groups can be inactive and go unnoticed, however, having a negligible effect on group processes (Lau & Murnighan, 1998). When testing these propositions, researchers therefore should not only consider the objective demographics of team members, but also examine whether members perceive and behave as if they were members of two separate subgroups. The underlying assumption of current faultline research, which generally focuses on potential faultlines, is that demographic characteristics, such as gender and age, represent meaningful social groups with which individuals identify (Li & Hambrick, 2005; Thatcher et al., 2003). This assumption should, however, be tested. Future research should also determine whether these demographic characteristics are indeed relevant faultline triggers or if there might be other attributes (e.g., family situation, hobbies) or organizational features (e.g., an empowerment policy for senior employees; a positive action hiring policy for women and cultural minorities) or particular occasions (e.g., organized meetings for technicians) that can activate faultlines.

Finally, future research should further investigate which other factors can potentially moderate the relationship between demographic faultlines and team learning. In this chapter, we introduced psychological safety and error management culture as moderators of the relationship between social-category faultlines and informational faultlines; however, other moderators should be taken into account as well, such as group identity and task type (Bezrukova, Thatcher, & Jehn, in press).

CONCLUSION

Only recently, researchers have begun to conceptualize and examine the concept of team learning. In this chapter, we reviewed past typologies and definitions of team learning and found that in past definitions, the subject of team learning remains largely unclear. To address this shortcoming in past research, we proposed a new team learning typology: task, process, and social learning. This distinction of team learning types may help scholars to deepen their fundamental understanding of the concept of team learning, and identify important factors, such as psychological safety and error management culture, that can facilitate team learning in teams with various group compositions.

REFERENCES

Alagna, S., Reddy, D., & Collins, D. (1982). Perceptions of functioning in mixed sex and male medical training groups. *Journal of Medical Education, 57*, 801–803.

Alderfer, C. P. (1987). An intergroup perspective on organizational behavior. In J. W. Lorsch (Ed.), *Handbook of organizational behavior* (pp. 190–222). Englewood Cliffs, NJ: Prentice-Hall.

Allen, V. L., & Levine, J. M. (1971). Social support and conformity: The role of independent assessment of reality. *Journal of Experimental Social Psychology, 7*(1), 48–58.

Allport, G. (1954). *The nature of prejudice*. Cambridge, MA: Addison-Wesley.

Amabile, T. (1998). A model of creativity and innovation in organizations. In B. Staw, & L. Cummings (Eds.), *Research in organizational behavior* (Vol. 10, pp. 123–167). Greenwich, CT: JAI Press.

Amason, A. C. (1996). Distinguishing the effects of functional and dysfunctional conflict on strategic decision making: Resolving a paradox for the top management teams. *Academy of Management Journal, 39*, 123–148.

Ancona, D. G., & Caldwell, D. (1992). Bringing the boundary: External activity and performance in organizational teams. *Administrative Science Quarterly, 37*, 634–665.

Anderson, S. E., Coffey, B. S., & Byerly, R. T. (2002). Formal organizational initiatives and informal workplace practices: Links to work-family conflict and job-related outcomes. *Journal of Management, 28*, 787–810.

Argote, L., Gruenfeld, D., & Naquin, C. (2001). Group learning in organizations. In M. E. Turner (Ed.), *Groups at work: Advances in theory and research* (pp. 369–411). New York: Erlbaum.

Argyris, C., & Schön, D. (1978) *Organizational learning: A theory of action perspective*. Reading, MA: Addison-Wesley.
Baer, M., & Frese, M. (2003). Innovation is not enough: Climates for initiative and psychological safety, process innovations, and firm performance. *Journal of Organizational Behavior, 24*, 45–68.
Bantel, K. A., & Jackson, S. E. (1989). Top management and innovation in banking: Does the composition of the top team make a difference? *Strategic Management Journal, 10*, 107–124.
Behfar, K. J., Mannix, E. A., Peterson, R. S., & Trochin, W. M. K. (2005). *A multi-faceted approach to intra-group conflict: Issues of theory and measurement*. Evanston, IL: Northwestern University Press.
Bettencourt, B. A., Dill, K. E., Greathouse, S., Charlton, K., & Mulholland, A. (1997). Evaluations of ingroup and outgroup members: The category-based expectancy violation. *Journal of Experimental Social Psychology, 33*, 244–275.
Bezrukova, K., Thatcher, S. M. B., & Jehn, K. A. (in press). Group heterogeneity and faultlines: Comparing alignment and dispersion approaches to group composition. In L. Thompson (Ed.), *Conflict in organizational teams*. Evanston, IL: Northwestern University Press.
Blau, P. (1977). *Inequality and heterogeneity*. New York: Free Press.
Bragg, B. W., & Allen, V. (1972). The role of the public and private support in reducing conformity. *Psychonomic Science, 29*(2), 81–82.
Byrne, D. (1971). *The attraction paradigm*. New York: Academic Press.
Cannon, M. D., & Edmondson, A. C. (2001). Confronting failure: Antecedents and consequences of shared beliefs about failure in organizational work groups. *Journal of Organizational Behavior, 22*, 161–177.
Cramton, C. D., & Hinds, P. J. (2005). Subgroups dynamics in internationally distributed teams: Ethnocentrism or cross-national learning? *Research in Organizational Behavior, 26*, 231–263.
Cox, T., Lobel, S., & McLeod, P. (1991). Effects of ethnic group cultural differences on cooperative and competitive behavior on a group task. *Academy of Management Journal, 34*, 827–847.
Crossan, M. M., Lane, H. W., & White, R. E. (1999). An organizational learning framework: From 'intuition to institution.' *Academy of Management Review, 24*, 522–537.
De Dreu, C. K. W., & Weingart, L. R. (2003). Task versus relationship conflict, team performance, and team member satisfaction: A meta-analysis. *Journal of Applied Psychology, 88*, 741–749.
De Dreu, C. K. W., & West, M. (2001). Minority dissent and team innovation: The importance of participation in decision making. *Journal of Applied Psychology, 86*, 1191–1201.
Dougherty, D. (1992). Interpretive barriers to successful product innovation in large firms. *Organization Science, 3*(2), 179–202.
Drach-Zahavy, A., & Somech, A. (2001). Understanding team innovation: The role of team processes and structures. *Group Dynamics: Theory, Research, and Practice, 5*(2), 111–123.
Earley, P. C., & Mosakowski, E. (2000). Creating hybrid team cultures: An empirical test of transnational team functioning. *Academy of Management Journal, 43*(1), 26–49.
Edmondson, A. (1999). Psychological safety and learning behavior in work teams. *Administrative Science Quarterly, 44*, 350–383.

Edmondson, A. (2002). The local and variegated nature of learning in organizations: A group-level perspective. *Organization Science, 13*, 128–146.
Edmondson, A. C., Bohmer, R. M., & Pisano, G. P. (2001). Disrupted routines: Team learning and new technology implementation in hospitals. *Administrative Science Quarterly, 46*, 685–716.
Ellis, A. P. J., Hollenbeck, J. R., Ilgen, D. R., Porter, C. O. L. H., West, B. J., & Moon, H. (2003). Team learning: Collectively connecting the dots. *Journal of Applied Psychology, 88*, 821–835.
Ely, R. J., & Thomas, D. A. (2001). Cultural diversity at work: The effects of diversity perspectives on work group processes and outcomes. *Administrative Science Quarterly, 46*, 229–273.
Frone, M. R., Yardley, J. K., & Markel, K. S. (1997). Developing and testing an integrative model of the work-family interface. *Journal of Vocational Behavior, 50*, 145–167.
Gibson, C. B. (2001). From knowledge accumulation to accommodation: Cycles of collective cognition in work groups. *Journal of Organizational Behavior, 22*, 121–134.
Gibson, C., & Vermeulen, F. (2003). A healthy divide: Subgroups as a stimulus for team learning behavior. *Administrative Science Quarterly, 28*, 202–239.
Goff, S. J., Mount, M. K., & Jamison, R. L. (1990). Employer supported child care, work- family, and absenteeism: A field study. *Personnel Psychology, 43*, 793–809.
Gruenfeld, D. H. (1995). Status, ideology, and integrative complexity on the United States Supreme Court: Rethinking the politics of politics decision. *Journal of Personality and Social Psychology, 68*(1), 5–20
Gruenfeld, D. H., Mannix, E. A., Williams, K. Y., & Neale, M. A. (1996). Group composition and decision making: How member familiarity and information distribution affect process and performance. *Organizational Behavior and Human Decision Processes, 67*, 1–15.
Hackman, J. R. (1987). The design of work teams. In J. Lorsch (Ed.), *Handbook of organizational behavior* (pp. 315–342). Englewood Cliffs, NJ: Prentice-Hall.
Hackman, J. R., & Morris, C. G. (1975). Group tasks, group interaction process, and group performance effectiveness: A review and proposed integration. In L. Berkowitz (Ed.), *Advances in experimental social psychology*, vol. 8 (pp. 45–99). Greenwich, CT: JAI Press.
Halfhill, T., Sundstrom, E., Lahner, J., & Calderone, W. (2005). Group personality composition and group effectiveness: An integrative review of empirical research. *Small Group Research, 36*(1), 83–105.
Hallinan, M., & Smith, S. (1985). The effects of classroom racial composition on students' interracial friendliness. *Social Psychology Quarterly, 48*, 3–16.
Hambrick, D., Cho, T., & Chen, M. (1996). The influence of top management team heterogeneity on firms' competitive moves. *Administrative Science Quarterly, 41*, 659–684.
Hambrick, D., Li, J. T., Xin, K., & Tsui, A. S. (2001). Compositional gaps and downward spirals in international joint venture management groups. *Strategic Management Journal, 22*(11), 1033–1053.
Harrison, D., Price, K., & Bell, M. (1998). Beyond relational demography: Time and the effects of surface- and deep-level diversity on work group cohesion. *Academy of Management Journal, 41*, 96–107.

Harrison, D. A., Price, K. H., Gavin, J. H., & Florey, A. T. (2002). Time, teams, and task performance: Changing effects of surface- and deep-level diversity on group functioning. *Academy of Management Journal, 45*, 1029–1045.

Hinsz, V. B., Tindale, R. S., & Vollrath, D. A. (1997). The emerging conceptualization of groups as information processors. *Psychological Bulletin, 121*, 43–64.

Hoffman, E. (1985). The effect of race-ration composition on the frequency of organizational communication. *Social Psychology Quarterly, 48*, 17–26.

Hogg, M. A., Turner, J. C., & Davidson, B. (1990). Polarized norms and social frames of reference: A test of self-categorization theory of group polarization. *Basic and Applied Social Psychology, 11*, 77–100.

Huber, G. P. (1991). Organizational learning: The contributing processes and the literatures. *Organizational Science, 2*(1), 88–115.

Jackson, S. (1992). Team composition in organizations. In S. Worchel, W. Wood, & J. Simpson (Eds.), *Group process and productivity* (pp. 1–12). London: Sage.

Jackson, S. E., Joshi, A., & Erhardt, N. L. (2003). Recent research on teams and organizational diversity: SWOT analysis and implications. *Journal of Management, 29*(6), 801–830.

Jackson, S., May, E., & Whitney, K. (1995). Understanding the dynamics of diversity in decision-making teams. In R. Guzzo, E. Salas, & associates (Eds.), *Team decision making effectiveness in organizations* (pp. 204–261). San Francisco: Jossey-Bass.

Jehn, K. A. (1995). A multimethod examination of the benefits and detriments of intragroup conflict. *Administrative Science Quarterly, 40*, 256–282.

Jehn, K. A. (1997). A qualitative analysis of conflict types and dimensions in organizational groups. *Administrative Science Quarterly, 42*, 520–557.

Jehn, K. A., Bezrukova, K., & Thatcher, S. M. B. (in press). Conflict, diversity and faultlines in work groups. In C. K. W. De Dreu, & M. J. Gelfand (Eds.), *The psychology of conflict and conflict management in organizations*. New York: Lawrence Erlbaum Associates.

Jehn, K. A., Chadwick, C., & Thatcher, S. M. B. (1997). To agree or not to agree: The effects of value congruence, individual demographic dissimilarity, and conflict on workgroup outcomes. *International Journal of Conflict Management, 8*(4), 287–306.

Jehn, K., & Mannix, E. (2001). The dynamic nature of conflict: A longitudinal study of intragroup conflict and group performance. *Academy of Management Journal, 44*(2), 238–251.

Jehn, K. A., Northcraft, G., & Neale, M. (1999). Why differences make a difference: A field study of diversity, conflict, and performance in workgroups. *Administrative Science Quarterly, 44*, 741–763.

Kramer, R. M. (1991). Intergroup relations and organizational dilemmas: The role of categorization processes. In L. L. Cummings, & B. M. Staw (Eds.), *Research in organizational behavior* (Vol. 13, pp. 191–227). Greenwich, CT: JAI Press.

Kolb, D. A. (1984). *Experiential learning*. Englewood Cliffs, NJ: Prentice Hall.

Lau, D., & Murnighan, J. K. (1998). Demograhpic diversity and faultlines: The compositional dynamics of organizational groups. *Academy of Management Review, 23*(2), 325–340.

Lau, D. C., & Murnighan, J. K. (2005). Interactions within groups and subgroups: The effects of demographic faultlines. *Academy of Management Journal, 48*(4), 645–659.

Levine, J. L., & Moreland, R. L. (1999). Knowledge transmission in work groups: Helping newcomers to succeed. In L. L. Thompson, J. M. Levine, & D. M. Messick (Eds.). *Shared cognition in organizations: The management of knowledge* (pp. 267–296). Mahwah, NJ: Lawrence Erlbaum.

Li, J. & Hambrick, D. C. (2005). Factional groups: A new vantage on demographic faultlines, conflict, and disintegration in work teams. *Academy of Management Journal, 48,* 794–813.

Liang, D. W., Moreland, R., & Argote, L. (1995). Group versus individual training and group performance: The mediating role of transactive memory. *Personality and Social Psychology Bulletin, 21,* 384–393.

Mannix, E. A., & Neale, M. A. (2005). What differences make a difference? The promise and reality of diverse teams in organizations. *Psychological Science in the Public Interest, 6*(2), 31–55.

Marks, M. A., Mathieu, J. E., & Zaccaro, S. J. (2001). A temporally based framework and taxonomy of team processes. *Academy of Management Review, 26,* 356–376.

McGrath, J. E. (1998). A view of group composition through a group-theoretic lens. In M. A. Neale, E. A. Mannix, & D. H. Gruenfeld (Eds.), *Research on managing groups and teams* (Vol. 1, pp. 255–272). Stamford, CT: JAI Press.

Messick, D. M., & Mackie, D. M. (1989). Intergroup relations. *Annual Review of Psychology, 40,* 45–81.

Milliken, F., & Martins, L. (1996). Searching for common threads: Understanding the multiple effects of diversity in organizational groups. *Academy of Management Review, 21,* 402–433.

Moreland, R. L. (1999). Transactive memory: Learning who knows what in work groups and organizations. In L. L. Thompson, J. M. Levine, & D. M. Messick (Eds.), *Shared cognition in organizations: The management of knowledge* (pp. 3–32). Mahwah, NJ: Lawrence Erlbaum Associates.

Moreland, R. L., & Levine, J. M. (1992). The composition of small groups. In E. J. Lawler, B. Markovsky, C. Ridgeway, & H. A. Walker (Eds.), *Advances in group processes* (Vol. 8, pp. 237–280). Greenwich, CT: JAI Press.

Moreland, R. L., & Myaskovsky, L. (2000). Exploring the performance benefits of group training: Transactive memory or improved communication? *Organizational Behavior and Human Decision Processes, 82,* 117–133.

Nemeth, C., & Kwan, J. (1987). Minority influence, divergent thinking, and detection of correct solutions. *Journal of Applied Social Psychology, 17,* 786–797.

O'Reilly, C. A., Williams, K., & Barsade, S. (1997). Group demography and innovation: Does diversity help? In E. A. Mannix, & M. Neale (Eds.), *Research in the management of groups and teams* (Vol. 1, pp. 183–207). Greenwich, CT: JAI Press.

Orlikowski, W. J., & Hofman, J. D. (1997). An improvisational model for change management: The case of groupware technologies. *Sloan Management Review, 38*(2), 11–21.

Pelled, L. H. (1996). Demographic diversity, conflict, and work group outcomes: An intervening process theory. *Organization Science, 17,* 615–631.

Pelled, L. H., Eisenhardt, K. M., & Xin, K. R. (1999). Exploring the black box: An analysis of work group diversity, conflict, and performance. *Administrative Science Quarterly, 44,* 1–28.

Peterson, R. S., & Nemeth, C. J. (1996). Focus versus flexibility: Majority and minority influence can both improve performance. *Personality and Social Psychology Bulletin, 22* (1), 14–23.
Phillips, K. W. (2003). The effects of categorically based expectations on minority influence: The importance of congruence. *Personality and Social Psychology Bulletin, 29,* 3–13.
Phillips, K. W., & Loyd, D. L. (2006). When surface and deep-level diversity collide: The effects on dissenting group members. *Organizational Behavior and Human Decision Processes, 99*(2), 143–160.
Phillips, K. W., Mannix, E. A., Neale, M. A., & Gruenfeld, D. H. (2004). Diverse groups and information sharing: The effects of congruent ties. *Journal of Experimental Social Psychology, 40,* 497–510.
Polzer, J. T., Milton, L. P., & Swann, W. B. (2002). Capitalizing on diversity: Interpersonal congruence in small work groups. *Administrative Science Quarterly, 47*(2), 296–324.
Prentice, D. A., & Miller, D. T. (2002). The emergence of homegrown stereotypes. *American Psychologist, 57,* 352–359.
Rink, F., & Ellemers, N. (in press). Diversity as a basis for shared organizational identity: The norm-congruity principle. *British Journal of Management.*
Rispens, S. (2006). *Multiple interdependencies and workgroup effectiveness.* Unpublished doctoral dissertation, Leiden University, the Netherlands.
Rupert, J., & Jehn, K. A. (2006, September). *Team learning: The development and validation of a new typology.* Paper presented at the 10th International Workshop on Teamworking, Groningen, the Netherlands.
Sarin, S., & McDermott, C. (2003). The effect of team leader characteristics on learning, knowledge application, and performance of cross-functional new product development teams. *Decision Sciences, 34*(4), 707–739.
Shah, P., & Jehn, K. (1993). Do friends perform better than acquaintances? The interaction of friendship, conflict, and task. *Group Decision and Negotiation, 2,* 149–165.
Smith, C. M., Tindale, R. S., & Dugoni, B. L. (1996). Minority and majority influence in freely interacting groups: Qualitative versus quantitative differences. *British Journal of Social Psychology, 35,* 137–149.
Stasser, G., & Stewart, D. D. (1995). Expert roles and information exchange during discussion: The importance of knowing who knows what. *Journal of Experimental Social Psychology, 31*(3), 244–265.
Stevenson, W. B., Pearce, J. L., & Porter, L. W. (1985). The concept of "coalition" in organizational theory and research. *Academy of Management Review, 10,* 256–268.
Stewart, G. L. (2006). A meta-analytic review of relationships between team design features and team performance. *Journal of Management, 32*(1), 29–54.
Swann, W. B., Polzer, J. T., Seyle, D. C., & Ko, S. J. (2004). Finding value in diversity: Verification of personal and social self-views in diverse groups. *Academy of Management Review, 29*(1), 9–27.
Tajfel, H., & Turner, J. C. (1986). The social identity theory of intergroup behavior. In S. Worchel, & W. G. Austin (Eds.), *Psychology of intergroup relations* (pp. 7–24). Chicago: Nelson-Hall.
Thatcher, S. M. B., Jehn, K. A., & Zanutto, E. (2003). Cracks in diversity research: The effects of faultlines on conflict and performance. *Group Decision and Negotiation, 12,* 217–241.

Thomas, L. T., & Ganster, D. C. (1995). Impact of family supportive work variables on work-family conflict and strain: A control perspective. *Journal of Applied Psychology, 80,* 6–15.

Thompson, C. A., Jahn, E., Kopelman, R., & Prottas, D. (2004). The impact of perceived organizational and supervisory family support on affective commitment: A longitudinal and multi-level analysis. *Journal of Managerial Issues, 16,* 545–565.

Tjosvold, D., Yu, Z., & Chun, H. (2004). Team learning from mistakes: The contribution of cooperative goals and problem solving. *Journal of Management Studies, 41,* 1223–1245.

Tsui, A. S., & Gutek, B. A. (1999). *Demographic differences in organizations: Current research and future directions.* Lanham, MD: Lexington Books.

Turner, J. C. (1987). *Rediscovering the social group: A self-categorization theory.* Oxford, U.K.: Basil Blackwell.

Van der Bossche, P., Van Gennip, G. W. H., & Segers, M. S. R. (2006). *Harvesting diversity.* Unpublished manuscript, Leiden University.

Van der Vegt, G. S., & Bunderson, J. S. (2005). Learning and performance in multidisciplinary teams: The importance of collective team identification. *Academy of Management Journal, 48,* 532–547.

Van Dyck, C., Frese, M., Baer, M., & Sonnentag, S. (2005). Organizational error management culture and its impact on performance: A two-study replication. *Journal of Applied Psychology, 90*(6), 1228–1240.

Van Knippenberg, D., De Dreu, C. K. W., & Homan, A. C. (2004). Work group diversity and group performance: An integrative model and research agenda. *Journal of Applied Psychology, 89*(6), 1008–1022.

Von Glinow, M. A., Shapiro, D. L. & Brett, J. M. (2004). Can we talk, and should we? Managing emotional conflict in multicultural teams. *Academy of Management Review, 29* (4), 578–592.

Webber, S., & Donahue, L. (2001). Impact of highly and less job-related diversity on work group cohesion and performance: A meta-analysis. *Journal of Management, 27,* 141–162.

Wegner, D. M. (1986). Transactive memory: A contemporary analysis of the group mind. In G. Mullen, & G. Goethals (Eds.), *Theories of group behavior* (pp.185–208). New York: Springer-Verlag.

Williams, K. Y., & O'Reilly, C. A. (1998). Demography and diversity in organizations: A review of 40 years of research. *Research in Organizational Behavior, 20,* 77–140.

Wittenbaum, G. M., & Stasser, G. (1996). Management of information in small groups. In J. L. Nye, & A. M. Brower (Eds.), *What's social about social cognition? Social cognition research in small groups* (pp. 3–28). Thousand Oaks, CA: Sage.

Zenger, T. R., & Lawrence, B. S. (1989). Organizational demography: The differential effects of age and tenure distributions on technical communication. *Academy of Management Journal, 32,* 353–376.

CHAPTER

7

A Multilevel, Multiconceptualization Perspective of Goal Orientation in Teams

CHRISTOPHER O. L. H. PORTER
Texas A&M University

INTRODUCTION

Businesses today rely on teams to accomplish tasks because teams are perceived as being more creative, responsive, productive, efficient, and effective than individuals working alone. In fact, Sundstrom (1999) noted that few managers question the potential benefits of teams. What underlies this is both a recognition that the workplace represents an important learning and achievement context for employees and the assumption that in responding to the challenges that such a context creates, employees can reach higher levels of performance when organized into teams. Understanding how groups and teams respond to the challenges in the workplace should therefore be an important topic of study for both organizational scholars and practitioners.

In this chapter, I explore the goal-orientation construct in teams because goal orientation has been useful in understanding how individuals interpret, learn from, and respond (or adapt) to situations and challenges (e.g., Brett & VandeWalle, 1999; Dweck, 1989; Dweck & Elliott, 1983). Building on LePine (2005), goal orientation can be thought of as a representation of the nature of the desires and reactions of an individual, group or team, or organization in an achievement context (a context in which the goal is learning, performance, or both). Across these multiple organizational levels, a learning goal orientation is a focus on achievement through learning and mastery. Learning goals are often pursued via experimentation and exploration. A performance orientation is a focus on achievement through performance and meeting and/or exceeding performance expectations in an attempt to demonstrate competence. Performance goals are often pursued via incremental changes and exploitation (see also Gully & Phillips, 2005). To date, little attention has been devoted to fully exploring the potential of goal orientation at levels other than the individual level. However, evidence is emerging that suggests that goal orientation explains adaptation, learning, and achievement in teams (e.g., Bunderson & Sutcliffe, 2003; LePine, 2005; Porter, 2005). Similar to other scholars (e.g., Gully & Phillips, 2005) who have recently suggested that increased attention be devoted to exploring goal orientation at higher organizational levels (e.g., groups and organizations), I suggest that goal orientation has considerable promise for explaining individual and collective behavior in team settings. However, this chapter is a departure from previous work in at least two regards.

First, in this chapter, I explicitly discuss some of the conceptual ambiguities that have emerged in previous research examining goal orientation among individuals working alone. In doing so, I hope to prevent these problems from hindering future theory and research on goal orientation at higher levels. Of particular importance are two issues regarding the nature of the goal-orientation construct: (a) whether goal orientation is a trait or a state and (b) the dimensionality of the goal-orientation construct.

Second, I explicitly propose and outline an important avenue for future research on goal orientation in teams. Specifically, the multilevel, multiconceptualization perspective developed here highlights a number of potential interactive effects among various dimensions of goal orientation, across multiple conceptualizations of goal orientation, and across multiple levels of analyses. Although previous work on goal-orientation among individuals has failed to systematically develop and test theory regarding how the various dimensions of goal orientation may work in tandem, I believe that future theory and research on goal orientation in teams must devote specific attention to understanding these effects.

The chapter begins by first providing a general, albeit brief, overview of the goal-orientation construct. Admittedly, this section draws heavily on the research on goal orientation among individuals largely because little attention has been devoted to understanding goal orientation in groups and teams. Next, I discuss a number of deficiencies that have emerged in the previous work on goal orientation. I hope that an explicit recognition of these conceptual ambiguities will mitigate their potentially negative effects on future goal orientation research as scholars shift their attention to exploring goal orientation in teams. Next, I discuss and compare three distinct conceptions of goal orientation in team settings: (a) dispositional goal orientation among team members, (b) composition goal orientation, and (c) collective goal orientation. It is here that I suggest that each of these conceptualizations of goal orientation in teams has the potential to uniquely explain how teams respond to achievement situations. Finally, I present a taxonomy that integrates each of the conceptualizations of goal orientation in teams and suggest the types of questions that future research on goal orientation in teams should attempt to explore.

AN INTRODUCTION TO GOAL ORIENTATION

Although first introduced into the organizational literature in the early 1990s (Farr, Hofmann, & Ringenbach, 1993), goal orientation has quite a rich history dating back to its inception by educational psychologists almost two decades earlier. Early work on goal orientation focused on children in educational settings, in particular, on their approach to educational achievement (e.g., Dweck & Elliott, 1983; Eison, 1981, 1982). Of particular interest among those scholars was explaining differences in the extent to which students were concerned with increasing personal competence (e.g., learning goals) versus obtaining favorable judgments from others regarding their personal competence (e.g., performance goals).

Scholars working in this area appear to have taken two distinct approaches to examining the differences observed in children's goals in achievement situations. The first approach viewed goal orientation as a stable, trait-like individual difference much like personality (e.g., Eison, 1979, 1981, 1982; Eison, Pollio, & Milton, 1982). The second approach focused not only on outcomes of goal orientation but also on predicting goal orientation (e.g., Dweck, 1986; Nicholls, 1984). Of particular importance, Dweck and her colleagues proposed that these differences (e.g., being learning oriented or performance oriented) could be explained by the extent to which children maintained implicit theories. Specifically, these researchers believed that different implicit theories led to different concerns which, in turn, oriented individuals toward different goals in achievement situations. Dweck and her colleagues proposed that those holding an implicit theory that his or her intelligence was fixed tended to adopt performance goals. On the other hand, those holding an implicit theory that his or her ability was malleable tended to adopt learning goals. In sum, the first approach viewed goal orientation as an individual difference whereas the second approach viewed goal orientation as a state that could be induced, but was caused largely by one's belief system.

Although these two approaches to understanding what underlies goal orientation differ, scholars mainly agreed that (a) differences in goal orientation represented different approaches individuals could take when faced with achievement or learning situations, (b) learning orientation tended to be associated with more positive outcomes than performance orientation, and (c) goal orientation could be succinctly thought of in terms of learning and performance goal orientation (or what Ames & Archer, 1987, labeled mastery and performance goals, respectively). Of particular interest in this chapter are two issues that were raised by this early research on goal orientation. Both of these issues continue to influence work on goal orientation in the organizational literature and have become increasingly more complex as theory and research on goal orientation evolve in an attempt to better understand individuals' interpretations of and experiences in learning and achievement settings (e.g., Elliot, 1999; Elliot & Church, 1997; Elliot & Harackiewicz, 1996; VandeWalle, 1997). More important here is that both of these issues have the potential to impede our extending of theory and research on goal orientation to higher organizational levels, and thus have implications for understanding learning and achievement in group and team settings. The first of these issues concerns whether goal orientation is a trait or a state. The second concerns the dimensionality of the construct.

Trait Versus State Conceptualizations

Early work by Dweck and her colleagues (which arguably has had the most influence on goal-orientation research in the organizational literature) focused on goal orientation as a state. While goals are often dependent on the nature of the task situation (e.g., one can foster a learning orientation by stressing the importance of learning task strategies or by rewarding learning), most efforts to explore goal orientation in the organizational literature have instead focused on dispositional goal orientation. When conceptualized as a dispositional characteristic, goal orientation is generally believed to be a relatively stable individual difference. In other words, it is assumed that an individual who is, for example, high on performance orientation at one time (e.g., at the onset of organizational entry) will be remain relatively high on performance orientation at some later time (e.g., a year after the beginning of employment).

A recent meta-analytic investigation conducted by Payne, Youngcourt, and Beaubien (2007) of almost 10 years of research on goal orientation (178 independent samples from 141 published and unpublished studies) suggested that goal orientation is both a trait and a state. Payne et al. argued that similar to other psychological variables, goal orientation may function as a trait that, in turn, manifests itself as a state, which has more direct effects on other variables. Consistent with their arguments, they demonstrated that goal orientation had a "moderate degree of stability over time," at least in the short term, confirming previous arguments (e.g., Button, Mathieu, & Zajac, 1996) that goal orientation is in fact relatively stable. Payne and her colleagues found that trait goal orientation was also a significant predictor of state goal orientation. That is, they found support for their notion that trait goal-orientation dimensions had large effects (ranging from .55 to .58) on their respective state goal orientation dimensions. Unfortunately, they did not examine whether state goal orientation explained the effects of trait goal orientation on outcomes, thereby providing a test of their implied hypothesis that trait goal orientation leads to state goal orientation, which, in turn, leads to outcomes. Nevertheless, their findings make it clear that goal orientation can also be meaningfully conceptualized as a state (or what some have referred to as a quasi-trait, e.g., DeShon & Gillepsie, 2005). The implications of this on conceptualizations of goal orientation in groups and teams are discussed later.

Dimensionality

The second issue that continues to influence organizational scholars' thinking about goal orientation concerns the dimensionality of the goal orientation construct. Here, the question arises as to whether goal orientation is best conceptualized as a single dimension or as a multidimensional construct. When introduced into the organizational literature, significant attention was devoted to whether or not learning and performance goal orientation represented opposite ends of a single continuum or if they were in fact two distinct dimensions (e.g., Button et al., 1996; see also Farr et al., 1993). Much of this discussion was the result of the early influence that Dweck's work had on organizational scholars' thinking about goal orientation. As previously mentioned, Dweck proposed that individuals (in her case children) focused on either learning goals or performance goals largely as a result of their implicit theories. The distinction that Dweck and others (e.g., Ames & Archer, 1987; Diener & Dweck, 1978) drew between learning goals and performance goals clearly suggested that individuals focused on one or the other. The perspective this work tended to take regarding the dimensionality of goal orientation can be gleaned from the following question: "What leads individuals to favor performance goals over learning goals or vice versa?" (Dweck & Leggett, 1988). Clearly, individuals were assumed to be learning oriented or performance oriented, but not both. Those researchers who based their understanding of goal orientation on implicit theories of intelligence were obviously those most likely to adopt the thinking that goal orientation consisted of a single dimension because it was difficult to imagine a situation in which one would believe that ability or intelligence was both fixed and malleable.

Despite the suggestion made by scholars who did early work on goal orientation in organizational settings that the two types of goal orientation were neither mutually exclusive nor contradictory (Button et al., 1996; Farr et al., 1993), many scholars continue to have difficulty accepting that an individual can, in fact, be concurrently high or low on both learning and performance goal orientation. The frequency with which researchers make opposing predictions for learning orientation and performance orientation (recent examples include Davis, Carson, Ammeter, Treadway, 2005; Gong & Fan, 2006) in addition to the paucity of research examining their potential interactive effects provides direct evidence that scholars have yet to fully accept that the two dimensions are not polar opposites.

Payne et al.'s (2007) recent meta-analysis again provides valuable insight regarding the dimensionality of the goal orientation construct. Somewhat consistent with arguments proposed in early work by organizational scholars on goal orientation (e.g., Button et al., 1996), Payne and her colleagues demonstrated learning goal orientation and performance goal orientation (what Payne et al. labeled performance-prove goal orientation) are only weakly related ($p = .15$). Thus, they provided clear empirical evidence that an individual can be concurrently high or low on both of these dimensions. These findings suggest that the nomological network of relationships among learning and performance goal orientations and other learning and achievement variables are more complex than the questions posed by most scholars suggest. Just as important, their findings suggest that scholars' failure to fully consider how learning and performance goal orientation may work in tandem is quite possibly a major shortcoming of the previous work on goal orientation. Thus, there may be a significant void in our understanding of how individuals behave in learning and achievement contexts due to our failure to systematically examine these potential interactions.

An Integration and Reconciliation

Although a number of scholars have treated these two issues (e.g., trait vs. state and single vs. multiple dimensions) separately, the two issues are not entirely unrelated. Each issue gives rise to the other. Organizational scholars' failure to reconcile divergent perspectives regarding whether or not goal orientation should be conceptualized as a state or trait and goal orientation's dimensionality has greatly hindered understanding about the value of the individual goal orientation (cf. DeShon & Gillepsie, 2005). More important, it has the potential to inhibit our ability to fully explore what value goal orientation holds for understanding cognition, affect, behavior, and—of particular interest here—learning in group and team settings.

There is little doubt that goal orientation is a meaningful construct that has utility in explaining attitudes and behavior in organizations. Previous research, for example, has shown goal orientation to be related to attention (Fisher & Ford, 1998), self-esteem (Button, Mathieu, & Zajac, 1996), motivation (Colquitt & Simmering, 1998; Steele-Johnson, Beauregard, Hoover, & Schmidt, 2000), self-efficacy (Bell & Kozlowski, 2002; Kozlowski, Gully, Brown, Salas, Smith, & Nason, 2001; Phillips & Gully, 1997), and performance (Bell & Kozlowski, 2002; Brett & VandeWalle, 1999; Kozlowski et al., 2001; Steele-Johnson et al., 2000) to name a few of the outcomes predicted by goal orientation.

When conceptualized as an individual difference, goal orientation is a meaningful trait-like construct, much like personality. Moreover, like personality, goal orientation may be influenced by both biological and environmental factors. This would perhaps explain why goal orientation can be conceptualized as both a trait and a state. I suggest that goal orientation is best conceptualized as a relatively stable phenomenon, but one that can also be influenced as a state (cf. Button et al., 1996). Put another way, consistent with recent research (e.g., Payne et al., 2007), I believe that goal orientation should be thought of as a quasi-trait (DeShon & Gillepsie, 2005).

To debate whether goal orientation is a trait or a state is similar to debating whether conscientiousness is a trait, a state, or both. Further exploring this analogy, conscientiousness has been shown to be an excellent predictor of employee performance across a wide range of employment contexts (e.g., Barrick & Mount, 1991; Salgado, 1997). An individual may enter an achievement situation high on conscientiousness, which may, in turn, positively influence that individual's behavior (e.g., work performance). However, an individual who is low on conscientiousness may enter an achievement situation that demands and supports high levels of conscientiousness. External influences such as job demands, coworker and managerial support, work-role transitions over time, and the proper incentive systems may evoke behaviors from this individual similar to those one might expect from an individual who is high on conscientiousness. In this example, that conscientiousness is both a trait and a state. Goal orientation is no different, as evidenced by previous research examining dispositional goal orientation (e.g., Button et al., 1996) and previous research that successfully manipulates goal orientation (e.g., Steele-Johnson et al., 2000). Of particular importance is that it may be no more fruitful to question what causes goal orientation (implicit theories of intelligence or biological factors) than it is to question what causes conscientiousness.

Indeed, in the absence of research using methodological designs that allow one to determine the direction of causality between implicit theories of intelligence and the goal orientation dimensions, one cannot rule out the possibility that the relationships found between the goal orientation and the tendency to hold one of these theories are no more than just spurious relationships. Perhaps more important, the magnitudes of these relationships suggest that even if they are causal, they are relatively weak (see Payne et al., 2007). Therefore, if we cannot conclude that implicit theories of ability or intelligence cause goal orientation, then researchers should not be "practically" bound to the assumption that goal orientation dimensions cannot work in tandem (e.g., have additive and/or multiplicative effects). Researchers should therefore discontinue the practice of making relatively simplistic, opposing predictions for learning and performance goal orientation except in situations in which there is strong theory suggesting that learning and performance goal orientation will indeed have opposite effects.

Once scholars accept that, like other individual differences, goal orientation is a relatively stable trait that can also be influenced as a state, we can more fully explore goal orientation in team settings as teams are collections of individuals who possess their own individual traits (or dispositions). These dispositions can have meaningful functions in team settings. They can also exert "bottom-up" influences (Kozlowski & Klein, 2000) on the teams to which the individuals belong. Finally, because goal orientation can also be a state or state-like phenomenon, it can be influenced by both bottom-up and top-down processes and team members who share similar experiences may share a perception of the state of their team. In the next section, I describe various conceptualizations of goal orientation across multiple levels of analyses in team settings resulting from these various processes.

Before doing so, however, it is important to note that although the research questions scholars continue to explore and those that they continue to avoid suggest that we have yet to realize the full potential that a multidimensional perspective of goal orientation construct provides, most scholars maintain that goal orientation is in fact a multidimensional construct. What remains unresolved, however, are questions regarding how many dimensions are necessary to adequately capture goal orientation. Both Elliot and his colleagues (Elliot, 1994, 1999; Elliot & Church, 1997; Elliot & Harackiewicz, 1996) and VandeWalle (1997) proposed that goal orientation was better represented by decomposing performance orientation into two separate dimensions, both of which are concerned with external judgments: (a) performance-prove orientation (a concern with demonstrating one's competency) and (b) performance-avoid orientation (a concern with avoiding displays of incompetence). In this conceptualization, performance goal orientation is made up of two separate factors thus yielding a three-factor model of goal orientation. Recently, some scholars have suggested that there are two separate aspects of learning orientation as well and that goal orientation should be represented by four dimensions: (a) learning-prove orientation (a concern with gaining task mastery and skill acquisition), (b) learning-avoid orientation (a concern with maintaining, or not losing, one's task mastery skills) in addition to (c) performance-prove and (d) performance-avoid orientations (e.g., Elliot, 1999; Elliot & McGregor, 2001; Pintrich, 2000). Currently, research on goal orientation utilizes all three of these perspectives; thus, there continues to be much discussion and debate about the exact dimensionality of goal orientation.

Although it is beyond the scope of this chapter to attempt to resolve these conceptual differences, the following discussion and the taxonomy proposed here are relevant regardless of the perspective (two- vs. three- vs. four-factor models) one subscribes. While it may prove fruitful for future research on goal orientation to move toward more complex conceptualizations of goal orientation, it is premature to call for a moratorium on research that utilizes more simplistic conceptualizations and operationalizations of the goal-orientation construct until there is more agreement among scholars about its dimensionality. As discussed next, there is still much that we do not know about the effects of the various goal orientation dimensions, namely their joint, interactive effects. Efforts to systematically examine and understand these effects are likely to yield valuable insight about learning and achievement in groups and teams.

GOAL ORIENTATION: A MULTILEVEL PERSPECTIVE

Despite the interest that goal orientation has generated among organizational researchers as it relates to individuals in work organizations, few published empirical studies have explored the utility of goal orientation at higher organizational levels. This is somewhat surprising because organizational scholars readily accept the notion that teams, business units, and organizations can be goal oriented. Although research on goal orientation in team settings is just beginning to emerge, the findings that have emerged from this research suggest that the goal-orientation construct may be especially promising as it relates to understanding how teams learn and respond to achievement situations. For example, previous research has found that goal orientation is related to team members' reactions to individual-level and team-level feedback (DeShon, Kozlowski, Schmidt, Milner, & Wiechmann, 2004), the team's engaging in adaptive responses (e.g., backing up behavior; Porter, 2005), adaptability over time in response to unexpected communication failures (LePine, 2005), and team performance over time (Bunderson & Sutcliffe, 2003).

Without exception, scholars examining goal orientation in teams have assumed that it is an isomorphic construct. Isomorphic constructs are those that, at higher levels of analyses (e.g., team-level) have the same meaning and should demonstrate similar patterns of relationships as they do at the individual level (e.g., Kozlowski & Klein, 2000; Morgeson & Hofmann, 1999). Team goal orientation scholars have assumed that team-level goal orientation is relatively similar in function to individual-level goal orientation (e.g., LePine, 2005; Porter, 2005). Although it may be the case that goal orientation in teams is very similar to goal orientation among individuals, some unique issues result from team settings that deserve special attention as researchers begin to conceptualize goal orientation at higher levels. In this section, I explore some additional issues regarding the conceptualization of goal orientation in teams.

I propose a multilevel, multiconceptualization perspective clarifying three conceptualizations of goal orientation in group and team settings: (a) as a dispositional variable among team members, (b) as a team-level composition variable, and (c) as a team-level collective variable. In doing so, I argue that because team settings may provide a social context sufficiently unique from that of nonteam settings, they warrant further investigation regarding the effects of dispositional goal orientation. I also acknowledge that researchers examining goal orientation at the team level have taken multiple, seemingly contradictory perspectives of team goal orientation (e.g., compare Bunderson & Sutcliffe, 2003 to Porter, 2005). Rather than arguing for one approach over another, I propose that each team-level conceptualization provides a valid and meaningful approach to understanding the influence of goal orientation in group and team settings. Moreover, the multilevel, multiconceptualization perspective I advocate suggests that each conceptualization may provide unique insight regarding learning and achievement in groups and teams.

Dispositional Goal Orientation Among Team Members

As previously discussed, goal orientation is best thought of as a relatively stable individual difference, or disposition, that can also be manipulated across situations. Thus, dispositional goal orientation among team members is trait goal orientation among members of a team. When individuals enter groups or teams, they bring their own individual goal orientations to the work arrangement. Dispositional goal orientation among members of a team is important because, like other individual differences (e.g., conscientiousness; Porter et al., 2003; cognitive ability; LePine, Hollenbeck, Ilgen, & Hedlund, 1997; etc.), goal orientation among team members may have important influences on individual behavior, the behavior of other team members, and the team's behavior as a whole. Kozlowski and Klein (2000) referred to these latter influences as bottom-up influences.

Research has examined goal orientation among individuals in organizations with much of this work examining goal orientation as an individual difference variable similar to how one would examine the effects of dispositional goal orientation among team members. Although a complete review of the findings of this work is beyond the scope of this chapter (for a review, see Payne et al., 2007), goal orientation has been linked to important learning- and performance-related outcomes including goals (e.g., Brett & VandeWalle, 1999) and feedback-seeking (e.g., VandeWalle & Cummings, 1997) and efficacy beliefs (e.g., Bell & Kozlowski, 2002; Phillips & Gully, 1997), and motivation (e.g., Colquitt & Simmering, 1998).

Unfortunately, little of this research has been specifically focused on the effects of individual level dispositional goal orientation among members of groups and/or teams. A study conducted by DeShon et al. (2004) was a noteworthy exception. DeShon et al. examined the effects of dispositional goal orientation among members in addition to team goal orientation among three-person teams working on a radar-tracking task. Among their findings, they found that members who were high on performance orientation were less committed to individual goals when the feedback they received was aimed at the team rather than the individual level.

As interest in teams continues to increase among both scholars and practitioners, researchers should further examine the effects of dispositional goal orientation when individuals are organized into groups and teams. It is reasonable to expect that team-level phenomena have effects on relationships occurring at lower levels. In fact, given the saliency of work groups and teams, it is likely that such effects are stronger than those from higher levels (e.g., organization level, industry level). We currently know very little about how group and team phenomena may impact the effects of dispositional goal orientation. In addition, because teams provide a social context in which social comparisons may be more easily made among team members (cf. Porter, 2001), dispositional goal orientation may have effects in team settings that are quite different from those found in previous research. For example, research at the individual level has been somewhat mixed in regard to the predictive validity of dispositional performance orientation. In contrast, DeShon et al. (2004) found that dispositional performance orientation positively affected members' goal commitment when they received either individual feedback only or individual and team feedback. Performance orientation had a negative effect on member's commitment when they received team feedback only. Although they did not make any formal predictions regarding these effects, their findings speak to the potential boundary condition (e.g., the moderating role) that the team context may have on the effects of dispositional goal orientation. It may be the case that when individuals are organized into groups and teams, it facilitates between-person comparisons. Perhaps work arrangements that encourage between-person (e.g., between-member) comparisons (e.g., ego involvement) change the nature of the effects of the various dispositional goal orientation dimensions on learning and achievement outcomes. This would certainly seem to be an issue worthy of future research.

Composition Goal Orientation

To date, scholars have taken two different approaches in examining goal orientation at the team level. A first group of scholars examined goal orientation as a team composition variable. When taking this approach, team goal orientation represents a descriptive measure of the lower level, individual goal orientations of the members who make up the team (Porter, 2005). This approach is very similar to the approach taken by a number of scholars in examining team personality (e.g., Barrick, Stewart, Neubert, & Mount, 1998). In particular, the approach assumes that the characteristics of the individuals within the team can be combined in some fashion (e.g., mean scores, etc.) to describe the team as a whole. Although Kozlowski and Klein (2000) argued that such conceptualizations are relatively simplistic ways of examining team-level phenomena, research on team personality (e.g., Barrick et al., 1998; Ellis et al., 2005; Porter et al., 2003), team cognitive ability (Ellis et al., 2003; LePine et al., 1997), and more important, emerging research on team-goal orientation suggests that this is an empirically valid approach for predicting group and team behavior (e.g., LePine, 2005; Porter, 2005).

Composition goal orientation emerges via bottom-up processes in which the goal orientations of individual team members combine to represent the goal orientation of the team as a whole. Using the analogy of how genes function within individuals in that they combine to make up the traits that an individual possesses, Stewart (2003) argued that the individual traits (e.g., dispositions) of members of a group or team combine to make up the traits a team possesses. This suggests that members' dispositional goal orientation can be used to meaningfully represent the collective pool of dispositional goal orientation the team has at its disposal. Stated another way, when the dispositional goal orientation of a team's members are aggregated to create a summary of the collective pool of disposition, this summary statistic represents the composition of the team as a whole. Chan (1998) suggested that such operationalizations are valid to the extent to which they can be shown to have predictive validity.

I published one of the first studies examining goal orientation as a team composition variable (Porter, 2005). In this study, I demonstrated that team learning orientation was positively related to backing up behavior, efficacy beliefs, and commitment. These findings are especially relevant here because backing up behaviors are often evoked in an attempt to adapt, or learn. In addition, I found support for my hypothesis that team performance orientation had a more complex relationship with team outcomes (e.g., efficacy and commitment) such that its effects became clear once team performance was also taken into account. Specifically, I found that team performance orientation was positively associated with commitment when teams performed well and negatively associated with efficacy beliefs when teams performed poorly. My findings suggested that to better understand the effects of performance orientation in teams, it may be useful to also take into account task performance.

LePine (2005) also demonstrated the predictive validity of goal orientation in teams as a team composition variable. Of particular interest was team adaptation. Specifically, he found that among teams experiencing difficult goals, those that were high on learning orientation were more likely to adapt to unforeseen changes in the team task (in this case the gradual failure of a communication link between two of the teams' members) than those that were low on learning orientation. As he predicted, LePine found the opposite as it related to team-performance orientation—teams that were low on performance orientation were more likely to adapt to unforeseen change than teams that were high on performance orientation.

Although these studies suggest that goal orientation can be meaningfully conceptualized as a composition variable, it is important to note that when conceptualized this way, it is critical that the researcher determine the most theoretically appropriate method of aggregating individual level, dispositional goal orientation among the members of the team. To date, researchers examining goal orientation as a team composition variable have conducted their studies using teams working on tasks that are primarily additive in nature (for a complete discussion of different task types, see Steiner, 1972). The task I used (Porter, 2005), for example, was one in which each member's contribution was equally weighted. I argued that what each team member contributed in terms of dispositional trait goal orientation added to the collective pool of goal orientation that the team had at its disposal. Both my and LePine's (2005) findings suggest the utility of mean scores to represent goal orientation as a team composition variable much like previous research on cognitive ability in teams (Devine & Phillips, 2001) suggests the utility of mean scores in predicting team behaviors and outcomes. Nevertheless, researchers should at least consider the nature of the team task when determining the most appropriate aggregation method for operationalizing goal orientation at the team level (cf. Barrick et al., 1998).

Collective Goal Orientation

Another group of scholars has examined goal orientation as a collective, emergent state (e.g., Bunderson & Sutcliffe, 2003; DeShon et al., 2004). While equally valid, research of this nature is based on very different assumptions about the emergent properties of goal orientation in team settings. Scholars examining goal orientation from this perspective assume that goal orientation is a shared, team-level perception that emerges over time (cf. Gully & Phillips, 2005). Collective goal orientation likely emerges as a team-level variable via a number of processes with some of these processes occurring at the team level while others being top-down and bottom-up processes.

Top-down processes have been used to describe the manner in which higher-level phenomena influence lower-level phenomena (Kozlowski & Klein, 2000). Collective goal orientation is likely to be influenced by a number of features of the organizations in which they are embedded (e.g., reward systems, culture, climate, etc.; Gully & Phillips, 2005). For example, Gully and Phillips (2005) proposed that the functional role the team plays should influence the development of collective goal orientation in teams. They suggested that teams charged with meeting specific performance goals may develop a high performance orientation. Similarly, teams required to develop new methods of performing a task may develop a learning orientation.

In contrast, bottom-up processes have been used to describe the manner in which lower-level phenomena influence higher-level phenomena (Kozlowski & Klein, 2000). Examples include when member interaction is such that it cultivates a climate focused on either learning or performance, both, or neither. For example, Gully and Phillips suggested that team leaders are likely to influence the development of collective goal orientation. Similarly, Dragoni (2005) proposed that leaders directly and indirectly (via individual team members themselves) shape the achievement climate of a group or team via their interactions with team members. Specifically, she suggested that leaders influence collective goal orientation through modeling behaviors, signaling expectations, and providing feedback and the degree to which they emphasize learning and performance goals.

Regardless of the directional nature of the processes involved, what is central to this conception of goal orientation is that it is a shared perception among team members. In this way, collective goal orientation is a climate-like construct. Bunderson and Sutcliffe (2003) examined the effects of collective learning orientation among management teams. They found that team learning orientation had somewhat curvilinear effects on team performance (as measured by both actual profitability relative to target profitability and actual profitability relative to units sold) such that team learning orientation had some positive effects on team performance up to a point, then the effect became negative. Additionally, they found that previous performance moderated the effects of team learning orientation on future performance such that poor performing teams benefited more from being high on learning orientation than high performing teams.

Another study that examined the effects of collective goal orientation was conducted by DeShon et al. (2004). DeShon et al. examined the effects of team learning orientation and team performance orientation on regulatory behavior in teams in response to various types of performance feedback (e.g., individual level, team-level, and individual- and team-level feedback). They found that team learning orientation had interactive effects with feedback such that learning orientation had the most positive effects on goal commitment among teams that received team-level feedback and teams that received both individual- and team-level feedback compared to teams receiving only individual-level feedback. They further found that both team learning and performance orientation had interactive effects with feedback on efficacy beliefs (although they did not develop a priori hypotheses regarding the effects of team performance orientation). As with goal commitment, learning orientation had the most positive effects on efficacy among teams receiving team-level feedback or both individual- and team-level feedback. Team performance orientation was positively associated with efficacy beliefs across teams, but its effects were strongest for teams receiving team-level feedback or individual-level feedback only compared to its effects for teams receiving both team- and individual-level feedback.

It should be mentioned that the study conducted by DeShon et al. (2004) was a multilevel study in that they examined the independent effects of both dispositional goal orientation among team members and collective goal orientation. In addition, their methodology allowed them to examine the extent to which there was evidence of homologous effects for goal orientation across the individual and team levels of analysis. Overall, their results suggested moderate functional equivalence across the two levels of analyses.

Finally, it should be pointed out that researchers have acknowledged the increased complexity inherit in conceptualizing goal orientation as a collective construct and correctly have considered this increased complexity in their measurement of collective goal orientation. For example, Bunderson and Sutcliffe (2003) were able to assess learning orientation as a collective construct because their study utilized intact teams that performed together for no less than two years prior to their data collection. This does not suggest, however, that research on collective goal orientation must be done with actual work teams (e.g., that this research cannot be conducted in laboratory settings). DeShon et al. (2004), for example, recognized that the teams in their study that were comprised of individuals who were together only to work on the laboratory-based experimental task. These team members needed to first have substantial opportunity to interact with one another and work on the team task prior to completing a collective goal orientation measure. Therefore, they measured collective goal orientation at the end of their 2 1/2-hour experimental session. It is important for those interested in examining collective goal orientation to ensure that there are sufficient opportunities for shared beliefs to develop in teams for collective goal orientation to be meaningful in teams (e.g., validly and reliably measured).

Summary

In team settings, goal orientation can be conceptualized at two levels of analysis: individual and team. When conceptualized at the individual level, goal orientation in teams represents trait goal orientation among members of a team. It is likely that research examining dispositional goal orientation among team members may find that its effects in teams are distinct from those found in nonsocial contexts. At the team level, goal orientation can be conceptualized either as a team composition variable or a collective construct. The former represents a description of the characteristics of the individuals who make up the team; the latter represents a shared perception regarding the team climate. Each conceptualization is based on different assumptions about how goal orientation emerges at the team level (thus, there are some obvious conceptual and measurement issues unique to each). Although it might be tempting to conclude that composition goal orientation and collective goal orientation represent competing approaches, the developing literature on both suggests that they are equally valid approaches to examining goal orientation at higher organizational levels and that both have the potential to promote our understanding of achievement and learning in groups and teams. Moreover, rather than argue for the validity of one approach over the other, I propose a multilevel, multiconceptualization perspective that suggests a number of potential directions for future research on goal orientation in group and team settings when each of the approaches is jointly considered. In other words, I advocate that these various conceptualizations are complementary, and this is the focus of the final section of this chapter.

IMPLICATIONS OF THE MULTILEVEL, MULTICONCEPTUALIZATION PERSPECTIVE OF GOAL ORIENTATION

The multilevel, multiconceptualization perspective of goal orientation in teams just discussed should help researchers recognize both the utility and validity of multiple conceptualizations of goal orientation in teams. Another important implication of this perspective is that it suggests a number of important directions for future research, namely the examination of potential interactive effects among the various dimensions and conceptualizations of goal orientation. To date, studies on goal orientation, including those on goal orientation in teams, have emphasized the independent effects of the goal orientation dimensions (Bunderson & Sutcliffe, 2003, are a noteworthy exception at the team level; however, they did not formulate any a priori hypotheses regarding the potential interactive effects of learning and performance goal orientations).

Although scholars readily acknowledge that the various goal orientation dimensions can be independently measured, few researchers have attempted to articulate potential patterns of interaction among the various dimensions of goal orientation. For example, Gully and Phillips (2005) acknowledged that collective learning and performance orientation were independent dimensions and offered a number of excellent propositions regarding how each might have effects across multiple levels in organizations. However, they offered no propositions regarding their potential interactive effects. In fact, a review of the extant literature on goal orientation among individuals and in teams suggests a number of ways researchers avoid exploring these potential effects. In teams, some researchers, while acknowledging that learning orientation and performance orientation are not opposing dimensions, formulate opposing hypotheses for the two different goal orientation dimensions (e.g., LePine, 2005, assuming that a two-dimensional operationalization of goal orientation is utilized). Rather than formulate opposing hypotheses, other researchers focus on only one goal orientation dimension instead of multiple goal orientation dimensions (e.g., Bunderson & Sutcliffe, 2003). Others simply state that in the absence of theory regarding the nature of these interactive effects in their particular study, they will not test for those effects (e.g., Porter, 2005).

As I argued earlier, the failure of previous research to systematically examine interactions among the various dimensions of goal orientation in individual contexts is a major shortcoming of the extant literature on goal orientation. It would be unfortunate for researchers examining goal orientation in team settings to allow the same gap to emerge in our understanding of how goal orientation operates in teams. Moreover, the multilevel, multiconceptualization perspective of goal orientation in teams suggests additional avenues for future research on goal orientation in teams. These research questions are unique to team settings as the perspective suggests that there is the possibility that there may be interactions both within and between goal orientation dimensions as they are conceptualized both within and across levels. Thus, the multilevel, multiconceptualization perspective proposed here suggests that the examination of goal orientation in team settings provides team scholars with a unique opportunity to explore a number of potential research questions, many of which cannot be examined in regard to goal orientation among individuals. In the next sections, I outline a taxonomy of interactions that deserve research attention given a multilevel, multiconceptualization perspective of goal orientation in teams (see Table 7.1).

Within-Level Effects

One important, broad type of interaction suggested by a multilevel, multiconceptualization perspective of goal orientation in teams is that within a single level (what I refer to here as within-level interaction). Simply stated, within-level interaction effects examine interactions between goal orientation dimensions conceptualized at the same level of analysis (e.g., interactions among multiple individual-level variables or interactions among multiple team-level variables). The multilevel, multiconceptualization perspective of goal orientation makes salient two types of within-level interactions that have yet to be systematically explored.

Within-level, single-conceptualization interactions. Within-level, single-conceptualization interactions examine the interactive effects of similarly conceptualized goal orientation dimensions. For example, research examining within-level, single-conceptualization interactions in teams should examine the interactive effective of dispositional goal orientation

TABLE 7.1 Taxonomy of Interactions Based on a Multilevel, Multi-conceptualization of Goal Orientation

×	**Dispositional**	**Composition**	**Collective**
Dispositional	Within-Level Single-conceptualization		
Composition	Cross-Level Multi-conceptualization	Within-Level Single-conceptualization	
Collective	Cross-Level Multi-conceptualization	Within-Level Multi-conceptualization	Within-Level Single-conceptualization

dimensions among individuals working in team settings. Because dispositional goal orientation in team settings may yield effects unique from those generated in nonsocial contexts, it is possible that the joint effects of various goal orientation dimensions may be distinct from those in nonsocial settings.

With few exceptions, to date, goal-orientation research in nonsocial settings has virtually ignored these potential effects despite calls from scholars to examine these effects (e.g., Button et al., 1996). Yeo and Neal (2004) found that dispositional learning and dispositional performance orientation interacted to explain additional variance in performance over time among individuals working on an air-traffic control task. According to these authors, individuals who were low on performance orientation should have performed better over time (e.g., learned faster) than those who were high on performance orientation. They found that, over time, the relationship between performance orientation and performance became negative for individuals who were high on learning orientation. They found the highest levels of performance at later performance trials for those who were low on performance orientation and high on learning orientation. They concluded that contrary to arguments suggesting that a combination of both high learning orientation and high performance orientation may yield the highest levels of performance (e.g., Button et al., 1996), low levels of learning orientation may prevent the realization of the potential benefits of low levels of performance orientation. It should be noted that these researchers did not specify, a priori, the nature of this interaction. However, they did formally predict that the nature of the interaction would increase over time.

Janssen and Van Yperen (2004) also examined the interactive effects of dispositional learning and dispositional performance orientation without making formal predictions regarding the nature of these interactive effects. Similar to Yeo and Neal, they found that the effects of performance orientation depended on learning orientation. However, the pattern of this interaction was quite different from that described by Yeo and Neal. Specifically, Janssen and Van Yperen found the lowest levels of in-role job performance among individuals who were high on performance orientation but low on learning orientation. They concluded that high levels of learning orientation are necessary to buffer the negative effects of high levels of performance orientation. Research such as this needs to be conducted at the team level with single conceptualizations of goal orientation (e.g., interactive effects of dispositional learning orientation and dispositional performance orientation among team members).

Future research should also test for interactions between various dimensions of composition goal orientation and various dimensions of collective goal orientation. To my knowledge, no studies have examined such effects; however, one study lends some insight regarding the nature of these effects. Bunderson and Sutcliffe (2003) found evidence of low levels of performance among teams that focused too heavily on learning (e.g., that were too learning oriented), leading them to suggest that some teams need to focus on both learning and performance to be successful. This is contrary to the findings of Yeo and Neal (2004) and Janssen and Van Yperen (2004) and suggests that learning and performance orientation in group and team settings may have some important interactive effects that are unique from their interactive effects among individuals.

Additional support for contextual differences that may give rise to unique patterns of interactions among goal orientation dimensions in team settings compared to individual settings lies in the fact that teams are typically performance oriented. Ilgen (1999) stated that performance is perhaps the primary reason why individuals are organized into teams. Therefore, it may be the case that high levels of performance orientation may not have the negative effects on team outcomes that such levels have on individual outcomes. In addition, perhaps the nature of the potential interactive effects of various goal orientation dimensions depends on the nature of the team task, the availability of resources to focus on more than one goal, and time among other aspects of the task or environment. Considerable attention has been devoted to understanding differences across team tasks (e.g., Smolek, Hoffman, & Moran, 1999) and previous research has suggested that team-task type often has an important moderating influence on the effects of team composition (e.g., Barrick et al., 1998). Therefore, it is quite possible that there may be situations in which the extent to which and/or the nature of the interaction between goal orientation dimensions depends largely on the type of task a team faces. This also seems like an important direction for future research.

Within-level, multiconceptualization interactions. Within-level, multiconceptualization interactions have also yet to be explored by researchers interested in goal orientation in team settings. These interactions are concerned with how the effects of a team's goal orientation climate on team processes or outcomes may depend on the composition of the team. These interactions may also be concerned with how the effects of a team's composition may depend on the team's climate. Because collective and composition goal orientation measure different phenomena with different emergent properties, they should each capture some unique variance given rise to the potential for interactive effects. To my knowledge, no research exists that examines such effects.

Cross-Level Effects

The multilevel, multiconceptualization perspective proposed here makes salient the fact that individuals working in groups and teams do not exist in a vacuum, but rather exist in a social context. As a result, individuals are influenced by higher-level influences (e.g., their team and/or organization) while teams are influenced by the organization itself. According to Kozlowski and Klein (2000), higher-level influences such as those of the team on individuals typically have an effect in one of two ways. First, the team-level phenomena may have a direct effect on the members. Second, team-level phenomena may shape or moderate the effects that occur at the individual level. Similarly, it is also possible for individual-level phenomena to have a direct effect on teams and for individual-level phenomena to shape or moderate effects that occur at the individual level. Whether the moderating effects of team-level phenomena on individual-level relationships or the moderating effects of individual-level phenomena on team-level relationships, the multilevel, multiconceptualizations perspective of goal orientation in groups and teams suggests a number of potential cross-level interactions that future research should explore.

Cross-level, multiconceptualization interactions. Future research should examine the interactive effects between goal orientation at the team-level (composition and/or collective) and dispositional goal orientation among team members. By definition, cross-level interactions are multiconceptualization interactions. Research exploring cross-level interactions needs to address two broad types of research questions. First, to what extent does team goal orientation influence the relationship between members' dispositional goal orientation and outcomes? Second, to what extent does the dispositional goal orientation of some subset, or all team members, influence the relationship between team goal orientation and outcomes. To date, no research has examined such effects. However, there is research examining similar types of relationships in team settings. For example, Porter et al. (2003) examined the moderating role of legitimacy of need (a team-level phenomenon) on the effects of personality characteristics (dispositional variables) among subsets of team members on the extent to which they provided and received backing-up behavior from other members of their team. Research such as this is needed to determine to what extent composition goal orientation and collective goal orientation have interactive effects with dispositional goal orientation among members of a team.

A number of theoretical perspectives suggest how cross-level effects may operate and any of these could be used to explain interactions between team-level goal orientation and dispositional goal orientation among members. One interesting perspective, which has yet to receive much empirical attention by group and team scholars, is Hackman's (1992) discussion of how teams can exert influence on members via ambient and discriminatory stimuli. Simply stated, Hackman suggested a number of mechanisms through which teams can encourage/discourage certain behaviors among their members. Building on this theoretical perspective, researchers could explore, for instance, whether or not the presumed negative effects of high dispositional performance orientation for some subset of members could be mitigated by lower levels of performance orientation among the team as a whole.

CONCLUSION

In this chapter, I argued that the goal orientation construct has much promise for understanding team processes and effectiveness outcomes. I discussed three conceptualizations of goal orientation in team settings that are all meaningful and have the potential to explain unique variance in how teams response to learning and achievement situations. Specific emphasis was placed on a number of potential interactions, both within and across levels of analyses, that become apparent when approaching goal orientation from a multilevel, multiconceptualization perspective. Central to this discussion was the assumption that each conceptualization is complementary and no one conceptualization is more valid than another. Indeed, a number of the interactive effects I suggested that deserve specific attention as researchers begin to explore goal orientation in teams are those in which the effects of multiple conceptualizations of goal orientation are simultaneously considered. In no way were the research questions I suggested meant to provide an exhaustive list of the potential questions that could be asked from this perspective. Rather, I suggested some areas for future theory and research as scholars extend their work on goal orientation beyond goal orientation among individuals to goal orientation in groups and teams. I hope that the multilevel, multiconceptualization perspective I proposed in this chapter provides a useful framework for identifying gaps in our understanding about how goal orientation influences learning and achievement in teams. I also hope that it helps group and team scholars avoid some of the pitfalls that have and continue to plague researchers examining goal orientation among individuals.

REFERENCES

Ames, C., & Archer, J. (1987). Mothers' beliefs about the role of ability and effort in school learning. *Journal of Educational Psychology, 79,* 409–414.

Barrick, M. R., Stewart, G. L., Neubert, M. J., & Mount, M. K. (1998). Relating member ability and personality to work-team processes and team effectiveness. *Journal of Applied Psychology, 83,* 377–391.

Bell, B. S., & Kozlowski, S. W. J. (2002). Goal orientation and ability: Interactive effects on self-efficacy, performance, and knowledge. *Journal of Applied Psychology, 87,* 497–505.

Brett, J. E., & VandeWalle, D. (1999). Goal orientation and goal content as predictors of performance in a training program. *Journal of Applied Psychology, 84,* 863–873.

Bunderson, J. S., & Sutcliffe, K. M. (2003). Management team learning orientation and business unit performance. *Journal of Applied Psychology, 88,* 552–560.

Button, S. B., Mathieu, J. E., & Zajac, D. M. (1996). Goal orientation in organizational research: A conceptual and empirical foundation. *Organizational Behavior and Human Decision Processes, 67,* 26–48.

Chan, D. (1998). Functional relationships among constructs in the same content domain at different levels of analysis: A typology of composition models. *Journal of Applied Psychology, 83,* 234–246.

Colquitt, J. A., & Simmering, M. S. (1998). Conscientiousness, goal orientation, and motivation to learn during the learning process: A longitudinal study. *Journal of Applied Psychology, 83,* 654–665.

Davis, W. D., Carson, C. M., Ammeter, A. P., & Treadway, D. C. (2005). The interactive effects of goal orientation and feedback specificity on task performance. *Human Performance, 18,* 409–426.

DeShon, R. P., & Gillepsie, J. Z. (2005). A motivated action theory account of goal orientation. *Journal of Applied Psychology, 90,* 1096–1127.

DeShon, R. P., Kozlowski, S. W. J., Schmidt, A. M., Milner, K. R., & Wiechmann, D. (2004). A multiple-goal, multilevel model of feedback effects on the regulation of individual and team performance. *Journal of Applied Psychology, 89,* 1035–1056.

Devine, D. J., & Phillips, J. L. (2001). Do smarter teams do better? A meta-analysis of cognitive ability and team performance. *Small Group Research, 32,* 507–532.

Diener, C. I., & Dweck, C. S. (1978). An analysis of learned helplessness: Continuous changes in performance, strategy, and achievement cognitions following failure. *Journal of Personality and Social Psychology, 39,* 940–952.

Dragoni, L. (2005). Understanding the emergence of state goal orientation in organizational work groups: The role of leadership and multilevel climate perceptions. *Journal of Applied Psychology, 90,* 1084–1095.

Dweck, C. S. (1986). Motivational processes affecting learning. *American Psychologist, 41,* 1040–1048.

Dweck, C. S. (1989). Motivation. In A. Lesgold, & R. Glaser (Eds.), *Foundations for a psychology of education* (pp. 87–136). Hillsdale, NJ: Erlbaum.

Dweck, C. S., & Elliott, E. S. (1983). Achievement motivation. In P. Mussen (Ed.) & E. M. Hetherington (Vol. Ed.), *Handbook of child psychology* (Vol. 4, pp. 643–691). New York: Wiley.

Dweck, C. S., & Leggett, E. L. (1988). A social-cognitive approach to motivation and personality. *Psychological Review, 95*, 256–273.
Eison, J. A. (1981). A new instrument for assessing students' orientations towards grades and learning. *Psychological Reports, 48*, 919–924.
Eison, J. A. (1982). Educational and personal dimensions of learning- and grade- oriented students. *Psychological Report, 51*, 867–870.
Eison, J. A., Pollio, H., & Milton, O. (1982). *LOGO II: A user's manual*. Knoxville, TN: University of Tennessee Early Learning Center for Research and Practice (ELC).
Elliot, A. J. (1994). *Approach and avoidance achievement goals: An intrinsic motivation analysis*. Unpublished doctoral dissertation, University of Wisconsin-Madison, Madison, WI.
Elliot, A. J. (1999). Approach and avoidance achievement goals. *Educational Psychologist, 34*, 169–189.
Elliot, A. J., & Church, M. A. (1997). A hierarchical model of approach and avoidance achievement motivation. *Journal of Personality and Social Psychology, 72*, 218–232.
Elliot, A. J., & Harackiewicz, J. M. (1996). Approach and avoidance goals and intrinsic motivation: A mediation will analysis. *Journal of Personality and Social Psychology, 70*, 461–475.
Elliot, A. J., & McGregor, H. A. (2001). A 2 × 2 achievement goal framework. *Journal of Personality and Social Psychology, 80*, 501–519.
Ellis, A. P. J., Hollenbeck, J. R., Ilgen, D. R., Porter, C. O. L. H., West, B. J., & Moon, H. (2003). Team learning: Collectively connecting the dots. *Journal of Applied Psychology, 88*, 821–835.
Farr, J. L., Hofmann, D. A., & Ringenbach, K. L. (1993). Goal orientation and action control theory: Implications for industrial and organizational psychology. *International Review of Industrial and Organizational Psychology, 8*, 193–232.
Fisher, S. L., & Ford, J. K. (1998). Differential effects of learning effort and goal orientation on two learning outcomes. *Personnel Psychology, 51*, 392–420.
Gong, Y., & Fan, J. (2006). Longitudinal examination of the role of goal orientation in cross-cultural adjustment. *Journal of Applied Psychology, 91*, 176–184.
Gully, S. M., & Phillips, J. M. (2005). A multilevel application of learning and performance orientations to individual, group, and organizational outcomes. In J. J. Martocchio (Ed.). *Research in personnel and human resource management* (Vol. 24). Greenwich, CT: Elsevier.
Hackman, J. R. (1992). Group influences on individuals in organizations. In M. D. Dunnette, & L. M. Hough (Eds.), *Handbook of industrial organizational psychology: Vol. 3* (2nd ed. 199–267). Palo Alto, CA: Consulting Psychologists Press, Inc.
Ilgen, D. R. (1999). Teams embedded in organizations: Some implications. *American Psychologist, 54*, 129–139.
Janssen, O., & Van Yperen, N. W. (2004). Employees' goal orientations, the quality of leader-member exchange, and the outcomes of job performance and job satisfaction. *Academy of Management Journal, 47*, 368–384.
Kozlowski, S. W. J., Gully, S. M., Brown, K. G., Salas, E., Smith, E. A., & Nason, E. R. (2001). Effects of training goals and goal orientation traits on multi-dimensional training outcomes and performance adaptability. *Organizational Behavior and Human Decision Processes, 85*, 1–31.

Kozlowski, S. W. J., & Klein, K. J. (2000). A multilevel approach to theory and research in organizations: Contextual, temporal, and emergent processes. In K. J. Klein, & S. W. J. Kozlowski (Eds.), *Multilevel theory, research, and methods in organizations: Foundations, extensions, and new directions* (pp. 3–90). San Francisco: Pfeiffer

LePine, J. A. (2005). Adaptation of teams in response to unforeseen change: Effects of goal difficulty in team composition in terms of cognitive ability and goal orientation. *Journal of Applied Psychology, 90*, 1153–1167.

LePine, J. A., Hollenbeck, H. R., Ilgen, D. I., & Hedlund, J. (1997). Effects of individual differences on the performance of hierarchical decision-making teams: Much more than g. *Journal of Applied Psychology, 82*, 803–811.

Morgeson, F. P., & Hofmann, D. A. (1999). The structure and function of collective constructs: Implications for multilevel research and theory development. *Academy of Management Review, 24*, 249–265.

Nicholls, J. G. (1984). Achievement motivation: Conceptions of ability, subjective experience, task choice, and performance. *Psychological Review, 91*, 328–346.

Payne, S. C., Youngcourt, S. S., & Beaubien, J. M. (in press). A meta-analytic examination of the goal orientation nomological net. *Journal of Applied Psychology.*

Phillips, J. M., & Gully, S. M. (1997). Role of goal orientation, ability, need for achievement, and locus of control in the self-efficacy and goal-setting process. *Journal of Applied Psychology, 82*, 792–802.

Pintrich, P. R. (2000). Multiple goals, multiple pathways: The role of goal orientation in learning and achievement. *Journal of Educational Psychology, 92*, 544–555.

Porter, C. O. L. H. (2001). Singled out: Task and social implications of providing individual level performance feedback in teams. *Dissertation Abstracts International, 62*(12-A). (UMI No. AAI3036733)

Porter, C. O. L. H. (2005). Goal orientation: Effects on backing up behavior, performance, efficacy, and commitment in teams. *Journal of Applied Psychology, 90*, 811–818.

Porter, C. O. L. H., Hollenbeck, J. R., Ilgen, D. R., Ellis, A. P. J., West, B. J., & Moon, H. (2003). Backing up behaviors in teams: The role of personality and legitimacy. *Journal of Applied Psychology, 88*, 391–403.

Smolek, J., Hoffman, D., & Moran, L. (1999). Organizing teams for success. In E. Sundstrom (Ed.), *Supporting work team effectiveness: Best management practices for fostering high performance* (pp. 24–62). San Francisco: Jossey-Bass Publishers.

Steele-Johnson, D., Beauregard, R. S., Hoover, P. B., & Schmidt, A. M. (2000). Goal orientation and task demand effects on motivation, affect, and performance. *Journal of Applied Psychology, 85*, 724–738.

Steiner, I. D. (1972). *Group process and productivity.* New York: Academic Press.

Stewart, G. L. (2003). Toward an understanding of the multilevel role of personality in teams. In M. R. Barrick, & A. M. Ryan (Eds.), *Personality and work: Reconsidering the role of personality in organizations* (pp. 183–204). San Francisco: Jossey-Bass Publishers.

Sundstrom, E. (1999). The challenges of supporting work team effectiveness. In E. D. Sundstrom (Ed.), *Supporting work team effectiveness: Best management practices for fostering high performance* (pp. 3–23). San Francisco: Jossey-Bass Publishers.

VandeWalle, D. (1997). Development and validation of a work domain goal orientation instrument. *Education and Psychological Measurement, 57,* 995–1015.

VandeWalle, D., & Cummings, L. L. (1997). A test of the influence of goal orientation on the feedback-seeking process. *Journal of Applied Psychology, 82,* 390–400.

Yeo, G. B., & Neal, A. (2004). A multilevel analysis the effort, practice, and performance: Effects of ability, conscientiousness, and goal orientation. *Journal of Applied Psychology, 89,* 231–247.

CHAPTER

8

Navigating Across Culture and Distance: Understanding the Determinants of Global Virtual Team Performance

NORHAYATI ZAKARIA
Faculty of International Studies, Universiti Utara Malaysia

ANDREA AMELINCKX
Faculty of Management, University of Lethbridge

DAVID WILEMON
Whitman School of Management, Syracuse University

INTRODUCTION

In this chapter, we examine the nature, structure, and composition of global virtual teams and consider how the cultural complexities of these teams impact team dynamics and group learning. We then propose a framework called "effectiveness of global virtual teams" to create and manage global virtual teams. Subsequently, we discuss several key questions that are important to ask when assessing the performance of effective global virtual teams. We conclude by discussing new patterns of communication and positive social exchange that may emerge in computer-mediated team environments giving multinational corporations' (MNCs) important competitive advantages.

As globally distributed collaborations become more important to MNCs, so does the need to effectively manage global virtual teams. Organizations use global virtual teams for different purposes; some are short-term and temporary groups while others are permanent units. Global virtual teams tend to share three main characteristics: (a) teams are comprised of heterogeneous members with diverse cultural backgrounds, (b) team members work together across geographical/national boundaries, and (c) teams use technology to facilitate communication and collaboration (Lipnack & Stamps, 1997; Montoya-Weiss, Massey, & Song, 2001; Zakaria, Amelinckx, & Wilemon, 2004).

Effective information and communication technologies are crucial for building a virtual workplace and creating successful global virtual teamwork. Communication and knowledge-sharing processes are difficult and in some cases impossible without computer-facilitated communication technologies. Thus, effective information and communication technologies are crucial for building a virtual workplace and having successful teamwork. Nonetheless, such technologies are not straightforward tools; they are inadequate unless well-integrated and aligned with team design, behavior, and collaboration and communication processes (Anderson & Shane, 2002; Prasad & Akhilesh, 2002; Zakaria, Amelinckx, & Wilemon, 2004).

Group collaboration is often complex, with or without electronic technology. Teamwork requires members to learn and share a common framework, have clear purposes and goals, and work together effectively. The dispersed and diverse nature of global teams accentuates group complexity and cultural differences and can exacerbate miscommunication and conflict unless it is well managed and has strong leadership and organizational support (Kayworth & Leider, 2001/2002; Pauleen, 2003). The human component in the global virtual environment largely facilitates or hinders teamwork.

As global virtual teams present new modes of learning, team members need to develop new patterns of knowledge sharing, communication, and social exchange in a computer-mediated team environment. In order to be effective, they also need to work on building and maintaining intrateam-member relationships and trust (Jarvenpaa, Shaw, & Staples, 2004) to facilitate team learning. Team learning is defined as "…a relatively permanent change in the team's collective level of knowledge and skill produced by the shared experience of the team members (Ellis et al., 2003, p.3). Ellis et al. further argued that team learning must take place at the individual level before it can be strengthened at the group level. In a similar vein, not only is it crucial for members to acquire knowledge individually (Weiss, 1990), they also need to share this information with their team members. Usually, learning takes place when there are contributive factors such as cohesiveness, cooperation, trust, leadership, and infrastructure. These factors provide competencies that enable members to learn to share information as well as knowledge. When working in teams, team members learn from their own experiences as well as from those of others (Ellis et al., 2003).

WHAT IS A GLOBAL VIRTUAL TEAM?

In order to better understand the intricate aspects of global virtual teams, we first define what we mean by teams and teamwork. For the purposes of this chapter, we make a clear distinction between *group* and *team*. According to Hellriegel, Slocum, and Woodman (2001), a team is defined as a small number of employees comprising between 2 and 10 members working on objective-oriented assignments or tasks, whereas groups tend to be larger, less-structured entities with less-specific mandates, comprised of more than 20 members. Katzenbach and Smith's (1993) further defined *team* as "…a small number of people with complementary skills who are committed to a common purpose, et of performance goals, and approach for which they hold themselves mutually accountable" (p. 112).

Organizational structure and configuration differentiates the two constructs. The distinction between "group" and "team" may be less clear in other languages and cultures, however, as the notion of what a team is and what it does is not universally shared. How teams are perceived will differ due to the cultural constructs of team members and the organization itself (Gibson & Zellmer-Burhn, 2001). Similarly, teamwork is also a culturally bounded concept, the meaning of which varies by culture and language. Studies on teamwork across cultures have found significant variance in defining team membership and team-leader functions (Pillai & Meindl, 1998), team-goal setting (Erez & Earley, 1987), intrateam conflict, and social loafing (Earley, 1989; Montoya-Weiss et al., 2001).

In examining global virtual teams, we look at two different yet overlapping aspects of team structure: (a) global and (b) virtual. Global teams are defined as "individuals who are globally dispersed, meet face-to-face rather infrequently, members are from different cultures, and speak different languages" (McDonough & Cedrone, 2000, p. 3). They also differ due to functional expertise and complexity (Wheatley & Wilemon, 1999). *Global teams* are usually heterogeneous and bond by electronic communications capabilities, while traditional teams are often homogenous and nonelectronic groups. Like global teams, a *virtual team* is seen as a "...culturally diverse, geographically dispersed, electronically communicating work group" (Kristof, Brown, Sims, & Smith, 1995). A virtual team is considered global when members' backgrounds are culturally diverse, and members are able to work within the diversity of a global environment (DeSanctis & Poole, 1994; Jackson, Aiken, Vanjani, & Hasan, 1995). We define *global virtual teams* as a distinct entity whose members come from different geographical locations, may not have a common background, are organizationally dispersed, collaborate using asynchronous and synchronous technologies, and often assemble on an ad hoc basis. Global virtual teams can also be considered collocated when the virtual work environment is considered collocated space.

Collocation is a powerful term that illustrates the dynamics of global virtual teams (Lipnack & Stamps, 1997). Historically, *collocated teams* are defined as team members that work side by side in the same project area or work space (Crow, 1996), for instance, in the same building, department, organization, or geographic location. Collocated members that are assigned to develop new products within a timeframe are said to develop better ways of collaboration, communication, coordination, and working relationships (Crow, 1996). Members contribute different levels of knowledge and expertise that are shared in order to develop a product or service. Collocation can also occur in the virtual sense when members are geographically distributed yet connected to each other with computer-mediated communication tools (Mark, Grudin, & Poltrock, 1999) as emphasized by us with the concept of global virtual teams. It is important to note that global virtual teams that work together but are geographically apart face greater challenges than traditional collocated teams.

FRAMEWORK FOR CREATING EFFECTIVE GLOBAL VIRTUAL TEAMS

As previously mentioned, it is challenging to create effective group learning, particularly when the composition of group members is heterogeneous and culturally different. Therefore, in order to ensure effective performance from global virtual teams, MNCs need to understand several factors regarding how to develop an effective environment conducive to global virtual team performance. Particularly, teams need to learn and engage in collective efforts rather than merely bringing in individual expertise. Based on the following framework (see Fig. 8.1), there are six main factors for establishing a global virtual team: (a) enabling environment, (b) members, (c) purpose, (d) process, (e) communication, and (f) resources.

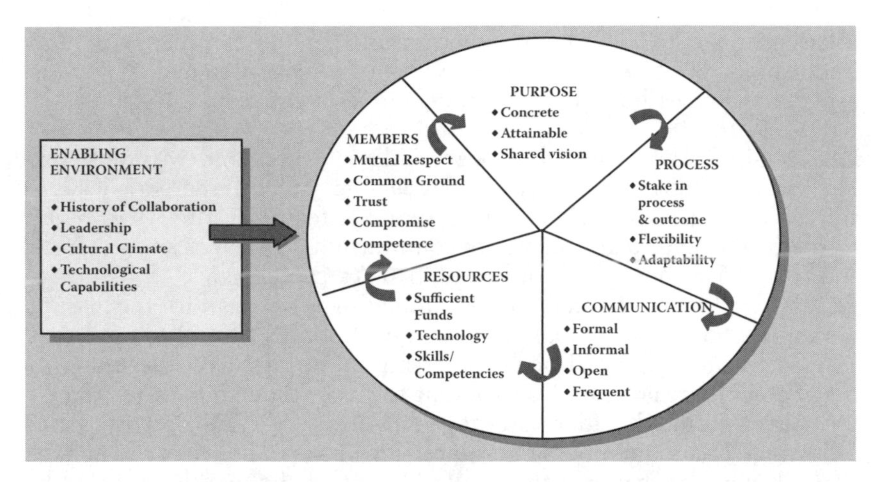

Figure 8.1 Framework for understanding the determinants of effective global virtual teams.

Enabling Environment

In order for global virtual teams to work effectively, it is essential to create an enabling environment such as history of collaboration, leadership, cultural climate, and technological capabilities. This environment serves as the initial infrastructure for members to operate on a global basis. Such an environment also helps facilitate team learning. The first two factors—cultural climate and technological capabilities—are required since these factors not only signify and define global virtual teams but also differentiate them from other types of teams such as problem-solving, self-managed, and internal cross-functional teams.

History of collaboration. It is challenging to work with strangers. Most of the time, a global virtual team is used on ad-hoc projects without a history of collaboration (Allred, Snow, & Miles, 1996; Sundstrom, McIntyre, Halfhill, & Richards, 2000). Members may be assigned to new projects where the project duration can be as short as 2 to 6 months or longer such as within 1 to 3 years. If group members have collaborated with others before, any future projects will facilitate their ability to work together and increase the likelihood of learning from each other. A history of collaboration can take place among team members or within the larger organization. More often than not, members do not have the opportunity to work together again. Yet, this does not prevent team members from learning and sharing their knowledge. For example, once they have acquired the right competencies and learn as much as they can with their present task, those experiences and knowledge will enhance their level of expertise and ability to work as effective teams in future projects. Effective collaboration requires team members to build relationships with other team members and become familiar with, and understand, what needs to be done with the tasks assigned. All these aspects will contribute to the learning curve of the team as a whole.

Leadership. According to Yoo and Alavi (2002) and Misiolek and Heckman (2005), a new type of leadership called "emergent leadership" is often present in many global virtual teams. Rather than being formally assigned, team members voluntarily take charge and perform the role of leader to help ensure high team performance. This emergent leadership form often rotates among members as different issues are encountered by a global virtual team. Robbins (2003) argued that teams continuously need both leadership and structure. Therefore, in many global virtual teams, a different form of leadership, other than a formally appointed leader, is required. Robbins (2003) suggested the following: " Team members must agree on who is to do what and ensure that all members contribute equally in sharing the workload. In addition, the team needs to determine how schedules will be set, what skills need to be developed, how the group will resolve conflicts, and how the group will make and modify decisions" (p. 267).

We emphasize that leadership is pivotal and that MNCs need to develop effective leaders that can instruct, guide, and manage teams so that high team performance and learning result. As noted in the context of global virtual teams, leaders are not necessarily appointed, but rather emerge voluntarily. Also, in cases where leaders are not appointed, they often will emerge within a team's structure in a relatively short time. While this type of emergent leadership seems to operate effectively, the issue of accountability can be a source of challenge to those organizations opting for global virtual teams and where the managers are used to managing and supporting formally appointed team leaders.

Several studies concur that emergent leadership can result in effective, high-performing teams (Misiolek & Heckman, 2005; Yoo & Alavi, 2002) since emergent leaders can direct members toward the team's mission and goals and help teams reach agreement on the specifics of project teamwork. Such leadership can create synergy among team members' expertise, rather than relying primarily on individual contributions, which may not result in synergistic performance.

Cultural climate. Global virtual teams operate in a cultural diversity platform. This means people come from different geographical locations and nationalities. Therefore, MNCs need to build a working structure and create conditions that produce a positive climate for its teams. *Conducive cultural climate* implies that team members are motivated to work in a high culturally diverse environment. In short, the members share a common culture in which they eventually build trusting relationships with each other. In order to establish a common culture and conducive climate, Chen and Starosta (1996) suggested three key competencies: (a) cognitive, (b) affective, and (c) adroitness. These competencies allow team members to first recognize, become aware, and learn about the differences, and then become more sensitive to the differences, and finally learn to behave in accordance to the cultures that they need to deal with.

Consequently, only a conducive cultural climate is likely to promote a trusting environment for teams. For example, in the early stage of learning, trust is often difficult to achieve. Since trust is a culturally determined behavior (Fukuyama, 1995), culture can affect the way information is used to make decisions (Triandis, 1972). Triandis (1995) further noted that people from different cultures have differing requirements for establishing trust. For example, high-context people who rely heavily on nonverbal and subtle situational cues trust only the in-groups, which include spouse, family, and friends. On the other hand, they hardly trust out-group members, such as acquaintances or strangers (Hall, 1990). This concept of in-group and out-group establishes the cultural boundary for determining what information and knowledge are disclosed and shared among team members. Low-context people, who rely heavily on words to convey meanings in communication, seldom make the distinction between people inside and outside of their network. Their willingness to share knowledge and disclose information depends on whether their actions serve instrumental goals. Thus, by taking into account the cultural boundaries that facilitate trust, learning, and sharing behaviors, MNCs can provide the needed intercultural training (Zakaria, 2000).

Technological capabilities. Besides interpersonal, communication, and leadership skills, technological competence is needed when teams collaborate in a distributed working structure. As such, it is crucial for MNCs to invest in computer-mediated communication technologies that can be fully optimized by team members. MNCs also need to introduce a "technology" culture in which people have a positive regard for technology. However, organizations must also understand that not all types of technologies are appropriate to a team due to cultural preferences. For instance, Lee (2002) found that patterns of e-mail use vary among eastern and western cultures due to cultural differences. Differences also exist in communication styles between team members when they use e-mail, such as using a direct and an indirect tone in messages when making decisions as well as succinct and ambiguous messages (Zakaria, 2006). Likewise, Massey, Montoya-Weiss, Hung, and Ramesh (2001) found significant differences in the perception of task technology fit between virtual team members from the United States, Asia, and Europe. Once the appropriate technology is identified, organizations must ensure that people are fully prepared to use the technology selected. One way to develop and enhance the competence level is to provide training on the "what-to" and "how-to" operate using different types of technologies so that teams are fully competent and confident to perform effectively in their assigned projects.

Members

Global virtual team members, individually and as a group, cope with very different challenges than do their traditional team counterparts. Potter and Balthazard (2002) compared conventional and virtual teams and found that on all outcome measures, virtual teams were not as successful as face-to-face teams. Similarly, Warekentin, Sayeed, and Hightower (1997) indicated that teams that relied wholly on virtual communication reported less satisfaction with group interaction.

So, what does it take for a global virtual team to succeed? It certainly requires more than information-communication technologically savvy participants. In part, it requires group members to continually exhibit both a willingness and an ability to learn from and share with one another—even when separated by geography, time, and culture.

At a minimum, global virtual teams must have appropriate membership and technology to function (Zakaria, 2000). By appropriate, we mean members who are motivated, have both technical and cross-cultural competencies, and have the ability and willingness to compromise. It has been shown that those working in a virtual environment are more likely to experience information overload and social isolation (Rogers & Albritton, 1995), so in the selection of members, temperament and personality should be considered along with technical expertise. While the choice and variety of information communication technology media does play a role in global virtual teams, it is the frequency and intensity of human interaction that tends to be a deciding factor in knowledge transfer processes, team coherence, and performance and work output.

Intrateam social-relationship construction in global virtual teams is challenging, however, as it takes significant time, commitment, and effort. For team members, building and maintaining social relationships with others too distant to actually socialize with in meaningful ways may flatten or restrict the emotive aspects of such relations; in turn, making social relationship building and knowledge sharing more difficult. Conversely, certain team members may feel less inhibited with disclosure if their cultural biases are challenged in a more ambiguous virtual setting.

While team output and productivity do not automatically follow when positive intrateam relations are established, they nonetheless remain necessary in fostering productivity. Without the existence and maintenance of intrateam respect, mutual trust, reciprocity, and positive individual and group relationships, global virtual teams will not be successful.

Purpose

The process of establishing a common team vision, collectively agreed-upon goals, and attainable objectives has the capacity to foster positive team relations—particularly if team members come from individualistic, less hierarchical cultures. While it is often assumed that team members should be included in setting team direction in order for the organization and team leadership to gain team endorsement and support (Goodbody, 2005), in cross-cultural teams where certain members value more hierarchical and rigid decision-making structures, such members may feel uncomfortable voicing dissent, particularly if they believe it will not be welcome.

Individuals from different cultures vary in terms of their communication and group behaviors. These variances include the motivation to seek and disclose individuating information and the need to engage in self-categorization (Gudykunst, 1997). One major dimension of cultural variability is individualism-collectivism (Hofstede, 1980). Research suggests that people from individualistic cultures tend to be less influenced by group membership, have greater skills in entering and leaving new groups, and engage in more open and precise communication than individuals from collectivist cultures (Hall, 1976; Hofstede, 1980). In addition, the willingness to respond to ambiguous messages, interpreted by Pearce (1974) to be a trusting behavior, has been shown to be higher among members of individualistic cultures than among members of collectivist cultures (Gudykunst, 1997). These findings suggest that individuals from individualistic cultures might be more ready to trust others than individuals from collectivist cultures in computer-mediated communication environments, be more open in voicing differences of opinion, and expect to be involved in goal-setting exercises. If this is so, it is imperative for global virtual teams to insure that members from more collectivist cultures are comfortable and engaged in the goal-setting process and vision determination and not intimidated or resentful of it.

One possible positive aspect of the virtual environment is that it may actually diminish positional bias and status perceptions among team members (Pollard, 1996). Thus, lower-status team members from the large power-distance cultures might be more willing or prefer to participate in computer-mediated discussions since the member status ambiguity may be more salient. For global virtual teams, being both heterogeneous cultural entities and geographically dispersed virtual entities, the risk of potential misunderstandings and mistrust is heightened so effective team management is required.

Both intrateam trust and trust between the team and the organization are equally important in establishing concrete attainable goals. The ability to collaborate depends heavily upon open reciprocity and trust—the sharing of information and knowledge will not freely occur without it (Scott, 2000). Duarte and Snyder (1999) recommended a "microclimate" as a possible solution to supporting effective norms and values. In such an environment, team members with various cultural backgrounds create a working culture that takes into account cultural variance and promotes a compatible decision-making and goal-setting process.

Process

Successful global virtual teams do certain things right—they develop their own dynamics and shared culture and more actively focus on relationship building and trust establishment (Maznevski & Chudoba, 2000). But how? One means is by actively encouraging regular and frequent reciprocal cross-cultural exchange of ideas and team-created solutions. Members need to be invested in the process and outcome, be flexible, and learn to work together. As mentioned earlier, face-to-face meetings between members at the global virtual team formation process and periodically thereafter may help. Certainly, understanding how information communication technology usage impacts virtual teams' social context and performance remains critical. Gallupe, Cooper, Grise, and Bastianutti (1994) showed that without anonymity, parallel input, and brainstorming memory input, electronic groups performed more poorly than nonelectronic groups.

However, the degree of technological sophistication among team members is not an accurate predictor of global virtual team success. Duarte and Snyder (1999) emphasized that technology is only one factor in global virtual teams' success and such teams rarely indicate that technology was a principal reason for success or failure (Nunamaker, Briggs, Romano, & Mittleman, 1997). It is important to note that there are also challenges that arise from intrateam processes such as incompatibility between cultural fit and technology fit, stress and conflict, and loss of momentum when working together. As for the team-boundary-management processes, challenges like marketing team's product to key stakeholders and maintaining management support are also significant factors for MNCs to manage.

Though global virtual teams offer enormous prospective utility, they need to be well managed to realize their potential. Ensuring that team processes incorporate culturally appropriate intrateam knowledge sharing and communication and relationship patterns and that global virtual team membership has a stake in both process and outcome is a principal step toward realizing the opportunities present in global team dynamics.

Communication

For a global virtual team, the processes of both knowledge sharing and team learning are dependant on maintenance of successful communication processes and protocols. Knowledge sharing, however, is not unrelated to the social and human locale from which it arises (Thomas, Kellogg, & Erikson, 2001). Knowledge is shaped, evaluated, discarded, or embraced based upon people's social and cultural assumptions. A rank ordering of knowledge (from most to least important) occurs after such knowledge is filtered through cultural lenses, whether we are aware of such filters or not. Research on the nature of knowledge also recognizes differences in tacit versus codified knowledge (Nelson & Winter, 1982; Polanyi, 1966).

As Sole and Edmondson (2002) noted,, whereas codified knowledge is generally viewed as readily transferable, social, or tacit, knowledge is not and may depend on both proximity and interpersonal interaction. Thus, for globally dispersed teams, soft or relationship knowledge may be less salient and more difficult to learn than is factual knowledge. Notwithstanding, even factual knowledge may not be as objective as we might assume, and the transmission of such knowledge, both in the process by which it is conveyed, as well as the information itself, should not be deemed to be culture free.

As noted, communication between team members is primarily based on computer-mediated communication technology; organizations therefore need to ensure that each member is not only comfortable with but also competent in using communication tools. Moreover, the technology must be compatible with members' different communication preferences. Hall (1976) suggested that communication styles allow people to forecast the behaviors of others through two aspects—(a) high context—nonverbal such as tone of voice, hand gestures and movements, and facial expressions, and (b) low context—verbal aspects such as spoken and written words. Empirically, it is established that the communication styles will impact the way people relate and perform managerial tasks, such as decision-making activities (Zakaria, 2006).

Organizations must develop a more open, frequent communication link (both formal and informal) to establish effective intercultural communication between members. Jarvenpaa and Leidner (2004) suggested that teams need to meet face to face before they embark on any distributed working structure. The meeting should be set at the initial stage where the members can communicate clearly on aspects such as the goals, mission, and vision of the organization, describe and outline the tasks to be performed, institutionalize key rules, regulations, and procedures, as well as develop rapport and working relationships.

Resources

Collaboration among team members relies largely on social-technical infrastructure (Cogburn, Zhang, & Khothule, 2002). The infrastructure can be identified as having three dimensions of resources: (a) people to technology, (b) people to people, and (c) people to organizations. The perspective of people to technology illustrates the need for team members to confluence with the technological capability. Lipnack and Stamps (1997) strongly argued that in the virtual work design, technology is not the only answer to team effectiveness. Instead, people are the main drivers of team success (Katzenbach, 2001). Without the human element, large investments in technology will be of limited value. Technology is no more than a tool that facilitates the processes within organizations. Acceptance level, which includes factors like perceived ease of use and perceived usefulness, determines whether people prefer to use technology or not (Venkatesh, Morris, Davis, & Davis, 2003).

For the people-to-people dimension, teams need to establish a rapport as well as develop a trusting relationship. Each team member needs to work effectively by taking into consideration the values, attitudes, and perceptions of others. Moreover, organizations must strategically identify and retain highly qualified people, prepare managers to deal with cultural differences, and ensure that people possess both the technical and managerial capabilities to compete (Brake, Walker, & Walker, 1995). Additionally, people need to acculturate and adapt to new working structures and environments, tolerate and understand cultural diversity among team members, and inculcate competencies such as interpersonal skills, leadership abilities, and an awareness of the importance of effective intercultural communication. If team members face cultural clashes, the challenges of working together will be intensified.

The last dimension deals with people to organizations and highlights the creation of an effective organizational culture. Organizations need to choose team members from the best pool of talent. When selecting talent, organizations need to undergo systematic processes of screening, selection, and hiring. Organizations also need to acquire people with different levels of expertise. This expertise, in turn, can offer diverse range of competencies and knowledge. Only then can organizations benefit from the synergistic effect that teams create for a better learning environment. Consequently, such an organizational culture is based not only on members' expectations but also on members' cultural values. The main resources here center on (a) organizational resources that include sufficient funds for recruitment, and (b) human resources with appropriate cross-cultural competencies.

ASSESSING GLOBAL VIRTUAL TEAMS PERFORMANCE

An important part of global virtual team management is an understanding of performance and how it is appraised. Only then effective group learning can be created in MNCs. Earlier, we developed a "global virtual team effectiveness framework" (see Fig. 8.1). In order to assess overall performance, we suggest that global virtual teams use this framework as a platform for appraising performance and taking corrective action. The appraisal process we recommend is not a one-time occurrence; rather it is done several times during the life of the global virtual team (Thomsett, 2002; Kerth, 2001; Carmel, 1999). We pose the following performance assessment questions based on our global virtual team effectiveness framework as follows:

Members

- Is there mutual respect?

- Is there trust among the members?
- Is the team able to deal with conflicts and disagreements?
- Do the members have the relevant expertise?
- Are they capable and willing to work in a global virtual team environment?

Purpose
- Is there a shared vision of the project?
- Are the team's objectives clear?
- Are the team's objectives attainable?

Processes
- Are the processes the teams use effective?
- Is there an emphasis on continual improvement of the team's processes?
- Are the processes adaptable to changing circumstances?
- Are the team's decision-making processes clear?

Communication
- Is the formal communication clear, timely, and accurate?
- Is there productive open informal communication?
- Is the frequency of formal and informal communication adequate?
- Are cultural differences in communication preferences understood?

Resources
- Are resources sufficient for the team to accomplish its task?
- Does the time have the right technologies and skills to perform?
- Is the team capable of forecasting its resource needs?

Overall Performance
- Is the team meeting its performance objectives?
- Is the team meeting its schedule objectives?
- Is the team meeting its cost/budget objectives?
- Is learning captured for future projects?
- Is the team effectively marketing its product to stakeholders and users?
- Are there opportunities for professional growth?
- Is team members' satisfaction at a productive level?

As noted, we recommend that any global virtual team periodically assess its performance—a far cry from the way many teams assess their effectiveness. By this continual review of performance, corrective action can be taken to get the global virtual team back on track when needed, and team learning is more likely to be realized.

CONCLUSION

Creating effective global virtual teams is challenging, particularly when such teams often take longer to make decisions, tend to experience greater stress and uncertainty, and have more frequent conflicts among team members. All these challenges arise from the cultural complexities and the technological sophistication needed to make such teams effective. As we have noted, individuals from different cultures vary in terms of their communication and group behaviors (Gudykunst, 1997, Kerber & Buono, 2004). Additionally, cross-cultural misunderstandings can be exacerbated in information communication technology usage when cultural differences are not acknowledged and addressed. As a result, cultural divergence between group members needs to be recognized in order to establish constructive intra and interteam communication and interaction, particularly when using information communication technologies.

Global virtual teams need to be committed to developing new patterns of knowledge sharing, communication, and social exchange in their computer-mediated team environments. Argote, McEvily, and Reagans (2003) observed that situational context, social relationships, and individual ability, motivation, and opportunity all play a role in knowledge management. "[S]ocial relationships provide individuals with the opportunity to create, retain, and transfer knowledge...and also provide individuals with the incentives to participate in the process" (p. 575). The future of global virtual teams depends, in part, on whether such teamwork is productive and sustainable. In a nutshell, if global virtual teams are to become an integral component of the global work environment, organizations need to understand the cultural complexities of such teams and provide the sociotechnical infrastructure, intercultural training, and support for team success.

REFERENCES

Allred, B., Snow, C., & Miles, R. (1996). Characteristics of managerial careers in the 21st century. *Academy of Management Executive, 10,* 17–27.

Anderson, F., & Shane, H. (2002). The impact of netcentricity on virtual teams: The new performance challenge. *Team Performance Management, 8*(1/2), 5–13.

Argote, L., McEvily, B., & Reagans, R. (2003). Managing knowledge in organizations: An integrative framework and review of emerging themes. *Management Science, 49,* 571–582.

Brake, T., Walker, D., & Walker, T. (1995). *Doing business internationally: The guide to cross-cultural success.* New York: Irwin.

Carmel, E. (1999). *Global software teams.* Upper Saddle River, NJ: Prentice Hall, Inc.

Chen, G., & Starosta, W. (1996). Intercultural communication competence: A synthesis. In B.R. Burleson, & A.W. Kunkel (Eds.), *Communication yearbook* (Vol. 19, pp. 353–383). Thousand Oaks, CA: Sage.

Cogburn, D., Zhang, L., & Khothule, M. (2002). Going global, locally: The socio-technical influences on performance in distributed collaborative learning teams. *ACM International Conference Proceedings Series,* South Africa, *30,* 52–64.
Crow, K. (1996). Enabling product development teams with collocation. Retrieved September 27, 2006, from http://www.npd-solutions.com/collocation.html
DeSanctis, G., & Poole, M. S. (1994). Capturing the complexity in advanced technology use: Adaptive structuration theory. *Organization Science,* 5,121–147.
Duarte, D., & Snyder, N. (1999). *Mastering virtual teams: Strategies, tools, and techniques that succeed.* San Francisco: Jossey-Bass.
Earley, P. (1989). Social loafing and collectivism: A comparison of the United States with the People's Republic of China. *Administrative Science Quarterly, 34,* 565–581.
Ellis, P., Hollenbeck, J., Ilgen, D., Porter, C., West, B., & Moon, H. (2003). Team learning: Collectively connecting the dots. *Journal of Applied Psychology, 5,* 821–835.
Erez, M., & Earley, P. C. (1987). Comparative analysis cultures. *Journal of Applied Psychology, 72*(44), 658–665.
Fukuyama, F. (1995). *Trust: The social virtues and the creation of prosperity.* New York: Free Press.
Galuppe, R., Cooper, W., Grise, M., & Bastianutti, L. (1994). Blocking electronic brainstorms. *Journal of Applied Psychology, 79,* 77–86.
Gibson, C., & Zellmer-Bruhn, M. (2001). Metaphor and meaning: An intercultural analysis of the concept of teamwork. *Administrative Science Quarterly, 46,* 274–303.
Goodbody, J. (2005). Critical success factors for global virtual teams. *Strategic Communication Management, 9,* 18–22.
Gudykunst, W. (1997). Cultural variability in communication. *Communication Research,* 24, 327–349.
Hall, E. (1976). *Beyond culture.* Garden City, NY: Anchor Press.
Hall, E. T., & Hall, M. R., (1990). *Understanding cultural differences: Germans, French, and Americans.* Intercultural Press.
Hellriegel, D., Slocum, J., Woodman, R. (2001). *Organizational Behavior* (9th ed.). Cincinnati: South Western.
Hofstede, G. (1980). *Culture's consequences.* Beverly Hills, CA: Sage.
Jackson, N., Aiken, M., Vanjani, M., & Hasan, B. (1995). Support group decisions via computer systems. *Quality Progress, 28,* 75–78.
Jarvenpaa, S., & Leidner, D. (1999). Communication and trust in global virtual teams. *Organizational Science, 10,* 791–815.
Jarvenpaa, S., Knoll, K., & Leidner, D. (1998). Is anybody out there? Antecedents of trust in global virtual teams. *Journal of Management Information Systems, 14*(4), 29–64.
Jarvenpaa, S. L., Shaw, T. R., & Staples, D. S. (2001). Toward contextualized theories of trust: The role of trust in global virtual teams. *Information Systems Research, 15*(3), 250–267.
Katzenbach, J. (2001). *The discipline of teams.* New York: John Wiley & Sons.
Katzenbach, J., & Smith, D. (1993, March/April). The discipline of teams. *Harvard Business Review,* 111–120.

Kayworth, D., & Leidner, D. (2001/2002). Leadership effectiveness in global virtual teams. *Journal of Management Information Systems, 18*(3), 7–41.

Kerber, K., & Buono, A. (2004). Intervening in virtual teams: Lessons from practice. In A. F. Buono (Ed.), *Creative consulting: Innovative perspectives on management consulting.* Greenwich, CT: Information Age Publishing.

Kerth, N. (2001). *Project retrospectives: A handbook for team reviews.* New York: Dorset House Publishing.

Kristof, A. L., Brown, K. G., Sims, H. P., Jr., & Smith, K. A. (1995). The virtual team: A case study and inductive model. In M. M. Beyerlein, D. A. Johnson, & S. T. Beyerlein (Eds.), *Advances in interdisciplinary studies of work teams: Knowledge work in teams* (Vol. 2, pp. 229–253). Greenwich, CT: JAI Press.

Lee, O. (2002). Cultural differences in e-mail use of virtual teams: A critical social theory perspective. *Cyberpsychology & Behavior,* 5(3), 227–232.

Lipnack, J., & Stamps, J. (1997). *Virtual teams: Reaching across space, time, and organizations with technology.* New York: John Wiley & Sons.

Mark, G., Grudin, J., & Poltrock, S. E. (1999). Meeting at the desktop: An empirical study of virtually collocated teams. In S. Bodker (Ed.), *ECSCW '99: The 6th European Conference on Computer Supported Cooperative Work* (pp. 159–178). New York: Kluwer Academic Publishers.

Massey, A., Montoya-Weiss, M., Hung, C., & Ramesh, V. (2001). Cultural perceptions of task-technology fit. *Communications of the ACM, 44*(12), 83–84.

Maznevski, M., & Chudoba, K. (2000). Bridging space over time: Global virtual-team dynamics and effectiveness. Organizational Science, *11,* 273–492.

McDonough, E., & Cedrone, D. (2000). Meeting the challenges of global team management. *Research Technology Management, 43*(4), 12–18.

Misiolek, N., & Heckman, R. (2005). *Patterns of emergent leadership in virtual teams.* Paper presented at the 38th Hawaii International Conference on System Sciences. Retrieved (September 2006), from http://www.hicss.hawaii.edu/home.htm

Montoya-Weiss, M., Massey, A., & Song, M. (2001). Getting it together: Temporal coordination and conflict management in global virtual teams. *Academy of Management Journal, 44,* 1251–1262.

Nelson, R., & Winter, S. (1982). *An evolutionary theory of economic hange.* Cambridge, MA: Harvard University Press.

Nunamaker, J., Jr., Briggs, R. O., Romano, N., Jr., & Mittleman, D. (1997). The virtual office workspace: Group systems web and case studies. In D. Coleman (Ed.), *Groupware: Collaboration strategies for corporate LANs and Intranets.* Upper Saddle River, NJ: Prentice Hall.

Pillai, R., & Meindl, J. R. (1998). Context and charisma: A meso level approach to the relationship of organic structure, collectivism, and crisis to charismatic leadership. *Journal of Management, 24*(5), 643–671.

Pauleen, J. (2003). An inductively derived model of leader initiated relationship building in virtual teams. J*ournal of Management Information Systems, 20*(3), 227–256.

Polanyi, M. (1966). *The tacit dimension.* Garden City, NY: Doubleday.

Pollard, C. (1996). Electronic meeting systems: Specifications, potential, and acquisition strategies. *Journal of Systems Management, 47,* 22–38.

Potter, R., & Balthazard, P. A. (2002). Understanding human interactions and performance in the virtual team. *Journal of Information Technology Theory & Application, 4,* 1–23.

Prasad, K., & Akhilesh, K. (2002). Global virtual teams: What impacts their design and performance? *Team Performance Management, 8*(5/6), 102–113.

Robbins, S. P. (2003). *Organizational Behavior.* (10th Ed.) Upper Saddle River, NJ: Prentice Hall.

Rogers, E., & Albritton, M. (1995). Interactive communication technologies in business organizations. *Journal of Business Communication, 32*(2), 177.

Scott, J. (2000). Facilitating interorganizational learning with information technology. *Journal of Management Information Systems, 2,* 81–113.

Sole, D., & Edmondson, A. (2002). Situated knowledge and learning in dispersed teams. *British Journal of Management, 13,* 17–34.

Sundstrom, E., McIntyre, M., Halfhill, T., & Richards, H. (2000). Work groups: From the Hawthorne studies to work teams of the 1990s and beyond. *Group Dynamics, 4,* 44–67.

Thomas, J., Kellogg, W., & Erickson, T. (2001). The knowledge management puzzle: Human and social factors in knowledge management. *IBM Systems Journal, 40*(4), 863–884.

Thomsett, R. (2002). *Radical project management.* Upper Saddle River, NJ: Prentice Hall.

Triandis, H. C. (1972). *The analysis of subjective culture.* New York: Wiley-Interscience.

Triandis, H. C. (1995). *Individualism & collectivism.* Boulder, CO: Westview Press.

Venkatesh, V., Morris, M., Davis, G., & Davis, F. (2003). User acceptance of information technology: Toward a unified view. *MIS Quarterly, 27*(3), 425–478.

Warekentin, M., Sayeed, L., & Hightower, R. (1997). Virtual teams versus face-to-face teams: An exploratory study of a Web-based conference system. *Decision Sciences, 28*(4), 975–996.

Weiss, H. (1990). Learning theory and industrial and organizational psychology. In M. Dunnette, & L. Hough (Eds.), *Handbook of industrial and organizational psychology* (2nd ed., pp. 171–221). Palo Alto, CA: Consulting Psychologists Press.

Wheatley, K. K., & Wilemon, D. (1999). *Global innovation teams: A requirement for the new millennium.* Paper presented at the International Conference on the Management of Engineering & Technology Management (PICMET), Portland, OR.

Yoo, Y., & Alavi, M. (2002). Electronic mail usage pattern of emergent leaders in distributed teams. *Sprouts: Working papers on information environments, systems, and organizations, 3*(3), 140–159.

Zakaria, N. (2000). The effects of cross-cultural training in the process of acculturation of the global workforce. *International Journal of Manpower, 21*(6), 492–510.

Zakaria, N. (2006). *Culture matters?: The impact of context on globally distributed civil society decision making processes during WSIS.* Unpublished doctoral dissertation, Syracuse University, Syracuse, NY.

Zakaria, N., Amelinckx, A., & Wilemon, D. (2004). Working together apart? Building a knowledge-sharing culture for global virtual teams. *Creativity and Innovation Management, 13*(1), 15–29.

CHAPTER

9

The Leader's Role in Group Learning

STEPHEN J. ZACCARO
George Mason University

KATHERINE ELY
George Mason University

MARISSA SHUFFLER
University of North Carolina, Charlotte

Several realities confront today's organizations that heighten the need for group-level continuous learning. First, as many researchers have noted (e.g., Devine, Clayton, Philips, Dunford, & Melner, 1999; Ilgen, 1999; Guzzo, 1995; Sundstrom, McIntyre, Halfhill, & Richards, 2000), groups have been assigned a greater share of work in organizations. Most organizational tasks have grown in complexity (Katzenbach & Smith, 1999), incorporating more sophisticated technology, becoming more diverse in functional requirements, requiring greater information processing, and accordingly, straining the capacities of any individual to complete them. Thus, organizations have determined that more team-based organizational structures provide an effective response to this increased complexity (Ellis et al., 2003; Katzenbach & Smith, 1999). Along this line, Stagl, Burke, Salas, and Pierce (2006) noted, "teams are ubiquitous in modern organizations because they can be used to create synergies, streamline workflow, deliver innovative services, satisfy incumbent needs, maximize the benefits of technology connecting distributed employees, and seize market opportunities in a global village" (p. 117). This means, however, that work-related learning must also occur more often at the group level (Argote, Gruenfeld, & Naquin, 2001).

The dynamic nature of today's operating environment for organizational work groups presents a second reality driving the need for group learning (Argote et al., 2001; Bunderson & Sutcliffe, 2003). Today's work environment is quicker to change and often presents new and different kinds of challenges to work incumbents (Kozlowski & Ilgen, in press; Kozlowski, Gully, Nason, & Smith, 1999). This pace and degree of change, in turn, renders existing knowledge and skills more quickly obsolete. Also, the boundaries of work have extended globally, and the teams that are completing this work have members who are often geographically dispersed (Sessa & London, 2006; Jarvenpaa & Leidner, 1999). The globally dispersed and dynamic aspects of current organizational environments present requirements for tactical and strategic adaptation (Pulakos, Arad, Donovan, & Plamondon, 2000), where individuals and teams need to combine existing knowledge structures in novel ways and develop innovative solutions to changing problems (Smith, Ford, & Kozlowski, 1997). Such adaptive problem solving thrives more successfully in a psychologically safe environment (Edmondson, 1999) that encourages continuous exploration and learning (Ilgen, Hollenbeck, Johnson, & Jundt, 2005). Also, organizations may respond to such environmental dynamism and skill obsolescence by creating temporary project teams composed of members with the individual skills to address rising challenges (Sundstrom et al., 2000). Ellis et al. (2003) noted that because members of such teams move repeatedly to different tasks, often involving unfamiliar components, they need to engage in continuous learning. For more permanent teams, organizations can respond to organizational dynamism by replacing particular team members with new members possessing updated skills (Klimoski & Zukin, 1999). However, these members then need to help the team collectively acquire new understandings.

These realities of organizational life indicate that to gain and retain competitive advantage, organizations need to adopt policies that encourage a continuous training and learning environment (Sessa & London, 2006), particularly at the group level (Ellis et al., 2003). Group learning can be construed as more difficult than individual learning because it involves both individual and shared cognitive and social processes (Van den Bossche, Segers, & Kirschner, 2006). According to Van den Bossche et al. (2006), collaborative learning entails the integration of individual knowledge structures, experiences, and perspectives into a coherent shared understanding, as well as a "social context that nourishes the willingness to engage in the (joint) effort to build and maintain mutually shared cognition" (p. 493). Accordingly, in creating an effective group-learning environment, organizations need to facilitate and enable both of these social and cognitive processes within and across group members.

Organizational leadership represents a critical parameter that can leverage effective group learning (Bunderson & Sutcliffe, 2003). At the team or group level, leadership processes act as important drivers of collective effectiveness (Zaccaro, Rittman, & Marks, 2001; Burke et al., 2006). Zaccaro et al. argued that leadership activities influence cognitive, motivational, affective, and coordination processes within the team, which in turn influence several indicators of team performance. The primary role of team leadership is to foster the integration of individual member resources and capabilities that creates the most effective *synergy* for maximum team performance (Zaccaro, Heinen, & Shuffler, in press; Zaccaro et al., 2001). An extension of this argument suggests, then, that in team-learning situations, leaders need to foster the synergistic processes that maximize collective learning. Along these lines, Kozlowski and his colleagues have argued that team leaders serve an additional function—to engage team-performance regulation processes (goal setting, performance monitoring, feedback, goal-strategy adjustment) and help teams develop task-related capabilities pertaining to different parts of the team task cycle (Kozlowski, Gully, McHugh, Salas, & Cannon-Bowers, 1996; Kozlowski, Gully, Salas, & Cannon-Bowers, 1996). Team leaders also shift developmental roles at different phases of a group's tenure (Kozlowski, Gully, Salas, et al., 1996). These perspectives highlight the role of leadership processes in group learning.

While a number of other researchers have alluded to the importance of organizational and team leadership processes for effective group learning (e.g., Black, Oliver, Howell, & King, 2005; Edmondson, 2003; Tannenbaum, Smith-Jentsch, & Behson, 1998; Vera & Crossan, 2004), there has not been a systematic summary and integration of these contributions. Further, some researchers have noted the relative lack of research on the precise means by which leadership contributes to group learning. For example, Vera and Crossan (2004) noted, "researchers have not delineated the specific behaviors and mechanisms through which leaders impact learning" (p. 222). Bunderson and Sutcliffe (2003) also called for more research and understanding into how leaders influence the specific processes of team learning. The purpose of this chapter is to provide a framework that summarizes and integrates various contributions in the literature and specifies several means by which team leaders determine and facilitate processes of collective and collaborative learning.

In the next section of this chapter, we examine three different definitional perspectives of group learning. The particular perspective that is adopted influences how one specifies the central pathways by which a leader can influence group learning. Rather than endorsing one perspective, we will describe each of these pathways. Then, in the subsequent sections of the chapter, we examine three sets of leadership activities that are purported to facilitate team learning. The first set refers to the development of a learning climate within the team (Bunderson & Sutcliffe, 2003; Edmondson, 1999). The second refers to the development of individual and team-level learning tools that enable group learning (Day, Gronn, & Salas, 2004; Kozlowksi, Gully, Salas, et al., 1996; Zaccaro et al., in press). The third set refers to the leader's actions as a learning partner (Edmondson, 2003; Hackman & Wageman, 2005).

DEFINITIONS OF GROUP LEARNING

Considerable ambiguity exists in the extant literature regarding the definition of group learning (Wilson, Goodman, & Cronin, in press). Specifically, a survey of this literature yields three distinct, although related, perspectives. First, group learning has been defined by some as a process by which individual team members gain new understandings and knowledge, and share these gains with the group as a whole (Ellis et al., 2003; Wilson et al., in press). Group learning occurs when this sharing produces an expansion of the group's behavioral capabilities (Wilson et al., in press). Note that there are three components to this collective learning process: (a) individuals gain new skills, knowledge, and understanding; (b) these individuals share that learning with other team members; and (c) the sharing process results in the group changing its shared knowledge states and potential behavior patterns. For example, Ellis et al. (2003) noted that "any conceptualization of the learning at the team level needs to include each team member's ability to individually acquire knowledge and skill as well as their ability to collectively share that information with their teammates" (pp. 821–822). A similar process can occur when new members rotate through the team. Such "itinerant group members" (Gruenfeld, Martorana, & Fan, 2000, p. 46) can influence group learning by bringing new expertise into the group and sharing it with existing members, or by changing how the group is framing or thinking about existing group problems (Gruenfeld et al., 2000; Van der Vegt & Bunderson, 2005); the latter effect may simply take the form of having new members prompt existing members to consciously reevaluate habitual ways of solving group problems (Louis & Sutton, 1991).

Two key implications become apparent in this perspective of group learning. First, the process of group learning can break down at any of its three phases—individuals may fail to learn (or not bring any new expertise to the team), they may fail to share it with the team, and team as a whole may not learn from the experiences of particular individuals. Arguably, then, to foster effective group learning, leaders need to attend to all three parts of this process. However, the second implication defines the quality of this learning, or key linking pin which alters it from an individual to a group process, as being essentially reflected in the process of *sharing* new knowledge (Wilson et al., in press). Accordingly, while leaders can influence group learning through any of the three aforementioned stages, perhaps the most critical of interventions may be to facilitate the sharing process.

The aforementioned perspective of group learning emphasizes a process of individuals gaining a full understanding of a task, situation, event, or problem and then conveying that learning to other team members. However, a second and slightly different perspective examines group learning as deriving from the collective or synergistic information processing that occurs as a group acquires new understanding or knowledge (Day et al., 2004; Hinsz, Tindale, & Vollrath, 1997; Kayes, Kayes, & Kolb, 2005). The emphasis of this approach is clearly on the group as a whole working through the processes of learning as they seek to evaluate and understand shared experiences. Learning may still begin at the level of individuals providing information, but these are only pieces of the larger understanding needed for the group to be effective. This full understanding, or emergent knowledge state (Marks, Mathieu, & Zaccaro, 2001), occurs after members interact and integrate their individual, and incomplete, pieces of information. Thus, the learning process occurs at the group level, entirely through group member interaction.

The key to this perspective of group learning lies in the collective information processing members engage in to acquire new knowledge and understanding. Edmondson (1999) characterized this form of collective learning:

> as an ongoing process of reflection and action, characterized by asking questions, seeking feedback, experimenting, reflecting on results, and discussing errors or unexpected outcomes of actions. For a team to discover gaps in its plans and make changes accordingly, team members must test assumptions and discuss differences of opinions openly rather than privately or outside the group. (p. 353)

Note that the emphasis is on knowledge gains that derive from joint or collaborative learning activities. As in the first perspective of group learning, member sharing is important to the learning process. However, the key aspect of this perspective is that members must overtly engage in behavioral activities that are necessary for all to gain new understanding. Accordingly, from this perspective the most crucial leadership task may be to provide members with the tools to engage in such interactive learning processes, and providing a safe climate (Edmondson, 1999) to use these tools.

The third perspective of group learning emphasizes group members learning how to work with one another (Kozlowski, Gully, Salas, et al., 1996; London, Polzer, & Omoregie, 2005; Sessa & London, 2006: Vera & Crossan, 2004). Sessa and London (2006) noted, "group members need to learn to be a group—that is, move from a collective of individuals to a cohesive unit focused on the same goals and understanding the methods of achieving those goals. The group needs to learn how to structure itself, communicate, conduct work processes, make decisions, and put these decisions into action" (p. 2). Thus, this form of group learning emphasizes that individual members must learn how to work collaboratively. Indeed, Kayes et al. (2005) defined team learning in part as "the ability of individual team members to learn teamwork skills" (p. 330).

The central learning task in this perspective, reflecting several models of group development (Gersick, 1988; Tuckman, 1965), is members learning how to substitute individual forms of action for collective or collaborative ones (Kayes et al., 2005). Such individuals need to learn *teamwork* as well as *task work* skills (Salas, Dickinson, Converse, & Tannebaum, 1992; Salas, Sims, & Burke, 2005). The primary responsibility for team leaders in such group learning, then, is to promote the learning of teamwork and help members form an effective and integrated unit (Zaccaro et al., 2001).

While we have delineated three distinct group-learning perspectives in the literature, they can be entwined as reflecting the various forms of learning occurring at different points in the group's cycles of development, learning, and performance. These forms arguably work reciprocally in both a sequential and integrated fashion, occurring within and across team members (Ellis et al., 2003). Thus, the formative stages of group development, where members learn how to become a cohesive group and work well together can also entail the development of group norms that foster collective learning processes. These might include norms for openness in group conversation as well as for constructive cognitive conflict without such exchanges becoming affective conflict (Amason, 1996; Amason & Sapienza, 1997; Edmondson, 2003; Ellis et al., 2003). Such norms and developmental processes may increase the likelihood that individuals will seek opportunities to learn more on behalf of group goals (e.g., a team-learning orientation; Bunderson & Sutcliffe, 2003), and share acquired knowledge with other group members. Finally, a collective-learning orientation coupled with a group environment that encourages discovery learning should result in members exploring, questioning, reflecting upon, and debating new ideas and concepts (Edmondson, 1999). Such an environment makes it easier for new members to bring new expertise and ideas to the group and for existing members to share new insights and discoveries with other group members. Thus, the norms and collective-learning orientations that are established as the group forms can influence both the likelihood that individual members will seek new understandings and expertise on behalf of the group, and that the group as a whole can engage successfully in synergistic learning processes. Likewise, the act of individuals sharing their own expertise with the rest of the group will be facilitated by groups who can collectively engage and explore this new understanding. And the successful learning accomplishments from these experiences, in turn, foster group learning norms and prescriptions.

Thus, group learning should be construed as a multifaceted, multi-componential, and continuous process that changes in quality at different stages of group development and action. This means that leadership processes can influence group learning through myriad pathways. We propose that group leaders engage in three sets of activities that encourage and promote collaborative learning in teams and groups. These are (a) developing, promoting, and maintaining a learning climate within the team; (b) helping members develop and use particular learning tools, both individually and collectively; and (c) acting as learning partners for group members at different stages of group development, learning, and performance. Fig. 9.1 provides a summary of these leadership activities and their influences on different forms of group learning. We describe these activities in more detail in the next sections of this chapter.

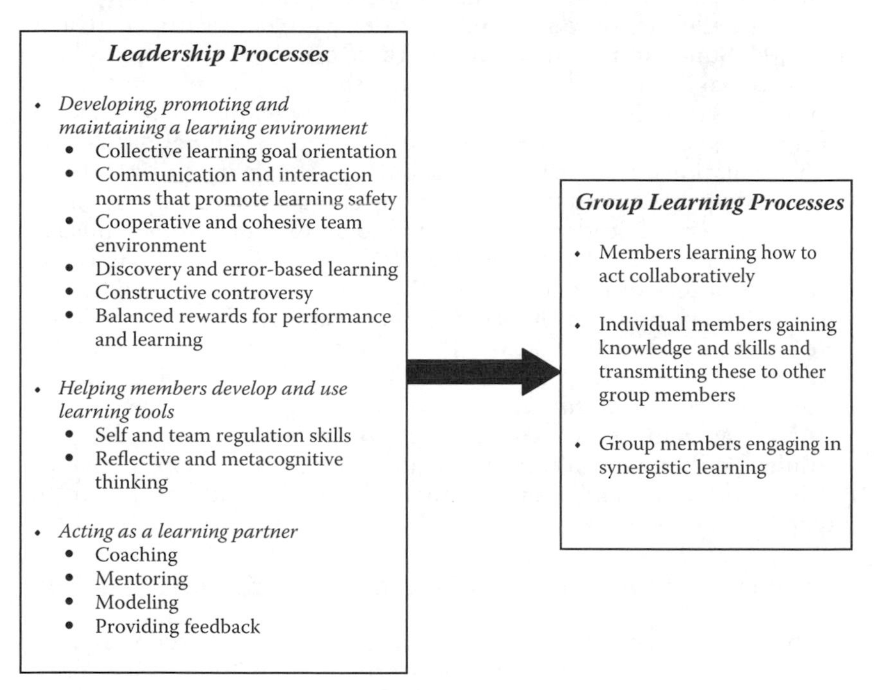

Figure 9.1 A simplified model of leadership and group learning.

GROUP LEADERSHIP PROCESSES AND GROUP LEARNING

The role of leadership in group learning can be specified from the conceptual framework of the functional leadership perspective (Hackman & Walton, 1986). This perspective argues that team leaders are responsibile for creating, fostering, and maintaining the conditions for teams and groups to function effectively (Fleishman et al., 1991; Hackman, 2002; Hackman & Walton, 1986; Lord, 1977; Mumford, Zaccaro, Harding, Jacobs, & Fleishman, 2000; Roby, 1961; Zaccaro et al., 2001). Mumford et al. (2000; see also Fleishman et al., 1991; Zaccaro et al., 2001) described functional leadership as a problem-solving process entailing the diagnosis of team problems and the generation and implementation of team solutions. As team environments become more dynamic and complex, such problem solving would necessarily entail more creative and novel solution formulation and correspondingly increased needs for effective and creative group learning (Basadur, 2004). However, even in more routine (or at least less dynamic) contexts, resolving existing team problems may require an infusion of new expertise into a team, requiring a reshuffling of existing team membership, or even the creation and staffing of a smaller, more specialized temporary project team (e.g., Day et al., 2004; Sundstrom et al., 2000). In these contexts, the responsibility of functional leaders will be to foster the sharing of new expertise that can lead to group learning, or in the case of new teams, to facilitate the emergence and maintenance of an effective learning climate.

The functional leadership approach does not specify a particular set of leadership behaviors that are appropriate across all team-problem situations. Instead, leaders are expected to do "what *needs to be done* for effective performance" (Hackman & Walton, 1986, p. 77), giving rise to a large variety of leadership functions that would be defined by the details of team problem situations (Hackman & Walton, 1986; Mumford, 1986; Zaccaro et al., 2001). By the same argument, functional leadership in collective-learning contexts would entail doing *whatever needs to be done for effective learning* within the group. As shown in Fig. 9.1, the leadership functions that are largely required for most group learning would be facilitating a learning climate, developing collaborative learning tools, and acting as learning partners and enablers in the group learning process.

Developing, Promoting, and Maintaining a Learning Climate

Establishing a learning climate may begin with the attitudes and values regarding learning that members bring to the group. Goal orientation represents a key belief system that influences how individuals respond to learning situations (Dweck, 1986; Elliott & Dweck, 1988). A *learning* goal orientation reflects an emphasis on gaining new competencies and demonstrating mastery of new tasks (Bell & Kozlowski, 2002; Dweck, 1986; Porter, 2005). Individuals with a high learning goal orientation believe that "ability is malleable and can be developed with effort, practice, or both" (Porter, 2005, p. 811). Accordingly, they will react favorably to and exert strong effort and persistence in situations that provide opportunities to learn new skills and abilities (Bell & Kozlowski, 2002; Sessa & London, 2006). A *performance* goal orientation reflects an emphasis on demonstrating competence, being evaluated positively by others, and avoiding failure (Bell & Kozlowski, 2002; Bunderson & Sutcliffe, 2003; Porter, 2005; Sessa & London, 2006). Individuals with a high-performance orientation tend to believe that ability is relatively unchanging and "often see little utility in devoting effort on tasks in which they perceive they have low levels of ability" (Porter, 2005, p. 811; see also Dweck, 1986; Sessa & London, 2006).

These differences suggest that groups composed mostly of members holding high levels of learning goal orientation are likely to appreciate and nourish a learning climate than groups composed of members with a high performance goal orientation (Bunderson & Sutcliffe, 2003; DeShon, Kozlowski, Schmidt, Milner, & Wiechmann, 2004; Porter, 2005). Although empirical research on group-level goal orientation is fairly limited, recent studies have shown that an aggregated learning-goal orientation in teams has resulted in more backing-up behavior in teams (Porter, 2005), where members monitor and correct errors by other members (Marks et al., 2001; Porter, 2005; Hollenbeck, Ilgen, Ellis, West, & Moon, 2003), better performance (although, up to a point of decreasing returns; Bunderson & Sutcliffe, 2003), and greater efficacy and commitment regarding the team task (Porter, 2005).

Because goal orientation represents a fairly stable individual difference (Dweck, 1986), leaders will likely have little success in altering it in individual group members. However, group leaders can influence the collective-learning climate by staffing the group with members who have displayed behaviors and attitudes denoting a learning goal orientation rather than a performance one. Also, group leaders can provide cues that a learning orientation would be emphasized or rewarded in a particular team context, raising the likelihood that members will pursue individual and collaborative learning (Bunderson & Sutcliffe, 2003). Thus, the leader's establishment of a learning climate within teams begins with the staffing of the team with individuals possessing high learning goal orientations, and signaling that the team's environment will be conducive to such an orientation.

Part of this signaling process entails establishing communication and interaction norms that promote a noncritical exchange of ideas, comments, and observations. At the onset of collaborative action, and indeed through most of a team's tenure, team members generally display a reluctance to "speak up" even when such interaction is crucial for the success and actual survival of the team (Edmondson, 2003). Indeed, several studies have documented tragic consequences of members failing to voice alarms or concerns as groups hurtle toward a destructive end (Prince, Chidester, Bowers, & Cannon-Bowers, 1992; Weick, 1993). Edmondson (2003) noted that leaders can coach more speaking-up behavior in teams engaged in learning by minimizing perceived power differences in groups and delivering the message that members' input is "explicitly needed and desired by others" (p. 1424). In groups with strong power differentials, low-power members may feel inhibited and threatened for speaking up. Leaders can address such inhibitions by noting the need for feedback from everyone in the team, rewarding such behavior, and not judging or punishing even those speaking-up behaviors that do not appear to advance team goals. Edmondson found that when leaders encourage such speaking-up behaviors in interdisciplinary action teams, the results lead to successful implementation of new technology and innovative practices.

Because speaking up can be interpersonally threatening, especially when the input includes critical commentary or the admission of errors and possibly failure, leaders need to establish a "psychologically safe" climate (Edmondson, 1999) for such communications. Edmondson (1999) defined team psychological safety as "a shared belief that the team is safe for interpersonal risk taking" (p. 354). Note that such beliefs represent a team-level construct, with strong homogeneity across team members, and characterizing part of the team climate that is transmitted to new members. Edmondson also noted, "team psychological safety should facilitate learning behavior in work teams because it alleviates excessive concern about others' reactions that have the potential for embarrassment or threat, which learning behaviors often have" (p. 355).

Because of these learning advantages, and because of the leaders' high salience to other team members, they have the responsibility of establishing a psychologically safe environment for group learning (Edmondson, 1999). We have noted how the leader can encourage speaking-up behavior by rewarding it and emphasizing the need for it. Psychological safety pertains more specifically to the content of voice, particularly when such content is critical or risky. Accordingly, the leader needs to coach and encourage such content, placing a positive value on risky interpersonal content, even when it may be directed at the team leaders or central team goals. Indeed, Edmondson (1999; Edmondson, Bohmer, & Pisano, 2001a) found that leader encouragement and coaching fostered team safety, which, in turn, increased the incidents of such team learning behaviors as seeking feedback and discussing errors.

Encouraging psychological safety as part of the context for effective group learning highlights the importance of "constructive controversy" (Ellis et al., 2003; Tjosvold & Deemer, 1980) and "cognitive conflict" (Amason, 1996). A vibrant atmosphere for group learning should entail a vigorous exchange of different ideas and perspectives, especially in teams where members bring diverse functional expertise to the table (Bunderson & Sutcliffe, 2002; Van der Vegt & Bunderson, 2005; Murray, 1989). In fact, Van der Vegt and Bunderson (2005) noted, "scholars have long recognized that exposure to individuals with different expertise, knowledge and experience is a key source of individual and collective learning. Interaction with dissimilar others promotes learning and innovation by exposing individuals to new paradigms and perspectives and by enabling (and often requiring) the cross-fertilization of ideas" (p. 534; see also Ellis et al., 2003, p. 823). However, the task of the team leader is to ensure that such cognitive conflict does not become affective conflict. Amason (1996) defined cognitive conflict as "generally task-oriented and focused on judgmental differences about how best to achieve common objectives" (p. 127). Affective conflict "tends to be emotional and focused on personal incompatibilities or disputes" (Amason, 1996, p. 129). Such conflict does not have to occur across all members of the team to be corrosive. If the exchange of different ideas leads to acrimony and personal conflict between just two team members, the overall psychological safety of the group's climate is impaired. Also, to the degree both members are prominent in the structure of the team, such conflict can result in coalitions forming around each member and the eventual psychological splintering of the team.

Research has suggested several means by which leaders can retain cognitive conflict without it degenerating into affective conflict. One is to maintain a "superordinate perspective" where the emphasis is always on cooperation and the larger team goals (Sherif & Sherif, 1953; Tjosvold & Deemer, 1980). Indeed, in one experiment, Tjosvold and Deemer (1980) noted that when norms were created that stated team members should "confront their differences squarely, pursue mutual benefits, and avoid trying to 'win'" (p. 591), these norms produced better acceptance of counterarguments and more decisions that integrated different ideas and perspectives than norms in which team members were to try and win arguments. Indeed, the "constructive" forms of controversy "induced security, expectations of assistance and openness toward the discussion" (Tjosvold & Deemer, 1980, p. 593), in other words, greater psychological safety. Thus, an emphasis on mutual gain and superordinate goals can allow constructive conflict in group-learning situations without fostering competitive and destructive arguments.

Leaders can also foster constructive controversy by developing the collective identification and cohesiveness of the team. Van der Vegt and Bunderson (2005) found that in multidisciplinary teams, *collective team commitment,* defined as "the emotional significance that members in a social group attach to their membership in that group" (p. 533), inverted the relationships between expertise diversity and team-learning behavior and performance, respectively. When collective identification was high, team-learning behaviors and performance were highest at moderate levels of expertise diversity—too much diversity or too little reduced team learning. Group cohesion, a construct similar to collective-team identification, should also reduce the likelihood of cognitive exchanges leading to acrimony. Cohesion has been defined as the members' attraction and desire to remain in the group (Cartwright, 1968; Festinger, 1950)—the stronger the group's cohesion, the more members want to belong to the group, and the more disconcerting is the possibility of being removed from the group. Accordingly, group cohesion can restrain members from moving cognitive conflict into personal acrimony. However, as the "groupthink" literature suggests (Janis, 1972), group cohesion is not sufficient because it can reduce the likelihood that members will exchange differing ideas. Accordingly, leaders need to build up both the cohesion of the group and the norms for perspective sharing and idea exchange. Indeed, to the degree that such norms become integral to the group, as they often do in effective learning groups, greater cohesion increases the likelihood that members will adhere to these prescriptions (Festinger, 1950).

In sum, establishing a learning climate that promotes a safe exchange of ideas represents a prime means by which leaders foster effective group learning. However, two caveats must be considered. First, leaders need to ensure that the learning climate does not constrain or interfere with the group's performance effectiveness. Bunderson and Sutcliffe (2003) reported that an overemphasis on learning can result in at best diminishing gains in performance efficiency, and losses in teams that are already performing well. They argued,

> Team leaders face at least two significant challenges in attempting to manage a team's learning orientation. First they much determine how strongly to emphasize learning.... Second, team leaders must understand the symbolic, structural , demographic and processual levels that affect a team's learning orientation, and be able to use these levels to maintain an appropriate emphasis on learning with the team. (p. 559)

Thus, team leaders need to very carefully manage the learning climate of the team. Another caveat, however, is that, even with the existence of an appropriate learning climate, members must have the tools necessary to engage in effective learning. Team leaders can help members gain and use these tools.

Helping Members Develop and Use Learning Tools

Several learning tools, when used collaboratively, can enhance potential gains from group learning exercises. The learning process begins with an assessment of one's strengths and weaknesses in order to identify learning or training goals (Goldstein & Ford, 2002; London & Smither, 1999; London, 2002). These goals become the basis for establishing learning strategies and monitoring these strategies to assess learning progress. Thus, *self-regulation processes* become an important tool in any learning exercise, especially those that are informal or self-directed (Cortina et al., 2004; London, 2002; Sessa & London, 2006). Accordingly, Sessa and London (2006) noted, "self-regulated learners structure their environment to be conducive to learning, set goals, and plans, seek needed information, organize and transform the information, rehearse and memorize, keep records of their performance, and monitor others reactions to them" (p. 56). Effective self-regulation in learning domains requires accurate self-information stemming from skill in conducting self-appraisals, an ability to establish and use appropriate learning standards, skill in establishing appropriate learning curricula, a monitoring capacity that provides accurate assessments of environmental events and personal goal progress, and the willingness and ability to switch learning goal strategies when existing ones are yielding insufficient progress (Cortina et al., 2004; London, 2002).

For group learning, similar processes need to occur collaboratively among team members. A few studies have examined *collective regulation,* or the extension of self-regulation activities to the group or team level (e.g., DeShon et al., 2004; Prussia & Kinicki, 1996; for a review, see Kozlowski & Ilgen, in press). Kane, Zaccaro, Tremble, and Masuda (2002) examined the leader's use of regulation processes on behalf of the group. Thus, a team leader established team goals and goal strategies and was primarily responsible for monitoring and adjusting team goal progress. Day et al. (2004) noted, however, that when team members rely too much on individual leaders to provide goals and solutions, particularly in complex situations requiring adaptation and learning, they "may not be able to learn or lead collectively with any consistency or effectiveness" (p. 872). Thus, the readiness of team members to engage in collective learning may rest on their aggregate ability to define their own learning goals and strategies and monitor their own learning progress. Their capacity to use collective regulation processes in the context of learning would enhance their adaptive capabilities. Indeed, Day et al. noted,"having the collective capacity to face an adaptive challenge in an open and learning-oriented manner broadens the resources of the team, which should contribute to greater adaptability and effectiveness" (p. 873).

This recommendation does not obviate the leaders from having a role in collective regulation. As members of the group, they contribute to collaborative regulatory processes. However, their prime role may be in helping members develop norms and procedures for collective regulation early in the group's formation, and coaching these activities throughout their subsequent learning and performance activities. Kozlowski and his colleagues (1999; Kozlowski, Gully, McHugh, et al., 1996; Kozlowski, Gully, Salas, et al., 1996) noted that in team learning and team training, as the process of skill acquisition moves to demonstration of performance skills, leaders have the responsibility of helping teams acquire self-regulation and self-management capabilities. They argued that leaders help teams develop coherence, defined as the "sharing, compatibility, and alignment of affect and knowledge—skill across individual team members" (Kozlowski, 1999, p. 134), by fostering a learning cycle that is synchronized with team action cycles. The learning cycle includes the steps in collective regulation—setting learning objectives and strategies, monitoring team behavior and progress, diagnosing errors, and using process feedback to make adjustments (Kozlowski, 1999; Kozlowski, Gully, Salas, et al., 1996). Kozlowski and colleagues argued that leaders engage in defining learning goals and goal strategies. During high-intensity phases, the leader is monitoring and diagnosing learning errors and failures. Afterwards, during another low-intensity phase, the leader uses process feedback ("how to" rather then "how well"; Kozlowski,

1998, p. 135) to guide the team in a reflective analysis of the learning and performance errors. Kozlowski (1998) noted, "Although the leader guides this process, *it is the team and its members who must diagnosis the reasons for their lack of mastery* [italics added]" (p. 135). Thus, the leader has the role of fostering collective regulatory learning processes in the team. As the team learns to collectively set learning objectives and diagnosis learning errors through several learning cycles, these activities are likely to become part of the normative structure and basis for coherence within the team—the team has acquired for effective tools to engage in collective learning.

Another learning tool that is also part of this process needs to be especially highlighted—*metacognitive thinking.* Metacognition refers to a process of reflecting upon one's own cognitive processes and approaches to decision making and problem solving (Flavell, 1979; Davidson, Deuser, & Sternberg, 1994). Some researchers have specified a collective form of metacognitive that occurs within and across team members. Hinsz et al. (1997) defined such thinking as "what group members know about the way groups process information" (p. 58). Zaccaro et al (2001) suggested that such metacognition "refers to individual and collective reflection upon how members constructed team problems, evaluated possible solutions, and implemented selected solutions" (p. 360). They also argued that while metacognitive thinking occurs within individual team members, it also appears in the interactions among team members. For example, such thinking is represented when individual members verbalize how the team as a whole is thinking about or approaching a problem ("We seem to defining the problem this way—Is that correct?"), and other members overtly reflect upon these observations. Edmondson (1999) included such reflection as a key part of group-level learning. Team leaders can foster the development of such thinking as a learning tool when early in the team's tenure, or during the low-intensity action phases noted by Kozlowski (1998; Kozlowski, Gully, Salas, et al., 1996), they prompt the team to reconsider how members are processing information during both team learning and team action. Again, as teams become familiar with such thinking, it becomes part of the normative team processes that guide subsequent team learning and performance.

Acting as Learning Partners

In this chapter, we have noted how leaders need to act as coaches to help establish a psychologically safe environment for learning exploration and to help team members learn how to collectively regulate their learning progress. In this section, we want to elaborate on this leadership role, and describe ways leaders can serve as learning partners and enablers for collaborative learning. Specifically, group leaders can act as models, mentors, and coaches at various stages of the collaborative learning process (cf. Kozlowski, Gully, Salas, et al., 2006). Most of all, leaders enable group learning by providing feedback at these different stages.

Early in the group's tenure, members are learning how to work and learn collaboratively (Kozlowski, Gully, Salas, et al., 1996; Tuckman, 1965). At this stage, team leaders can effectively enable early learning by modeling several of the behaviors that need to become learning norms within the group. Along this line, Edmondson (1999) noted, "team leaders themselves can engage in learning behaviors, demonstrating the appropriateness of and lack of punishment for [interpersonal] risks [associated with learning]" (p. 356). Thus, leaders can demonstrate the kind of exploration and reflective thinking necessary for effective learning. They can model use of self- and team-regulation processes and ask team members for input to facilitate monitoring processes, conveying an atmosphere of openness and safety (Day et al., 2004; Edmondson, Bohmer, & Pisano, 2001a). Leaders can model the types of communication norms necessary for learning by reacting nondefensively to questions and challenges posed by other team members (Edmondson, 1999), and by supportively inviting responses to such questions by others (Edmondson et al., 2001a). In addition, Basadur (2004) noted that leaders can model "open-minded thinking" (p. 107) that fosters group-level creativity, and the active exploration of new and innovative ideas. Edmondson, Bohmer, and Pisano (2001b) also suggested that leaders can indicate their own need for learning by conveying their own mistakes and errors to the team (called the "fallibility model," p. 132; see also Tannenbaum, Smith-Jentsch, & Behson, 1998). In this way, they model the initial stages of self-regulated learning by engaging in self-appraisal and establishing learning objectives.

Several researchers have noted the importance of leaders acting as mentors and coaches during group-learning processes (Edmondson, 1999, 2003; Hackman & Wageman, 2005; Koslowski, Gully, Salas, et al. 1996). Hackman and Wageman (2005) defined three different forms of leadership coaching—(a) motivational coaching, (b) consultative coaching, and (c) educational coaching (p. 273). The latter form of coaching, defined in part as directed toward the "development of members' knowledge and skills" (p. 273), appears most closely linked to group learning. However, we would argue that the effects of team leadership in group learning, as modeled in Fig. 9.1, would also implicate the other two forms of coaching as well for different types of group learning. According to Hackman and Wageman (2005), motivational coaching is intended to "minimize free-riding or 'social loafing' and to build shared committed to the group and its work" (p. 273). Such coaching should increase the effort members will contribute to group learning. Also, recall that constructive controversy is more likely to occur in groups whose members identify with and are commitment to the group (Ellis et al., 2003; Tjosvold & Deemer, 1980). Thus, this form of coaching that is likely to produce such commitment facilitates the exchange of differing perspectives within group-learning processes.

The purpose of consultative coaching is "to minimize mindless adoption or execution of task performance routines in uncertain and changing environments and to foster the invention of ways of proceeding with the work that are especially well aligned with task requirements" (Hackman & Wageman, 2005, p. 273). This suggests a role of coaching in *initiating* group-learning processes. Need for group learning increases in dynamic and uncertain environments that require adaptation (Day et al., 2004; Ilgen et al., 2005). We interpret this aspect of leadership coaching as involving, in part, the signaling of cues to group members about a growing discrepancy between changing environmental conditions on one hand, and existing group strategies and members' knowledge and skills on the other. The magnitude of this discrepancy should, in turn, trigger perceptions of learning needs that, in groups with high learning climates, should lead to the specification of learning objectives and strategies.

Giving feedback represents an integral aspect of the leadership mentoring and coaching role in group learning—it represents perhaps the most effective and direct intervention of leaders in collaborative learning (Tannenbaum et al., 1998). "Feedback" is a limited term in this case, because Tannenbaum et al. pointed to the utility of providing information *before* (e.g., "prebriefs") as well as after learning and performance trials. They describe a team-learning cycle in which prebriefs are used to articulate team plans and performance strategies, clarify members' roles, and focus members' collective attention on team learning needs. These prebriefs are followed in the team-learning cycle by performance or practice trials, which, in turn, lead to a period of performance diagnosis, and a post-action review in which members evaluate and summarize lessons learned. This diagnostic and post-performance review becomes the grist for future performance and learning prebriefs. Thus, the provision of performance information provides an impetus to group-learning processes both early and later in the learning episode. Tannenbaum et al. (1998, pp. 253–259) offered several leadership prescriptions to facilitate the team-learning cycle including some that match those offered earlier in this chapter. Other prescriptions refer to the leader offering specific types of feedback, such as task-focused vs. person-focused, and information about teamwork as well as task work. They urge leaders to refer to previous prebriefs and post-performance reviews as a means of linking lessons from different learning episodes, and they suggest encouraging active feedback giving and review by all members of the team.

Bell and Kozlowski (2002) noted that the provision of feedback needs to be paired with "adaptive guidance," defined as a learning approach "that provides trainees with diagnostic and interpretive information that helps them make effective learning decisions" (p. 269). According to Bell and Kozlowski, adaptive guidance is intended to help learners enhance learning self-regulation, determine appropriate learning goals, and focus their attentional resources in appropriate areas of knowledge and skill development. Thus, such guidance, when deployed as part of the prebrief stage of group learning, helps learners make effective use of information and feedback about prior performance. These effects of adaptive guidance were confirmed in a empirical study by Bell and Kozlowski on individual learning—however, further research is necessary to demonstrate these effects on team learning.

Marks, Zaccaro, and Mathieu (2000) demonstrated positive effects of prebrief information, in the form of leader "intent" statements, on shared cognition and subsequent adaptive performance in teams. Leaders provided information about expected team actions and members' roles under different situational contingencies—such information helped team members form more shared and accurate mental models (presumably, an index of group learning), which in turn facilitated performance in a novel performance context. Burke (1999) extended this study by demonstrating that performance in novel contexts improved significantly when leaders embellished prebrief performance information with further information on why certain goals and strategies should result in better team actions (e.g., "sense-giving"). These studies demonstrate the value of preperformance information in an adaptive performance setting that required teams to learn and apply new performance strategies.

SUMMARY AND CONCLUSIONS

We have noted that group learning thrives when members (a) share a high learning goal orientation, (b) have norms that promote exploration and learning in a psychologically safe environment, (c) develop a climate that permits all members voice in discovery learning, (d) develop a cooperative and cohesive team environment, (e) allow constructive controversy without affective conflict, (f) use self- and team-regulation skills, and (g) use skills in metacognitive and reflective thinking. We have suggested that groups can engage in three focal learning activities—(a) learning how to work collaboratively, (b) having individual members teach the whole group specific knowledge and skills, and (c) engaging in synergistic learning. The aforementioned strategies for learning apply across all three forms of learning. We have also noted the responsibility of group leaders to help facilitate group learning by developing, promoting and maintaining a learning climate, helping members develop and use learning tools, and acting as learning partners. These leadership activities reflect a functional approach to team learning (cf. Hackman & Walton, 1986; Hackman & Walton, 2005), where leaders are tasked with providing the team whatever it needs to learn effectively.

We have summarized a number of ideas and perspectives in the extant literature about the effects of team leadership on team learning. We would note, however, that these contributions are mostly conceptual in nature, with few empirical tests, even of principles of team learning in general (Kozlowski & Ilgen, in press). We have articulated three pathways by which leaders facilitate different forms of group learning. Further empirical research is necessary to confirm some of the ideas, prescriptions, and assertions made here and in the extant literature. Also, we need such research to uncover which leadership behaviors are most efficacious for each form of group learning, and when in the group learning cycle such behaviors are most effectively deployed. Finally, we need to investigate more thoroughly the contextual factors (both team and organizational), as well as individual and group compositional variables that moderate different aspects of group learning (Sessa & London, 2006). Such a research effort, based on the rich conceptual foundation emerging in the current literature, can greatly enhance the quality of leadership in team learning that is vital in today's complex organizational environments.

Author Note: Some of the ideas expressed in this chapter came from research funded by the Army Research Institute (Contract Numbers: DASW01-98-K-005 and W74V8H-05-K-0004). These ideas are those of the authors and do not reflect the official policy or positions of the U.S. Army, Department of Defense, or the U.S. Government.

REFERENCES

Amason, A. C. (1996). Distinguishing the effects of functional and dysfunctional conflict on strategic decision making: Resolving a paradox for top management teams. *Academy of Management Journal, 39,* 123–148.

Amason, A. C., & Sapienza, H. J. (1997). The effects of top management team size and interaction norms on cognitive and affective conflict. *Journal of Management, 23,* 495–516.

Argote, L., Gruenfeld, D., & Naquin, C. (2001). Group learning in organizations. In M. E. Turner (Ed.), *Groups at work: Advances in theory and research* (pp. 369–411). New York: Lawrence Erlbaum Associates.

Basadur, M. (2004). Leading others to think innovatively together: Creative leadership. *Leadership Quarterly, 15,* 103–121.

Bell, B. S., & Kozlowski, S. W. J. (2002). Adaptive guidance: Enhancing self-regulation, knowledge, and performance in technology-based training. *Personnel Psychology, 55,* 267–306.

Black, J. A., Oliver, R. L., Howell, J. P., & King, J. P. (2005). A dynamic system simulation of leader and group effects on context for learning. *The Leadership Quarterly, 17,* 39–56.

Bunderson, J. S., & Sutcliffe, K. M. (2003). Management team learning orientation and business unit performance. *Journal of Applied Psychology, 88,* 552–560.

Bunderson, J. S., & Sutcliffe, K. M. (2002). Comparing alternative conceptualizations of functional diversity in management teams: Process and performance effects. *Academy of Management Journal, 45,* 875–893.

Burke, C. S. (1999). *Examination of the cognitive mechanisms through which team leaders promote effective team processes and adaptive performance.* Unpublished doctoral dissertation, George Mason University, Fairfax, VA.

Burke, C. S., Stagl, K. C., Klein, C., Goodwin, G. F., Salas, E., & Halpin, S. (2006). What type of leadership behaviors are functional in teams: A meta-analysis. *The Leadership Quarterly, 17,* 288–307.

Cartwright, D. (1968). The nature of group cohesiveness. In D. Cartwright, & A. Zander (Eds.), *Group dynamics: Research and theory* (pp. 91–109). New York: Harper & Row.

Cortina, J., Zaccaro, S., McFarland, L., Baughman, K., Wood, G., & Odin, E. (2004). *Promoting realistic self-assessment as the basis for effective leader self-development* (ARI Research Note 2004-05). Crystal City, VA: United States Army Research Institute for the Behavioral and Social Sciences.

Davidson, J. E., Deuser, R., & Sternberg, R. J. (1994). The role of metacognition in problem solving. In J. Metcalfe & A. P. Shimamura (Eds.), *Metacognition: Knowing about knowing* (pp. 207–226). Cambridge, MA: MIT Press.

Day, D. V., Gronn, P., & Salas, E. (2004). Leadership capacity in teams. *Leadership Quarterly, 15,* 857–880.

DeShon, R. P., Kozlowski, W. J., Schmidt, A. M., Milner, K. R., & Wiechmann, D. (2004). A multiple-goal, multilevel model of feedback effects on the regulation of individual and team performance. *Journal of Applied Psychology, 89*(6), 1035–1056.

Devine, D. J., Clayton, L. D., Philips, J. L., Dunford, B. B., & Melner, S. B. (1999). Teams in organizations: Prevalence, characteristics, and effectiveness. *Small Group Research, 30,* 678–711.

Dweck, C. S. (1986). Motivational processes affecting learning. *American Psychologist, 41,* 1040–1048.

Edmondson, A. (1999). Psychological safety and learning behavior in work teams. *Administrative Science Quarterly, 44,* 350–383.

Edmondson, A. C. (2003). Speaking up in the operating room: How team leaders promote learning in interdisciplinary action teams. *Journal of Management Studies, 40,* 1419–1452.

Edmondson, A. C., Bohmer, R. M., & Pisano, G. P. (2001a). Disrupted routines: Team learning and new technology implementation in hospitals. *Administrative Science Quarterly, 46,* 685–716.

Edmondson, A. C., Bohmer, R. M., & Pisano, G. P. (2001b, October). Speeding up team learning. *Harvard Business Review,* 125–132.

Elliot, E. S., & Dweck, C. S. (1988). Goals: An approach to motivation and achievement. *Journal of Personality and Social Psychology, 54,* 5–12.

Ellis, A. P. J., Hollenbeck, J. R., Ilgen, D. R., Porter, C. O. L. H., West, B. J., & Moon, H. (2003). Team learning: Collectively connecting the dots. *Journal of Applied Psychology, 55,* 929–948.

Festinger, L. (1950). Informal social communication. *Psychological Review, 57,* 271–282.

Flavell, J. H. (1979). Metacognition and cognitive monitoring: A new area of cognitive-developmental inquiry. *American Psychologist, 34,* 906–911.

Fleishman, E. A., Mumford, M. D., Zaccaro, S. J., Levin, K. Y., Korotkin, A. L., Hein, M. B., et al. (1991). Taxonomic efforts in the description of leader behavior: A synthesis and functional interpretation. *Leadership Quarterly, 2*(4), 245–287.

Gersick, C. J. G. (1988). Time and transition in work teams: Toward a new model of group development. *Academy of Management Journal, 31*(1), 9–41.

Goldstein, I. L., & Ford, J. K. (2002). *Training in organizations* (4th ed.). Belmont, CA: Wadsworth.
Gruenfeld, D. H., Martorana, P. V., & Fan, E. T. (2000). What do groups learn from their worldliest members? Direct and indirect influence in dynamic teams. *Organizational Behavior and Human Decision Processes, 82*, 45–59.
Guzzo, R. A. (1995). Introduction: At the intersection of team effectiveness and decision making. In R. A. Guzzo, E. Salas, & associates (Eds.), *Team effectiveness and decision making in organizations* (pp. 1–8). San Francisco: Jossey-Bass.
Hackman, J. R. (2002). *Leading teams: Setting the stage for great performances.* Boston: Harvard Business School Press.
Hackman, J. R., & Wageman, R. (2005). A theory of team coaching. *Academy of Management Review, 30*, 269–287.
Hackman, J. R., & Walton, R. E. (1986). Leading groups in organizations. In P. S. Goodman, & associates (Eds.), *Designing effective work groups* (pp. 72–119). San Francisco: Jossey Bass.
Hinsz, V. B., Tindale, R. S., & Vollrath, D. A. (1997). The emerging conceptualization of groups as information processors. *Psychological Bulletin, 121*, 43–64.
Ilgen, D. (1999). Teams embedded in organizations. *American Psychologist, 54*, 129–139.
Ilgen, D. R., Hollenbeck, J. R., Johnson, M., & Jundt, D. (2005). Teams in organizations: From input-process-output models to IMOI models. *Annual Review of Psychology, 56*, 517–543.
Janis, I. L. (1972). *Victims of groupthink*. Boston: Houghton Mifflin.
Jarvenpaa, S., & Leidner, D. (1999). Communication and Trust in Global Virtual Teams. *Organization Science, 10*, 791–815.
Kane, T. D., Zaccaro, S. J., Tremble, T. R., & Masuda, A. D. (2002). An examination of the leader's regulation of groups. *Small Group Research, 33*(1), 65–120.
Katzenbach, J. R., & Smith, D. K. (1999). *The wisdom of teams: Creating the high-performance organization*. New York: Harper-Perennial.
Kayes, A. B., Kayes, D. C., & Kolb, D. A. (2005). Experiential learning in teams. *Simulation and Gaming, 36*, 330–354.
Klimoski, R. J., & Zukin, L. B. (1999). Selection and staffing for team effectiveness. In E. Sundstrom, & associates (Eds.), *Supporting work team effectiveness: Best management practices for fostering high performance* (pp. 63–91). San Francisco: Jossey-Bass.
Kozlowski, S. W. J. (1998). Training and developing adaptive teams: Theory, principles, and research. In J. A. Cannon-Bowers, & E. Salas (Eds.), *Descision making under stress: Implications for training and simulation* (pp. 115–153). Washington, DC: American Psychological Association.
Kozlowski, S. W. J., Gully, S. M., McHugh, P. P., Salas, E., & Cannon-Bowers, J. A. (1996). A dynamic theory of leadership and team effectiveness: Developmental and task contingent leader roles. *Research in Personnel and Human Resources Management, 14*, 253–305.
Kozlowski, S. W. J., Gully, S. M., Nason, E. R., & Smith, E. M. (1999). Developing adaptive teams: A theory of compilation and performance across levels and time. In D. R. Ilgen, & E. D. Pulaokos (Eds.), *The changing nature of performance* (pp. 240–292). San Francisco: Jossey-Bass.

Kozlowski, S. W. J., Gully, S. M., Salas, E., & Cannon-Bowers, J. A. (1996). Team leadership and development: Theory, principles, and guidelines for training leaders and teams. In M. M. Beyerlein, D. Johnson, & S. T. Beyerlein (Eds.), *Interdisciplinary studies of work teams, Vol. 3. Team Leadership* (pp. 253–291). Greenwich, CT: JAI Press.

Kozlowski, S. W. J., & Ilgen, D. R. (2006). Enhancing the effectiveness of work groups and teams. *Psychological Science in the Public Interest, 7,* 77–124.

London, M. (2002). *Leadership development: Paths to self-insight and professional growth.* Mahwah, NJ: Lawrence Erlbaum Associates.

London, M., Polzer, J. T., & Omoregie, H. (2005). Interpersonal congruence, transactive memory, and feedback processes: An integrative model of group learning. *Human Resource Development Review, 4,* 114–135.

London, M., & Smither, J. W. (1999). Career-related continuous learning: Defining the construct and mapping the process. In G. R. Ferris (Ed.), *Research in Human Resources Management, 17,* 81–121.

Lord, R. G. (1977). Functional leadership behavior: Measurement and relation to social power and leadership perceptions. *Administrative Science Quarterly, 22,* 114–133.

Louis, M. R., & Sutton, R. I. (1991). Switching cognitive gears from habits of mind to active thinking. *Human Relations, 44,* 55–76.

Marks, M. A., Mathieu, J., & Zaccaro, S. J. (2001). A temporally based framework and taxonomy of team processes. *Academy of Management Review, 26,* 356–376.

Marks, M., Zaccaro, S. J., & Mathieu, J. (2000). Performance implications of leader briefings and team interaction training for team adaptation to novel environments. *Journal of Applied Psychology, 85,* 971–986.

Mumford, M. D. (1986). Leadership in the organizational context: A conceptual approach and its application. *Journal of Applied Social Psychology, 16,* 212–226.

Mumford, M. D., Zaccaro, S. J., Harding, F. D., Jacobs, T. O., & Fleishman, E. A. (2000). Leadership skills for a changing world: Solving complex social problems. *Leadership Quarterly, 11,* 11–35.

Murray, A. I. (1989). Top management group heterogeneity and firm performance. *Strategic Management Journal, 10,* 125–141.

Porter, C. O. L. H. (2005). Goal orientation: Effects on backing up behavior, performance efficacy and commitment in teams. *Journal of Applied Psychology, 90,* 811–818.

Porter, C. O. L. H., Hollenbeck, J. R., Ilgen, D. R., Ellis, A. P. J., West, B. J., Moon, H., et al. (2003). Backing up behaviors in teams: The role of personality and legitimacy of need. *Journal of Applied Psychology, 88,* 391–403.

Prince, C., Chidester, T. R., Bowers, C., & Cannon-Bowers, J. (1992). Aircrew coordination – Achieving teamwork in the cockpit. In R. W. Swezey, & E. Salas (Eds.), *Teams: Their training and performance* (pp. 329–353). Norwood, NJ: Ablex Publishing Co.

Prussia, G. E., & Kinicki, A. J. (1996). A motivational investigation of group effectiveness using social cognitive theory. *Journal of Applied Psychology, 81,* 187–198.

Pulakos, E. D., Arad, S., Donovan, M. A., & Plamondon, K. E. (2000). Adaptability in the workplace: Development of a taxonomy of adaptive performance. *Journal of Applied Psychology, 85,* 612–624.

Roby, T. B. (1961). The executive function in small groups. In L. Petrullo, & B. M. Bass (Eds.), *Leadership and interpersonal behavior* (pp. 118–136). New York: Holt, Rinehart and Winston.

Salas, E., Dickinson, T. L., Converse, S., & Tannenbaum, S. I. (1992). Toward an understanding of team performance and training. In R. W. Swezey, & E. Salas (Eds.), *Teams: Their training and performance* (pp. 3–29). Norwood, NJ: Ablex Publishing Co.

Salas, E., Sims, D., & Burke, C. S. (2005). Is there a "Big 5" in teamwork? *Small Group Research, 36*, 555–599.

Sessa, V. I., & London, M. (2006). *Continuous leaning in organizations*. Mahwah, NJ: Lawrence Erlbaum Associates.

Sherif, M., & Sherif, C. W. (1953). *Groups in harmony and tension*. New York: Harper & Row.

Smith, E., Ford, J. K., & Kozlowski, S. W. J. (1997). Building adaptive expertise: Implications for training design. In M. A. Quinones, & A. Ehrenstein (Eds.), *Training for a rapidly changing workplace: Applications of psychological research* (pp. 89–118). Washington, DC: American Psychological Association.

Stagl, K. C., Burke, C. S., Salas, E., & Pierce, L. (2006). Team adaptation: Realizing team synergy. In C. S. Burke, L. G. Pierce, & E. Salas (Eds.), *Understanding adaptability: A prerequisite for effective performance within complex environments* (pp. 117–141). Amsterdam: Elsevier, Ltd.

Sundstrom, E., McIntyre, M., Halfhill, T., & Richards, H. (2000). Work groups: From the Hawthorne Studies to work teams of the 1990s and beyond. *Group Dynamics: Theory Research and Practice, 4*, 44–67.

Tannenbaum, S. I., Smith-Jentsch, K. A., & Behson, S. J. (1998). Training team leaders to facilitate team learning. In R. W. Swezey, & E. Salas (Eds.), *Teams: Their training and performance* (pp. 247–270). Norwood, NJ: Ablex Publishing Co.

Tjosvold, D., & Deemer, D. K. (1980). Effects of controversy within a cooperative or competitive context on organizational decision making. *Journal of Applied Psychology, 65*, 590–595.

Tuckman, B. W. (1965). Developmental sequences in small groups. *Psychological Bulletin, 63*, 384–399.

Van den Bossche, P., Segers, M., & Kirschner, P. A. (2006). Social and cognitive factors driving teamwork in collaborative learning environments. *Small Group Research, 37*, 490–521.

Van der Vegt, G. S., & Bunderson, J. S. (2005). Learning and performance in multidisciplinary teams: The importance of collective team identification. *Academy of Management Journal, 48*, 532–547.

Vera, D., & Crossan, M. (2004). Strategic leadership and organizational learning. *Academy of Management Review, 29*, 222–240.

Weick, K. E. (1993). The collapse of sensemaking in organizations: The Mann Gulch Disaster. *Administrative Science Quarterly, 38*, 628–652.

Wilson, J. M., Goodman, P. S., & Cronin, M. A. (in press). Group learning. *Academy of Management Review.*

Zaccaro, S. J., Heinen, B., & Shuffler, M. (in press). Team leadership and team effectiveness. In E. Salas, J. Goodwin, & C. S. Burke (Eds.), *Team effectiveness in complex organizations: Cross-disciplinary perspectives and approaches*. San Francisco: Jossey-Bass.

Zaccaro, S. J., Rittman, A. L., & Marks, M. A. (2001). Team leadership. *The Leadership Quarterly, 12*(4), 451–483.

SECTION

III

Learning Interventions

In this section, we begin to address group-learning interventions. Some of the chapters consider learning "in situ" while others address more "offline" group training interventions, and still others fall somewhere in between.

Burke, Salas, and Granados (chapter 10) examine group learning "in situ." They place group learning within their team-adaptation model. Team adaptation is an outcome, and they define it as "a change in team performance, in response to a salient cue or cue stream, which leads to a functional outcome for the entire team." The cycle leading up to the adaptation includes four phases: (a) assessing the situation and recognizing the need for adaptation, (b) formulating a plan, (c) executing a plan, and (d) team learning. In this chapter, they further delineate what exactly they mean by team learning. They cross processes involved in group learning (thinking that includes framing and reframing, action that includes crossing boundaries and experimentation, and integration) with cycles of team learning as learning moves from more individual based learning to actual team learning. Finally, they address the question, "How can this information be used to delineate the methods and tools by which teams can learn from ongoing experience and in the process move one step closer to adaptive team performance and the corresponding distal outcome of team adaptation?" While they acknowledge that a number of methods and tools can be used, they concentrate on three determined to be more novel: (a) storytelling, (b) action learning, and (c) communities of practice.

Rouwette and Vennix (chapter 11) discuss procedures that foster learning as groups engage in so-called messy problems—complex problems about which group members have different ideas about the nature of the problem and how to solve it. Group learning is especially important under these conditions because members depend on each other and must collaborate to arrive at a solution. Problem structuring methods (PSMs) are group-decision-support procedures that promote group learning as they help the group solve problems and make decisions. As an example, the authors discuss a model-building intervention that is a step-by-step process for conceptualizing the problem, identifying knowledgeable participants to work on the problem, designing the meeting space and communication media, and building an agenda with process orchestrated by a facilitator. Members provide their individual input in analyzing the causes, consequences, or elements of the problem, and examining each other's ideas about causes and effects. As the group works though these steps, the members learn how to address messy problems, establishing a memory system for handling such problems in the future.

Brandon and Hollingshead (chapter 12) show how group processes unfold using information and communications technologies. They outline a model of collaborative learning in organizational online groups. The model includes four classes of inputs (social behavioral, social cognitive, course technology fit, and learner variables) moderated by leader and computer-mediated communication variables that affect cognitive and behavioral processes at the group and individual level, and, in turn, learning outcomes. Brandon and Hollingshead suggest that learning is a product of the people involved, how well the technology used supports learning, and whether there is the chance for needed learning processes to occur.

Cannon-Bowers, and Sanchez (chapter 13) describe synthetic-learning environments (SLEs) as methods of group training. SLEs are simulations and games that provide realistic-yet-safe situations for group learning. They offer propositions about how best to structure SLE-based training to impart crucial teamwork competencies.

In the final chapter of this section, authors concentrate less on training intervention and more on when to intervene and for what reason. Silberstang and Diamante (chapter 14) outline different interventions for different phases of group process. Early on, the group needs interventions that help the group members get to know each other, understand group goals, and recognize the constraints and pressures under which they will operate. The members may need to be motivated to participate actively and get excited about the group task. As the group progresses, learning interventions are consultative and aimed at helping the group establish task processes and structures. Mid-way goals may be especially helpful for teams lacking a clearly defined deadline (e.g., research and development) or whose work is continuous (e.g., customer service). As the group achieves its objectives, interventions can prompt group reflection about impediments to effective team performance, how the group handled specific situations, and possible alternative approaches the group might try in the future. This is also a time to reward group efforts and encourage members to be proud of their accomplishments.

CHAPTER

10

The Role of Team Learning in Facilitating Team Adaptation Within Complex Environments: Tools and Strategies

C. SHAWN BURKE, EDUARDO SALAS,
AND DEBORAH DIAZ
University of Central Florida

> The most successful corporation of the 1990s will be something called a learning organization, a consumatively adaptive enterprise. (Domain, 1989, pp. 48–62)

Organizations are being faced with increased complexity in their operating environments. While this complexity arises from many sources (e.g., increased operational tempo, cultural diversity, distribution, and dynamic competition), the end result is an increasing need for organizations to possess the capacity to adapt. As organizations increasingly turn to the implementation of work teams as a design strategy, the importance of adaptive team performance, and correspondingly team adaptation, cannot be overlooked. In order to understand the end state of team adaptation, the concept of teams must first be defined. Building off prior work (e.g., Beyerlein, Johnson, & Beyerlein, 2003; Guzzo & Dickson, 1996; Ilgen, Major, Hollenbeck, & Sego, 1993; Swezey & Salas, 1992), teams have been defined as consisting of

> (1) two or more individuals, (2) who interact socially, (3) adaptively, (4) have shared or common goals, (5) hold meaningful task, feedback and goal interdependencies, (6) are hierarchically structured, (7) have a limited life-span, (8) whose expertise and roles are distributed and (9) are embedded within an organizational / environmental context which influences and is influenced by ongoing enacted competencies, processes, emergent states and performance outcomes. (Salas, Stagl, Burke, & Goodwin, in press, p. 5)

Within teams, where coordinated action is required, adaptation is needed not only to remain competitive and viable within the broader organization, but also to effectively and consistently coordinate within team interaction. Teams must be able to adapt not only to external cues, but also to cues internal to the team that arise out of moment-to-moment, dynamic team-member interaction. In this context, team adaptation is defined as, "a change in team performance, in response to a salient cue or cue stream, which leads to a functional outcome for the entire team" (Burke, Stagl, Salas, Pierce, & Kendall, 2006, pp. 1189–1190).

Despite researchers and practitioners arguing for the increasing importance of team adaptation (Burke et al., 2006; Pulakos, Dorsey, & White, 2006; Zaccaro & Bader, 2003), little is known about the individual and team-level processes that comprise it or the antecedents that enable it. Recently, researchers have begun to try to better understand team adaptation. While the work of Pulakos et al. (2006) began to identify the types of adaptive performance within work teams, other researchers have taken a more general approach to understanding team adaptation (see Burke et al., 2006; LePine, 2003; Kozlowski, 1998; Zaccaro & Bader, 2003). In this later vein, Burke et al. (2006) proposed a multilevel model that begins to identify the processes and emergent states that comprise adaptive team performance, as well as those antecedents leading to adaptive team performance and team adaptation.

While researchers have just begun to systematically examine team adaptation, many would explicitly or implicitly argue for the importance of team learning in promoting team adaptation. Team learning can be defined as the process by which relatively permanent changes occur in the behavioral potential of the group because of group-interaction activities through which members acquire, share, and combine knowledge (Edmondson, 1999). The process of team learning, and its relation to team adaptation, is especially important for those teams that are operating in the "wild." Traditionally, teams have either attended classroom training or become proficient at new tasks or processes over time; however, this is a luxury that few teams have in the current organizational environments. Within the dynamic environments characterizing today's work organizations and those of the future, it will not be a team's ability to work together and coordinate its actions that make it effective. In dynamic environments, the ability to work together as a team must be combined with an ability to continuously learn at both the individual and team level. Despite the importance of team learning, researchers are only beginning to understand its relation to team adaptation, the processes that comprise it, or the methods by which team learning can be promoted in real-time environments. Therefore, the purpose of this chapter is four-fold. First, a model of team adaptation is briefly reviewed to set the context and delineate the role of team learning. Second, the initial model is expanded by briefly reviewing the literature on team learning to better understand the components comprising this process. Third, using the information gained, propositions concerning the tools and methods that can be used to promote team learning outside the classroom are delineated. Finally, areas of future research are proposed.

ESTABLISHING THE CONTEXT FOR TEAM LEARNING: CONCEPTUALIZING TEAM ADAPTATION

In an effort to begin to delineate the components comprising team adaptation, Burke et al. (2006) presented a cross-level mixed-determinants model that incorporates constructs from a range of subdisciplines within psychology and management (see Fig. 10.1). The core of the model lies within the specification of an adaptive cycle comprised of four process-orientated phases: (a) situation assessment, (b) plan formulation, (c) plan execution, and (d) team learning, as well as emergent cognitive states, which serve as both proximal outcomes and inputs to this cycle. The adaptive cycle and corresponding emergent states (e.g., situation awareness, shared mental models, and psychological safety) comprise adaptive team performance. Within the model, adaptive team performance is an antecedent to team adaptation and is defined as "an emergent phenomenon that compiles over time from the unfolding of a recursive cycle whereby one or more team members utilize their resources to functionally change current cognitive or behavioral goal-directed action or structures to meet expected or unexpected demands" (Burke et al., 2006, p. 1192).

While specification of the adaptive cycle and corresponding emergent states comprise the core of the model, the authors also delineate variables that represent distal forces with respect to the adaptive cycle (e.g., individual characteristics, job-design characteristics). Taken together, the model components, representing individual and team-level process variables and the resulting emergent cognitive and attitudinal states, directly and interactively determine team adaptation. Given the focus

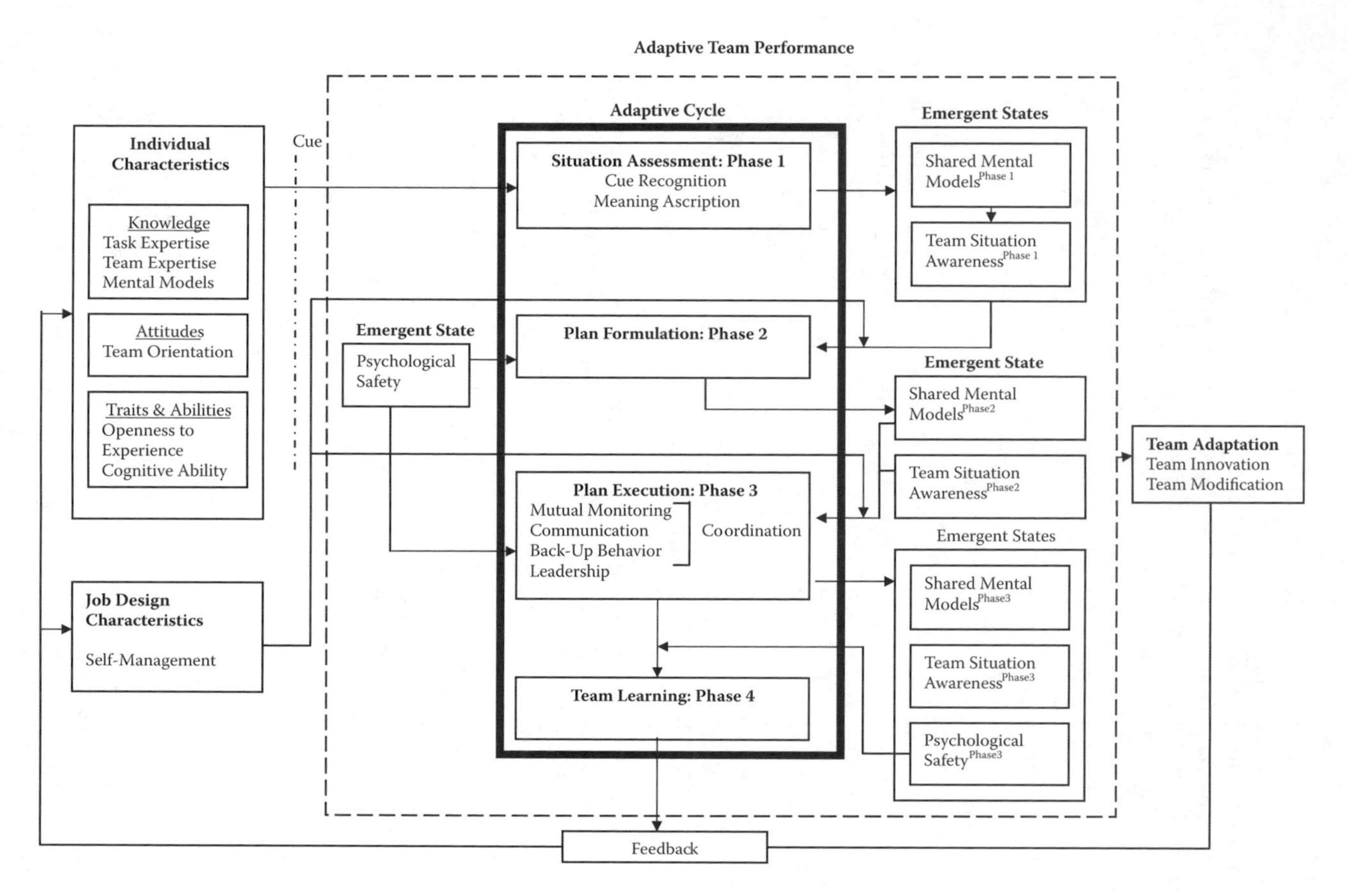

Figure 10.1 ITO model of team adaptation (Burke et al. (2006).

of the current chapter, the components that comprise adaptive team performance are briefly described, as they are the most proximal to the outcome of team learning. The processes and emergent states that comprise the core model will serve to set the context for better understanding the role of team learning within team adaptation (for a detailed description of the model, see Burke et al., 2006).

Phase 1: Situation Assessment

Situation assessment is defined using Gutwin and Greenberg's (2004) definition, "the human processes of gathering information (e.g., attention, pattern recognition, communication)" (p. 181). Burke et al. (2006) explained that this individual-level cognitive process begins the adaptive cycle and involves at least one team member searching the environment in order to identify cue(s) that could impact the success of the team's mission. The criteria for identifying cues that are deemed relevant are based on past experiences and cognitive frameworks. Teams have to work against their habitual routines in order to identify these cues. Once a cue or cue pattern is perceived, meaning has to be assigned. This step is more complex when dealing with teams, since the information gathered needs to be communicated to the rest of the team. Team members would need to develop the situation awareness and mental models residing at the individual level to the corresponding team-level emergent states, shared mental models, and team-situation awareness.

Burke et al. (2006) explained that at this phase adaptive team performance is promoted in at least two ways. First and foremost, the team must be aware that a change is needed. Situation assessment is the process by which the team can recognize a cue that indicates a need for change. Research has suggested that the rate with which changes are recognized and appropriate responses are enacted is related to subsequent team adaptability (Waller, 1999). Second, this phase affords the opportunity for team members to develop a compatible view of equipment, tasks, and roles and responsibilities that allow members to adapt proactively.

Phase 2: Plan Formulation

The emergent states that occur as a result of Phase 1 (e.g., shared mental models and team-situation awareness) and provide the input to the second phase of the adaptive cycle, plan formation. Planning has been defined by Stout and Salas (1993) to involve deciding on a course of action (COA), setting goals, clarifying member roles and responsibilities with respect to the COA, discussing relevant environmental characteristics and constraints, prioritizing tasks, clarifying performance expectations, and sharing information related to task requirements.

In Fig. 10.1, Burke et al. (2006) pulled from the human factors and management literature to identify two constructs that are fundamental to plan formation. The first, team-situation awareness (TSA), refers to a shared understanding of the current situation at a given time (Salas, Prince, Baker, & Shrestha, 1995). During this phase, team members must maintain a shared perspective regarding which environmental elements are appropriate to the team's goals. According to Endsley (1995), TSA does not require that each member possess identical pieces of information; rather, what is important is that the members' situational awareness overlaps to create a shared mental model in the context of the team's objectives. The second construct is psychological safety. Psychological safety is defined as the shared belief that the team is safe for interpersonal risk taking (Edmonson, 1999). Psychological safety contributes to plan development by fostering a climate where members are free to question suggestions or decisions.

The importance of this phase in the adaptive cycle is represented by the arrow depicting plan formulation as a proximal input to shared mental models. It is at this step that the information gathered and created during the first phase is given meaning in relation to the team's objective.

Phase 3: Plan Execution

In Fig. 10.1, it is noted that plan execution involves an assortment of related processes. During plan execution, a combination of individual and team-level behaviors such as monitoring, back-up, communication, leadership and coordination are involved in order to engage in adaptive team performance. Specifically, the implementation of a new plan requires communication and coordination of actions, while monitoring and back-up behavior assist team members when cognitive or physical resources become depleted (Burke et al., 2006). Leadership is also essential during this phase as the leader enacts processes that serve to structure member action, develop members, and assist members in maintaining and recreating the shared coherence (e.g., affect, behavior, cognition) needed to be adaptive (Kozlowski, 1998).

Just as there are two proximal inputs in the plan-formulation phase (e.g., shared mental models, psychological safety) that impact plan execution, shared mental models, which revolve around the task, equipment, and team members, provide the conceptual basis for actions such as monitoring and back-up behavior. Psychological safety, in turn, impacts plan execution via the degree to which mutual performance monitoring and back-up behavior is offered and accepted by members. Low levels of psychological safety within the team serve to work against teamwork behaviors such as mutual-performance monitoring and back-up behavior as members may not feel comfortable providing suggestions for fear of retribution and, in turn, the actions may be viewed as spying vs. helping.

Team-member interaction during this phase serves to update existing affective and cognitive states (e.g., shared mental models, TSA, psychological safety). In addition, the nature of team interaction during plan execution impacts existing levels of psychological safety. For example, if positive interactions occur, then the level of psychological safety will either remain the same or essentially increase, but if interactions turn negative, psychological safety may begin to decrease.

Phase 4: Team Learning

While team learning is the final phase in the adaptive cycle, it is no less important than the other four phases. Teams and their members can cycle through the first three phases, yet if teams do not learn during the adaptive cycle, consistent adaptive team performance will not occur. Levitt and March (1988) delineated learning as the outcome of a process that consists of encoding inferences from history into the routines that guide behavior. Team learning warrants the development of knowledge and also contributes to the ability of team members to improve their collective understanding of their situation. Team members then understand the consequences of their actions, how any unintended consequences can be prevented, and how a course of action can be revised. This completes the adaptive cycle and the process begins again as members scan their environment for change.

While the Burke et al. (2006) model of team adaptation presented team learning as an important phase in the adaptive cycle, the model did not delineate the processes that comprise team learning. Without further delineation, the specification of methods and tools by which team learning can be promoted within teams striving to be adaptive cannot be specified. Therefore, within this section, the nature of team learning is further explicated.

TEAM LEARNING: DELINEATING THE PROCESS

Although human learning has received much attention in the literature, the nature of team learning or learning at the team level is a fairly recent development in the literature on teams. Team learning has been defined in many ways, including "a process through which a group creates knowledge for its members, for itself as a system and for others" (Dechant, Marsick, & Kasl, 2000, p. 5); and "the process of aligning and developing the capacity of a team to create the results its members truly desire" (Senge, 1990, p. 236). Edmondson (1999) and Edmondson, Bohmer, and Pisano (2001) offered a definition with a more concrete description. These authors argued that knowledge gained through this process occurs by members openly testing assumptions and discussing differences. This was echoed by West (in press), who argued that team learning involves members' joint reflection about team processes and behaviors.

Processes Involved in Team Learning

While the definitions previously offered begin to provide a picture of team learning, a small subset of researchers have moved beyond definitions to delineate the nature of the team-learning cycle (e.g., Kasl, Marsick, & Dechant, 1997; Edmondson, 2001). Kasl et al. (1997) argued that the processes involved in team learning can be divided into two component parts—thinking and action—and integration. The thinking component is comprised of framing and reframing, while the action component consist of crossing boundaries and experimentation. Integration is a process that cuts across these components and pulls thinking and acting together, resulting in team learning.

The learning process begins with the act of framing comprised of the team's initial perception of a situation or action, based on prior experience. This initial act of framing is akin to the processes that happen in the early stages of sensemaking (see Burke, Priest, Upshaw, & Salas, Weick, 1979; under review). Through interaction with other team members and the larger organizational environment (e.g., the action component), members reframe their initial perceptions through experimentation and boundary crossing in which they listen to others' perspectives and use this information to examine their own perceptions in a different light. Specifically, through the dialogue and inquiry that occurs because members actively cross boundaries, individuals are able to adjust and reframe their cognitive frameworks (e.g., schemas, mental models). Experimentation in the form of deliberate interventions (Mezirow, 1991), or that which is more exploratory in nature (see Schon, 1983), also serves to provide the impetus for reframing. While the actions of experimentation and crossing boundaries provide the impetus for reframing, learning at the team level only occurs when reframing consists of dialogue, in which team members are not only willing to listen to the perspectives of others, but also integrate and share these views such that learning is shared or a collective process.

Coming from a slightly different perspective Gibson (2001) identified cycles of collective cognition in work groups (e.g., accumulation, interaction, examination, accommodation). As collective cognition can be defined as "the group processes involved in the acquisition, storage, transmission, manipulation, and use of information" (Gibson, 2001, p.123), this work also contributes to understanding the team-learning cycle. As team learning takes place at both an individual and team level, many of the processes involved in collective cognition are intricately tied to team learning. Specifically, while the cycles identified by Gibson all have a place within the team-adaptation model (and as such will be briefly described), those most relevant to our understanding of team learning within the model are the latter two (e.g., examination, accommodation). The first identified phase, accumulation, consists of activities such as perceiving cues and corresponding information, filtering that information, and storing the filtered information. Going back to the Burke et al. (2006) model of team adaptation, this sounds very similar to the first phase of the adaptive cycle (e.g., situation assessment). Given the iterative nature of the adaptive cycle, the later part of the activities that encompass accumulation (e.g., filtering information, storing information) would also be expected to appear as activities within the framing portion of the team-learning cycle (see Fig. 10.2).

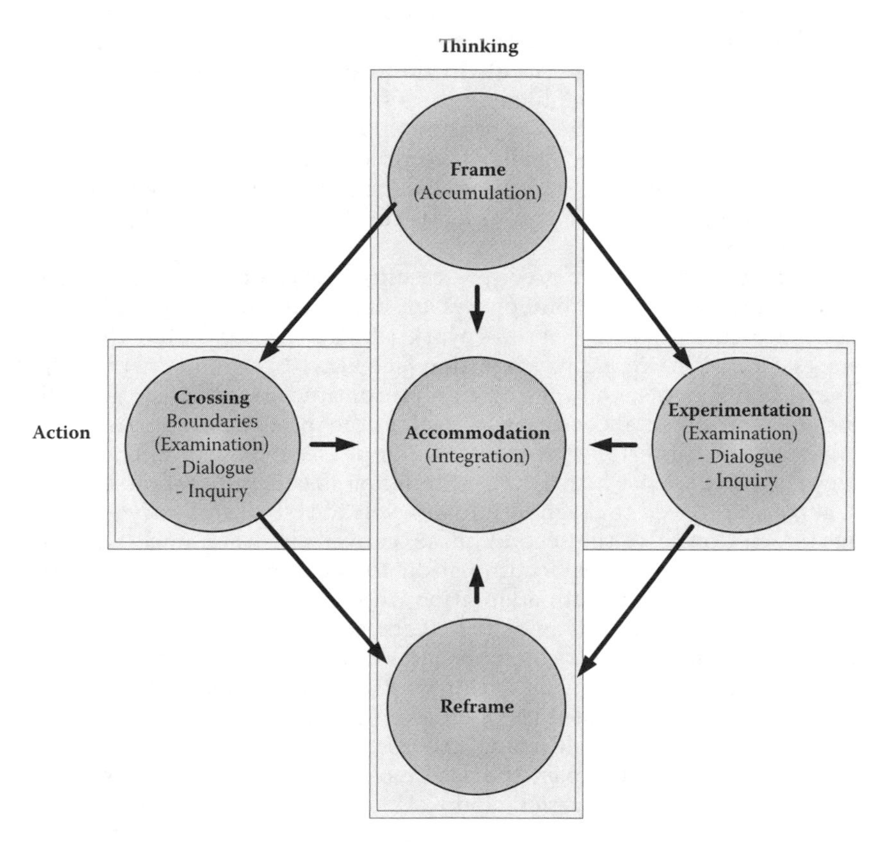

Figure 10.2 Team learning process.

The next identified phase, interaction, consists of activities such as retrieving, exchanging, and structuring information. The activities involved in this phase would be inserted into the team-adaptation model at phases two (plan formulation) and three (plan execution).

Most important for the current discussion on team learning are the last two phases identified by Gibson (2001, e.g., examination, accommodation). Examination consists of activities such as negotiating, interpreting, and evaluating. Within this phase the interaction and discussion that occurs within the team serves to create collectively negotiated impressions and views. Through open discussion, members influence one another's perceptions and opinions. Discussion at this phase may be dominated by higher-status members. Examination, as described by Gibson, is integrated within the team-learning process when members are crossing boundaries and conducting experimentation (see Fig.10.2). The last stage, accommodation, involves team members integrating viewpoints and opinions, thereby creating new team-mental models, deciding, and acting. Gibson argued that mutual-perspective is important at this stage because it aids in the learning process. Gibson contended that this last stage likely occurs simultaneously with reframing or shortly thereafter—the key within this stage is the common team-learning outcomes. Specifically, accommodation represents the integration of the thinking and action components depicted within the team-learning cycle (see Fig. 10.2). It is this final integration that results in team learning.

In an attempt to more precisely specify how the team-learning process occurs across different phases or iterations within the adaptive cycle, we turn back to Gibson's work (2001). Gibson noted that the stages comprising collective cognition (see Fig. 10.2) are not necessarily linear. Teams may spend varying amounts of time on each stage depending on environmental conditions as well as the maturity of the team. For example, task uncertainty impacts which phases of collective cognition are relied upon most heavily. Accumulation is generally the first phase that teams proceed through, but high levels of task uncertainty encourage interaction to be the second phase; conversely, when uncertainty is lower, teams jump from accumulation to accommodation. Tying this back to the model of team adaptation, in Fig. 10.1, task uncertainty is greater under conditions in which team adaptation is represented as team innovation (e.g., novel solution) rather than team modification (e.g., modified solution made within routine environment). While Gibson's work pointed to how task or environmental conditions may impact the nature of the team-learning process, information related to how team maturity might impact the nature of team learning can be seen in the work of Dechant, Marsick, and Kasl (1993).

Cycles of Team Learning

While it has been previously argued within this chapter that there are five primary processes involved in team learning that are cyclical in nature (see Fig. 10.2), they are not the only manner in which team learning is cyclical. Dechant et al. (1993) noted the cyclical nature by arguing that the process of team learning can be delineated into four phases: (a) fragmented, (b) pooled, (c) synergistic, and (d) continuous. These stages vary both in their complexity and in the level (individual or team) at which they occur. Specifically, the first two phases primarily occur at an individual level, while the latter two reflect true team-level phenomena.

The first phase argued for by Dechant et al. (1993), fragmented learning, is characterized by members who frame their understanding of team interaction, but are not likely to engage in dialogue or inquiry. As such, any reframing is not based on the perspective of other team members, but tends to be highly ethnocentric. Team members are primarily operating as individuals with respect to any learning that takes place. As such, although Dechant et al. characterized this as a phase within team learning, we will not discuss it any further as it is more reflective of individual than team learning. During the next phase, pooled, subsets, or clusters of team members engage in learning, but not the entire team. At this stage, knowledge begins to become pooled among team members, but there is little attempt at integration as only a few members begin to experiment and cross boundaries. While reframing begins at an individual level based on the pooled knowledge, this phase still reflects primarily an individual-level process in terms of learning.

Beginning with the third phase of team learning, synergistic, the learning process truly becomes a team-level phenomenon. During the synergistic phase, team-member schemas are often changed as a result of collective reframing that occurs through dialogue and collaborative inquiry. At this phase, team experimentation begins to occur regularly, as does boundary spanning, which serves to bring in additional perspectives as members interact with those outside their initial circle. These perspectives are then shared and often contribute to the processes of collective reframing and accommodation. Finally, within the final phase, continuous learning, crossing boundaries, and experimentation have become the norm for the team in an effort to continuously gain new knowledge by examining situations in different orientations and integrating these perspectives into existing schemas and mental models. Diversity is both valued and sought after at this stage in an effort to keep the team adaptive and engaged in a continuous cycle of learning. While other researchers have also acknowledged the cyclical nature of team learning, often the team-learning phases seem indicative of team development at a broader level (e.g., Tompkins, 2000).

Now that the processes involved and the phases of team learning have been further delineated, the remaining question is, How can this information be used to delineate the methods and tools by which teams can learn from ongoing experience and in the process move one step closer to adaptive team performance and the corresponding distal outcome of team adaptation?

METHODS FOR PROMOTING TEAM LEARNING "IN SITU"

Given the delineation of team learning offered earlier and its place within the team-adaptation model, team learning can be promoted "in situ" using a variety of methods and tools. Here we take a multidisciplinary view in identifying three methods and corresponding propositions that can be used in more natural settings, as opposed to traditional training settings: (a) storytelling, (b) action learning (e.g., team self-correction), and (c) communities of practice. While we do not argue that these are the only methods that can be used to promote team learning in naturalistic settings, we do argue that these or the manner in which we suggest they be used are among the more novel.

Storytelling

In many ways, views on storytelling are much like views on team training in general (e.g., assuming that it is a natural ability). While storytelling is a fundamental aspect of being human, Denning (2005) argued that it is a rare skill (e.g., few do it effectively). However, stories are a natural way by which humans learn. Individuals use stories to make sense of complex situations (Bruner, 1990). Stories are one manner in which information can be transmitted (e.g., intellectual capital, tacit knowledge) and learning targeted within organizations. Storytelling has been described as a social experience, a means to connect to others and develop professional identities (Shank, 2006). Often in an attempt to make sense of an event we attempt to provide it with surrounding context and essentially build a story. It is a method that is increasing in popularity and can be used to ensure that learning is tied back to the organizational context and tends to heighten participant engagement. It allows the transmittal of information and building of knowledge, sometimes tacit, in a method that is grounded in context and experience.

Proposition 1: To Foster Team Learning at Any Phase of the Learning Process Storytelling Must Be Grounded in Context, Experience, and Contain Authentic Questions

Storytelling is often used at the individual or organizational level, but may also be a powerful tool for team learning. Research has shown that when stories are grounded in experience, contain authentic questions, and are sustained, they may serve an important means for both creating and learning within a collaborative space. Shank (2006) found that the use of storytelling within cross-disciplinary teaching groups helped teachers see themselves in new ways, connect their private worlds of practice to those of others and to broader educational issues, and develop shared norms of good teaching practice. In preparing a story version of an experience the content must first be leveled and sharpened to foster engagement. While details from the actual experience are included, often the whole experience is not described and is often embellished with potentially fictional details. However, these details must be believable, relevant to the audience, and engaging.

Proposition 2: The Phase of Team Learning Targeted Will Drive the Structure of the Story

All stories will and should facilitate the accumulation of information and initial framing that takes place as a result of that accumulation no matter what phase of team learning is being targeted. However, as one moves toward the later phases of team learning (e.g., synergistic, continuous), stories must be structured so that they facilitate the need to engage in learning actions (e.g., crossing boundaries, experimentation). In other words, the story has to be engaging enough and complex enough that the immediate resolution or learning point is not obvious. This, in turn, will cause members to engage in dialogue and active inquiry.

Langellier (1989) argued for five theoretical orientations to storytelling: (a) story-text, (b) storytelling performance, (c) conversational interaction, (d) social process, and (e) political praxis. For the purposes of the present discussion, the most relevant forms include storytelling performance and social process. Within the storytelling-performance orientation, stories represent personal communication that takes place in a social context to affect the immediate audience in a certain way. It is expected that stories within this orientation would primarily target the early phases of team learning focusing primarily on thinking components as depicted in Fig. 10.1. Conversely, stories told within the social-process orientation represent a means to link private and public discourse, allowing tacit knowledge to be revealed. Specifically, Shank (2006) argued that stories told in this orientation serve to connect members to both the immediate social context, as well as broader social and cultural contexts. As such, it is expected that stories within this orientation would enable both thinking and action components and may be used to target learning objectives within the later phases of team learning.

Proposition 3: The Structure of the Story Is Not Only Dictated by the Phase of Learning the Team Is in, But Also by the Learning Objective

Denning (2004) argued that although stories can be a very effective tool for team leaders, they must be carefully matched to the objective one is trying to achieve. In this vein, Denning argued for seven different objectives (sparking action, communicating who you are, transmitting values, fostering collaboration, taming the grapevine/rumors, sharing knowledge, and leading people into the future) that stories may serve.

Of importance is that the format and what will need to be done to tell the story effectively differs depending on purpose. The following section is a brief review of those objectives most relevant to team learning (e.g., transmitting values, fostering collaboration, and sharing knowledge) as well as the structure that stories targeted to increase team learning along each objective may take.

Transmitting values. Stories that transmit values often take the form of parables, which are usually grounded in a generic past and have few contextual details. While the facts can be hypothetical, they must be believable and relevant to the audience. While transmitting values does not necessarily embody team learning, within teams the transmission of values such that a core set is established provides the basis for collaboration and teamwork—a necessary ingredient for team learning and team adaptation.

Fostering collaboration. Denning (2005) argued that a story crafted around a team's concerns and goals can serve to foster collaboration. In essence, this is similar in form to the method used by Shank (2006). One member of the team shares a concern in the form of a story, which ideally sparks another. This, in turn, begins to promote a shared perspective. When this form of storytelling is combined with dialogue and active inquiry, it may go beyond fostering collaboration and shared perspectives to truly facilitating team learning through crossing boundaries and experimentation.

Proposition 4: Dialogue Is Essential for Team Learning to Occur When the Targeted Objective Is to Foster Collaboration (e.g., Teamwork)

Within this context, dialogue has been defined as "a free-flowing meaning through a group, allowing the group to discover insights not attainable individually" (Senge, 1990, p. 10). Within dialogue, team members suspend their positions and probe others for their reasoning to discover new possibilities. In order to promote team learning, listening without judgment is necessitated (Levine, 1994). With dialogue, the sharing of different perspectives around a common team problem or concern provides the impetus for new information that can be incorporated during reframing.

The act of dialogue is essential for truly collaborative team learning (e.g., learning at the team level). In order to enable the type of dialogue necessary for team learning three conditions must be present (Senge, 1990). First, team members must suspend their assumptions. Second, participants must regard one another as colleagues. Third, there must be a facilitator who holds the context of dialogue and keeps team members focused. A fourth is argued for in that team members must suspend their ethnocentric views in addition to suspending assumptions.

Sharing knowledge. Stories delivered for the purpose of sharing knowledge are probably the most related to our purpose of facilitating team learning. Knowledge-sharing stories are typically told to incite team learning with regard to anomalies. Given the task uncertainty often found with regard to anomalies, team members will often progress through all of the processes (thinking, action; see Fig. 10.2) as opposed to going from accumulation to integration as is the case in more certain environments. This method is one avenue through which weak signals in terms of errors or lapses can be exploited as learning opportunities. These stories are told with considerable contextual detail, as opposed to those that transmit values and include a description of the problem, setting, solution, and explanation. The inclusion of an explanation, something often left out of traditional stories, is what enables this form to be a learning opportunity. Without the explanation, members are just left with facts and contextual details, but not the underlying strategic knowledge as to causal factors. Denning (2005) argued that to build an explanation, the beginning and end state must be defined and causal factors identified. Finally, an action sequence must be provided to tie all elements together, thereby forming the explanation.

Proposition 5: Team Learning as Accomplished Through Knowledge Sharing Stories May Be Difficult for Teams Who Are in the Early Phases of Team Learning Due to a Lack of Psychological Safety at These Phases

Denning (2005) argued that knowledge-sharing narratives lack a hero or even a detectable plot, yet must still be made interesting in order to motivate listeners. Knowledge stories must be crafted such that they touch upon the listener's frame of reference, which, in turn, helps him or her imagine being in the story. Often these stories have a negative tone as they are highlighting a problem or challenge. Although important avenues for team learning, team members may initially resist because the basis of these stories is often the admittance of a mistake or lapse. However, the establishment of psychological safety within the team will often mitigate any trepidation

Action Learning

A second method by which team learning can be promoted "in situ" is through action learning. *Action learning* is a "method to generate learning from human interaction occurring as learners engage together in real-time work problems" (Raelin, 2006, p. 152).

Proposition 6: The Unfamiliar Nature of the Problems Often Tackled Within Action Learning Will Cause the Team to Progress Through the Entire Team-Learning Process

Within action learning, learning occurs not just from the representation of material, but also from questioning and collective reflection among team members as they tackle unfamiliar problems (Revans, 1982). The unfamiliar situations are comparable in some aspects to the "stretch assignments" commonly used within leader and employee development. In the current case, unfamiliar problems that provide the stretch conditions often found within action learning include (a) keeping methods and practices the same, but varying the normal setting and (b) keeping the team setting the same, but varying the methods or practices.

Action learning has many variants, but all seem to share three common principles (Raelin, 2000). First, learning is acquired in the midst of action and dedicated to the task at hand. Second, knowledge creation and utilization are seen as collective activities in which learning is everyone's job. Third, a learning-to-learn aptitude exists such that members are free to question the underlying assumptions of practice. Making this broad method extremely viable as a team-learning method at all phases of team learning is that action learning is typically applied in a group setting that seeks to generate learning from human interaction arising from engagement in the solution of real-time work problems (Marquardt, 1999; Pedler, 1991; Raelin, 2000). Action learning theorists contend that the best way to test theories and make them actionable is through real experience.

Actions taken are subject to inquiry about their effectiveness, including a review of how any related theories were applied in practice. Participants learn as they work by taking time to reflect with their colleagues who offer insights into their workplace problems (Raelin, 1997). The reflection that occurs within this method is bolstered by feedback from mutual learners who participate in a real-time debriefing of the learners' workplace experience. In this way, action learning has been argued to address the pitfalls within conventional training by surfacing tacit knowledge and converting it to learning (Raelin, 2006). By having peers serve as a sounding board to one another regarding the operational assumptions underlying project interventions, participants become more equipped to produce the desired outcome (Argyris & Schon, 1996). From each other, they learn how to overcome the blocks that they themselves and others erect to deter project accomplishment (Coghlan & Brannick, 2001). Tsoukas and Mylonopoulos (2004) argued that learning is tied to knowledge collectively and concurrently constructed in the service of action.

Proposition 7: Team Self-Correction Is a Form of Action Learning that Targets Both Individual and Team-Level Learning

Team self-correction. The description of action learning previously offered, perfectly illustrates why team self-correction (Smith-Jentsch, Zeisig, Acton, & McPherson, 1998) can be viewed as a form of action learning. The premise underlying the notion of team self-correction is to structure a team's natural tendency to review its performance. Effective teams tend to debrief themselves after a significant performance event in that they will review what went right and what went wrong and why. Teams will then use this information to discuss what should be done differently next time (Blickensderfer, Cannon-Bowers, & Salas, 1997). Team self-correction allows team members to learn to diagnose the team's problems and develop effective solutions in near real time (during periods of low workload) and thus can be seen as a form of action learning.

Proposition 8: Team Learning Is Facilitated When Members Discuss Both Positive and Negative Performance Aspects During Team Self-Correction

Team self-correction has been effectively used to promote team learning within military environments and student population where the context is team debriefings, which can be done by the team members or team leaders themselves (Smith-Jentsch et al., 1998; Smith-Jentsch, Blickensderfer, Salas, & Cannon-Bowers, 2000). It entails team members monitoring their own and others' behavior during an event followed by a nonaccusatory discussion of positive and negative examples of teamwork that occurred. As a part of the self-correction process, members provide, seek, and accept constructive feedback to and from others. Providing feedback on the positive and negative aspects of the task at its completion allows team members to reflect on what was done correctly and what needs to be improved to ensure safety of the workplace (Ellis, Mendel, & Nir, 2006). The exact distribution or sampling of these instances depends on whether performance on the specific event was successful or unsuccessful. More specifically, Ellis et al. (2006) reported that after successful events, the most effective review was one that discussed wrong actions; conversely, unsuccessful events benefited from reviewing both what went right as well as that which went wrong. The authors argued that discussing both positive and negative events for those teams that were successful may lead to complacency, while for those teams that need improvement, the mix of both positive and negative critical incidents serves as a way to further build and elaborate mental models and plan for improvement.

Proposition 9: Both Structure and the Presence of an Internal Facilitator Are Essential to the Enabling Team Self-Correction as a Team-Learning Method

Smith-Jentsch et al. (2000) identified several guidelines for the implementation of team self-correction. First, prior to a team self-correction discussion, members should be trained in the use of effective, diagnostic-feedback skills. Discussions should be diagnostic and focus on how to change behavior rather than offering generic "do-better" feedback. Second, teams should be provided with sufficient time (e.g., no less than 30 minutes) to go through the team self-correction process. Third, sessions should begin with a high-level overview of the events that transpired in order to trigger team members' recall. Fourth, discussions should be structured around targeted learning objective(s); in most cases these revolve around teamwork dimensions. Sixth, discussions should be guided (e.g., instructor, team leader, team member) and establish a psychologically safe and open climate where differences of opinion can be voiced without retribution or harm. As teams mature, the degree of psychological safety present will further enable the success of team self-correction. In facilitating the discussion, positive events as well as negative events should be reviewed. Finally, the outcome of the discussions should be specific improvement goals for the next performance session.

Communities of Practice

Taking a slightly different approach from that presented above is the use of communities of practice to enhance both individual and team learning. Communities of practice (COPs) have commonly been defined as joint enterprises that are continually renegotiated and produce a shared repertoire of resources that members have developed over time (Wenger, 1998). COP refers to "groups of people informally bound by their shared competence and mutual interest in a given practice, which makes it natural for them to share their individual experiences and knowledge in an informal and creative way" (Choi, 2006, p. 143). They typically represent an emergent property of a community or operational specialty that arises based on an unmet need. COPs are not stable, static entities, but evolve over time as new members join and others leave. While it has been argued that COPs cannot be formed (Roberts, 2006), the conditions that support COP emergence can be fostered by organizational teams or human-resource departments. Once emerged, further support can be offered to facilitate their presence.

While recent conceptualizations suggest that COPs can be cultivated and leveraged for strategic advantage (Saint-Onge & Wallace, 2003; Wenger et al., 2002), they have not traditionally been used to promote team learning as they are often unstructured and promote informal individual learning and a sense of community. Choi (2006), however, suggested a constructivist learning strategy perspective to COPs to explore them as an alternative learning model for performance training in corporations.

COPs can be utilized to promote team learning as they directly tie back to the processes outlined by both Gibson (2001) and Kasl et al. (1997) as comprising team learning. The information shared within COPs allows the fostering of new perspectives and new ways of responding to problems that arise. Furthermore, they contain a repository of contextually based knowledge that could serve as an impetus for team learning depending on the exact nature of the content and structure. Wenger (1998) argued that meaning within COPs is negotiated through a process of participation and reification. Wenger (1998) argued, "any community of practice produces abstractions, tools, symbols, stories, terms, and concepts that reify something of that practice in a congealed form" (p. 59). The abstractions, terms, concepts, and symbols are often engrained within stories that form the basis of the practice and contribute to an engaging form of knowledge distribution (e.g., the first step to team learning).

Proposition 10: While Traditionally an Emergent Property, COPs Can Be Used to Facilitate Experiential Learning Within Teams at Both an Individual and Team Level

Burke et al. (in press) argued that COPs could be structured by those who create them in such a manner as to facilitate the growth of experiential learning and the development of breadth and flexibility within members' mental models, which, in turn, contribute to team learning. For example, communities of practice pertaining to emergency response could be designed such that the main page links to various themes (e.g., working with local populace, working within the political structure, and working with joint operations) where users can submit questions, experiences, and answers with regard to a specific theme within the broader community or occupational specialty. This use encompasses team learning at more of an individual level. Within the cycles/phases of team learning identified earlier, this might be representative of the pooled phase of team learning.

A second possibility is for a community or occupational specialty to form a Web site where visitors could post key information regarding essential coordination processes and workarounds. The site could be structured such that a team might pick several critical incidents around a common theme (or teamwork dimensions) that other teams in the organization faced and each member of the team would provide his or her perspective on that incident. This information is then available to those within that specialty as well as to internal team members. Not only does this provide a way to document team history (as new members rotate in), but allows multiple perspectives to be examined both at an individual level (e.g., role) and team level. Furthermore, perspectives can be offered up in a nonthreatening manner for those who might possess cultural or personal values that prohibit them from calling attention to themselves within the team. By examining various perspectives categorized around a common theme and extracting key cue-response linkages, this method provides an avenue by which tacit and contextual knowledge may be built.

CONCLUSION AND FUTURE RESEARCH

Within the dynamic environments that work teams now find themselves in, a team's ability to be adaptive is becoming a necessity in order for continued viability, productivity, and competitiveness. However, theoretical and empirical work surrounding this construct is in its infancy as models and frameworks are just beginning to emerge (e.g., Burke et al., 2006; Hildebrand, K., Zaccaro, S. J., & Shuffler, M. L. 2006). Within the work that now exists, many processes and emergent states have been argued to contribute to team adaptation. However, when one looks to teams "in the wild" and asks how they are able to consistently manage to be adaptive in both their performance and outcomes a consistent theme emerges—they are engaging in continuous learning at both an individual and team level. In an attempt to better understand team adaptation, Burke et al. (2006) argued that consistent, long-term team adaptation is not possible without team learning, yet the model of team adaptation that was put forth failed to delineate the processes that comprise team learning.

In an effort to better understand the process of adaptive team performance and the outcome of team adaptation within naturally existing teams, this chapter has taken a multidisciplinary view to further delineate the processes involved in team learning and specify how they might relate to Burke et al.'s (2006) team-adaptation model. Once delineated, this information was then utilized to facilitate the identification of methods, tools, and corresponding propositions that can be used to facilitate team learning at different phases of the learning cycle. In identifying methods and tools, the authors sought to leverage not only what has been proposed about team adaptation and the role that team learning has in achieving this outcome, but also what is known about team interaction in general. In addition, we attempted to push the envelope by examining tools and methods that may not have been traditionally applied to teams (e.g., story telling, communities of practice), but with some modification we believe could be very viable and forward-looking tools. It is the hope that the ideas put forth within this chapter will serve to provoke thought and continue to advance knowledge about the role that team learning occupies in team adaptation within work teams. However, it is also useful to highlight a few areas where research is needed. What follows is a brief description of some of these areas.

While this chapter acknowledges and actually highlights the cyclical nature of team adaptation as well as the process of team learning occurring within the adaptive team-performance cycle, the investigation of this facet of the model is underrepresented. While many have talked about the importance of examining and measuring teams over time and at multiple points in development (Harrison, Price, Gaven, & Florey, 2002; Harrison, Mohammed, McGrath, Florey, & Vanderstoep, 2003; McGrath, 1991) to better understand the cyclical nature of team processes (e.g., those comprising team adaptation), this area of research is often neglected due to its complexity. While several assertions were made within the chapter concerning how different aspects of the team-learning process might play out at different points within the adaptive cycle, future research needs to not only examine such assertions, but also examine the nature of the cycles housed within adaptive team performance. Are there set cycles? How are they characterized according to developmental stage? How does the cyclical nature or different phases of learning correspond?

In terms of more practical applications, research needs to examine the types of tools and methods that can be best used to promote team learning in context as applied to each stage of team development as well as for each stage of team learning. While the current chapter begins to suggest how various tools or methods might be more or less amenable to use during the various stages of team learning, these are only initial propositions. Moreover, there exist a wide variety of methods and tools that team researchers have at their disposal. Researchers and practitioners should begin to examine how some of these may be used in unique ways as well as how some tools traditionally used for individual learning may be able to be modified to facilitate team learning in context. Along these lines, more applied research can begin to be conducted to examine the myriad actions or behaviors that can be used to gather additional information during the action phases of team learning (e.g., crossing boundaries, experimentation) above and beyond dialogue and active inquiry. This, in turn, will serve to highlight additional tools that can be used to promote team learning in context. The importance of facilitating a team's ability to learn in context at all stages of the learning cycle is paramount, for no longer do teams have the resources to continuously be pulled "off the line" to attend training. Teams can no longer afford to view team learning as a single event, but must change their view to see it as a continuous process that must be engaged in to remain adaptive.

ACKNOWLEDGMENT

The views expressed in this work are those of the authors and do not necessarily reflect official U.S. Army policy. This work was supported by funding from the Army Research Laboratory's Advanced Decision Architecture Collaborative Technology Alliance (Cooperative Agreement DAAD19-01-2-0009).

REFERENCES

Argyris, C., & Schon, D. A. (1996). *Organisational learning II: Theory, method, and practice*. Reading, MA: Addison-Wesley.

Beyerlein, M., Johnson, D., & Beyerlein, S. (2003). *Team based organizing: Advances in interdisciplinary studies of work teams* (Vol. 9). Oxford, U.K.: Elsevier Science.

Blickensderfer, E., Cannon-Bowers, J. A., & Salas, E. (1997, April). *Training teams to self-correct: An empirical investigation*. Paper presented at the 12th Annual Meeting of the Society of Industrial and Organizational Psychology, St. Louis, MO.

Bruner, J. S. (1990). *Acts of meaning*. Cambridge, MA: Harvard University Press.

Burke, C. S., Priest, H. A., Upshaw, C. L., & Salas, E. (under review). A sensemaking approach to understanding multicultural teams: An initial framework. In D. I. Stone, E. F. Stone-Romero, & E. Salas (Eds.), *Cultural diversity and human resource practices*. New York: Lawrence Erlbaum Associates.

Burke, C. S., Salas, E., Estep, S., & Pierce, L. (in press). Facilitating team adaptation 'in the wild': A theoretical framework, instructional strategies, and research agenda. In R. Hoffman (Ed.), *Expertise out of context*. New York: Lawrence Erlbaum Associates

Burke, C. S., Stagl, K. C., Salas, E., Pierce, L., & Kendall, D. (2006). Understanding team adaptation: A conceptual analysis and model. *Journal of Applied Psychology, 91*, 1189–1207.

Choi, M. (2006). Communities of practice: An alternative learning model for knowledge creation. *British Journal of Educational Technology, 37*(1), 143–146.

Coghlan, D., & Brannick, T. (2001). *Doing action research in your own organization*. London: Sage.

Dechant, K., Marsick, V. J., & Kasl, E. (1993). Toward a model of team learning. *Studies in Continuing Education, 15*(1), 1–14.

Dechant, K., Marsick, V. J., & Kasl, E. (2000). Team learning: A model for effectiveness in high performing teams. *Team Development, 7*, 1–19.

Denning, S. (2005). *The leader's guide to storytelling: Mastering the art and discipline of business narrative*. San Francisco: Jossey-Bass Publishers.

Denning, S. (2004, May). Telling tales. *Harvard Business Review*, 122–129.

Domain, B. (1989). What leaders of tomorrow see. *Fortune, 120*(1), 48–62.

Edmondson, A. (1999). Psychological safety and learning behavior in work teams. *Administrative Science Quarterly, 46*, 685–716.

Edmondson, A., Bohmer, R., & Pisano, G. (2001, October). Speeding up team learning. *Harvard Business Review*, 125–132.

Ellis, S., Mendel, R., & Nir, M. (2006). Learning from successful and failed experience: The moderating role of kind of after-event review. *Journal of Applied Psychology, 91*(3), 669–680.

Endsley, M. R. (1995). Toward a theory of situation awareness in dynamic systems. *Human Factors, 38*, 232–250.

Gibson, C. B. (2001). From knowledge accumulation to accommodation: Cycles of collective cognition in work groups. *Journal of Organizational Behavior, 22*, 121–134.

Gutwin, C., & Greenberg, S. (2004). The importance of awareness for team cognition in distributed collaboration. In E. Salas, & S. Fiore (Eds.), *Team cognition: Understanding the factors that drive process and performance* (pp. 177–201). Washington, DC: American Psychological Association.

Guzzo, R. A., & Dickson, M. W. (1996). Teams in organizations: Recent research on performance and effectiveness. *Annual Review Psychology, 47,* 307–338.

Harrison, D. A., Price, K. H., Gavin, J. H., & Florey, A. (2002). Time, teams, and task performance: Changing effects of surface- and deep-level diversity on group functioning. *Academy of Management Journal, 45,* 1029–1045.

Harrison, D. A., Mohammed, S., McGrath, J. E., Florey, A. T., & Vanderstoep, S. W. (2003). Time matters in team performance: Effects of member familiarity, entrainment, and task discontinuity on speed and quality. *Personnel Psychology, 56,* 633–669.

Hildebrand, K., Zaccaro, S. J., & Shuffler, M. L. (2006). Adaptive team leadership. Paper presented at the 21st Annual Meeting of the Society for Industrial/Organizational Psychology, Dallas, TX.

Ilgen, D. R., Major, D. A., Hollenbeck, J. R., & Sego, D. J. (1993). Team research in the 1990s. In M. M. Chemers, & R. Ayman (Eds.), *Leadership theory and research: Perspectives and directions.* San Diego, CA: Academic Press, Inc.

Kasl, E., Marsick, V. J., & Deschant, K. (1997). Teams as learners: A research-based model of team learning. *Journal of Applied Behavioral Science, 33*(2), 227–246.

Kozlowski, S. W. J. (1998). Training and developing adaptive teams: Theory, principles, and research. In J. A. Cannon-Bowers, & E. Salas (Eds.), *Making decisions under stress: Implications for individual and team training* (pp. 15–153). Washington, DC: American Psychological Association.

Langellier, K. M. (1989). Personal narratives: Perspectives on theory and research. *Text and Performance Quarterly, 9,* 243–276.

LePine, J. A. (2003). Team adaptation and postchange performance: Effects of team composition in terms of members' cognitive ability and personality. *Journal of Applied Psychology, 88,* 27–39.

Levine, L. (1994). Listening with spirit and the art of team dialogue. *Journal of Organizational Change Management, 7*(1), 61–73.

Levitt, B., & March, J. G. (1988). Organizational learning. *Annual Review of Sociology, 14,* 319–340.

Marquardt, M. (1999). *Action learning in action.* Palo Alto, CA: Davies-Black.

McGrath, J. E. (1991). Time, interaction, and performance (TIP): A theory of groups. *Small Group Research, 22,* 147–174.

Mezirow, J. (1991). *Transformative dimensions of adult learning.* San Francisco: Jossey-Bass.

Pedler, M. (Ed.). (1991). *Action learning in practice* (2nd ed.). Brookfield, VT: Gower.

Pulakos, E. D., Dorsey, D. W., & White, S. (2006). Adaptability in the workplace: Selecting an adaptive workforce. In S. Burke, L. Pierce, & E. Salas (Eds.), *Understanding adaptability: A prerequisite for effective performance within complex environments.* Cambridge, MA: Elsevier Science.

Raelin, J. A. (1997). Action learning and action science: Are they different? *Organizational Dynamics, 26*(1), 21–34.

Raelin, J. A. (2000). *Work-based learning.* Upper Saddle River, NJ: Prentice-Hall.

Raelin, J. A. (2006). Does action learning promote collaborative leadership? *Academy of Management Learning & Education, 5*, 152–168.

Revans, R. (1982). *The origins and growth of action learning.* Kent, U.K.: Chartwell-Bratt.

Roberts, J. (2006). Limits to communities of practice. *Journal of Management Studies, 43*(3), 623–639.

Saint-Onge, H., & Wallace, D. (2003). *Leveraging communities of practice for strategic advantage.* London: Butterworth Heinemann.

Salas, E., Prince, C., Baker, D. P., & Shrestha, L. (1995). Situation awareness in team performance: Implications for measurement and training. *Human Factors, 37*, 123–136.

Salas, E., Stagl, K. C., Burke, C. S., & Goodwin, G. F. (in press). Fostering team effectiveness in organizations: Toward an integrative theoretical framework of team performance. In W. Spaulding, & J. Flowers (Eds.), *Modeling complex systems: Motivation, cognition, and social processes.* Lincoln, NE: University of Nebraska Press.

Schon, D. A. (1983). *The reflective practitioner.* New York: Basic Books.

Senge, P. M. (1990). *The fifth discipline: The art and practice of the learning organization.* New York: Doubleday.

Shank, M. J. (2006). Teacher storytelling: A means for creating and learning within a collaborative space. *Teaching and Teacher Education, 22*, 711–721.

Smith-Jentsch, K. A., Blickensderfer, E., Salas, E., & Cannon-Bowers, J. A. (2000). Helping team members help themselves: Proposition for facilitating guided team self-correction. In M. M. Beyerlein, D. A. Johnson, & S. T. Beyerlein (Eds.), *Team performance management* (pp. 55–72). Stamford, CT: JAI Press.

Smith-Jentsch, K. A., Zeisig, R. L., Acton, B., & McPherson, J. A. (1998). Team dimensional training: A strategy for guided team self-correction. In J. A. Cannon-Bowers, & E. Salas (Eds.), *Making decisions under stress: Implications for individual and team training* (pp. 271–297). Washington, DC: American Psychological Association.

Stout, R. J., & Salas, E. (1993). The role of planning in coordinated team decision making: Implications for training. *Proceedings of the Human Factors and Ergonomics Society 37th Annual Meeting* (pp. 1238–1242). Santa Monica, CA: Human Factors and Ergonomics Society.

Swezey, R. W., & Salas, E. (Eds.). (1992). *Teams: Their training and performance.* Norwood, NJ: Ablex.

Tompkins, T. C. (2000). Developing mature teams: Moving beyond team basics. *Team Development, 7*, 207–222.

Tsoukas, H., & Mylonopoulos, N. (Eds.). (2004). *Organizations as knowledge systems: Knowledge, learning, and dynamic capabilities.* Basingstoke, U.K.: Palgrave Macmillan.

Waller, M. J. (1999). The timing of adaptive group responses to nonroutine events. *Academy of Management Journal, 42*, 127–137.

Weick, K. E. (1979). *The social psychology of organizing* (2nd ed.). Reading, MA: Addison-Wesley.

Wenger, E. (1998, June). Communities of practice: Learning as a social system. *Systems Thinker, 9*(5), 1–10.

Wenger, E., McDermott, R., & Snyder, W. M. (2002). *Cultivating communities of practice*. Boston: Harvard Business School Press.

Zaccaro, S. J., & Bader, P. (2003). E-leadership and the challenges of leading e-teams: Minimizing the bad and maximizing the good. *Organizational Dynamics, 31*, 377–387.

CHAPTER

11

Team Learning on Messy Problems

E. A. J. A ROUWETTE AND J. A. M. VENNIX
Radboud University Nijmegen, the Netherlands

In this chapter, we concentrate on procedures used to foster group learning for a particular type of problem, the so-called messy problem. The distinctive feature of messy problems is that the people involved have different ideas on what the problem is or whether there even is a problem. Nevertheless, those involved in the problem depend on one another as some form of cooperation is needed to improve the situation. In other words, a process of group learning is required. In the last few decades, different procedures have been developed to support group learning of managers and experts involved in a messy problem. This chapter describes the shared features of these methods and tries to group effective elements by relating them to the phases in a generic information-processing model. For each phase, we survey recent research with an emphasis on expert and naturalistic decision making. We then consider how group-decision support procedures try to influence group activities in each phase. We conclude this chapter by summarizing the areas where theories on group learning can benefit from methods for supporting group learning in messy problems and vice versa.

BACKGROUND

Since the end of the 1970s, researchers in management science and systems science have called attention to ill-defined problems that are particularly difficult to manage. The type of problem that lends itself well to analysis was described by Rosenhead (1989) as one that has "unambiguous objectives, firm constraints, and establishable relationships between causes and effects. It will also, as a result of this specificity, have one clear solution" (p. 5). Rittel and Webber (1973) referred to this as a "tame" problem, in contrast to "wicked" problems that are more difficult to define. In this information age (Hinsz, Tindale, & Vollrath, 1997), more problems are becoming wicked as interconnections between and within organizations increase (Mason & Mitroff, 1981; Napuk, 1993; Friedman, 2005). The basic feature of a complex problem is a lack of knowledge on the part of the individual or group trying to describe the problem (Mitroff & Sagasti, 1973; Vriens, 1998). Ackoff (1981) drew attention to the difficulty of disentangling a specific problem from the "mess" of problems an organization faces. According to Vennix (1996), the essential feature of a messy problem is that it is defined differently by different members of the organization, and some members might even deny there is a problem at all. In the remainder of this chapter, we will use the terms ill-defined problem and messy problem interchangeably.

Since the 1970s, researchers have developed a set of practical procedures to help groups cope with messy problems. These procedures are known as soft-operational research or Problem Structuring Methods (PSMs; Eden, 1995; Morton, Ackermann, & Belton, 2003). PSMs aim to structure and integrate information and aid in the negotiation process between meeting participants. Their ultimate goal is to help a group reach a decision and create commitment to actions (Eden, 1995). PSMs have a background in operational research (Rosenhead, 1989; Morton et al., 2003). Traditionally, operational research works by constructing a model of the decision/problem, which is then used to find the optimal solution (Checkland, 1981). Using a PSM, the model serves both as an integrated view of the problem and a negotiation device. In PSMs, the model is thus no longer seen as a description of reality as in traditional operational research, but instead as a coherent combination of problem perceptions. PSMs have been used in many applied projects to the satisfaction of problem owners and researchers (Mingers & Rosenhead, 2004). Some projects address high-profile problems in litigation (Cooper, 1980), multiparty engineering projects (Williams, Ackermann, & Eden, 2003), organizational change in hospital care (Winch & Derrick, 2006), or national criminal justice policies (Rouwette, Jongebreur, Van Hooff, Heijmen, & Vennix, 2004). PSMs have largely developed on the basis of a design-test-redesign approach using action research. This means that in many instances, at first a practical approach is discovered that works for groups dealing with messy problems, but only later is this practical connected to theories and insights from group decision making or related disciplines. Practitioners in the field of PSMs recognize that their approaches have largely developed on the basis of intuition (Eden, 1995) and are sometimes more art than science (Andersen, Richardson, & Vennix, 1997). Thus, from the perspective of PSM practitioners, it is relevant to compare their practice to relevant theory, in order to see if there are general insights that could increase their methods' effectiveness or efficiency. Uncovering and testing hidden assumptions of practitioners is likely to refute some of their intuitions and improve their approach. From the perspective of theories and research on group learning, this comparison is relevant as we are assessing whether insights also apply to the extreme case of groups working on messy problems.

In the remainder of this chapter, we describe PSM approaches in more depth. We then address phases of information sharing in groups and summarize the main results of studies for each phase. Next, we describe how PSMs guide participants through these phases and consider the empirical evidence for the effectiveness of PSMs. We conclude by listing insights for PSM practice and theory on group learning.

PROBLEM STRUCTURING METHODS

Researchers working in the PSM tradition are concerned with the understanding of a phenomenon in its context and from the perspective of participants. Research is interpretivistic in nature and often takes the form of action research. Finlay (1998) pointed to subjective idealism and normativism as the underlying philosophy of PSMs. Besides understanding the perspective of the participants, PSM proponents aim to help a group in deciding how to act and support the creation of commitment to future actions (Eden, 1995). PSMs do not so much offer a product as "... model-driven researchers are more likely to see themselves as offering a 'problem structuring' (...) or 'problem consultation' (...) *service*, a vital component of which is the skill of the change agent" (Morton et al., 2003, p. 115). This service is highly dependent on the context encountered and the facilitator plays a central role as he or she guides the group process. The facilitator interacts directly with the group, asking questions and eliciting ideas for constructing the model. An important issue in the evaluation of model-based approaches is the transferability of the approaches, the "transmission of [...] to tacit knowledge to potential practitioners of the method" (Morton et al., 2003, p. 115). The effects of model-based approaches have been documented in numerous case studies, and reviews are beginning to appear (Mingers, 2000; Rouwette, Vennix, & Van Mullekom, 2002; Mingers & Rosenhead, 2004).

Electronic meeting systems (EMS) are another type of intervention that also aims to support all phases of group decision making (DeSanctis & Gallupe, 1987; Briggs, Vreede, & de Nunamaker, 2003). PSM and EMS differ in regard to their field of origin, focus of research, and aim of interventions (Morton et al., 2003). EMS originated in the field of information science, which, according to Morton et al., makes the underlying computer system the central focus of research. The use of formal propositions, quantifiable measures of variables, and sampling procedures point to a positivist philosophical orientation favoring comparability of situations and experimental studies on effectiveness (e.g., Zigurs, 1993). Studies on EMSs share a meta-analytical framework (Pinsonneault & Kraemer, 1989; Stevens & Finlay, 1996) that makes results easy to compare. An important aim of EMS is effective and efficient data collection (Eden, 1995), although Finlay (1998) extended their goals to supporting decision making. Studies on PSM and EMS are thus frequently different in the variables studied and research design used, which in practice leads to little contact or synergy between the two fields (Morton et al., 2003).

A practical example of a particular model-based intervention may clarify the process followed. We use an example of a group model building intervention. Group model building is the construction of a system dynamics model (Forrester, 1961) in close participation with problem owners.[1] The starting point for a group model building intervention is a problem perceived by one or more managers in an organization. Although this may seem trivial, the initial problem "label" functions as a focus for the intervention. Typically, the problematic behavior is depicted in a graph over time. In system dynamics terms, the historical problem behavior is known as the reference mode of behavior. Based on the initial problem statement, a decision is made whether group model building is an appropriate method for this problem. This involves questions such as the following: Is the problem dynamically complex? Does it entail short- and long-term effects?

If the method turns out to be suitable for the problem, the next step is to identify participants in the modeling process. Two criteria are employed. Managers that are knowledgeable about the problem area, as well as managers involved in implementing actions, are asked to participate in the project.

After the applicability of the approach and who is involved are decided, participants are invited for the first meeting. The meeting space is set up to allow maximum involvement of all participants. Each

[1] Although on the surface this seems identical to the practice of other PSMs, Mingers and Rosenhead (2004; Rosenhead & Mingers, 2001; Rosenhead, 1996) see system dynamics as falling outside the category of PSMs but similar in some of its modes of use. Andersen, Vennix, Richardson, and Rouwette (2007) concluded that, in the mode of group-model building, there is a very close similarity, but they did not categorize the method as a PSM.

attendant should be able to see the other participants from his or her seat as well as a whiteboard or projection screen. A group model building session is generally conducted in the so-called chauffeured style, where only the facilitator uses electronic support and projection equipment, while participants do not have access to electronic communication media (Nunamaker, Dennis, Valacich, Vogel, & George, 1991). The facilitator has the most important role in the session since he or she guides the group process. As the model is visible to all participants, it serves as a group memory that at each moment reflects the content of the discussion up to that point.

Typically, the first modeling session will start with a brief introduction of the goal of the sessions, the central problem, and the method to be employed. In general, it is emphasized that participants are invited for the sessions based on their expertise or responsibilities in the problem. The facilitator interacting with the group therefore focuses on the group process, while participants are content experts. After the members of the facilitation team and participants have briefly introduced themselves, attention shifts to the problem to be modeled.

If an initial problem statement is agreed upon and the reference mode of behavior is identified, the facilitator asks group members to write down their ideas on the problem individually. Causes, consequences, or elements of the problem are all ideas that may be written down. Participants are then asked one by one to name their most important idea. Each contribution is noted on the central screen and clarified. This is similar to the first steps of Nominal Group Technique (Delbecq, Ven, & van de Gustafson, 1975). The last phase of Nominal Group Technique, prioritization of elements is usually not included here, as most elements will later be incorporated into the model. After several rounds of gathering problem variables, a sizable list will have resulted. The construction of the model then starts by placing the problem variable in the center of the projection screen. The facilitator invites participants to look at the list of variables and identify causes for changes in the problem variable. In group model building, the model is visually depicted using variables and arrows indicating relations between variables. (Note that in system dynamics and in other PSMs other types of models are also used.) A positive relation indicates that both variables change in the same direction: If the independent variable increases, the dependent variable also increases, or if the independent variable decreases, the dependent variable also decreases (see also Richardson, 1986). Variables in a negative relationship change in opposite directions. Apart from variables and relations, the model also contains feedback loops. Feedback loops are the main elements of any system dynamics model, as they are primarily responsible for dynamic behavior. A feedback loop is formed when a variable influences other variables in the model, which ultimately have an impact again on that variable. We illustrate relationships and loops with an example from a group model building case.

The diagram is constructed with representatives from organizations involved in criminal justice in the Netherlands. The Dutch Prison Administration has been faced with a shortage of prison capacity for years. The lower part of Fig. 11.1 shows required detention capacity, which is calculated by multiplying the number of prison sentences with the average time served. If required detention capacity is greater than available detention capacity, a shortage of capacity results. In 2000, the Prison Administration initiated a policy that made prisoners who are serving time for infractions and have completed 90% of their sentence eligible for early release. In 2003, the strictness of norms for early release was reduced and prisoners who had completed 70% of their sentence were eligible for early release. This increased the potential number of early releases and actual releases: In 2000, 200 prisoners were released early, rising to 446 in 2001 and 4,837 in 2002 (Prison Administration Annual Report, 2002). By reducing the average time served by a reduction time, the early release policy frees up capacity for new prisoners. A judge participating in the modeling project recalled that he became aware of the policy after he recognized a suspect as someone recently convicted and imprisoned for an earlier crime. He then became concerned that the suspect's sentence passed for the earlier crime was not served to completion. He foresaw that when judges would perceive an increase in the difference between duration of the sentence and time

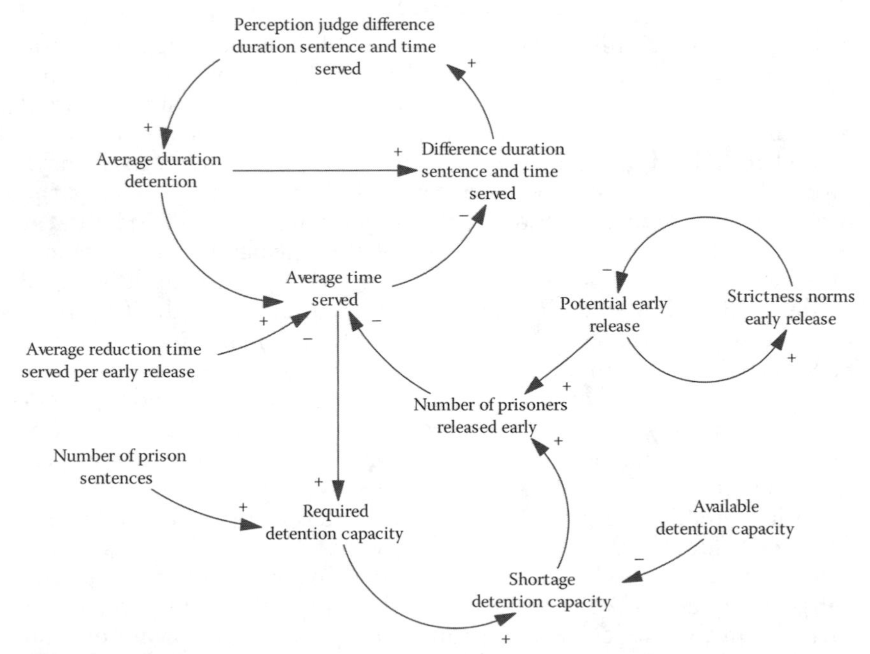

Figure 11.1 Causal loop diagram on early release of prisoners. (Adapted from Rouwette et al., 2004.)

served (upper part of Fig. 11.1) they would compensate by increasing the duration of sentences. Thus, there are three negative feedback loops in the causal loop diagram above. Negative-feedback loops lead to balancing behavior. In the loop at the bottom of the figure, an increase in required detention capacity leads to more prisoners released early. This reduces the average time served and thereby reduces required detention capacity. In this way, an initial increase is compensated by a decrease. The example shows how feedback effects play out over different parts of the criminal-justice system.

The results of a modeling session are captured in a workbook containing the diagram and a short description of the model. The workbook usually also contains questions that serve as a preparation for the following session. While the project progresses, the model increases in complexity until the group of participants feels that all important variables and relations are included. An important check with regard to completeness is whether the model structure, in particular the loops, can explain the reference mode of behavior. A number of other validity tests are discussed in the literature (see Forrester & Senge, 1980). The model just described is qualitative and was in later stages of the project translated into a formal, quantified model and simulated. Simulated model behavior was compared to the historical data contained in the reference mode. The ultimate goal of model construction is to identify interventions that change behavior in the preferred direction. This involves identifying the policy levers in the model—those variables that can be influenced by the client organization. In the model just discussed, the strictness of norms for early release are under the control of the Prison Administration. Using a formal model, different values for strictness could be tested for their effect on the behavior of other variables in the model.

Usually, a group model building intervention is closed by handing over the final model and an accompanying report to the client. However, some of the most important outcomes of group model building and PSMs are the creation of a consensus view on the problem and commitment to actions in the problem. The creation of these outcomes is a gradual process that takes place during the complete intervention.

PHASES OF INFORMATION EXCHANGE SUPPORTED BY PSMS

In this section, we compare insights from group learning to the practice of Problem Structuring Methods (PSMs). To structure our argument, we use the generic information-processing model depicted in Fig. 11.2. The model, described by Hinsz et al. (1997), distinguishes different components of information processing. Although the model was originally developed for individual decision making (e.g., Anderson, 1990), the authors found this model useful because it allows them to use individual behavior as a comparison for group behavior. In addition,

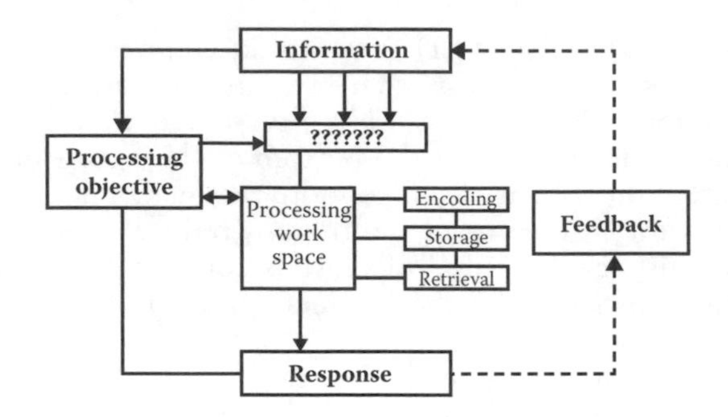

Figure 11.2 Generic information-processing model. (From Hinsz et al., 1997, p. 44, reprinted with permission.)

cognitive metaphors seem useful to theorize about groups. The authors argued that the processes in group learning span virtually all the phases they discuss (Hinsz et al., 1997, p. 53).

The model consist of the following eight phases. Interactions with the world provide the basis for individual information acquisition. Interactions with the world take place in a context that provides a *processing objective* for the information. Perception of the information forms the *attention* phase of information processing. Transformation by structuring, evaluating, and interpreting information to form a representation is the *encoding* phase. *Storage* is then the process of information entering memory, which may be brought into awareness again by *retrieval*. Encoding, storage, and retrieval involve the *processing workspace* in which information is integrated and processed on the basis of different rules and strategies. Processing on the basis of objectives may lead to a *response* such as stating an opinion or idea, or making a judgment or choice. The response may lead to *feedback* about changes in the world and thereby provide new information. For each information processing phase, Hinsz et al. (1997) reviewed research on information processing by groups performing cognitive tasks. In the following, for each phase, we briefly list the most important topics raised in Hinsz et al.'s article and then review research that is particularly relevant for groups of experts working on messy problems. This means that where possible we describe results from a field or naturalistic setting and review studies showing how experts differ from novices in the way they process information.

Processing Objective

Processing objectives for groups include tasks, missions, and collective goals and are an important part of the social reality of group members working on a task. Instructions, task characteristics, procedural factors, member perspectives, roles, and norms may be sources of processing objectives (Hinsz et al., 1997, p. 45). The research reviewed by the authors showed that a processing objective emphasizing group relations (e.g., mutual consideration) leads to more normative influence, whereas a task-oriented processing objective (e.g., provide the most correct response) leads to more informational influence. Task cues may influence the degree of fairness that group members prefer. Procedural factors, including organizational culture, also influence the way in which groups in organizations perform tasks. Dissimilar perspectives concerning background, gender, or demographic characteristics lead members to approach tasks in different ways and process information differently. Stasser, Stewart, and Wittenbaum (1995) found that assigning different roles to team members influences the type of information a person brings up in a discussion. Finally, Hinsz et al. (1997) cited several studies showing that groups may set their own objective (e.g., with regard to productivity) depending on the group norm. Kerr and Tindale (2004) reviewed studies that indicate that in particular situations, groups set more challenging goals than individuals can (p. 630).

Two areas of research may further clarify how the issues just discussed play out with regard to expert teams working on messy problems. First, since messy problems are of great importance to the organizations and groups involved, research on groups grappling with urgent problems is especially relevant. This type of problem is addressed in research on groupthink (Janis, 1972, 1982), which focuses on the extreme case of cohesive groups that find themselves in a highly challenging context. A second important area of study concerns the time aspect. The consequences of messy problems play out over a long time and interact with management policies that have been implemented in the past. The literature on escalation of commitment addresses this issue. Groupthink has been termed the most influential theory in the group-decision field (Turner & Pratkanis, 1998). Janis' (1982) adapted model featured two antecedents of groupthink: (a) structural faults such as a cohesive group and lack of norms for methodical procedures, and (b) a provocative context involving external threats and low self-esteem. These antecedents lead to a situation of groupthink, characterized by an overestimation of the group's capabilities, closed-mindedness, and uniformity pressure. This situation is expected to lead to defective decision making, and thus a low probability of a successful outcome. The empirical support for the groupthink model is mixed (Turner & Pratkanis, 1998; Curşeu, 2003; Kerr & Tindale, 2004). In some studies, good decisions are made in situations in which the model would predict groupthink and disastrous consequences. Turner and Pratkanis (1998) found three directions in recent studies on groupthink: (a) studies that use Janis' model without changes (a minority), (b) those who reformulate the model, and (d) those who reject it outright. According to Kerr and Tindale (2004), the main contribution of the model is its clarification of how aspects of groups that are usually seen as positive (e.g., cohesiveness) do not always lead to positive outcomes. The second field of study, escalation of commitment (Staw, 1976; Staw & Ross, 1980), refers to the situation in which an individual or group continues a course of action despite evidence of its negative consequences. In his initial study, Staw (1976) showed that escalation of commitment increases with a sense of responsibility for the decision. Recent studies extend the results to a wide variety of situations, such as interpersonal situations, waiting times, gambling, and investments (Curşeu, 2003, p. 142). Escalation of commitment has also been found to operate in group decisions (Bazerman, Giuliano, Appelman, 1984; Whyte, 1991; Seibert & Goltz, 2001).

The influences listed by Hinsz et al. (1997), as well as the insights from the studies on groupthink and escalation of commitment, clearly apply to members of expert teams focusing on messy problems. The example on criminal justice shows that these teams are heterogeneous with regard to member perspectives and roles. Participants are invited based on the different expertise they can contribute, and frequently managers from different hierarchical levels work together in a session. The dominant norms in an organization (or multiple organizations) and the complexity of the task are givens with which a PSM practitioner will have to work. If a team has a history of working on a messy problem together, the antecedents of groupthink and escalation of commitment may be present. The question then becomes how instructions and procedures may be used to prevent detrimental effects of differences between members as well as extreme situations as groupthink and escalation of commitment. How do PSMs try to influence processing objectives? Here it is useful to distinguish objectives in the intervention process (from first to last contact with the client, which may span a period of weeks or months) from objectives in a single face-to-face session (lasting a few hours or days). Handbooks on PSMs underline the importance of expectation management, a clear definition of roles, and explicit recognition of differences in goals between participants (Eden, 1995; Vennix, 1996). Eden (1995) saw management of the client-consultant relation as one of the prerequisites for a successful intervention. Schein (1987b) referred to this as the psychological contract between client and consultant. An important part of the contract is that the client remains the problem owner throughout the intervention process. The intervener has the role of a facilitator who helps in diagnosing the problem, but the client makes the final choice for an action that will be implemented. The roles of the interveners and clients were further refined by Richardson and Andersen (1995) and Eden and Ackermann (1996). Part of the contract is also that the client is committed to the process and will spend the time needed to analyze the problem. The commitment and time devoted to the process hinges upon the importance the client organization and the participants in the PSM sessions attach to the problem: "If you want to achieve changes in an organization as a result of your corporate modeling work, the problem or opportunity that you select must be important to the client. Otherwise, that client will neither pay much attention to the modeling effort, nor bother with its resulting recommendations" (Roberts, 1978, p. 79). Analysts focusing on power in organizations emphasize the importance of information as a power base. Lieshout (1995) and Scheper (1991) assumed that a participant would only contribute information in a collective decision-making process if he or she expects to profit more by sharing information. This viewpoint draws attention to differences between individual and collective goals in groups dealing with messy problems. McGrath (1984) argued that in an organizational setting there is always a degree of competition as well as an interdependence between individuals (p. 94). In these settings, it is difficult to disentangle conflicts of interest from conflicts of viewpoints. In messy problems where the exact problem is unclear, these aspects are particularly hard to separate. Clarifying the nature of the problem may then be a necessary step to show where the real conflict of interests is, if any actually exists. PSM practitioners (e.g., Vennix, 1995, 1999) argue that what seems to be a difference of interest often turns out to be a difference of viewpoint. Frequently, more consensus exists about the preferred course of action than expected before structuring the problem.

With regard to a PSM meeting, we discuss three aspects of the processing objective: (a) the effect of process structure, (b) the impact of the model on the discussion theme, and (c) the effect of group interaction. The facilitator is neutral with regard to content but has an expert role in structuring a meeting. Thus, he or she chooses particular techniques in line with the group task at that moment. Mixing processing objectives such as generating and evaluating information decreases the productivity of a group (Osborn, 1953). Thus, the agenda of a group meeting typically starts with information generation using, for instance, brainstorming (Osborn, 1953) or Nominal Group Technique (Delbecq et al., 1975) followed by a convergence task using a technique such as construction of a qualitative model.

In a typical PSM session discussion and model construction go hand in hand and inform each other. Scheper and Faber (1994; Scheper, 1991) drew attention to the meaning of terms used in the discussion process. They used a semiotic perspective to understand the creation of shared meaning. Scheper (1991) noted that a clear discussion theme is helpful in fostering convergence of meaning and reducing ambiguity of terms among participants. The model is an important device in this as it shows how different concepts (variables or means/ends) relate to one another.

Practical guidelines for PSM projects emphasize the importance of participant attendance. Although the results of a session are captured in a workbook, participants that miss a session usually have to be brought up to speed again in the next session (e.g., Vennix, Akkermans, & Rouwette, 1996). Apparently, even though the written workbook contains the resulting model and the main elements of the discussion, it fails to capture the essence of a discussion. This may be due to the fact that the context of a face-to-face discussion evokes a different implicit processing objective than reading a report of the same discussion. Scheper (1991) took this group-process effect (the additional effect beyond the "pure" exchange of information) to be the most important effect of a

PSM intervention (p. 212). Curşeu (2003) showed that information on the processing objective is in part implicit and may have a different impact depending on the medium of information exchange that is used: face-to-face discussion allows for more exchange of implicit information than a computer-mediated discussion. This is in line with Daft and Lengel's (1986) hypothesis that media allow a particular "richness" of information to be exchanged: text-based media allow only verbal interaction, while a face-to-face exchange allows for exchange of both verbal and nonverbal cues. In complex situations involving negotiation, face-to-face interaction may be crucial to achieve a satisfactory outcome. Kenis (1995) found some evidence for this in research on an electronic Delphi procedure (p. 141). In the absence of face-to-face discussion, participants need an informal channel in addition to a text-based discussion of their task. This is supported by Kerr and Murthy (2004), who found that face-to-face groups perform worse than computer-mediated groups in the divergence phase of discussion but perform better in the convergence phase. Their conclusion is that computer-mediated communication "may not be appropriate for performing highly ambiguous tasks or in situations involving conflicts of interest where it may be more difficult for the team to converge on a solution" (Kerr & Murthy, 2004, p. 396).

Attention

Hinsz et al. (1997) focused on three topics in their discussion of attention: (a) whether group members focus their attention internally or externally, (b) how the distribution of information impacts what information becomes the center of attention, and (c) how group interactions focus attention on particular information. In our discussion, we concentrate on the role of conscious attention and its relation to biases and heuristics in decision making. Hinsz et al. (1997) started their review of research on attention with the statement: "Group members must attend to information in order to process it" (p. 46). Recently, however, "unconscious processing" of information has received more and more attention in psychological research (Mandler, 1984; Oatley, 1992; Damasio, 1994; Wilson, T. D., 2002; Dijksterhuis, Bos, Nordgren, & Van Baaren, 2006). T. D. Wilson (2002) illustrated the crucial part unconscious information plays with an example of a man who loses his sense of proprioception (p. 19). With a great deal of effort, the patient had to replace unconscious proprioception with conscious control of his body. Whenever his concentration was lost, he would lose control over his body and end up "in a heap of tangled limbs on the floor." Based on experimental as well as real-world purchase decisions, Dijksterhuis et al. (2006) concluded that unconscious thinkers are better able to make the best choice among complex products. Conscious thinkers are better able to make the best choice among simple products. Popular books such as *Blink* (Gladwell, 2005) maintain that expert decision making is often instantaneous, difficult to access by conscious processes, and in specific circumstances leads to high-quality decisions. A classic example of expert decision making, reported by Simon (1957), already has many of these features. Simon studied a chess player who tried to decide on the next move in a game, an activity that involves a highly analytical approach. Expert chess players indicate that good moves usually come to mind after a few seconds of looking at the board, after which they spend considerable time verifying that the move does not have hidden weaknesses (Simon, 1987, p. 59). So, although a decision comes to mind almost immediately, chess players use a more analytical and time-consuming process to check this first option. This analysis may reveal that the first option is biased. Simon (1987) described how in a situation of stress, for example, intuitive decisions may be based on "primitive urges" such as the need to reduce embarrassment or guilt. Research in the biases and heuristics program (e.g., Tversky & Kahneman, 1971, 1974; Gilovich, Griffin, & Kahnemann, 2002) shows convincingly that human judgment is biased in systematic ways. We discuss the generalizibility of these studies to the domain of decision making on ill-defined problems in the section on processing. A conclusion that directly bears on the role of attention in this domain comes from the paradigm of naturalistic decision making (e.g., Lipshitz, Klein, Orasanu, & Salas, 2001). Naturalistic decision making focuses on decision makers with some degree of expertise in real-life contexts. In several fields of expertise, decision makers confronted with time pressure and uncertainty typically carried out the first course of action that came to mind. This idea is similar to Simon's (1987) assertion that "intuition and judgment—at least good judgment—are simply analyses frozen into habit" (p. 63). This process, termed recognition-primed decision making, actually consists of a range of strategies. In its simplest form, the strategy comes down to sizing up the situation and responding with the initial option identified. If the situation is not clear, the decision maker may supplement this strategy by mentally simulating the events leading up to the situation. In a situation that is shifting continuously, the decision maker may apply a different kind of simulation. Here the proposed plan of action is mentally simulated to see if unintended consequences arise that are unacceptable. In a review of these studies, Klein (1998) considered the conditions under which recognition-primed decision making applies. Decision makers use these strategies when they have considerable expertise relevant to the situation at hand, are under time pressure, and the goals are uncertain and/or ill defined. Recognition-primed decision making is less likely to be used with highly combinatorial problems, when a justification for the decision is required, and when the views of different stakeholders have to be taken into account. From our previous description, it is clear that decision making in messy problems falls into the latter category: different stakeholders are involved and asked to explain (or justify) their decisions to each other. The situation is complex and is certainly a highly combinatorial problem. Thus, it seems likely that for individual decision makers confronted with a messy problem, a course of action will immediately come to mind, but this proposal will be analyzed, rethought, and discussed with others before it is implemented.

In an organizational setting, the studies by Argyris and Schön (1978; Argyris, 1992) showed how the context in which information is evoked determines the answers of subjects. When asked to comment on a videotaped interaction between a superior and his or her subordinate, subjects clearly pointed out the mistakes the superior makes that cause the conversation to go awry. When the same subjects were then asked to convey their ideas to the superior in person, they made mistakes similar to the ones they just pointed out in the supervisor's behavior. Argyris and Schön coined the term "espoused theory" for a person's verbalized beliefs and "theory in use" for the actual beliefs underlying one's behavior. As their research pointed out, the espoused theory and the theory in use need not be similar (see also Bella, King, & Kailin, 2003). Thus, it seems that observing other people interact (the videotape) evokes reactions on the basis of the espoused theory, while actual interaction evokes the theory in use. In addition, whereas the first reaction involves conscious attention, the second involved less deliberation and is much more intuitive. The difference between more and less deliberative information processing is brought up again when we discuss System 1 and 2 as proposed by Kahneman and Frederick (2002) (e.g., Gilovich et al., 2002). As the previously discussed group model building case shows (see Fig. 11.1), models constructed in PSM interventions frequently include information on decisions of participants: the judge describes how he is confronted with an undesirable situation (a decrease in time served) and reacts to this (by increasing the duration of sentences). Since the information discussed in PSM meetings is frequently on a participant's own behavior, it may be questioned how information on theories in use is brought to the surface.

How do PSM approaches try to manage attention of participants? In particular, how does one reconcile the instantaneous character of expert decision making with the need to analyze the problematic situation in depth? Again, this question may be answered for the intervention as a whole as well as for a particular session. The attention of participants to the intervention as a whole is clearly also dependent on the psychological contract, the importance the client attaches to the problem and individual versus collective goals which were discussed in the previous section. Mintzberg, Raisinghani, and Théorêt (1976) and Hickson, Butler, Cray, Mallory, and D. C. Wilson (1986) showed that decision makers in an organization only select a problem from the myriad issues they are dealing with daily, if it exceeds a certain threshold of urgency. Thus, it may happen that some people in an organization consider a problem to be urgent while others would not define it as a problem at all (Vennix, 1996). Problem urgency may lead to a feeling of stress in participants, an issue that will be discussed further under the section on processing work space.

In a particular meeting, the facilitator has an important role in focusing attention. To some extent, the facilitator acts as a role model in a PSM meeting (e.g., Richardson & Andersen, 1995; Vennix, 1996). Freely interacting task groups can be plagued by nonproductive norms such as departmental bias (Hall & Menzies, 1983), defensive routines (Argyris, 1990), or groupthink (Janis, 1972). The role of the facilitator is to guard against these processes and foster open sharing and analysis of information. Thus, in part, the facilitator sets a norm for the way in which information is processed. Postmes, Spears, and Cihangir (2001) showed that a critical-thinking norm increases the quality of decisions in a hidden-profile condition (a situation where part of the information is initially unshared but all information needs to be combined to arrive at an optimal decision). Setting a critical thinking norm may be seen as a process of priming, where the behavior shown by the facilitator makes a certain category of behavior more accessible for participants and may be inadvertently taken over by participants. In this way, the facilitator may check participants' assumptions, including those about causes of their own behavior. In the section on feedback, three other ways of checking espoused theories are discussed: (a) feedback from other participants, (b) external data, or (c) model simulations. Lastly, the fact that the facilitator attends to the process and procedure used in the discussion provides him or her with an important tool to focus attention. By summarizing the discussion at key points, the facilitator can steer attention to points of agreement or disagreement. For instance, Andersen and Richardson (1997) proposed to summarize key insights at the close of a session and "end with a bang." In this way, participants' recollection of key insights is hopefully improved and their chance of showing up at a future session increased.

Encoding

Encoding raises the question of how members' individual representations of information are combined into a meaningful representation by the group (Hinsz et al., 1997, p. 47; Wilson, M., & Canter, 1993). Hinsz et al. (1997) discussed three topics with regard to encoding: (a) complexity of individual vs. group representations, (b) the formation of shared representations, and (c) the relation of encoding to other phases of group information processing. Groups and individuals may form mental representations of the same information with different levels of complexity. Research is inconclusive as to whether groups process information with more or less dimensions than individuals.

When group members encode information, this information is subject to individual representations, and the information may mean different things to different members. Differences in meaning may not become clear until the group begins to discuss the issue. According to Hinsz et al. research had begun to address the impact of shared representations, but the amount of convincing evidence was still meager (p. 48). Encoding is clearly related to other phases of information processing, such as processing objectives. A shared representation is less likely to develop if the group's objective is to give a common response. The authors wonder if groups that are given a process objective develop representations with a greater degree of similarity. Encoding may also impact the group's response. A high-level map with few dimensions may be easier to understand and implement for group members than a map with more dimensions.

In expert decision making on complex problems, an important type of representation is the mental model (e.g., Johnson-Laird, 1995; Rouse & Morris, 1986). If a group of individuals works together, shared mental models consist of the shared understanding of knowledge, skills, and attitudes related to the group's task and to the team (Curşeu, 2003, p. 27; Mohammed & Dumville, 2001; Cannon-Bowers & Salas, 2001). The antecedents and consequences of shared representations were among Hinsz et al.'s (1997) pertinent questions for future research. With regard to antecedents of shared representations, we look at one aspect of the group's processing objective: the role of active information processing. With regard to consequences, we focus on the influence of shared representations on group process and effectiveness. A number of studies have shown that active and deliberate processing of information leads to better understanding and (individual) decision-making performance (Cosmides & Toobey, 1996: Lee & Hutchinson, 1998; Stern, Aprea, & Ebner, 2003; Wadey & Frank, 1997). In these studies, subjects are asked to construct a graphical display of the information presented. Compared to a group that passively uses graphical displays or text, people in the active graphical representation group answer more questions on the task presented correctly. Natter and Berry (2005) reviewed a number of similar studies in the area of risk communication and investigated the impact of active processing on both understanding and affective ratings. They found that active processing leads to better understanding and influences affective judgments such as likelihood of experiencing side effects (of the medication described in the task information), satisfaction with the information given, and the estimated health risk from taking the medication. Natter and Berry (2005) interpreted their results in the light of dual-process theories of persuasion (further addressed in the section on processing workspace). Thus, it seems that individuals who can be made to use more active ways of processing information achieve a better understanding and experience a greater impact on affective factors. We may speculate that the same process is operational in groups.

With regard to consequences of shared representations, a number of studies find positive effects on group process and effectiveness. Mathieu, Heffner, Goodwin, Salas, and Cannon-Bowers (2000) studied 56 two-person teams in a flight simulator. They found evidence for a positive influence of task-mental-model convergence and team-mental-model convergence on team process. Team process, in turn, has a positive influence on team performance. Rentsch and Klimoski (2001) studied 41 teams of 2–27 members in a naturalistic setting. They found that teamwork agreement is strongly related to all team-effectiveness measures. Other studies using a naturalistic setting found that shared mental models lead to better communication and planning, which, in turn, improves decision-making performance (Volpe, Cannon-Bowers, Salas, & Spector, 1996; Stout, Cannon-Bowers, Salas, & Milanovich, 1999). Curşeu (2003) studied 72 three- or four-person teams and found evidence that a group's representation of teamwork is represented in narrative fashion. In order to study task information at the group level, Curşeu asked groups to jointly develop a cognitive map of their group's work. A second measurement 2 weeks after the map was constructed shows that the relation between concepts at a great distance in the original map takes longer to discuss than the relation between two close concepts. Curşeu (2003) interpreted this as support for the stability of the map (p. 102). The complexity of the shared task model (diversity and number of relations between concepts in the map) is positively related to group performance.

Encoding is an important topic in PSM research and practice. Mental models and ways to improve them are central topics in the system dynamics literature (Forrester, 1961; Doyle & Ford, 1998; Morecroft, 2004). PSM practitioners operate on the assumption that modeling and facilitation foster learning (Morton et al., 2003; Rouwette, Vernix, & Felling, in press). For example, Shields (2002) assumed that visualization and discussion used in a typical modeling session support one another because each draws on different memory systems (p. 5). A model influences visual memory while discussion influences phonetic memory. Thus, using a model to support a group discussion may also make it easier to arrive at a shared perspective on the information exchanged. Several authors (e.g., Vennix, 1996) underlined the importance of a shared perspective by pointing to the fact that two members of an organizational task group may use the same term but often interpret it in different ways. Richmond (1997) pointed to an important benefit of modeling in this respect. The symbols used in system dynamics models work as a unified language that can help in bridging differences between organizational departments. In addition to the format of models, the elements of the respective models used in PSMs deserve attention as well. Scheper and Faber (1994) pointed to several difficulties of using models to represent individual or shared meaning. In their view, when using a correct representation, a model can be used to represent individual meaning. Most types of maps discussed in the literature cannot, however, represent shared meaning (defined as similarity among semantic networks), most importantly because they treat the concepts in the maps as labels and do not identify their properties. Cognitive maps, as used in the approach by Eden and Ackerman (2001b), do not suffer from this shortcoming, but the authors wondered what happens when individuals after discussion still do not agree on essential concepts in the map. Scheper and Faber expected that, in this case, more general concepts might be chosen that are acceptable to all group members. These general concepts may be interpreted differently by group members, so that shared meaning in a semiotic sense has not been reached. The same comments apply to models constructed in group model building sessions, where differences in opinion are also brought to the surface and discussed, but agreement on a specific level is not always attainable. At a more fundamental level, the question can be raised: What is the epistemological status of a model? Zagonel, Rohrbaugh, Richardson, and Andersen (2004) concluded that system dynamics models have a dual identity: at some points in the modeling process they are seen as descriptions of the real world (microworlds) and at other times they are viewed as socially constructed artifacts (boundary objects, see also Morecroft, 2004). In other PSMs, models are generally seen as representations of an individual group member's view on the situation of interest. This leads us to the conclusion that modeling may have an effect on team- and task-mental-model convergence (Fogel, 2005).

Storage

The studies reviewed by Hinsz et al. (1997) showed that groups are able to store more information than individuals are but are not as efficient as they could be (p. 53). Hinsz (1990) estimated that groups use only about 70% of their storing capacity. He expected that the collaboration required to remember at the group level could be responsible for this. An important perspective on implicit strategies for storing information is the *transactive memory model* (Wegner, 1987): a set of implicit strategies for storing information. The transactive memory allows different members of the group to process information, so they remember information that is directly related to their areas of expertise. Implicit strategies are available for encoding, storing, and retrieving information. During the encoding stage, group members learn about each other and especially about each other's field of expertise. Storing and retrieving is facilitated since members know "who knows what." A limited number of studies support the model's assumptions (Curşeu, 2003, p. 40). Liang, Moreland, and Argote (1995) and Moreland, Argote, and Krishnan (1998) showed that members of a group who are trained together perform better than group members who are separately trained. Rulke and Rau (2000) and Yoo and Kanawattanachai (2002) shed more light on the development of transactive memory, while Brandon and Hollingshead (2004) looked at the development of transactive memory in an organizational context.

In PSMs the model is often referred to as a *repository of group knowledge* and expected to have an impact on decision making. The model reflects the content of the group discussion up to that point. In between sessions, it is temporarily "frozen" in workbooks. Vennix (1996) mentioned that visualization helps keep track of complex structures (p. 34; Larkin & Simon, 1987, Lippitt, 1983, Anderson, 1990). In the previous section, the question was addressed whether the model is a reflection of the outside world, an individual's view, or a group view on the situation at hand. If the model made in the session is close to an individual or group's point of view, one would expect that elaborating the model would result in more understanding and improved decision making. Several studies using so-called management-flight simulators address this issue. These studies aim to mimic the important characteristics of decision making in complex, dynamic problems, and test the effectiveness of various decision aids. Participants are placed in a simulated-decision environment and asked to manipulate available decision variables, receive feedback on outcomes, and enter a new round of decisions (Sterman; 1994; Hsiao & Richardson, 1999; Rouwette et al., 2004). Richardson, Andersen, Maxwell, and Stewart (1994) studied the impact of modeling on three types of mental models: (a) means, (b) ends, and (c) means-ends models. The ends model contains goals, while the means model consists of strategies, tactics, and policy levers. The means-ends model contains the connection between the two former types of models and may contain either detailed "design" logic or more simple "operator" logic. The three types of models are derived from the psychological research by Brunswik (1955; Hammond & Stewart, 2001). Based on management-flight-simulator studies (Richardson & Rohrbaugh, 1990; Andersen, Maxwell, Richardson, & Stewart, 1994), the authors conclude that operator logic, or high-level heuristics, is a necessary condition for improving system performance. Therefore, providing managers with operator knowledge is the key to implementation of system changes. The model constructed in a system dynamics session in itself (without supporting decision heuristics) reflects how the system functions and is thus close to design logic. A limited number of studies in the review by Rouwette et al. (2004) showed that groups provided with decision rules and a transparent model outperform groups using only a transparent model. However, model transparency has an independent effect on performance as well.

Retrieval

Hinsz et al. (1997) listed a number of studies that report on the superior ability of groups to recall information in comparison to individuals (p. 49). Reasons for the greater ability of groups to recall information are an easier recognition of errors in memory because there is a greater pool of memories to draw from, a division of roles for remembering information, and the stimulation of memory by cues from another person's recollections. Diehl and Stroebe (1987) found that retrieving and uttering information by one group member could interfere with another person's retrieval processes. Clearly, there is a trade-off between stimulation and interference from other persons' ideas.

Recent research provides more insight into variables influencing retrieval. Nijstad, Stroebe, and Lodewijkx (1999) showed that dyads combine minimal productivity loss with high levels of persistence and satisfaction. Nijstad, Stroebe, and Lodewijkx (2003) revisited the detrimental effect of production blocking on productivity loss in brainstorming groups. They showed that relatively long delays disrupt the organization of ideas, while unpredictable delays reduce the flexibility of idea generation. While all previous studies focus on idea generation, Rietzschel, Nijstand, and Stroebe (2006) focused on idea selection. Interacting groups generated fewer ideas than nominal groups, and ideas generated in interacting groups were less original and more feasible. Quality of ideas was not different between the two types of groups. Research in the hidden profile or information sampling tradition (e.g., Stasser & Titus, 1985; Curşeu, 2003) reveals a number of additional factors that influence recall. Larson, Foster-Fishman, and Keys (1994) showed that group interaction often starts with a discussion of shared information, while distributed information is addressed in the later part of long discussions or not at all in short discussions. In recently formed groups, pressure for conformity seems to be higher than in groups with a longer history, leading members of recently formed groups to chiefly mention shared information (Worchel, Wood, & Simpson, 1992). Wittenbaum, Stasser, and Merry (1996) found that tacit coordination of group interaction influences information exchange: members anticipating a group decision focus on information that they assume everybody knows. Most research in the information sampling tradition is done in laboratory settings, using inexperienced groups making decisions of little relevance to them (Larson, Christensen, Franz, & Abbott, 1998). Larson, Christensen, et al. (1998; Larson, Foster-Fishman, & Franz, 1998) introduced some level of reality by asking teams of physicians to make a decision on hypothetical medical cases. In line with other research, Larson, Christensen, et al. (1998; Larson, Foster-Fishman, et al., 1998) found that shared information is discussed more than unshared information and is also brought into the discussion earlier.

The studies by Larson, Christensen, et al. (1998; Larson, Foster-Fishman, et al., 1998) were also interesting because they pointed to interventions that improve information recall in groups. In their studies, team leaders repeated more information than other group members did; in addition, over time they steadily increased the rate in which they repeated unshared information. Team leaders were also more likely to ask questions about shared as well as unshared information, thereby integrating new information with already shared knowledge and keeping information alive during discussion. Other interventions that increase the likelihood of recalling and mentioning unshared information are increasing the salience of unique information before discussion (Stasser, 1992), using a structured decision procedure (Hollingshead, 1996), facilitation (Wheeler & Valacich 1996), and encouraging group members to assess information critically (Postmes et al., 2001; Liljenquist,

Galinsky, & Kray, 2004). Clearly, the structured and facilitated decision process in group model building incorporates these factors to some extent. Another important element of a PSM intervention, the model, is addressed in recent research on group memory. Paul, Haseman, and Ramamurthy (2004) and Haseman, Nazareth, and Paul (2005) found that presence of a group memory (a rank-ordered list of alternatives, attributes of alternatives, and selections and weights of attributes by previous groups) increases speed of decision making and contrary to expectations decreases thoroughness of task analysis. Although groups using a collective memory needed less decision iterations to reach agreement, no effect on group agreement in the final round of decision making was found. Perceived quality of decisions also did not differ between conditions.

Many of the elements of PSMs discussed earlier help in retrieval processes, most notably the use of a structured procedure, facilitation, encouraging critical thinking, and the use of a group memory. Other elements of PSMs have not been explicitly mentioned before but relate to factors just discussed. Since PSMs bring experts together for an extended period of time in multiple sessions, we can expect there is ample time to express unique information and that pressure of confirmation is low. By emphasizing the expert role of each participant, we expect that unique information is made salient at the outset of the group decision process.

Processing Workspace

Hinsz et al. (1997) discussed information processing at the group level with regard to strategies used, differences in processing by groups and individuals and describe how group processing is influenced by member expectations (p. 49). We first discuss strategies for information processing with an emphasis on processing in expert teams. Second, we describe differences between the individual and group level. Third, we address the role of stress. Much recent work on information processing is founded on dual-process models of cognition (Gilovich et al., 2002, p. 16). Dual-process models assume one set of mental processes that are effortless and quick, and a second set of processes that are more deliberate and require more effort. In social psychology, two-dual process models describe the formation and change of attitudes: the elaboration-likelihood model (Petty & Cacioppo, 1986) and the heuristic-systematic model (Chaiken, Liberman, & Eagly, 1989). Both assume that when judgments are unimportant and motivation is lacking, people use effortless and quick processes. When a judgment is important, people use more taxing and deliberate processes. This perspective is sometimes characterized as the "cognitive-miser view" on information processing. Another type of dual-process model does not fall into the cognitive miser perspective. These models, often called "two-systems models," assume two processes that work in parallel. One is a quick and inaccessible process, similar to intuition. The second is a rule-governed, controllable system akin to reasoning. The intuitive process is labeled System 1 and the reason-based process is called System 2 (Stanovich & West, 2002; Kahneman & Frederick, 2002). Although System 1 is older, it is capable of operations at least as complex as those performed by System 2. Similar to Simon (1957) and Dijksterhuis et al. (2006), Kahneman and Frederick (2002) assumed that complex cognitive operations transfer from System 2 to System 1 as skill and expertise develop. The systems cooperate in the sense that "System 1 quickly proposes intuitive answers to judgmental problems as they arise, and System 2 monitors the quality of these proposals, which it may endorse, correct, or override" (Kahneman & Frederick, 2002, p. 51). The authors attempted to understand the biases and heuristics identified in earlier research (e.g., Kahneman, Slovic, & Tversky, 1982) by raising two questions: (a) What features of System 1 created the error? and (b) Why was the error not detected and corrected by System 2? They then attempt to answer these questions by reviewing empirical work in the biases and heuristics tradition. Several conditions and variables reduce biases. The representativeness heuristic is, for example, diminished when subjects' attention is directed to critical variables, or when statistically sophisticated subjects are asked to compare two options (without filler items in between). Several contributions in Gilovich et al. (2002) focused on biases and heuristics in expert judgment. The conclusion seems warranted that expertise judgment is prone to biases. Expert estimates on issues in physics, demographics, or energy consumption consistently show overconfidence (Fischhoff, 2002, p. 744). These estimates were made by both individuals and groups. Research shows that the quality of expert judgments (e.g., weather forecasters; Murphy & Winkler, 1984) increases with immediate, unambiguous feedback and incentives for performance, conditions similar to those found in the laboratory for lay subjects (Fischhoff, 2002, p. 743). Koehler, Brenner, and Griffin (2002) showed that experts are likely to predict outcomes correctly only when discriminability is high and base rates are moderate; otherwise probabilities are over- or underrated. Dawes, Faust, and Meehl (2002) compared human-clinical judgment to actuarial judgment, in which a statistical method is used based on empirically established relations between data and relevant conclusions. In the domain of diagnosing and predicting human behavior, the actuarial approach is generally found to be more correct than the clinical approach. A review by Grove, Zald, Lebow, Snitz, and Nelson (2000) looked at 136 comparisons and found the actuarial approach to be equal or superior to the clinical approach in all but eight cases.

A limited number of studies contrast the impact of biases and heuristics at the group and individual level. A study by Curşeu (2003) illustrated the operation of System 1 and 2 at the group level. Groups trying to solve a murder mystery using the task proposed by Stewart and Stasser (1998) first discussed a shared implicit stereotype. Only by examining all of the evidence could a group determine the guilt of another suspect (the correct answer). Groups under time pressure chose the stereotypical murderer more often than groups operating without time constraints. Thus, it seems that group decision making System 1 offers a first response, which will only be checked by System 2 if adequate time is available. Studies on naturalistic decision making show an essential part of group-information processing is team-situation awareness. Team-situation awareness is created when group members engage in information collection, exchange, and closed-loop communication (Lipshitz et al., 2001, p. 341). Kerr, MacCoun, and Kramer (1996) used a more direct approach to compare individual and group processing. Kerr et al. addressed the question whether individual or group decision making is more biased. In a theoretical analysis, they show that this question cannot be answered without specifying group size, initial individual judgments, magnitude of bias among individuals, the type of bias considered and the social decision scheme (Davis, 1973) used for the group decision-making process. The social-decision scheme is also used to explain processes of collective induction (inferring general principles or rules from data; see Kerr & Tindale, 2004, p. 631).

Stress is a feature of many important decisions that often increases simplified, heuristic processing. The relation between stress and performance at the individual and group level is complex (Joëls, Pu, Wiegert, Oitzl, & Krugers, 2006; Ellis, 2006). In the field of decision making, Janis and Mann (1971) described how stress evokes hot cognitive processing. Stressful decisions may be coped with using one of five patterns, such as defensive avoidance of cues associated with the decision situation. Only one of five patterns (vigilance) results in decisions of high quality. Kerr and Tindale (2004, p. 630; see also Collyer & Malecki, 1998) reviewed research that showed groups under stress tend to increase in performance quantity with an accompanying decline of quality, to narrow attention to more vital parts of their task and to use more heuristic information processing. Kruglanski, Shah, Pierro, and Mannetti (2002) argued that stressful conditions increase the need for closure (specific, unambiguous solutions). Increased need for closure prompts attempts to influence deviating opinions and/ or increases the readiness to yield to others, which both lead to more centralized information exchange (centered on a few influential group members).

The support of PSMs to group decision making is often related to information processing. Vennix (1996; 1999) related the construction of a system dynamics model to individual perception and retention processes. The human information processing capacity cannot deal adequately with complex systems, as humans are biased in their decision making and fail to see feedback processes (Sterman, 1994). A model helps participants structure the problem and enables them to put their problem definitions to the test. Vennix et al. (1996) expected that the main effect of group model building on decision making to be its increase in the ability to process information, which fosters systematic processing (Petty & Cacioppo, 1986). Sterman's (2000) assertion that one of the most important goals of system dynamics is to "speak truth to power" (p. 85) also demonstrates the importance of the systematic route in PSMs. The ability to process information is fostered in a number of ways. A facilitator systematically asks participants to explain their contibution to the discussion, by reformulating ideas into variables, and relating them to previously discussed information by placing the variables in the model. When this happens, we can expect that message comprehensibility is increased. When the facilitator does this, he or she uncouples ideas from persons and reduces cues such as source credibility, in favor of more equal information sharing. Thus, the facilitator helps to distinguish cognitive from interpersonal conflict (Vennix, 1996). The model allows for hypothesis testing (see the section on information feedback). The work of Fischhoff (2002) in the biases and heuristics tradition had some similarities to PSM practice. Fischhoff (2002) noted that in real-world applications, people have many beliefs and infer other beliefs that influence their judgments. Studies reveal that people use flexible templates (also referred to as *mental models* or *substantive heuristics*) to organize their beliefs on particular topics. Templates might, for example, order beliefs on how the respiratory system functions, or how fishing-boat capacity and fish stock interact. These studies contrast beliefs with a normative standard. In complex, ill-structured problems, the normative standard can be captured in influence diagrams that show the factors that determine the probabilities of events and outcomes. The diagrams show what is worth knowing about a problem for individuals who are not knowledgeable on the topic of interest. The difference between these diagrams and existing beliefs show *what is worth saying,* in order to best guide persons to relevant information (Fischhoff, 2002, p. 756). As described earlier, when using PSMs, members of decision-making groups combine their unique and initially unshared information in the construction of a model. It follows that each group member is influenced in unique ways by the information exchanged in the modeling session, a conclusion also reached by Rouwette, Vernix, and Felling (in press).

Response

Hinsz et al. (1997) structured their discussion of group response in the following categories: (a) the type of task involved, (b) the procedures used to derive the group response, (c) the nature of the response mode and, (d) the selection of a response that best reflects the group's opinion. We follow the same approach here but start by discussing task and the nature of response mode together. An influential typology of tasks was developed by McGrath (1984). McGrath distinguished four general processes: (a) generate (alternatives), (b) choose (alternatives), (c) negotiate, and (d) execute. Then, each of the processes is subdivided into two task types. For example, the choose process is subdivided into intellective tasks (with one correct answer) and decision-making tasks (with an agreed upon answer). Rohrbaugh (1988) criticized this last element of McGrath's model, on the grounds that both types of tasks easily become blurred. Indeed, in a review of group support system studies, Fjermestad and Hiltz (1998) observed that authors sometimes place tasks in two or three different categories. The effect of task type on group response is often assumed. Poole, Siebold, and McPhee (1985) suggested that it accounts for 50% of the variance of group performance. Osborn (1953) proposed this as one of the cornerstones of brainstorming: Group members generate more ideas when they feel free of evaluation and criticism. He also asserted that "quantity breeds quality," meaning that a high number of ideas would also boost the number of good ideas. According to Rietzschel et al. (2006), there is some support for the effect of task separation on idea quantity, but the effect on quality of ideas remains an open question. The literature on group-decision support points to the influence of more subtle elements of the task, which are closely related to the response mode. Vennix (1996; 1999) referred to the work of Kahneman et al. (1982) and others on the effect of framing on choice and discussed self-fulfilling prophecies created by expected outcomes of tests (Rosenthal & Jacobson, 1968).

With regard to procedures used to derive the group response, four strands of research can be distinguished. First, there is research on procedures (or better techniques) that support only one or a few phases of decision making. Examples are well-known techniques such as brainstorming (Osborn, 1953) and Nominal Group Technique (Delbecq et al., 1975). The development of these techniques prompted research into their effectiveness and led to further questions. Osborn's original claim, for example, was that brainstorming groups produce more and better ideas than nonbrainstorming groups. This claim has prompted a line of research (e.g., Diehl & Stroebe, 1987, 1991; Nijstad et al., 2003; Rietzschel et al., 2006; Nijstad & Stroebe, 2006) that has highlighted the benefits of nominal vs. interacting groups.

Second, there is research on methods that purport to support most or all phases of decision making. Examples are technology-based group support systems (e.g., Fjermestad & Hiltz, 1998), model-based group support systems (e.g., Mingers & Rosenhead, 2004), or Delphi (Rowe & Wright, 1999). In studying the effects of these broader methods, context factors play an even more important role than in studying techniques. It is instructive that authors researching different methods come to the same conclusion: effects are a function of both method and context variables (McGrath & Hollingshead, 1994, p. 78; Rowe & Wright, 1999). The dependent variable in most of these studies is some measure for group performance, such as quantity or quality of ideas (e.g., Fjermestad & Hiltz, 1998). Rohrbaugh and colleagues have consistently drawn attention to the decision process and use the Competing Values Approach to assess process effectiveness (Quinn & Rohrbaugh, 1983; Rohrbaugh, 1989). An important conclusion of their line of research is that managerial openness is central to the implementation of results of an intervention (McCartt & Rohrbaugh, 1995).

The third form of research focuses on elements of procedures, such as facilitation, process structure, or group memory. The effect of facilitation is, for example, studied by Kaplan (1979), Offner, Kramer, and Winter (1996), and Oxley, Dzindolet, and Paulus (1996). Process structure (Rietzschel et al., 2006) and group memory (Paul et al., 2004; Haseman et al., 2005) are discussed in other sections of this chapter.

The fourth form of research on procedures focuses on aspects of procedures that apply to all decision-making phases. Examples are procedural justice (e.g., Korsgaard, Schweiger, & Sapienza, 1995; Hui, Au, & Zhao, 2007), which is found to increase commitment to decisions, and the effects of active processing (Natter & Berry, 2005) discussed earlier.

The selection of a response that best reflects the group members' shared point of view is an important topic in teams of experts working on ambiguous and urgent problems. In a number of traditional strands of research on group decision making, the effect of the group in individual decisions is framed in a negative context. Examples are the group-polarization model (Lamm, 1988; Curşeu, 2003, p. 139) and studies on escalation of commitment (Staw, 1976; Seiber & Goltz, 2001; Curşeu, 2003, p. 141). In research on decision support, the effect of the group on individual decision making has a more positive connotation. Most decision support methods underline the importance of eliciting and integrating group members' ideas on the problem, not only for gathering relevant information but also for creating commitment to conclusions. Some support for this idea exists. In naturalistic decision making, Orasanu (1994) saw beneficial consequences of shared problem assessment. Sauquet (2004) maintained that learning of professionals is directed by previous knowledge and individual purpose (p. 378). He also drew attention to the fact that subgroups in organizations use and allow different forms of argumentation, which underlines the importance of language (p. 384). Several authors stressed the importance of an incremental changing of minds through scaffolding (Van der Heijden, 2000; Sauquet, 2004) building on the idea of situated learning (Vygotski, 1978). In decision support, group reactions include not only cognitive change but also attitudinal and behavioral change. Rouwette (2003; Rouwette & Vennix, in press) described the argumentation exchange in group discussion using theories of persuasion and the relation between cognitions, attitudes, and behavior (see also Spaargaren, 2006). In Ajzen's (1991; 2001) theory of planned behavior, cognitions underlie the attitude toward behavior and subjective norm and perceived behavioral control. These three variables, in turn, influence intentions and, finally, behavior. Ajzen (1991) maintained that changes in intention and behavior operate through change in beliefs and attitude, norm, and control. Dual-process theories of persuasion (Petty & Cacioppo, 1986; Chaiken, Giner-Sorolla, & Chen, 1996; Petty & Wegener, 1998) specify two routes through which beliefs may be changed: (a) by understanding and evaluation of arguments and (b) by using simple decision rules or heuristics. In situations where both motivation to process information and ability to process information are high, the first route is most influential in changing beliefs (Petty & Cacioppo, 1986). Vennix et al. (1996) maintained that as participants in group model building sessions are invited on the basis of their managerial responsibilities or expertise in the problem, motivation to process information is generally high. The most important contribution of PSMs is then to increase the ability to process information, and, in doing so, ultimately influence behavior. Huz (1999) and Rouwette (2003) found evidence for an effect of model-based approaches on beliefs, attitude, norm, control, and intentions. An important mediating factor is the level at which conclusions are formulated: conclusions have the strongest impact on behavior when both are formulated at the same level of generality (Rouwette, 2003; see also Koppert, 2005).

How do PSMs influence the response of participants in the intervention? Again, it is useful to distinguish a single meeting from the intervention as a whole. The management of responses in a single meeting makes up the major part of guidelines covered in PSM handbooks. The expertise of the PSM practitioner is not related to the content area of a particular messy problem, but concerns the structure and process of participant interaction. In general, PSM practitioners follow a process consultation model (Schein, 1987) in which the consultant is neutral with regard to content, but focuses attention on choosing a structure for the group interaction and the resulting process. In a PSM intervention, parts of the process may be structured using already existing methods or techniques. Examples are Delphi and Nominal Group Technique (Delbecq et al., 1975), which are used as part of group model building (Vennix, 1996). Individual interviews are a widely used part of interventions.

PSM interventions as a whole are expected to lead to particular client responses. PSM approaches aim to foster participant learning, increase consensus, and create commitment to a joint course of action (Vennix, 1996; Morton et al., 2003).

> In group decision making we expect to see a shift in emotional attitudes as well as a cognitive shift to the problem situation. Changes in emotional attitude reflect, in part, the role of intuition and hunch which leads to a feeling of comfort about the path ahead [...] Cognitive shifts are about someone "changing their mind"—changed beliefs, changed values, and changes in the salience of particular values. (Eden, 1992, p. 208)

Eden (1992) drew attention to two ways of influencing participants that do not involve exchange of information related to the task at hand. The first is transparency of the procedure in which individual client contributions are combined into a model and result in recommended actions. This factor is based on the theory of procedural justice (Korsgaard et al., 1995). The second is the creation of a commitment package, consisting of verbal descriptions, models, and pictures of the interacting group of participants, which Eden (1992) expected are crucial for the creation of commitment. The commitment package seems a conscious effort to use heuristic route in the dual-process theories of persuasion (e.g., Petty & Cacioppo, 1986). As we have seen in the section on information storage, operator knowledge or strategic heuristics were instrumental in improving performance in a management-flight simulator (Richardson et al., 1994). The heuristic route, however, refers to a broader set of heuristics than the strategic heuristics described by use in simulators. Strategic heuristics are based on the content of a particular domain and seem similar to substantive heuristics (Fischhoff, 2002, p. 746). We may, thus, conclude that a range of heuristic cues is used in group-decision support (e.g., operator knowledge and the commitment package), but their beneficial effect has only been shown for a subset of cues in a controlled environment (e.g., operator knowledge).

Feedback

With regard to feedback, Hinsz et al. (1997) found a paucity of research in group settings. One possible reason for this is the complexity of providing feedback to groups. In research on managerial decision making, feedback has a more prominent role. Ignoring feedback effects leads to suboptimal decisions (e.g., Hall, 1984), but is the rule rather than the exception in controlled as well as field settings (Axelrod, 1976; Vennix, 1990; Sterman, 1989). As discussed before, Vennix (1996) underlined the importance of self-fulfilling prophecies in social situations. The system dynamics literature offers a range of studies on the influence of feedback on managerial decision making. Many of these studies involve a management flight simulator discussed earlier (Sterman 1994; Hsiao & Richardson, 1999; Rouwette et al., 2004). Although most of these studies involve individual decision makers, several outcomes point to possible improvements in the design of interventions in groups. A couple of results from this field relevant to group decision making are the following. Research on management-flight simulators shows that performance improves when the model is more transparent, for instance, when decision makers are provided with a diagram or a lecture on the model used in the simulator. Subjects receiving decision cues or strategic heuristics increase their performance, and in one study they even outperformed subjects that received information on model structure. Studies using management-flight simulators indicate that procedural knowledge (cf. Anderson, 1990) has a separate and possibly more important role in dynamic decision making than declarative knowledge. Other research shows that decision makers have trouble manipulating very simple structures, consisting of one inflow and outflow and no feedback (Sweeney & Sterman, 2000). This result supports the attention given by some modelers to decision makers' appreciation of accumulation of resources (e.g., Warren, 2000).

In PSMs feedback may take three forms: (a) giving feedback on an action proposal from other participants in the intervention; (b) simulating the effects of a planned action in the problem or (c) formulating some form of action plan. The facilitated group process is used to create an open atmosphere in which actions can be proposed and discussed freely. Simulating the effects of a planned action may consist of using a qualitative model to assess expected consequences. The cognitive maps constructed in COPE/Journey-making interventions consist of interconnected means and ends, which allows for a qualitative estimation of effects of planned actions. In group model building, qualitative models may be used in the same fashion. The feedback loops contained in system dynamics models often include decision maker's actions: a decision maker perceives values of certain variables in the system (e.g., current inventory), observed values are used to instantiate a policy (e.g., if the difference between current and desired inventory surpasses a maximum value, order new inventory), which leads to an action (e.g., ordering a certain amount of new inventory) that changes the values of variables in the system. Formal system dynamics models can be used for policy experiments in which effects of variable changes are simulated over time. In this way, hypotheses on effects of changes can be tested (Richmond, 1997), at the same time debunking organizational myths and theories on (own and others') behavior (Vermaak, 2006, p. 189). Computer simulation can supplement mental simulation, which is an important part of recognition-primed decision making on ambiguous problems (Klein, 1998).

Feedback both from other participants and the (qualitative or quantitative) model involve safe environments; recommendations are not tried out in the real world and, thus, do not involve information feeding back from actual results. These interventions are in a sense one-shot operations: actions are formulated once and not revised on the basis of real-world results. The last form of feedback does use real-world information. The last form of feedback consists of devising an action plan and having evaluation meetings some time after the first modeling meetings. This is, however, not the main part of the intervention. For group model building, for example, Rouwette (2003) noted that the intervention typically ends with identifying strategic levers for intervening in a messy problem. Implementation of actions is not part of the group model building intervention but may be planned as an additional activity.

CONCLUSION

In this chapter, we revisited Hinsz et al.'s (1997) model of groups as information processors. For each phase of information processing, we

TABLE 11.1 Needs of Decision-Making Groups and Corresponding Elements of Group Decision Support

	Group needs	Intervention	Session
Processing objective	Prevention of groupthink and escalation of commitment	Expectation management, clarification roles, attention to differences between goals of participants	Process structure, the impact of the model on the discussion theme, (implicit and explicit) effect of group interaction on information exchange
Attention	Surfacing and testing nonconscious processing and recognition-primed decision making, exploration of differences between theory in use and espoused theory	Similar to processing objective, attention to differences in perceived urgency problem	Facilitator acts as model for critical thinking, summarizes discussion
Encoding	Exploration of differences in meaning terms, use active information processing, formation shared (team and task) mental model	Use shared language, model as boundary object	Use discussion to influence phonetic memory and model to influence visual memory
Storage	Creation of transactive memory		Use operator knowledge
Retrieval	Optimization stimulation from other group members for retrieval, limit pressure for confirmation, improvement information recall, creation group memory	Use a structured procedure, emphasize unique information group members, use ample time for discussion	Facilitation, encourage critical thinking, use of a group memory

(Continued)

TABLE 11.1 (continued)

Processing work space	Allow for check on system 1 by system 2, feedback on quality decision, diminish the impact of stress on divergent thinking	Optimize ability to process by separating ideas from persons, use model for hypothesis testing	Probe information by asking questions
Response	Choose procedures in accordance with group tasks, facilitate use of arguments for persuasion, use transparent process	Use existing techniques to support phases in decision making, use transparent process	Create commitment package
Feedback	Identification of feedback relations in problem, need for scaffolds	Generate feedback from action plan	Generate feedback from other participants, simulation

described research on expert and naturalistic decision making. Next, we discussed how Problem Structuring Methods (PMSs) try to influence the group activities outlined in each phase. Table 11.1 summarizes the needs that confront teams striving to make high-quality decisions and the support offered by PSMs in the intervention as a whole and a particular session.

Two themes in recent research on group decision making seem to be especially relevant to expert decision making on messy problems: (a) the degree to which information processing is conscious (processing ranges from unconscious to using heuristics to explicit argumentation) and (b) the use of multiple modes of encoding and processing. Most notably in the phase of providing feedback, research originating in group-decision support seems to make a promising contribution to general studies on group decision making.

In a recent review of studies on group model building, Rouwette and Vennix (2006) concluded that further development of theory is the most important condition for the advancement of research on effectiveness of PSMs (see also Morton et al., 2003). Aiming for a unified and consistent theoretical framework that combines all relevant process, outcome, and context variables is probably too ambitious. They suggested developing several partial theories and to distinguish the following theoretical areas: (a) participants' contribution of information in a modeling session; (b) the impact of exchanged information and other cues on participants; (c) the relation of group model building to decision-making biases and shortcomings, and (d) the impact of the intervention on the wider organization. Clearly, the discussion in the foregoing has provided a number of suggestions to flesh out these areas.

REFERENCES

Ackoff, R. L. (1981). *Creating the corporate future.* Chichester, U.K.: Wiley and Sons.

Ajzen, I. (1991). The theory of planned behavior. *Organizational Behavior and Human Decision Processes, 50,* 179–211.

Ajzen, I. (2001). Nature and operation of attitudes. *Annual Review of Psychology, 52,* 27–58.

Andersen, D. F., Maxwell, T. A., Richardson, G. P., & Stewart, T. R. (1994). Mental models and dynamic decision making in a simulation of welfare reform. *Proceedings of the 1994 International System Dynamics Conference: Social and public policy,* Sterling, Scotland, 11–18.

Andersen, D. F., & Richardson, G. P. (1997). Scripts for group model building. *System Dynamics Review, 13*(2), 107–130.

Andersen, D. F., Richardson, G. P., & Vennix, J. A. M. (1997). Group model building: Adding more science to the craft. *System Dynamics Review, 13*(2), 187–203.

Andersen, D. F., Vennix, J. A. M., Richardson, G. P., & Rouwette, E. A. J. A. (2007). Group model building: Problem structuring, policy simulation and decision support. *Journal of the Operational Research Society, 58*(5), 691–694.

Anderson, R. (1990). *Cognitive psychology and its implications.* New York: W. H. Freeman and Co.

Argyris, C. (1990). *Overcoming organizational defenses and facilitating organizational learning.* Boston: Allyn and Bacon.

Argyris, C. (1992). *On organizational learning.* Cambridge,U.K.: Blackwell.

Argyris, C., & Schön, D. A. (1978). *Organizational learning: A theory of action perspective.* Reading, MA: Addison-Wesley.

Axelrod, R. (1976). *Structure of decision: The cognitive maps of political elites.* Princeton, NJ: Princeton University Press.

Bazerman, M. H., Giuliano, T., & Appelman, A. (1984). Escalation of commitment in individual and group decision making. *Organizational Behavior and Human Performance, 33,* 141–152.

Bella, D. A., King, J. B., & Kailin, D. (2003). The dark side of organizations and a method to reveal it. *Emergence, 5,* 66–82.

Brandon, D. P., & Hollingshead, A. B. (2004). Transactive memory systems in organizations: Matching tasks, expertise, and people. *Organization Science, 15*(6), 633–644.

Briggs, R. O., Vreede, G. J., & de Nunamaker, J. F. J. (2003). Collaboration engineering with ThinkLets to pursue sustained success with group support systems. *Journal of Management Information Systems, 19,* 31–63.

Brunswik, E. (1955). Representative design and probabilistic theory in a functional psychology. *Psychological Review, 62,* 193–217.

Cannon-Bowers, J. A., & Salas, E. (2001). Reflection on shared cognition. *Journal of Organizational Behavior, 22,* 195–202.

Chaiken, S., Giner-Sorolla, R., & Chen, S. (1996). Beyond accuracy: Defense and impression motives in heuristic and systematic information processing. In

P. M. Gollwitzer, & J. A. Bargh (Eds.), *The psychology of action: Linking cognition and motivation to action* (pp. 553–578). New York: Guilford Press.

Chaiken, S., Liberman, A., & Eagly, A. H. (1989). Heuristic and systematic processing within and beyond the persuasion context. In J. S. Uleman, & J. A. Bargh (Eds.), *Unintended thought* (pp. 212–252). New York: Guilford Press.

Checkland, P. B. (1981). *Systems thinking, systems practice.* Chichester, U.K.: Wiley.

Collyer, S. C., & Malecki, G. S. (1998). Tactical decision making under stress: History and overview. In J. A. Cannon-Bowers, & E. Salas (Eds.), *Decision making under stress: Emerging themes and applications* (pp. 107-15). Aldershot, U.K.: Ashgate Publishing Company.

Cooper, K. G. (1980). Naval ship production: A claim settled and a framework built. *Interfaces, 10*(6), 20–36.

Cosmides, L., & Toobey, J. (1996). Are humans good intuitive statisticians after all? Rethinking some conclusions from the literature on judgment under uncertainty. *Cognition, 58*, 1–73.

Curşeu, P. L. (2003). Formal group decision-making: A social-cognitive approach (Doctoral dissertation, Tilburg University, 2003). Cluj-Napoca, Romania: ASCR Press.

Daft, R. L., & Lengel, R. (1986). Organizational information requirements, media richness, and structural design. *Management Science, 32*(5), 554–571.

Damasio, A. R. (1994). *Descartes' error. Emotion, reason, and the human brain.* New York: Putnam Berkley Group.

Davis, J. H. (1973). Group decision and social interaction: A theory of social decision schemes. *Psychological Review, 80*, 97–125.

Dawes, R. M., Faust, D., & Meehl, P. E. (2002). Clinical versus actuarial judgment. In T. Gilovich, D. Griffin, & D. Kahneman (Eds.), *Heuristics and biases. The psychology of intuitive judgment* (pp. 716–729). Cambridge, U.K.: Cambridge University Press.

Delbecq, A. L., Ven, A. H., & van de Gustafson, G. H. (1975). *Group techniques for program planning: A guide to nominal group and delphi processes.* Glenview, IL: Scott, Foresman, and Co.

DeSanctis, G., & Gallupe, R. B. (1987). A foundation for the study of group decision support systems. *Management Science, 33*, 589–609.

Diehl, M., & Stroebe, W. (1987). Productivity loss in brainstorming groups – toward the solution of a riddle. *Journal of Personality and Social Psychology, 53*(3), 497–509.

Diehl, M., & Stroebe, W. (1991). Productivity loss in idea-generating groups – tracking down the blocking effect. *Journal of Personality and Social Psychology, 61*(3), 392–403.

Dijksterhuis, A., Bos, M. W., Nordgren, L. F., & Van Baaren, R. B. (2006). On making the right choice: The deliberation-without-attention effect. *Science, 311*, 1005–1007.

Doyle, J. K., & Ford, D. N. (1998). Mental models concepts for system dynamics research. *System Dynamics Review, 14*(1), 3–29.

Eden, C. (1992). Strategy development as a social process. *Journal of Management Studies, 29*(6), 799–811.

Eden, C. (1995). On evaluating the performance of 'wide-band' GDSS's. *European Journal of Operational Research, 81*, 302–311.

Eden, C., & Ackermann, F. (1996). "Horses for courses": A stakeholder approach to the evaluation of GDSSs. *Group Decision and Negotiation, 5*, 501–519.
Eden, C., & Ackermann, J. (2001b). SODA—The principles. In J. Rosenhead, & J. Mingers (Eds.), *Rational analysis for a problematic world revisited. Problem structuring methods for complexity, uncertainty and conflict.* Chichester: Wiley: 21–41.
Ellis, A. P. J. (2006). System breakdown: The role of mental models and transactive memory in the relationship between acute stress and team performance. *Academy of Management Journal, 49*(3), 576–589.
Finlay, P. N. (1998). On evaluating the performance of GSS: Furthering the debate. *European Journal of Operational Research, 107*(1), 193–201.
Fischhoff, B. (2002). Heuristics and biases in application. In T. Gilovich, D. Griffin, & D. Kahneman (Eds.), *Heuristics and biases. The psychology of intuitive judgment* (pp. 730–748). Cambridge, U.K.: Cambridge University Press.
Fjermestad, J., & Hiltz, S. R. (1998). An assessment of group support systems, experimental research, methodology, and results. *Journal of Management Information Systems, 15*(3), 7–149.
Fogel, J. (2005). Learning to see a brighter future for Morgan County, TN. In J. Sterman, N. P. Repenning, R. S. Langer, J. I. Rowe, & J. M. Yanni (Eds.), *Proceedings System Dynamics Conference.* Boston. Retrieved June 7, 2007, from http://www.systemdynamics.org/conferences/2005/proceed/papers/FOGEL197.pdf
Forrester, J. W. (1961). *Industrial dynamics.* Williston, VT: Pegasus Communications.
Forrester, J. W., & Senge, P. M. (1980). Tests for building confidence in system dynamics models. *TIMS Studies in the Management Sciences, 14*, 209–228.
Friedman, T. L. (2005). *The world is flat. The globalized world in the twenty-first century.* London: Penguin Books.
Gilovich, T., Griffin, D., & Kahnemann, D. (Eds.). (2002). *Heuristics and biases. The psychology of intuitive judgment.* New York: Cambridge University Press.
Gladwell, M. (2005). *Blink: The power of thinking without thinking.* New York: Time Warner Book Group.
Grove, W. M., Zald, D. H., Lebow, B. S., Snitz, B. E., & Nelson, C. (2000). Clinical versus mechanical prediction: A meta-analysis. *Psychological Assessment, 12*(1), 19–30.
Hall, R. I. (1984). The natural logic of management policy making: Its implications for the survival of an organization. *Management Science, 30*(8), 905–927.
Hall, R. I., & Menzies, W. B. (1983). A corporate system model of a sports club: Using simulation as an aid to policy making in a crisis. *Management Science, 29*(1), 52–64.
Hammond, K. R., & Stewart, T. R. (Eds.). (2001). *The essential Brunswik: Beginnings, explications, and applications.* New York: Oxford University Press.
Haseman, W. D., Nazareth, D. L., & Paul, S. (2005). Implementation of a group decision support system utilizing collective memory. *Information & Management, 42*, 591–605.

Hickson, D. J., Butler, R. J., Cray, D., Mallory, G. R., & Wilson, D. C. (1986). *Top decisions: Strategic decision making in organizations.* Oxford, U.K.: Basil Blackwell.

Hinsz, V. B. (1990). Cognitive and consensus processes in group recognition memory performance. *Journal of Personality and Social Psychology, 59*(4), 705–718.

Hinsz, V. B., Tindale, R. S., & Vollrath, D. A. (1997). The emerging conceptualization of groups as information processors. *Psychological Bulletin, 121*(1), 43–64.

Hollingshead, A. B. (1996). The rank-order effect in group decision making. *Organizational Behavior and Human Decision Processes, 68*(3), 181–193.

Hsiao, N., & Richardson, G. P. (1999). In search of theories of dynamic decision making: A literature review. In R. Y. Cavana, et al. (Eds.), *Systems thinking for the next millennium: Proceedings of the 17th International Conference of the System Dynamics Society.* Wellington, New Zealand. Retrieved June 7, 2007, from http://www.systemdynamics.org/conferences/1999/PAPERS/PLEN16.PDF

Hui, M. K., Au, K., & Zhao, X. (in press). Interactional justice and the fair process effect: The role of outcome uncertainty. *Journal of Experimental Social Psychology.*

Huz, S. (1999). *Alignment from group model building for systems thinking: Measurement and evaluation from a public policy setting.* Unpublished doctoral dissertation, SUNY, Albany, NY.

Janis, I. L. (1972). *Victims of groupthink: A psychological study of foreign-policy decisions and fiascoes.* Boston: Houghton Mifflin Company.

Janis, I. L. (1982). *Groupthink: Psychological studies of policy decisions and fiascoes* (2nd ed.). Boston: Houghton Mifflin Company.

Janis, I. L., & Mann, L. (1977). *Decision making: A psychological analysis of conflict, choice, and commitment.* New York: Free Press.

Joëls, M., Pu, Z. W, Wiegert, O., Oitzl, M. S., & Krugers, H. J. (2006). Learning under stress: How does it work? *Trends in Cognitive Sciences, 10*(4), 152–158.

Johnson-Laird, P. N. (1995). *Mental models: Towards a cognitive science of language, inference, and consciousness* (6th ed.). Cambridge, MA: Harvard University Press.

Kahneman, D., & Frederick, S. (2002). Representativeness revisited: Attribute substitution in intuitive judgment. In T. Gilovich, D. Griffin, & D. Kahneman (Eds.), *Heuristics and biases: The psychology of intuitive judgment* (pp. 49–81). Cambridge, U.K.: Cambridge University Press.

Kahneman, D., Slovic, P., & Tversky, A. (1982). *Judgement under uncertainty: Heuristics and biases.* Cambridge, U.K.: Cambridge University Press.

Kaplan, R. E. (1979). On the conspicuous absence of evidence that process consultation enhances task performance. *Journal of Applied Behavioral Science, 15,* 346–360.

Kenis, D. G. A. (1995). *Improving group decisions. Designing and testing techniques for group decision support systems applying Delphi principles.* Unpublished doctoral dissertation, University of Utrecht, the Netherlands.

Kerr, N. L., MacCoun, R. J., & Kramer, G. P. (1996). Bias in judgment: Comparing individuals and groups. *Psychological Review, 103*(4), 687–719.

Kerr, D. S., & Murthy, U. S. (2004). Divergent and convergent idea generation in teams: A comparison of computer-mediated and face-to-face communication. *Group Decision and Negotiation, 13,* 381–399.

Kerr, N. L., & Tindale, R. S. (2004). Group performance and decision making. *Annual Review of Psychology, 55,* 623–655.

Klein, G. A. (1998). Sources of power: How people make decisions. Cambridge, MA: MIT Press.

Koehler, D. J., Brenner, L., & Griffin, D. (2002). The calibration of expert judgment : Heuristics and biases beyond the laboratory. In T. Gilovich, D. Griffin, & D. Kahneman (Eds.), *Heuristics and biases. The psychology of intuitive judgment* (pp. 686–715). Cambridge, U.K.: Cambridge University Press.

Koppert, T. (2005). Het broeikaseffect. Een probleem van iedereen? [The greenhouse effect. Everyone's problem?]. Unpublished master's thesis, Wageningen University, The Netherlands.

Korsgaard, M. A., Schweiger, D. M., & Sapienza, H. J. (1995). Building commitment, attachment, and trust in strategic decision making teams: The role of procedural justice. *Academy of Management Journal, 38,* 60–84.

Kruglanski, A. W., Shah, J. Y., Pierro, A., & Mannetti, L. (2002). When similarity breeds content: Need for closure and the allure of homogeneous and self-resembling groups. *Journal of Personality and Social Psychology, 83*(3), 648–662.

Lamm, H. (1988). A review of our research on group polarisation: Eleven experiments on the effect of group discussion on risk acceptance, probability estimation, and negotiation positions. *Psychological Reports, 62,* 807–813.

Larkin, J. H., & Simon, H. A. (1987). Why a diagram is (sometimes) worth ten thousand words. *Cognitive Science, 11,* 65–99.

Larson, J. R., Christensen, C., Franz, T. M., & Abbott, A. S. (1998). Diagnosing groups: The pooling, management, and impact of shared and unshared case information in team-based medical decision making. *Journal of Personality and Social Psychology, 75*(1), 93–108.

Larson, J. R., Foster-Fishman, P. G., & Franz, T. M. (1998). Leadership style and the discussion of shared and unshared information in decision-making groups. *Personality and Social Psychology Bulletin, 24*(5), 482–495.

Larson, J. R., Foster-Fishman, P. G., & Keys, C. B. (1994). Discussion of shared and unshared information in decision-making groups. *Journal of Personality and Social Psychology, 67*(3), 446–461.

Lee, A. Y., & Hutchinson, L. (1998). Improving learning from examples through reflection. *Journal of Experimental Psychology: Applied, 4,* 187–210.

Liang, D. W., Moreland, R. L., & Argote, L. (1995). Group versus individual training and group performance: The mediating role of transactive memory. *Personality and Social Psychology Bulletin, 21,* 384–393.

Lieshout, R. H. (1995). *Between anarchy and hierarchy: A theory of international politics and foreign policy.* Aldershot, U.K.: Edward Elgar.

Liljenquist, K. A., Galinsky, A. D., & Kray, L. J. (2004). Exploring the rabbit hole of possibilities by myself or with my group: The benefits and liabilities of activating counterfactual mind-sets for information sharing and group coordination. *Journal of Behavioral Decision Making, 17*(4), 263–279.

Lippitt, G. L. (1983) *A handbook for visual problem solving: A resource guide for creating change models* (Rev. ed.). Bethesda, MD: Development Publications.
Lipshitz, R., Klein, G., Orasanu, J., & Salas, E. (2001). Taking stock of naturalistic decision making. *Journal of Behavioral Decision Making, 14,* 331–352.
Mandler, G. M. (1984). *Mind and body. Psychology of emotion and stress,* New York: W.W. Norton.
Mason, O. M., & Mitroff, I. I. (1981). *Challenging strategic planning assumptions: Theory, cases, and techniques.* New York: Wiley.
Mathieu, J. E., Heffner, T. S., Goodwin, G. F., Salas, E., & Cannon-Bowers, J. A. (2000). The influence of shared mental models on team process and performance. *Journal of Applied Psychology, 85*(2), 273–283.
McCartt, A. T., & Rohrbaugh, J. (1995). Managerial openness to change and the introduction of GDSS: Explaining initial success and failure in decision conferencing. *Organization Science,* 6(5), 569–584.
McGrath, J. E. (1984). *Groups: Interaction and performance.* Englewood Cliffs, NJ: Prentice Hall.
McGrath, J. E., & Hollingshead, A. B. (1994). *Groups interacting with technology.* London: Sage.
Mingers, J. (2000). Variety is the spice of life: Combining soft and hard OR/MS methods. *International Transactions in Operational Research, 7,* 673–691.
Mingers, J., & Rosenhead, J. (2004). Problem structuring methods in action. *European Journal of Operational Research, 152,* 530–554.
Mintzberg, H., Raisinghani, D., & Théorêt, A. (1976). The structure of "unstructured" decision processes. *Administrative Science Quarterly, 21,* 246–275.
Mitroff, I. I., & Sagasti, F. (1973). Epistemology as general systems theory. An approach to the design of complex decision-making experiments. *Philosophy of the Social Sciences* (Vol. 3, pp. 117–134). Aberdeen, U.K.: Aberdeen University Press.
Mohammed, S., & Dumville, B. C. (2001). Team mental models in a team knowledge framework: Expanding theory and measurement across disciplinary boundaries. *Journal of Organizational Behavior, 22,* 89–106.
Morecroft, J. D. W. (2004). Mental models and learning in system dynamics practice. In M. Pidd (Ed.), *Systems modeling: Theory and practice* (pp. 101–126). Chichester, U.K.: Wiley.
Moreland, R. L., Argote, L., & Krishnan, R. (1998). Training people to work in groups. In R. S. Tindale, L. Heat, J. Edwards, E. J. Posavac, F. B. Bryant, Y. Suarez-Balcazar, et al. (Eds.), *Theory and research on small groups* (pp. 37–60). New York: Plenum Press.
Morton, A., Ackermann, F., & Belton, V. (2003). Technology-driven and model-driven approaches to group decision support: Focus, research philosophy, and key concepts. *European Journal of Information Systems, 12,*110–126.
Murphy, A. H., & Winkler, R. L. (1984). Probability forecasting in meteorology. *Journal of the American Statistical Association, 79,* 489–500.
Napuk, K. (1993). *Managing change in an uncertain world.* Maidenhead, U.K.: McGraw-Hill.
Natter, H. M., & Berry, D. C. (2005). Effects of active information processing on the understanding of risk information. *Applied Cognitive Psychology, 19,* 123–135.

Nijstad, B. A., & Stroebe, W. (2006). How the group affects the mind: A cognitive model of idea generation in groups. *Personality and Social Psychology Review, 10*(3), 186–213
Nijstad, B. A., Stroebe, W., & Lodewijkx, H. F. M. (1999). Persistence of brainstorming groups: How do people know when to stop? *Journal of Experimental Social Psychology, 35*(2), 165–185.
Nijstad, B. A., Stroebe, W., & Lodewijkx, H. F. M. (2003). Production blocking and idea generation: Does blocking interfere with cognitive processes? *Journal of Experimental Social Psychology, 39*(6), 531–548.
Nunamaker, J. F., Dennis, A. R., Valacich, J. S., Vogel, D. R., & George, J. F. (1991). Electronic meetings to support group work. *Communications of the ACM, 34*(7), 40–61.
Oatley, K. (1992). *Best laid schemes. The psychology of emotions.* Cambridge, U.K.: Cambridge University Press.
Offner. A. K., Kramer, T. J., Winter, J. P. (1996). The effects of facilitation, recording, and pauses on group brainstorming. *Small Group Research, 27*(2), 283–298.
Orasanu, J. (1994). Shared problem models and flight-crew performance. In N. Johnston, N. McDonald, & R. Fuller (Eds.), *Aviation psychology in practice* (pp. 255–285). Aldershot, U.K.: Ashgate.
Osborn, A. F. (1953). *Applied imagination: Principles and procedures of creative problem-solving.* New York: Charles Scribner's Sons
Oxley, N. L., Dzindolet, M. T., & Paulus, P. B. (1996). XXX of brainstorming groups. *Journal of Social Behavior and Personality, 11,* 1–14.
Paul, S., Haseman, W. D., & Ramamurthy, K. (2004). Collective memory support and cognitive-conflict group decision-making: An experimental investigation. *Decision Support Systems, 36,* 261–281.
Petty, R. E., & Cacioppo, J. T. (1986). The elaboration likelihood model of persuasion. *Advances in Experimental Social Psychology, 19,* 123–205.
Petty, R. E., & Wegener, D. T. (1998). Attitude change: Multiple roles for persuasion variables. In D. T. Gilbert, S. T. Fiske, & G. Lindzey (Eds.), *The handbook of social psychology* (4th ed., Vols. 1–2). Boston: McGraw-Hill.
Pinsonneault, A., & Kraemer, K. L. (1990). The effects of electronic meeting support on group processes and outcomes: An assessment of the empirical research. *European Journal of Operational Research, 46,* 143–161.
Poole, M. S., Siebold, D. R., & McPhee, R. D. (1985). Group decision-making as a stucturational process. *Quarterly Journal of Speech, 71,* 74–102.
Postmes, T., Spears, R., & Cihangir, S. (2001). Quality of decision making and group norms. *Journal of Personality and Social Psychology, 80*(6), 918–930.
Prison Administration Annual Report. (2002). *Terugblik en toekomst DJI Jaarverslag 2002* [DJI Annual report 2002]. The Netherlands, Ministry of Justice.
Quinn, R. E., & Rohrbaugh, J. (1983). A spatial model of effectiveness criteria: Toward a competing values approach to organizational analysis. *Management Science, 29,* 363–377.
Rentsch, J. R., & Klimoski, R. J. (2001). Why do 'great minds' think alike?: Antecedents of team member schema agreement. *Journal of Organizational Behavior, 22,* 107–120.
Richardson, G. P. (1986). Problems with causal loop diagrams. *System Dynamics Review, 2,* 158–170.

Richardson, G. P., & Andersen, D. F. (1995). Teamwork in group model building. *System Dynamics Review, 11*(2), 113–137.
Richardson, G. P., Andersen, D. F., Maxwell, T. A., & Stewart, T. R. (1994). Foundations of mental model research. *Proceedings of the 1994 International System Dynamics Conference: Problem solving methodologies*, Scotland, 181–192.
Richardson, G. P., & Rohrbaugh, J. (1990). Decision making in dynamic environments: Exploring judgments in a system dynamics model-based game. In K. Borcherding, O. I. Larichev, & D. M. Messick (Eds.), *Contemporary issues in decision making* (pp. 463–472). Amsterdam: North-Holland.
Richmond, B. (1997). The strategic forum: Aligning objectives, strategy, and process. *System Dynamics Review, 13*(2), 131–148.
Rietzschel, E. F., Nijstad, B. A., & Stroebe, W. (2006). Productivity is not enough: A comparison of interactive and nominal brainstorming groups on idea generation and selection. *Journal of Experimental Social Psychology, 41*(2), 244–251.
Rittel, H. W. J., & Webber, M. M. (1973). Dilemmas in a general theory of planning. *Policy Sciences, 4*, 155–169.
Roberts, E. B. (1978). Strategies for effective implementation of complex corporate models. In E. B. Roberts (Ed.), *Managerial applications of system dynamics* (pp. 77–85). Cambridge, MA: Productivity Press.
Rohrbaugh, J. (1988). Cognitive conflict tasks and small group processes. In B. Brehmer, & C. R. B. Joyce (Eds.), *Human judgment: The SJT view* (pp. 199–226). Amsterdam: Elsevier Science Publishers.
Rohrbaugh, J. (1989). Demonstration experiments: Assessing the process, not the outcome, of group decision support. In Benbasat (Ed.), *Experimental methods in information systems*. Cambridge, MA: Harvard Business School.
Rosenhead, J. (Ed.). (1989). *Rational analysis for a problematic world*. Chichester, U.K.: Wiley.
Rosenhead, J. (1996). What's the problem? An introduction to problem structuring methods. *Interfaces, 26*(6), 117–131.
Rosenhead, J., & Mingers, J. (Eds.). (2001). *Rational analysis for a problematic world revisited. Problem structuring methods for complexity, uncertainty and conflict*. Chichester, U.K.: Wiley.
Rosenthal, R., & Jacobson, L. (1968). *Pygmalion in the classroom, teacher expectations, and pupils' intellectual development*. New York: Holt, Rinehart and Winston, Inc.
Rouse, W. B., & Morris, N. M. (1986). On looking into the black box: Prospects and limits in the search for mental models. *Psychological Bulletin, 100*, 349–363.
Rouwette, E. A. J. A. (2003). Group model building as mutual persuasion (Doctoral dissertation, Radboud University, 2003). Nijmegen, the Netherlands: Wolf Legal Publishers.
Rouwette, E. A. J. A., Jongebreur, W., Van Hooff, P., Heijmen, T., & Vennix, J. A. M. (2004). Modeling crime control in the Netherlands [electronic version]. In M. Kennedy, G. W. Winch, R. S. Langer, J. I. Rowe, & J. M. Yanni (Eds.), *Proceedings of the system dynamics conference*. Oxford, U.K. Retrieved June 7, 2007, from http://www.systemdynamics.org/conferences/2004/PAPERS/270ROUWE.pdf

Rouwette, E. A. J. A., & Vennix, J. A. M. (2006). System dynamics and organizational interventions. *Systems Research and Behavioral Science, 23*(4), 451–466.

Rouwette, E. A. J. A., Vennix, J. A. M., & Felling, A. J. A. (in press). On evaluating the performance of problem structuring methods: An attempt at formulating a conceptual framework. *Group Decision and Negotiation*.

Rouwette, E. A. J. A., Vennix, J. A. M., & Van Mullekom, T. (2002). Group model building effectiveness: A review of assessment studies. *System Dynamics Review, 18*(1), 5–45.

Rowe, G., & Wright, G. (1999). The Delphi technique as a forecasting tool: Issues and analysis. *International Journal of Forecasting, 15*, 353–375.

Rulke, D. L., & Rau, D. (2000). Investigating the encoding process of transactive memory development in group training. *Group and Organization Management, 25*(4), 373–396.

Sauquet, A. (2004). Learning in organizations: Schools of thought and current challenges. In J. Boonstra (Ed.), *Dynamics of organizational change and learning* (pp. 371–388). Chichester, U.K.: Wiley.

Schein, E. H. (1987a). *Process consultatio* (Vol. 2). Boston: Addison-Wesley.

Schein, E. H. (1987b). *The clinical perspective in fieldwork*. Beverly Hills, CA: Sage.

Scheper, W. J. (1991). *Group decision support systems: An inquiry into theoretical and philosophical issues.* Unpublished doctoral dissertation, University of Utrecht, the Netherlands.

Scheper, W. J., & Faber, J. (1994). Do cognitive maps make sense? *Advances in Managerial Cognition and Organizational Information Processing, 5*, 165–185.

Seibert, S. E., & Goltz, S. M. (2001). Comparison of allocations by individuals and interacting groups in an escalation of commitment situation. *Journal of Applied Social Psychology, 31*(1), 134–156.

Shields, M. (2002). The role of group dynamics in mental model development. *Proceedings of the 20th International Conference of the System Dynamics Society*, Palermo, Italy.

Simon, H. A. (1957). *Administrative behavior. A study of decision making processes in administrative organization*. New York: Macmillan.

Simon, H. A. (1987). Making management decisions: The role of intuition and emotion. *The Academy of Management Executive, 1*(1), 57–64.

Spaargaren, G. (2006). Milieu-innovaties in alledaagse gedragspraktijken. [Innovations in everyday environmental behavior]. Working paper, Wageningen University, the Netherlands.

Stanovich, K. E., & West, R. F. (2002). Individual differences in reasoning: Implications for the rationality debate?. In T. Gilovich, D. Griffin, & D. Kahneman (Eds.), *Heuristics and biases. The psychology of intuitive judgment* (pp. 421–440). Cambridge, U.K.: Cambridge University Press.

Stasser, G. (1992). Information salience and the discovery of hidden profiles by decision-making groups: A thought experiment. *Organizational Behavior and Human Decision Processes, 52*(1), 156–181.

Stasser, G., Stewart, D. D., & Wittenbaum, G. M. (1995). Expert roles and information exchange during discussion: The importance of knowing who knows what. *Journal of Experimental Social Psychology, 31*(3), 244–265.

Stasser, G., & Titus, W. (1985). Pooling of unshared information in group decision making: Biased information sampling during discussion. *Journal of Personality and Social Psychology, 48,* 1467–1478.
Staw, B. M. (1976). Knee-deep in big muddy: A study of escalating commitment to a chosen future of action. *Organizational Behavior and Human Performance, 16*(1), 27–44.
Staw, B. M., & Ross, J. (1980). Commitment in an experimenting society: A study of the attribution of leadership from administrative scenarios. *Journal of Applied Psychology, 65*(3), 249–260.
Sterman, J. D. (1989). Misperceptions of feedback in dynamic decision making. *Organizational Behavior and Human Decision Processes, 43*(3), 301–335.
Sterman, J. D. (1994). Learning in and about complex systems. *System Dynamics Review, 10*(2–3), 291–330.
Sterman, J. D. (2000). *Business dynamics.* Boston: McGraw-Hill.
Stern, E., Aprea, C., & Ebner, H. G. (2003). Improving cross-content transfer in text processing by means of graphical representation. *Learning and Instruction, 13,* 191–203.
Stevens, C. A., & Finlay, P. N. (1996). A research framework for group support systems. *Group Decision and Negotiation, 5*(4–6), 521–543.
Stewart, D. D., & Stasser, G. (1998). The sampling of critical, unshared information in decision-making groups: The role of an informed minority. *European Journal of Social Psychology, 28*(1), 95–113.
Stout, R. J., Cannon-Bowers, J. A., Salas, E., & Milanovich, D. M. (1999). Planning, shared mental models, and coordinated performance: An empirical link is established. *Human Factors, 41*(1), 61–71.
Sweeney, L. B., & Sterman, J. D. (2000). Bathtub dynamics: Initial results of a systems thinking inventory. *System Dynamics Review, 16*(4), 249–286.
Turner, M. E., & Pratkanis, A. R. (1998). Twenty-five years of groupthink theory and research: Lessons from the evaluation of a theory. *Organizational Behavior and Human Decision Processes, 73*(2–3), 105–115.
Tversky, A., & Kahnemann, D. (1971). Belief in the law of small numbers. *Psychological Bulletin, 76,* 105–110.
Tversky, A., & Kahnemann, D. (1974). Judgment under uncertainty: Heuristics and biases. *Science, 185,* 1124–1131.
Van der Heijden, H. (2000). Scenarios and forecasting: Two perspectives. *Technological Forecasting and Social Change, 65*(1), 31–36.
Vennix, J. A. M. (1990). *Mental models and computer models: Design and evaluation of a computer-based learning environment for policy making.* Unpublished doctoral dissertation, University of Nijmegen, the Netherlands.
Vennix, J. A. M. (1995). Building consensus in strategic decision making: Insights from the process of group model building. *Group Decision and Negotiation, 4*(4), 335–355.
Vennix, J. A. M. (1996). *Group model building: Facilitating team learning using system dynamics.* Chichester, U.K.: Wiley.
Vennix, J. A. M. (1999). Group model-building: Tackling messy problems. *System Dynamics Review, 15*(4), 379–401.
Vennix, J. A. M., Akkermans, H. A., & Rouwette, E. A. J. A. (1996). Group model building to facilitate organizational change: An exploratory study. *System Dynamics Review, 12*(1), 39–58.
Vermaak, J. G. (2006). Interactief werken met causale diagrammen. [Interactive working with causal diagrams.] *M&O,* 3–4, 182–199.

Volpe, C. E., Cannon-Bowers, J. A., Salas, E., & Spector, P. E. (1996). The impact of cross-training on team functioning: An empirical investigation. *Human Factors, 38*(1), 87–100.

Vriens, D. (1998). *Constructief beslissen: Een cybernetische verkenning van het individuele beslisproces. Constructive decision making: A cybernetical analysis of the individual decision making process.* Unpublished doctoral dissertation, Radboud University, the Netherlands.

Vygotski, L. S. (1978). *Mind in society: The development of higher psychological processes.* Cambridge, MA: Harvard University Press.

Wadey, V., & Frank, C. (1997). The effectiveness of patient verbalization on informed consent. *Canadian Journal of Surgery, 40,* 124–128.

Warren, K. D. (2000). *Competitive strategy dynamics.* Chichester, U.K.: Wiley.

Wegner, D. (1987). Transactive memory: A contemporary analysis of the group mind. In G. Mullen, & G. Goethals (Eds.), *Theories of group behavior* (pp. 185–208). New York: Springer Verlag.

Wheeler, B. C., & Valacich, J. S. (1996). Facilitation, GSS, and training as sources of process restrictiveness and guidance for structured group decision making: An empirical assessment. *Information Systems Research, 7*(4), 429–450.

Whyte, G. (1991). Diffusion of responsibility: Effects on the escalation tendency. *Journal of Applied Psychology, 76*(3), 408–415.

Williams, T., Ackermann, F., & Eden, C. (2003). Structuring a delay and disruption claim: An application of cause-mapping and system dynamics. *European Journal of Operational Research, 148,* 192–204.

Wilson, M., & Canter, D. (1993). Shared concepts in group decision-making: A model for decisions based on qualitative data. *British Journal of Social Psychology, 32,* 159–172.

Wilson, T. D. (2002). *Strangers to ourselves. Discovering the adaptive unconsciousness.* Cambridge, MA: Harvard University Press.

Winch, G., & Derrick, S. (2006). Flexible study processes in 'knotty' system dynamics projects. *Systems Research and Behavioral Science, 23*(4), 497–507.

Wittenbaum, G. M., Stasser, G., & Merry, C. J. (1996). Tacit coordination in anticipation of small group task completion. *Journal of Experimental Social Psychology, 32*(2), 129–152.

Worchel, S., Wood, W., & Simpson, J. A. (1992). *Group process and productivity.* Newbury Park, CA: Sage.

Yoo, Y., & Kanawattanachai, P. (2002). Dynamic nature of trust in virtual teams. *Journal of Strategic Information Systems, 11*(3–4), 187–213.

Zagonel, A. A., Rohrbaugh, J., Richardson, G. P., & Andersen, D. F. (2004). Using simulation models to address "what if" questions about welfare reform. *Journal of Policy Analysis and Management, 23*(4), 890–901.

Zigurs, I. (1993). Methodological and measurement issues in group support systems research. In L. M. Jessup, & J. S. Valacich (Eds.), *Group support systems. New perspectives* (pp. 112–122). New York: Macmillan.

CHAPTER

12

Collaborative Knowledge and Training in Online Groups

DAVID P. BRANDON
University of Illinois at Urbana-Champaign

ANDREA B. HOLLINGSHEAD
University of Southern California

Learning in organizational groups using commonplace information and communication technologies is a collaborative outcome, a product of group-member interactions and negotiations. The need to apply collaborative-learning concepts to online organizational groups arises from three broad trends: (a) the widespread interest in organizational learning, (b) the now commonplace use of information and communication technologies for training and other purposes of the organization, and (c) the ubiquitous presence of groups in modern organizations.

Organizational learning represents a general belief by organizations that learning efforts at all levels—inter and intra-organization efforts, learning networks, and communities—are essential to helping the organization become more adaptive and efficient in response to marketplace and technological changes (Bogenrieder & Nooteboom, 2004; Dodgson, 1993; Knight & Pye, 2005; Polito & Watson, 2002). In short, organizations must have the capacity to learn, at all levels, if they are to survive. As organizations struggle to learn, use of information and communication technologies (ICTs) has continued to grow. In the year 2000, 74.6% of manufacturing organizations provided Internet access, and 68.7% had a local-area network, and 40.4% an intranet (U.S. Bureau of the Census, 2002). Educational manifestations of information and communication technologies (e.g., virtual classrooms, computer-based learning, etc.) are also the foundation through which many organizations deliver training to their membership (Allen & Seaman, 2005; DeRouin, Fritzsche, & Salas, 2005; Trierweiler & Rivera, 2005).

In the midst of these technological and learning efforts are work groups of various types, with nearly half of all organizations using one or more types of groups for work purposes (Devine, Clayton, Philips, Dunford, & Melner, 1999; Dumaine, 1994; Yan & Louis, 1999). As with all other levels of the organization, to be and remain effective work groups need to be able to learn, preferably in the most efficient and productive manner possible. Collaborative learning—a pedagogical method built around the use of groups—engages learners in the active processing of information needed for learning to occur and is associated with greater learning and academic performance, increased student responsibility, initiative, and interaction with others (Althaus, 1997; Barkley, Cross, & Major, 2005; Johnson & Johnson, 1991; King, 1994; McComb, 1994).

In sum, there is a great need for organizations to have the capacity to learn, and as organizations rely heavily on groups using various ICTs, there is a great need to understand how learning occurs in technology-supported groups. As collaborative learning appears to be effective in promoting knowledge development in traditional groups, this approach may, in turn, inform the development of effective learning in technology-supported groups.

This chapter explores collaborative learning in organizational work groups using ICTs. It applies and extends a model describing collaborative learning in online groups in academic settings (Brandon & Hollingshead, 1999) to those in organizational settings, such as training or project teams. Our model of collaborative learning in organizational online groups posits four classes of inputs: (a) social-behavioral, (b) social-cognitive, (c) course-technology fit, and (d) learner variables. These variables are then moderated by managerial- and computer-mediated communication variables. Group behavioral and individual cognitive processes that emerge then influence learning and other outcomes.

The model suggests that learning is a product of the people involved, how well the technology used supports learning, and whether there is the chance for needed learning processes to occur. Managerial influences, and how much the technology used affects communication, are further issues, all of which influence how much the actual collaborative-learning processes occur, and, in turn, learning outcomes. We hope that the model will serve both as an overview of significant conceptual factors and issues to be considered when designing collaborative-learning programs for organizational groups using ICTs. While the model and discussion does emphasize fully online groups, the concepts should also be useful to more mixed efforts, such as where a collaborative, online component combines with other instructional methods.

DEFINING GROUPS AND TECHNOLOGY

As a first step, we define basic terms for groups and technologies. Groups, their goals and context, and the technology that supports them can be defined in many ways. In this chapter, we use the term *online group* to refer to an entity comprised of people having interdependent goals, who are acquainted with each other, interact with each other, and who have a sense of belonging associated with their membership (Hollingshead & Contractor, 2002). As the focus of this volume is on work groups, we assume that the group's goals are defined in whole or part by their member organization(s), that member interdependence distinguishes them from other groups, and that technology is used to support their learning goals (Covert & Thompson, 2001). We also assume (or recommend) that the group size is kept small as possible (three to four members, which is the size common to classroom collaborative efforts and a size suggested for online-learning groups (Harasim, 1991; Sharan & Sharan, 1994; Slavin, 1988), and that the group is relatively long-term in its lifespan (e.g., at least several months). An example is a three-person team, with members distributed geographically across three regional offices, using e-mail and online video conferencing over a period of 6 months to learn about local consequences of changes in federal health insurance policies.

Gone already are the days when a particular information or communication technology served a single purpose and offered a single channel. Just yesterday phones were for audio, and e-mail was for text messages. Now people e-mail via their phones, and attach audio files to their e-mail or use Internet phone systems. Here, the general term *information and communication technologies*, or ICTs, will be used to refer to both commonplace Internet communication technologies (e-mail, Web sites, newsgroups) and more specialized information/knowledge management tools (groupware, intranets, Lotus Notes). A subset of ICTs are technologies specifically tailored for learning purposes (DeRouin et al., 2005; Miyake & Koschmann, 2002; van Bruggen & Kirschner, 2003), such as a software program that helps teach mathematical reasoning.

The discussion that follows assumes that online groups are using one or more ICTs for their interaction and perhaps using ICTs tailored to a learning purpose. In addition, we assume that the group uses some form of ICT for at least the collaborative aspects of its learning, and perhaps to substitute, supplement, or complement other aspects of learning (Brandon & Hollingshead, 1999).

DEFINING COLLABORATIVE LEARNING IN ORGANIZATIONAL ONLINE-LEARNING GROUPS

As in defining groups and technology, there are several ways to view collaborative learning. Concepts applicable to collaborative learning in online groups come from a variety of disciplines ranging from research on collaborative instruction in the traditional classroom (Johnson & Johnson, 1991) to work on computer-mediated communication and work (Borghoff & Schlichter, 2000; Harasim, 1991; Koschmann, Myers, Feltovich, & Barrows, 1994) to a field in its own right, computer-supported collaborative learning (Blumenfeld, Marx, Soloway, & Krajcik, 1996; Koschmann, Hall, & Miyake, 2002).

Our model borrows primarily from classroom models of collaborative learning and applies them to groups in the online context, and this literature makes a distinction between group learning that is either primarily about sharing workload or developing shared meaning. In other words, the work is cooperation based (group members share a divided workload) or collaboration based (group members develop shared meanings) (Webb & Palincsar, 1996). For example, suppose group members are writing a paper. They can either coordinate contributions of separately written chapters (cooperation) or provide a single paper where each section represents the group's shared thoughts and conclusions (collaboration) (Anderson, Mayes, & Kibby, 1995). As compared to cooperation, collaborative learning emphasizes knowledge generated by group members and the development of thinking skills, which is likely to be better suited to more mature learners (Barkley et al., 2005). This perspective on knowledge as being socially created emphasizes that meaning cannot be delivered prepackaged for memorization; rather it is negotiated by group members (Pea, 1996; Roschelle, 1992).

In this chapter, collaborative learning is defined as the acquisition by individuals of knowledge, skills, or attitudes through group interaction in which group members share work and develop shared meanings (Derycke & D'Halluin, 1995). As such, learning evolves from the creation and interpretation among individuals and groups (Gay & Lentini, 1995). As applied to online groups, this means that learning will evolve primarily from online interactions among group members.

APPLICABILITY OF COLLABORATIVE LEARNING TO THE ORGANIZATIONAL CONTEXT

Many organizations use online courses from higher-learning institutions for their training purposes, given that the course content meets or can be adjusted to meet their goals. Graduate-level university programs incorporating online learning continue to grow, with over a billion dollars in revenues in recent years (Huber & Lowry, 2003; Trierweiler & Rivera, 2005). Collaborative learning is one reason organizations utilize online learning (Garrett & Vogt, 2003).

Another perspective on the suitability of a classroom-based approach is to view collaborative learning within the larger framework of organizational learning. Theorists have argued for the distinction between individual and organizational learning, with organizational learning often discussed as a macrofeature or cultural value that supports learning by individuals and groups (Dodgson, 1993; Fiol & Lyles, 1985). Even so, the processes underlying organizational learning have a foundation in individual-learning theory (Akgun, Lynn, & Byrne, 2003; Dodgson, 1993; Ghosh, 2004; Polito & Watson, 2002), and the means by which organizations bridge learning from individuals to the organization is often via various types of groups, where knowledge transmission occurs via interaction (cf. Bogenrieder & Nooteboom, 2004; Senge, 1990). Other researchers suggested that use of teams is a characteristic of a learning organization (Marquardt & Reynolds, 1994). Collaborative-learning methods as utilized in small groups thus represent both a knowledge generation and a knowledge transmission venue for collaborative learning.

VARIABLES THAT IMPACT ONLINE GROUPS AND COLLABORATIVE-LEARNING OUTCOMES

Collaborative-learning theory argues that social context inherently influences learning, whether or not a communication technology mediates the associated interaction over space/time (Davies, 1995; Salaberry, 1996). However, while online-learning environments now have an extensive research history, their efficacy in creating the needed social context for learning remains a matter of some debate (Johnson & Aragon, 2003). Still, while adding communication technologies may add to the complexity of the learning tasks . . . it does encourage learning about the technology itself, and learning a technology itself tends to promote group cooperation (Johnson & Johnson, 1994).

Further, agreement on a theoretical approach for describing collaborative-online learning has been elusive, in part due to resolving how to incorporate all the theory that may apply, such as learning theory, instructional design, social-interaction theory, person-technology fit, and so on (Koschmann et al., 1994). A shift in focus from individually focused, content-based instruction to group-focused, process-based instruction does appear under way, yet there is still a lack of conceptual and pragmatic direction on how educational programs can make this adjustment (Andriessen, Baker, & Suthers, 2003).

The model described next does not purport to resolve these issues, but rather to describe major variables for consideration in the design of collaborative learning for online groups. Three models of group effectiveness—(a) the Webb and Palincsar (1996) description of group processes in the classroom, (b) the O'Donnell and O'Kelly (1994) classification of collaborative-learning theory, and (c) the McGrath and Hollingshead (1994) model of the impact of communication technologies on interacting groups—in combination provide the foundation of the model. As shown in Fig. 12.1, social-behavioral, social-cognitive, technology fit, and participant variables are inputs, subsequently modified by computer-mediated communication channel(s) and variables associated with any facilitators, instructors, or managers involved in the group's learning. Social and behavioral processes arising from the interactions of the online group stimulate individual intellectual activity that in turn contributes to knowledge, attitudinal and organizational outcomes.

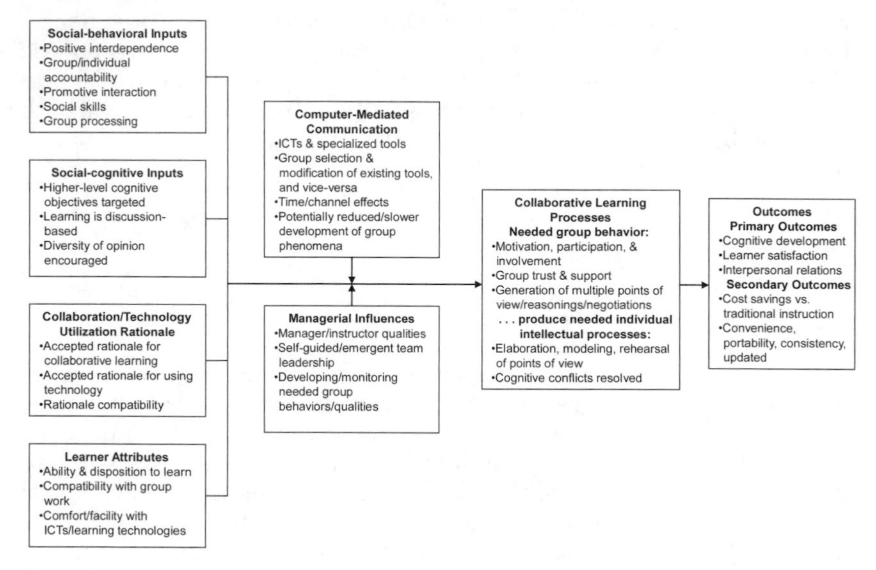

Figure 12.1 Collaborative learning influences and outcomes.

INPUTS TO THE MODEL

Social-Behavioral Inputs

A first set of inputs to the model are *social-behavioral inputs,* a term meant to encompass both social-motivation and social-cohesion theories of collaborative learning (O'Donnell & O'Kelly, 1994). From the social-cohesion perspective, efforts to learn arise from identification with the group; for this reason (and for other reasons benefiting online groups), managers will want group members to have a strong commitment to the group. From the social-motivation perspective, collective goals and rewards motivate collaborative learning. That is, working with peers motivates the individual to learn.

Structurally, group goals, commitment to those goals, and individual accountability are prerequisites of this approach. Included here within the social-behavioral umbrella is the well-researched area of social interdependence theory, which suggests that interdependence exists when individuals share common goals, and success is contingent on the actions of others (Johnson & Johnson, 1991, 2004; Johnson, Johnson, & Smith, 1991). Building on social interdependence, Johnson and Johnson (2004) described five basic elements required for collaborative learning: (a) positive interdependence, (b) individual and group accountability, (c) promotive interaction, (d) demonstration of appropriate social skills by participants, and (e) group-processing discussions about achieving group goals. These elements are included in the model as part of the broader social-behavioral perspective. Individual accountability is an important aspect of social motivation theory, while promotive interaction, social skills, group processing, and group accountability are important aspects of social cohesion theory. Notably, qualities such as accountability, feedback, and trust are often discussed as characteristic of a learning organization (Marquardt & Reynolds, 1994; Park, Ribière, & Schulte Jr., 2004; Popper & Lipshitz, 1998)—an indication that the classroom learning concepts are applicable to organizational online groups.

Promotive interaction (group members facilitate and encourage one another in the completion of group tasks), group processing discussions (members discuss their task achievement and working relations—see Johnson & Johnson, 1991; Johnson et al., 1991; Johnson, Johnson, & Smith, 1995), and demonstration of social skills are interpersonal processes that contribute to the social context important to the success of online groups (cf. Martins, Gilson, & Maynard, 2004). Similarly, task interdependence and accountability are structures that can influence virtual-team outcomes (Bell & Kozlowski, 2002; Martins et al., 2004), which again indicates an overlap of collaborative learning and online group concepts.

It can be assumed that these elements are likely to influence each other; for example, task type and associated interdependence will influence interaction (Driskell, Radtke, & Salas, 2003). All of the five elements will be relevant and present throughout the group's history, but they are mentioned here as inputs with the perspective that they can be structured to occur within the group. Perhaps more so than face-to-face groups, online groups need a clear direction for the group and associated individual goals and guidelines for appropriate group behavior (Bell & Kozlowski, 2002). Building in these elements benefits learning goals.

An online-learning group's design can include some or all of the five elements. To establish accountability and common goals, a manager organizing a self-managed online group to learn about new markets overseas could have the group generate a single report on the topic for distribution in the organization, but at the same time a manager might have each member write a subreport providing more detail on how his or her home department should respond. Goal, reward, resource, and role interdependence structures can foster positive interdependence. An example of the latter is to give each member a duty within the group (Johnson & Johnson, 1991; Johnson & Johnson, 1994; Johnson et al., 1991). To encourage social skills, at a launch meeting, the manager may wish to review with the group corporate expectations about appropriate behavior, such as avoiding flaming and other disruptive online behaviors (Berge, 1995; McGlaughlin, Osborne, & Smith, 1995) during conversation and responding in a timely fashion to online queries. Other getting acquainted activities may benefit an online group as well; introductions and the sharing of contact information at the start of the group can encourage the development of needed social conventions (Feenberg, 1989; Scalia & Sackmary, 1996). As needed, managers should encourage group-processing discussions (cf. Johnson, Johnson, & Holubec, 1994).

Further means of implementing collaborative structures in formal training groups are possible by applying classroom collaborative-learning techniques to the online environment, such as the Group Investigation (Sharan, 1995; Sharan & Sharan, 1994) and Structured Academic Controversy (Johnson & Johnson, 1994; Johnson et al., 1995). These methods essentially have many of the necessary characteristics for collaborative learning (e.g., interdependence, accountability) built into them, but they were developed for face-to-face groups and thus will require translation into online forms (e.g., face-to-face assumptions, time frame, sequence and number of steps involved may need modification).

Other methods with a collaborative-learning foundation may already exist in the workplace, and be built upon. Szarka, Grant, and Flannery (2004), for example, described the use of intergroup competition to motivate 34 project-based teams in the design of quality-improvement processes, a design not dissimilar to the Teams-Games-Tournaments collaborative-learning method (Slavin, 1988; Webb & Palincsar, 1996) and other techniques (Moshaiov, 2003).

Social-Cognitive Inputs

While social cognition has been described as underlying organizational learning (Akgun et al., 2003), our emphasis is on theories tailored to collaborative learning. Specifically, the social-cognitive perspective refers to how social interaction encourages learning, and includes theories of Vygotsky, Piaget, and the cognitive-elaboration theory (O'Donnell & O'Kelly, 1994). The Vygotskian view of cognitive development asserts that individual's cognitive structures develop through a process of mediation and modeling of other's cognitive structures as demonstrated during interaction. However, the cognitive structures of others must be within the individual's range of comprehension or zone of proximal development (Vygotsky, 1978). That is, one should not have a group of learners from the marketing department of a pharmaceutical company learn advanced organic chemistry; it is more than likely out of their range of comprehension.

The Piagetian view (starting from Piaget, 1932) of learning suggests that cognitive structures develop through the resolution of cognitive conflicts, with such conflicts arising during the natural process of peer interaction; multiple perspectives lead to conflicts the individual must then resolve cognitively. Similar to both theories, in cognitive-elaboration theory peer-interaction drives learning. Interaction encourages active processing of information by the individual, with subsequent modifications of the individual's cognitive structures. The use of specific examples to illustrate concepts, multiple representations (of charts, figures, pictures, etc.) to explain concepts, generation of analogies, translations of terms, detailed descriptions of how to perform tasks, descriptions of difference between concepts, justifications of problem solving, use of evidence, and the like are all examples of elaborations that benefit learning. In sum, group members need encouragement to discuss the subject(s) at hand, as a means of driving them to generate then resolve multiple perspectives and as a result learn.

The emphasis of the social-cognitive perspective is that learning requires interaction. As applied to online groups, this essentially recommends not exporting simpler learning tasks to an environment typified by communication tools. One means of classifying learning task complexity is Bloom's (1956) taxonomy of six increasingly difficult levels of cognitive objectives—(a) knowledge, (b) comprehension, (c) application, (d) analysis, (e) synthesis and (f) evaluation. Only the last three levels involve complex cognitive tasks, such as separating or combining concepts or making judgments based on evidence and thus would be suitable to online learning. Learning that involves a high degree of memorization, or mastering a specific skill, may not be suitable for online-group learning (Berge, 1995; Hiltz, 1994). Developing an online group with the goal of helping group members memorize new product codes would be a poor approach.

On the other hand, complex content that involves debate, controversy, and multiple points of view is better suited to an online-group environment. For example, consider an online group tasked with learning about a new series of federal regulations potentially affecting various parts of an organization's manufacturing process. Having the group meet online just to start reading the regulations or about how the regulations would apply within each member's area of specialty would be of little benefit. More benefit would accrue from having group members discuss more complex topics online, such as how to reconcile conflicting federal and state regulations, prioritize the organization to respond to the new regulations, or estimate the financial impact of the new regulations.

Collaboration/Technology Utilization Rationale

Simply put, if group members do not see the point in working together and/or using a particular ICT for learning, the online-learning project is likely to fail. Encouraging discussion within organizational groups is challenging enough (cf. Sense, 2005), and this challenge is unlikely to diminish with the transition of discussion to the online environment. Collaborative learning agendas will need to provide a strong rationale for both the use of a collaborative pedagogy and the use of a technology to carry out the collaboration. Of the two factors, researchers are fairly uniform in stating that pedagogy and course design are more important than any ICT used to deliver that instruction (Johnson & Aragon, 2003; Russell, 1999). Still, designers of online groups will want to carefully consider the ICT to be used; the technology used to support the collaboration (e.g., ICT or a more specialized tool) should be selected for its ability to facilitate collaborative work (Yoon, 2003).

Rationales provided by managers or administrators for online groups should be obvious and motivating to participants. Learners may reject online discussions if they feel they are not sufficiently relevant to course goals, dismissing them as technological busy work (Nalley, 1995; Witmer, 1998). Perhaps more so than higher-education students, adult learners are likely to assess if a course is going to benefit them personally and if the course format will work for them (Yoon, 2003). Such assessments will extend to the technology utilized for the online collaboration; some may see the technology as unneeded, others may see direct benefits to the course organization and content, and yet others may see benefit to learning about the technology itself (Lerouge, Blanton, & Kittner, 2004). Even with a solid rationale in place, it cannot be guaranteed that group members will use a given ICT or will always stay on the group's assigned topic (Kreijns, Kirschner, & Jochems, 2003).

Some organizational circumstances may themselves help provide the rationale for utilizing collaborative learning and online groups. Having group members use new communication software that is about to become standard in the organization may be motivating or a group of managers in an online group might use a groupware package, so that they can understand how their subordinates might use the program (cf. Nalley, 1995). Organizational plans to make greater use of distributed work teams (Lipnack & Stamps, 1997; Martins et al., 2004) will almost certainly influence participants to want to learn the ICTs the distributed teams are likely to use or the already commonplace use of groupware may encourage its use (cf. Hiltz, 1994). Other organizational circumstances may also provide compelling rationales such as extensive business travel or telework necessitating ICT use. Interinstitutional learning programs (Gay & Lentini, 1995; Wheeler, Valacich, Alavi, & Vogel, 1995), or the formation of interorganizational alliances that require learning among distributed groups (Ghosh, 2004), for example, can require collaborative learning and ICT use by teams. The broader and stronger the ties to organizational imperatives, the more likely an online-learning program will be successful.

In addition to having a macrolevel organizational culture that supports learning (cf. Dodgson, 1993), online-learning programs will benefit from management involvement, connections between the learning program and technology support within the organization, and tying the learning to the organization's overall business strategy (Garrett & Vogt, 2003). Consider an online course on leadership in distributed work groups offered to members of an organization that rarely uses such teams, does not intend to expand their use, is geographically consolidating once dispersed satellite offices into fewer units, and is planning to adopt a new, comprehensive feature ICT/intranet in several months. Learners will likely see little utility in attending such an undersupported training venture.

Learner Attributes

Characteristics of learners are another set of inputs likely to influence the utility and success of collaborative learning in an online group. These characteristics include general skills, aptitudes, cognitive and learning styles, academic maturity, positive attitudes toward the learning, and an active and visual learning style will influence learner participation and outcomes, some of which may be set early in life (Hiltz, 1993; Johnson & Aragon, 2003; Martins et al., 2004; Meyer, 2002; Selwyn, Gorard, & Furlong, 2005). Comfort with group work, and with technology, can also vary by participant in ways that ultimately influence learning (Hiltz, 1993, 1994; Johnson & Johnson, 2004).

Additionally, research on collaboration in the traditional classroom environment finds that some learners are inclined to cooperate and function well in collaborative activities, while others tend to prefer to work on their own and do best in individual or whole-class settings (Webb & Palincsar, 1996). Such preferences may extend to participation in online groups as well, with learners being resistant to group-oriented software that requires information sharing (Scalia & Sackmary, 1996). Qualities that predispose a person to be successful in distributed work teams, such as willingness to trust, trustworthiness, interpersonal skills that facilitate collaborative work, and skills in communicating in a virtual environment (Shin, 2004), may also encourage online-group participation.

And since an online group is, after all, a group, composition variables argued to impact virtual-group behavior—group size, member demographics, overall group diversity—also stand to influence learning outcomes (Martins et al., 2004). Classroom studies indicate that both homogeneous and heterogeneous groups can benefit from collaborative learning, but that the greatest benefits may accrue in the heterogeneous groups, as such groups tend to stimulate the needed kind of discourse more than their homogenous counterparts (Johnson & Johnson, 2004).

Thus, when putting together online-learning groups, managers need to consider which members of their organization are likely to be able to participate constructively in an online group, yet at the same time not end up with groups so homogenous the possibility of active discussion diminishes. Assuring that the overall pedagogy includes both individual and collaborative-group activities and that learning is to some degree self-directed (Johnson & Aragon, 2003; Rovai, 2004) may also be productive. Such decisions can mean tradeoffs in making assignments. For example, when assigning someone to an online group, it may be more beneficial to assign a member who has the skills to be an effective online-group member in place of someone higher in the organizational hierarchy who does not have these skills.

MODERATING VARIABLES—ICT EFFECTS AND MANAGERIAL BEHAVIORS

Having discussed inputs into collaborative learning in online groups, the next step is to consider what factors might modify the connections between the inputs and the desired learning outcomes. The model indicates that the ICT(s) used and leadership in the group moderates the relation between the aforementioned inputs, resulting behavioral and cognitive processes, and subsequent outcomes. Technology has the curious distinction of being both an input and a moderator in the model, although this is not uncommon in discussions of virtual and distributed work teams (cf. Driskell et al., 2003; Martins et al., 2004). Essentially, this is an indication that the characteristics of a technology will tend to influence online interaction, but also suggests that how the group makes use of and exploits the technology is an ongoing process that will moderate group interaction.

Qualities of ICTs that may influence collaborative learning are identified via three areas of research: (a) studies of communication channels, (b) models describing virtual teams, and (c) studies of specialized learning tools. Managerial behaviors is used as an umbrella term in the following discussion, for both circumstances in which there is a leader (e.g., a trainer, facilitator, or manager) for the online group, and for more "leaderless" situations such as self-managed teams.

ICT Effects—Communication Channels Research

Early studies of various ICTs used for group learning emphasized providing multiple channels to learners, reflecting concerns about system usability and channel capacity, and a perhaps optimistic view that online learning would encourage overall participation. Asynchronous computer conferencing, providing message posting/responding as found in basic online newsgroups, was initially the commonplace ICT tool for both colocated and distant learners (O'Malley, 1995). However, it soon became apparent that online groups desired and could make use of multiple channels, including audio and video options. A study of academic groups using multiple channels (chat tools, drawing tools, and video/audio conferencing) found that each group used the available channels in idiosyncratic ways to increase the depth and breadth of their understanding, suggesting that multiple-communication modalities can make groups more productive (Gay & Lentini, 1995).

Related arguments posited that courses requiring visual material, manipulation of physical objects, or audio interaction needed to provide those options to learners (Hiltz, 1994). Online collaborative learning seemed unlikely to advance until multimedia options providing for multiple representations and nontext transmissions (Pea, 1996) were available to groups. Still, researchers were hopeful that use of ICTs for learning would increase participation by reducing some barriers found in face-to-face interaction, and consequently increase learner satisfaction and engagement in the learning process (Bannon, 1995; Koschmann, 1994). For example, status tends to affect one's participation in face-to-face groups; to the extent that the salience of demographically based status indicators are reduced by the online environment, more group members may feel comfortable participating in processes that provide cognitive gains (Bonito & Hollingshead, 1997; Kiesler & Sproull, 1992).

Current thinking on how ICT use may influence group interaction (and vice versa) has emerged from a number of prior theories (Hollingshead & Contractor, 2002), including social presence (ICTs reduce one's salience/social presence to others), and media richness (ICTs vary in their ability to reduce uncertainty and equivocality). Where these theories suggest selection of an ICT(s) based on its channel effects, the social-influence model suggests that media selection reflects a number of social factors rather than solely objective media characteristics, such as using e-mail over audio conferencing out of habit. Another perspective is media effects, which argues that use of ICTs influences group interaction such that social and psychological processes are substantially different than found in face-to-face groups (Hollingshead & Contractor, 2002). Included in the media effects perspective is the notion that ICTs provide a narrower bandwidth of information than face-to-face communication. Lastly, the theory of adaptive structuration asserts that while a communication technology may impose certain rules, the rules do not bind the group, and the group will adopt the technology to its own occasionally ironic purposes in a way that affects group outcomes.

For the designer of an online-collaborative-learning plan, this research suggests that online groups will need more time to complete their work than comparable colocated groups, even when using real-time communication tools (McGrath & Hollingshead, 1994). Some groups may only produce two to three well-articulated points per month via their discussions (Berge, 1995) and may experience coordination problems that managers can assist by establishing milestones and deadlines (Harasim, 1991; Scalia & Sackmary, 1996), though inevitably groups will to some degree go their own way in their use of ICTs. Further, while even deep social relationships can emerge from online interaction (McKenna & Green, 2002), initially groups may experience some social discord due to the constraints on interaction imposed by the online environment. For example, a course designer hoping to translate an organization's 2-hour in-person ethics course into an online unit based in a particular groupware package may find that the online version is distributed over a much longer timeframe and that course members largely ignore their groupware in favor of phone and e-mail interactions.

ICT Effects—Virtual Teams Research

The growing literature on virtual and distributed work teams also suggests a moderating influence of ICTs on learning in online groups. One model of virtual teams posits that the type of ICTs used, the type of task, and temporal factors, moderate the effect of the computer-mediated environment on mediating group processes (cohesiveness, status processes, counternormative behavior, and communication), and then again moderate the impact of these group processes on team performance (Driskell et al., 2003). The overall conclusion of research using this model is that ICTs can have a negative impact on a number of group phenomena, such as lower cohesiveness, reduced-status cues that may hinder the positive influence of higher-status individuals, more counternormative behavior, and greater difficulty in communication. However, the type of task, the type of ICT(s) used, and how long the groups are together moderates these effects. The combined interactions of the inputs, moderators, and mediating process variables then influence team performance.

Findings within this model point to task type as the most influential moderator, with less-rich media tending to aggravate the negative effect of using computer-mediated channels. However, given sufficient time, groups might be able to overcome problems caused by the online environment. Designers of online-collaborative efforts should build sufficient time into the agenda for the group to accomplish its goals (e.g., more time than one would allot for a face-to-face group), provide the group with as many media channels as possible, and require that the group engage in activities that both develop and monitor internal social phenomena.

A second model of virtual-team functioning again describes team inputs, processes, and outcomes, and with a set of variables influencing team processes (Martins et al., 2004). Team size, individual and team characteristics, task, and technology are inputs influencing team processes of goal setting, communication, participation, and various interpersonal phenomena (e.g., conflict, trust). Moderating variables of task type, time, and social context influence the development of the team processes. Team outcomes include member satisfaction, time required, and decision quality. More so than the prior model, this model emphasizes social factors in team processes as influencing team outcomes, suggesting that designers of online programs must not view online groups as something they start, leave running on their own, and then return to for a final product. Instead, ongoing monitoring of group interaction has to be part of the learning architecture.

Specialized Tools for Learning

While online-learning efforts can utilize commonplace ICTs, more specialized tools may also be used, such as software designed to structure collaboration in a particular fashion, via providing guidance through text or representational interfaces or scripts that regulate interaction (Jermann, Soller, & Lesgold, 2004). Learning-management systems such as WebCT© and Blackboard© essentially combine into a single package common ICTs along with online presentation, content management, and assessment tools (Garrett, 2003; WebCT, 2006). The learning-management system genre of software can provide benefits to learning, although this can depend on qualities of the technology (e.g., reliable, easy to learn, sufficient options), critical mass in use by an online group, and individual assessments of the tool—all generating a sense of use quality (e.g., informed and effective use) (Lerouge et al., 2004). If targeted at a learning audience, the learning-management tools are still essentially compilations of generic tools, and don't have collaborative pedagogy inherently built into the design (Yang & Wang, 2005). Thus, instructors using these tools for collaborative purposes will still face the issues described in this chapter, such as the need for a pedagogy underlying use of the tool, training for instructors, motivating use of the tool by participants, individual differences in use, and so on (Hoskins & van Hoof, 2005; Samarawickrema & Benson, 2004).

Other specialized tools for collaborative learning build upon the notion of interaction contributing to learning, but seek to guide or capture learning more distinctively than provided via standard learning software tools. Software tools designed to produce learning outcomes are designed under a variety of theoretical perspectives (Blumenfeld et al., 1996; Harasim, 1991; Johansson & Gardenfors, 2005; Koschmann et al., 1994; Stahl, 2004). Collaborative software tools may combine computer-mediated channels with features that structure interactions, provide argument representations, and actively guide argumentation in ways that encourage collaborators to produce discourse and subsequent learning, such as through stimulating group negotiation (Andriessen et al., 2003).

For example, software written to help students learn physics concepts requires students to first develop their own solutions to a question, then enter into conversation with other students, with the students evaluating each other's reasoning via required verifications (Baker, 2003). Another tool provides students with the ability to construct diagrams of their argument structure (Veerman, 2003), another provides feedback mechanisms intended to enhance group well-being during problem-based learning (Zumbach & Reimann, 2003), and there are other examples (Andriessen et al., 2003; Bravo, Redondo, Ortega, & Verdejo, 2006; Jermann et al., 2004; Wasson, Ludvigsen, & Hoppe, 2003).

Compelling as it may be to organizations that they can plug online groups into a software package that will then train them without consuming further resources, in reality familiar issues about using a collaborative technology will arise. For example, specialized packages may or may not suit training goals and learners may or may not be easily adaptable to other, perhaps similar, tasks. Specialized packages may require more initial training than commonplace technologies, groups will still require ongoing monitoring (via an instructor or software), and there is no guarantee online groups will use the feedback a software produces (Jermann et al., 2004).

For example, consider a software package designed to teach technicians the algorithm underlying a computer-driven manufacturing process via genesis of diagrams of workflow produced and discussed by group members and then tested periodically against the actual model by the software. Still there would be issues of motivation and suitability to the user group (e.g., some may wish for more information, others may wish for less, and still others may wish for information in a different format). Group members would also need training to use the diagramming features and the group would need to be monitored to make sure that there is participation, and so forth. The chance also exists that the algorithm will change, making the software superfluous unless it is reasonably adaptable.

In sum, standard productivity and specialized learning tools will raise concerns related to the reliability, learnabilty, and usability of the course software. If the technology is too hard to use, has a high learning curve, and is generally hard to access, it is unlikely that learners will make use of the system (cf. Chiu, Hsu, Sun, Lin, & Sun, 2005; Scalia & Sackmary, 1996). And, whatever mix of commonplace or specialized ICT tools may be available, the most success will come from designers of online groups adapting existing tools to match the learning tasks and processes the group faces (Beise, Niederman, & Mattord, 2004) and from providing training to instructors (cf. Samarawickrema & Benson, 2004).

Managerial Influences

The phrase *moderating managerial influences* as used in the model refers both to the presence of a manager serving as an instructor or facilitator for the online group and to the development of self-organized, intragroup development of culture/behaviors that facilitate the collaborative-learning process. With regards to direct management, theory on virtual-team leadership suggests that leaders should focus on a group's relational aspects, such as more team building upfront, setting standards for interaction, providing structure, and providing ongoing relational development (Zhang, Fjermestad, & Tremaine, 2005; Zigurs, 2003). Generally, online group leaders or managers will need to create more structures across a number of areas for the group, to engage in more monitoring of the group, help the group anticipate problems, focus on either or both short- and long-term team building, and develop clear goals and directions for the group (Bell & Kozlowski, 2002).

In terms of instructional approaches, support from an instructor/manager should be "scaffolded" to the intellectual level of the group. It should be intense in the early stages of the group, and then tapered off as group members achieve learning goals (Smagorinsky & Fly, 1993). An instructor's role in an online group is not a matter of taking a traditional academic position of the expert presenting information to the passive receivers, but rather a role as discussion facilitator and manager (Berge, 1995). A conversational tone tends to be more effective than posing questions or making statements, and some participants may need coaching on their communication skills (Ahern, Peck, & Laycock, 1992; Berge, 1995; Harasim, 1987). Summarizing the state of a discussion by identifying unifying themes and/or areas of disagreement can stimulate cognitive processing as well (Feenberg, 1989). Another method suggests that managers should ask all participants to respond individually to a question before asking new questions, assign debates within the group, and initiate free association (Eisley, 1991). Responding to group-member questions, clarifying subject matter, and asking follow-up questions may also help (Gilbert & Dabbagh, 2005). Facilitating groups in such a fashion may best be suited for instructors who can provide examples from real-life experience, demonstrate openness, concern, flexibility, and sincerity, have good communication skills, are advocates of online learning, value critical thinking, and have training in online instruction (Huber & Lowry, 2003).

There is also the prospect for leadership to emerge from within the online group itself (Misiolek & Heckman, 2005; Zigurs, 2003), in a particular group member, or in some other fashion be shared across group members (Johnson, Suriya, Yoon, Berrett, & La Fleur, 2002). With some initial training in instructional design, facilitating discussions, and direct instruction, leadership functions can manifest in peer teams (Rourke & Anderson, 2002), suggesting that after initial phases, instructors may be able to taper support. A knowledgeable manager training leading remote sales personnel on new legal mandates might begin attending every online session held by the group until they have sized up the problem, established goals, set an agenda, demonstrated communication skills, and so on. Should the online group demonstrate organized and functional behavior on its own, the manager might then gradually only drop in on the group perhaps every third or fourth session.

Part of the ability of an online group to manage its learning process may be the group's adoption of values that foster both organizational learning and that support self-managed teams, such as trust, respect, reciprocity, and awareness of cultural, communication, and participation barriers (Zakaria, Amelinckx, & Wilemon, 2004). Formal and informal learning mechanisms, supported by related organizational values supporting learning (Popper & Lipshitz, 1998), might help develop these qualities in an online group. For example, an online group may adopt an action-learning approach, repeating stages of problem identification, individual reflection and group discussion, identifying and enacting solutions, and evaluating outcomes to learn about a particular issue (Faull, Hartley, & Kalliath, 2005). However, neither emergent leadership nor structured learning procedures provide organizations with a "plug-and-play" method for organizing learning groups; each approach requires some level of initial management from a lead figure (cf. Rourke & Anderson, 2002).

COLLABORATIVE-LEARNING PROCESSES IN ONLINE GROUPS

The goal of the inputs described in the model, and of the moderating variables, is to help the group generate the behavior and cognitive processes argued by collaborative-learning theory to foster cognitive development, at both the group and individual levels. At the group level are the behaviors that the preceding factors intend to generate, including participation and involvement, demonstration of social skills, helping behavior, group-processing discussions, generation of multiple points of view, and display of multiple patterns of reasoning. At the individual level are the enactment of cognitive processes, stimulated by the group behavior, that produce learning, including cognitive elaboration, rehearsal, modeling, and the resolution of cognitive conflict. If listed separately, the processes in action are likely highly interwoven. For example, as one group member expresses a perspective on a particular problem, that action will, in turn, stimulate cognitive conflict in another member, who by expressing that conflict may raise conflict in another group member. Alternatively, in the act of explaining a perspective, a group member may elaborate in more detail, enhancing the understanding of one or more group members, and so on.

Because collaborative-learning theory has its foundation in face-to-face interaction, it is reasonable to wonder if online interaction is different from this traditional format, in a way that influences group behaviors. Research indicates that online discussions encourage sharing of ideas, greater breadth and depth of participation (Ruberg, Moore, & Taylor, 1996), and while online discussions may take longer, the exchanges can be richer and more complex than in face-to-face interaction

(Salaberry, 1996; Scalia & Sackmary, 1996). Additionally, learners have the opportunity to use asynchronous tools to provide links to course-related materials and make more in-depth comments, while more interactive channels can carry initial reactions and social interaction (Davidson-Shivers, Tanner, & Muilenburg, 2000; Irvine, 2000). A comparison of face-to-face and online threaded discussions found evidence of higher-order learning in the online discussions, as well as student perceptions that the online tool increased their time spent on course objectives, and that both venues contributed to learning (Meyer, 2002). Conclusions regarding the ability of online discussion to generate useful pedagogical material are not limited to a particular learning perspective; an analysis of online discussions using a number of different theoretical frames repeatedly found high-level interaction in the exchanges (Meyer, 2004).

OUTCOMES

In the traditional classroom setting, collaborative learning affects numerous cognitive and affective outcomes, such as academic achievement, cognitive development, schemata and deeper understanding, intergroup relations, self-esteem, motivation, and anxiety (Ahern et al., 1992; Alavi, 1994; Barkley et al., 2005; Courtney, Courtney, & Nicholson, 1994; Johnson & Johnson, 1991, 2004; Johnson et al., 1991; Slavin, 1991; Webb & Palincsar, 1996). The questions then are these: (a) Given that conditions necessary for collaborative learning to occur in online groups exist, will learning in fact occur? (b) And, are there other outcomes or benefits associated with this format of learning in comparison to traditional formats and other options? Next, we discuss primary and secondary outcomes, where primary outcomes refer to intellectual development, willingness to learn, and learner satisfaction, and secondary outcomes encompass ancillary results, such as gaining experience with ICT software or economic savings from the design of training programs.

Identifying the outcomes of online-collaborative learning can pose a number of methodological challenges—a number of studies describe methodological issues in obtaining credible outcome results, including a need for more accurate methods for obtaining detailed information, and needs for methods and instruments higher in both validity and reliability (Valcke & Martens, 2006). Use of multiple methodologies for evaluation would seem a logical response, but there are many combinations of methodologies that might be used, possibly leading to more confusion (Valcke & Martens, 2006; Yang & Wang, 2005). At the same time, there is a general perception by many education leaders that evaluating an online course is no more difficult than evaluating traditional instruction (Allen & Seaman, 2005).

General reviews of online-learning efforts do present somewhat qualified support for the efficacy of online learning for delivering primary learning outcomes. An initial review found no significant difference between online and face-to-face learning (Russell, 1999). Another review (Welsh, Wanberg, Brown, & Simmering, 2003) indicated that online learning can be superior to traditional learning in some circumstances, but the review shies away from prior review notions that online learning is on average superior to traditional learning (Kulik & Kulik, 1991; Russell, 1999). Yet another review suggested that the presence of moderating variables complicates the connection between online learning and outcomes, making it difficult to conclude whether online learning is superior, inferior, or equal to traditional instruction in providing learning outcomes (DeRouin et al., 2005).

Given equivocal results about the efficacy of online vs. traditional groups, organizations may find motivation to use online groups in secondary outcomes associated with online learning, such as cost savings versus the organization's standard training practices. For example, consider the cost of flying in four remote account supervisors to a single location for 3 hours of training from an instructor for a seminar on foreign tax laws, vs. having them remain onsite for 3 hours of individual and 3 hours of collaborative online training on the same topic. The time saved just by not having to go through the airport would alone suggest the greater practicality of the online program.

Several researchers have suggested secondary outcomes associated with online learning that may influence the propagation of such programs. One researcher indicates organizations may pursue online learning to "(1) provide consistent, worldwide training; (2) reduce delivery cycle time; (3) increase learner convenience; (4) reduce information overload; (5) improve tracking; and (6) lower expenses" (Welsh et al., 2003, p. 247). Secondary outcomes such as reduction in travel costs, access to better educational resources, ability to make real- or just-in-time adjustments to course material, more individual tailoring of instruction and responsibility by the learner may also be of interest (Burgess & Russell, 2003). Overall benefits to the organization, commonly described in broad financial terms, describe the bottom line as a motivator—if financial savings are likely or found, the online approach is validated and maintained, without much consideration of other organizational variables such as turnover, burnout, or productivity (Burgess & Russell, 2003; DeRouin et al., 2005).

CONCLUSION

An undeniable result of organizational and technological trends, online-learning efforts will inevitably make use of collaborative-learning techniques, an approach to learning having a solid conceptual and empirical background from use in the traditional classroom. However, successful utilization of collaborative-learning methods in online groups requires consideration of a number of variables moderating between the learner and subsequent outcomes. The intellectual content targeted for development in the individual has to be amenable to this approach, requiring input from others, a course designed to encourage such input, and a meaningful rationale for the group effort. Individuals also vary in how open they are to such an online approach, as do instructors tasked with managing the learning group. Technologies used to support the collaborative effort will vary in their specialization to the group task, and while always influencing the group's progress to some degree, are ultimately less influential than the overall instructional strategy. While intellectual and other traditional-learning outcomes are likely to be about as substantial as those delivered by face-to-face methods, secondary outcomes—financial savings, practical issues in delivering content, and the like may also be motivators to begin and support an online group using collaborative methods. Prior research does provide some positive support for both learning and other outcomes in online-learning efforts, but measurement of any of the outcomes poses a challenge.

Other trends that may affect online groups have not been discussed for the sake of simplicity. For example, collaborative-learning efforts could supplement, complement, or substitute for the content of a traditional class, a notion that now appears realized in the form of "blended" instructional efforts (Brandon & Hollingshead, 1999; DeRouin et al., 2005; Rovai, 2004). For example, corporate training efforts may include Web-facilitated courses utilizing a minimum of online content (1–30% online, e.g., an online syllabus), blended/hybrid efforts (30–70% online content, some face-to-face interaction), and online courses (80% or more online; Allen & Seaman, 2005). The discussion here has focused primarily on the fully online case, not because the model offered does not have applicability to the other cases, but because it will be most useful to the fully online circumstance. And as complicated as the model may make collaborative-learning efforts in online groups appear, designers should take comfort in the number of guidelines and heuristics that researchers and practitioners have made available in the extant literature (cf. DeRouin et al., 2005).

Areas for future research are present in any area of the overall model, whether it be refining the social-behavioral inputs needed in an online versus face-to-face environment, or perhaps identifying which topics are poor candidates for social-cognitive development in online groups. Future research should include developing measures to help select candidates who are likely to be successful in an online group, further exploring instructor and technological influences, and determining how to best measure primary and secondary outcomes associated with an online-collaborative-learning effort.

We recommend that both researchers and practitioners consider the place of the online group in the larger knowledge structure of the organization. That is, the group and the media they use can be viewed as a knowledge network, a set of nodes and relations between these nodes, describable in terms of their communication patterns and the actual and perceived distribution of knowledge within the network (Hollingshead & Contractor, 2002). The ability of members of the online group and others within the organization(s) to access the information generated during the learning experience is influenced by this knowledge-network structure. For example, consider a cross-functional team put together from several organizational units to learn about opening markets in South America. As team members proceed through their learning, a system of transactive memory will develop naturally, with members remembering more information based on their area of expertise than in other areas, which they leave to others to remember (Wegner, 1986). If the group disbands after the learning experience, consequent loss of the transactive memory system will impair all group members' ability to access acquired knowledge. Consider a group of engineers with similar expertise. Each group member is given access to a specialized system of software that helps train him or her to use a new piece of complex machinery through a series of structured discussions on underlying scientific concepts. If afterwards the engineers or other organizational members cannot access their learning discussions (e.g., licensing restricts use of the software), some amount of the knowledge gained will be lost. In sum, just how the organization intends to make use of the knowledge generated by the online group is required to make the most out of the collaborative-learning effort.

REFERENCES

Ahern, T. C., Peck, K., & Laycock, M. (1992). The effects of teacher discourse in computer-mediated discussion. *Journal of Educational Computing Research, 8*(3), 291–309.

Akgun, A. E., Lynn, G. S., & Byrne, J. C. (2003). Organizational learning: A socio-cognitive framework. *Human Relations, 56*(7), 839–868.

Alavi, M. (1994). Computer-mediated collaborative learning: An empirical evaluation. *MIS Quarterly, 18*(2), 159–174.

Allen, I. E., & Seaman, J. (2005). *Growing by degrees: Online education in the United States, 2005*. Needham, MA: The Sloan Consortium.

Althaus, S. L. (1997). Computer-mediated communication in the university classroom: An experiment with on-line discussions. *Communication Education, 46*(3), 158–174.

Anderson, A., Mayes, J. T., & Kibby, M. R. (1995). Small group collaborative discovery learning from hypertext. In C. O'Malley (Ed.), *Computer supported collaborative learning* (pp. 23–28). New York: Springer-Verlag.

Andriessen, J., Baker, M., & Suthers, D. (2003). *Arguing to learn: Confronting cognitions in computer-supported collaborative learning environments*. London: Kluwer Academic Publishers.

Baker, M. (2003). Computer-mediated argumentative interactions for the co-elaboration of scientific notions. In J. Andriessen, M. Baker, & D. Suthers (Eds.), *Arguing to learn: Confronting cognitions in computer-supported collaborative learning environments* (pp. 47–78). London: Kluwer Academic Publishers.

Bannon, L. J. (1995). Issues in computer collaborative learning. In C. O'Malley (Ed.), *Computer supported collaborative learning* (pp. 267–287). New York: Springer-Verlag.

Barkley, E. F., Cross, K. P., & Major, C. H. (2005). *Collaborative learning techniques: A handbook for college faculty*. San Francisco: Jossey-Bass.

Beise, C. M., Niederman, F., & Mattord, H. (2004). IT project managers' perceptions and use of virtual team technologies. *Information Resources Management Journal, 17*(4), 73–88.

Bell, B. S., & Kozlowski, S. W. (2002). A typology of virtual teams. *Group & Organization Management, 27*(1), 14–49.

Berge, Z. L. (1995). Facilitating computer conferencing: Recommendations from the field. *Educational Technology, 35*(1), 22–30.

Bloom, B. S. (1956). *Taxonomy of educational objectives. Handbook 1: Cognitive domain*. New York: McKay.

Blumenfeld, P. C., Marx, R. W., Soloway, E., & Krajcik, J. (1996). Learning with peers: From small group cooperation to collaborative communities. *Educational Researcher, 25*, 37–40.

Bogenrieder, I., & Nooteboom, B. (2004). Learning groups: What types are there? A theoretical analysis and an empirical study in a consultancy firm. *Organization Studies, 25*(2), 287–313.

Bonito, J. A., & Hollingshead, A. B. (1997). Participation in small groups. *Communication Yearbook, 20*, 227–261.

Borghoff, U. M., & Schlichter, J. H. (2000). *Computer-supported cooperative work: Introduction to distributed applications*. New York: Springer.

Brandon, D. P., & Hollingshead, A. B. (1999). Collaborative learning and computer-supported groups. *Communication Education, 48*(2), 109–126.

Bravo, C., Redondo, M. A., Ortega, M., & Verdejo, M. F. (2006). Collaborative environments for the learning of design: A model and a case study in Domotics. *Computers & Education, 46*, 152–173.

Burgess, J. R. D., & Russell, J. E. A. (2003). The effectiveness of distance learning initiatives in organizations. *Journal of Vocational Behavior, 63*, 289–303.

Chiu, C., Hsu, M., Sun, S., Lin, T., & Sun, P. (2005). Usability, quality, value and e-learning continuance decisions. *Computers & Education, 45*, 399–416.

Courtney, D. P., Courtney, M., & Nicholson, C. (1994). The effect of cooperative learning as an instructional practice at the college level. *College Student Journal, 28*(4), 471–477.

Covert, M. D., & Thompson, L. F. (2001). *Computer supported cooperative work: Issues and implications for workers, organizations, and human resource management*. London: Sage.

Davidson-Shivers, G., Tanner, E., & Muilenburg, L. (2000, April). *Online discussion: How do students participate?* Paper presented at the annual meeting of the American Educational Research Association, New Orleans, LA.

Davies, D. (1995). Learning network design: Coordinating group interactions in formal learning environments over time and distance. In C. O'Malley (Ed.), *Computer supported collaborative learning* (pp. 101–124). New York: Springer-Verlag.

DeRouin, R. E., Fritzsche, B. A., & Salas, E. (2005). E-learning in organizations. Journal of management, *31*(6), 920–940.

Derycke, A. C., & D'Halluin, C. (1995). Co-operative learning in the distance education of adults: Why, how, and first results from the Co-Learn Project. In B. Collis, & G. Davies (Eds.), *Innovative adult learning with innovative technologies* (pp. 101–122). New York: Elsevier.

Devine, D. J., Clayton, L. D., Philips, J. L., Dunford, B. B., & Melner, S. B. (1999). Teams in organizations: Prevalence, characteristics, and effectiveness. *Small Group Research, 30*(6), 678–711.

Dodgson, M. (1993). Organizational learning: A review of some literatures. *Organization Studies, 14*(3), 375–394.

Driskell, J. E., Radtke, P. H., & Salas, E. (2003). Virtual teams: Effects of technological mediation on team performance. *Group Dynamics, 7*(4), 297–323.

Dumaine, B. (1994, September 5). The trouble with teams. *Fortune, 130,* 86.

Eisley, M. E. (1991, June). Guidelines for conducting instructional discussions on a computer conference. In A. J. Miller (Ed.), *Applications of computer conferencing to teacher education and human resource development.* Proceedings from an International Symposium on Computer Conferencing, Columbus, OH (pp. 35–39). (ERIC Document Reproduction Service No. ED 337705)

Faull, K., Hartley, L., & Kalliath, T. (2005). Action learning: Developing a learning culture in an interdisciplinary rehabilitation team. *Organization Development Journal, 23*(3), 39–52.

Feenberg, A. (1989). The written world. In R. Mason, & A. R. Kaye (Eds.), *Mindweave: Communication, computers, and distance education* (pp. 22–39). New York: Pergamon Press.

Fiol, C. M., & Lyles, M. A. (1985). Organizational learning. *Academy of Management. The Academy of Management Review, 10,* 803.

Garrett, L. A., & Vogt, C. L. (2003). Meeting the needs of consumers: Lessons from business and industry. *New Directions for Adult and Continuing Education, 100,* 89–101.

Garrett, R. E. (2003). Product review of WebCT Vista. *Internet in Higher Education, 7,* 165–168.

Gay, G., & Lentini, M. (1995). Use of collaborative resources in a networked collaborative design environment. *Journal of Computer-Mediated Communication, 1,* 1–12.

Ghosh, A. (2004). Learning in strategic alliances: A Vygotskian perspective. *The Learning Organization, 11*(4/5), 302–311.

Gilbert, P. K., & Dabbagh, N. (2005). How to structure online discussions for meaningful discourse: A case study. *British Journal of Educational Technology, 36*(1), 5–18.

Harasim, L. (1987). Teaching and learning on-line: Issues in computer-mediated graduate courses. *Canadian Journal of Educational Communication, 16*(2), 117–135.

Harasim, L. (1991, June). *Applications of computer conferencing to teacher education and human resource development*. Proceedings from an International Symposium on Computer Conferencing, Columbus, OH (pp. 25–34). (ERIC Document Reproduction Service No. ED 337705)

Hiltz, S. R. (1993). Correlates of learning in a virtual classroom. *International Journal of Man-Machine Studies, 39*(1), 71–98.

Hiltz, S. R. (1994). *The virtual classroom: Learning without limits via computer networks*. Norwood, NJ: Ablex Publishing.

Hollingshead, A. B., & Contractor, N. S. (2002). New media and organizing at the group level. In L. A. Lievrouw, & S. Livingston (Eds.), *Handbook of new media: Social shaping and consequences of ICTs* (pp. 221–235). London: Sage Publications.

Hoskins, S. L., & van Hoof, J. C. (2005). Motivation and ability: Which students use online learning and what influence does it have on their achievement. *British Journal of Educational Technology, 36*(2), 177–192.

Huber, H. E., & Lowry, J. C. (2003). Meeting the needs of consumers: Lessons from postsecondary environments. *New Directions for Adult and Continuing Education, 100*, 79–88.

Irvine, S. E. (2000). What are we talking about? The impact of computer-mediated communication on student learning. In D. A. Willis, J. D. Price, & J. Willis (Eds.), *Society for Information Technology & Teacher Education International Conference: Proceedings of SITE 2000* (Vols. 1–3, pp. 354–358). Charlottesville, VA: Association for the Advancement of Computing in Education.

Jermann, P., Soller, A., & Lesgold, A. (2004). Computer software support for CSCL. In J. Strijbos, P. A. Kirschner, & R. L. Martens (Eds.), *What we know about CSCL and implementing it in higher education* (pp. 141–166). London: Kluwer Academic Publishers.

Johansson, P., & Gardenfors, P. (2005). Introduction to cognition, education, and communication technology. In P. Gardenfors, & P. Johansson (Eds.), Cognition, education, and communication technology (pp. 1–20). London: Lawrence Erlbaum Associates.

Johnson, D. W., & Johnson, R. T. (1991). *Learning together and alone. Cooperative, competitive, and individualistic learning* (3rd ed.). Englewood Cliffs, NJ: Prentice Hall.

Johnson, D. W., & Johnson, R. T. (1994). Structuring academic controversy. In S. Sharan (Ed.), *Handbook of cooperative learning methods* (pp. 66–81). Westport, CT: Greenwood Press.

Johnson, D. W., & Johnson, R. T. (2004). Cooperation and the use of technology. In D. H. Jonassen (Ed.), *Handbook of research on educational communications and technology* (pp. 785–811). London: Lawrence Erlbaum Associates.

Johnson, D. W., Johnson, R. T., & Holubec, E. (1994). *Cooperative learning in the classroom*. Alexandria, VA: Association for Supervision and Curriculum Development.

Johnson, D. W., Johnson, R. T., & Smith, K. A. (1991). *Cooperative learning: Increasing college faculty instructional productivity (ASHE-ERIC Higher Education Report No. 4)*. Washington, DC: George Washington University.

Johnson, D. W., Johnson, R. T., & Smith, K. A. (1995). Cooperative learning and individual student achievement in secondary schools. In J. E. Pedersen, & A. D. Digby (Eds.), *Secondary schools and cooperative learning: Theories, models, and strategies* (pp. 3–54). New York: Garland.

Johnson, S. D., & Aragon, S. R. (2003). An instructional strategy framework for online learning environments. *New Directions for Adult and Continuing Education, 100.*

Johnson, S. D., & Aragon, S. R. (2003). An instructional strategy framework for online learning environments. *New Directions for Adult and Continuing Educational Leadership, 100,* 31–43.

Johnson, S. D., Suriya, C., Yoon, S. W., Berrett, J. V., & La Fleur, J. (2002). Team development, and group processes of virtual learning teams. *Computers & Education, 39,* 379–393.

Kiesler, S., & Sproull, L. (1992). Group decision making and communication technology. *Organizational Behavior and Human Decision Processes, 52,* 96–123.

King, K. M. (1994). Leading classroom discussions: Using computers for a new approach. *Teaching Sociology, 22,* 174–182.

Knight, L., & Pye, A. (2005). Network learning: An empirically derived model of learning by groups of organizations. *Human Relations, 58*(3), 369–392.

Koschmann, T. D. (1994). Toward a theory of computer support for collaborative learning. *Journal of the Learning Sciences, 3*(3), 219–225.

Koschmann, T. D., Hall, R., & Miyake, N. (2002). *CSCL 2: Carrying forward the conversation.* Mahwah, NJ: Lawrence Erlbaum.

Koschmann, T. D., Myers, A. C., Feltovich, P. J., & Barrows, H. S. (1994). Using technology to assist in realizing effective learning and instruction: A principled approach to the use of computers in collaborative learning. *Journal of the Learning Sciences, 3*(3), 227–264.

Kreijns, K., Kirschner, P. A., & Jochems, W. (2003). Identifying the pitfalls for social interaction in computer-supported collaborative learning environments: A review of the research. *Computers in Human Behavior, 19,* 335–353.

Kulik, C. C., & Kulik, J. A. (1991). Effectiveness of computer-based instruction: An updated analysis. *Computers in Human Behavior, 7,* 75–94.

Lerouge, C., Blanton, J. E., & Kittner, M. (2004). A causal model for using collaborative technologies to facilitate student team projects. *The Journal of Computer Information Systems, 45*(1), 30–37.

Lipnack, J., & Stamps, J. (1997). *Virtual teams.* New York: John Wiley & Sons.

Marquardt, M., & Reynolds, A. (1994). *The global learning organization: Gaining competitive advantage through continuous learning.* Burr Ridge, IL: Irwin.

Martins, L. L., Gilson, L. L., & Maynard, M. T. (2004). Virtual teams: What do we know and where do we go from here? *Journal of Management, 30*(6), 805–835.

McComb, M. (1994). Benefits of computer-mediated communication in college courses. *Communication Education, 43*(2), 159–170.

McGlaughlin, M., Osborne, K., & Smith, C. (1995). Standards of conduct on Usenet. In S. Jones (Ed.), *Cybersociety: Computer-mediated communication and community* (pp. 90–111). Thousand Oaks, CA: Sage.

McGrath, J. E., & Hollingshead, A. B. (1994). *Groups interacting with technology: Ideas, evidence, issues, and an agenda.* Newbury Park, CA: Sage Publications.

McKenna, Y. A., & Green, A. S. (2002). Virtual group dynamics. *Group Dynamics: Theory, Research, and Practice, 6*(1), 116–127.

Meyer, K. A. (2002). *Quality in distance education.* Washington, DC: ERIC Clearinghouse on Higher Education.

Meyer, K. A. (2004). Evaluating online discussions: Four different frames of analysis. *Journal of Asynchronous Learning Networks, 8*(2), 101–114.

Misiolek, N. I., & Heckman, R. (2005). *Patterns of emergent leadership in virtual teams.* Paper presented at the 38th Hawaii International Conference on System Sciences, Honolulu, HI.

Miyake, N., & Koschmann, T. D. (2002). Realizations of CSCL conversations: Technology transfer and the CSILE project. In T. Koschmann, R. Hall, & N. Miyake (Eds.), *CSCL 2: Carrying forward the conversation* (pp. 3–10). Mahwah, NJ: Lawrence Erlbaum.

Moshaiov, A. (2003). New breed of computer supported student contests: Learning by and for tele-collaboration. In B. Wasson, S. Ludvigsen, & U. Hoppe (Eds.), *International Conference on Computer Support for Collaborative Learning 2003. Designing for change in learning environments* (pp. 135–141). London: Kluwer Academic Publishers.

Nalley, R. (1995). Designing computer-mediated conferencing into instruction. In Z. L. Berge, & M. P. Collins (Eds.), *Computer-mediated communication and the online classroom* (Vol. 2). Cresskill, NJ: Hampton Press.

O'Donnell, A. M., & O'Kelly, J. (1994). Learning from peers: Beyond the rhetoric of positive results. *Educational Psychology Review, 6*(4), 321–349.

O'Malley, C. (1995). *Computer supported cooperative learning.* New York: Springer-Verlag.

Park, H., Ribière, V., & Schulte, W. D., Jr. (2004). Critical attributes of organizational culture that promote knowledge management technology implementation success. *Journal of Knowledge Management, 8*(3), 106–117.

Pea, R. D. (1996). Seeing what we build together: Distributed multimedia learning environments for transformative communications. In T. Koschmann (Ed.), *CSCL: Theory and practice of an emerging paradigm* (pp. 171–186). Mahwah, NJ: Erlbaum.

Piaget, J. (1932). *The moral judgement of the child.* New York: Harcourt Brace Jovanovich.

Polito, T., & Watson, K. (2002). Toward an interdisciplinary organizational learning framework. *Journal of American Academy of Business, 2*(1), 162.

Popper, M., & Lipshitz, R. (1998). Organizational learning mechanisms: A structural and cultural approach to organizational learning. *Journal of Applied Behavioral Science, 34*(2), 161–179.

Roschelle, J. (1992). Learning by collaborating: Convergent conceptual change. *Journal of the Learning Sciences, 2*(3), 235–276.

Rourke, L., & Anderson, T. (2002). Using peer teams to lead online discussions. *Journal of Interactive Media in Education, 1,* 1–21.

Rovai, A. P. (2004). A constructivist approach to online college learning. *Internet and Higher Education, 7,* 79–93.

Ruberg, L. F., Moore, D. M., & Taylor, C. (1996). Student participation, interaction, and regulation in a computer-mediated communication environment: A qualitative study. *Journal of Educational Computing Research, 14*(3), 243–268.

Russell, T. L. (1999). *The no significant difference phenomenon*. Raleigh: North Carolina State University.
Salaberry, M. R. (1996). A theoretical foundation for the development of pedagogical tasks in computer mediated communication. *CALICO Journal, 14*, 5–34.
Samarawickrema, G., & Benson, R. (2004). Helping academic staff to design electronic learning and teaching approaches. *British Journal of Educational Technology, 35*(5), 659–662.
Scalia, L. M., & Sackmary, B. (1996). Groupware in the classroom: Applications and guidelines. *Computers in the Schools, 12*(4), 39–53.
Selwyn, N., Gorard, S., & Furlong, J. (2005). *Adult learning in the digital age*. London: Routledge Falmer.
Senge, P. (1990). *The fifth discipline: The art and practice of the learning organization*. New York: Doubleday.
Sense, A. J. (2005). Facilitating conversational learning in a project team practice. *Journal of Workplace Learning, 17*(3/4), 178–193.
Sharan, S. (1995). Group investigation: Theoretical foundations. In J. E. Pedersen, & A. D. Digby (Eds.), *Secondary schoos and cooperative learning: Theories, models, and strategies* (pp. 251–280). New York: Garland Publishing.
Sharan, Y., & Sharan, S. (1994). Group investigation in the cooperative classroom. In S. Sharan (Ed.), *Handbook of cooperative learning methods* (pp. 66–81). Westport, CT: Greenwood Press.
Shin, Y. (2004). A person-environment fit model for virtual organizations. *Journal of Management, 30*(5), 725–743.
Slavin, R. E. (1988). *Student team learning: An overview and practical guide* (2nd ed.). Washington, DC: National Education Association.
Slavin, R. E. (1991). Synthesis of research on cooperative learning. *Educational Leadership, 48*, 71–82.
Smagorinsky, P., & Fly, P. K. (1993). The social environment of the classroom: A Vygotskian perspective on small group process. *Communication Education, 42*(2), 159–171.
Stahl, G. (2004). Building collaborative knowing: Elements of social theory of CSCL. In J. Strijbos, P. A. Kirschner, & R. L. Martens (Eds.), *What we know about CSCL and implementing it in higher education* (pp. 53–86). London: Kluwer Academic Publishers.
Szarka, F. E., Grant, K. P., & Flannery, W. T. (2004). Achieving organizational learning through team competition. *Engineering Management Journal, 16*(1), 21–31.
Trierweiler, C., & Rivera, R. (2005). Is online higher education right for corporate learning? *T + D, 59*(9), 44.
U.S. Bureau of the Census. (2002). *E-stats: Detailed tabulations of manufacturing e-business process use in 2000*. Washington, DC: Author and Economics and Statistics Administration.
Valcke, M., & Martens, R. (2006). The problem arena of researching computer supported collaborative learning: Introduction to the special edition. *Computers & Education, 46*, 1–5.
van Bruggen, J. M., & Kirschner, P. A. (2003). Designing external representations to support solving wicked problems. In J. Andriessen, M. Baker, & D. Suthers (Eds.), *Arguing to learn: Confronting cognitions in computer-supported collaborative learning environments* (pp. 177–204). London: Kluwer Academic Publishers.

Veerman, A. (2003). Constructive discussions through electronic dialogue. In J. Andriessen, M. Baker, & D. Suthers (Eds.), *Arguing to learn: Confronting cognitions in computer-supported collaborative learning environments* (pp. 117–143). London: Kluwer Academic Press.

Vygotsky, L. (1978). *Mind in society*. Cambridge, MA: Harvard University Press.

Wasson, B., Ludvigsen, S., & Hoppe, U. (2003). Designing for change in networked learning environments. *Proceedings of the International Conference on Computer Support for Colaborative Learning*. London: Kluwer Academic Publishers.

Webb, N. M., & Palincsar, A. S. (1996). Group processes in the classroom. In D. Berliner & R. Calfee (Eds.), *Handbook of educational psychology* (pp. 841–873). New York: Macmillan.

WebCT. (2006). WebCT campus edition, 2006. Retrieved March 15, 2006, from http://www.webct.com/software/viewpage?name=software_virtual

Wegner, D. M. (1986). Transactive memory: A contemporary analysis of the group mind. In B. Mullen, & G. R. Goethals (Eds.), *Theories of group behavior* (pp. 185–208). New York: Springer-Verlag.

Welsh, E. T., Wanberg, C. R., Brown, K. G., & Simmering, M. J. (2003). E-learning: Emerging uses, empirical results, and future directions. *International Journal of Training and Development, 7*(4), 245–258.

Wheeler, B. C., Valacich, J. S., Alavi, M., & Vogel, D. (1995). A framework for technology-mediated inter-institutional telelearning relationships. *Journal of Computer-Mediated Communication, 1*, 1–13.

Witmer, D. F. (1998). Introduction to computer-mediated communication: A master syllabus for teaching communication technology. *Communication Education, 47*(2), 162–173.

Yan, A., & Louis, M. R. (1999). The migration of organizational functions to the work unit level: Buffering, spanning, and bringing up boundaries. *Human Relations, 52*(1), 25.

Yang, Y., & Wang, G. (2005, September). *An evaluation model for Web-based learning support systems*. Paper presented at the 2005 IEEE/WIC/ACM International Conference on Web Intelligence, Compiegne, France.

Yoon, S. (2003). In search of meaningful online learning experiences. *New Directions for Adult and Continuing Education, 100*.

Zakaria, N., Amelinckx, A., & Wilemon, D. (2004). Working together apart? Building a knowledge-sharing culture for global virtual teams. *Creativity and Innovation Management, 13*(1).

Zhang, S., Fjermestad, J., & Tremaine, M. (2005). *Leadership styles in virtual team context: Limitations, solutions, and propositions*. Paper presented at the 38th Hawaii International Conference on System Sciences, Honolulu, HI.

Zigurs, I. (2003). Leadership in virtual teams: Oxymoron or opportunity? *Organizational Dynamics, 31*(4), 339–351.

Zumbach, J., & Reimann, P. (2003). Influence of feedback on distributed problem based learning. In B. Wasson, S. Ludvigsen, & U. Hoppe (Eds.), *Designing for change in networked learning environments* (pp. 219–228). London: Kluwer Academic Publishers.

CHAPTER

13

Using Synthetic Learning Environments to Train Teams

JANIS A. CANNON-BOWERS,
CLINT A. BOWERS, AND ALICIA SANCHEZ
School of Film and Digital Media & Institute for Simulation and Training, University of Central Florida

INTRODUCTION

The reliance on teams to perform crucial functions has become increasingly evident in the modern workplace. Interdependency between individual tasks, particularly in complex work environments, has necessitated teams with members who have a wide range of knowledge and skill. Moreover, the increasing pace of change and technological sophistication common in many organizations has led to increased reliance on interdisciplinary teams in order to provide viable solutions. Not surprisingly, a concomitant need to provide efficient, effective team training has also developed.

The science of team training has considerably evolved over the last 15 years, as evidenced through viable research into the factors that contribute to team effectiveness, team-training methodologies, and the ability of teams to become self sufficient (see Salas & Cannon-Bowers,

2001). At the same time, the evolution of technology now provides an opportunity to advance the existing toolset for team training by using simulations, games, and virtual environments that can be designed to enhance team performance. In order to realize the potential of technologies, however, design guidelines must be generated to increase their chances of success.

To this end, the goal of this chapter is to highlight the potential use of Synthetic Learning Environments (SLEs)—particularly simulations and games—in team training. To accomplish this, we first provide definitions of teams and team learning, and briefly review the literature into the set of competencies found to underlie effective teamwork. We then discuss the emerging area of Synthetic Learning Environments (SLEs) and highlight the opportunities this technology provides in delivering high-quality team training. Following this, we offer a set of propositions regarding how best to structure SLE-based training to impart crucial teamwork competencies.

THE NATURE OF TEAMS AND TEAM PERFORMANCE

Before beginning the discussion of team performance, we first must define relevant terms. We define *teams* in keeping with Salas, Cannon-Bowers, and Johnston (Salas et al., 1997) as "a distinguishable set of two or more people who interact, dynamically, interdependently, and adaptively toward a common and valued goal/objective/ mission, who have each been assigned specific roles or functions to perform, and who have a limited life-span of membership" (p. 4). We believe that *team learning* occurs when team members acquire the competencies (e.g., knowledge, skills, and attitudes) necessary to effectively perform as part of a team. This notion implies that team members must acquire underlying declarative and procedural knowledge that enables them to understand teamwork and the nature of the team within which they are functioning, the skills necessary to perform team-level functions, and team-related attitudes necessary to optimize team performance.

Much has been written in recent years regarding the competencies necessary for teamwork (e.g., Cannon-Bowers, Tannenbaum, Salas, & Volpe, 1995). Rather than revisit this work, we provide Table 13.1 (based largely on the work of Cannon-Bowers et al., 1995), which describes what we consider to be a comprehensive set of competencies required for effective teamwork. Our goal in this table is simply to summarize and describe the competencies that we believe are most relevant for teams so that we can better understand how to develop SLEs that can impart them.

TABLE 13.1 Team Competencies that Must be Trained

TEAM COMPETENCIES	DEFINITION	CITATIONS
KNOWLEDGE		
Shared Mental Models	Preexisting knowledge and expectations about how the team must perform in order to cope with task demands, organized in a way that makes it useful to team members in task situations.	Cannon-Bowers, Salas, & Converse, 1993; Mathieu, Heffner, Godwin, Salas, & Cannon-Bowers, 2000
Interpositional knowledge (IPK)	Extent to which team members hold accurate knowledge about the role responsibilities of other members. High degrees of IPK allow team members to have a better understanding of their roles within the team, as well as to anticipate the needs of their teammates.	Beck-Jones, 2004
Understanding of teamwork skills	Conceptual understanding of the nature of teamwork skills that are required to perform successfully and how these contribute to successful team performance.	Morgan, Salas, & Glickman, 1993
Understanding of team context	Understanding of context, including the overall team goals and objectives, the team's mission, and other team-level constructs such as norms and resources. This contextual understanding also requires that team members have knowledge of the "boundary spanning" role.	Sundstrom, de Meuse, & Futrell, 1990; Lanzetta & Roby, 1960

(Continued)

TABLE 13.1 (continued)

TEAM COMPETENCIES	DEFINITION	CITATIONS
Knowledge of teammates	Knowledge and understanding team members' hold regarding the particular strengths, weakness, preferences, and desires of teammates that enables them to better adjust their behavior to meet task objectives.	Hirschfeld, Jordan, Field, Giles, & Armenakis, 2006; Smith-Jentsch, Campbell, Milanovich, & Reynolds, 2001
Cue->Strategy Associations	Knowledge of action-outcome contingencies that exist under various task conditions that enable team members to recognize the task and environmental cues that trigger specific strategy changes. Team members learn to recognize *when* particular interaction processes are appropriate.	Mohammed & Dumville, 2001; Rentsch & Klimoski, 2001; Smith-Jentsch, Mathieu, & Kraiger, 2005
SKILLS		
Adaptability	Knowledge and expectations about how the team must perform in order to cope with task demands, organized in a way that makes it useful to team members in task situations.	Kozlowski et al., 2001
Shared Situational Awareness	Extent to which team members hold accurate knowledge about the roles responsibilities of other members. High degrees of IPK allow team members to have a better understanding of their role within the team and enables them to anticipate the workload and capabilities of their teammates.	Banks & McKeran, 2005

(Continued)

TABLE 13.1 (continued)

TEAM COMPETENCIES	DEFINITION	CITATIONS
Performance Monitoring and Feedback	Conceptual understanding of the nature of teamwork skills required to perform successfully, and how these contribute to successful team performance.	Marks & Panzer, 2004
Leadership/Team Management	Understanding of context, including the overall team goals and objectives, the team's mission, and other team-level constructs such as norms and resources. This contextual understanding also requires that team members have knowledge of the "boundary spanning" role and relationship to the larger organization.	Burke et al., 2006; Marks, Zaccaro, & Matheiu 2000
Interpersonal	Knowledge and understanding of team members' hold regarding the particular strengths, weakness, preferences and desires of teammates that enables them to better adjust their behavior to meet task objectives.	Golden & Veiga, 2005; Jentsch & Smith-Jentsch, 2001
Coordination	Knowledge of action-outcome contingencies that exist under various task conditions that enable team members to recognize the task and environmental cues that trigger specific strategy changes. Team members learn to recognize *when* particular interaction processes are appropriate, as well as *how* they must be implemented.	Klein, 2001

(Continued)

TABLE 13.1 (continued)

TEAM COMPETENCIES	DEFINITION	CITATIONS
Communication	The process by which information is clearly and accurately exchanged between two or more team members in the prescribed manner and by using proper terminology; closed loop communication, such as the ability to clarify or acknowledge the receipt of information.	Bowers, Jentsch, Salas, & Braun, 1998
Decision Making	The ability to (a) gather and integrate information, (b) use sound judgments, (c) identify alternatives, (d) select the best solution, and (e) evaluate the consequences. In team context, emphasizes skill in pooling information and resources in support of a response choice.	Cannon-Bowers & Salas, 1998
ATTITUDES		
Attitudes Toward Teamwork	Beliefs (positive or negative) team members hold regarding the importance of teamwork in accomplishing their task objectives.	Helmreich et al., 1986 ; Gregorich, Helmreich, & Wilhelm, 1990
Collective Efficacy	Belief that team members hold regarding the ability of their team to effectively perform as a unit given some set of specific task demands; individual team member's assessment of his or her team's collective ability to perform the task at hand.	Bandura, 1986; Shamir, 1990; Guzzo, 1986; Lent, Schmidt, & Schmidt, 2006; Chen, Thomas, & Wallace, 2005

(Continued)

TABLE 13.1 (continued)

TEAM COMPETENCIES	DEFINITION	CITATIONS
Collective Orientation	Involves an attraction to the team (versus the individual) as a means of task accomplishment, and includes the capacity to take others' behavior into account during group interaction, as well as the belief that a team approach is superior to an individual one.	Driskell & Salas, 1997
Cohesion	The sense of "teamness" within the team; team morale; also considered the total field of forces which act on members to remain in the group.	Peterson & Martens, 1972

THE POTENTIAL OF SLES IN TEAM TRAINING

Now that we have specified the targeted competencies associated with effective team performance, we can turn our attention to understanding the opportunities to improve it using Synthetic Learning Environments. We use the term *Synthetic Learning Environments (SLEs)* to refer to simulations, games, and virtual worlds that together comprise a subset of technology-enabled instructional systems (Cannon-Bowers & Bowers, in press). We define SLEs as systems that provide instruction by augmenting, replacing, creating, and/or managing the actual experiences a learner has with the world. Hence, SLEs provide realistic content, but go further by embedding deliberate synthetic experiences and instructional features targeted at enhancing learning and performance on specific tasks.

Obviously, the notion of using simulation in training is not new; indeed, considerable evidence from the cognitive and learning sciences exists to suggest that the process of moving from novice to expert in a domain occurs as learners build appropriate knowledge structures through experience in the world (see Bransford, Brown, & Cocking, 1999). Hence, one of the theoretical bases to justify the use of simulations in training is that providing novices with realistic experience should accelerate the process of expertise development (see Cannon-Bowers & Bowers, in press). Other justification stems from the fact that simulations provide stimuli that closely mimic the actual task, increasing the likelihood of transfer of training (reference). In the area of team training, a body of work conducted by Cannon-Bowers, Salas, and colleagues (e.g., Cannon-Bowers & Salas, 1998; Dwyer, Fowlkes, Oser, &

Salas, 1997; Fowlkes, Lane, Salas, Franz, & Oser, 1994) began to demonstrate that well-conceived simulation-based training can be an effective means to improve team performance.

Further effort is needed to build on and expand this foundational work into simulation-based training. One relatively new area of simulation-based training that is gaining attention is using video games as instructional devices, in part at least, due to the overwhelming popularity of them. The Entertainment Software Association (ESA) reports that 50% of all Americans play video games, with the average age of game players being 33 years. Game play per week averages 7.6 hours for men and 7.4 hours for women, who represent 38% of game players. The popularity of video games is undeniable, as the industry has surpassed all other entertainment industries including movies, netting roughly 7 billion dollars in 2005. Hence, there appears to be a natural opportunity to capitalize on the popularity of computer games for learning (see Gee, 2003). In fact, the term *serious games* refers to games that are developed for purposes other than entertainment, including training and education.

From a pedagogical standpoint, games inherently force players to learn, as they must understand and abide by rules and conditions in order to succeed (Gee, 2003). Games can also intrinsically be motivating and stimulating, and can increase time on task (Garris, Ahlers, & Driskell, 2002; Prensky, 2002; Lieberman, 2006) as evidenced by their popularity. Moreover, games can easily accommodate multiple players, making them well-suited as a potential team training intervention. For example, Massively Multiplayer Online Games (MMOGs) are played online or in a networked environment and make up 22% of the games commonly played online (ESA, 2006). Popular MMOGs can have millions of players, even when there is a fee for participation.

There is also emerging interest in using persistent *virtual worlds* as training environments. These environments typically involve a large number of geographically distributed players who all interact with and within a shared cue set (the virtual world). Virtual worlds are persistent in the sense that actions continue, and the world changes whether or not any given player is involved. Interest in these environments for learning applications is likely to increase in the coming years (cf. Dickey, 2005).

A graphic example of the potential for team learning in video games is documented in a somewhat infamous video clip nicknamed "Leroy Jenkins." The Leroy Jenkins video is a screen capture from a popular online game, World of Warcraft, that has been widely shown at gaming conferences. In the video, a team of characters named "Pals for Life" stand outside a chamber that is known to have a specific type of enemy force within it. One of the players demonstrates strong leadership skills by discussing with a group of 10–12 players whether or not they need to enter the chamber. Since the chamber holds resources that several players need, the team begins to formulate a plan for entering the chamber that will increase their chances for survival. One team member even calculates survival rates. As they discuss what resources they will need to expend in order to maximize their safety, a single player, Leroy Jenkins, suddenly and unexpectedly shouts out a battle cry and runs into the chamber. The rest of the team, shocked at the bravado of this player, run in after him. They are immediately attacked and most of the players die during the confrontation. The clip ends with team members angrily denouncing Leroy for his actions.

Whether or not this event was staged is debatable. Nonetheless, it demonstrates the potential for team members to develop and practice advanced coordination, teamwork, and leadership skills through online games. In fact, games such as this often spawn teams of strangers who, through practice and exposure, demonstrate high levels of teamwork-related behaviors. Often strangers in real life, these teams can be diverse in age, race, and gender. Moreover, such games are often are played with headphones and microphone systems that allow team members to communicate with one another via voice transmissions, increasing their ability to coordinate in real time. Additionally, players can become enveloped in communities surrounding a single game that exist solely in the virtual world. These communities often exist in chat rooms and blogs where players debrief game play, share their experiences and lessons learned, provide strategies to one another, and trade or sell their resources.

OPPORTUNITIES AFFORDED BY USING SLES FOR TEAM TRAINING

Taken together, the features of games and simulations discussed thus far indicate that they may provide a perfect backdrop for effective team training. The challenge for learning scientists is to find ways to harnesses these environments so that they can be tailored to specific team-training needs. To begin this process, we must apply the science of learning to better understand the features of SLEs that may make them particularly effective as team-training interventions. The following sections outline our propositions in this regard.

Proposition 1: SLEs Provide Authentic Learning Experiences

It has been argued that learning is more efficient when the learning environment is constructed to be "authentic." Shaffer and Resnick (1999) recently reviewed the construct of authenticity, arguing that there are four aspects of authenticity; SLEs can be effective in increasing each of these. The first type of authenticity described by Shaffer and Resnick occurs when learning is *personally meaningful* for the learner. SLEs are well-suited to improve this type of authenticity since learning objectives can be cast in a variety of narratives or scenarios that are meaningful to the learners. In addition, actual tasks or work environments can be modeled so that trainees are engaging in simulations that are perceived to be directly meaningful to their job success.

The second type of authenticity occurs when the learning environment is constructed in a way that supports transfer of training to the real world outside of the classroom. Again, this is more easily accomplished using SLEs (as compared with traditional training) since they can be developed to mimic real world processes. This definition of authenticity is similar to the construct of "fidelity." It seems apparent that one way to improve transfer of training is by increasing the degree to which the training environment resembles the real world, such as "physical fidelity" (Allen, Hays, & Buffardi, 1986). SLEs can leverage this effect by creating a learning environment that has greater physical fidelity than traditional classrooms.

The effects of physical fidelity are especially salient in skill-based training in domains that require intensive use of technology. For example, use of computer games has been effective in improving the training of pilots (Roessingh, 2005). Similar effects have been obtained for medical procedures (Gerling & Thomas, 2005; Scerbo, Bliss, Schmidt, & Thompson, 2006) and crane operations (Huang & Gau, 2003), among others. In these cases, the effectiveness of the training is thought to be tied to the similarity of the interface in the game to those of the real world. By engaging in the simulated environment, trainees can acquire complex skills in the relatively safe, inexpensive context afforded by modern technology.

The third type of authenticity discussed by Shaffer and Resnick (1999) is achieved when the learning environment enables the student to think in the modes that characterize a particular discipline. In this regard, Jonassen (2000) argued that the notion of authenticity does not necessarily mean that the instruction is developed around specific, real-world tasks. Rather, authenticity (in this sense) can best be thought of as the degree to which the learning environment causes learners to engage in cognitive processes that are similar to those in the real world (see Honebein, Duffy, & Fishman, 1993; Petraglia, 1998).

In SLEs, the learner can be cast into realistic roles that are actually a part of the operational task or more abstract ones that draw on competencies that are similar to those used in the real world. This concept has also been labeled "psychological fidelity" (Bowers & Jentsch, 2001; Driskell & Salas, 1992). In these cases, the effectiveness of the training environment is not a result of the similarity between the physical elements of the SLE with the real world. Rather, the goal is to create a psychological experience that is similar that which will ultimately be experienced, even if the physical stimuli are quite different from those in the operational environment.

Paramount to creating high psychological fidelity is accurately representing the informational cues that are likely to exist in the actual performance environment. For example, O'Neil and Fisher (2004) described an approach that used computer games to augment leadership training. Similarly, Nemitcheva (1994) described how the additional fidelity of computer games can add to the effectiveness of foreign language training. Alternatively, SLEs might also be effective in creating cognitive "states" that are likely to be present in the real world. For example, one might use elements of an SLE to create a higher level of stress than is typically found in traditional classrooms (Schneider, Lang, Shin, & Bradley, 2004). By learning new skills in the stressful game environment, it is likely that these skills will better transfer to the actual environment (Morris, Hancock, & Shirkey, 2004). For example, novice pilots who participated in a challenging flight-simulation game were better able to deal with the demands of actual flight (Gopher, Weil, & Baraket, 1994).

The final type of authenticity reviewed by Shaffer and Resnick (1999) occurs when the means of assessment or evaluation in learning reflects the actual learning process (as opposed to artificial devices, e.g., paper-and-pencil tests; for similar arguments, see Kraiger et al., 1995). SLES represent an important new capability in this regard. By leveraging intelligent agent technology, it is possible to build feedback systems that monitor the progress of the learner and give them feedback relevant to their current cognitive state (Anderson & Shunn, 2000). In other words, rather than simply waiting for a "right" or "wrong" answer, SLEs can dynamically assess performance (based on embedded models of effective performance) and give feedback that will allow the learner to adjust their mental model "on the fly," presumably leading to better and faster learning (Gott & Lesgold, 2000).

Proposition 2: SLEs Provide Flexible, Effective Practice Environments for Teams

The importance of practice and feedback in learning cannot be overemphasized (for a comprehensive review, see Kozlowski et al., 2001). SLEs offer several advantages in building effective practice environments as compared to more traditional training methods. These include the following:

The opportunity to provide guided practice. According to Bell and Kozlowski (2002), adaptive (guided) practice is necessary to aid learners in complex environments. For example, Bell and Kozlowski improved outcomes by providing adaptive (performance-based) guidance to trainees that helped them to understand how to improve their performance on a simulated task. SLEs provide an excellent environment in which to allow learners to actively participate in the learning process while receiving performance-enhancing feedback as they progress.

The opportunity to dynamically assess performance. As noted, SLEs offer unprecedented opportunities to collect and interpret ongoing performance data. According to Anderson and Shunn (2000) there is vast potential for applying cognitive theory to the issue of measuring and diagnosing learner performance. More work in this area is needed, particularly with respect to developing unobtrusive methods to collect and interpret data such as keystrokes, button or mouse actions, eye movements, verbal responses, protocol analysis, and even facial expression and gesturing.

Flexibility with respect to roles and scenarios. An aspect of SLEs that makes them well-suited to team training is that they offer flexibility with respect to the role that the individual trainee can play in the environment. This feature is essential for cross-training, which has been found to be an effective mechanism for developing shared knowledge among team members (Volpe, Cannon-Bowers, Salas, & Spector, 1996; Cannon-Bowers & Salas, 2001). Specifically, team members in SLEs can be allowed to play the role of a teammate so that they build interpositional knowledge and an appreciation of the teammate's perspective on the task.

SLEs also offer flexibility with respect to the number and type of scenarios or problems that confront the trainee (Cannon-Bowers & Salas, 1998). In keeping with the research on developing expertise, this capability means that it is possible to construct many variations of a single problem structure, enabling the trainee to build up a repertoire of instances of the task (learning, for example, important cue-strategy associations). Scenarios can also be tailored to a particular teamwork competency (e.g., communication or decision making) or crafted to address several competencies at once. In fact, the use of trigger events to stimulate trainees to engage in targeted teamwork skills has been well tested (see Dwyer et al., 1997; Fowlkes et al., 1994).

The opportunity for team members to practice on their own. SLEs offer several types of flexibility in this regard. First, the advent of Web-based games and simulations means that trainees can access training content for a variety of places (including the workplace, their home, hotels, etc.). This feature vastly increases the potential exposure that trainees can have to team training as compared with traditional (face-to-face) training. Second, depending on the training objectives, team members can remotely train with their real teammates (e.g., who can all participate from their own location), or with other live players who can fill the roles of their teammates (but who are not their actual teammates).

Finally, when appropriate (see below), team members may be able to practice with synthetic or computer-generated teammates. The technology underlying simulated teammates—human performance modeling—is just beginning to mature to the point where it can be applied in actual training settings. While further work is needed to validate this capability, it seems likely that application of this approach is not more than a few years away. What this means for team training is that individual team members will be able to receive viable practice on teamwork skills in the absence of other live trainees. This capability—though not applicable to all team training situations—will certainly enhance the potential exposure that team members have to team training.

The opportunity to embed instructional features. Besides measurement and feedback, SLEs can be used as a vehicle to embody instructional features that are likely to improve performance. For example, research has demonstrated that providing examples and working out examples in training can aid comprehension (see Cannon-Bowers & Bowers, in press). Likewise, the notion of scaffolding—such as providing hints, clues, or other devices to aid novices early in training—has been studied extensively (see Cannon-Bowers & Bowers, in press). Either of these techniques can be incorporated into an SLE. Moreover, it may be possible to trigger effective metacogntive strategies in learners (see Kozlowski et al., 2001, for a review) by manipulating features in the SLE. For example, inducing trainees to self-assess (as part of the game) early in training may trigger self-regulatory processes (Cannon-Bowers & Bowers, in press).

Proposition 3: SLEs Can Motivate Additional Time-on-Task and Engagement

It is generally believed that one of the potential benefits of SLEs—particularly, games—for training is that they are inherently interesting and motivating. Thus, SLE-based learning is believed to be more fun and engaging than traditional learning, leading in turn, to greater time on task and mastery (Garris, Ahlers, & Driskell, 2002). An emerging body of evidence suggests that this is, in fact, the case. For example, Schwabe and Goth (2005) designed a mobile game intended to teach learners the spatial orientation of a college campus. The data indicated that the game was not only perceived as more fun, but lead to positive learning outcomes. Positive motivational effects of gaming have also been found in teaching music (Simms, 1998) and health (Lieberman, 1997).

There is good reason to believe that the motivational aspects of games as learning tools are at least as relevant when applied to group tasks. In fact, social contact has been demonstrated to be one of the most reinforcing aspects of multiplayer gaming (Jansz & Martens, 2005). Further, game-based education has been demonstrated as an effective way to teach some group skills such as collaborative problem solving (Keys, 1997; Wolfe, 1997).

Another motivational feature of SLEs that might be important to group learning is that they create a sense of *presence* or immersion. Both of these psychological constructs are associated with the feeling of "really being there," and are often discussed as being a key variable in virtual environments (Sadowski & Stanney, 2002). It has also been hypothesized that training effectiveness in virtual environments may be influenced by the degree to which trainees experience feelings of immersion or engagement (Knerr, Breaux, Goldman, & Thurman, 2002). Indeed, several studies suggest that immersive experiences are associated with positive learning outcomes. For example, Jones and her colleagues (Jones, Minogue, Tretter, Negshi, & Taylor, 2006) reported that adding haptic feedback to an online learning aid created a more immersive experience and was, in turn, associated with more positive learning outcomes.

The relationship between presence and positive learning outcomes has also been shown in the teaching of spatial knowledge (Finkelstein, 2000) and in elementary schools (Selverian, 2005). Interestingly, the Selverian study also demonstrated the effects of not just physical presence (the physical sensation of "being there,") but also of social presence. Social presence is defined as the ability of players to project themselves (socially and emotionally) into a virtual community (Rourke, Anderson, Garrison, & Archer, 1999). In this regard, Manninen (2003) described the inventive approaches that players take to increase their ability to communicate and coordinate in collaborative social environments. These behaviors are consistent with the notion of social presence. Combined with the anecdotal evidence from observations of multiplayer games, it certainly seems that this is a potentially important area for future study.

Another feature of SLEs that can potentially contribute to motivation is narrative or story. As noted, the story cannot only increase the relevance and meaningfulness of learning content; it may also contribute to factors such as presence, engagement, and meaningfulness of material. Moreover, when the training situation is instructorless (e.g., where there is not a teacher or coach present to provide guidance), narrative elements might be an important factor in guiding the learner through the experience (Laurillard, Stratford, Luckin, Plowman, & Taylor, 2000; Plowman, 2005). Although the research is this area is only beginning to be conducted, there are some data to suggest that specific narrative elements can aid in computer-presented learning (Plowman, 2005; Wolfe, 2002).

GUIDELINES FOR USING SLES TO TRAIN TEAMWORK COMPETENCIES

To this point, we have made a rather general case that SLEs can be effective for team training. However, the specific application of SLEs in team training requires a more detailed analysis, especially if practical guidelines are sought. Some work along these lines has already been accomplished—at least theoretically—and guidelines are beginning to emerge (see Kozlowski et al., 2001, for an excellent summary). Table 13.2, Table 13.3, and Table 13.4 highlight our propositions in this regard. Specifically, these tables link specific SLE features and strategies to particular teamwork competencies, a focus which has not been taken in past work. The particular features/strategies we focus on include (a) the nature of the problem set being presented in training, (b) the specific events or triggers needed in the scenario or story, (c) the types of instructional features that need to be embedded in the SLE, (d) the nature of feedback needed to impart the competency, (e) the measures of performance and metrics that need to be collected, (f) the need for flexibility in roles, (g) the requirement to include live team members or synthetic ones; and (h) any other specific requirements that may arise. Our rationale for the entries in each table is summarized in the following sections.

Guidelines for Imparting Teamwork Knowledge

Shared mental models. Shared mental models are specific to a particular task and team; therefore, actual teammates should train together. Trainees should be forced to use shared knowledge by reducing their ability to strategize. Examples of effective knowledge sharing may help novice teams. Shared knowledge should be measured (see Kraiger & Wenzel, 1997; Mathieu et al., 2005), and feedback regarding accuracy given to trainees. Allowing team members to experience the task from multiple perspectives (roles) might be helpful.

Interpositional knowledge. Interpositional knowledge is specific to a task (or job), but not necessarily to a particular set of team members; therefore, using simulated teammates is appropriate. Scenarios should highlight the contribution of various team members, as well as trigger the trainee to understand the roles. Allowing team members to adopt different roles (cross-training) is an effective strategy. Knowledge of member roles should be measured and feedback delivered based on the accuracy of trainee's knowledge of teammate's roles.

Understanding of teamwork skills. Understanding teamwork is foundational knowledge for trainees; therefore, controlling the behavior of teammates is best done by modeling correct team behavior in simulated teammates. Events should demonstrate effective teamwork and indicate why it is necessary. Allowing team members to adopt different roles can strengthen this understanding. Understanding of teamwork skills should be measured and feedback given on trainee knowledge of these.

Understanding of team context. Team context is specific to a task and may be to a specific set of team members (particularly in the case of norms); hence, simulated teammates can be used only if they accurately reflect this context. Trainees need to gain an appreciation of how their

TABLE 13.2 Guidelines for Imparting Team Knowledge In SLEs

KNOWLEDGE DIMENSION	COMPONENTS	SLE STRATEGIES
Shared Mental Models	• Shared task knowledge • Shared team models • Shared equipment models	• Provide complex problems that require knowledge sharing • Script events that mitigate against overt communication • Provide examples of effective knowledge sharing • Measure shared knowledge • Provide feedback on accuracy of shared knowledge • Present flexible role perspectives to allow cross-training • Require live (actual) teammates to participate
Interpositional knowledge	• Role of each team member • Responsibilities of each member • Information/ resource needs of each member	• Provide scenarios that highlight the roles and responsibilities of each team member • Script events that provide information about roles in the team • Measure interpositional knowledge • Provide feedback on accuracy of IPK • Present flexible role perspectives • Allow synthetic or live teammates
Understanding of teamwork skills	• Understand requirements of teamwork • Contribution of teamwork to task success	• Provide scenarios that highlight the need for teamwork and consequences of poor teamwork • Script events that display correct teamwork behaviors • Measure trainee's knowledge of teamwork skills • Provide feedback on accuracy of teamwork knowledge • Allow team members to play multiple roles • Provide simulated teammates (who model correct behavior)

(Continued)

TABLE 13.2 (continued)

KNOWLEDGE DIMENSION	COMPONENTS	SLE STRATEGIES
Understanding of team context	• Overall team goals and objective • Team mission • Norms • Resources • Boundary spanning • Relationship to larger organization	• Provide scenarios that incorporate the team's role in the larger organization • Script evens that focus trainee's attention on the importance of understanding the team's mission, goals and objectives • Measure trainee's knowledge of team context • Provide feedback regarding accuracy of knowledge • Allow team members to play specific roles • Use live or simulated teammates (but ensure that they accurately reflect the team context)
Knowledge of teammates	• Knowledge of strengths • Knowledge of weaknesses • Knowledge of preferences • Knowledge of desires	• Provide a variety of scenarios that force teammates to rely on each other • Script events that cause team members to anticipate the needs of other members • Provide hints regarding the needs of teammates and to trigger discussion • Measure knowledge of teammates • Provide feedback regarding the accuracy of teammate knowledge • Use live (actual) teammates

(Continued)

TABLE 13.2 (continued)

KNOWLEDGE DIMENSION	COMPONENTS	SLE STRATEGIES
Cue–Strategy Associations	• Action-outcome contingencies • When strategy is appropriate • How strategy is executed • Triggers for strategy change	• Provide many scenarios that have similar, but slightly different input conditions (cues) • Script events that clearly demonstrate the consequences of strategies the trainee employs • Highlight triggers that should cue trainees to change strategies, especially early in training • Measure trainee's ability to recognize cues and act appropriately • Provide feedback that highlights the relationship among cues and appropriate teamwork processes • Use synthetic or live teammates

team fits into the larger organizational setting; therefore, scenarios need to be written to highlight this. Allowing team members to play specific roles (e.g., boundary spanning) can enhance their appreciation for these positions. Measurement and feedback should focus on the trainee's understanding of how his or her team functions in the larger context.

Knowledge of teammates. Knowledge of teammates is specific to both the task and team and therefore requires actual teammates in training. Scenarios should be developed to span a variety of conditions, and events scripted that specifically require trainees to anticipate the needs of teammates (e.g., by increasing time pressure so that there is not time to strategize). Hints and other devices can be provided to encourage trainees to think about their teammate's needs and to trigger dialogue among team members to clarify resource needs if necessary. Teammate knowledge should be measured and feedback given. Cross-training (having teammates switch roles) may help trainees have a better understanding of their teammates' perspectives.

Cue–strategy associations. Expert performance is distinguished from novice performance because experts can make fine distinctions among cue (input) sets; hence, many variations of a scenario should be provided and the consequences of the trainee's actions clearly provided. Hints and other methods to highlight important cues can be useful to novices. Measurement and feedback can be incorporated into transfer scenarios that do not include hints. Live or simulated teammates can be used; however, simulated teammates are probably best used early in training, since their behavior can be controlled. Later in training, the addition of live teammates heightens the fidelity with respect to the actual environment.

GUIDELINES FOR TRAINING TEAMWORK SKILLS

Adaptability. The ability of teams to adapt to changing conditions is a hallmark of effectiveness. To develop adaptability, trainees should be provided with many variations of a specific scenario or problem. Events should be included that force trainees to back each other up and reallocate function on the fly. A capability that allows team members or trainers to quickly script their own scenarios would be useful. Hints can be provided to more novice trainees to aid them in understanding how to adapt behavior, and effective back up and load balancing can be modeled by simulated teammates. Feedback should specifically address the trainee's ability to recognize triggers for strategy change and selection of appropriate course of action.

Shared situational awareness. Since shared situational awareness is highly specific to both a task and team, the level of fidelity must be high, and real teammates are required in training. Scenarios should incorporate rapidly changing and evolving problem sets and be developed to require information sharing. The assessment of shared situational awareness can be incorporated into the scenario (e.g., by asking trainees to report on their current situation), and feedback on the accuracy of this assessment should be given. Early in training, there may be opportunities to provide hints or cues that will help shared SA develop.

Performance monitoring and feedback. Intrateam performance monitoring and feedback can be accomplished with simulated or live teammates. Early in training, simulated teammates should be scripted to make errors and require assistance. Likewise, criticism or input from other team members to the trainee can be provided. A requirement to debrief and self-correct can also be included in the scenario. Early in training, hints or other devices can be included that help the trainee to monitor her or his teammates (and remind the trainee to do this). Both intrateam monitoring (and error correction) and giving and receiving feedback can be measured and feedback provided.

Leadership/team management. Leadership and team management skills transcend a particular team situation and therefore can be trained with live or simulated teammates. Scenarios should require the trainee to make resource-allocation decisions, to plan for contingencies, to

TABLE 13.3 Guidelines for Training Teamwork Skills In SLEs

SKILL DIMENSION	COMPONENTS	SLE STRATEGIES
Adaptability	• Flexibility in strategy • Compensatory (back up) behavior • Provide/ask for assistance • Dynamic reallocation of function	• Provide many variations of a fundamental problem structure • Script events that force team members to back each other up • Develop rapid scenario authoring capability • Provide scaffolds, hints in novel situations • Measure ability to adapt across problems/events • Provide feedback with respect to the efficacy of various approaches • Allow for flexible roles (cross-training) • Allow live or simulated teammates
Shared Situational Awareness	• Information seeking • Shared problem model development • Common situational understanding	• Provide scenarios that contain rapidly changing, evolving problems • Script triggers that require information sharing • Present many varied problems or scenarios • Provide hints early in training • Measure momentary understanding of situation • Measure shared situational awareness • Provide feedback with respect to current problem understanding • Require actual teammates

(Continued)

TABLE 13.3 (continued)

SKILL DIMENSION	COMPONENTS	SLE STRATEGIES
Performance Monitoring and Feedback	• Intramember feedback • Mutual performance monitoring • Team self correction	• Script errors by other team members into scenarios • Require trainees to debrief as part of the scenario • Script criticism and/or feedback from other members into scenarios • Provide opportunities to monitor and/or assess team functioning (bird's-eye view) • Measure extent of intrateam monitoring • Measure feedback giving and receiving • Provide feedback based on measurements • Allow for live or simulated teammates
Leadership/ Team Management	• Task structuring • Resource management • Goal setting • Mission analysis • Motivating others	• Provide resource allocation scenarios/problems • Script complex problems that require extensive analysis and planning • Provide triggers that require the trainee to direct activities of other team members • Measure ability to organize/ prioritize resources • Measure team management functions • Provide feedback on leadership and management skills • Allow for live or simulated teammates

(Continued)

TABLE 13.3 (continued)

SKILL DIMENSION	COMPONENTS	SLE STRATEGIES
Interpersonal	• Conflict resolution • Cooperation • Assertiveness • Morale building • Boundary spanning	• Provide scenarios/problems that require assertiveness • Provide scenarios/problems that require conflict resolution • Demonstrate the impact/ consequences of poor interpersonal skills • Measure task-related assertiveness • Measure conflict-resolution skills • Provide feedback regarding interpersonal style • Use simulated teammates to model correct behavior early in training; live teammates to heighten fidelity later
Coordination	• Task organization • Coordination of task sequence • Coordinated task interactions/ inputs • Timing and activity pacing	• Provide realistic problems that require precise task sequencing and pacing • Script in events that contain cues which require strategy changes • Allow for flexible roles (ability to cross-train) • Measure procedural knowledge • Measure trainee's ability to appropriately respond to important cues • Provide feedback regarding task execution and procedures • Provide feedback regarding cue recognition and actions taken • Use simulated teammates to model correct behavior early in training; live teammates to heighten fidelity later

(Continued)

TABLE 13.3 (continued)

SKILL DIMENSION	COMPONENTS	SLE STRATEGIES
Communication	• Information exchange • Closed loop communication • Information sharing • Volunteer/ request information • Consulting with others • Open exchange of relevant interpretations	• Provide problems that require communications with other team members • Provide the opportunity to exchange verbal information (e.g. voice over IP) • Record and code verbal communications • Measure degree to which team members use close-loop communication and proper phraseology • Measure anticipation ratio (providing information before being asked) • Provide feedback with respect to how communication skills need to be improved • Use live teammates
Decision Making	• Problem assessment • Problem solving • Information processing and evaluation • Planning/ contingency development • Metacognitive behavior	• Provide problems that require pooled informational resources • Script events that require extensive information gathering and diagnosis • Script opportunities for trainees to discuss strategies with teammates • Script events that trigger metacognitive decision making processes • Measure decision making strategy • Assess planning skills and soundness of plan • Measure accuracy, timeliness, latency of decisions • Provide feedback with respect to specific aspects of the decision making process • Use live teammates

prioritize and assign tasks to other members, and to direct the activities of teammates. Early in training, hints and cues can be provided to aid the trainee in successfully managing the team. These skills can be measured via transfer scenarios, and feedback should be delivered. Either live or simulated team members can be used.

Interpersonal skills. This skill area actually represents several related yet distinct skill sets. Scenarios should be scripted to allow practice of important dimensions such as task-related assertiveness and conflict resolution. Early in training, simulated team members can be used to model correct behaviors; later in training, live teammates provide heightened fidelity. Prompts or hints early in training can be beneficial. Measurement and feedback should be geared specifically toward helping trainees to improve their ability to recognize when interpersonal skills are important and how to express them.

Coordination. Subtleties in task inputs, including when and how action should be taken, must be practiced by team members in scenarios with high task fidelity. Trainees should be required to recognize and react to cues that trigger important strategy changes and specific feedback given in this regard. Early in training, simulated teammates can be used to provide examples of correct behavior and reduce variability. Later in training, using live team members is useful to provide more realistic practice.

Communication. In order to practice communication skills, team members must be able to communicate with each other in a manner that is consistent with the real task (including verbally). Scenarios should be written to emphasize the need for team members to communicate, and verbal exchanges must be recorded and scored (a practice that is very labor intensive, but necessary). Team members should be given feedback regarding their use of closed-loop communication, phraseology, and the extent to which they provide information before it is requested of them (anticipation ratio). Since natural-language-processing technology is not mature enough to allow for simulated teammates who can verbally communicate, live teammates should be used for communication training except very early in training when correct behaviors can be demonstrated with simulated teammates.

Decision making. Team decision making can be trained in an SLE by presenting team members with complex, evolving problems that require extensive diagnosis and planning. In addition, they should require team members to pool resources and provide opportunities for trainees to strategize with teammates. Measures of performance should include indicators of the soundness of the process used by the team to arrive at its decisions (e.g., information exchange, strategy and plan formation, metacognitive awareness) as well as the outcome of the decision (e.g., accuracy, timeliness, latency, quality, etc.). Early in training, performance can be scaffolded by providing hints that aid the trainee in making the decision.

IMPROVING TEAMWORK ATTITUDES

Attitudes toward teamwork. Changing trainee's attitudes toward teamwork in a simulation or game may best be done by demonstrating the impact of poor teamwork on task outcomes (e.g., the Leroy Jenkins vignette previously described). Also, providing scenarios in which the trainee must depend on his or her teammates to succeed can be useful. This can be done by presenting emergency or stressful events where the trainee is overloaded and forced to rely on team members to succeed. Using simulated teammates is effective for this category since it is desirable for correct behaviors to be modeled.

Collective efficacy. To build collective efficacy, early scenarios should be developed to be easy enough to ensure success and gradually build in difficulty. Ample hints should be provide early in training to increase the likelihood that the team is successful. In addition, successes should be highlighted and reinforced so that team members can use this information to increase collective efficacy. Because collective efficacy is team specific (e.g., it changes depending on the configuration of the team), actual teammates should be used in training.

Collective orientation. Early exposure to team-level scenarios may be useful in developing collective orientation in trainees. Scenarios should explicitly reinforce collective behavior and display the consequences of poor teamwork. Collective efficacy should be measured over the course of training, with positive changes reinforced. Early in training, simulated teammates can be used to model correct behavior; later in training, live teammates can heighten realism.

Cohesion. Game players often spontaneously develop strong senses of "teamness" by repeatedly confronting difficult situations, but coping with them effectively. Real teammates can be exposed to simulations that both challenge them to perform effectively as a team and reward them for such behavior (e.g., by giving them extra resources, providing advantages or hints for future play, providing public reward, incorporating competition, etc.). Game-playing teams are also encouraged to personalize their team (e.g., with names, graphics, etc.), a practice that could be useful in training as well.

TABLE 13.4 Guidelines for Improving Team-Related Attitudes In SLEs

ATTITUDE DIMENSION	COMPONENTS	SLE STRATEGIES
Attitudes toward Teamwork	• Importance of teamwork skills • Appreciation of teamwork processes	• Provide demonstrations of the consequences of effective and ineffective teamwork • Script events in which the trainee cannot succeed without aid from teammates • Include emergency and nonroutine events in the scenario that force effective teamwork • Measure attitudes toward teamwork • Provide feedback regarding attitude change • Use simulated teammates to model correct behaviors
Collective Efficacy	• Beliefs of team-level competence • Confidence in team resources • Potency • Beliefs in team's leadership, powerbase, structure	• Provide increasingly difficult scenarios that build on one another • Script events that can provide positive reinforcement early in training • Scaffold early performance to ensure success • Measure collective efficacy as trainee gains experience • Reinforce successes through reward/recognition • Use live teammates so that attitudes transfer
Collective Orientation	• Team concept • Attraction to team situations • Empathy with respect to teammates	• Provide problems that allow for practice/familiarity in being on a team • Script events that demonstrate consequences of poor team work • Measure collective orientation • Measure attitudes toward teamwork • Reinforce effective teamwork • Reinforce positive attitude change • Use simulated teammates to model correct behavior early; then live teammates later in training

(Continued)

TABLE 13.3 (continued)

ATTITUDE DIMENSION	COMPONENTS	SLE STRATEGIES
Cohesion	• Esprit de corps • Team morale • "Teamness"	• Provide problems that emphasize the dependency of teammates on one another • Script events that allow team to succeed • Measure cohesion • Reinforce/reward team successes • Encourage team to develop its own identity • Use live teammates

CONCLUSIONS

In this chapter, we have attempted to describe the tremendous promise that synthetic learning environments hold for the important area of team training. It is important to note, however, that while there are many compelling arguments to suggest that SLEs *could* work as a training modality, there is not a substantial body of literature evaluating whether they *do* work. This is an important area of research, and it is hoped that the community of team researchers will recognize and respond to this need.

In the meantime, our theoretical arguments, combined with the empirical results that currently exist, lead us to conclude that effective SLEs can be developed for team training immediately. Instead of identifying a subset of team competencies that are ripe for training in SLEs, however, we would argue that nearly all of the competencies identified can be trained in this way if design of the SLE is carefully managed. As a starting point, we recommend developing SLEs in which actual team members are present, since the challenge of developing realistic simulated teammates is not fully solved. We also recommend focusing on competencies that do not rely on sophisticated interfaces (e.g., psychomotor skills) since these add considerable complexity to the design. Hence, focusing on knowledge competencies, higher order skills and attitudes is advised. Finally, we recommend that manual procedures be used in place of automated ones to augment the SLE. For example, our vision of an SLE that can automatically record performance and provide feedback will probably not be realized in the short term; however, creating observational assessment protocols that can be used by human instructors in conjunction with an SLE is certainly a viable alternative.

REFERENCES

Allen, J., Hays, R., & Buffardi, L. (1986). Maintenance training simulator fidelity and individual differences in transfer of training. *Human Factors, 28*(5), 497–509.

Anderson, J. R., & Schunn, C. D. (2000). Implications of the ACT-R learning theory: No magic bullets. In R. Glaser (Ed.), *Advances in instructional psychology: Educational design and cognitive science* (Vol. 5, pp. 1–33). Mahwah, NJ: Lawrence Erlbaum Associates.

Bandura, A. (1986). *Social foundations of thought and action: A social cognitive theory.* Englewood Cliffs, NJ: Prentice-Hall.

Banks, A., & McKeran, W. (2005). Team situation awareness: Shared displays and performance. *International Journal of Cognitive Technology, 10*(2), 23–28.

Beck-Jones, J. (2004). The effect of cross-training and role assignment in cooperative learning groups on task performance, knowledge of accounting concepts, teamwork behavior, and acquisition of interpositional knowledge. *Dissertation Abstracts International Section A: Humanities and Social Sciences, 64*(7-A), 2378.

Bell, B., & Kozlowski, S. (2002). Adaptive guidance: Enhancing self-regulation, knowledge, and performance in technology-based training. *Personnel Psychology, 55*(2), 267–306.

Bowers, C., & Jentsch, F. (2001). Use of commercial, off-the-shelf simulations for team research. In E. Salas (Ed.), *Advances in human performance and cognitive engineering research* (pp. 293–317). Oxford, U.K.: Elsevier Science, JAI Press.

Bowers, C., Jentsch, F., Salas, E., & Braun, C. (1998). Analyzing communication sequences for team training needs assessment. *Human Factors, 40*(4), 672–679.

Bransford, J. D., Brown, A. L., & Cocking, R. R. (Eds.). (1999). *How people learn: Brain, mind, experience, and school.* Washington, DC: National Academy Press.

Cannon-Bowers, J. A., & Bowers, C. (in press). Synthetic learning environments: On developing a science of simulation, games, and virtual worlds for training. In S. Koslowski, & E. Salas (Eds.), *Frontiers of industrial-organizational psychology.*

Cannon-Bowers, J. A., & Salas, E. (Eds.). (1998). *Making decisions under stress: Implications for individual and team training.* Washington, DC: APA.

Cannon-Bowers, J.A., & Salas, E. (2001). Reflections on shared cognition. *Journal of Organizational Behavior, 22,* 195–202.

Cannon-Bowers, J.A., Salas, E., & Converse, S. (1993). Shared mental models in expert team decision making. *Individual and group decision making: Current issues* (pp. 221–246). Mahwah, NJ: Lawrence Erlbaum Associates.

Cannon-Bowers, J. A., Tannenbaum, S. I., Salas, E., & Volpe, C. E. (1995). Defining team competencies and establishing team training requirements. In R. Guzzo & E. Salas (Eds.), *Team effectiveness and decision making in organizations* (pp. 333–380). San Francisco, CA: Jossey-Bass.

Chen, G., Thomas, B., & Wallace, J. (2005). A multilevel examination of the relationships among training outcomes, mediating regulatory processes, and adaptive performance. *Journal of Applied Psychology, 90*(5), 827–841.

Dickey, M. (2005). Three-dimensional virtual worlds and distance learning: Two case studies of active worlds as a medium for distance education. *British Journal of Educational Technology, 36*(3), 439–451.

Driskell, J., & Salas, E. (1992). Can you study real teams in contrived settings? The value of small group research to understanding teams. In R. Swezey, & E. Salas (Eds.), *Teams: Their training and performance* (pp. 101–124). Greenwich, CT: Ablex Publishing.

Driskell, J., & Salas, E. (1997). Collective behavior and team performance. In R. Litrell & E. Salas (Eds.), *Human resource development review: Research and implications* (pp. 206–222). Thousand Oaks, CA: Sage Publications, Inc.

Dwyer, D., Fowlkes, J., Oser, R., & Salas, E. (1997). Team performance measurement in distributed environments: The TARGETs methodology. In M. T. Brannick, E. Salas, & C. Prince (Eds.), *Team performance assessment and measurement: Theory, methods, and applications* (pp. 137–153). Mahwah, NJ: Lawrence Erlbaum Associates.

Finkelstein, N. (2000, June). Charting the retention of tasks learned in synthetic virtual environments. *Dissertation Abstracts International: Section B: The Sciences and Engineering, 60*(11-B), 5702.

Fowlkes, J. E., Lane, N. E., Salas, E., Franz, T., & Oser, R. (1994). Improving the measurement of team performance: The TARGETs methodology. *Military Psychology, 6*, 47–61.

Garris, R., Ahlers, R., & Driskell, J. (2002). Games, motivation, and learning: A research and practice model. *Simulation & Gaming, 33*(4), 441–467.

Gee, J. P. (2003). *What video games have to teach us about learning and literacy.* New York: Palgrave Macmillan.

Gerling, G. J., & Thomas, G. V. (2005). Augmented, pulsating tactile feedback facilitates simulator training of clinical breast examinations. *Human Factors, 47*(2), 670–681.

Gopher, D., Weil, M., & Bareket, T. (1994). Transfer of skill from a computer game trainer to flight. *Human Factors, 36*(3), 387–405.

Gott, S. P., & Lesgold, A. M. (2000). Competence in the workplace: How cognitive performance models and situated instruction can accelerate skill acquisition. In R. Glaser (Ed.), *Advances in instructional psychology: Educational design and cognitive science* (Vol. 5, pp. 239–327). Mahwah, NJ: Lawrence Erlbaum Associates.

Gregorich, S., Helmreich, R., & Wilhelm, J. (1990). The structure of cockpit management attitudes. *Journal of Applied Psychology, 75*(6), 682–690.

Guzzo, R. (1986). Implicit theories and the evaluation of group process and performance. *Organizational Behavior and Human Decision Processes, 37*(2), 279–295.

Hirschfeld, R., Jordan, M., Feild, H., Giles, W., & Armenakis, A. (2006). Becoming team players: Team members' mastery of teamwork knowledge as a predictor of team task proficiency and observed teamwork effectiveness. *Journal of Applied Psychology, 91*(2), 467–474.

Honebein, P. C., Duffy, T. M., & Fishman, B. J. (1993). Constructivism and the design of learning environments: Context and authentic activities for learning. In T. M. Duffy, J. Lowyck, & D. H. Jonassen (Eds.), *Designing environments for constructive learning* (pp. 87–108). New York: Springer-Verlag.

Huang, J., & Gau, C. (2003). Modelling and designing a low-cost high-fidelity mobile crane simulator. *International Journal of Human-Computer Studies, 58*(2), 151–176.

Jansz, J., & Martens, L. (2005). Gaming at a LAN event: The social context of playing video games. *New Media & Society, 7*(3), 333–355.

Jentsch, F., & Smith-Jentsch, K. (2001). Assertiveness and team performance: More than "just say no". In E. Salas, C. Bowers, & E. Edens (Eds.), *Improving teamwork in organizations: Applications of resource management training* (pp. 73–94). Mahwah, NJ: Lawrence Erlbaum Associates.

Jonassen, D. (2000). Revisiting activity theory as a framework for designing student-centered learning environments. In D. H. Jonassen & S. Long (Eds.), *Theoretical foundations of learning environments* (pp. 89–121). Mahwah, NJ: Lawrence Erlbaum Associates.

Jones, M. G., Minogue, J., Tretter, T., Negshi. A., & Taylor, R. (2006). Haptic augmentation of science instruction: Does touch matter? *Science Education, 90*(1), 111–123.

Keys, J. (1997). Strategic management games: A review. *Simulation & Gaming, 28*(4), 395–422.

Klein, G. (2001). Features of team coordination. In M. McNeese, E. Salas, & M. Endsley (Eds.), *New trends in cooperative activities: Understanding system dynamics in complex environments* (pp. 68–95). Santa Monica, CA: Human Factors and Ergonomics Society.

Knerr, B., Breaux, R., Goldberg, S., & Thurman, R. (2002). National defense. In K. Stanney (Ed.), *Handbook of virtual environments: Design, implementation, and applications* (pp. 857–872). Mahwah, NJ: Lawrence Erlbaum Associates.

Kozlowski, S., Toney, R., Mullins, M., Weissbein, D., Brown, K., & Bell, B. (2001). Developing adaptability: A theory for the design of integrated-embedded training systems. In E. Salas (Ed.), *Advances in human performance and cognitive engineering research* (pp. 59–123). Oxford, U.K.: Elsevier Science/JAI Press.

Kraiger, K., Salas, E., & Cannon-Bowers, J. (1995). Measuring knowledge organization as a method for assessing learning during training. *Human Factors, 37*(4), 804–816.

Kraiger, L. F., & Wenzel, L. C. (1997). Conceptual development and empirical evaluation of measures of shared mental models as indicators of team effectiveness. In M. T. Brannick, E. Salas, & C. Prince (Eds.), *Team performance assessment and measurement: Theory, methods, and applications* (pp. 45–84). Mahwah, NJ: Lawrence Erlbaum Associates.

Lanzetta, J., & Roby, T. (1960). The relationship between certain group process variables and group problem-solving efficiency. *Journal of Social Psychology, 52*, 135–148.

Laurillard, D., Stratfold, M., Luckin, R., Plowman, L., & Taylor, J. (2000). Affordances for learning in a non-linear narrative medium. *Journal of Interactive Media in Education, 00*(2).

Lent, R., Schmidt, J., & Schmidt, L. (2006). Collective efficacy beliefs in student work teams: Relation to self-efficacy, cohesion, and performance. *Journal of Vocational Behavior, 68*(1), 73–84.

Lieberman, D. A. (1997). Interactive video games for health promotion: Effects on knowledge, self-efficacy, social support, and health. In R. L. Street, Jr., W. R. Gold, & T. Manning (Eds.), *Health promotion and interactive technology: Theoretical applications and future directions*. Mahwah, NJ: Lawrence Erlbaum Associates.

Lieberman, D. (2006). What can we learn from playing interactive games? *Playing video games: Motives, responses, and consequences* (pp. 379–397). Mahwah, NJ: Lawrence Erlbaum Associates.

Manninen, T. (2003). Interaction manifestations in multi-player games. In G. Riva, S. Davide, W. Usselsteijn (Eds.), *Being there: Concepts, effects, and measurements of user presence in synthetic environments* (pp. 295–304). Amsterdam: IOS Press.

Marks, M., & Panzer, F. (2004). The influence of team monitoring on team processes and performance. *Human Performance, 17*(1), 25–41.

Mathieu, J., Heffner, T., Goodwin, G., Salas, E., & Cannon-Bowers, J. (2000). The influence of shared mental models on team process and performance. *Journal of Applied Psychology, 85*(2), 273–283.

Mathieu, J. E., Heffner, T. S., Goodwin, G. F., Cannon-Bowers, J. A., & Salas, E. (2005). Scaling the quality of teammates' mental models: Equifinality and normative comparisons. *Journal of Organizational Behavior, 26*, 37–56.

Mohammed, S., & Dumville, B. (2001). Team mental models in a team knowledge framework: Expanding theory and measurement across disciplinary boundaries. *Journal of Organizational Behavior, 22*, 89–106.

Morgan, B., Salas, E., & Glickman, A. (1993). An analysis of team evolution and maturation. *Journal of General Psychology, 120*(3), 277–291.

Morris, C., Hancock, P., & Shirkey, E. (2004). Motivational effects of adding context relevant stress in PC-based game training. *Military Psychology, 16*(2), 135–147.

Nemitcheva, N. (1995). The psychologist and games in the intensive foreign language game-based course. In D. Crookall & K. Arai (Eds.), *Simulation and gaming across disciplines and cultures: ISAGA at a watershed* (pp. 70–74). Thousand Oaks, CA:Sage Publications.

O'Neil, H., & Fisher, Y. (2004). A technology to support leader development: Computer games. In D. Day, S. Zaccaro, & S. Halpin (Eds.), *Leader development for transforming organizations: Growing leaders for tomorrow* (pp. 99–121). Mahwah, NJ: Lawrence Erlbaum Associates.

Peterson, J., & Martens, R. (1972). Success and residential affiliation as determinants of team cohesiveness. *Research Quarterly, 43*(1), 62–76.

Petraglia, J. (1998). *Reality by design: The rhetoric and technology of authenticity in education*. Mahwah, NJ: Lawrence Erlbaum Associates.

Plowman, L. (2005). Getting the story straight: The role of narrative in teaching and learning with interactive media. *Cognition, education, and communication technology* (pp. 55–76). Mahwah, NJ: Lawrence Erlbaum Associates.

Prensky, M. (2002). The motivation of gameplay or the real 21st century learning revolution. *On the Horizon, 10*(1).

Rentsch, J., & Klimoski, R. (2001). Why do 'great minds' think alike? Antecedents of team member schema agreement. *Journal of Organizational Behavior, 22*, 107–120.

Roessingh, J. (2005). Transfer of manual flying skills from PC-based simulation to actual flight-comparison of in-flight measured data and instructor ratings. *International Journal of Aviation Psychology, 15*(1), 67–90.

Rourke, L., Anderson, T., Garrison, D. R., & Archer, W. (1999). Assessing social presence in asynchronous, text-based computer conferencing. *Journal of Distance Education, 14*(3), 51–70.

Sadowski, W., & Stanney, K. (2002). Presence in virtual environments. In K. Stanney (Ed.), *Handbook of virtual environments: Design, implementation, and applications* (pp. 791–806). Mahwah, NJ: Lawrence Erlbaum Associates.

Salas, E., & Cannon-Bowers, J. (2001). The science of training: A decade of progress. *Annual Review of Psychology, 52*, 471–499.

Salas, E., Cannon-Bowers, J., & Johnston, J. (1997). How can you turn a team of experts into an expert team?: Emerging training strategies. In G. Klein (Ed.), *Naturalistic decision making* (pp. 359–370).

Scerbo, M., Bliss, J., Schmidt, E., & Thompson, S. (2006). The efficacy of a medical virtual reality simulator for training phlebotomy. *Human Factors, 48*(1), 72–84.

Schneider, E., Lang, A., Shin, M., & Bradley, S. (2004). Death with a story: How story impacts emotional, motivational, and physiological responses to first-person shooter video games. *Human Communication Research, 30*(3), 361–375.

Schwabe, G., & Göth, C. (2005). Mobile learning with a mobile game: Design and motivational effects. *Journal of Computer Assisted Learning, 21*(3), 204–216.

Selverian, M. (2005). Being there in the VLE: A pan-pedagogical model for enhanced learning through perceptual states of 'presence'. *Dissertation Abstracts International Section A: Humanities and Social Sciences*, 66(5-A). 1617.

Shaffer, D. W., & Resnick, M. (1999). "Thick" authenticity: New media and authentic learning. *Journal of Interactive Learning Research, 10*(2), 195–215.

Simms, B. (1998). The effects of an educational computer game on motivation to learn basic musical skills: A qualitative study. *Dissertation Abstracts International Section A: Humanities and Social Sciences, 59*(3-A), 0766.

Smith-Jentsch, K., Campbell, G., Milanovich, D., & Reynolds, A. (2001). Measuring teamwork mental models to support training needs assessment, development, and evaluation: Two empirical studies. *Journal of Organizational Behavior, 22*, 179–194.

Smith-Jentsch, K., Mathieu, J., & Kraiger, K. (2005). Investigating linear and interactive effects of shared mental models on safety and efficiency in a field setting. *Journal of Applied Psychology, 90*(3), 523–535.

Sundstrom, E., de Meuse, K., & Futrell, D. (1990). Work teams: Applications and effectiveness. *American Psychologist, 45*(2), 120–133.

Volpe, C., Cannon-Bowers, J., Salas, E., & Spector, P. (1996). The impact of cross-training on team functioning: An empirical investigation. *Human Factors, 38*(1), 87–100.

Wolfe, J. (1997). The effectiveness of business games in strategic management course work. *Simulation & Gaming, 28*(4), 360–376.

Wolfe, C. (2002). Learning and teaching on the World Wide Web. *Applied Cognitive Psychology, 16*(7), 863–864.

CHAPTER

14

Phased and Targeted Interventions: Improving Team Learning and Performance

JOYCE SILBERSTANG
Adelphi University School of Business

THOMAS DIAMANTE
Marist College School of Management

Fortune 500 companies rely extensively on teams; in fact nearly 80% reportedly do so (Robbins, 2003). Team decisions and actions significantly impact a firm's performance, whether these performance metrics focus on morale, productivity, turnover, profitability, growth, or market share. The expectation is that people will be more energized when working in a group (Sodenkamp, Schmidt, & Kleinbeck, 2005) and that the collective expertise of team members makes teams more effective than individuals working alone (Mathieu, Goodwin, Heffner, Salas, & Cannon-Bowers, 2000). This, however, is not always the case.

Despite the extensive use of teams to carry out mission critical activities, teams derail; rather than enhance organizational value, poorly performing teams detract from it. Team *ineffectiveness* derives from a variety of sources, as does team *effectiveness*. That said, this chapter focuses on how to improve team learning and performance. Such a focus necessitates the exploration of "learning" as a process of change and growth.

The importance of group learning cannot be overstated. For instance, companies spend billions of dollars to improve one type of team skill alone—collaboration (Weiss & Hughes, 2005). This chapter provides actionable intelligence on the types of team competencies groups need to improve their effectiveness. A Diagnostic Team Learning Model, introduced in this chapter, provides guidance on when and how to address team impediments through Phased and Targeted Interventions. These interventions are designed to optimize group processes and improve team effectiveness, thereby enhancing tangible business outcomes.

Throughout this chapter the terms *group* and *team* are used interchangeably in accordance with research in the field (Hackman, 2000). Both terms refer to an interdependent work unit of two or more who share a common goal or objective.

IMPROVING TEAM LEARNING AND PERFORMANCE

In fast-paced or knowledge-intensive business environments, team learning is critically important (Argote, Gruenfeld, & Naquin, 2001). Our definition of learning is not limited to the acquisition of knowledge. It also incorporates changes in attitudes and behaviors. To learn, teams must have the opportunity to experiment with new ideas and approaches, work through interpersonal and task related issues, seek feedback, discuss errors, and reflect on group performance. Above all, there must be a mutual openness among team members that enables nurturance, knowledge exchange, and growth. We view team learning as the group's ability to develop job or task related competencies, so teams are able to meet a defined goal.

Acquiring Team Competencies

For teams to learn, they must become proficient in both context-driven and transportable competencies (Chen et al., 2002). Context-driven competencies are specific to a team and their task. For example, disaster response teams sent to the Middle East require training in Muslim customs. Many context specific competencies can be taught, although it is unrealistic to expect that teams can obtain training in every situation or issue that might arise.

In contrast, transportable competencies are generic to all types of teams and tasks across a wide variety of settings (Canon-Bowers, Tannenbaum, Salas, & Volpe, 1995), countries, and cultures. Transportable competencies enable groups to understand *how* they operate as a team and *what* they should accomplish. Stevens and Campion (1999; 1994) identified five dimensions of transportable team competencies that predict team performance, effectiveness, and overall organizational performance. Three of these competencies, conflict resolution, collaborative problem solving, and communication, focus on *interpersonal* knowledge, skills, and abilities. The other two competencies, goal setting and performance management, and planning and task coordination, focus on *self-management* knowledge, skills, and abilities.

Team Learning Interventions: Three Phases

Team interventions provide learning opportunities for individual group members and the group as a whole. Interventions enable a team to acquire and make better use of context-driven and transportable competencies. As a result, teams are better able to examine how they are doing day-to-day as they use or modify past practices and accomplish short-term goals. Learning interventions also provide information on *what* the team is doing; this macro-orientation focuses on the team's goals and processes (Lant & Hewlin, 2002). Such tactical and strategic insights enable individuals and groups to learn effective patterns of interaction and approaches to the work that can be repeated later in their groups or in other groups. Unfortunately, many groups lack the skills to assess, modify, and improve their performance. This section presents the "phases" of a team's life cycle, and provides guidelines on the type of intervention teams can use during each cycle.

A team can be viewed as having three phases in its life cycle, inertia, a midpoint, and completion. These phases, originally developed by Gersick (1988), were modified by Hackman and Wageman (2005), yet still retain their original elements. Groups develop through a "punctuated equilibrium" (Gersick, 1988, p. 32), not a smooth, imperceptible transition. They alternate between bursts of activity and relative inertia where progress seems to be extremely slow moving (Gersick, 1989).

Groups significantly transform as they move from phase to phase, and have different developmental needs, dynamics, and behaviors (Agazarian & Gantt, 2003). Indeed, a team's main focus shifts as different behaviors and issues emerge (Gersick, 1989). Consequently, there may be a greater frequency of certain types of behaviors in each phase of a group's development, as behavior that is expected in one phase may be inappropriate in another phase (Agazarian & Gantt, 2003). During each phase, there is an optimal window of opportunity during which time intervention efficacy is heightened. Fig. 14.1 depicts the three phases along with the optimal windows for change.

Phase One

In Phase One, characterized as "inertia," the newly formed team is launched (Hackman & Wageman, 2005; Gersick, 1988; 1989). Many of the characteristics required for effective group performance emerge in

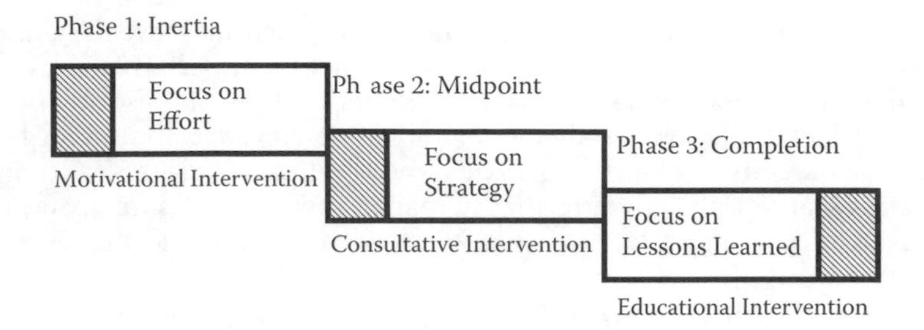

Figure 14.1 Timing of team learning interventions for the three phases of group development. Shaded boxes indicate when a phased intervention will have the greatest impact.

Phase One and remain important throughout the team's life cycle. These include a stable (rather than frequently changing) membership, a collective team identity, and frequent team member contact. If team members have difficulty getting to know one another and communicating, there can be a negative spillover to other processes (Jehn & Mannix, 2001).

During Phase One, team members discuss and clarify the team's "structural" characteristics (the goals, roles, and tasks), begin to plan, and determine how best to communicate, collaborate, and coordinate. They also establish behavioral norms that promote openness and the exchange of ideas (Sala, 2003). Each team has a unique approach to carrying out their work which remains relatively stable until Phase Two (Gersick, 1988).

Phase One interventions are motivational and occur during the early stages of team development. They are designed to assist the group's efforts to form and develop, thereby establishing the groundwork for an effective launch. A newly formed group must know who is on the team, and clearly understand team goals and deadlines. Managers often "intervene" to clarify these or similar issues.

Team progress is not always apparent during Phase One. Teams make false starts; they often review and rethink decisions, develop and modify timelines, and disagree on how to proceed. Differing perceptions of how best to accomplish the team's goals, delegate tasks (e.g., to the group as a whole, to specific individuals) and make decisions can cause discomfort. Some members may want to immediately start working while others insist on creating detailed plans. Members may jockey for power or position, especially if the team chooses its own leader. Personality clashes, disagreements, expectations, anxieties (regarding other projects or work)—even indifference, can cause confusion and conflict.

It is this very process that enables the team to gel and find ways to productively communicate, coordinate, and collaborate. The manager must allow the team to find its own direction and work through its own issues. In essence, the manager stands by, ready to help. The manager should only intercede if asked, or if conflict threatens to derail team functioning.

The establishment of healthy, productive behavioral norms is paramount to team success. Building team capabilities through training is a proactive approach, and one that we highly recommend. When the team or task is new, providing training in team skills (transportable competencies) when the team *first forms* enables a group to become more proficient in solving problems, coordinating tasks, planning, and communicating (Ellis, Bell, Polyhart, Hollenbeck, & Ilgen, 2005).

When teams require specialized skills or knowledge to complete their tasks (i.e., context-driven competencies), the input, advice, or assistance of other managers, personnel, subject matter experts, and even customers and suppliers can be helpful. The focus should be on the specific knowledge and skills required for their present job, *not* for their next job. Preparing team members for their next jobs while they are still performing their present job has been linked to a 5.6% decrease in shareholder value (Pfau & Cohen, 2003).

A summary of Phase One interventions, designed to be carried out at the beginning of the phase, is presented in Table 14.1. These interventions are designed to help the group create an identity, develop ways to communicate and coordinate, and begin to focus on the team's goals, roles, and tasks. Interventions that focus on strategy (e.g., devising or

TABLE 14.1 Phase One Interventions—Motivational Activities

Phase One	Situation	How to Intervene
Form Team	Group lacks 'teamwork skills'	Provide training in teams skills (transportable competencies)
	Group lacks task specific skills	Provide training in specific skills (context-driven competencies)
First Meeting	Team forms	Define membership, goals, timelines, decision making authority, resources and support
Next Meetings	Roles and tasks uncertain	Only intervene if help is needed
	Behavioral norms developed	Only intervene if help is needed
	Data collected	Provide information, as needed
	Decisions reached	Review and/or approve solution
	Group loses direction	Do not intervene

implementing a long-term plan) should not be attempted during Phase One, as they will not be accepted by the team (Hackman & Wageman, 2005). Strategic interventions should take place during Phase Two.

Phase Two

Phase Two, characterized as the "midpoint," functions as a temporal and task milestone. It marks a transition between the group's early formation activities and their urgent need to complete the work (Gersick, 1989). Groups feel pressure to perform, and are acutely aware of the dwindling amount of time to completion. Consequently, at this time, teams often experience a surge of energy, usually accompanied by anxiety (Hackman & Wageman, 2005).

During Phase Two, groups reexamine existing assumptions and redefine their situation and approach to the work (Gersick, 1988). Groups with an effective strategy continue on to the next task. Other groups drop approaches that did not work, search for help, and develop new ways to achieve their goals.

Phase Two interventions are consultative and take place halfway between the group's first meeting and their deadline. For teams that lack a clearly defined deadline (e.g., research and development), or whose work is continuous (e.g., customer service), performance benchmarks that allow time for reflection can serve as the midpoint. Phase Two interventions help groups develop strategies to successfully complete their work. Thus, the main emphasis is on how groups will accomplish their goals.

Some managers automatically intervene by providing training to floundering groups. Training is not recommended for Phase Two, as it can result in a performance deficit. Teams must focus on accomplishing the work. Groups that need assistance examining existing strategies, or that fail to adequately change ineffective strategies, benefit from the use of trained facilitators to help them develop frameworks and structure decisions (Mohrman & Quam, 2000). Teams may also require additional resources, such as time, tools, equipment, and information.

Groups are most open to guidance during the beginning of Phase Two, when they are actively seeking new ways to reach their goals. Once groups have developed new strategies, they focus on performing their work, thereby precluding the need to continue this type of intervention. Phase Two Interventions, which focus on assessing team progress, developing new strategies, and deciding how to proceed, are summarized in Table 14.2.

Phase Three

In Phase Three, known as "completion," groups focus on completing their goals in a timely and satisfactory manner. As the deadline nears, they become reenergized in anticipation of a successful outcome.

TABLE 14.2 Phase Two Interventions—Consulting Activities

Phase Two	Situation	How to Intervene
Work Review	Progress assessed	Provide feedback if required
Team Direction	Group seeks direction	Assist team only if required
	Difficulty reaching decisions	Facilitator assists with process
Team Strategy	Assumptions examined	Manager/facilitator assists if needed
	New strategies developed	Manager/facilitator assists if needed
	Ineffective strategy continued	Provide feedback and assistance
		Do not provide training

During this burst of energy, group members concentrate on the tasks at hand. This is not the time to introduce new and creative ideas. Doing so could cause frustration, resulting in decreased levels of team learning and diminished project quality (Ford & Sullivan, 2004).

Once a project has been completed, most teams do not take the initiative to reflect on their work. If left to themselves, teams are likely to celebrate successes and misattribute failures. Even when teams examine their own performance without assistance from others, their views are likely to be biased (Hackman & Wageman, 2005). This is why it is so important for managers to conduct a team learning intervention at the end of Phase Three.

Phase Three interventions are educational and are conducted at the end of the project. The team reflects on past performance with the goal of identifying lessons learned. During the debriefing session, the team and team leader identify impediments to effective team performance, discuss whether and how the team handled specific situations, and propose alternative approaches. The team should also examine how they facilitated team performance, and take pride in their accomplishments.

This review of teamwork and the team's work provides an opportunity to assess individual and team strengths and areas requiring improvement. Examining how well (or poorly) the team did with regard to transportable team competencies can help structure discussions and track progress. Thus, at a minimum, teams should examine how goals were set, tracked and reached, how well team members coordinated and communicated, how they structured and solved problems, whether team members felt free to express their opinions, and how conflict was

TABLE 14.3 Phase Three Interventions—Educational Activities

Phase Three	Team Issues	How to Intervene
Nears Goal	Focus on work	Do not intervene or provide training
Goal Reached	Examine lessons learned	Review team strengths/ weaknesses
	Team failures ignored	Discuss 'difficult' issues with team
	Team accomplishments	Celebrate team successes

handled and resolved. The knowledge gained from these interventions can be applied to subsequent team efforts.

Conflicts can still appear at this stage, as personalities clash, egos are threatened, professional jealousies arise, and political maneuvers occur. Even personal issues play a role, as resentment of another's job, salary, status, or life—or dissatisfaction with one's own life or work satisfaction can hinder constructive dialogue. Managers should intervene to ensure that the team focuses on issues and events, not personalities. Blame is not the game; rather the intent is to gain insight.

It is the manager's responsibility to provide objective feedback, bring up difficult issues, involve all team members, and ensure that discussions remain constructive. If the manager was part of the team, or was the team leader, objectivity can be compromised. If this is the case, a facilitator would be helpful.

Although this intervention should occur *after* a group has completed its work, this is not always feasible, as some projects or teams are ongoing. For projects that are continuous, "any natural or imposed milestone (e.g., midpoint, anniversary, completion of major part of a project)" provides an especially apt time to conduct an intervention (Morgeson, 2005, p. 498). Lessons learned should be incorporated into future team projects and activities. The major issues addressed in Phase Three are presented in Table 14.3.

Targeted Interventions

As noted earlier, the "Phased Interventions" address team formation efforts (Phase One), changes to team strategy (Phase Two), and lessons learned (Phase Three). There are, however, opportunities *within these phases of a team's life cycle* to address other types of team challenges. These opportunities, which we call "Targeted Interventions," also help teams learn. They "target" specific incidents, situations, or events, and have a smaller scope than Phased Interventions.

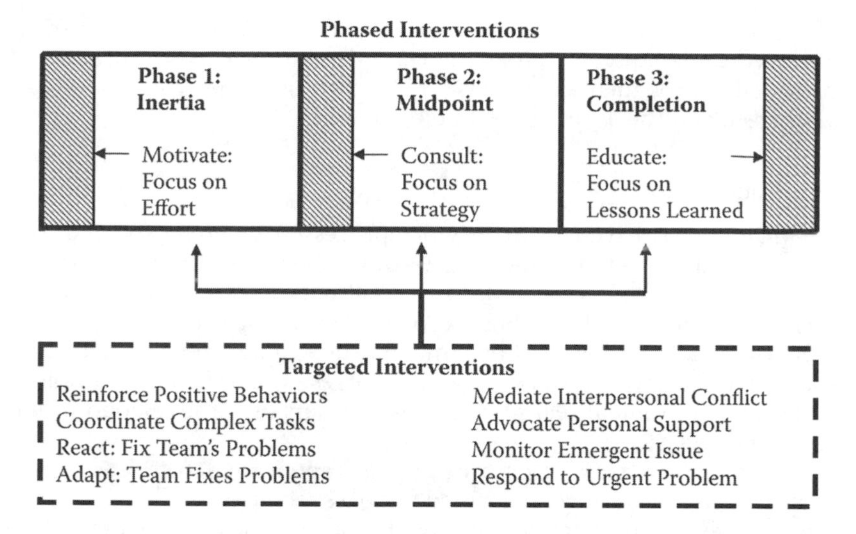

Figure 14.2 Phased and targeted interventions. Shaded boxes depict the best time to conduct a phased intervention.

The eight Targeted Interventions presented here address ineffective team behaviors, coordination challenges, and disruptions to a work routine. They also tackle interpersonal conflict and personal issues, as well as slowly emerging and urgent problems. If not addressed, these issues can derail team performance. Fig. 14.2 depicts the relationship between Targeted and Phased Interventions. The Targeted Interventions described below can be conducted during all three phases of a team's life cycle.

Reinforce and Coordinate

The first Targeted Intervention *reinforces* rarely occurring behaviors deemed beneficial to team effectiveness. The purpose of this intervention is to shape team behavior by increasing desired behaviors, thereby decreasing undesired behaviors. This intervention is relatively simple. The team leader or manager must first identify the behavior, describe the behavior, and then commend the team. This feedback process can be formal or informal, depending on the situation. For example, the manager can simply point out the effectiveness of an action or approach.

The second Targeted Intervention helps a team manage and *coordinate* complex tasks and activities. This is especially effective for inexperienced teams and team members (Hackman & Wageman, 2005). Some teams may become overwhelmed by logistics and require the appropriate tools or techniques to structure their work. For example, a wall chart listing tasks and timelines, or an Excel spreadsheet, helps some groups organize their activities and track deadlines. The type of support provided is dependent on the task, the timeframe, the group members' skill level, and the available technology.

React and Adapt

Some groups have repetitive work processes, whereby specific routines are performed over and over until they become almost automatic (Morgeson & Hoffman, 1999). In these situations, team members perform the same set of functions day after day. These routines, known as "event-cycles," are bounded by time and task, and often occur in production and customer service teams (Morgeson, 2005). For example, a call center fulfillment team, which takes orders over the telephone, has set event-cycles.

Many of these teams lack preexisting responses (Marks, Zaccaro, & Mathieu, 2000), as they are trained to do a specific task. They therefore react poorly to problems or changes. Because these teams cannot adequately respond, discontinuous events *interrupt* the work routine and disrupt team performance (LePine, 2003).

When a repetitive work process is interrupted, two types of interventions are possible. The first intervention, which is *reactive*, ensures that the obstacle is overcome so team members can resume their work. In this situation, the manager intervenes by fixing the problem. The team then continues to perform the same routine. The second type of intervention, which is *adaptive*, helps teams break out of their routine, and adapt new patterns of behavior (LePine, 2003). In this circumstance, team members are encouraged to fix the problem, adapt new behaviors, and develop new work routines.

In contrast, other teams, such as planning teams, rarely have event-cycles, as they engage in unique, nonrepetitive work. In these types of groups (e.g., management planning teams, and academic committees), new ideas are expected and creative approaches valued. Discontinuous occurrences are the *norm* for these teams, as their approach to work is adaptive and changeable, not fixed.

Mediate and Advocate

This pair of Targeted Interventions addresses interpersonal conflict and personal problems. The former issue has the potential to destroy team cohesion and productivity, while the latter issue can render the group member, or even the group, unproductive.

Team conflict is to some extent not only necessary for effective decision-making and team functioning, but extremely important (Weiss & Hughes, 2005). Part of the team's work is the team process, and managers should take care to help, not hinder team functioning. Therefore, the manager should *mediate* team conflicts only if they appear to get out of hand. Managers must be careful not to overreact by interceding too soon.

When the group climate is healthy, most team member behaviors are functional and within acceptable norms. A proliferation of strange or destructive behaviors may be symptomatic of an unhealthy and dysfunctional group.

Managers must be careful to differentiate between *healthy* conflicts, which facilitate team functioning, and *unhealthy* conflicts, which inhibit team functioning and destroy cohesion. If it appears that the conflict is due to a personality clash, and focuses on people rather than issues, an outside mediator or facilitator is recommended. Immediate action must be taken to minimize ill will, and rebuild group communication and cohesion.

We have found that team conflict, communication breakdowns, and performance deficits are often caused by confusion about individual and group goals, roles, and behavioral norms. Therefore, to remedy these problems, the learning intervention should focus on these issues, rather than on interpersonal relationships. In many situations, clarifying the group's goals and roles, and developing a mix of task and goal interdependence (Van der Vegt, Van de Vliert, & Oosterhof, 2003) improves team performance. While group members may enjoy learning about the personality preferences, communication styles and attitudes of themselves and their leader, this feel-good practice does little, if anything, to improve team performance.

According to Hackman (2000), there is no compelling evidence to support the practice of improving team performance through individual interventions. Rather, the intervention must take place at the group level. An exception to this rule is when a team member has personal, family, health, or other problems unrelated to the group or work. These issues can affect performance, and should be discussed in a private setting.

A manager may have to *advocate* for a team member when a personal issue threatens to impedes team performance. Sometimes the group member just needs a supportive manager to listen. In more severe cases, counseling, coaching, referral to human resources, special accommodations, or other responses might be required. Whatever the issue, the manager should not solve the employee's problem, nor act as a therapist, but assist the employee and keep the team on track. If necessary, the individual should leave the team on a temporary or permanent basis.

Monitor and Respond

One of the most difficult interventions involves *mediating* emerging issues, because managers must be able to discern between team process and team problems. In general, when assessing team progress, managers must be careful not to mistakenly diagnose team "problems." Teamwork is a process and must be allowed to unfold. Often, when issues emerge, they provide an opportunity for the team to learn, find a new or creative approach, or overcome the impediment, and in so doing, become stronger and more adept. No matter when an emergent issue arises, managers must wait and let the team address it. An emergent intervention should only take place if the team becomes overwhelmed and needs assistance; if the issue potentially threatens anyone's health, safety, or life; or if there are other negative consequences that must be avoided.

For example, when a group first forms, managers may expect quick results. It may appear as if the team is achieving little, if anything. What the manager views as wasted time and energy, could in actuality be the *best use of the team's time*. Allowance has to be made for team development activities, as the team gels, formulates a plan, works out coordination and communication issues, and engages in other seemingly "invisible" activities. These activities help ensure the successful development and maintenance of teams (Morgeson, Reider, & Campion, 2005).

In contrast to emergent issues, rapidly developing problems have the potential to significantly derail team performance and negatively impact others. The manager should *respond* rather than wait for the group to resolve the matter. If the group lacks the ability (e.g., time, resources, or skills) to rapidly fix a critical issue or problem, the manager must intercede. Whenever possible, the team should be included in the solution, and at the very least, receive periodic progress reports.

Timing of Targeted Interventions

Targeted Interventions are most effective when teams are open to feedback, have the time to focus on the intervention, and can do so without a significant performance deficit. The three phases of a team's life cycle provide many opportunities to conduct Targeted Interventions. However, the beginning of Phase Two is generally not an opportune time to intervene (unless the problem prevents the team from functioning), as teams are focused on strategy and experience extreme pressure to accomplish their goals.

The "work-cycle" provides an ideal time to conduct a Targeted Intervention. A work-cycle refers to the smallest meaningful unit of a team's work performance that is capable of being evaluated. Work-cycles can be thought of as the focal point of the team's mission; they represent the tasks that must be performed to successfully reach their goals. During short work-cycles, when every second matters, such as in the response to an unfolding disaster, there is usually no time to reflect, discuss, correct mistakes, monitor, or coach team members (Devine, 2002). In this situation, team learning and improvement is heavily dependent on post hoc analysis, and an attempted intervention would be destructive to team effectiveness.

It is the long work-cycle, where time is less critical, that provides favorable conditions in which to improve team learning and effectiveness. For example, when the team is engaged in open-ended tasks, such as developing a new process or product, brainstorming ideas, or developing a proposal, the team has the time to attend to the intervention, and benefit from it.

There are some exceptions. For example, *reactive interventions* are designed for repetitive work processes, whether long or short. Conflicts that occur during a short work-cycle and significantly impact performance may require a *mediation intervention*. Managers should *intervene to advocate* for team members whose personal issues prevent them from carrying out their responsibilities, whatever the work-cycle. In most cases, longer work-cycles provide more opportunities for improvement than short work-cycles. The Diagnostic Team Learning Model (see Table 14.4) summarizes the type, purpose and best time to intervene using both Phased Interventions and Targeted Interventions. This model is based on the work of Gersick (1988), Hackman and Wageman (2005), LePine (2003), Morgeson (2005), and the present authors.

TABLE 14.4 Diagnostic Team Learning Model: Phased and Targeted Interventions

Type	Purpose	Best Time to Intervene
Phased Interventions		
Phase One	Motivate Team's Effort	When team first forms
Phase Two	Consult on Strategy	Midpoint of team's work
Phase Three	Educate Using Lessons Learned	When team reaches goal
Targeted Interventions		
Reinforce	Reinforce Positive Behaviors	During a long work-cycle
Coordinate	Coordinate Complex Tasks	During a long work-cycle
React	React—Fix Team's Problem	Disrupted repetitive work process
Adapt	Adapt—Team Fixes Problem	Disrupted repetitive work process
Mediate	Mediate Interpersonal Conflict	When conflict overwhelms team
Advocate	Support for Personal Issue	When personal problems interfere
Monitor	Monitor Emerging Issue	Emerging issue overwhelms team
Respond	Respond to Urgent Problem	Critical issue or problem occurs

Although "groups differ in many ways, what is true for one team may not be true for another" (Devine, 2002, p. 292). The intervention guidelines must be tailored to the team, the task, the timing, and the situation. For example, when a team is performing well, conducting an intervention that focuses on learning may result in a *decline* in short-term performance, as team members direct their attention to *learning* a task, rather than *working* on additional tasks. They must be allowed to complete their work, or risk compromising productivity (Bunderson & Sutcliffe, 2003).

Interventions are not an exact science. They are a business necessity (Wetlaufer, 1994), and must be conducted if the team is to learn and succeed. A team must be ready for coaching (Hackman & Wageman, 2005) and the correct intervention must be conducted. As Morgeson (2005) so aptly observed, an "inappropriate ... intervention will have deleterious effects on team functioning" (p. 498). When a team fails to learn from its mistakes, the process loss can lead to personal disappointment, team failure, and in extreme circumstances, organizational decline.

HELPING TEAMS LEARN

Ideally, team interventions serve as a positive catalyst to promote group learning. As group members become more knowledgeable, and groups more mature, they can assume a greater role in assessing and correcting their own performance. Eventually, teams can learn to effectively intervene on their own behalf. This knowledge and experience base can then transfer to other situations, whether in the present group or the next. As a result, team interventions build individual, group, and organizational capabilities. The team leader, manager, and facilitator play important roles in enhancing team learning, as discussed below.

Team Leader

Effective team leaders cultivate trust, delegate responsibilities (Maruping & Agarwal, 2004), and facilitate group coordination and communication. Team leaders, whether appointed by the manager or chosen by the team, are instrumental in mobilizing teams to take self-correcting measures to address process or work issues. However, team leaders may not be in the best position to impartially observe the team's performance, as they are enmeshed in daily activities (Morgeson, 2005). This lack of distance or even perspective may provide a barrier to effective team monitoring. When the team leader cannot adequately assist the team, the manager should be called in to diagnose and guide team interventions. In those cases where the manager does not have adequate diagnostic skills, or where the manager is also the team leader, a facilitator should assist the team.

Team leaders play a significantly greater role in self-managing teams, whose autonomy over their work processes and decisions often precludes a manager from intervening on the team's behalf. In most cases, a manager should refrain from conducting interventions with self-managing teams, for to do so would negatively impact team functioning (Morgeson, 2005). If an event becomes disruptive, the manager should confer with the team and team leader before intervening.

Team Facilitator

Facilitators assist teams with the group process, and act as a catalyst for team learning and growth. Facilitators help teams diagnose issues and determine appropriate and inappropriate behaviors for each phase of a team's life cycle (Agazarian & Gantt, 2003). They also help teams structure the decision making process, prioritize goals and objectives, and manage conflict.

Many organizations use internal facilitators. When there is low trust, high conflict, or politically sensitive issues, teams require an impartial outsider to mediate issues. In these cases, we recommend the use of an external facilitator so the outcome can be perceived as fair.

Team Manager

In effect, the manager serves as the team's coach. "Coaching is about building teamwork, not about doing the team's work" (Hackman, 2000, p. 167). When managers coach a team, they must let go of the propensity to solve all of the team's issues and do the team's work (Mohrman & Quam, 2000). Their role is to allow the team to learn from their mistakes, and reward and recognize team growth and accomplishments. They help a team learn by listening, observing, and providing feedback, and encouraging the group to work through routine problems and accept new challenges.

Managers may abdicate responsibility to the team, but should not relinquish accountability. Managers are advised to schedule periodic meetings with their teams to monitor group outcomes and processes. The type of task, and the amount of support or oversight needed should determine the frequency of the meetings. For virtual teams, it may be more effective to assess progress on projects and results, rather than focus on activities and time (Cascio, 2000). Preferably, results should be tied to value drivers, which align specific performance goals with organizational objectives (Pfau & Cohen, 2003). As managers cannot simply observe a virtual team at work (Pearlson & Saunders, 2001), they must rely on team leader and member feedback to determine when an intervention is required.

Overall, managers are instrumental in helping groups and their members learn by conducting Phased and Targeted Interventions. As teams mature, the balance shifts; team learning precludes the need for some interventions, and teams begin to conduct many of their own interventions. Yet effective managers stand by, ready to help groups improve their performance.

CONCLUSION

Despite the wide variety of team types, goals, circumstances, and contexts, the timing or need for team corrective actions is remarkably similar (Gersick, 1988). These similarities allow for a planned, systematic approach to team learning and team development. In this chapter, we provide such an approach.

The foregoing describes how groups learn, describes key team competencies, and offers guidelines on the design of suitable learning interventions. These interventions provide opportunities to enhance creativity, growth, and the exchange of knowledge. The Diagnostic Team Learning Model introduced in this chapter depicts three Phased Interventions: inertia, the midpoint, and completion, and specifies appropriate actions to accelerate learning during each phase. The model also includes eight Targeted Interventions that address team behaviors, work processes, group conflict and other issues. By following the recommendations provided, managers can significantly enhance individual, group, and organizational learning and performance.

As individual group members learn, they acquire to the ability to assess and improve team efforts, whether with their present team or with subsequent teams. As teams mature, they become more capable of identifying learning opportunities and conducting many of the interventions themselves. This critical and sustainable transfer of learning brings returns on additional team ventures for years to come.

Knowledge of team processes is useful for understanding how teams learn. Knowledge provides valuable tools, techniques, and actionable recommendations. However, to optimize group outcomes, behaviors must be shaped (Bartram, 2004). *Understanding must lead to action.* The challenge is twofold. Arm teams with the tools to enable learning. Deploy the Diagnostic Team Learning Model to guide teams toward higher goals.

REFERENCES

Agazarian, Y., & Gantt, S. (2003). Phases of group development: Systems-centered hypotheses and their implications for research and practice. *Group Dynamics: Theory, Research, and Practice, 7*(3), 238–252.

Argote, L., Gruenfeld, D., & Naquin, C. (2001). Group learning in organizations. In M. E. Turner (Ed.), *Groups at work: Advances in theory and research* (pp. 369–411). Hillsdale, NJ: Erlbaum.

Bartram, D. (2004). Assessment in organizations. *Applied Psychology: An International Review, 53*(2), 237–259.

Bunderson, J. S., & Sutcliffe, K. M. (2003). Management team learning orientation and business unit performance. *Journal of Applied Psychology, 88*(3), 552–560.

Canon-Bowers, J. A., Tannenbaum, S. I., Salas, E., & Volpe, C. E. (1995). Defining competencies and establishing team training requirements. In R. A. Guzzo, & E. Salas (Eds.), *Team effectiveness and decision making in organizations* (pp. 333–380). San Francisco: Jossey-Bass.

Cascio, W. F. (2000). Managing a virtual workplace. *Academy of Management Executive, 14*(3), 81–90.

Chen, G., Webber, S. S., Bliese, P. D., Mathieu, J. E., Payne, S. C., Born, D. H., et al. (2002). Simultaneous examination of the antecedents and consequences of efficacy beliefs at multiple levels of analysis. *Human Performance, 15*, 381–409.

Devine, D. J. (2002). A review and integration of classification systems relevant to teams in organizations. *Group Dynamics: Theory, Research, and Practice, 6*(4), 291–310.

Ellis, A. P. J., Bell, B. S., Polyhart, R. E., Hollenbeck, J. R., & Ilgen, D. R. (2005). An evaluation of generic teamwork skills training with action teams: Effects on cognitive and skill-based outcomes. *Personnel Psychology, 58*(3), 641–672.

Ford, C., & Sullivan, D. M. (2004). A time for everything: How the timing of novel contributions influences project team outcomes. *Journal of Organizational Behavior, 25*, 279–292.

Gersick, C. J. G. (1988). Time and transition in work teams: Toward a new model of group development. *Academy of Management Journal, 31*(1), 9–41.

Gersick, C. J. G. (1989). Marking time: Predictable transitions in task groups. *Academy of Management Journal, 32*(2), 274–309.

Hackman, J. R. (2000). *Leading teams: Setting the stage for great performances.* Boston: Harvard Business School Press.

Hackman, J. R., & Wageman, R. (2005). A theory of team coaching. *Academy of Management Review, 30*(2), 269–287.

Jehn, K. A., & Mannix, E. (2001). The dynamic nature of conflict: A longitudinal study of intragroup conflict and group performance. *Academy of Management Journal, 44*, 238–251.

Lant, T. K., & Hewlin, P. F. (2002). Information cues and decision making: The effects of learning, momentum, and social comparison in competing teams. *Group & Organization Management, 27*(3), 374–398.

LePine, J. A. (2003). Team adaptation and postchange performance: Effects of team composition in terms of members' cognitive ability and personality. *Journal of Applied Psychology, 88*(1), 27–39.

Marks, M. A., Zaccaro, S. J., & Mathieu, J. E. (2000). Performance implications of leader briefings and team-interaction training for team adaptation to novel environments. *Journal of Applied Psychology, 85*, 971–986.

Maruping, L. M., & Agarwal, R. (2004). Managing team interpersonal processes through technology: A task-technology fit perspective. *Journal of Applied Psychology, 89*(6), 975–990.

Mathieu, J. E., Goodwin, G. F., Heffner, T. S., Salas, E., & Cannon-Bowers, J. A. (2000). The influence of shared mental models on team process and performance. *Journal of Applied Psychology, 85*(2), 273–283.

Mohrman, S. A., & Quam, K. (2000). Consulting to team-based organization: An organizational design and learning approach. *Consulting Psychology Journal: Practice and Research, 52*(1), 20–35.

Morgeson, F. P. (2005). The external leadership of self-managing teams: Intervening in the context of novel and disruptive events. *Journal of Applied Psychology, 90*(3), 497–508.

Morgeson, F. P., & Hoffman, D. A. (1999). The structure and function of collective constructs: Implications for multilevel research and theory development. *Academy of Management Review, 24*, 249–265.

Morgeson, F. P., Reider, M. H., & Campion, M. A. (2005). Selecting individuals in team settings: The importance of social skills, personality characteristics, and teamwork knowledge. *Personnel Psychology, 58*(3), 583–611.

Pearlson, K. E., & Saunders, C. S. (2001). There's no place like home: Managing telecommuting paradoxes. *Academy of Management Executive, 15*(2), 117–128.

Pfau, B. N., & Cohen, S. A. (2003). Aligning human capital practices and employee behavior with shareholder value. *Consulting Psychology Journal: Practice and Research, 55*(3), 169–178.

Robbins, S. P. (2003). *Organizational behavior.* Upper Saddle River, NJ: Prentice Hall.

Sala, F. (2003). Executive blind spots: Discrepancies between self- and other-ratings. *Consulting Psychology Journal: Practice and Research, 55*(4), 222–229.

Sodenkamp, D., Schmidt, K. H., & Kleinbeck, U. (2005). Self-management of work groups through corporate values: From theory to practice. *International Journal of Manpower, 26*(1), 67–79.

Stevens, M. A., & Campion, M. J. (1994). The knowledge, skill, and ability requirements for teamwork: Implications for human resource management. *Journal of Management, 20*, 503–530.

Stevens, M. A., & Campion, M. J. (1999). Staffing work teams: Development and validation of a selection test for teamwork settings. *Journal of Management, 25*, 207–228.

Van der Vegt, G. S., Van de Vliert, E., & Oosterhof, A. (2003). Informational dissimilarity and OCB: The role of interteam interdependence and team identification. *Academy of Management Journal, 46*, 715–727.

Weiss, J., & Hughes, J. (2005). Want collaboration? *Harvard Business Review, 83*(3), 93–101.

Wetlaufer, S. (1994). The team that wasn't. *Harvard Business Review, 72*(6), 22–26.

SECTION

IV

Assessment of Group Learning

This final section of the book addresses how to assess group learning. Stagl, Salas, and Day (chapter 15) describe alternative criteria for group learning—variables that should be measured to reflect the amount and type of learning that has taken place as the group process unfolded. They discuss the emergent nature of group process as distinguished from group outcomes. Most attempts to measure group learning infer measurements from changes in group outcomes rather that through direct measures of learning. They describe ways to measure shared skills (e.g., situational-judgment tests), team knowledge (e.g., asking members to specify the relationships between concepts).

Gessner, Langkamer, and Klimoski (chapter 16) argue for rigorous measures and research designs to evaluate group learning and outcomes. They provide some examples of group-learning interventions and their evaluation. They note that group-learning interventions are instructional strategies used to introduce new behaviors and patterns of interactions. They address how different interventions are appropriate for different situations. Research designs need to take into account the type of group, temporal factors affecting the group's functioning, and reasons why the intervention is being used. In selecting a research design, they outline questions to determine the adequacy of the sample, the group task, the intervention and its delivery, measurement, research design, and statistics.

CHAPTER

15

Assessing Team Learning Outcomes: Improving Team Learning and Performance

KEVIN C. STAGL
Department of Psychology & Institute for Simulation & Training, University of Central Florida

EDUARDO SALAS
Department of Psychology & Institute for Simulation & Training, University of Central Florida

DAVID V. DAY
Lee Kong Chian School of Business, Singapore Management University

During the first half of gestation, hundreds of millions of neurons form an intricate web within a "dynamic learning machine," said Dr. Carla Shatz, Chair of the Neurobiology Department at Harvard Medical

School (http://www.dana.org). The machine, of course, is a baby, and as its neural network mushrooms, its nervous system is busy at work, checking and rechecking established connections. At this early stage, genetics largely dictate the complex connections being made; however, soon after the balance of influence shifts to nurture and via learning, a toddler continuously undergoes changes in the synapses or linkages between neurons. Over time, learning leads to biochemical and possibly genetic changes that, in turn, give rise to memory.

While amazing in its own right, the brain of a child is qualitatively different from that of an adult team member. For example, the frontal lobes, which are critical for organizational tasks, do not reach maturation until year 20. Also, in parts of the adult brain such as the hippocampus, generic stem cells can miraculously morph into new neurons via the process of neurogenesis. The news is not all positive, however, as even the most health-conscious reader has already lost about half of the synaptic pathways that he commanded at age 2. Moreover, the plasticity of these connections erodes over time, making it difficult to forge new pathways in adulthood.

The neurosciences have undoubtedly advanced our understanding about the genetic, cellular, and molecular mechanisms that underlie growth and decline in "dynamic learning machines." Unfortunately, this body of research provides less practical insight at other levels of analysis, such as those pertinent to designing a suite of assessment tools that can be used to measure, track, and manage the learning process and its outcomes in work settings. Yet, assessing team learning and its effects in the workplace is important because the use of teams as a preferred performance arrangement is often predicated upon the assumption that collectives can develop and draw upon a broader array of competencies and response processes to address the complex problems that typify modern operations (Ilgen, Hollenbeck, Johnson, & Jundt, 2005).

When it comes to scaling learning and its effects in the workplace, the theories and findings of the behavioral sciences are paramount. According to this body of science, teams are often used as a preferred performance arrangement to structure work because their members can lean on and learn from one another before, during, and after task-performance episodes. Thus, team learning is both a precursor to, and an outcome of, routine team performance and effectiveness judgments. In fact, research findings suggest that learning is vital to the performance of a wide range of teams, including (a) research and development teams in the energy industry (Van Der Vegt & Bunderson, 2005), (b) enterprise resource planning system implementation teams (Yeh & Chou, 2005), (c) command and control project teams (Ellis et al., 2003), and (d) uninhabited air vehicle control teams (Cooke, Kiekel, & Helm, 2001).

Team learning is also an input and an outcome of adaptive team performance and team adaptation. For example, a recently advanced theory of team adaptation frames team learning as one core component of a recursive cycle of adaptive team performance that ultimately culminates in team adaptation (Burke, Stagl, Salas, Pierce, & Kendall, 2006). Research findings support this theory, suggesting that learning was a precursor to team members developing the strategic knowledge and situation-assessment skills required to effectively engage in change in a complex context (Fritzsche, Stagl, Burke, & Salas, under review). Team learning has also been found to be an important driver of the adaptation of routines that ultimately resulted in the adoption of an innovative technology by cardiac-surgery teams (Edmondson, Bohmer, & Pisano, 2001). Moreover, recent empirical evidence suggests that learning facilitates adaptive performance at both the individual member and team levels of analysis (Chen, Thomas, & Wallace, 2005). For all of these reasons, the team learning process can be considered as an ongoing and dynamic one that takes on varied forms. Thus, our preferred label is of "dynamic learning teams" in discussing the team learning process and how it might be assessed.

This chapter leverages some of the theories, measurement techniques, and lessons learned in the behavioral sciences to advance a set of assessment tools that can be used to measure learning and its outcomes in teams embedded in organizations. We begin by distinguishing the process of learning from its outcomes, discussing its emergent nature, and by bracketing this phenomenon in a hierarchical nomological network. Next, a sample of learning outcomes is presented, often operationalized in terms of learning measures in the workplace. Finally, a set of assessment tools is advanced that can be used by practitioners to measure growth and decline in "dynamic learning teams."

THE PROCESS OF TEAM LEARNING

Team learning is a process whereby knowledge, skills, and affective states are acquired via dyadic interactions and shared experience (Kozlowski & Ilgen, in press). The process of team learning is multifaceted, manifesting in myriad specific behaviors such as (a) information sharing, (b) joint reflection, (c) asking questions, (d) seeking feedback, (e) experimentation, (f) the discussion of errors and differences, (g) testing assumptions, (h) forming new routines, and (i) adjusting strategies (Edmondson, 1999; Edmondson et al., 2001). When team members learn, they experience growth in the form of differentiation from and integration with the systems in which they are embedded. Teams "at higher levels of development are able to use a greater number of knowledge principles to construct their experiences (differentiation), make more interconnections among these principles (integration). This results in a broader perspective" (Day & Lance, 2004, p. 43). Thus, learning activities culminate in an increased capacity to engage in the transition, action, and interpersonal processes that comprise team performance and lead to valued team outcomes (see Marks, Mathieu, & Zaccaro, 2001).

Team learning is a team-level phenomenon that is distinct in nature from both individual (Argyris & Schön, 1978; Halpern, 2004) and organizational learning (Levitt & March, 1988). As a team-level property rooted in individual learning, team learning can emerge in a number of qualitatively different ways (Kozlowski & Klein, 2000). For example, team learning can manifest at the team level via a convergent emergence process, which is a type of *isomorphic composition*. Composition processes describe the coalescence of identical, lower level properties that yield a similar, higher level property. Learning can be conceptualized at the team level via a convergent emergence model if, for example, the three members of a team all engaged in an identical set of learning behaviors (e.g., each member shared equally relevant ideas about implementing a new standard operating procedure).

In most work settings, however, team learning is not a process of synchronized, identical actions; rather, it emerges from the unique configuration or pattern of social interactions and dyadic exchanges that characterize efforts to navigate complex challenges. A *configural compilation* emergence model is based on the assumptions of discontinuity, whereby functionally equivalent, but not identical, phenomena unfold over time to compile across levels (Kozlowski & Klein, 2000). For example, one member of a sales support team may be actively experimenting with various strategies of influence with a senior representative of their team's client. Concurrently, three other team members share information with a second client representative about pricing points. This kind of compatible, yet distinct, set of actions can culminate in common ground about what tactics and services are desirable for use with a given client.

The preceding examples suggest that the process of learning can be conceptualized at the team level in a variety of different ways. Similarly, the outcomes of team learning can manifest at the team level via unique emergence processes. For example, knowledge often becomes embedded in a team as a result of learning activities, but the nature of this knowledge can change depending upon the specific learning behaviors enacted, the communication of information within a team, and/or contextual constraints. In the previous example about isomorphic composition processes, all team members were involved in a joint discussion of a major error that resulted in the establishment of a new standard operating procedure. Because the team possessed shared knowledge of the new policy at the conclusion of the meeting, they held a collected shared mental model (see Klimoski & Mohammed, 1994) of how the new policy would shape future interactions in regards to this issue. Conversely, the previous example about configural compilation processes illustrates how a team might develop a compatible mental model, or unique knowledge held by individual team members that forms a congruent whole (Kozlowski, Gully, Salas, & Cannon-Bowers, 1996; Kozlowski & Klein, 2000).

The most important point raised in the preceding examples of different types of processes that result in team learning is that the elemental contributions of individual-level activities and outcomes have important implications for how team-level phenomena manifest and are ultimately measured in the workplace. Mapping the myriad paths via which team learning and its outcomes can emerge is beyond the scope of this chapter; however, it should be noted that the manner in which a particular emergence process is conceptualized is directly relevant to subsequently selecting elicitation methods, combination rules, and metrics to measure learning and its outcomes at the team level. This speaks to the importance of aligning constructs, models of emergence, metrics, and ultimately, the research designs and analyses that are employed to generate construct validity evidence in support of the interpretations and actions taken on the basis of psychological assessments (Kozlowski & Klein, 2000).

The remainder of this chapter is divided into two sections. The next section introduces a set of outcomes that result from team learning. A discussion of learning outcomes may seem counterintuitive, given that team learning was previously framed in this chapter as a behavioral process. The emphasis on team learning outcomes rather than the actual activities underpinning learning is purposeful, however, as most attempts to measure learning in the workplace infer team learning from changes in team outcomes rather than via the direct measurement of the team learning construct (see Kozlowski & Ilgen, in press). This chapter seeks to incrementally inform current organizational practice, while noting that additional theory building and testing is warranted to continue to develop reliable process measures of team learning.

THE OUTCOMES OF TEAM LEARNING

The unfolding behavioral process of team learning is rarely assessed directly (for exceptions, see Edmondson, 1999; Ellis et al., 2003). Rather, the outcomes of growth are often measured as proxies for team learning (Kozlowski & Ilgen, in press). The specific outcomes of team learning discussed in this chapter were selected for review because they are consistent with theories and frameworks of team performance and development (see Burke, Stagl, Salas, Pierce, & Kendall, 2006; Campion, Medsker, & Higgs, 1993; Dickinson & McIntyre, 1997; Hackman, 1987; Marks et al., 2001; Morgan, Salas, & Glickman, 1994; Salas, Stagl, Burke, & Goodwin, in press; Tannenbaum, Beard, & Salas, 1992). For example, Burke and colleagues' theory of team adaptation proposes a model of the shared cognitive states that emerge from the process of team learning, such as shared mental models, team situation awareness, and psychological safety.

Many of the team learning outcomes discussed in this chapter are also consistent with taxonomic efforts undertaken to classify the outcomes of developmental initiatives (see Kraiger, 2002; Kraiger, Ford, & Salas, 1993). Kraiger and colleagues suggested that learning outcomes can be classified into three broad taxons: (a) affective, (b) behavioral, and (c) cognitive—the *ABCs of Learning.* These taxonomies are grounded in learning research that has been conducted in the field of education since the 1950s (see Bloom, 1956), but also draw heavily upon recent instructional design principles (see Jonassen & Tessmer, 1996). Together, the previously noted theories of team performance and the taxonomies of learning outcomes provide insight into the assessment tools that can be used by stakeholders to measure the outcomes of team learning in the workplace.

Affective Outcomes of Team Learning

The importance of affect in teams is just beginning to garner serious attention as part of a broader "affective revolution" in the behavioral sciences (Ashkanasy, 2003). Theories of team performance and taxonomies of learning outcomes suggest that affective states such as team efficacy, potency, and cohesion are vital to cultivating effectiveness. These affective states emerge as a result of team learning and can serve to drive team performance. For example, *team efficacy* (Lindsley, Brass, & Thomas, 1995)—or *collective efficacy,* when the team is the referent (Bandura, 1997)—has been defined as a shared belief that a team can successfully execute its specific tasks. In contrast to task-specific beliefs, potency has been defined as a set of generalized beliefs about a team's capability to execute across varying tasks and contexts (Guzzo, Yost, Campbell, & Shea, 1993). Cohesion has been defined as the result of the forces acting on team members to remain in the team (Festinger, 1950).

Mounting empirical research findings support the pivotal role of shared affect in teams. For example, meta-analytic findings suggest that team efficacy (P = .41) and potency (P = .37) are moderately related to team performance (Gully, Incalcaterra, Joshi, & Beaubien, 2002). Meta-analytic findings also support the relationships between the three facets of cohesion proposed by Festinger (1950) and team performance (Beal, Cohen, Burke, & McClendon, 2003). Collectively, these meta-analytic findings underscore the importance of emergent affective states for executing team performance and achieving team effectiveness.

Behavioral Outcomes of Team Learning

Team-level, skill-based learning outcomes include a wide range of latent competencies that are enacted as manifest performance processes during task episodes. These interdependent activities comprise the core of teamwork. As teams recursively display these behavioral processes and draw upon and update shared emergent cognitive states, team performance compiles over time (Stagl, Salas, & Burke, 2006). Teams can learn to more effectively coordinate member exchanges, distribute their workload, solve social problems, and make decisions (Campbell & Kuncell, 2002). Teams can also learn to construct higher quality solutions to challenges (Marshall-Mies et al., 2000), formulate and execute plans more effectively (Burke, Stagl, Salas, et al., in press), regulate their attention and effort (DeShon, Kozlowski, Schmidt, Milner, & Wiechmann, 2004), collaborate to process information (Ellis & Bell, 2005), and enhance their leadership capacity (Day, Gronn, & Salas, 2004). These team skills are acquired, compiled, automatized, and tuned (Kraiger, 2002). For example, team leaders provide expert coaching from which teams learn to coordinate their actions (Burke, Stagl, Klein, Goodwin, Salas, & Halpin, 2006; Stagl, Salas, & Burke, 2006).

Cognitive Outcomes of Team Learning

The third class of outcomes that result from team learning are cognitive in nature. Teams can acquire declarative knowledge (e.g., information about *what*), procedural knowledge (e.g., information about *how*), and strategic or tacit knowledge (e.g., information about *why* and *when*; Anderson, 1985). When this knowledge becomes shared via sensemaking and communication, teams can develop clusters of knowledge structures such as team mental models and transactive memory systems. Team mental models refer to team member knowledge that is either shared (Cannon-Bowers, Salas, & Converse, 1993) or compatible (Kozlowski, Gully, McHugh, Salas, & Cannon-Bowers, 1996). Conversely, transactive memory systems refer to knowledge of the distribution of information within teams (e.g., *who* knows *what;* Wegner, 1995).

These cognitive structures provide a common conceptual framework that enables teams to perceive, represent, interpret, and respond to dynamic environments in a synchronized, adaptive fashion (Endsley & Pearce, 2001). Teams acquire these cognitive reservoirs from their ongoing experiences. Of note, however, shared cognitive states can also be developed via a leader's efforts to synchronize task and learning cycles (Kozlowski, Gully, Salas, & Cannon-Bowers, 1996) and by providing verbal briefings (Marks, Zaccaro, & Mathieu, 2000; Smith-Jentsch, Zeisig, Acton, & McPherson, 1998). Research evidence also suggests that team mental models can be developed via team-interaction training (Marks et al., 2000), cross training (Marks, Sabella, Burke, & Zaccaro, 2002), and team self-correction training (Blickensderfer, Cannon-Bowers, & Salas, 1998).

ASSESSMENT OF TEAM LEARNING

The previous section introduced the *ABCs of Learning,* highlighting some of the affective, behavioral, and cognitive outcomes that are often measured as proxies of team learning. This section introduces basic measurement concepts in order to set the stage to advance a set of assessment tools that can be used to scale the outcomes of team learning in the workplace. Although the discussion is predominantly concerned with assessment tools that can scale the proximal effects of learning (e.g., questionnaires, paired comparisons), some of the techniques (e.g., behavioral anchored rating scales) advanced in the following section can also be designed and adopted to capture the actual behavioral activities that are indicative of the team learning construct itself. When feasible, practitioners are advised to measure both learning activities and the outcomes of learning in order to better gauge team development.

Measurement and Scaling

Determining whether a team has developed affective, behavioral, and cognitive outcomes as a result of its learning activities is a matter of measurement. As noted by Nunnally and Bernstein (1994), "measurement consists of rules for assigning symbols to objects so as to (a) represent quantities of attributes numerically (scaling) or (b) define whether the objects fall in the same or different categories with respect to a given attribute (classification)" (p. 3). The concern in this chapter is with scaling the learning outcomes of teams. Regardless of whether classical or modern psychometric theory is applied to scale team learning outcomes, team members or other stakeholders with pertinent information about the team are asked to provide their judgments (e.g., when there is a correct response) or sentiments (e.g., when measuring attitudes, values). Member responses are then combined in some manner to reflect team-level outcomes.

The major requirement in scaling team outcomes is that alternative scalings be monotonically related to one another, such that different scalings rank order teams in the same way. In order to meet this requirement, practitioners are advised to develop a scaling model or internally consistent plan that specifies how to construct and apply an assessment tool. A scaling model makes testable predictions about a set of observations that are used to generate one or more dimensions (e.g., cohesion, psychological safety). Specifically, a scaling model establishes a hypothesis suggesting that if a given scale is working, subsequent data should support it. If accumulated observations fit a scaling model (e.g., transitivity), the model accurately determines the scale value that should be assigned to each observation.

Four types of psychometric models can be used to scale people, and thereby, the learning outcomes, of teams: (a) nonmonotone deterministic models, (b) nonmonotone probabilistic models, (c) monotone probabilistic models with specified distribution forms, and (d) monotone probabilistic models with unspecified distribution forms (Nunnally & Bernstein, 1994). In practice, the first two types of models are infrequently used. Moreover, while monotone probabilistic models, which assume ogival item trace lines or item characteristic curves serve as the basis for modern psychometric theory (e.g., item response theory), they are also seldom found in the workplace. These first three types of models are therefore only briefly introduced in this chapter, and the emphasis is placed on the use of monotone probabilistic models with unspecified distribution forms for scaling the learning outcomes of teams.

Nonmonotone deterministic models are characterized by trace lines that are step functions because they assume there is no error. For example, Guttman scales consisting of dichotomously scored items assume that if a person passes an item with a given difficulty, then that person will pass all easier items on the measure. Likewise, if a person fails an item of a given difficulty, then that person will fail all of the more difficult items presented. Similarly, these models assume that if an item is passed by a person with a given level of ability, then that item will also be passed by all other individuals with higher ability. Unfortunately, infinite discrimination at the threshold is an assumption rooted in psychophysics and is much less realistic under the conditions in which measurement is typically conducted in the workplace.

Nonmonotone probabilistic models are similar to nonmonotone deterministic models in that both types of models assume that trace lines change slope from positive to negative or from negative to positive. In contrast to deterministic models, however, all probabilistic models assume that trace lines are not step functions (Nunnally & Bernstein, 1994). Specifically, nonmonotone probabilistic models assume item curves in the shape of the normal distribution. These models have been used to develop Thurstone scales of attitudes. In general, however, nonmonotone items are difficult to construct, as they are often characterized by double-barreled item stems (Nunnally & Bernstein, 1994). Moreover, in particular, Thurstone scales are tricky to design because raters often have difficulty distancing themselves from their own beliefs and attitudes when rating the favorability of these items during development (Nunnally & Bernstein, 1994).

Monotone probabilistic models with specified distribution forms make assumptions about the fit of item trace lines to specific statistical functions (Nunnally & Bernstein, 1994). As noted above, those models that assume ogival trace lines are increasingly prevalent as they provide the basis for modern psychometrics. Perhaps the defining characteristic of most of these models is their implication for calculating scale scores. When using monotone probabilistic models with ogive item characteristic curves scale scores are calculated from the pattern of responses instead of the sum of the number of items answered correctly (e.g., in the alpha direction). Despite the convenient mathematical properties that characterize these models, the conventional approach of summing items answered in the alpha direction remains the simplest model for scaling people or the learning outcomes of teams, as discussed next (Nunnally & Bernstein,1994).

As noted, *monotone probabilistic models with unspecified distribution forms* such as the linear model are the most popular means of constructing assessment tools. The linear, centroid, or summative model is so labeled because scale scores are a function of the linear combination or sum of item responses (Nunnally & Bernstein, 1994). Given monotonic item trace lines and a unitary attribute as the focus of measurement, the linear model proves versatile, as it can be used to guide the construction of weighted and unweighted multicategory and dichotomous items. The intuitive appeal and widespread applicability of the linear model makes a compelling case for use when scaling the learning outcomes of teams. For example, the linear model can be used as a basis for constructing Likert scales to measure shared affect (e.g., cohesion), or when designing behaviorally anchored rating scales for measuring team processes (e.g., coordination). The linear model underpins the multi-item assessment tools that are discussed in this chapter.

Measuring Shared Affect

One set of outcomes that arises from the learning activities in which teams engage is affective in nature. Shared affective states such as trust, collective orientation, potency, collective efficacy, and cohesion originate in the individual level affect of team members and via communication, shared experience, and dyadic interactions, manifest as collective phenomena that can be scaled as outcomes of team learning. A growing base of empirical evidence supports the importance of affective states such as collective efficacy beliefs to cultivating team effectiveness (e.g., Campion et al., 1993; Campion, Papper, & Medsker, 1996; Gibson, 1999; Gully et al., 2002; Lindsley, Mathieu, Heffner, & Brass, 1994).

In practice, affective outcomes are often measured via the use of inventories and questionnaires that ask respondents to make ratings about their (dis)agreement to a set of statements presented on a Likert scale (Gregorich, Helmreich, & Wilhelm, 1990). The items of these scales often reference the team as the unit of interest, and given sufficient perceptual agreement, individual responses are aggregated to the team level. Conversely, a consensus approach involves a single response to an item from the entire team that has been determined via joint discussion. A consensus approach is a less common approach to measuring affective states (Gully et al., 2002), but evidence suggests that consensus ratings explain significantly greater variance in team effectiveness than aggregate indices (Kirkman, Tesluk, & Rosen, 2001).

Although Kirkman et al. (2001) research findings suggested that a consensus approach may be a viable alternative to aggregating individual data when measuring team-level phenomena, there are several caveats to consider before applying this technique. For example, a consensus approach to measuring team-level constructs is subject to the problems inherent to most team decisions such as groupthink, polarization, and status differences that lead to conversation domination and subordinate conformity. Moreover, teams and their employers lose time and money when they are asked to assemble for nonperformance-related activities. Fortunately, research on the decision making of distributed teams suggests that many of these issues can be largely circumvented by encouraging anonymous contributions (Stagl, Salas, Rosen, Priest, Burke, & Goodwin, in press). Current information technologies such as IBM's Lotus Workplace Team Collaboration and Microsoft's Team Collaboration Tool combine instant messaging, presence awareness, discussion forums, and web conferencing, allowing for anonymous real time decision making by members evaluating team-level phenomena.

The widespread use of inventories and questionnaires suggests some additional commentary on these tools may be valuable. The use of self-report measures can be traced back 150 years to Sir Francis Galton's investigations of mental imagery. Galton believed that character, conceptualized as a respondent's inner world of perception and emotion, was a definite and durable phenomenon that could be measured. To this end, Galton developed standardized questionnaires. A measure is standardized to the extent it has clear rules for assigning numbers to attributes, is practical to apply, does not demand extensive skill to administer, and produces results that are not administrator specific (Nunnally & Bernstein, 1994). Standardized assessment tools are advantageous, as they facilitate observation, replication, and generalization; provide finer distinctions than those afforded by subjective judgments; permit the use of more powerful analytics; and provide an economical means of assessing large numbers of respondents (Nunnally & Bernstein, 1994). Today, self-report inventories and questionnaires are the most widely used form of assessment (Hough & Ones, 2001). In fact, their abundance prompted Cattell (1963) to characterize these diagnostic devices as the "rabbits" of the psychometric world.

A variety of inventories, questionnaires, and surveys (e.g., checklists, scaled response, multiple choice / forced choice) can be utilized to assess attitudes (Guion, 1998). For example, checklists are comprised of a list of words or phrases that respondents check off as applicable. Scaled-response inventories are characterized by three or more options that are arranged in an ordered sequence. Many of the instruments for scaling shared affective states include a five point scale to which respondents rate whether they (a) "strongly disagree," "disagree," "cannot say," "agree," or "strongly agree" that a given item stem is descriptive of their own internal states or those of their team. A third type of inventory utilizes a multiple/forced-choice approach. A *forced-choice approach* is characterized by multiple response options from which respondents must chose which stimuli is most descriptive and which is least descriptive.

Although self-report inventories and questionnaires provide a number of advantages, their use comes with a few notable caveats. For instance, the use of self-report measures assumes that respondents have the awareness to accurately assess their own or their team's attributes, which is sometimes a questionable assumption. Inventories and questionnaires are also subject to scrutiny because of an inherent vulnerability to contrived response protocols. A response set is a tendency to adopt a certain style in responding to stimuli (Guion, 1998). Self-report inventories and questionnaires are susceptible to a number of possible response sets, including socially desirable responding and acquiescence (Kurtz & Parrish, 2001). This is an important issue, because as noted by Guion (1998): "A response set contributing variance to scores intended for inferences about something else is a validity-reducing contaminant" (p. 596).

A social-desirability response set is characterized by intentional distortion (e.g., faking) on the part of respondents in order to look good to the administrators or other stakeholders making decisions based in part on the information provided by the administration of a given measure. Examining this issue, Messick (1960) identified nine distinct social-desirability factors apparent in one commonly used self-report instrument. Self-report scales are particularly subject to social-desirability response sets because they are often comprised of items that are translucent to respondents with regards to which option is organizationally valued. Thus, when encountering the item stem, "How confident do you feel that your team is able to recognize complex problems?" those respondents adopting a social-desirability response set will be more likely to answer "extremely confident" rather than admitting that they are "somewhat confident." Moreover, faking will be more likely to occur when respondents hold the expectation that distortion is instrumental in achieving valued outcomes, as would be the case when a team is assessed at the conclusion of certification training conducted to shape a team's attitudes about the provision of exemplary customer service. These issues warrant consideration when measuring shared affect.

Measuring Shared Skills

The second set of outcomes that compile from team learning are shared behavioral and cognitive skills. Latent team skills are enacted episodically as performance processes during the transformation of raw materials to goods and services. Teams can learn to more effectively coordinate their exchanges, cooperate when dynamically allocating their resources, and communicate to make better decisions as they navigate their internal and external challenges (Campbell & Kuncell, 2002; Kozlowski & Bell, 2003; Salas et al., 2004). Team skills that result from learning are often assessed during performance tests, which typically include supervisor, peer, subject-matter expert, or administrator ratings. Of note, however, situational judgment tests (SJTs) given as a type of performance test require respondents to identify what they should or would do in response to a posed scenario, rather than actually acting out a chosen response.

Performance tests encapsulate a wide range of stimuli that (a) can be cognitive or noncognitive in nature, (b) require paper and pencil or hands on responses, and (c) use a forced choice or constructed response format (Guion, 1998). Even though a wide range of performance tests exist, all of these devices generally simulate key aspects of a work situation, such as contextual forces and complex problems to be solved. Performance tests are typically used to measure proficiency, skill, or understanding. Although prediction is implied, the emphasis is placed on current rather than future performance (Cascio, 1998). These assessment tools are therefore most often associated with capturing samples of behavior (e.g., extant examples) rather than signs of behavior (e.g., indicators of different behavioral constructs).

Historically speaking, performance tests were one of the earliest measurement strategies adopted to assess skills, as seen by Münsterberg's (1912) use of these tools to select trolley-car operators almost a century ago. Not long after, Max Simoneit pioneered the use of performance tests to help the German army select officers during World War II, a practice that was quickly benchmarked by both Britain's War Office Selection Board and in the United States by the Office of Strategic Services (OSS; Highhouse, 2002). For example, the OSS used the Construction Test to select spies and saboteurs.

The approach adopted by the OSS and other governmental organizations exemplified how situational exercises could be designed to prompt individual assesses, or even entire teams, to display their skills. Once enacted, assessors would form overall impressions about a candidate's capabilities. Specifically, assessors captured relevant information, recorded it in some manner, and recalled it later to form an impression about a candidate. Unfortunately, the process of attention, encoding, recalling, and integrating information in order to form judgments is susceptible to a number of random and systematic errors (Guion, 1998). For example, ratings are subject to distributional errors in mean levels (e.g., leniency, severity) and variance (e.g., restriction of range). Furthermore, ratings are subject to a host of other errors such as illusory halo and similar-to-me error. In retrospect, the approach employed in these early assessment centers was holistic by design and afforded little attention to psychometric concerns. The assessment process was characterized by (a) an active orientation whereby assesses acted out their responses to contrived scenarios; (b) a limited concern for psychometric issues, as instruments were often modified on the fly to test a particular assessor's hunches about a given candidate; and (c) a scoring process that was heavily dependent upon the idiosyncrasies inherent to the intuitive clinical judgment of a given assessor or assessment team (Highhouse, 2002).

By the 1960s, personnel psychologists had successfully lobbied both the public and private sectors of the value of testing in the workplace. It was during this historical period that the military's initial approach to performance assessment via the use of situational tests was revamped by government scientists and their private-sector colleagues. This massive effort was undertaken to address some of the serious psychometric concerns raised about performance testing as typified by the holistic assessment process utilized by the OSS. Modifications made to situational tests emphasized standardization of testing conditions and scoring procedures (Flanagan, 1954). Rater errors were reduced via the use of error-resistant forms, rater error training, and frame-of-reference training. For example, assessor ratings were enhanced via the use of checklists of behavior to make performance ratings. Moreover, the use of graphic rating scales (Meister, 1985), behavioral-anchored rating scales (Smith & Kendall, 1963), and behavioral-observation scales (Tziner, Joanis, & Murphy, 2000) helped reduce errors because they served to minimize assessor idiosyncrasies, thereby making ratings more standardized and increasing cross-rate comparability. Furthermore, these new rating-scale formats were easy to understand and use in fluid settings and thereby contributed to their widespread acceptance, frequent application, and timely completion.

Today, many governments and their affiliated industries used performance tests to assess teams as part of training, development, and certification initiatives (e.g., Baker, Prince, Shrestha, Oser, & Salas, 1993; Bell, 1995; Bowers, Salas, Prince, & Brannick, 1992; Jentsch & Bowers, 1998; Smith-Jentsch, Salas, & Baker, 1996). Although performance tests have proven most useful for assessing team skills that have compiled from learning activities, research has continued to examine a wide range of issues inherent to the application of these assessment tools. For example, research has been undertaken to investigate the optimal fidelity required of performance tests (Marks, 2000). The evidence that has accumulated from this research suggests that the physical fidelity of an environment created within a simulation is of secondary concern relative to psychological reality or fidelity. Performance tests that simulate operational settings should be designed to trigger similar psychological processes as those experienced in the work context. Specifically, Marks' (2000) research suggested that the fidelity of a performance test should match the level of complexity typically experienced by an individual or team during their performance episodes. Thus, in some circumstances, the use of high-fidelity performance tests to provide an immersive experience may be warranted. Of note, however, as workers increasingly interact via e-mail and voicemail, lower fidelity simulations that only require written or oral responses may sufficiently mirror the cognitive processes that actually occur during work. These findings suggest that lower fidelity, computer-based performance tests may be a cost-effective and psychometrically sound solution for organizations seeking to assess team skills.

A lower fidelity alternative to hands on performance tests for assessing team skills is offered by situational judgment tests (SJTs; see Weekley & Ployhart, 2006). SJTs are lower fidelity assessment tools that are comprised of item stems, response instructions, standardization rules, and when a forced-choice format is used, a set of response alternatives. SJTs can be administered via paper-and-pencil, video, or orally. According to Fritzsche, Stagl, Salas, and Burke (2006), the use of SJTs is predicated upon the assumption that those respondents: "[W]ho can identify more effective and less effective responses to job-related situations, have greater job-relevant knowledge or better job-related judgment and reasoning skills and are thus expected to have higher levels of job performance than those who are less able to identify appropriate responses to job-related situations" (p. 301).

SJTs are quite versatile, as they can be used to assess a wide range of team skills that result from team learning, including crew resource-management skills (Hedge, Borman, & Hanson, 1996), judgment skills (Hunter, 2003), problem-solving skills (Motowidlo, Dunnette, & Carter, 1990), decision-making skills (Stagl, Fritzsche, Salas, Wooten, & Burke, under review), and interpersonal skills (Olson-Buchanan et al., 1998). One example of a paper-and-pencil-based SJT is the Tacit Knowledge for Military Leadership (TKML; Sternberg et al., 2000). Sternberg et al. developed the TKML as a low-fidelity simulation to measure the tacit knowledge underlying practical intelligence. Although the TKML was designed to measure knowledge, rather than skill per se, Sternberg et al. suggested that SJTs designed with an extended case study format can be utilized to assess the specific cognitive and decision making skills inherent to problem formulation and solution generation (Cianciolo, Antonakis, & Sternberg, 2004). An extended case-study exercise incorporates (a) a detailed overview, (b) additional documentation, and (c) a constructed response format. Thus, an SJT with an extended case-study format may provide a more cost-effective means of assessing team skills than more expensive and time-consuming, hands-on performance tests.

Measuring Team Knowledge

The third set of team-level outcomes that emanate from team learning are shared cognitive structures such as team mental models. Although team mental models manifest in a variety of specific forms (e.g., task, equipment, team member, team interaction), each of these models serves the similar purpose of facilitating the organization and acquisition of information in a task domain, which, in turn, helps team members predict the need for and subsequently execute coordinated actions (Cannon-Bowers et al., 1993). Thus, team knowledge provides an infrastructure for enacting episodic team processes (Mathieu & Schulze, in press).

The assessment of team mental models is concerned with both the degree of convergence amongst team members on the components of a given model and the relationships between these components (Mohammed, Klimoski, & Rentsch, 2000). With regard to assessment, the first of these two issues is concerned with *elicitation*, or techniques that are used to determine the content of a team mental model (Klimoski & Mohammed, 1994). The second issue is concerned with *representation*, or tools that can be used to illuminate the relationships between components. This subsection includes a discussion of pairwise relatedness ratings as an elicitation technique and the use of Pathfinder and UNICET as tools for representing data obtained from these similarity ratings. We also discuss the use of card sorting and concept mapping as approaches that combine elicitation and representation.

The underlying assumption of pairwise-relatedness ratings for scaling team learning outcomes is that the closer raters perceive two concepts to be, the closer those concepts are in their knowledge structures (Kraiger et al., 1993). Regarding this issue, Thurstone's Law of Comparative Judgments provides a basis for deriving an interval level index of this ordinal scaling approach. The process consists of presenting each rater with all possible pairs of stimuli. Raters are then asked whether stimulus A is similar to stimulus B on some attribute in question. Observed ratings are then analyzed to determine the proportion of times stimulus A is deemed similar to stimulus B, and so forth. These proportions are converted to z-scores to form a matrix of normal deviate units. Matrix entries are then summed and averaged for each column in order to reduce measurement error. The lowest average is subtracted from itself and the remaining averages to obtain an interval level scaling of ordinal data obtained from paired comparisons.

In practice, relatedness ratings are often postprocessed via the use of statistical software programs such as Pathfinder Associate Networks (Schvaneveldt, 1990). For example, the Pathfinder algorithm has been utilized to scale the knowledge structure coherence of trainees exposed to mastery or performance-training goals (see Kozlowski et al., 2001). Pathfinder converts paired comparisons to nodes (e.g., concepts) and node linkages (e.g., relations between concepts) in order to assess cognitive structure. A related algorithm, UNICET, has also been utilized to scale team mental models (see Mathieu, Heffner, Goodwin, Cannon-Bowers, & Salas, 2005; Mathieu, Heffner, Goodwin, Salas, & Cannon-Bowers, 2000). UNICET provides indices of both centrality and convergence of mental models via the use of QAP correlations between two matrices (Borgatti, Everett, & Freeman, 1992).

Two other techniques for scaling team mental models are card sorting and concept mapping. The card-sorting approach requires raters to cluster concept cards together based on their perceived similarities and differences. When concept mapping is used, respondents are asked to specify the relationships between concepts. Concepts maps are comprised of the previously described nodes and links along with the additional component of propositions, which describe the meaning of the linkage between two nodes. A recently developed software tool, TPL-KATS, can be used to automatically administer and score both card sorts and concept maps (Hoeft et al., 2002). TPL-KATS thus provides a relatively quick and cost-efficient means of scaling a team's mental models, as well as comparing these knowledge structures to an expert's models.

CONCLUSION

The use of teams as a preferred performance arrangement is increasingly prevalent in the workplace. Teams are a popular means of structuring work because their members can lean on and learn from one another during performance episodes. In fact, an accumulating base of research findings suggest learning is vital to routine and adaptive team performance. Teams that learn, operate from a broader perspective and therefore are more likely to be effective at enacting the processes comprising performance episodes. Thus, in order to enhance team effectiveness, it is first necessary to cultivate a clear understanding of both how teams learn and the effects of these activities. To this end, this chapter leveraged some of the theories, measurement methods, and lessons learned in the behavioral sciences to define team learning and advance a set of assessment tools that can be used to measure team learning and its outcomes in the workplace.

Throughout this chapter, we have noted that team learning is a multifaceted process that unfolds over time from the cognitive and behavioral activities undertaken by team members as individuals, in dyads, and collectively. This speaks to the multilevel nature of team learning, it is a team-level property rooted in individual action that emerges in qualitatively different ways. Given the circumstances that characterize typical work settings, team learning usually compiles from a unique pattern of social interactions and exchanges, or via a configural compilation process. This is an important point, because the nature of the emergence process bears upon the methods that can be used to elicit, combine, and measure learning and its outcomes in teams.

The process of team learning is often measured via the use of proximal proxies, or outcome operationalizations. More specifically, in order to gauge team learning, affective, behavioral, and cognitive outcomes, or the *ABCs of Learning*, are typically measured. When the opportunity and resources are available, we suggest that practitioners should make every effort to measure both the core learning activities and the outcomes of these actions in order to better triangulate team development. Ascertaining whether a given team has developed the affective, behavioral, and/or cognitive outcomes that flow from learning involves measurement. Some basic concepts in measurement were reviewed in order to advance a set of assessment tools built upon the linear model that can be used to scale the outcomes of team learning in the workplace. Inventories, questionnaires, surveys, performance tests, situational-judgment tests, pairwise-relatedness ratings, card sorts, and concept maps were all discussed as appropriate techniques to measure phenomena under specific conditions. We hope that the advanced set of assessment tools will help practitioners measure growth and decline in "dynamic learning teams."

REFERENCES

Anderson, J. P. (1985). *Cognitive psychology and its implications* (2nd ed.). New York: Freeman.

Argyris, C., & Schon, D. (1978). *Organizational learning: A theory of action perspective.* Reading, MA: Addison-Wesley.

Ashkanasy, N. M. (2003). Emotions in organizations: A multilevel perspective. In F. Dansereau, & F. J. Yammarino (Eds.), *Research in multi-level issues: Vol. 2: Multi-level issues in organizational behavior and strategy* (pp. 9–54). Oxford, U.K.: Elsevier Science.

Baker, D. P., Prince, C., Shrestha, L., Oser, R., & Salas, E. (1993). Aviation computer games for crew resource management training. *The International Journal of Aviation Psychology, 3,* 143–156.

Bandura, A. (1997). *Self-efficacy: The exercise of control.* New York: W.H. Freeman.

Beal, D. J., Cohen, R. R., Burke, M. J., & McClendon, C. L. (2003). Cohesion and performance in groups: A meta-analytic clarification of construct relations. *Journal of Applied Psychology, 88,* 989–1004.

Bell, H. H. (1995). The engineering of a training network. *Proceedings of the Human Factors and Ergonomics Society 39th Annual Meeting* (pp. 1311–1315). Santa Monica, CA: Human Factors and Ergonomics Society.

Blickensderfer, E., Cannon-Bowers, J. A., & Salas, E. (1998). Cross-training and team performance. In J. A. Cannon-Bowers, & E. Salas (Eds.), *Making decisions under stress: Implications for individual and team training* (pp. 299–311). Washington, DC: APA.

Bloom, B. S. (1956). Taxonomy of educational objectives handbook 1: Cognitive domain. New York: Longman, Green, & Co.

Borgatti, S. P., Everett, M. G., & Freeman, L. C. (1992). Ucinet IV: Network analysis software. *Connections, 15,* 12–15.

Bowers, C. A., Salas, E., Prince, C., & Brannick, M. (1992). Games teams play: A method for investigating team coordination and performance. *Behavior Research Methods, Instruments, & Computers, 24,* 503–506.

Burke, C. S., Stagl, K. C., Klein, C., Goodwin, G. F., Salas, E., & Halpin, S. (2006). What types of leader behaviors are functional in teams?: A meta-analytic integration. *Leadership Quarterly.*

Burke, C. S., Stagl, K. C., Salas, E., Pierce, L., & Kendall, D. (2006). Understanding team adaptation: A conceptual analysis and model. *Journal of Applied Psychology.*

Campbell, J. P., & Kuncel, N. R. (2002). Individual and team training. In N. Anderson, D. S. Ones, H. K. Sinangil, & C. Viswesvaran (Eds.), *Handbook of industrial, work, and organizational psychology* (pp. 272–312). London: Sage.

Campion, M. A., Medsker, G. J., & Higgs, A. C. (1993). Relations between work group characteristics and effectiveness: Implications for designing effective work groups. *Personnel Psychology, 46,* 823–850.

Campion, M. A., Papper, E. M., & Medsker, G. J. (1996). Relations between work team characteristics and effectiveness: A replication and extension. *Personnel Psychology, 49,* 429–452.

Cannon-Bowers, Salas, E., & Converse, S. A. (1993). Shared mental models in expert team decision making. In N. J. Castellan, Jr. (Ed.), *Current issues in individual and group decision making* (pp. 221–246). Hillsdale, NJ: Lawrence Erlbaum Associates.
Cascio, W. F. (1998). *Applied psychology in human resource management.* Upper Saddle River, NJ: Prentice Hall
Cattell, R. B. (1963). Theory of fluid and crystallized intelligence: A critical experiment. *Journal of Educational Psychology, 54,* 1–22.
Chen, G., Thomas, B., & Wallace, J. C. (2005). A multilevel examination of the relationships among training outcomes, mediating regulatory processes, and adaptive performance. *Journal of Applied Psychology, 90,* 827–841.
Cianciolo, A. T., Antonakis, J., & Sternberg, R. J. (2004). Practical intelligence and leadership: Using experience as a mentor. In D. Day, S. J. Zaccaro, & S. M. Halpin (Eds.), *Leader development for transforming organizations.* Mahwah, NJ: Lawrence Erlbaum Associates.
Cooke, N. J., Kiekel, P. A., & Helm, E. (2001). Measuring team knowledge during skill acquisition of a complex task. *International Journal of Cognitive Ergonomics: Special Section on Knowledge Acquisition, 5,* 297–315.
Day, D. V., Gronn, P., & Salas, E. (2004). Leadership capacity in teams. *The Leadership Quarterly, 15,* 857–880.
Day, D., & Lance, C. (2004). Understanding the development of leadership complexity through latent growth modeling. In D. Day, S. J. Zaccaro, & S. M. Halpin (Eds.), *Leader development for transforming organizations.* Mahwah, NJ: Lawrence Erlbaum Associates.
DeShon, R. P., Kozlowski, S. W. J., Schmidt, A. M., Milner, K. R., & Wiechmann, D. (2004). A multiple goal, multilevel model of feedback effects on the regulation of individual and team performance in training. *Journal of Applied Psychology, 89,* 1035–56.
Dickinson, T. L., & McIntyre, R. M. (1997). A conceptual framework for team measurement. In M. T. Brannick, E. Salas, & C. Prince (Eds.), *Team performance and measurement: Theory, methods, and applications* (pp. 19–43). Mahwah, NJ: Lawrence Erlbaum Associates.
Edmondson, A. C. (1999). Psychological safety and learning behavior in work teams. *Administrative Science Quarterly, 44*(2), 350–383.
Edmondson, A. C., Bohmer, R. M., & Pisano, G. P. (2001). Disrupted routines: Team learning and new technology implementation in hospitals. *Administrative Science Quarterly, 46*(4), 685–716.
Ellis, A. P. J., & Bell, B. S. (2005). Capacity, collaboration, and commonality: A framework for understanding team learning. In L. L. Neider, & C. A. Schriesheim (Eds.), *Understanding teams: A volume in research management* (pp. 1–25). Greenwich, CT: Information Age.
Ellis, A. P. J., Hollenbeck, J. R., Ilgen, D. R., Porter, C. O., West, B. J., & Moon, H. (2003). Team learning: Collectively connecting the dots. *Journal of Applied Psychology, 88*(5), 821–835.
Endsley, M. D., & Pearce, C. L. (2001). Shared cognition in top management teams: Implications for new venture performance. *Journal of Organizational Behavior, 22,* 145–160.
Festinger, L. (1950). Informal social communication. *Psychological Review, 57,* 271–282.

Flanagan, J. C. (1954). The critical incident technique. *Psychological Bulletin, 4,* 327–359.

Fritzsche, B. A., Stagl, K. C., Burke, C. S., & Salas, E. (under review). Developing adaptability and adaptive performance: The benefits of active learning. *Journal of Applied Psychology.*

Fritzsche, B. A., Stagl, K. C., Salas, E., & Burke, C. S. (2006). Enhancing the design, delivery, and evaluation of scenario-based training: Can situational judgment tests contribute? In J. A. Weekley, & R. E. Ployhart (Eds.), *Situational judgment tests.* Mahwah, NJ: Lawrence Erlbaum Associates.

Gibson, C. B. (1999). Do they do what they believe they can? Group efficacy and group effectiveness across tasks and cultures. *Academy of Management Journal, 42,* 138–152.

Gregorich, S. E., Helmreich, R. L., & Wilhelm, J. A. (1990). The structure of cockpit management attitudes. *Journal of Applied Psychology, 6,* 682–690.

Guion, R. M. (1998). *Assessment, measurement, and prediction for personnel decisions.* Mahwah, NJ: Lawrence Erlbaum Associates.

Gully, S. M., Incalcaterra, K. A., Joshi A., & Beaubien, J. M. (2002). A meta-analysis of team efficacy, potency, and performance: Interdependence and level of analysis as moderators of observed relationships. *Journal of Applied Psychology, 87,* 819–832.

Guzzo, R. A., Yost, P. R., Campbell, R. J., & Shea, G. P. (1993). Potency in groups: Articulating a construct. *British Journal of Social Psychology, 32,* 87–106.

Hackman, J. R. (1987). The design of work teams. In J. Lorsch (Ed.), *Handbook of organizational behavior* (pp. 315–342). Englewood Cliffs, NJ: Prentice-Hall.

Halpern, D. F. (2004). The development of adult cognition: Understanding constancy and change in adult learning. In D. V. Day, S. J. Zaccaro, & S. M. Halpin (Eds.), *Leadership development for transforming organizations: Growing leaders for tomorrow* (pp. 125–152). Mahwah, NJ: Erlbaum Associates.

Hedge, J. W., Borman, W. C., & Hanson, M. A. (1996, March). *Videotaped crew resource management scenarios for selection and training applications.* Paper presented at the 38th Annual Conference of the International Military Testing Association.

Highhouse, S. (2002). Assessing the candidate as a whole: A historical and critical analysis of individual psychological assessment for personnel decision making. *Personnel Psychology, 55,* 363–387.

Hoeft, R. M., Jentsch, F. G., Harper, M. E., Evans, A. W., Berry, D. G., Bowers, C., et al. (2002). Structural knowledge assessment with the Team Performance Lab's knowledge analysis test suite (TPL-KATS). *Proceedings of the Human Factors and Ergonomics Society 46th annual meeting.*

Hough, L. M., & Ones, D. S. (2001). The structure, measurement, validity, and use of personality variables in industrial, work, and organizational psychology. In N. Anderson, D. S. Ones, H. K. Sinangil, & C. Viswesvaran (Eds.), *Handbook of industrial, work, and organizational psychology.* Thousand Oaks, CA: Sage Publications, Inc.

Hunter, D. R. (2003). Measuring general aviation pilot judgment using a situational judgment technique. *The International Journal of Aviation Psychology, 13,* 373–386.

Ilgen, D. R., Hollenbeck, J. R., Johnson, M., & Jundt, D. (2005). Teams in organizations: From Input-Process-Output models to IMOI models. *Annual Review of Psychology, 56,* 1–19.

Jentsch, F., & Bowers, C. A. (1998). Evidence for the validity of PC-based simulations in studying aircrew coordination. *International Journal of Aviation Psychology, 8,* 261–276.

Jonassen, D. H., & Tessmer, M. (1996). An outcomes-based taxonomy for instructional systems design, evaluation and research. *Training Research Journal, 2,* 11–46.

Kirkman, B. L., Tesluk, P. E., & Rosen, B. (2001). Alternative methods of assessing team-level variables: Comparing the predictive power of aggregation and consensus methods. *Personnel Psychology,* 54, 645–667.

Klimoski, R., & Mohammad, S. (1994). Team mental model: Construct or metaphor? *Journal of Management, 20,* 403–437.

Kozlowski, S. W. J., & Bell, B. S. (2003). Work groups and teams in organizations. In W. C. Borman, D. R. Ilgen, & R. J. Klimoski (Eds.), *Handbook of psychology: Industrial and organizational psychology* (Vol. 12, pp. 333–375). London: Wiley.

Kozlowski, S. W. J., Gully, S. M., Brown, K. G., Salas, E., Smith, E. M., & Nason, E. R. (2001). Effects of training goals and goal orientation traits on multidimensional training outcomes and performance adaptability. *Organizational Behavior and Human Decision Processes, 85,* 1–31.

Kozlowski, S. W. J., Gully, S. M., McHugh, P. P., Salas, E., & Cannon-Bowers, J. A. (1996). A dynamic theory of leadership and team effectiveness: Developmental and task contingent leader roles. In G. R. Ferris (Ed.), *Research in personnel and human resources management* (Vol. 14, pp. 253–305). Greenwich, CT: JAI Press.

Kozlowski, S. W. J., Gully, S. M., Salas, E., & Cannon-Bowers, J. A. (1996). Team leadership and development: Theory, principles, and guidelines for training leaders and teams. In M. Beyerlein, S. Beyerlein, & D. Johnson (Eds.), *Advances in interdisciplinary studies of work teams: Team leadership* (Vol. 3, pp. 253–292). Greenwich, CT: JAI Press.

Kozlowski, S. W. J., & Ilgen, D. R. (in press). Enhancing the effectiveness of work groups and teams. *Psychological Science in the Public Interest.*

Kozlowski, S. W. J., & Klein, K. J. (2000). A multilevel approach to theory and research in organizations: Contextual, temporal, and emergent processes. In K. J. Klein, & S. W. J. Kozlowski (Eds.), *Multilevel theory, research, and methods in organizations: Foundations, extensions, and new directions* (pp. 3–90). San Francisco: Jossey-Bass.

Kraiger, K. (2002). Decision-based evaluation. In K. Kraiger (Ed.), *Creating, implementing, and maintaining effective training and development: State-of-the-art lessons for practice* (pp. 331–375). Mahwah, NJ: Jossey-Bass.

Kraiger, K., Ford, J. K., & Salas, E. (1993). Application of cognitive, skill-based, and affective theories of learning outcomes to new methods of training evaluation. *Journal of Applied Psychology, 78,* 311–328.

Kurtz, J. E., & Parrish, C. L. (2001). Semantic response consistency and protocol validity in structured personality assessment: The case of the NEO-PI-R. *Journal of Personality Assessment, 76,* 315–332.

Levitt, B., & March, J. G. (1988). Organizational learning. *Annual Review of Sociology, 14,* 319–340.

Lindsley, D. H., Brass, D. J., & Thomas, J. B. (1995). Efficacy-performance spirals: A multilevel perspective. *Academy of Management Review, 20,* 645–678.

Lindsley, D. H., Mathieu, J. E., Heffner, T. S., & Brass, D. J. (1994, April). *Team efficacy, potency, and performance: A longitudinal examination of reciprocal processes.* Paper presented at the 9th annual conference of the Society for Industrial and Organizational Psychology, Nashville, TN.

Marks, M. A. (2000). A critical analysis of computer simulations for conducting team research. *Small Group Research, 31,* 653–675.

Marks, M. A., Mathieu, J. E., & Zaccaro, S. J. (2001). A temporally based framework and taxonomy of team process. *Academy of Management Review, 26,* 356–376.

Marks, M. A., Sabella, M. J., Burke, C. S., & Zaccaro, S. J. (2002). The impact of cross-training on team effectiveness. *Journal of Applied Psychology, 87,* 3–13.

Marks, M. A., Zaccaro, S. J., & Mathieu, J. E. (2000). Performance implications of leader briefings and team-interaction training for team adaptation to novel environments. *Journal of Applied Psychology, 85,* 971–986.

Marshall-Mies, J. C., Fleishman, E. A., Martin, J. A., Zaccaro, S. J., Baughman, W. A., & McGee, M. L. (2000). Development and evaluation of cognitive and metacognitive measures for predicting leadership potential. *Leadership Quarterly, 11,* 135–153.

Mathieu, J. E., Heffner, T. S., Goodwin, G. F., Cannon-Bowers, J. A., & Salas, E. (2005). Scaling the quality of teammates' mental models: Equifinality and normative comparisons. *Journal of Organizational Behavior, 26,* 37–56.

Mathieu, J. E., Heffner, T. S., Goodwin, G. F., Salas, E., & Cannon-Bowers, J. A. (2000). The influence of shared mental models on team process and performance. *Journal of Applied Psychology, 85,* 273–283.

Mathieu, J. E., & Schulze, W. (in press). The influence of team knowledge and formal plans on episodic team process → performance relationships. *Academy of Management Journal.*

Meister, D. (1985). *Behavioural foundations of system development.* Malabar, FL: Robert E. Krieger.

Messick, S. (1960). Dimensions of social desirability. *Journal of Consulting Psychology, 24,* 279–287.

Mohammed, S., Klimoski, R., & Rentsch, J. (2000). The measurement of team mental models: We have no shared schema. *Organizational Research Methods, 3,* 123–165.

Morgan, B. B., Salas, E., & Glickman, A. S. (1994). An analysis of team evolution and maturation. *The Journal of General Psychology, 120,* 277–291.

Motowidlo, S. J., Dunnette, M. D., & Carter, G. W. (1990). An alternative selection procedure: The low-fidelity simulation. *Journal of Applied Psychology, 75,* 640–647.

Münsterberg, H. (1912). *Vocation and learning.* St. Louis, MO: The Peoples University.

Nunnally, J., & Bernstein, I. (1994). *Psychometric theory.* New York: McGraw Hill.

Olson-Buchanan, J. B., Drasgow, F., Moberg, P. J., Mead, A. D., Keenan, P. A., Donovan, M. A. (1998). Interactive video assessment of conflict resolution skills. *Personnel Psychology, 51,* 1–24.

Salas, E., Stagl, K. C., & Burke, C. S. (2004). 25 years of team effectiveness in organizations: Research themes and emerging needs. In C. L. Cooper, & I. T. Robertson (Eds.), *International review of industrial and organizational psychology*. New York: John Wiley & Sons.

Salas, E., Stagl, K. C., Burke, C. S., & Goodwin, G. F. (in press). Fostering team effectiveness in organizations: Toward an integrative theoretical framework of team performance. In J. W. Shuart, W. Spaulding, & J. Poland, (Eds.), *Modeling complex systems: Nebraska Symposium on Motivation,* (p. 52). Lincoln, NE: University of Nebraska Press.

Schvaneveldt, R. W. (Ed.). (1990). *Pathfinder associative networks: Studies in knowledge organization*. Norwood, NJ: Ablex Publishing Corp.

Smith, P. C., & Kendall, L. M. (1963). Retranslation of expectations: An approach to the construction of unambiguous anchors for rating scales. *Journal of Applied Psychology, 47,* 149–155.

Smith-Jentsch, K., Salas, E., & Baker, D. P. (1996). Training team performance-related assertiveness. *Personnel Psychology, 49,* 909–936.

Smith-Jentsch, K. A., Zeisig, R. L., Acton, B., & McPherson, J. A. (1998). Team dimensional training: A strategy for guided team self-correction. In J. A. Cannon-Bowers, & E. Salas (Eds.), *Making decisions under stress* (pp. 271–297). Washington, DC: APA.

Stagl, K. C., Burke, C. S., Salas, E., & Pierce, L. (2006). Team adaptation: Realizing team synergy. In C. S. Burke, L. Pierce, & E. Salas (Eds.), *Understanding adaptability: A prerequisite for effective performance within complex environments* (pp. 117–141). Oxford, U.K.: Elsevier Science.

Stagl, K. C., Fritzsche, B. A., Salas, E., Wooten, W., & Burke, C. S. (under review). The construct validity of a situational judgment test in a maximum performance context. *International Journal of Selection & Assessment.*

Stagl, K. C., Salas, E., & Burke, C. S. (2006). Best practices in team leadership: What team leaders do to facilitate team effectiveness. In J. A. Conger, & R. E. Riggio (Eds.), *The practice of leadership* (pp. 172–197). New York: John Wiley & Sons.

Stagl, K. C., Salas, E., Rosen, M. A., Priest, H. A., Burke, C. S., Goodwin, G. F., et al. (in press). Distributed team performance: A multilevel review of distribution, demography, and decision-making. In F. Yammarino, & F. Dansereau (Eds.), *Research in multi-level issues: Vol. 5. Multi-level issues in organizations*. Oxford, U.K.: Elsevier.

Sternberg, R. J., Forsythe, G. B., Hedlund, J., Horvath, J. A., Wagner, R. K., Williams, W. M., et al. (2000). Practical intelligence: An example from the military. *Practical intelligence in everyday life*. Cambridge, U.K.: Cambridge Press.

Tannenbaum, S. I., Beard, R. L., & Salas, E. (1992). Team building and its influence on team effectiveness: An examination of conceptual and empirical developments. In K. Kelley (Ed.), *Issue, theory, and research in industrial/organizational psychology* (pp. 117–153). Amsterdam: Elsevier.

Tziner, A., Joanis, C., & Murphy, K. R. (2000). A comparison of three methods of performance appraisal with regard to goal properties, goal perception, and ratee satisfaction. *Group and Organization Management, 25,* 175–190.

Van Der Vegt, G. S., & Bunderson, J. S. (2005). Learning and performance in multidisciplinary teams: The importance of collective team identification. *Academy of Management Journal, 48*(3), 532–547.

Weekley, J. A., & Ployhart, R. E. (2006). (Eds.). *Situational judgment tests.* Mahwah, NJ: Lawrence Erlbaum Associates.
Wenger, D. M. (1995). A computer network model of transactive memory. *Social Cognition, 13,* 319–339.
Yeh, Y. J., & Chou, H. W. (2005). Team composition and learning behaviors in cross-functional teams. *Social Behavior and Personality, 33,* 391–402.

CHAPTER

16

Research Designs for Assessing Group Learning

THEODORE L GESSNER,
KRISTA L. LANGKAMER,
AND RICHARD J. KLIMOSKI

George Mason University

INTRODUCTION

This chapter is about the logic, choices, and operations that we would recommend for the systematic evaluation or assessment of team learning interventions. The approach builds on well-developed models and practices associated with social-science research. From this perspective, strong inference is the investigator's capacity to make firm conclusions from his or her efforts to evaluate a theory, a hypothesis, or a team-training intervention. Strong inference means that we can have confidence in our findings, but it is also about understanding that certain methods and measures insure that what is observed is "real" (can be reliably reproduced) and to explain why we get the results that we do.

We will use the logic of strong inference through out the chapter; however, the point of view and language will be geared to the human resources (HR) professional (the perspective of the latter will be the recurring "voice" of this chapter). The major points that we will cover will parallel those of a good methods text. Strong inference is accomplished through careful attention to choices of design or methods, and the practitioner will have to be sensitive to the conditions that are set up in a team-training evaluation for purposes of informative comparisons or contrasts. Strong inference is also more plausible when employing good measures.

CHAPTER ORGANIZATION

Because the chapter (and indeed, the book) is oriented around "team learning," we will begin with a brief treatment of the type of teams often found in work organizations. Type of team often implies the establishment of differing learning goals or calls for alternative interventions. Importantly, type of team (and its context) usually demands different approaches to program evaluation, design, and execution. Thus, we will argue the best evaluation plan must be appropriate to team type.

We then move to the task of reviewing our approach to thinking about implementing team learning interventions. Here we discuss the politics, the pragmatics, and the practices associated with evaluations in terms of the I-P-O (input-process-outcome) framework. We advise giving attention to processes and defining team learning as effective change in these processes. We are also interested in the outcomes. Here we will stress not only the proximal outcomes associated with learning and improved team performance, but also indicate that evaluators may need to find a method to examine the more distal outcomes.

We next move to a discussion of strategy and provide three cases or examples of team learning interventions and their evaluations. Each example will serve to illustrate one of the key strategies and some choices that evaluators must make. We will also point out the capacity and limits of each study for making firm conclusions as to the impact of a learning intervention. All of the cases have been published in reputable sources and will therefore serve to make another point: no evaluation plan is perfect. If many of the principles that we advocate in this chapter are followed, however, the team learning evaluation that will result can provide incremental knowledge of specific training-program merits and liabilities, as well as offer useful guidance to training policy decision makers.

TEAM TYPE AND TEAM EFFECTIVENESS

The premise of this chapter is that learning interventions are usually implemented to improve team effectiveness. Team learning interventions are instructional strategies provided to a team that introduce a new method of behavioral effectiveness. As discussed by Day, Gronn, and Salas (2004), there are different classes of learning interventions (some geared toward the individual and some for the team setting), each of which may serve a different need. An abbreviated version of their classification system is provided in Table 16.1. Just as one type of learning intervention may be more appropriate for one learning need than it is for another, the type of learning intervention chosen should also align with the type of team to which the intervention is introduced; not all work teams are the same. Different types of teams have different needs when it comes to improving effectiveness. The kinds of interventions called for should relate to both team type and context, and certainly, both team type and context present opportunities and challenges when it comes to performing a credible evaluation of a team learning intervention. There are several contingencies that evaluators must consider when studying the effects of a learning intervention. These include the type of team being examined, the temporal factors that impact the team's functioning, and the reasons why the intervention is being implemented. This section will review these by characterizing team types, team effectiveness, and the key processes that underlie effectiveness in terms of the concepts of teamwork and taskwork.

Type of team. It is important that the evaluator consider type of team before contemplating an evaluation plan. With different types of teams, the team processes and behaviors of interest will vary, as well as what is deemed effective team behavior. In this chapter, we focus on a typology of teams delineated by Sundstrom (1999). He classified teams into six different types based upon the kind of work that they do: (a) production teams, (b) service teams, (c) management teams, (d) project teams, (e) action or performing teams, and (f) parallel teams. These teams differ from one another on factors such as the time that members are together as a team, physical location of team members, and the type of work that they must perform. Because each type of team engages in a different type of work, each will have different criteria for success. For example, a production team normally has a tangible finished product, one that could be used as a criterion of performance and effectiveness, whereas the evaluation of an action team (e.g., an athletic team) may focus on intangible products such as team coordination (Sundstrom, 1999).

TABLE 16.1 Team Training and Developmental Instructional Strategies

Instructional Strategy	Level	Description
Cross Training	Team	Strategy targets team members interposition knowledge and shared mental models; increases team coordination and reduces process loss
Metacognitive Strategy	Individual	Training develops metacognitive skills which in turn regulate cognitive abilities
Team Coordination Training	Team	Targets mutual performance monitoring and back-up behavior
Self-guided Correction Training	Individual and Team	Generates instructive feedback so that team members can review performance episodes and correct deficiencies
Assertiveness Training	Individual	Provides multiple practice and feedback opportunities for trainees
Stress Exposure Training	Individual and Team	Develops trainee insight into the link between stressors, perceived stress and individual affect and performance
Scenario-based Team Training	Individual and Team	Provides guidelines for training objectives, trigger events, measures of performance, scenario generation, exercise conduct and control, data collection and feedback
Team Building	Team	Targets role clarification, goal setting, problem solving or interpersonal relations for improvement

Adapted from Day et al. (2004)

With a production team, it is often the case that a learning intervention aimed at improved functioning will focus on developing task knowledge or equipment-utilization skills. For an action team, deficiencies relative to interpersonal or coordination skills among the members may often be a root cause of poor performance. Thus, it should be clear that although Sundstrom's team classification scheme gives us an important starting point when considering training goals and the evaluation plan, understanding why teams differ in their functioning is essential in selecting and designing an intervention that is effective and useful (Kozlowski & Bell, 2003). To put it another way, not just team type, but also an understanding of functional and dysfunctional team processes, will be required for better program design and a stronger evaluation.

Time in team. Another variable that impacts the evaluation of a learning intervention is where the team is in light of its own history. Because teams exist within an organization, which must respond to a dynamic environment, teams must change and adapt over time to remain congruent with their surroundings (Sundstrom, de Meuse, & Futrell, 1990). Kozlowski and colleagues (Kozlowski, Gully, McHugh, Salas, & Cannon-Bowers, 1996; Kozlowski, Gully, Salas, & Cannon-Bowers, 1996) have put forth a model of groups indicating that leadership processes should change as the stage of group development changes. While such work does not speak directly to the specific targets for team learning, it does imply that the conditions needed for a team to be effective will vary with different stages of development.

Marks, Mathieu, and Zaccaro (2001) speak to the importance of temporal considerations in their discussion of performance episodes. *Episodes* refer to action phases that are characterized by goal-oriented behavior; these action phases are coupled with transition phases where more planning behavior takes place to form a complete performance episode. From a practical perspective, it would appear that the ideal time to introduce learning interventions to a team would be during a transition phase. If a learning intervention is implemented during transitions, performance will not be interrupted, and the intervention can be a part of the planning for the next action phase. This model also has implications for the evaluation of the learning intervention. Thus, a learning intervention might best be evaluated at the end of an entire performance episode (e.g., after both an action and transition phase) in order to be able to fully examine the impact of the intervention on the team.

A more global set of temporal factors that will impact both design and evaluation relates to the history of the group. If the focus of the learning intervention is on a well-established team, one that has members who have an extensive prior history and way of conducting their tasks, then a part of the learning intervention may well call for unlearning past protocols or procedures. The evaluation plan should not only show evidence of new learning, but also of the reduction or elimination of dysfunctional patterns and practices.

Reason for intervention. Some team learning interventions are introduced because the teams are not performing as well as they could; therefore, the goal of the learning intervention is to improve team performance and efficiency. Other learning interventions are implemented to deal with performance failures. These two reasons can be distinguished by the fact that the former deals with enhancing successful team processes, whereas the latter seeks to replace unsuccessful processes. Apart from performance deficiencies, learning interventions may also be imposed for more fundamental reasons. Perhaps a team is performing well, but it is thought that there is a better way of functioning; in this case, an intervention might introduce new work-flow processes. Finally, a learning intervention may be implemented because of major changes in managerial philosophy that seek to transform the working environment. For example, in moving toward the goal of becoming a high performance organization (e.g., Muldrow, Buckley, & Schay, 2002), management may seek to implement self-managing teams. To sum up, the reason for the intervention is important to the evaluator because it will have an impact on several factors, including training goals, the way that effectiveness is defined, the kind of intervention that may be chosen, and thus, the design and conduct of any evaluation.

Learning Interventions and Team Effectiveness

The I-P-O framework. Team theory and research has frequently employed an Input-Process-Outcome (I-P-O) framework (McGrath, 1964) to examine the complexity of team functioning. The I-P-O model indicates that while group inputs (e.g., member skills) impact outcomes (e.g., performance), this relationship is mediated by group processes. Marks et al. (2001) defined team processes as "members' interdependent acts that convert inputs to outcomes through cognitive, verbal, and behavioral activities directed toward organizing taskwork to achieve collective goals" (p. 357). They delineated 10 specific team processes (e.g., strategy formulation, backup behavior, conflict management) that are important for groups to function in a synergistic manner; these 10 processes are grouped into three superordinate categories of (a) transition processes, (b) action processes, and (c) interpersonal processes. While past research has highlighted the fact that the inputs that proceed team processes are indeed important (e.g., Ellis et al., 2003), failures in team performance can often be traced to ineffective team process. Thus, it is not uncommon for learning interventions to be designed to alter or improve some aspect of team process. The I-P-O model further assumes that process is the proximal predictor of outcomes, and therefore, "direct enhancement of team processes via training is the most prevalent team effectiveness intervention" (Kozlowski & Bell, 2003, p. 354).

The importance of team processes has been discussed for many years. Steiner (1972) focused on the phenomena of process loss and process gain. From this point of view, effective processes create a synergistic feeling to make a team perform better than a solitary individual performs; however, if team members have all of the necessary individual skills, but they have not learned to coordinate those skills, the team will not be able to capitalize on those skills and will experience process loss. To be clear, learning interventions can be focused on individual or group knowledge, skills, and abilities (KSAOs), attitudes, or behaviors. Improved team processes that support the combining of these individual level inputs, however, are likely to be the target of a learning intervention, and importantly, may also be the major indicators of group learning as a result of a learning intervention. Thus, for the purposes of this chapter, we will consider changes in team process to be a primary indicator of team learning.

Team learning as a process. Team learning is a difficult concept to disentangle from other related concepts (e.g., errors, performance), and such concepts are often used as proxy measures for learning (Kozlowksi & Bell, 2003). Measures of learning and performance, however, are often not substitutable (Druskat & Kayes, 2000). At an individual level, learning is easy to conceptualize in terms of improvement in KSAOs. At the team level, however, showing gains in KSAOs among members is not enough. Individual qualities still need to be woven into new team level capabilities. This usually implies the activation of better team processes.

We are in agreement with Edmondson (1999) that team learning involves more than just improving member task-related KSAOs. She has defined team learning as "an ongoing process of reflection and action, characterized by asking questions, seeking feedback, experimenting, reflecting on results, and discussing errors or unexpected outcomes of actions" (p. 353). Note that here, learning at the individual level is described as involving processes, but processes that can have a potential impact on teamwork. At the group level, learning-based changes in teamwork can be used to establish the impact of an intervention. When implementing a learning intervention, we recommend that the evaluator look for evidence of both individual learning and team-level process improvements. A firm knowledge of group theory would advantage those who design as well as those who evaluate team learning interventions.

Taskwork and teamwork. When describing team learning, there are at least two areas of focus: (a) taskwork and (b) teamwork (Marks et al., 2001). *Taskwork* can be defined in terms of the more concrete tasks that team members must perform to be effective; it describes *what* the team's members are doing. *Teamwork* gets at *how* the teams are accomplishing their work. For example, if a team plans a reception for a conference, the actual planning tasks of the reception (e.g., calling the caterers, booking the venue, etc.) would constitute the taskwork, but how this taskwork got completed (e.g., in a coordinated manner with good communication) reflects members' competencies in teamwork. To put it another way, team training with a taskwork focus is more concerned with the competence of the individual team members, whereas team training with a teamwork focus is more concerned with effective processes, including work flow, coordination, and decision making among team members. It should also be noted that the type of team will affect the relative importance of taskwork and teamwork in the accomplishment of the team's goals. Thus, type of team should be a starting point for the diagnosis of team deficiencies.

Several other considerations relative to learning interventions should be taken into account. One consideration comes from the fact that teamwork and taskwork imply different forms of interventions. Similarly, they may invoke different temporal and function-form considerations when it comes to the acquisition of new learning (e.g., speed, implementation process). They certainly imply different measures and methods. Thus, team members' learning of new knowledge might be accomplished one way, while the development of the team members' individual and collective skills at managing team process may demand more creative efforts.

Assessing the impact of an intervention on teamwork may also take some patience. It often takes considerable time for team members to get better at managing process. Depending on the type of task or work to be done, the evidence of improvement may only be clear when all members (e.g., even the poorest performer) are functioning at some appropriate level. Measures of process are inherently complex, and it is usually more difficult to assess if the team is working effectively. The opportunities to demonstrate effective process may depend on certain contextual factors. While tests of knowledge are often seen as opportunities for "maximum performance," when it comes to teamwork, we are frequently interested in knowing how members operate under "typical" conditions.

As implied, the taskwork/teamwork distinction is important in the diagnosis of team learning deficiencies. Improper diagnosis can lead to the implementation of an ineffective intervention and the misapplication of resources. It will also reduce the credibility of those responsible for the initiative in the eyes of key stakeholders. The distinction between taskwork and teamwork is also important in establishing whether appropriate learning occurred. It guides instructional design, methods, and evaluation design. As an aside, for some managers, improved teamwork or taskwork itself is often the stated goal of the intervention (e.g., "we seek to improve team coordination"). As such, skill acquisition can be thought of as an important and proximal outcome of a team learning intervention (Campbell, McCloy, Oppler, & Sager, 1993). It is clear that the distinction is useful when selecting measures, methods, and design for any evaluation of the impact of the learning that might have taken place relative to enhancing team performance, and ultimately, organizational performance.

Summary

Before implementing and evaluating a learning intervention, several contextual considerations should be kept in mind as they may impact the choices to be made in both intervention program features and in the design of an assessment protocol:

- The type of team
- Stage of development and history of the focal team
- Reasons for the intervention
- Teamwork and/or taskwork as the focus of the intervention

EVALUATING TEAM LEARNING INTERVENTIONS

Knowledge of how different types of interventions are likely to affect the team's learning and eventual operational effectiveness constitutes the basic information needed to design an effective evaluation of team learning. Assembling basic information represents only a first step in the process of planning, designing, and implementing an evaluation. Evaluations in complex organizations involve balancing the demands from diverse stakeholders who need valid and usable information (Dionne, 1996). The task of evaluating a learning intervention involves mixing the pragmatics and politics of organizational life with the logic of evaluation research.

This section will focus on the realities of carrying out quality assessments of team learning interventions in organizational settings. We will focus on two sets of challenges: (a) the pragmatics and politics of evaluation, and (b) designing a context-appropriate approach to data collection and analysis, as well as drawing conclusions based on data.

The stakeholder perceptions of the intervention and involvement, cost, evaluation data security and data use, and appropriate selection of samples and settings are the primary pragmatic and political considerations. Dealing with practical and political issues during the design and planning phase is essential for success, and it will be much less frustrating than dealing with them during later phases of the evaluation. As in any evaluation that seeks to make strong conclusions, the methods used in the evaluation of a team learning intervention are also key. Major considerations in conducting a useful evaluation are (a) the design of the evaluation, (b) the selection of measures of taskwork and teamwork, (c) the methods of data analysis, and (d) the logic of interpretation and drawing valid conclusions from the data. The foundation for strong conclusions is comprised of (a) the strategy for data collection, (b) the quality of the data, and (c) the type of data analysis; the realities of politics and practice, however, are important determinants of the potential usefulness of the evaluation effort.

Pragmatics and Politics

Stakeholder relationship management. The implementation of any evaluation requires selecting a strategy that weaves constituent input with the demands of systematic data collection. The expectations of stakeholders and the logic of the evaluation are often at odds, and the evaluator must address and attempt to resolve these differences. We take the position that the best practice for evaluation involves developing a partnership among stakeholders to coordinate the different expectations during design, planning, and data collection phases. Ideally, an evaluation represents an attempt to obtain data which allow for strong conclusions that will be used by the organization. It is rare, however, that a training evaluation will not involve conflicting needs or goals among parties. In most cases, the stakes are high, there are financial risks, and there is the potential to erode social capital. Thus, the involvement of stakeholders becomes important; good relationship management can raise the profile of the evaluation, increase commitment of the stakeholders, and provide an audience for the results.

Perceptions of team learning interventions. As discussed in the previous section, there are considerations, such as type of team and reason for the intervention, that the evaluator must take into account when seeking to evaluate the effectiveness of a learning intervention. Under optimal conditions, the evaluator will not only be involved in the evaluation, but will have played a central role in such things as the training-needs analysis, the selection of training objectives, and the design of the actual intervention. Thus, the evaluator is able to control the quality of implementation and have a say on the measures reported to stakeholders. It is not that uncommon for an assessment to be requested after team training has been concluded, however, as well as to be dependent on data that are already available or easily accessible. In each case, the evaluator must entertain stakeholder perceptions and ascertain the anticipated benefits of a set of feasible evaluation plans while gathering enough information to have a high level of confidence in conclusions made from the data.

Stakeholders in the intervention. Identifying the relevant stakeholders and their perceptions and expectations for team learning and performance is a major consideration in evaluation design and implementation. Most team-training programs involve diverse stakeholders who inevitably have different perspectives. This includes thoughts about

(a) what the intervention means to them, (b) what the intervention means to others, (c) who is involved in and/or owns the intervention, (d) what the long-term and short-term cost and benefits are, and (e) who will have access to the data. The list of stakeholders is potentially long and includes top management, unit level manager, team lead, team members, other employees, unions, stockholders, customers, innovation champions, and consultants (Dionne, 1996; Phillips, 1997). It is important for the evaluator to be aware of the real and emotional investments that these potential stakeholders have in various aspects of the training program or its evaluation.

Stakeholder interests and concerns must be incorporated into the intervention and its assessment and are important to both the design and implementation phases of an effort. They are also critical to the acceptability of the results, and thus, to the likelihood that even a favorable evaluation will result in adopting the training as a basis for company practice. This last point should also serve to remind us that the power of different stakeholders is a nontrivial issue in stakeholder identification and relationship management. The evaluator must give greatest attention to the needs and views of the "key" people.

One practice in evaluation is to assemble stakeholders and conduct a forum that allows for discussion of how representatives of the different stakeholder groups perceive intervention-related issues, including the reasons for the intervention and its implications for them. Such cooperative efforts will increase an appreciation of the need for evaluation and the acceptability of specific features of an evaluation plan. While this approach may represent the ideal, it should be noted that differences among stakeholders are not always easily resolved. When collaborative efforts fail or are not feasible, the evaluator faces the dilemma of dealing with conflicting views of the purpose and usefulness of the evaluation. Under these conditions, power or authority within the organization to decide on evaluation features becomes an important issue. Thus, the evaluator's status and credibility may be brought to bear in order to influence powerful stakeholders' support. On the other hand, if the chief executive of the organization deems the intervention to be necessary, but must prove its worth, an evaluation will very likely be enabled. It is also more likely that the resources needed to design and execute a competent evaluation can be acquired.

Cost. Traditionally, three sets of costs must be considered, two of which fall under the cost of implementing the team based intervention and one component surrounding the costs of the evaluation. Under the implementation category, everything associated with program design and execution must certainly be considered, including purchased materials or consultant fees; however, there are opportunity costs as well. In particular, to the extent that current employees are to participate in the learning intervention, many companies are also concerned about the lost productivity of these people for the time that they are in training. The former are often covered as a separate budget item, but there must be some recognition "up front" of the latter and agreement as to who absorbs the cost of lost time at work. If this is not done, actually getting to deliver the training becomes problematic.

On the other hand, the costs of the evaluation are frequently seen as a part of the standard operating budget of the HR function and are not factored into the costs of the intervention. This may be a mistake, as it can result in poorly funded and less competent evaluation efforts. It is not uncommon, however, for major stakeholders to assume that the assessment process should not be costly because, based on the arguments of program "champions," the intervention is going to be effective and the benefits to the organization will be obvious. In reality, however, a competent evaluation requires a realistic budget. An evaluation may require new or modified methods of assessment, and the execution of the design may require additional personnel. The cost of an evaluation can also increase as such things as time frames needed (for training and criterion data gathering) expand or the number of participants or locations are increased. Evaluators may feel pressure to deliver the most cost-effective assessment possible (Tannenbaum & Yukl, 1992), however, they must learn to strike a balance between cost and quality of the evaluation. It is important to note that if an organization is willing to put forth monies to implement the intervention, it must also be willing to pay for a quality evaluation; after all, without a careful evaluation, one can never be sure of the effectiveness of the intervention, thus decreasing the worth of the intervention.

Another kind of cost is often not considered. This is the cost to "roll out" training to additional teams or locations. Many evaluations are done in anticipation of using the team learning intervention on a wide scale. The plan then is to expose all existing company work teams (e.g., of a given type) or all new teams coming "on line" to the training once it has been established as having the desired impact on learning or performance. It is obvious that such a plan has major cost implications.

Data security and use. Scientific research done under the rubric of program evaluation is frequently accompanied by a promise of anonymity or confidentiality. Participants are told that the data on their individual or collective learning and performance will only be reported under certain circumstances or only in certain forms (e.g., in the aggregate). They are often told that the information will be used for "research purposes" only. These conditions, however, cannot necessarily be assumed nor expected within most organizations where information about employee performance—in or outside of the context of training—is vital for managing and planning. In fact, usually, the information obtained about individual and team performance is the property of the organization and may be used in making individual personnel decisions, as well as decisions about the fate of administrative units.

Because of the importance of information in organizational settings, it is essential that the evaluator address and resolve the issues of how data will be gathered, stored, and used in any team learning evaluation. A shared understanding must be reached and conveyed to all participants. Most importantly, this understanding must be enacted and maintained as part of the evaluation. Not doing so will jeopardize the quality of the data gathered in the evaluation, and is also likely to reduce trust in any company representations of confidentiality/anonymity in future attempts to evaluate team learning.

Setting and samples. Access to different settings and samples is another pragmatic and political issue that will influence the quality of the evaluation. Many large organizations have a plethora of teams who are performing similar functions and are situated in multiple settings. For the evaluator, the availability of a large sample of teams in multiple settings provides the benefit of being able to make more comparisons, and ultimately, stronger conclusions regarding the effects of the intervention. Multiple settings can also present an opportunity for greater control over the implementation and timing of the presentation of the intervention. Problems associated with multiple settings come from the increased number of stakeholders and, as mentioned, the increased cost of the evaluation. When different settings and larger samples of teams are used, real and opportunity costs associated with gaining access to teams and collecting data are increased.

We have selected a set of considerations for evaluation planning that fall under the rubric of "pragmatics and politics," each of which has the potential to derail or frustrate an evaluation effort. While some things may be better left "unsaid," we strongly advise that the practical issues are covered (as well as others, such as clear lines of authority regarding expenditures) and woven into stakeholder discussions at the outset. Of course, this often means that the evaluator benefits from being "at the table" from the very beginning of any planning for a team learning intervention. Therein lies still another benefit of building and maintaining good working relationships with organizational leaders and operational managers when it comes to critical human-resource-management challenges—the evaluator will come to be seen as a partner rather than as an evaluation services provider.

METHODS FOR EVALUATING THE EFFECTIVENESS OF AN INTERVENTION

Planning and implementing a valid and useful evaluation while dealing with pragmatic and political considerations present challenges for the evaluator. The planning and implementation involves three interdependent steps: (a) selecting measures, (b) designing the evaluation, and (c) choosing methods for the analysis and synthesis of information.

The first step, deciding what to measure, requires knowledge of both the theory of and past research on the proposed intervention and its expected effects on team learning. Past work on the training/learning intervention should be "mined" for best practices associated with such things as what might be considered psychometrically valid measures, useful methods, and normative data. The second step of designing the evaluation involves choosing a strategy for collecting information about team learning and team performance. The process of systematically collecting information has received considerable attention over the years from organizational researchers (e.g., Campbell & Stanley, 1966) and is the core of research design books and courses. It should also be the key to the evaluator's choices of strategy because of its impact on the internal logic made possible by an evaluation and the strength of conclusions that can be made. The third step is to analyze and present the information so that useful conclusions about the intervention can be made and stakeholders can be convinced of the validity of these conclusions.

Deciding What to Measure

There are several issues to take into consideration when deciding upon the measures needed to assess the outcome of a learning intervention. The first decision involves *what* to measure and the second decision relates to *how* to measure it. We will discuss the first decision in terms of the I-P-O model and the latter in terms of levels and sources of information. Both of these decisions point to the complexity associated with actually assessing the learning that occurs within teams.

When making measurement decisions, the I-P-O model provides a useful framework because it serves as a reminder that inputs, processes, and outcomes should all be measured to help develop a fuller picture of what occurred in a team during the imposition of a learning intervention. Potential input measures, which include the initial characteristics of team members, the initial task structure adopted by the team, and the affordances of the organizational environment as related to team performance, are essential because they provide a starting point for the evaluator as to where the team was before the initiation of the learning intervention. It is our position here that team learning is reflected in changes in key team processes, and therefore, processes should be the focus of measurement. Process measures may be based on data systematically gathered from an assessment of the teamwork and taskwork occurring within the team. Even though improved processes serve as a measure of team learning, they should be assessed in regard to the relationship they have with outcome variables. Outcome measures are usually tied to the quality and the quantity of the products or services of the group. Although such outcomes may not be the primary focus of the evaluator, they are often the bottom line from an organizational perspective. If it can be demonstrated, however, that changes in processes result in positive outcomes for the team and the organization, such results may indicate to stakeholders that processes should be a primary concern in the implementation and evaluation of a team learning intervention.

Although the I-P-O rubric provides a starting point in terms of deciding what to measure, additional considerations must still be evaluated. Specifically, the evaluator must decide how the inputs, processes, and outcomes will be assessed, as well as who will be the source of measurement. To shed light on the possibilities associated with this measurement decision, we use Kirkpatrick's (1994) typology, which has identified four types of measures used as training-evaluation criteria: (a) reactions, (b) learning, (c) behavior, and (d) results. The type of information used in evaluation depends upon the objective of the training. The choice of criteria, however, goes beyond association with the training objective; a meta-analysis by Arthur, Bennett, Edens, and Bell (2003) indicated that the choice of the evaluation criteria does impact the observed effectiveness of the training program (to be subsequently discussed in more detail). These four types of measures can be placed on a continuum, going from subjective to objective, and each can be associated with any of the three parts of the I-P-O framework.

Participant reactions are the most subjective in that they are obtained directly from the individual trainee and represent perceptions and affect toward the training. The relationship between reaction measures and actual changes in learners has been questioned (Kraiger, 2002), and in their meta-analysis, Arthur et al. (2003) found that the relationship between training effectiveness and evaluation criteria was the smallest when reaction criteria were used; however, subcategories of reactions have been found to be measured reliably (Morgan & Casper, 2000). Interestingly, Arthur et al. reported that although reaction data is less commonly used for research purposes (comprising only 4% of the data points in their meta-analysis), it is very often used as training criteria in applied settings.

Measuring the amount of learning (in terms of newly acquired mental abilities) that takes place presents challenges. Recently, Kraiger (2003) reported work that builds on what we know about cognitive processing implications of learning and offers a framework that suggests the usefulness of measuring training-induced changes associated with such things as forming new concepts. An example of how new mental concepts may manifest themselves in team learning is improved situational awareness. Several choices are available for obtaining learning data, including self-generated data, as well as data gathered through trained observations of the trainees under standard conditions or in simulations. Determining the best way to effectively gather learning criteria, though, would be beneficial; Arthur et al. (2003) demonstrated that out of the four evaluation criteria, learning criteria have the largest relationship with training effectiveness.

In many cases, stakeholders in the evaluation of training interventions are focused on behavior or results, variables that may be difficult to disentangle from one another. In general, with learning interventions, we think of performance as behaviors as the observed manifestation of knowledge, skills, or attitudes. On the other hand, performance as results is usually thought of as results with economic consequences for the worker and firm. Performance in terms of behavior is a more proximal criterion, whereas performance in terms of results is more distal (Campbell et al., 1993). Due to the more distal nature of the results criteria and the longer time span results take to manifest themselves, it is not surprising that Arthur et al. (2003) reported these criteria being used the least in both research and applied setting.

The distinction between performance as behavior and performance as results becomes even more complex when the issue of "far transfer" is examined (e.g., Barnett & Ceci, 2002). Far transfer involves applying learned material to a dissimilar context; in other words, it involves having a deep understanding of the material that was learned so that it can be applied to a novel situation. In this case, performance becomes a function of more distal behavioral manifestations on later tasks and the results such behaviors can have for the organization. Perhaps deciding how to facilitate and asses far transfer should be the major goal of the evaluator. If far transfer really occurs, team learning has happened in a more cost-effective manner, and organizations will have a competitive edge.

In light of all the measurement choices described above, measurement choice is complex; however, it should be tied to what stakeholders believe to be the major drivers of performance (Campbell et al., 1993; Kozlowski & Bell, 2003; Kozlowski & Ilgen, 2006). It is important to note that performance is not often under the control of the focal individual or group. In certain situations (e.g., a team who is dependent upon technology to perform), contextual factors impact the evaluation and results. Several recent studies (Morgeson, Johnson, Campion, Medsker, & Mumford, 2006; Zellmer-Bruhn & Gibson, 2006) demonstrated the importance of examining the organizational context when assessing team learning. As demonstrated by their work, failure to take organizational context into account may lead an evaluator to erroneous conclusions regarding the learning that actually occurred. This research highlights the extreme diligence that must be used when making measurement decisions; measurement is one of the keys to establishing strong conclusions about the impact of an intervention on team learning.

Designing the Evaluation

It should be the goal of the evaluator to make the strongest possible conclusions about the value of the intervention, and the logic used to answer questions about a team learning intervention is essential to the process of making strong inferences. We will describe three basic strategies: (a) descriptive, (b) group comparison, and (c) randomized evaluation. Each of these design strategies can provide potential answers to the question of what the teams have learned and whether these process changes affect behavior and performance. The level of confidence in the conclusions that can be made will depend on both the content or nature of the measures used and the appropriateness of the evaluation design.

The differences between these three strategies can be seen in the way information is used to answer everyday questions about business practices. If the HR manager has been asked by top management to determine what human-resource policies are related to turnover within the company, the strategy selected to address the question will focus on different information and provide different answers. The descriptive strategy is focused on information about the characteristics of the employees who are leaving. The comparative strategy focuses on information about the differences between the employees who leave or stay, or information about the turnover rates of groups of employees who have been exposed to different HR policies. The third strategy of randomized evaluation focuses on information about the effects on turnover rates resulting from selectively changing HR policy in some units, but not in others. Each of these strategies will provide an answer for different but related questions, and each will result in differing levels of confidence as to our conclusions. We will discuss each of these strategies by presenting an exemplar of that strategy. Some of the choices made by the evaluators and their effects on the evaluation will be discussed. We will then discuss each design in more general terms and identify some of the other options available to the evaluator within the design.

The three exemplars are Mathieu, Gilson, and Ruddy (2006; descriptive), Cohen and Ledford (1994; group comparison), and Pearson (1992; randomized evaluation). These exemplars are published studies that have evaluated the effectiveness of self-managing/empowered teams in which team members have the authority and responsibility for their work environment and team functioning (Mathieu et al., 2006). Empowerment interventions are a good example of team learning because of their prevalence within the work place, because empowerment changes both teamwork and taskwork, and because empowerment produces changes in individuals, teams, and organizations.

Descriptive Strategies

Descriptive strategies can be a rich source of information to the extent that they describe the changes within teams or the differences in the pattern of relationships between aspects of team learning (e.g., knowledge vs. skills) and team performance. Descriptive strategies can suggest what is happening. They do not, however, provide a mechanism for elimination of alternative explanations, and they have limited value for explaining why team learning and performance are related. In discussing descriptive studies, we will first present a example of a well-designed descriptive study (Mathieu et al., 2006), and then examine general consideration which effect these types of studies.

The study by Mathieu et al. (2006) used a post-only descriptive design because all customer-services engineering teams in a large organization had already been exposed to the intervention. Although many of the pragmatic and political considerations are not specified in this paper, the evaluators appear to have been engaged to evaluate the intervention after the changes were either in progress or completed. The evaluators compensated for some of the limitations of the descriptive strategy by placing emphasis on selecting theoretically relevant input, process, and outcome measures. The data were collected using a relatively inexpensive mail survey that members of the customer-service teams completed on company time.

Mathieu et al. (2006) concluded that "team empowerment evidenced the anticipated positive relationship with team processes, which in turn, related significantly with both customer satisfaction and quantitative team performance" (p. 106). This study clearly benefited from the large number of teams sampled and from the theoretical based choice of measures. A limitation mentioned by the authors was that time of measurement was an important factor that was not controlled and that "inference would be strengthened by the use of a complete longitudinal design" (p. 106). In addition, it can be noted that the absence of comparison groups or pretest measures does not allow for conclusions about the changes within the empowered teams or how empowered teams compare with traditional teams.

The descriptive strategy is frequently selected because evaluator access is limited to all teams that have been exposed to the learning intervention. Despite being limited to the study teams, the evaluator can strengthen the study by not confining the measurement to the direct reports and observations of the affected teams but by including alternative sources of information about the teams' inputs, process, and outcomes such as team leaders, division managers, observers, company records, etc. Systematically gathering information from a broad range of sources, and not simply the reports and observations of team members, is one way to avoid some of the biases that result from using team member self-reports and behaviors as the sole source of data.

The choice of measures is important to the quality of all assessments, but they are especially important for descriptive studies. The question of what to measure and how to select measures has been treated earlier, but we suggest that using care in choosing the content and level of the assessment will strengthen the conclusions about the probable effects of the intervention. In this case study (Mathieu et al., 2006), the evaluators selected input, process, and outcome measures that were theoretically relevant to the intervention and which provided a picture of the team processes within groups and the relationship of team process measures to level of performance. Although the authors had no equivalent comparison groups, the internal comparisons between teams with different levels of learning allowed for stronger conclusions about the how the team learning intervention affected team processes within this situation.

In descriptive evaluations, the question of the best time to measure is often considered to be moot; it is common to take measures after the intervention has been completed (e.g., Mathieu et al., 2006). The decision about the time intervals between measures should be based on a review of the literature and resulting insights regarding how a given team learning intervention might affect team learning and performance.

There may be opportunities to gain additional information by the judicious timing of the assessment. As discussed earlier, some interventions may take longer to influence team learning. When there is uncertainty about how long it takes for an intervention to affect group process or group outcomes, there may be reason to systematically control the timing of the assessment. One choice would be to measure one half of the already trained groups at time one and the other half of the groups at a later time. Another choice would be to measure the team inputs and processes now, but measure the changes in team performance later. A third choice would be to measure both processes and outcomes over an extended period of time to observe not only immediate impact, but also impact of the intervention on subsequent learning (Barnett & Ceci, 2002).

Another choice in descriptive studies involves selecting the setting for measurement. These choices involve considerations of the quality of the data, its utility, and the cost. Two common approaches in descriptive evaluations are either to send a survey to respondents at their home or work place, or to administer measures on-site. The survey is relatively cost-efficient if it can be assumed that respondents are truly able to characterize the changes in processes and outcomes; however, the evaluator often has little control over whether and how people will respond to the survey. When measures are taken on-site, the evaluator has greater control over insuring both appropriateness of the sources of information and the quality of assessments, whether these be based on self-reports, interviews, observations, or company records.

Group-Comparison Strategy

The group-comparison strategy allows for stronger inference than the descriptive strategy because the evaluator has a standard against which teams exposed to the learning intervention can be measured. Assessing differences in processes and outcomes between the intervention and nonintervention groups allows for strong conclusion about how and why the intervention affected team performance. The limitation of the group-comparison designs is that the lack of control over the introduction of the team learning intervention does not allow for conclusions about direct cause-and-effect relationships.

Our exemplar of a group-comparison design is Cohen and Ledford (1994). This study was a post-only study with matched comparison groups. The self-managing work teams in a large telecommunications company had emerged without a systematic intervention, and the teams involved had a variety of functions (e.g., technical, customer service, sales, and clerical support). The evaluation was conducted with teams that were already functioning as self-managing teams. Management supported the idea that self-managing teams might improve team effectiveness and employee satisfaction, and this support allowed the evaluators extensive access to matched comparison groups. Personnel resources were provided to help identify appropriate teams and to facilitate data collection from team members, supervisors, and managers. Although most of the measures were self-report mail surveys, the evaluators also used team-performance records. The study found that the self-managing team intervention was successful for some types of teams but not for others. Cohen and Ledford concluded that, "self-managing team designs are most appropriate when the work technology creates a high level of interdependence and requires a high level of employee information processing" (p. 26). This study allows for strong inference about which types of teams benefit from a self-managing design because of the comparison between matched groups; however, the lack of control over how, when, and to whom the change occurred limited their ability to discern why empowered teams are successful.

Large organizations with a variety of settings and teams provide an opportune setting for a group-comparison design (Campbell, 1988), and the successful implementation of an intervention is closely related to the evaluator's level of access to the organization's HR planning and to resources. Even if the evaluator has not been actively involved in the design and implementation of the intervention, having access to a large number of teams along with organizational support provides an opportunity to use a group-comparison strategy. The advantage of this strategy is that those teams that have been exposed to the intervention can be compared and contrasted with teams that have not had such exposure.

As with descriptive strategies, the primary focus here is on assessing teams who have been exposed to the learning intervention, but the use of a group-comparison design allows for the assessment of similarities and differences with the comparable teams. In Cohen and Ledford (1994), there was no systematic intervention, but a great deal of effort was devoted to identifying matched comparison groups. In the optimal case, one set of teams is exposed to the learning intervention and an equivalent set of teams is not. The comparison between teams allows for relatively strong inferences about what changes are associated with the intervention. While equivalent groups are preferred, a number of other possibilities exist. Other comparison groups might be chosen because of pragmatic or political reasons, such as other teams with the same function, but in a different unit of the organization (hence a different culture), or teams with a slightly different function from the same setting (hence, a different performance objective).

Deciding what processes and outputs should be measured is similar for descriptive, group-comparison, and randomized-evaluation strategies. With the group-comparison design, an additional consideration is the inclusion of measures of some characteristics that are not relevant to the intervention, but which will help to calibrate the similarities and differences between the teams that experience the learning intervention and those who have not. When seeking to document the effects of team training, some authors (Haccoun & Hamtiaux, 1994) have suggested measuring some aspects of team functioning or performance that were explicitly not the focus of the intervention because self-reports under conditions of repeated measures often become contaminated as a result of generalized affect, response bias, or memory traces. By including off-focus elements, one can see from the pattern of the data if the findings are susceptible to such factors. Ideally, groups should differ on only those attributes that were addressed by the learning intervention, while the other attributes should show no such pattern.

The timing of the measurement for the intervention and comparison teams is one key to having confidence in results from a group-comparison evaluation. One option is to take measures of both sets of teams only after the intervention has been implemented (posttest only). This timing allows for a single set of comparisons between intervention and comparison teams and could inform us as to the status of each set of teams on key measures at the same point in time. A second option is a pretest/posttest strategy. Here, measures of process and outcomes might be taken on both the intervention and comparison teams and in parallel fashion, but synchronized to the experience of the former. When an intervention team is measured before and then again after the learning experience, a comparison team would be measured in the same time periods as well. The strength of this design is that it allows for two sets of comparisons: (a) across and within teams, and (b) before and after the learning intervention. It also has the potential for dealing with forces that are operating in the larger organizational context or even in society that might affect learning outcomes. The logic of the design would suggest that such externalities could serve to inflate or depress scores on measures in a similar fashion, reducing the likelihood that we would falsely conclude that the effects were due to the team intervention.

The choice of the settings for measurement involves options similar to those used in the descriptive strategy. If the evaluator has knowledge of which teams are going into training and when this will occur, it is possible that data can be gathered either (or both) in the training setting or once participants get back on the job. Surveys in training or administered on the job can offer a cost advantage, but on-site measurement (in a training setting or job setting) usually provides more options and often results in higher quality data.

Randomized Evaluation Designs

The randomized-evaluation strategy involves doing a controlled experiment in a field setting and allows for strong conclusions about cause and effect. The evaluator's control over *which* teams receive the intervention and *when* the teams receive the intervention helps to eliminate other possible explanations for team behavior or performance differences. From the standpoint of making causal conclusions, this method is preferred, but pragmatic and political considerations often make this strategy impractical. The reality is that the opportunity to implement this type of controlled design is low within organizational setting (Tannenbaum & Yukl, 1992),

The exemplar of the randomization evaluation is a study by Pearson (1992). This study was a pre-/posttest, randomized evaluation that conducted with approximately 30 teams in a facility that built and maintained trains. The political impetus for the intervention and evaluation came from union representatives, who wanted the employees to have greater opportunities to engage in decision making. This initiative was given tentative support by management, and the evaluator was given considerable control over both the implementation of the intervention and the evaluation. All teams were actively included in the evaluation process, and the teams that received the intervention were selected in a public lottery. The study unfolded over a one-year period, and data were collected every two months. Process and performance data were collected for four months prior to the intervention and eight months after the intervention. The nonempowered groups continued to operate as normal.

Pearson (1992) was able to conclude that within this setting, "the development of semi-autonomous teams was associated with changes in perceptual, affective and behavioral responses. A relatively simple work reform of weekly meetings between group members and their supervisors had substantial impact on perceived decision making, job scope, role clarity, job satisfaction, productivity, attendance, and led to a safer working climate" (p. 925). Despite the relative small number of teams, strong conclusions about the effectiveness of the empowerment intervention were made because of the control exercised over the design and execution of the evaluation.

In this optimal variation, the evaluator had access to all eligible teams and randomly selected which teams would and would not receive the learning intervention. This strategy reduces the threats of bias that might be introduced by other methods of selection into the learning program (e.g., "first come, first serve"). While random assignment of teams (if or when they get training) is one of the strengths of this strategy, there are often competing practical and political pressures that make this difficult. For example, organizational priorities may prevail in terms of when particular teams can be released from their work setting. If the intervention has been crafted with the goal of improving the performance of teams that are failing, these teams may be given the first chance at training. It is not that these are inappropriate reasons for giving priority access to the intervention, but these nonrandom methods of selection have the potential to introduce biases that show up in measures and scores, and, as a consequence, weaken the conclusions that can be made from the evaluation.

Deciding what to measure is similar to the decision-making process used with the other strategies, but the control that the evaluator has over the learning intervention allows certain opportunities. In this design, it is possible to more clearly identify the anticipated changes and to employ a narrower range of team process and outcome measures. The evaluator usually has influence over when and how the learning intervention will be implemented. This allows for the possibility of taking measures in a way that can serve to reduce the potential influence of factors other than those being introduced in the learning intervention. The potential to take such biases into account results in a strong logic or inferential basis for conclusions, and it helps to explain group differences in scores obtained with our measures; it can certainly give us greater confidence in our conclusions based on the study.

The two major temporal options for the randomized evaluation are (a) postintervention or (b) both pre- and postintervention. The pre- and postintervention design is often preferred because of the opportunity to make additional comparisons between groups before any intervention occurs, thus ensuring their empirical comparability. The randomized assignment of groups and the post-only design, however, allows us to be equally convincing at a lower cost.

As with the other two strategies, both surveys and on-site measures are appropriate. It is suggested, however, that on-site measures administered by the evaluator will improve the degree of control over the evaluation process and are consistent with the emphasis on control associated with the randomized evaluation strategy.

Statistics

The choice of measures, the design strategy, and the statistical tools are all part of an integrated system for making valid and persuasive inferences about the usefulness of a team learning intervention. Statistics are tools for make sense of the data from the evaluation, but the strength of conclusions from the data depends on matching the statistics with the evaluation strategy. Statistical techniques can be classified as either descriptive or inferential. Descriptive statistics are used to summarize information and assess the strength of relationships among measures of inputs, processes, and outcomes. Inferential statistics are used to assess the strength of differences between groups (Phillips, 1997). The inferences made from descriptive evaluations are dependent on descriptive statistics.

The most common descriptive statistics are means and standard deviations. These statistics indicate the level of functioning and the variability among the teams exposed to the learning intervention. In addition, correlational techniques are descriptive statistics that allow for the assessment of the strength of relations between input, process, and outcome measures. Although correlations do not allow for causal inferences, they can be very useful for dissecting the complex relationship between variables. Advanced correlational techniques such as structural equation modeling (SEM) can be especially useful in the process of making inferences. In situations where the number of teams is sufficiently large and the evaluator has clear expectations about how the intervention is expected to occur, these statistics allow for a comparison of the evaluation data with expectations from the literature and can lead to greater confidence in the results.

With the group comparison strategy and the randomized evaluation, both descriptive statistics and inferential statistics are needed. The descriptive statistics give an overall picture of functioning within and across teams and are a central component of presentation to stakeholders. Inferential statistics such as t-tests and analysis of variance provide additional evidence for making inferences about the impact of the intervention. The inferential statistics provide the evaluator with a way to assess the strength of the differences between teams. These statistic allow the evaluator to infer that the differences are tied to the learning intervention, and with the randomized evaluation design, the evaluator can be more confident in making conclusions about whether the intervention causes the changes in process and performance.

Descriptive and inferential statistics are the essential tools in any evaluation of team learning intervention. It should be noted, however, that there are other considerations in the understanding and presentation of evaluative information. Three additional considerations are (a) level of analysis, (b) practical and statistical significance, and (c) the importance of qualitative information.

The first consideration is to identify the level of analysis to be used. Although measures are frequently collected and analyzed at the individual level, it is recommended that data be aggregated and analyzed at the group level since the processes and outcomes of interest reside at the team level. All three of the case studies described above analyzed data at the group level.

A second consideration is that stakeholder perspectives must be taken into consideration when it comes to using and presenting statistics to describe or evaluate a learning initiative. Whereas the evaluator frequently relies on statistical significance to assess the effectiveness of the intervention in terms of a reliable (reproducible) impact, key stakeholders are typically interested in the expected benefits (often in relation to costs). The evaluator must not only be able to reassure the stakeholders that the intervention is effective, but that it will also contribute meaningfully to business objectives. While the issues associated with establishing the quantifiable benefits of a human-resource-management intervention are too complex to cover in this chapter, the interested reader can find a useful review of current thinking on this topic in Boudreau and Ramstad (2003). Thus, both statistical and "practical" significance (e.g., effect sizes, costs relative to gains) must be considered in any analysis and presentation. All this becomes even more salient should the evaluation uncover that the intervention appears to only have a modest impact. It is worth the effort?

The final consideration involves the use of quantitative versus qualitative information. We have focused on the analysis of quantitative data, but it should be noted that pairing quantitative and qualitative analyses is useful for highlighting the practical significance of quantitative data. For example, Cohen and Ledford (1994) based the majority of their conclusions regarding the intervention on quantitative statistics, but they also presented detailed qualitative information about the three different groups as they performed in the workplace. The qualitative information allowed them not only to gain further insight into the effectiveness of the intervention, but to also make more persuasive arguments about the intervention to the stakeholders.

MAKING STRONG INFERENCES

In our view, the goal of an evaluation is to be able to make strong inferences about the effects of an intervention. Simply stated, how *confident* are we that our findings are reliable? Can we explain them, and can we expect to see them occur in a context other than the context of our study? Having confidence in our inferences usually involves a process of systematic deduction from what we think we know about the intervention and its effects; the evaluator must anticipate the challenges associated with such an activity.

The deduction process we advocate requires a number of interrelated components. The first component is a deep understanding of team dynamics and the relationships of the features of the team learning intervention, team processes, and team performance. One must be quite knowledgeable about the phenomena of interest in order to enumerate the possible outcomes of the evaluation effort (including no effect or partial effects) and to prepare for addressing possible explanations for those outcomes. The second component involves the selection or development and skilled use of measures, which reflect key and relevant aspects of team functioning. In this regard, the assertion that valid or strong inferences about learning interventions can only be made when the measures used are reliable and valid is only partially true. As implied, it is also necessary to anticipate the need for deduction, and thus, to install in place a set of measures that are up to this task. The third component involves understanding the internal logic of evaluation and how the plan, its design, execution, the analysis of resulting data can be worked together to make strong inferences. In this regard, years ago, Runkel and McGrath (1972) proposed that knowledge is often "the knowledge of differences." For this chapter, the nostrum implies that both during the intervention and, certainly, during an evaluation of the learning that took place, we need the ability to compare and contrast, and explore the differences between teams in systematic ways in order to provide a clear picture of the extent and nature of effects detected.

The evaluator's primary responsibility, then, is to come to conclusions about how and why a team learning intervention works or does not work within context of the evaluation exercise, and to be able to anticipate just how it would play out if it were to be installed more broadly within the organization. Such conclusions can be offered with confidence if they are based on a good evaluation plan. They are only valid conclusions, however, if the inferences are shaped with attention and due diligence relative to addressing potential alternative explanations for any findings. In addition, this, in turn, requires both good design and careful execution of the kind of deductive-argumentative process that we advocate.

To illustrate this point, we offer as an example another recent effort to evaluate a team learning intervention. Morgeson et al. (2006) used a longitudinal quasi-experimental design to investigate a team-based intervention aimed at promoting greater team autonomy and empowerment in a printing company production setting. Their intervention was aimed at improving such things as team-member skills and team-level problem-solving processes. What is significant about this study for this chapter is the evaluation design that they used in support of being able to form strong inferences. Specifically, the authors intuited at the outset that certain aspects of the *organizational context* might make a difference in the impact that they might see coming out of the intervention. They set up their design and measurement platform accordingly. In fact, their findings about the intervention were substantially affected by the team's particular context when it came to such things as reward and feedback practices and the kind of information systems available to team members. When asked if the intervention worked, the authors would have to say that it depends. To put it differently, having knowledge of the team's context was important in order to make any strong conclusions.

In this regard, Morgeson et al. (2006) found that the team-based learning intervention had its effects on team process and performance for those work teams that had to function in contexts where supportive management systems were absent. On the other hand, when the local context provided such things as ample and timely information and where the feedback to team members met their needs, contrary to expectations, the team learning intervention did *not* have an appreciable impact. Thus, for the latter teams, redesigning work around a semiautonomous structure and training employees accordingly would not likely pay off.

To conclude this example, had the authors not invested in good evaluation design and suitable measures at the outset of their investigation (e.g., conditions for strong inference), they might have come to the wrong conclusion about the intervention. Depending on chance (the department where they chose to set up their study), they might have come to either of two false conclusions. One is that the intervention does not work, the other that the intervention does work (everywhere in the firm). Instead, because of their diligence, they could offer stakeholders a more valid and useful set of recommendations.

It is clear that in our view, the role of the evaluator is not that of a program champion, but a professional who employs empirical evidence about a proposed practice before supporting its widespread diffusion through out the organization. In this case, the evaluator must entertain the data and other evidence with some detachment. This will increase the likelihood that alternative explanations for the observed effects (causes, biases, mistakes) are addressed and ruled out. Although it is not possible to entertain all possibilities, reasonable counterarguments to a claim that the intervention is "working" should be considered. With the program designers in mind, what might constitute a "better" explanation for the impact of training (or lack thereof)? With the sample of participants in the study in mind, what might limit the potential value of the learning intervention for different teams, perhaps in different locations? Empathizing with shareholders, just what would you need to see by way of evidence that the program is worthy of company investment?

Toward the goal of stimulating a healthy skepticism for taking any set of results at face value, we offer Table 16.2. It presents some questions the critic should ask about the potential validity and utility of a learning intervention. As pointed out, while the questions have definite use in helping to make sense of any empirical findings, at the outset of any initiative, they can also serve as a set of considerations to be kept in mind when such things as the learning program design, the evaluation plan, and the measurement bed are initially being formulated.

To conclude, when it comes to convincing most stakeholders, it is always desirable to have empirical information that supports our initial (theoretical) expectations as to how, when, and where the intervention would be working. Similarly, evidence that is consistent across many teams in the evaluation study and points to improvements in teamwork, taskwork, or in individual or team-level performance will also be persuasive. In addition, having used a design or strategy that allows for systematic deduction in order to rule out reasonable explanations for findings also goes a long way toward enhancing our confidence that the team learning intervention did have value and is likely to have beneficial effects on work teams if implemented within the firm.

TABLE 16.2 Critical Questions Regarding Potential Threats to Strong Conclusions

Problem/Threat	Questions to Ask
Sample	Were the participants a part of a random sample? What type of teams was evaluated? Was there access to a variety of participants across a variety of jobs? Were there a large number of non-respondents? What was the demographic composition of the team and its members?
Task	Were the focal teams participating in teamwork or taskwork? Was the intervention aligned with the tasks performed by the team? Were there temporal factors involved in the task the team is performing that may impact the intervention?
Delivery	Was the intervention delivered at an appropriate time? Was the delivery of the intervention consistent across people and teams?
Setting	Was there something about the setting that could limit generalizability to other settings? Was the setting itself responsible for the effects of the intervention? Did stakeholder support within the setting limit conclusions that can be made?
Measurement	Were the measures focused on both teamwork and taskwork? Were the measures administered at appropriate times? Do the measures allow for inferences about inputs, processes, and outputs?
Design	Did the design allow comparisons to be made across people, teams, and organizations? Were the comparisons appropriate to the questions being asked? Were there any other comparisons that would provide useful information about the effectiveness of the intervention?
Statistics	At what level of analysis were the statistics assessed? Were the statistics appropriate for the design?

REFERENCES

Arthur, W. J., Bennett, W. J., Edens, P. S., & Bell, S. T. (2003). Effectiveness of training in organizations: A meta-analysis of design and evaluation features. *Journal of Applied Psychology, 88*(2), 234–245.

Barnett, S. M., & Ceci, S. J. (2002). When and where do we apply what we learn?: A taxonomy for far transfer. *Psychological Bulletin, 128*(4), 612–637.

Boudreau, J. W., & Ramstad, P. M. (2003). *Strategic industrial and organizational psychology and the role of utility analysis models.* In W. C. Borman, D. R. Ilgen, & R. J. Klimoski (Eds.), *Handbook of psychology* (Vol. 12, pp. 193–221). Hoboken, NJ: John Wiley & Sons.

Campbell, D. T., & Stanley, J. C. (1966). *Experimental and quasi-experimental designs for research.* Chicago: Rand McNally & Co.

Campbell, J. P. (1988). Training design for performance improvement. In J. P. Campbell, R. J. Campbell, & associates (Eds.), *Productivity in organizations* (pp. 177–216). San Francisco: Jossey-Bass.

Campbell, J. P., McCloy, R. A., Oppler, S. H., & Sager, C. E. (1993). A theory of performance. In N. Schmitt, & W. C. Bormon (Eds.), *Personnel selection in organizations* (pp. 35–70). San Francisco: Jossey-Bass.

Cohen, S. G., & Ledford, G. E. (1994). The effectiveness of self-managing teams: A quasi-experiment. *Human Relations, 47*(1), 13–43.

Day, D. V., Gronn, P., & Salas, E. (2004). Leadership capacity in teams. *Leadership Quarterly, 15*(6), 857–880.

Dionne, P. (1996). The evaluation of training activities: A complex issue involving different stakes. *Human Resource Development Quarterly, 7*(3), 279–286.

Druskat, V. U., & Kayes, D. C. (2000). Learning versus performance in short-term project teams. *Small Group Research, 31*(3), 328–353.

Edmondson, A. (1999). Psychological safety and learning behavior in work teams. *Administrative Science Quarterly, 44*(2), 350–383.

Ellis, A. P. J., Hollenbeck, J. R., Ilgen, D. R., Porter, C. O. L. H., West, B. J., & Moon, H. (2003). Team learning: Collectively connecting the dots. *Journal of Applied Psychology, 88*(5), 821–835.

Haccoun, R. R., & Hamtiaux, T. (1994). Optimizing knowledge tests for inferring learning acquisition levels in single group training evaluation designs: The internal reference strategy. *Personnel Psychology, 47,* 593–604.

Kirkpatrick, D. L. (1994). *Evaluating training programs: The four levels.* San Francisco: Berrett-Koehler.

Kozlowski, S. W. J., & Bell, B. S. (2003). Work groups and teams in organizations. In W. C. Borman, D. R. Ilgen, & R. J. Klimoski (Eds.), *Handbook of psychology: Industrial and organizational psychology* (Vol. 12, pp. 333–375). New York: John Wiley & Sons.

Kozlowski, S. W. J., Gully, S. M., McHugh, P. P., Salas, E., & Cannon-Bowers, J. A. (1996). A dynamic theory of leadership and team effectiveness: Developmental and task contingent leader roles. *Research in Personnel and Human Resources Management, 14,* 253–305.

Kozlowski, S. W. J., Gully, S. M., Salas, E., & Cannon-Bowers, J. A. (1996). Team leadership and development: Theory, principles, and guidelines for training leaders and teams. In M. M. Beyerlein, & D. A. Johnson, et al. (Eds.), *Advances in interdisciplinary studies of work teams: Vol. 3. Team leadership* (pp. 253–291). Greenwich, CT: Elsevier Science/JAI Press.

Kozlowski, S. W., & Ilgen, D. R. (2006). Enhancing the effectiveness of work groups. *Psychological Science in the Public Interest, 7*(3), 77–124.

Kraiger, K. (2002). Decision-based evaluation. In K. Kraiger (Ed.), *Creating, implementing, and managing effective training and development* (pp. 331–375). San Francisco: Jossey-Bass.

Kraiger, K. (2003). Perspectives on training and development. In W. C. Borman, D. R. Ilgen, & R. J. Klimoski (Eds.), *Handbook of psychology: Industrial and organizational psychology: Vol. 12* (pp. 171–192). New York: John Wiley & Sons.

Marks, M. A., Mathieu, J. E., & Zaccaro, S. J. (2001). A Temporally based framework and taxonomy of team processes. *Academy of Management Review, 26*(3), 356–376.

Mathieu, J. E., Gilson, L. L., & Ruddy, T. M. (2006). Empowerment and team effectiveness: An empirical test of an integrated model. *Journal of Applied Psychology, 91*(1), 97–108.

McGrath, J. E. (1964). *Social psychology: A brief introduction.* New York: Holt, Rinehart & Winston.

Morgan, R. B., & Casper, W. J. (2000). Examining the factor structure of participant reactions to training: A multidimensional approach. *Human Resource Development Quarterly, 11*(3), 301–317.

Morgeson, F. P., Johnson, M. D., Campion, M. A., Medsker, G. J., & Mumford, T. V. (2006). Understanding reactions to job redesign: A quasi-experimental investigation of the moderating effects of organizational context on perceptions of performance behavior. *Personnel Psychology, 59,* 333–363.

Muldrow, T. W., Buckley, T., & Schay, B. W. (2002). Creating high-performance organizations in the public sector. *Human Resource Management, 41*(3), 341–354.

Pearson, C. A. (1992). Autonomous workgroups: An evaluation at an industrial site. *Human Relations, 45*(9), 905–936.

Phillips, J. J. (1997). *Handbook of training evaluation and measurement methods* (3rd ed.). Woburn, MA: Butterworth-Heinemann.

Runkel, P. J., & McGrath, J. E. (1972). *Research on human behavior: A systematic guide to method.* New York: Holt, Rinehart & Winston.

Steiner, I. D. (1972). *Group process and productivity.* New York: Academic Press.

Sundstrom, E. (1999). The challenges of supporting work team effectiveness. In E. Sundstrom & associates (Eds.), *Supporting work team effectiveness: Best management practices for fostering high performance* (pp. 3–22). San Francisco: Jossey-Bass.

Sundstrom, E., de Meuse, K. P., & Futrell, D. (1990). Work teams: Applications and effectiveness. *American Psychologist, 45*(2), 120–133.

Tannenbaum, S. I., & Yukl, G. (1992). Training and development in work organizations. *Annual Review of Psychology, 43,* 399–441

Zellmer-Bruhn, M., & Gibson, C. (2006). Multinational organizational context: Implication for team learning and performance. *Academy of Management Journal, 49*(3), 501–518.

Author Index

Page references followed by *f* indicate figure.
Page references followed by *t* indicate table.
Page references followed by *n* indicate footnote.

B

C

D

E

F

G

H

I

J

L

Q

R

V

W

X

Y

Z

Subject Index

A

C

D

E

P

R

S

T